Praise for *The US Senate and the Commonwealth: Kentucky Lawmakers and the Evolution of Legislative Leadership*

"The names of Henry Clay, Alben Barkley, John Sherman Cooper, and Wendell Ford may be familiar to many Kentuckians for their political roles, but less so in relation to the evolution of leadership in Congress. And what about mostly forgotten figures such as John Brown, John Pope, James B. Beck, or J. C. S. Blackburn? A strength of this work is that it brings alive these significant players in the political past of the state and reminds us again of the importance of Kentucky in national affairs. But this work is more than that, for it also includes commentary by a Senate majority leader on the legislative body in which he serves. . . . An interesting read and an important look at politics, past and present."
—James C. Klotter, State Historian of Kentucky and coauthor of *A New History of Kentucky, Second Edition*

"*The US Senate and the Commonwealth* is an outstanding study of Senate leadership. Through a series of biographies, Senator McConnell and Mr. Brownell present vivid portraits of Kentucky senators who have stood in the front ranks of the institution—including Henry Clay (the great nineteenth-century statesman), Alben Barkley (the Senate's Democratic leader from 1937 to 1949), and Wendell Ford (the Democratic whip in the 1990s). Given the prominence of Kentuckians in the annals of the Senate, this book provides a window into the broader history of the institution. It is a fascinating read, grounded in an impressive command of the literature, a deep knowledge of original sources, and lively firsthand accounts of Congress in action. It is an essential source for anyone interested in the US Senate, its development, and its parties and leaders."
—Gerald Gamm, University of Rochester

The US Senate and the Commonwealth

THE US SENATE AND THE COMMONWEALTH

*Kentucky Lawmakers and the
Evolution of Legislative Leadership*

Senator Mitch McConnell
and
Roy E. Brownell II

UNIVERSITY PRESS OF KENTUCKY

Copyright © 2019 by The University Press of Kentucky

Scholarly publisher for the Commonwealth,
serving Bellarmine University, Berea College, Centre
College of Kentucky, Eastern Kentucky University,
The Filson Historical Society, Georgetown College,
Kentucky Historical Society, Kentucky State University,
Morehead State University, Murray State University,
Northern Kentucky University, Transylvania University,
University of Kentucky, University of Louisville,
and Western Kentucky University.
All rights reserved.

Editorial and Sales Offices: The University Press of Kentucky
663 South Limestone Street, Lexington, Kentucky 40508-4008
www.kentuckypress.com

Cataloging-in-Publication data available from the Library of Congress

ISBN 978-0-8131-7745-8 (hardcover : alk. paper)
ISBN 978-0-8131-7746-5 (pdf)
ISBN 978-0-8131-7747-2 (epub)

This book is printed on acid-free paper meeting
the requirements of the American National Standard
for Permanence in Paper for Printed Library Materials.
∞

Manufactured in the United States of America

Member of the Association
of University Presses

Contents

Note on Political Party Abbreviations

The following abbreviations have been used for political party names when designating party affiliations. The terminology reflects that found in the Congressional Biographical Directory: http://bioguide.congress.gov/biosearch/biosearch.asp. Some lawmakers switched parties during their careers; therefore, this book identifies the party that most accurately reflects the member's affiliation during the period under discussion. As a result, some lawmakers' party affiliations differ in different parts of the book.

Anti-Admin.	Anti-Administration (opposed to the Washington administration)
Anti-Jack.	Anti-Jacksonian (opposed to Andrew Jackson)
Cons.	Conservative Party
D	Democratic Party
Dem.-Rep.	Democratic-Republican Party (supporters of Thomas Jefferson)
Fed.	Federalist Party
Ind.	Independent
Jack.	Jacksonian (supporters of Andrew Jackson)
Nat. Rep.	National Republican Party (supporters of John Quincy Adams and Henry Clay)
Pro-Admin.	Pro-Administration (supporters of the Washington administration)
R	Republican Party
W	Whig Party

Introduction

Kentucky has long "punched above its weight" in the United States Senate.[1] Indeed, some of the nation's most distinguished senators have hailed from the commonwealth. Despite having a relatively small population for much of its history, Kentucky has produced the nation's greatest lawmaker in Henry Clay;[2] it is one of only five states that can claim two Senate majority leaders,[3] is the only state that has had three Senate majority whips, is the only state with four Senate caucus chairmen, and is one of only three states that has had four Senate party campaign chairmen.[4] In addition, Kentucky has been home to vice presidents, presidents pro tempore, and numerous other eminent members of the upper chamber.

At the beginning of the twentieth century, the *Baltimore Sun* observed that "Kentucky has played a leading and brilliant part in the Senate for more than a century. She has been represented there by Clay, Marshall, Breckinridge, Crittenden, Richard M. Johnson, Garrett Davis, Stevenson, Beck, Carlisle and Lindsay."[5] Yet no book exists that is devoted to Kentucky lawmakers.[6] This is the case even though at least six other states (with arguably less historically prominent lawmakers) have had works written about their most accomplished senators.[7]

Moreover, while the leadership of Congress has been subjected to much searching analysis, no book has focused on the development of Senate leadership.[8] This work aspires to address both shortcomings—discussing the lives and careers of distinguished Kentucky senators while using their experiences to highlight the evolution of leadership in the Senate in an accessible way. As such, this book examines the lives of selected Kentucky lawmakers and the development of Senate leadership institutions through several means: firsthand accounts by one who has held many of these positions, an exploration of primary source material, and a review of the relevant secondary literature.

The United States Senate is a uniquely American institution. It stands apart from other legislative bodies in the world in several ways.[9] First, no other legislative chamber grants such power to individual lawmakers and to the minority party.[10] This feature manifests itself in senators' broad leeway to debate public matters and to amend legislation. It maximizes the Senate's ability to consider issues in a deliberative fashion.[11] As Senator George F. Hoar (R-MA) observed in 1897, "the Senate . . . was created that . . . the sober second thought of the people might find expression."[12] This "cooling" effect of the Senate can frustrate ideological purists, as it often pushes legislation toward centrist solutions and away from political extremes.[13]

The uncommon authority the Senate assigns to individual members and the minority party also better ensures that all of the nation is represented in the law-making process.[14] At the same time, the emphasis on the rights of the minority party and individual senators can prove challenging to those trying to lead the institution.[15]

Second, no other legislative body in a separated system of government plays such a significant role in relation to the executive branch.[16] Treaties and nominations must receive the approbation of the upper chamber. Depending on the circumstances, with its advice and consent function, the Senate can act as a constitutional council offering recommendations to the president or as a check on perceived executive overreach.[17]

Third, virtually no other upper house stands on equal footing with its legislative counterpart, the lower chamber.[18] Indeed, with the exception of originating tax bills and articles of impeachment, the Senate can do everything the House of Representatives can do. In fact, the Senate both considers tax bills and votes on House-adopted articles of impeachment. Yet the Senate can do much that the House cannot, such as its aforementioned role in approving or rejecting treaties and nominations. Perhaps with the upper chamber's noteworthy relationship to both the presidency and the House in mind, James Madison characterized the Senate as "the great anchor of the Government."[19]

Finally, the Senate is remarkable because of its origins and development. The "Great Compromise" settled one of the most vexing issues facing the Framers at the Constitutional Convention of 1787: should the national legislature include representation based solely on population, or should it provide equal voting power to every state?[20] Ultimately, the Framers established representation based on the former in the House and based on the latter in the Senate.[21] The fact that every state is represented by two senators remains crucial to the modern chamber. Given that the successful operation of the Senate stems from mutual accommodation, it seems fitting that the body itself was born out of compromise.[22]

Much of the Senate's character and diversity of roles has been informed by the Constitution. The Framers created two different lawmaking institutions in the House and the Senate. The smaller size of the Senate accounts for many of its distinctive features: lengthy deliberation, protection of minority party rights, and the weighing of diverse viewpoints. Senators' six-year terms, along with staggered elections, provide electoral insulation, so the Senate is well situated to slow down a "rush to judgment" by the House, which might be responding with undue haste to momentary popular passions.[23]

One key difference between the two legislative bodies involves leadership. In 1922, *Washington Post* columnist George Rothwell Brown asserted, "the facts are that there has never been any leadership in the Senate."[24] That was not true in 1922—or even in 1822—and it is not true today. The Senate has always had leaders—both official and unofficial.[25] But the position known today as Senate majority leader is nowhere to be found in the Constitution or in early American history. It emerged slowly over time and is just over a century old. The same is true of the offices of Senate majority whip and chairman of the Senate party campaign committees. This leads to several questions: Where did these posts come from, and why did they emerge? Why have those holding the positions created by the Constitution not typically led the Senate? What factors contribute to some senators developing into leaders while others do not? What are some of the ways—institutional or otherwise—that senators can exercise leadership? This book answers these questions by using the experiences of notable Kentucky senators as a guide. It is hoped that these portraits will not only remind readers of many forgotten lawmakers but also humanize this discussion of institutional evolution.

Chapter 1 discusses the vice presidency. The president of the Senate (the vice president) is provided for in the Constitution and has been part of the Senate from the outset. On paper, the vice president is the formal leader of the Senate, although with few exceptions, this has not been the case in practice.[26] Vice presidents are not chosen by or accountable to the Senate, which has prevented them from leading the body except under rare circumstances.[27] Indeed, it was soon established that the Senate's leadership would come not from the presiding officer's chair—as it does in the House of Representatives—but from the floor.[28] Nonetheless, until the middle of the twentieth century, vice presidents spent most of their professional time in the Senate, presiding over the body. The lives and careers of Richard Mentor Johnson and John C. Breckinridge shed light on the limitations of the vice president's role in the Senate.[29]

Chapter 2 highlights the president pro tempore, an individual chosen by the Senate to fill in for the vice president as presiding officer. As already noted, for the first 150 years under the Constitution, vice presidents spent most of their professional time presiding over the Senate. At the same time, for the first century under the Constitution, the Senate elected a president pro tempore to serve only when the vice president was actually absent from the presiding officer's chair. As a result, presidents pro tempore were chosen only sporadically.[30]

Largely for this reason, the president pro tempore—like the vice president—did not develop into an independent power in the Senate.[31] This was true despite the president pro tempore's place in the line of presidential succession for much of American history. Thus, neither of the Senate's constitutional presiding officers evolved into a position of institutional leadership. Senators John Brown and John Pope both served as presidents pro tempore in the early nineteenth century. Their life stories serve as a backdrop to the development of this institution.

Early on, the lack of formal Senate leadership provided by the vice president and president pro tempore permitted individuals who enjoyed a close relationship with the incumbent president to serve essentially as administration spokesmen in the chamber.[32] In this manner, these lawmakers exercised a form of Senate leadership because they were known to represent the views of the president at a time when political norms dictated that the chief executive should not play an overt legislative role. A prime example of an early presidential spokesman is John Breckinridge (not to be confused with his grandson, the vice president). Breckinridge was President Thomas Jefferson's unofficial advocate in the Senate. His experience, discussed in chapter 3, demonstrates the role of the informal presidential lieutenant in the upper chamber.

In the era before formal floor leadership, senators with a major political following could, from time to time, assume de facto leadership of the body. No one better reflects this phenomenon than Henry Clay.[33] As a senator, Clay was the national leader of those who opposed President Andrew Jackson (a group that ultimately came to be known as the Whig Party).[34] His national standing was such that he helped drive the country's policy agenda from Capitol Hill.[35] Clay achieved this prominence even though he held no formal leadership slot in the Senate. His historic career is discussed in chapter 4.

The void in formal leadership in the nineteenth-century Senate was filled not only by presidential lieutenants and senators with national or regional followings but also by committee chairmen.[36] This was particularly true of those who chaired the most prestigious committees. One senator who chaired two such committees—Judiciary and Military Affairs—was John J. Crittenden. His life and the evolution of the role of committee chairmen are chronicled in chapter 5.

In the early 1790s, American political parties began to develop, and their presence was soon manifested in the Senate.[37] Virtually from the beginning, party members would meet away from the Senate floor to strategize privately about political and policy matters.[38] These gatherings were called "caucuses" (now referred to as "conferences"). In the mid-nineteenth century, the first records emerge of Senate party caucuses electing full-time chairmen.[39] Republican senators seem to have chosen caucus chairmen largely according to senior-ity.[40] By contrast, Democrats had no seniority rule and apparently chose their chairmen based at least in part on their political or legislative acumen.[41] Despite the title, early caucus chairmen were not officially responsible for setting legis-lative priorities, scheduling measures to be brought to the floor and determin-ing their order, enforcing party discipline, serving as public representatives of their party in the Senate, managing legislation on the floor, or coordinating or leading opposition to the president—all attributes of a modern-day Senate floor leader.[42] The initial responsibilities of caucus chairmen were generally more mundane. Three largely forgotten Kentuckians served as caucus chairmen in the pre–majority leader era: John W. Stevenson, James B. Beck, and Joseph C. S. Blackburn. Stevenson, in fact, is the first Democratic caucus chair on record.[43] The backgrounds of these three men frame the discussion of the institution in chapter 6.

The office of Senate majority leader evolved out of the caucus chairman position.[44] This occurred due to important external and internal political forces affecting the Senate.[45] On the external side, the position likely rose in stature partly to meet the growth of the activist presidency.[46] Moreover, the House of Representatives' decision to create the formal post of House majority leader in 1899 may have informed perceptions of de facto Senate leadership at the time.[47] On the internal side, the need for institutional innovation due to increased party competition within the Senate, the need for formal leadership given the body's increased size and workload, and the prestige brought to the caucus chair posi-tion by several prominent incumbents all contributed to the emergence of the Senate majority leader post.[48] Today, the Senate majority leader's main formal power is the right of "prior recognition."[49] This prerogative is not contained in Senate rules but dates back to a precedent established during the tenure of Sen-ate majority leader Alben Barkley, a historical event largely neglected in the lit-erature.[50] Barkley's career sets the stage for a historical analysis of the Senate majority leader position in chapter 7.

The office of Senate whip came into being during the same period as Senate majority leader. It first appeared just prior to World War I, as it became clear that the parties needed help rounding up votes and ensuring attendance to support their respective agendas.[51] Wendell Ford is one of three Kentuckians to have served as Senate majority whip.[52] Ford's life story in chapter 8 highlights the evolution of this vital Senate institution.

The origins of the Senate party campaign chairmanship are examined in chapter 9. This post was established by each party immediately after World War I.[53] The officeholders' main responsibility is to ensure the election of as many of their fellow partisans to the Senate as possible. Senators in this position are responsible for reelecting incumbents as well as renewing their parties' lifeblood by recruiting new candidates. Accordingly, over time, the institution has become an important aspect of Senate party leadership. Moreover, it has emerged as a platform from which to pursue other leadership slots.[54] Earle Clements and Thruston Morton are two of the four Kentuckians who have held this position, and their lives and careers are profiled.[55]

Finally, sometimes an individual senator develops the expertise and stature necessary to become a national leader on a specific issue, influencing the policy agenda for that subject even though he or she does not hold a formal Senate leadership post or serve as the chair or ranking member of the relevant committee. John Sherman Cooper was such a senator. He emerged as a national leader in the effort to halt and then reverse American military involvement in Southeast Asia in the late 1960s and early 1970s. His life story is the subject of chapter 10.

The lives and careers of a number of these notable Kentucky lawmakers have been sketched only briefly in reference texts or contemporary newspaper profiles. In this regard, chapters of this book constitute the first extended, published, modern treatment of the lives of Senators Brown, Beck, Blackburn, and Morton.[56] Similarly, Senators Stevenson, Ford, and Clements have been only briefly discussed in book segments focusing on their gubernatorial tenures, devoting little attention to their time in the Senate. This book provides the most detailed published biographical treatment of these seven senators.

While the lives and careers of other senators featured in this book, such as Henry Clay and Alben Barkley, may be more recognizable and familiar to readers, these chapters contain new material as well. For example, this book examines the origins and development of the vital Senate precedent of "prior recognition," which bolstered the institutional power of Senate floor leaders and took place during Barkley's tenure. In addition, the book provides fresh insights into the evolution of the caucus chair and majority leader positions from long-neglected floor debate. The scope of the vice president's authority as president of the Senate also receives updated treatment. Moreover, this book includes the first published discussion of the president pro tempore's purported role as the "acting vice president."

Finally, this work provides a firsthand account of what it is like to serve in a Senate leadership position. In this respect, although the book reflects the views of both authors, it uses the first-person singular voice and an italic font, where appropriate, to emphasize the personal recollections and observations of Senator McConnell.

Ultimately, this book tells the story of how leadership in the Senate has unfolded over the past two and a quarter centuries and how, through it all, Kentuckians have played an important role in this institutional development, their senatorial experience serving to mark this evolutionary path.[57] To this end, it is hoped that this book both illuminates and humanizes the Senate as an institution.

President of the Senate

Richard Mentor Johnson
and John C. Breckinridge

Looking solely at the text of the Constitution, there is every reason to believe that the vice president would be the actual leader of the upper chamber. After all, under Article I, he is the "President of the Senate."[1] Moreover, his constitutional counterpart in the House of Representatives—the Speaker—is today both the formal leader of the House and its leader in fact. Yet the vice president has not developed into the de facto leader of the Senate, even though, since 1789, the vice president spent much of his official time in the legislative branch.[2]

The vice president's standing in the Senate—like the other leadership roles discussed in this book—has followed an evolutionary path. Gradually—almost imperceptibly over time—the vice presidency has been transformed from a largely legislative branch position to a largely executive branch office.[3] In recent decades, it has become a rarity for the vice president to sit in the presiding officer's chair. Typically, a modern vice president attends Senate sessions only to break a tie vote or to perform ceremonial functions.

Because of this evolution, the reality of vice-presidential influence in the chamber (such as it is) has been transformed. Occasionally, in the first century and a half under the Constitution, vice presidents held some sway in the Senate based on their personal standing in the legislative branch and the exercise of their modest Senate powers. But these were fleeting occurrences owing much to context. In the years since, as vice presidents more clearly became part of the executive branch, they have exercised legislative influence somewhat more often but in different ways. On these occasions, vice presidents' impact on the Senate has typically been based not only on their personal relationships with senators and their formal Senate authority but also on their ability to speak for and to the president.

Kentucky can lay claim to four vice presidents: Richard Mentor Johnson, who served alongside President Martin Van Buren; John C. Breckinridge, who was vice president during the James Buchanan administration; Adlai Stevenson, who held the position during Grover Cleveland's second term; and Alben Barkley, who was elected vice president with Harry Truman. This chapter highlights the careers of Johnson and Breckinridge, whose tenures as vice president both reinforced and reflected the frustrations of premodern vice presidents. Chapter 7 examines the career of Barkley, who served at an important juncture in the evolution of the office as it became more of an executive branch position and a more meaningful part of American governance. Given that Stevenson did not represent Kentucky in public office, he is not discussed except in passing.

Origins of the Office

Exactly what the Framers had in mind when they created the vice presidency cannot be said with complete certainty.[4] In the deliberations that took place during the Constitutional Convention of 1787, the position of the president of the Senate actually appeared well before the vice presidency.[5] Indeed, some early drafts of the Constitution had the president of the Senate serving as the successor to the executive.[6] Later, the vice presidency emerged from the convention's Committee of Eleven as part of a broader mechanism for determining how presidents would be chosen.[7] At that point, the vice presidency was combined with the presidency of the Senate.[8]

With the vice presidency, the Framers wanted, among other things, to establish a clear successor to the president.[9] The question remained, however, what the vice president would do while the president remained alive and healthy. The presidency of the Senate seemed to offer a ready-made solution.[10] The vice president could preside over the upper chamber and break tie votes.[11]

Under the original Constitution, the vice president was the runner-up in the race for the presidency.[12] Indeed, the Framers considered the vice president to be pivotal to how presidents were chosen, helping to ensure that state electors would consider candidates of national stature and not vote only for "favorite sons."[13] In this regard, the Framers did not foresee the rise of political parties, which meant that individuals of different parties could be paired as president and vice president. The election of 1800 resulted in Thomas Jefferson—the Democratic-Republican presidential choice—receiving as many electoral votes as Aaron Burr—the same party's vice-presidential pick. The election was thrown into the House of Representatives, where it was resolved only after much haggling and controversy. This unsettling outcome convinced the nation to adopt the Twelfth Amendment in 1804 to recognize the reality of party politics and partisan national tickets.[14] Thereafter, individuals would run specifically for either president or vice president.[15]

In the beginning and for decades thereafter, the vice presidency was viewed largely as a legislative branch office.[16] As such, Vice President John Adams attempted to assume an open leadership role in the Senate based in no small part on his formal authority.[17] The chamber was a small body at the outset—for the first few months, it included only twenty senators—so deadlock was not uncommon.[18] As a result, Adams often held the balance of power. He broke twenty-nine tie votes—more than all but one of his successors.[19] Moreover, many of these votes decided vital public matters.

Senator William Maclay (Anti-Admin.–PA), who opposed the Washington administration as a general matter, kept a diary of the early years of the Senate. In it, Maclay described grousing among lawmakers at Adams's frequent exercise of his tiebreaking authority: "It was remarked that, as every question of moment was carried only by one majority, or for the most part by the casting vote of the Vice-President, it might be as well to vest the whole senatorial power in the President of the Senate. The fact really is as it was stated."[20]

In addition to breaking ties, Adams spoke from the chair with some regularity.[21] Maclay had this to say about Adams's participation in a debate in May 1789: "Up now got the Vice-President, and for forty minutes did he harangue us from the chair. He began first on the subject of order, and found fault with everything almost, but down he came to particulars, and pointedly blamed a member for disorderly behavior. . . . All this was only prefatory. On he got to his favorite topic of titles. . . . When he had exhausted this subject he turned a new leaf."[22]

Adams also helped manage the flow of Senate business and pushed for certain measures to be adopted.[23] On at least one occasion, he brought up a bill for consideration on his own accord.[24] Adams lobbied senators, and a number of them often followed his lead.[25] There was even an effort in 1791 to authorize the vice president to put forward committee appointments.[26] Finally, Adams was made responsible for a host of Senate administrative matters.[27] Due to these actions, Adams's early role has been likened to that of a majority leader.[28]

However, Adams's actions, coupled with his irascible personality and fixation on protocol, began to grate on senators' growing sense of institutional identification.[29] According to Maclay, only a few days into the First Congress, Senator William Paterson (Fed.-NJ) "passed censure on the conduct of the Vice-President . . . [saying] he made himself too busy."[30] Moreover, the vice president was informally advised by a friend to be less vocal.[31] Before long, one of the fundamental differences between the vice president and the Speaker began to manifest itself: the Speaker is chosen, and can be removed, by members of the House. The vice president bears no such relationship to the Senate.[32] He is chosen by the voters through the Electoral College. Thus, the vice president presides over the chamber irrespective of which party controls the Senate. He presides even if no one in the entire body would want him in the chair. Once senators asserted themselves, the potential for a legislatively powerful vice president began to recede.[33]

Unfortunately for the office, as the vice president's active involvement in the Senate diminished over the course of the 1790s, his potential for influence in the executive branch followed the same path.[34] Early on, President George Washington consulted with Adams on a handful of matters, but these requests became less frequent as the president's first term progressed.[35] In one case, Washington directed that the vice president be invited to participate in a cabinet session while he was away from the capital.[36] But Adams's attendance marked his only appearance at a cabinet meeting and the last formal participation by a vice president in such proceedings until the Civil War.[37]

Despite these constraints, a creative and talented vice president could leave a mark. Vice President Thomas Jefferson presided over a Senate made up of a Federalist majority that loathed him.[38] Yet, while in office he authored *A Manual of Parliamentary Practice,* a volume that has played an important role in Senate (and House) governance.[39] Vice President John C. Calhoun took advantage of Senate rules at the time to make committee assignments in a partisan fashion.[40] In addition, he informally guided Senator Robert Hayne (Jack.-SC) in his epic debate over the nature of the federal union with Daniel Webster (Anti-Jack.–MA).[41] Vice President Martin Van Buren was a close adviser to and advocate for President Andrew Jackson.[42]

Yet, such vice-presidential coups were rarities in the nineteenth century. The Senate did not want to be led by the vice president, and presidents consulted their vice presidents only occasionally.[43] As such, vice-presidential morale was often low, and some officeholders did not even preside regularly over the Senate.[44] As a result, during this period, many of the formal aspects of vice-presidential power—such as they were—began to atrophy. The vice president's authority to maintain order in the chamber—though exercised by Adams and Burr, among others—was disclaimed by Calhoun.[45] Even when the Senate later bolstered the vice president's standing in this area, the power remained largely dormant.[46]

Under the Constitution, a joint session of Congress is called every four years for the purpose of counting and confirming the validity of votes cast by the Electoral College. The Twelfth Amendment of the Constitution designates the vice president as presiding officer of such sessions. Over time, Congress passed legislation that essentially elbowed the vice president aside, and it assumed authority in this realm.[47]

The vice president is authorized to make parliamentary rulings as the presiding officer, but there has developed a strong expectation that he will follow the advice of the parliamentarian, an institution created in 1935.[48] The parliamentarian tacitly limits the vice president's leeway in making rulings, and vice-presidential parliamentary determinations can be overruled by the Senate.[49]

The one component of the vice president's formal Senate authority that has not suffered a diminution over time is his authority to break tie votes.[50] As discussed later in this chapter, this power has been interpreted broadly by vice presidents and the Senate alike. In fact, a vice president has never been rebuffed by the Senate in this regard, even though some have broken tie votes well outside the confines of routine lawmaking.[51]

Thus, by the mid-1830s, the state of the vice presidency was not promising. The experiences of two Kentuckians who served as vice president reflect the reality of this Senate leadership position for most of the nineteenth century: officeholders did not lead the chamber and, at best, enjoyed only sporadic influence.

Richard Mentor Johnson

Richard Mentor Johnson was born in 1780 in Jefferson County, Kentucky, the fifth child in a family of some means and social standing.[52] Virginia had been home to both sides of his family.[53] The future vice president's grandfather was a member of the Virginia House of Burgesses.[54] His father, Robert Johnson, served with General George Rogers Clark on military expeditions.[55] Equally brave was his mother, Jemima Suggett, who at great personal risk reportedly secured vital provisions for her community during an Indian siege.[56] Thus, the future vice president inherited the trait of courage under fire from both parents.

From his father, he also gained a love of politics.[57] Robert Johnson served in the state house, where he supported John Breckinridge's Kentucky Resolutions.[58] The state legislature would be the height of his public career, however, as he lost races for both Congress and lieutenant governor.[59]

Little is known of Richard Johnson's childhood. He grew up with several brothers, three of whom would figure prominently in Kentucky politics.[60] As a boy, Johnson apparently had a serious appetite. It was said that he would be served last during mealtimes to ensure that his siblings received sufficient portions.[61] Perhaps as a result of his eating habits, the future vice president developed "a robust constitution and excellent health."[62]

It does not appear that Johnson attended college.[63] Despite his family's standing, this is not surprising, as Johnson was not known for his intellectual curiosity. A contemporary noted dismissively that "his mind is not highly cultivated."[64] He did, however, study law under the tutelage of the eminent George Nicholas and struck out on his own as an attorney in 1802.[65] Johnson soon became active in public life and, like his father before him, served in the state house.[66] After two years in the legislature, Johnson was elected to the US House of Representatives in 1806, where he would remain until 1819.[67]

In addition to hailing from an accomplished family, one of the secrets to Johnson's rise was his affability. One authority has written that Johnson possessed "the rare quality of being personally liked by everyone."[68] A prominent female resident of the nation's capital at the time called him "the most tender hearted, mild, affectionate and benevolent of men. . . . [his] countenance beams with good will to all [and his] . . . soul seems to feed on the milk of human kindness!"[69] Commenting on Johnson's generous spirit, Martin Van Buren wrote that he "was the friend of the human race and all who needed his services in any honorable way could have them."[70]

The Kentuckian was a solid, though unspectacular, stump speaker. An observer noted at the time: "He is honest, fluent and open in debate. . . . There is nothing in his speeches either remarkable for eloquence or learning; but abundance of directness and honesty. Every body is pleased with the sentiments of this man, if they do not think him a first rate orator; it must however be acknowledged that there are those who think him remarkably eloquent."[71] Johnson himself conceded that "speaking is not my forte."[72]

Despite being in the public eye, Johnson seemed unconcerned about his appearance. It was commented that he "cares nothing about dress."[73] A woman who found herself seated near Johnson in later years at a White House dinner recalled, "If [Johnson] . . . should [himself] become President, he will be as strange-looking a potentate as ever ruled. His countenance is wild, though with much cleverness in it; his hair wanders all abroad, and he wears no cravat."[74] Another contemporary recalled viewing the Senate in action in 1838: "The lions were there—Clay, Webster, Calhoun, Wright, and Benton. . . . [At the same time], Vice-president Richard M. Johnson was in the chair. He was shabbily dressed, and to the last degree clumsy. What a contrast between him and Martin Van Buren, his urbane, elegant predecessor."[75]

Johnson in the House of Representatives

While Johnson was a congressman, relations between the United States and the United Kingdom reached a boiling point. Great Britain, in the midst of its titanic struggle with Napoleonic France, assumed an aggressive posture on the high seas and abroad and treated its former colony in high-handed fashion. This included impressing American sailors into British service, restricting US trade, and stoking tensions between Native American tribes and US citizens in the western states and territories.

Johnson supported President Jefferson's embargo to try to rein in Britain, but when the economic sanctions failed, he advocated stiffer measures.[76] As such, he backed a declaration of war against Britain as proposed by incoming Speaker of the House and fellow Kentuckian Henry Clay.[77] Johnson proclaimed at the time: "I feel rejoiced that the hour of resistance is at hand. We must now oppose the farther encroachments of Great Britain by war, or formally annul the Declaration of our Independence, and acknowledge ourselves her devoted colonies."[78]

The ensuing War of 1812 would dramatically raise Johnson's profile. He volunteered to command a Kentucky unit and, in this role, displayed great valor.[79] During the Battle of the Thames (in present-day Ontario, Canada) in 1813, Johnson not only exhibited bravery and élan but also reportedly killed Tecumseh, the fearsome Shawnee chief who had allied his tribe with the British.[80] Whether Johnson actually slew the great warrior is unclear.[81] When later asked whether he had indeed killed Tecumseh, Johnson replied: "I didn't stop to ask him his name."[82] Either way, it is beyond dispute that the Kentuckian proved his mettle during the military engagement and that the American victory relieved the commonwealth and its environs from the threat of Indian raids once and for all. It is also beyond dispute that Johnson's supposed slaying of Tecumseh brought him widespread acclaim.[83] For the Kentuckian, another lasting legacy from the battle was a partial disability from serious wounds to his arm and leg, causing him to walk with a limp for the rest of his days.[84]

While Johnson's military heroics helped propel his public career, one initiative he undertook upon his return to Congress almost ended it. In 1816, Johnson secured adoption of the Compensation Act, which changed the congressional pay rate from a per diem basis to an annual salary.[85] The so-called salary grab proved wildly unpopular among voters.[86] Johnson quickly recognized the serious political difficulty he was in, and with perhaps only some exaggeration, he later commented that the Compensation Act "excited more discontent than the alien or sedition laws, the quasi war with France, the internal taxes of 1798, the embargo, the late war with Great Britain, the treaty of Ghent, or any other measure of the Government from its existence."[87] Accordingly, Johnson beat a hasty retreat, promising to try to repeal the measure.[88] His about-face and his personal popularity saved his career, but the same could not be said of many of his fellow House members.[89] Sixty-six of the eighty-one who had voted for Johnson's compensation measure were defeated for reelection.[90]

In the following Congress, Johnson was true to his word. He was named to chair the House panel tasked with repealing the unpopular measure.[91] Legislation was ultimately adopted that returned congressional pay to the old per diem system.[92] Four decades would pass before members of Congress were provided with an annual salary.[93]

Not long after his return from the war, Johnson became chairman of the House Military Affairs Committee.[94] In this capacity, he helped secure legislation that provided pensions for those who had suffered lasting injuries from wartime service, as well as for military widows and orphans.[95] One claimant Johnson advocated for was the widow of Alexander Hamilton, although his efforts were ultimately unsuccessful.[96] At the same time, he rallied to the defense of Generals William Henry Harrison and Andrew Jackson, both of whom had been accused of malfeasance while in uniform.[97] Johnson's defense of Jackson would pit him against Speaker Clay but would earn him the gratitude of Old Hickory.[98]

During his tenure as committee chairman, Johnson also used his position in a much less edifying way: to enrich himself.[99] He encouraged the War Department to award transportation contracts to a family business in which Johnson himself held a stake.[100] He angled to secure these contracts to help outfit what came to be known as the "Yellowstone Expedition."[101] This 1819–1820 undertaking was supposed to result in the construction of a US military installation by the mouth of the Yellowstone River in what is today North Dakota.[102] The outcome was a debacle, replete with cost overruns and the inability of Johnson's company to transport military personnel to their final destination.[103] Moreover, Johnson's ill-fated venture left the Kentuckian's personal finances in complete disarray.[104] Clay, who was an attorney for a Johnson creditor, characterized the future vice president as "hopelessly insolvent . . . [hav]ing nothing which can be reached by execution."[105]

The Yellowstone Expedition was not the only endeavor Johnson encouraged the US government to undertake while he was a lawmaker. In 1822, he urged the Senate to authorize funds to explore the center of the earth.[106] Sometime earlier, an army captain had presented Johnson with a plan to accomplish this.[107] The officer hypothesized that a void existed at the earth's core, and to access the planet's interior, a team of explorers would need to enter a passageway that supposedly existed in the Arctic Circle.[108] The officer thought that 100 men "with Reindeer and sleigh" could travel to the North Pole and then descend into the earth's core, which he believed consisted of "a warm and rich land" with exotic flora and fauna.[109] As outlandish as this proposal seems, what is truly remarkable is that twenty-three senators joined Johnson in supporting it![110] The proposal was referred to a committee for consideration.[111] Ultimately, this Jules Verne–like plan failed in the Senate, and Johnson moved on to other matters.[112]

Following the Yellowstone Expedition, Johnson engaged in another venture to restore his financial standing, also at government expense.[113] In 1825, the War Department authorized him to establish an academy to educate Native American youths.[114] This institution, known as the Choctaw Academy, would prove a much more remunerative undertaking for Johnson than the transportation business had been.[115] The extent to which the academy was beneficial to its charges is less certain.[116]

The Kentuckian had other business interests as well. His enterprises included a resort and health spa, an inn, and a bar, all of which he opened a little over a decade after the Choctaw Academy.[117]

Johnson in the Senate and His Return to the House

Despite his self-dealing, Johnson was elected to the Senate in 1819 as a Democratic-Republican. He would serve in the upper chamber until 1829. While in the Senate, Johnson distinguished himself in several ways. He supported the Missouri Compromise and even sat on the joint committee formed by Clay to resolve a crucial aspect of the controversy—whether free African Americans could be prevented from settling in Missouri.[118]

Perhaps because of the fallout from his own failed financial dealings, Senator Johnson became a passionate advocate for ending the imprisonment of debtors.[119] Throughout much of the country at the time, citizens who owed delinquent bills could be jailed. Indeed, there is some evidence that the vice president at the time of Johnson's arrival in the Senate—Daniel Tompkins—was himself imprisoned for debt while in high office.[120]

Johnson relentlessly advocated for this cause for many years.[121] Ultimately, he secured some federal reforms in this area and convinced Kentucky to do away with the policy.[122] Moreover, his well-publicized efforts raised awareness of the issue, leading many other states to adopt comparable reforms.[123] For Johnson personally, advocacy on behalf of those imprisoned for debt raised his national profile and fostered his image as a tribune for the common man.[124]

In the early 1820s, Johnson pursued other initiatives to help the less fortunate. He teamed up with Senator Thomas Hart Benton (Dem.-Rep.–MO) to make the purchase of federal land more affordable.[125] This reform not only increased access to the West but also protected farmers from having their property confiscated.[126] Once again, this initiative reflected Johnson's concern for the downtrodden.

Another well-publicized issue Senator Johnson became associated with was the effort to maintain Sunday mail delivery.[127] At this time, Sabbatarians were mobilized to end Sunday delivery, believing that it interfered with religious observance.[128] Johnson successfully opposed this effort, arguing in part that the proposed policy violated the establishment clause of the Constitution.[129] This won him plaudits in many quarters.[130] Johnson also advocated for infrastructure spending to help Kentucky, even though federal support for internal improvements went against prevailing Jeffersonian dogma.[131] In addition, he proposed narrowing the authority of the Supreme Court, which garnered still more favorable attention for Johnson.[132]

Perhaps most important for his own advancement was that Johnson befriended fellow senator and future president Andrew Jackson, whom he had earlier defended in the House. Once it became clear that Clay would not win the 1824 presidential election, Johnson threw in his lot with Jackson and opposed John Quincy Adams, the ultimate victor.[133] Indeed, Johnson apparently informed Jackson that Clay had accepted Adams's offer to serve as secretary of state—the alleged "corrupt bargain."[134] As a result, Johnson became a member of the Jacksonians, who openly opposed the Adams administration.[135] Although Johnson's actions solidified his relationship with Old Hickory, Clay's followers never forgave him and worked to ensure that Johnson would not be reelected to the Senate.[136]

Due in large part to the work of Clay's allies, Johnson did not secure another term in the Senate.[137] Nonetheless, he was promptly elected to the US House, where he served until 1837 as a pro-Jackson Democrat.[138] In the House, the Kentuckian chaired the Committee on Post Offices and Post Roads from 1829 to 1833, where he continued his defense of the establishment clause.[139]

It appears that Johnson was not particularly diligent in his second stint as a congressman. As far back as 1816, Old Hickory had expressed concern that Johnson did "not possess sufficient capacity[,] stability or energy" to be secretary of war.[140] These worries were borne out on Capitol Hill. During one committee investigation in the 1830s, Johnson—who was a member of the panel—blithely conceded: "I never asked a question, or looked into a book, during the investigation; for the very great industry of others elicited everything desirable."[141] Nonetheless, Johnson's status remained undiminished in many quarters. In 1836—owing to his alleged slaying of Tecumseh, his reputation as a defender of the common man, his support for religious freedom, his relationship with Jackson, and his Kentucky roots, which brought geographic balance to the ticket—the Democratic Party nominated Johnson for vice president alongside Jackson's chosen successor, incumbent vice president Martin Van Buren.[142]

In the election canvass that year, Johnson's military heroics were extolled in an awkwardly titled campaign song: "Rumpsey, Dumpsey, Colonel Johnson Killed Tecumseh."[143] Ultimately, Van Buren and Johnson were elected on the coattails of the popular Jackson. In fact, the Little Magician would be the last vice president nominated for president until John C. Breckinridge in 1860, and he would be the last sitting vice president elected to the presidency until George H. W. Bush in 1988.[144]

Controversy and the 1836 Election

Despite the Democrats' success in the presidential election, all did not go smoothly for Johnson at the bottom of the ticket. His lifestyle was profoundly unpopular in the slaveholding South, a dominant part of the Democratic coalition at the time.[145]

Johnson remained a bachelor all his life.[146] It was said that when he was young, his mother had opposed his marrying a woman of lower social status, and Johnson thereafter refused to marry in response to his mother's actions.[147] Instead, Johnson openly cohabited with a slave mistress, Julia Chinn.[148] In fact, Chinn handled Johnson's business dealings while he was in the nation's capital.[149] The couple had two daughters, both of whom Johnson acknowledged as his own.[150]

Chinn passed away in 1833 following a bout of cholera.[151] At some point after her passing, Johnson reportedly started a relationship with a second female slave, Patience (or Parthene) Chinn, who may have been related to Julia.[152] Johnson may have had a liaison with Patience's sister as well.[153] While the fate of these two women remains unclear, one account contends that Johnson sold one of them.[154]

In addition to widespread criticism of his relationship with female slaves, there was growing anxiety about the Kentuckian's capabilities.[155] When rumors of a Johnson vice-presidential candidacy began to circulate, future Supreme Court justice John Catron wrote to President Jackson: "I pray you to assure our friends that the humblest of us do not believe that a lucky random shot, even if did it hit Tecumseh, qualifies a man for the Vice Presidency."[156] Van Buren himself was cool to the idea of Johnson being his party's nominee for vice president.[157] But Jackson was supportive of his friend, and Johnson was duly nominated.[158]

For these reasons, in the balloting of 1836, Democratic electors from Virginia voted for Van Buren but declined to vote for Johnson.[159] As a result, Van Buren secured 170 electoral votes, but Johnson received only 147, a single vote below the required majority threshold.[160] Consequently, the Senate was forced to decide the vice presidency for the first and only time to date.[161] That year, the Whig Party had put forward four regional nominees for president and vice president. Under the Twelfth Amendment, the Senate had to consider only the top two candidates, which meant that Johnson faced off against Whig vice-presidential candidate Francis Granger of New York, who had received the second-most electoral votes. In the end, the result was anticlimactic, as the Senate voted 33 to 16 for Johnson.[162]

Johnson and the Vice Presidency

Once Johnson became vice president, he did little to prove his detractors wrong. If a vice president has the confidence of senators or if he has the president's ear, he can achieve some standing in the upper chamber. Although this was not the norm in the nineteenth century, it had been the case with his predecessor; Van Buren had been on intimate terms with President Jackson.[163] But the Little Magician had not wanted Johnson on the ticket, and the Kentuckian never earned the president's trust.[164]

Nor was Johnson a particularly conscientious presiding officer.[165] He soon developed a reputation for truancy.[166] He spent much of his time as vice president away from the chamber, tending bar at the inn he owned in Kentucky.[167] The leading authority on the vice presidency has quipped, "Johnson seemed more interested in presiding over his tavern than over the Senate."[168] In general, Johnson was blasé about the office, describing his time as vice president as "pleasant and agreeable."[169]

Nevertheless, there were some notable occurrences during Johnson's time in office. In 1837, at Clay's request, Johnson was granted the authority on two occasions to assign senators to committees.[170] This constitutes one of the rare instances of a vice president being permitted to do so.[171]

Another noteworthy event was that Johnson broke new ground when it came to casting tiebreaking votes. Over the years, some have maintained that vice presidents may break tie votes only in the context of regular legislation.[172] The applicable clause of the Constitution, however, expresses no such limitation.[173] And the Senate votes on a wide array of matters that have nothing to do with legislation.[174] Thus, the question has arisen from time to time: what is the scope of the vice president's authority? Johnson's actions helped answer this question.

It could be maintained that vice presidents are not permitted to break ties in the context of treaties because the Constitution authorizes the Senate to give its "advice and consent" and does not mention voting per se.[175] Moreover, the vice president cannot break a tie vote on the final consideration of a treaty because a two-thirds supermajority is needed; anything less means that the treaty is defeated. Amendments to treaties, however, are subject to a simple majority vote. Therefore, when presented with the opportunity, Johnson broke three ties related to treaty amendments, establishing a precedent bolstering the vice president's authority when the Senate is deadlocked in this context.[176]

Johnson's actions fit into a broader body of precedent concerning the vice president's voting authority. Vice presidents have broken ties in a wide variety of instances, including whether to give advice and consent to executive branch nominations,[177] whether to confirm judicial nominations,[178] whether to adopt private relief bills,[179] whether to request information from the executive branch,[180] whether to adjourn,[181] whether to approve preliminary matters related to the seating of a potential senator,[182] whether to appoint Senate officers,[183] whether to adhere to a sense of the Senate,[184] whether to modify a concurrent resolution,[185] whether to sustain the vice president's own parliamentary ruling,[186] whether to create a joint congressional committee,[187] whether to conduct a committee investigation,[188] whether a party constitutes a majority for purposes of organizing the Senate,[189] whether to engross and read a measure a third time,[190] whether to table a measure,[191] whether to reconsider a vote on a measure,[192] and whether to proceed to executive session.[193] In sum, history provides no example of a vice president being denied the authority to break a tie vote on any matter.[194] For these reasons, a celebrated treatise on parliamentary procedure concluded that "the Vice-President votes on all questions wherein the Senate is equally divided."[195]

The vice president's power to break ties also includes the power not to vote at all.[196] Vice President John Nance Garner took this course on a tax measure in 1939; Charles Dawes did so in 1928, as did Calvin Coolidge in 1922.[197] Vice President Thomas Marshall opted not to vote on several occasions during the Wilson administration.[198] In one instance, Marshall was remarkably frank about his reason for not breaking the deadlock: "As the Vice President knows nothing about [the amendment], he refuses to vote."[199]

In addition, vice presidents have broken ties on important substantive issues. In 1789, Adams essentially decided whether the president could remove cabinet secretaries from office.[200] On another occasion, his vote determined whether the United States would adopt trade sanctions against Great Britain, a step that might have precipitated war.[201] George Dallas used his tiebreaking vote to secure enactment of key tariff legislation in 1846.[202] Millard Fillmore was prepared to cast his tiebreaking vote in favor of the Compromise of 1850, legislation with repercussions for the very existence of the Union.[203] (Ultimately, Fillmore did not have to do so because President Zachary Taylor died and Fillmore was elevated to the presidency.) Three times the vice president's vote has essentially decided which party controls the Senate.[204] Al Gore broke a tie to adopt President Bill Clinton's first budget.[205] Dick Cheney's vote ensured adoption of major tax legislation.[206]

The vice president can cast his tiebreaking vote in any way he chooses.[207] Although the modern vice president is politically and practically subordinate to the president, this is not true *constitutionally* when he presides over the upper chamber.[208] The vice president is legally independent of the president, and this extends to his role in the Senate.[209] Indeed, Vice Presidents Aaron Burr, George Clinton, John C. Calhoun, Henry Wilson, William Wheeler, and John Nance Garner all used their tiebreaking votes in ways that were contrary to the president's policies.[210] Of course, the modern political expectation is that the vice president will support the president. President Clinton recalled that Vice President Gore used to "joke that whenever he voted, we always won."[211] Breaking tie votes may not constitute Senate leadership; nonetheless, by definition, such an action decides the outcome in the upper chamber. And that is no small thing.

* * *

Being the leader of a narrow Senate majority, I can attest to the importance of having a vice president of the same party available to break tie votes. In many ways, it is like having a "101st senator."[212] In addition, it places a premium on coordination with the vice president's office. After all, the modern vice presidency is a full-time job, and the vice president is not sitting around all day waiting to cast votes in the Senate.[213] With little margin for error, it is essential to schedule votes for times when my party members can be present in the Senate. (As in any line of work, health issues and family concerns sometimes arise.) But if it looks like the vote is going to be close, I also need to factor in when the vice president can attend. That can make for challenging scheduling from time to time. These are just some of the many considerations that a majority leader must weigh when determining when to hold votes.

* * *

After the Vice Presidency

Despite Johnson's novel exercise of the power to break tie votes, his prospects for another four years as vice president were not promising. Due to the political baggage stemming from his relationships with slave women and his generally uninspired performance in office, Democrats plotted to remove Johnson from the ticket. Former president Jackson, who had backed Johnson in 1836, withdrew his support. Old Hickory wrote to President Van Buren, "I have great respect for Col. R. M. Johnson as a brave Soldier, and a Patriot. But . . . he will be dead weight upon your ticket."[214] John Quincy Adams observed, "Col. Richard M.['s] . . . Vice-Presidential chair, it is said, is [being] . . . gently drawn from under him."[215] Several challengers for the vice presidency emerged, including future president James K. Polk.[216]

To some degree, the Democratic scheming was successful, and the party did not renominate Johnson in 1840. The Democratic National Convention put Van Buren forward for another term but substituted *no one* in Johnson's place for vice president.[217] Despite the national convention's studied inaction regarding the naming of a vice-presidential candidate, a handful of state conventions placed Johnson on the ballot.[218] In the end, it did not matter, as the Whig ticket of William Henry Harrison and John Tyler triumphed in 1840. Van Buren secured only 60 electoral votes and Johnson 48.[219] After Johnson's defeat, Clay let bygones be bygones, and on the Senate floor, he graciously commended Johnson for his public service.[220] Tellingly, none of Johnson's fellow Democrats did the same.[221]

Johnson continued to play a minor role in public life after his vice presidency. Just a few months after leaving high office, he ran for and was elected to the state legislature.[222] As one might expect, after having served as vice president, such a station was hardly satisfying. "You never saw a more restless dissatisfied man in your life, than Dick is," commented Kentucky's governor to John Crittenden.[223] John C. Calhoun (D-SC), now a senator, utterly dismissed Johnson during this period, commenting, "the days of heroes are over. . . . [Johnson is] a mass of stupidity, vulgarity, and immorality."[224]

Johnson's discontent led him to take steps to run for the presidency in 1844.[225] Part of this effort involved an attempt in 1842 to return to the Senate.[226] Johnson was crushed, however, by John Crittenden in that contest.[227] Despite his Senate defeat, Johnson continued his long-shot pursuit of the presidency, embarking on a number of speaking tours.[228] He was courteously received, but there was no great outpouring of support.[229] At the 1844 Democratic Convention, Johnson polled third among presidential candidates on the first several ballots.[230] His delegate count peaked during the third round of voting, and Polk was ultimately nominated.[231] Afterward, Johnson beseeched the Polk administration for a federal job, but without success.[232]

Remarkably, even as 1848 approached, some Democrats were still calling for Johnson to be the party's presidential nominee.[233] However, little came of the boomlet. A similar result occurred when Johnson tried to regain a Senate seat, losing to Clay this time.[234] Johnson's only future electoral triumphs would be for the state house.[235] Moreover, age was taking its toll.[236] In Frankfort, even routine duties became difficult as Johnson evinced clear signs of deteriorating health.[237] Nonetheless, he still considered a run for governor.[238] This hope was dashed by a debilitating stroke that resulted in Johnson's death in November 1850.[239] Upon his passing, state senator and future Kentucky governor Beriah Magoffin described Johnson as "the poor man's friend."[240]

Even when factoring in the serious constraints under which vice presidents operated in the nineteenth century, Johnson's time in national office cannot be viewed as a success. He was often absent from the presiding officer's chair and could point to few substantive achievements during his time in office. Indeed, he reinforced stereotypes about the vice presidency that, though no longer applicable, endure in some quarters to this day.

The decade and a half after Johnson's tenure witnessed the elevation of two vice presidents—Tyler and Fillmore—to the presidency. Tyler originated and Fillmore reaffirmed the precedent that, following the death of the chief executive, the vice president actually became the president rather than merely the acting president.[241] While this development may have enhanced the attractiveness of the vice presidency to some degree, neither Tyler nor Fillmore was nominated for president by the party that had chosen him for the number-two spot.[242] The same would hold true for Andrew Johnson and Chester Arthur—the third and fourth vice presidents elevated to the White House following the death of a president.[243] Not until Theodore Roosevelt would a vice president who had succeeded to the presidency secure his party's nomination for a presidential term of his own.[244] On the eve of the Civil War, the vice presidency was still far from being a powerful and prestigious office.

John C. Breckinridge

In its long history, the commonwealth of Kentucky has produced a number of prominent political families. In the modern era, one thinks of the Chandlers and the Combses, for example. But the most distinguished family in Kentucky political history is the Breckinridges.[245] As one newspaper expressed a century ago, the Breckinridges "have been in American public life ever since there . . . [has been] an American public life."[246]

Future senator and vice president John C. Breckinridge was born in 1821 not far from Lexington, Kentucky.[247] He was named for his grandfather, the attorney general and senator (discussed in chapter 3). Politics was in the young boy's blood. His father, Joseph—like his father before him—had been Speaker of the Kentucky House of Representatives.[248] His uncle had been chaplain of the US House.[249] Unfortunately for young John C. Breckinridge, Joseph passed away at an early age, leaving his son to grow up essentially fatherless.[250]

Nor was this the only tragedy John C. would face as a youth. Two sisters died before he turned sixteen, and the two pillars of his upbringing—his mother Mary Clay Smith Breckinridge and his grandmother Mary Hopkins Cabell Breckinridge—had a major falling out.[251] Despite the break between his mother and paternal grandmother, the latter instilled in the boy the legacy of her husband.[252] She wrote: "Oh that he may inherit all the virtues of the one he is called for[,] that he may be a John Breckingridge [sic] in every whit."[253]

At age ten, Breckinridge attended school at the Kentucky Academy.[254] Following his secondary education, he matriculated at Centre College. There, he distinguished himself with his affable demeanor and elocution, two traits that would help Breckinridge immensely in his public career. A fellow student noted Breckinridge's "readiness of wit [which made him] a happy force."[255] The same colleague commended his "acuteness in argument and felicity of expression."[256]

After graduating from Centre in 1838, Breckinridge continued his studies at Princeton.[257] Thereafter he returned to the commonwealth and learned law at the knee of future Kentucky governor William Owsley, before rounding out his legal education at Transylvania University.[258] Breckinridge was soon admitted to the bar and would cross paths with esteemed Kentucky attorneys such as John Crittenden, whose law books he was known to borrow from time to time.[259] Following a brief period practicing law in Iowa, Breckinridge returned to Kentucky for good and put down permanent roots.[260] Not long afterward, in 1843, he married Mary Burch, the cousin of his law partner.[261]

Breckinridge's Rise to Prominence

Even in his mid-twenties, Breckinridge's skill at oratory was recognized in the community. In 1847, he was approached about speaking at a large military funeral in Frankfort for the Kentucky soldiers who had fallen during the Mexican-American War.[262] In front of at least 15,000 spectators, Breckinridge delivered a moving address.[263]

His reputation for public speaking grew markedly after the Frankfort speech.[264] One newspaperman wrote in the 1850s, "I have heard many speakers, [including] Daniel Webster . . . but for pure, soul stirring eloquence, John C. Breckinridge stands unrivalled."[265] Another journalist described his public speaking in similarly glowing terms: "His mind, thought and mode of expression are clear, explicit and intelligent, his manners dignified, courteous and pleasing. His diction is that of a scholar and man of taste, always selecting the appropriate word and placing it in the right position, all of which give to his speaking efforts the air of a finished and eloquent composition."[266]

In addition, Breckinridge had a pleasing personal demeanor.[267] Though not extroverted or charismatic, he had a genial quality that almost invariably left a favorable impression. It was said by one admirer that in his company you felt "you were in the presence of true greatness, and yet no one felt abashed for his manner was so charming and so natural that you liked him at once."[268]

He cut a dashing figure. Contemporaries repeatedly emphasized his striking appearance, which drew people to him.[269] One described Breckinridge while the Kentuckian was an officer during the Civil War: "Breckinridge [has a] knightly bearing and noble dignity—tall, strongly knit in bone and sinew, with a graceful carriage, an open, unreserved expression of countenance . . . he reminds one [of] a hero who has accidentally stepped out of one of Sir Walter Scott's poems."[270]

And of course, Breckinridge had the advantage of his distinguished pedigree. Clay once counseled the future vice president: "Be true to your name. Never forget that you are a Kentuckian and a Breckinridge, and the highest honors of the Republic . . . will be your glorious reward."[271]

Shortly after his 1847 Frankfort speech, Breckinridge joined the Mexican-American War as an officer, having been recommended for the position by Crittenden.[272] Breckinridge never saw action, however, and returned to Kentucky after spending almost nine months away.[273] He then made his initial foray into the political arena, winning a seat in the state house as a Democrat. He quickly established himself as a legislative leader.[274]

During this time, Breckinridge befriended a state lawmaker from Illinois who was staying with his in-laws in central Kentucky. That legislator was Abraham Lincoln.[275] In a decade and a half, these two men would vie for the presidency against each other, and not long thereafter, they would hold senior executive branch positions on opposite sides of the Civil War.

In the early 1850s, Breckinridge's star was on the rise. He was a pro-slavery Democrat who owned slaves himself.[276] Breckinridge vigorously contended that the federal government lacked the authority to impede slavery in the individual states, the territories, or the nation's capital.[277] Elected to Congress from Clay's old district, previously a bastion of the Whig Party, Breckinridge's victory propelled him into the national spotlight and forecast the overall decline of Whig fortunes.[278]

As was the case in Frankfort, Breckinridge's forensic ability stood him in good stead in the US House of Representatives. He quickly developed a reputation as one of its premier debaters.[279] Before long, reports were circulating that Breckinridge might be a candidate for Speaker.[280] Although that position ultimately went to fellow Kentuckian Linn Boyd, Breckinridge won a coveted seat on the powerful Ways and Means Committee.[281]

In Congress, Breckinridge was an important advocate of the Kansas-Nebraska Act of 1854, which upended Clay's Missouri Compromise of 1820.[282] (Opposition to this measure prompted the creation of the Republican Party.) The measure reflected a policy euphemistically known as "popular sovereignty." Under this approach, the people of a federal territory could determine for themselves whether that territory should be admitted into the Union as a free state or a slave state. With his newly acquired stature, Breckinridge labored hard to promote the Kansas-Nebraska legislation.[283] He even worked to convince a wavering President Franklin Pierce to sign the deeply divisive legislation.[284] Through his active stance on this controversial bill, Breckinridge emerged not only as a leading figure in the House but also as a prominent voice for the entire South.[285]

By 1856, Breckinridge's stature had grown to the point that he was selected as James Buchanan's running mate. The pairing of the Pennsylvanian Buchanan and the Kentuckian Breckinridge—"Buck and Breck"—provided geographic balance to the ticket.[286] (That same year, another native son of the commonwealth, former Illinois state lawmaker Abraham Lincoln, made a respectable showing in an attempt to gain the vice-presidential nomination of the newly formed Republican Party, but ultimately fell short.)[287] Breckinridge's popularity helped the Democrats carry Kentucky for the first time in more than a quarter century, and the Democratic ticket triumphed. The Kentuckian became the youngest vice president in American history, a distinction he still enjoys.[288]

Breckinridge and the Vice Presidency

Breckinridge's term as the nation's fourteenth vice president was not a happy one. Whereas the Kentuckian had benefited from a strong relationship with President Pierce when he had served in the House, he and Buchanan were not personally close.[289] Breckinridge supported Buchanan for president only after the Kentuckian's first two choices—Pierce and Senator Stephen Douglas (D-IL)—had been defeated for the nomination.[290] Nonetheless, the Democratic National Convention chose Breckinridge to run alongside the Pennsylvanian, reflecting the reality of vice-presidential selection at the time: by and large, party conventions and political bosses—not presidential candidates—chose vice-presidential nominees.[291] Such a practice led to many awkward pairings, including Buchanan and Breckinridge. Not until 1940 did the tradition of presidential candidates essentially choosing their own vice-presidential nominees start to take root.[292]

Since presidents did not typically select their vice presidents in the first century and a half under the Constitution, chief executives felt no "ownership" of their running mates and therefore had little reason to include them in decision making.[293] By the same token, vice presidents had little reason to "follow the company line," and on occasion, they acted contrary to administration policy.[294] Indeed, Breckinridge's public positions differed from Buchanan's from time to time. For example, the two men publicly disagreed on the rightful capital of Kansas, an important issue associated with the tragedy of "Bleeding Kansas" in the late 1850s.[295] The Kentuckian also supported Douglas—Buchanan's nemesis—for reelection to the Senate.[296]

The Buchanan-Breckinridge relationship, which had been cool to begin with, never fully recovered from an episode that occurred early in their term. In response to Breckinridge's request for a private meeting with the president, Buchanan encouraged the vice president to meet with his niece, who was acting as the bachelor president's hostess.[297] Whether Buchanan meant to frustrate or facilitate Breckinridge's request is unclear.[298] Either way, Breckinridge took umbrage at Buchanan's reply, and the relationship soured.[299]

Adlai Stevenson, Kentucky's third vice president, had a distant relationship with his own running mate, Grover Cleveland. Stevenson relayed an anecdote about Breckinridge that reflected his own experience in the second office: Later in life, someone inquired of Breckinridge if he had ever been asked to advise Buchanan on a public matter.[300] Breckinridge drolly replied: "He did consult me once. He sent for me one evening to come to the White House. As I was ushered into the library he solemnly drew a document from the inner pocket of his coat and said: 'Mr. Vice-President, I have here my Thanksgiving Proclamation, the phraseology of which I desire to submit to your critical opinion and judgment.'"[301] Apocryphal or not, the story reflects the strained relationship and that Breckinridge's advice was seldom sought.[302]

The single substantive executive branch assignment Breckinridge was asked to perform was not an enviable one: Buchanan urged the Kentuckian to request the resignation of Secretary of War John Floyd.[303] Breckinridge complied, and Floyd ultimately stepped down.[304] This task, however, was the exception that proved the rule. As was the case with most vice presidents in the nineteenth century, Breckinridge largely had to content himself with presiding over the Senate.

Breckinridge did participate in some notable events in his role as president of the Senate. For instance, in 1859, he gave the valedictory address in the old Senate chamber and then led the procession of lawmakers from there to the Senate's current location within the Capitol.[305] In so doing, he bade farewell to the old chamber and welcomed the Senate to its new home.[306]

Like Johnson, Breckinridge expanded the scope of the vice president's power to break ties. Whereas Johnson was the first vice president to break ties in the context of treaties, Breckinridge established the precedent of breaking ties related to modifications of potential constitutional amendments.[307] Although final passage of constitutional amendments requires a two-thirds vote in the Senate, proposed changes to constitutional amendments are decided by a simple majority and can end in deadlock (similar to the case with amendments to treaties).

Breckinridge's tiebreaking vote concerned a modification to a proposed constitutional amendment that would have made slavery permanent in the United States. The Kentuckian broke the tie, establishing a constitutional interpretation that the vice president can indeed cast a vote in this setting. Happily, the constitutional amendment Breckinridge voted to modify was never adopted. However, his actions would be followed decades later by Vice President James Sherman in consideration of what would later become the Seventeenth Amendment.[308]

Despite the dismal performance of the Buchanan administration, Breckinridge remained popular, particularly in the South.[309] There, the Kentuckian was widely seen as presidential timber.[310] By 1860, however, the nation was unraveling due to sectional discord. The Democratic Party reflected this reality and had essentially split in two. It held competing presidential nominating conventions, where Breckinridge was selected as the presidential standard-bearer for the southern wing and Douglas for the northern wing.

In the general election, Breckinridge faced not only Douglas but also John Bell of the Constitutional Union Party and another native Kentuckian, Abraham Lincoln.[311] The candidates split the vote four ways, and Lincoln prevailed. Breckinridge did not even carry his home state.

As a lame-duck vice president, Breckinridge did his best to head off civil war. He worked behind the scenes to promote the "Crittenden Compromise."[312] Using the prestige of his national profile, as well as his role as the Senate's presiding officer, Breckinridge convened a host of meetings with senators to try to arrive at an acceptable accommodation.[313] He also used his authority to name members to an ad hoc committee in an attempt to resolve the crisis.[314] Although these efforts were ultimately unsuccessful, they showed Breckinridge exercising (or trying to exercise) some measure of Senate influence.

One of the vice president's overlooked roles is presiding over the quadrennial joint session of Congress that counts the Electoral College votes in national elections.[315] Today, this is essentially a pro forma exercise, but given the great divisiveness following Lincoln's election, there was speculation that Breckinridge—as one of the losing candidates—might act to frustrate Lincoln's election.[316] Tensions ran so high ahead of the ceremony that Breckinridge felt the need to confer with General Winfield Scott about security.[317] Scott ringed the Capitol building with military personnel and assigned others to the chamber of the House where the counting was to take place.[318] As the process got under way, one southern lawmaker, in an incendiary move, formally requested that Breckinridge have Scott's troops removed from the chamber.[319] Breckinridge did not take the bait and calmly announced Lincoln's victory.[320]

Breckinridge in the Senate and the Confederate Army

As President Lincoln and Vice President Hannibal Hamlin took office, Breckinridge's tenure in the vice presidency ended, but his public career did not. Like Alben Barkley nearly a century later, Breckinridge served as a senator following his time as vice president.[321] Although defeated for the presidency in 1860, Breckinridge had managed to get himself elected to the Senate a few months earlier by the Kentucky legislature.[322] This led to an unusual sequence of events. On March 4, 1861, the outgoing vice president administered the constitutional oath to Hamlin, the incoming vice president, and then concluded the Senate session.[323] Vice President Hamlin then immediately convened a new session of the Senate and proceeded to swear in the class of newly elected senators, which included Breckinridge.[324]

The Kentuckian had managed to exercise some modest influence in the Senate as vice president, but as a senator, Breckinridge's standing in the chamber was greatly diminished. A major portion of the southern senators—his natural allies—had withdrawn from the chamber as their states seceded from the

Union.[325] The nation had begun its headlong plunge into civil war, and as a result, the Senate was far less receptive to the views of a southern supporter.[326] The immediate change in Breckinridge's Senate standing reflects the contextual nature of power in the upper chamber.

Breckinridge remained in the Senate for several months, even after hostilities began.[327] His southern sympathies prompted his removal from the Senate Committee on Military Affairs (the precursor to today's Armed Services Committee).[328] During this time, Breckinridge often took to the Senate floor to sharply criticize President Lincoln's efforts to preserve the Union.[329] This led to a dramatic, heated exchange between Breckinridge and Senator Edward Baker (R-OR), who had just returned to the Senate wearing his regiment's uniform after participating in military exercises at Fort Monroe.[330] This colloquy culminated when Baker asked if Breckinridge's eloquence did not constitute "words of brilliant, polished treason."[331] Not long afterward, Baker was cut down in a hail of Confederate gunfire at the Battle of Balls Bluff, the lone sitting senator to be killed in battle.[332]

Not long afterward, Breckinridge joined the Confederacy as a brigadier general, even though Kentucky remained loyal to the Union. He was expelled from the Senate in December 1861 by a 36–0 vote, one of fifteen senators to suffer this fate.[333] (Kentucky's other senator at the time, Democrat Lazarus Powell, was charged in 1862 with aiding the southern cause. At the behest of fellow Kentucky Democrat Garrett Davis, he was investigated but not expelled from the Senate and completed his term.)[334]

By most accounts, Breckinridge was an effective military officer.[335] He was courageous in battle and well regarded by his men.[336] He fought at the Battles of Shiloh, Chickamauga, and Chattanooga and won the respect of General Robert E. Lee.[337] Perhaps most notably, in 1864, Breckinridge and General Jubal Early led a Confederate invasion aimed at Washington, DC.[338] The unit reached the outskirts of the city, where the men could see the recently completed Capitol dome.[339] Confederate general John B. Gordon recalled that "General Early and his division commanders were considering in [a] jocular vein the propriety of putting General John C. Breckinridge at the head of the column and of escorting him to the Senate chamber and seating him again in the Vice-President's chair."[340] Ultimately, northern forces repulsed the rebel raid.

Despite his unsuccessful effort to take Washington, Breckinridge's military talents were sufficiently impressive for him to be elevated to Confederate secretary of war in 1865. In this post, he opposed the idea of the South conducting a guerrilla war against the North following General Lee's surrender at Appomattox.[341]

After the collapse of the Confederacy, Breckinridge—like many of his senior rebel colleagues—was a marked man. He eluded Union troops in dramatic fashion, making his way through Florida and then on to Cuba.[342] Breckinridge lived in exile in Cuba before moving to Europe and finally settling in Canada.[343] In 1868, in an effort to heal the wounds of war, President Andrew Johnson bestowed Christmas Day pardons on Breckinridge and scores of other former Confederates.[344]

The pardon permitted Breckinridge to return to Kentucky the next year, and he resumed the practice of law.[345] The former vice president and senator also became actively involved with promoting railroad construction.[346] In this capacity, he eschewed public matters, with the exception of condemning the violent actions of the Ku Klux Klan.[347] Less than a decade after the end of the Civil War, Breckinridge's health began to fail, and he passed away in 1875 from cirrhosis of the liver.[348]

In many ways, John C. Breckinridge's legacy is one of unfulfilled promise. Had he lived during quieter times, he might have become president. Instead, his career was cut short by his decision to support the Confederacy.

The Evolution of the Vice Presidency

Following Breckinridge's tenure, the vice presidency continued as a largely underutilized institution for several more decades. Although his immediate successor, Hannibal Hamlin, and later William Wheeler and Chester Arthur made the odd appearance at cabinet sessions, the "second office" did not achieve steady gains until after World War I.[349] The tenure of Thomas Marshall witnessed a significant development.[350] At the end of World War I, President Woodrow Wilson decided to attend the Versailles Peace Conference and determined that the vice president should join cabinet proceedings during his absence.[351] Marshall obliged and attended one such meeting.[352] In turn, President Warren Harding asked Calvin Coolidge to sit with the cabinet for the entirety of his term; since then, every vice president save one has participated in these meetings.[353]

Vice-presidential inclusion in the cabinet began the slow, steady trend of the office's greater involvement in the executive branch.[354] Gradually, vice presidents picked up new responsibilities.[355] The reciprocal of this trend was that vice presidents spent less time presiding over the Senate. One authority maintains that Senate action actually hastened—albeit unintentionally—this slow vice-presidential migration. Earl Shoup argues that the Senate's 1890 decision to permit presidents pro tempore to serve uninterrupted two-year terms, coupled with a few minor Senate rules changes a few years later, freed vice presidents to absent themselves more often from the chamber and take on more executive branch responsibilities.[356]

The vast expansion of the work of the executive branch following the New Deal and World War II provided an opportunity for presidents to assign more nonlegislative tasks to vice presidents.[357] Presidents needed help, and vice presidents were eager to provide it, happy to shed the tedium of presiding over the Senate.[358] John Nance Garner was an important adviser to President Franklin D. Roosevelt during the early years of the New Deal.[359] Henry Wallace, FDR's second vice president, chaired the Board of Economic Warfare, which was responsible for obtaining strategic materials for US efforts in World War II.[360]

National political campaigns evolved as well, which reinforced trends in governance that were already under way. To that end, presidential candidates increasingly began to choose their own running mates after 1940.[361] As such, chief executives developed a stake in vice-presidential success.[362] This enhanced the trend of vice presidents receiving favorable assignments from presidents.[363]

Greater vice-presidential participation in the executive branch also had the salutary effect of better preparing vice presidents should tragedy befall the chief executive. There seemed to be some recognition that Vice President Harry Truman's ignorance of the Manhattan Project at the time of his presidential elevation was not a good model to follow.[364] Truman therefore persuaded Congress to include Vice President Alben Barkley as a statutory member of the National Security Council (NSC).[365] The "Iron Man" from Paducah would in fact be the last officeholder to dedicate a considerable portion of his workday to serving as Senate presiding officer.[366]

President Dwight Eisenhower sent Vice President Richard Nixon on extensive overseas trips.[367] Nixon also presided at meetings of the cabinet and NSC during Eisenhower's health scares.[368] President John F. Kennedy granted Vice President Lyndon Johnson office space next to the White House.[369] The Twenty-Fifth Amendment, which was ratified in 1967, underscored the vice president's growing executive branch role.[370] For instance, the amendment authorized the vice president to work with the cabinet to determine presidential incapacity.[371] Subsequent vice presidents, such as Spiro Agnew, Gerald Ford, and Nelson Rockefeller, each gained perquisites, including a line item within the president's budget, enhanced staff resources, and regular private meetings with the president.[372]

The vice-presidential office reached new heights under Walter Mondale.[373] He was copied on the paper flow into the chief executive, was permitted to join all presidential meetings, and established himself as a high-profile adviser and problem solver.[374] Mondale's expanded role as vice president quickly became the norm for his successors.[375] Indeed, Vice President Richard Cheney took Mondale's model to an even greater level of influence, playing a leading role in a number of policy areas.[376]

Modern Vice-Presidential Influence in the Senate

Because contemporary vice presidents have assumed major executive branch responsibilities, they spend little time in the Senate chamber.[377] Yet, despite the vice president's declining participation in Senate proceedings, the officeholder can still be influential in formal legislative settings from time to time.[378] The vice president's power to break tie votes remains an important prerogative. For instance, Vice President Mike Pence's vote secured Senate advice and consent for a cabinet secretary.[379] Vice Presidents Gore and Cheney each helped ensure that their fellow partisans controlled the Senate during early 2001.[380]

In addition, the vice president's power to recognize legislators seeking the floor—though circumscribed by precedent and less broad in scope than that of the Speaker of the House—can still be important on occasion.[381] In part, this is true because the presiding officer's decision as to which senator to recognize cannot be appealed.[382] Vice President Rockefeller, for example, used his power of recognition in an assertive fashion during a 1975 debate.[383] He refused to recognize opponents of his position, which aroused considerable ire.[384] The power of the presiding officer in this regard also enabled Vice President Truman in 1945 to help secure the confirmation of former vice president Henry Wallace to serve as secretary of commerce.[385]

In addition, the vice president may make parliamentary rulings.[386] Although these rulings may be overturned by the Senate, they have occasionally proved important and enduring. Action by Vice President Garner formalized the authority of the Senate majority leader to command the floor if no other member is speaking.[387] This has become the most important formal power at the majority leader's disposal.[388] Furthermore, there is agitation from time to time for the vice president to change Senate interpretations of rules that favor certain policy outcomes.

Vice presidents also sign and authenticate passed bills.[389] Although this function is essentially ministerial, the Supreme Court has observed that this action by the vice president (or his stand-in as presiding officer) can help determine whether a measure has been properly adopted by Congress.[390] As such, in certain types of adjudication, the Supreme Court has viewed the act of authentication as a consideration when weighing the constitutionality of legislation.[391] Finally, the vice president has the authority to ensure order and decorum in the Senate.[392] As a practical matter, this authority is usually more theoretical than real.

* * *

Depending on his political skills, his relationship with the president, his ties with senators, and the context in which he operates, a vice president can assume an infor-

mal leadership role in the body from time to time.[393] *Indeed, I can recall this happening firsthand. On three occasions—in 2010 with the extension of the President George W. Bush–era tax rates, in 2011 with the Budget Control Act, and in 2012 with legislation to avert the "fiscal cliff" crisis—Vice President Joe Biden essentially assumed leadership of the Senate Democrats.*[394] *As a practical matter, Biden temporarily sidelined Senate majority leader Harry Reid (D-NV) and negotiated these three legislative deals with me to prevent the occurrence of potentially damaging economic consequences.*

* * *

Cheney was an important legislative player in the George W. Bush administration, particularly during the early years. With regard to the presiding officer's role, Cheney remarked that he "considered it an asset."[395] He was instrumental in securing tax-cut legislation in 2001 and 2003, helping to bridge the gap between the two houses when their relations had grown strained.[396] In addition, Cheney was a successful advocate on Capitol Hill with regard to the Iraq War authorization and the 2008 financial rescue package.[397]

Interestingly, Vice President Garner achieved a high level of legislative stature in the late 1930s in part due to his *independence from* the president.[398] Following the debacle of President Roosevelt's Court-packing scheme, in which he tried to expand the Supreme Court and fill it with ideological allies, the president's standing with Congress plummeted. To some extent, Garner stepped in to fill the void. The *Los Angeles Times* reported, "Vice-President Garner and not President Roosevelt emerges as the leader of the Democratic party in Congress, or at least the Senate, as a result of yesterday's court-fight developments. . . . [Regarding] future New Deal legislation he will have to be consulted beforehand, and . . . his veto is very apt to be final."[399]

As their second term progressed, and as Garner and Roosevelt drifted further away from each other, the vice president increasingly allied himself with disaffected conservative Democrats who held positions of influence in the Senate.[400] As such, Garner was a major force to be reckoned with in the chamber. For example, Garner was delegated the power to appoint senators to conference committees and ad hoc panels, and he was not afraid to exercise this authority independently from Roosevelt.[401]

Garner's quiet legislative opposition to the president is fairly rare in the modern era. More typical are vice presidents working as administration liaisons to Capitol Hill (as Garner had done during FDR's first term).[402] The vice president and his staff have office space right off the Senate floor. Cheney and Pence managed to secure office space on the House side of the Capitol, even though the vice president plays no formal role in the lower chamber.[403] Biden—a former senator—kept a locker at the Senate fitness center to facilitate his liaison role.[404]

* * *

Some vice presidents have been regular participants at the weekly lunches of senators from the same party. Vice Presidents Pence and Cheney have done this.[405] I have found it very useful to have Cheney and Pence at our lunches. It enhances information flow between the Senate and the executive branch.

* * *

From the prestigious (party lunches) to the prosaic (gym lockers), these links are all informal outgrowths of the vice president's formal role as presiding officer of the Senate. They make it easier for vice presidents to serve as legislative go-betweens for the executive branch. In this regard, many recent vice presidents have served as legislative liaisons and advocates for the administrations they served, as well as demonstrating some degree of influence in the Senate.

Vice-presidential success in the legislative arena is far from assured, however. Vice President Spiro Agnew had his difficulties, for example. At one point, while on the Senate floor, he attempted to lobby Senator Len Jordan (R-ID) on tax legislation.[406] Jordan was offended and replied: "You had . . . [my vote] until now."[407] Jordan promised to vote against any future measure Agnew approached him about.[408]

Vice-presidential power of this sort—like much of the power wielded in the chamber—is personal in nature. As Garner himself noted, "only if by his association with men [in the Senate] they come to have friendship for him and faith in and respect for his judgment can he [the vice president] be influential."[409] The examples of Biden, Cheney, and Garner demonstrate that the president of the Senate can, from time to time, exert influence and—on rare occasions—even assume a leadership role in the Senate for a brief period.

The vice presidencies of Richard Mentor Johnson and John C. Breckenridge reflect the unfulfilled promise of Senate leadership by nineteenth-century vice presidents. On paper, the president of the Senate has the potential to play a major role in Senate affairs; however, with a few modern exceptions, this has not been the case in practice. An impressive formal title is not sufficient to exercise real leadership in the chamber; there are simply significant limitations on the vice president's power in the Senate. In time, other institutions would fill this void.

2

President Pro Tempore

John Brown and John Pope

Article I, section 3, of the US Constitution provides that "the Senate shall chuse their other Officers, and also a President pro tempore, in the Absence of the Vice President, or when he shall exercise the Office of President of the United States."[1] As it does with regard to the vice presidency, the bare text of the Constitution holds out the promise that the position of president pro tempore could entail real Senate leadership.[2]

Indeed, the president pro tempore has some potential in this realm that the vice president lacks.[3] First, unlike the vice president, the president pro tempore is a senator (although, strictly speaking, he is not required to be).[4] Consequently, he can vote on all matters, serve on committees, speak on the floor, introduce bills, offer amendments, and make motions.[5] The vice president can vote only when there is a tie, and in the modern era, he speaks only with the indulgence of the Senate.[6] Second, because the president pro tempore is elected and can be removed by the Senate, he is accountable to the chamber.[7] Thus, unlike the vice president, he is not an outsider foisted upon the membership.[8] Moreover, the modern president pro tempore is a member of the Senate majority party, which may not be the case with the vice president.[9] Third, the president pro tempore has an acknowledged authority to delegate his responsibility. For instance, in the nineteenth and early twentieth centuries, the Senate established the principle that the president pro tempore could select a senator to preside temporarily in his absence, a prerogative the vice president does not enjoy.[10] However, despite these advantages enjoyed by the president pro tempore over the vice president, it did not take long for the Senate to determine that neither of them would lead the chamber in a true sense, except under unusual circumstances.[11]

Kentucky has produced two presidents pro tempore: John Brown and John Pope. Both were among the first senators from the commonwealth, and their life stories serve as a backdrop to discussion of the position of president pro tempore.

John Brown

John Brown was born in Virginia in 1757, thirty-five years before Kentucky became a state.[12] Brown was the son of a Presbyterian minister of the same name and Margaret Preston, who hailed from one of the Old Dominion's most venerable families.[13] Margaret's sister would marry Robert Breckinridge, father of future senator John Breckinridge, who is discussed in the next chapter.[14]

Unfortunately, much of Brown's upbringing is lost to history.[15] The death of his twin brother is one of the few scraps of information that has survived.[16] It is known that Brown was part of a large family with nine other siblings.[17] Apparently, he inherited an interest in public life from his parents, especially his father, who served in the House of Burgesses.[18] Young John would not be the only Brown sibling to rise to prominence in political circles. His brother James represented Louisiana in the US Senate from 1813 to 1817 and from 1819 to 1823, at one point chairing the Foreign Relations Committee.[19] Education was undoubtedly emphasized in Brown's youth. The Reverend Brown taught for two decades and played a role in the founding of Liberty Hall Academy, which would later become Washington College (and eventually Washington and Lee University).[20] John named his future home after his alma mater.[21]

Upon reaching adulthood, Brown became a man of sturdy build.[22] His son recalled that Brown was "not brought up in the lap of luxury, but in the vigorous nature of the western border[s], accustomed to labor in the field, to hunt in the forest and to excel in manly exercises. As a necessary consequence of such early habits [he] grew up with fine physical developments, and with a fearless and adventurous cast of character."[23] Yet his hearty exterior belied a reserved nature.[24] One historian described Brown as "shy and severely restrained, [and] sensitive to rebuffs."[25] Brown himself conceded that he had a "natural bashfulness."[26]

He was clearly a highly capable young man, attending Washington College, Princeton, and the College of William and Mary.[27] Following his studies, Brown was a teacher for a number of years.[28] During that time, he cultivated some powerful patrons in Virginia.[29] His legal training was conducted under the tutelage of the nation's first law professor, George Wythe; a future attorney general and secretary of state, Edmund Randolph; and a future president, Thomas Jefferson.[30]

Brown relished studying under the Sage of Monticello. The future Kentuckian resided only a short distance from Jefferson's home and found his time there was "as happ[y] as I could wish," as the president-to-be supplied him with "the necessary books and proper instructions."[31] In 1788, Brown wrote to Jefferson: "I must in Justice to my feelings express my gratitude for many favors I have rec'd from you; be assured that they have made a lasting impression upon my mind & that it is in a great measure to your friendship & Instruction that I am indebted for my success in life."[32] His relationship with Jefferson would become an important asset in future years.[33]

In 1783, Brown traveled westward to a relatively unspoiled part of Virginia that would eventually become Kentucky.[34] There, in Danville, he practiced law and became politically active.[35] Like many attorneys in early Kentucky, much of his business involved disputed land titles.[36] Lawful title was uncertain in the newly settled state, leading one contemporary to write that anyone buying property in Kentucky "buys a law-suit with every plot of unoccupied land."[37]

Brown's comportment and intellect impressed those around him. One contemporary wrote, "competent people tell me that in Virginia he is inferior only to Mr. Madison."[38] With such talents, Brown was soon encouraged to stand for public office. In 1784, he started his political career as a member of the Virginia state senate, where he served for four years.[39] Not long afterward, Brown was appointed to the Confederation Congress, where he was the youngest representative at the time.[40]

In the 1780s, many people in the western part of the state concluded that they should separate from Virginia.[41] These future Kentuckians felt that the government in Richmond was inattentive to their needs.[42] In particular, these western settlers placed a premium on defending themselves from Native American raids and securing navigation rights on the Mississippi River.[43] It was thought that only through statehood could these concerns be adequately addressed. But the split from Virginia was far from inevitable, and the statehood movement faced numerous setbacks.

During the late 1780s and early 1790s, Brown was unrelenting in his advocacy for statehood for Kentucky.[44] As a leading member of the Political Club in Danville, he agitated toward that end.[45] While in the Confederation Congress in 1788, Brown submitted a measure to authorize Kentucky's detachment from Virginia.[46] Though unsuccessful in this attempt, for the next few years, Brown remained dogged in his efforts.[47]

Also in 1788, Brown became a passionate supporter of another cause: ratifying the new federal Constitution that had been drafted the year before in Philadelphia. Although Brown himself was not elected to the Virginia ratifying convention, he wrote scores of letters to the delegates urging them to support the proposed charter, which, in Brown's words, would establish "a system of government upon which in my opinion the peace and glory of the United States depend."[48] This was not a popular position for the future Kentuckian to take, as the overwhelming majority of delegates from that region of Virginia voted against adoption of the Constitution.[49] Ultimately, by a vote of 89 to 79, the pro-ratification forces prevailed. Virginia, of course, would prove pivotal to the national process of ratifying the new Constitution.

Under the new national government, Brown was elected to serve in the first federal Congress as a representative from Virginia.[50] He advocated for Kentucky statehood with anyone in authority who would listen, including President George Washington and Secretary of War Henry Knox.[51] In this regard, Brown's friendship with Jefferson, who was secretary of state at the time, may have provided entrée into the upper echelons of the executive branch.[52]

In the House, he allied himself with fellow lawmaker James Madison, who had been impressed by Brown's advocacy for the Constitution.[53] Later in life, Madison recalled: "I owe it to Mr. Brown with whom I was in intimate friendship when we were associated in public life, to observe that I always regarded him, whilst steadily attentive to the interests of his constituents, as duly impressed with the importance of the Union, and anxious for its prosperity."[54]

Self-conscious about his abilities as an orator, Brown spoke infrequently in the House.[55] Regrettably, one of his few speeches as a congressman involved his support for the slave trade.[56] His views and actions in this regard, however, would soften over time.[57] On the positive side of the ledger, Brown made the procedural motion that ensured the House's consent to Kentucky becoming a state.[58] This marked the culmination of years of effort by Brown and his allies.

Brown in the Senate

Following Kentucky statehood in 1792, the legislature elected Brown to be one of the commonwealth's first two senators. The other was John Edwards (Anti-Admin.). On November 5, 1792, the two men were seated as senators, and four days later, they drew lots to see which of them would have to run immediately for reelection.[59] Brown "drew the short straw" and had to run again; nevertheless, he was duly reelected to the Senate in December 1792.[60]

Although parties were not as formalized as they are now, Brown was a Democratic-Republican. That group was composed of followers of Jefferson, and it dominated Kentucky politics for decades. Indeed, Kentucky elected only one member of the Federalist Party to the Senate: Humphrey Marshall, who served from 1795 to 1801.[61]

In the 1790s, Kentucky was still very much the frontier. It was sparsely settled by people of European and African descent, and those populations were vulnerable to attack by Native American tribes.[62] Establishing security for the fledgling state remained paramount, and Brown was a key player in trying to address the issue. President Washington regularly consulted with him about steps the federal government might take to protect the country's western border against Indian raids.[63] Congress created a board to examine various policy options, and Brown was named a member.[64] The panel recommended military action, which led to a disastrous campaign under the command of General

Arthur St. Clair.[65] It would take several years and repeated military interventions before Kentuckians felt safe from the threat of Native American attacks.

Even though Washington sought his advice on matters pertaining to Kentucky's security, Brown remained skeptical of many of the administration's initiatives. As a Jeffersonian, he did not support, for example, Secretary of the Treasury Alexander Hamilton's policies.[66] And he opposed the Jay Treaty.[67] Despite his opposition to many Federalist policies in the 1790s, Brown was well regarded for his moderation and his temperament.[68] Apparently in part for this reason, he was later elected to serve as president pro tempore from October 17 to December 6, 1803.[69] Senator John Taylor (D-VA) recalled an informal party gathering that facilitated Brown's election: "The evening before the Senate met, several members (whether designedly or accidentally I know not) fell in company and consulted as to a fit person for president pro tempore; it being understood that the vice president was absent."[70] The group chose Brown, and the Senate followed suit.[71] Brown presided over the Senate when it considered legislation to implement the Louisiana Purchase, a measure that would have a profound impact on Kentucky's fortunes and those of the nation as a whole.[72]

The Kentuckian's second election as president pro tempore proved more difficult. Many of Brown's fellow Democratic-Republicans considered his earlier rulings from the chair too nonpartisan, and they refused to support him for a second term.[73] Senator William Plumer (Fed.-NH) recalled: "After seven repeated trials John Brown was elected President pro temp. of the Senate. The senators from Virginia & others set up Mr. Franklin from North Carolina—& had not several of the Federalists voted for Brown, Franklin would eventually have been chosen. . . . The most *violent* censure the moderation of Mr. Brown, & were mortified at his election."[74] Episodes such as Brown's noncommittal posture on the impeachment of Federalist-appointed judge John Pickering suggest why Jeffersonians were cool toward Brown's candidacy the second time around. Senator Plumer reported, "Mr. John Brown . . . [was] said to be inclined to vote against convicting of the Accused; but being a Democrat, & unwilling to offend his party, obtained leave of absence for the residue of the session."[75] Brown was clearly less partisan than his cousin, John Breckinridge.[76] For instance, Brown had serious misgivings as to the wisdom of Breckinridge's efforts to repeal the Judiciary Act of 1801, though he ultimately held his nose and supported the measure.[77]

Brown served his second term as president pro tempore from January 23 to February 26, 1804.[78] During these two stretches of time, Brown was second in the line of succession to the presidency, behind only Vice President Aaron Burr.[79] Indeed, Burr was indisposed at the time of Brown's second election as president pro tempore.[80]

Brown's Marriage

John Brown married late in life. In 1799, at the age of forty-two, he wed Margaretta Mason, a highly cultivated New Yorker who was sixteen years his junior.[81] The two would have five children, although three died at a young age.[82] The couple appear to have been devoted to each other. Their bond is demonstrated by a heartfelt letter Margaretta sent to her husband in 1802, while he was in Washington and she remained in Kentucky: "Life is too short and too barren in happiness, to admit of such great deductions from the few joys it can boast; and conjugal felicity such as ours, is too rare, and too valuable to be sacrificed to anything but imperious necessity. It is my most earnest desire my love, that you may find our separation as painful as I do."[83] Margaretta was also a pious woman. In 1819, she established and taught at a Sunday school for girls and later published a book about religious terminology.[84]

Despite their personal closeness, the couple was known to have serious political disagreements. Margaretta did not share her husband's Jeffersonian philosophy. She opposed "the leveling principle of democracy even though her husband was a zealous democrat."[85] Brown, in turn, was critical of Margaretta's "aristocratic notions."[86]

Brown's Legacy

Brown was reelected to the Senate for a third time and sought a fourth term in 1804. Leading efforts to reelect Brown in his fourth race was a young state lawmaker named Henry Clay.[87] One suspects that Brown's moderation and hesitation to toe the Democratic-Republican Party line in the Senate worked against him in this final race.[88] For instance, Brown was criticized in some quarters for his "taciturnity in Congress."[89] Ultimately, Brown was defeated in the state legislature and never returned to federal office.[90]

Brown remained active, however, in the years after his Senate career. Returning to Frankfort, he continued his legal practice and played a prominent role in the local affairs of central Kentucky.[91] For a time, Brown served as county sheriff.[92] He was active on the board responsible for constructing the state capitol building (today called the Old State Capitol), and he participated in the establishment of the Kentucky Historical Society.[93] Brown was active in private ventures as well. He became a leading businessman and helped establish the Bank of Kentucky and the Frankfort Water Company.[94] In addition, he administered large landholdings in Kentucky and Ohio.[95]

When eminent figures stopped in Frankfort, they routinely visited Kentucky's aging patriarch.[96] Aaron Burr, the former vice president, visited Brown's home, Liberty Hall, in 1805.[97] In 1819, Brown and his wife had the rare honor of hosting a sitting president and two future chief executives simultaneously when they broke bread with President James Monroe, General Andrew Jackson, and Major Zachary Taylor.[98] Six years later, the Marquis de Lafayette met the couple at their home.[99]

As Brown grew older, his views toward slavery evolved. Although he owned slaves for much of his adult life, Brown's will included financial arrangements to assist one slave family and for the gradual manumission of the family's children.[100] In addition, Brown helped draft a document titled *An Address to the Presbyterians of Kentucky Proposing a Plan for the Instruction and Emancipation of Their Slaves,* which stated:

> Can any man believe that such a thing as this [the institution of slavery] is not sinful—that it is not hated by God—an[d] ought not to be abhorred and abolished by man?

> Not only has the slave no right to his wife and children, he has no right even to himself. His very body, his muscles, his bones, his flesh, are all the property of another. . . . Was the blood of our Revolution shed to establish a false principle, when it was poured out in defense of the assertion that, all men are created equal. . . .

> The sinfulness of slavery places it beyond all doubt, that it is the duty of every individual connected with the system to aid, vigorously and efficiently in its abolition, and thus free himself from all participation in its criminality.[101]

This document, which called for gradual emancipation, has been characterized as "the most significant found statement to date on the elimination of the system of slavery in Kentucky."[102] Regrettably, the church hierarchy did not endorse the declaration.[103]

When he passed away in 1837, Brown was the last surviving lawmaker from the Confederation Congress.[104] Throughout his public career, Brown advocated vigorously for Kentucky's interests. He focused in particular on three issues that were fundamental to the early commonwealth: statehood, American navigational rights on the Mississippi River, and protection against hostile Native American tribes.[105] Due in no small part to Brown, all three goals were realized during his public career. For these reasons, he has been considered one of the "founding fathers" of Kentucky.[106] Indeed, longtime friend John Beckley, who served as clerk of the US House of Representatives, wrote to Brown: "Emphatically you are one of the founders of Kentucky."[107] Professor Stuart Sprague similarly concluded that, "during his heyday, Brown was Kentucky's most important politician."[108]

Yet, Brown may have been led astray in pursuit of these goals. During the late 1780s, he had interactions with Spanish representatives who then controlled the Louisiana Territory.[109] The nature of these contacts is not altogether clear, but they do not appear to have been entirely honorable.[110] This seems true even after making allowances for the inchoate conception of the American Union at the time.[111] In addition, Brown may have had some business dealings with Burr during the latter's dubious western undertakings in the first decade of the nineteenth century.[112] The upshot is that these encounters may not have been altogether seditious, but neither do they paint Brown in a flattering light.

One lasting unambiguous legacy is Brown's home, Liberty Hall, which still stands in Frankfort as a national historic landmark.[113] Brown began building this residence in 1796 and apparently received architectural suggestions from his mentor, Thomas Jefferson.[114] He moved in five years later.[115] The Frankfort home remained in his family for generations and is today a popular tourist destination.[116]

The Early Office of President Pro Tempore

Brown's brief terms as president pro tempore reflect the limitations of the position as it was understood at the time. While he held the overt trappings of power as the chamber's presiding officer, real influence lay with others, such as his cousin John Breckinridge, who had joined him in the Senate in 1801.[117] Even at this early stage in Senate history, the constitutional presiding officer deferred to others with regard to legislative leadership.[118]

The position Brown's peers twice elected him to was first held by John Langdon (Pro-Admin.–NH), whom the Senate elected in one of its very first actions.[119] The body chose Langdon on April 6, 1789, while Vice President–elect John Adams remained in Massachusetts awaiting formal communication of his election to national office.[120] Thus, the first president pro tempore appeared in the Senate before the first vice president.[121]

It appears that Langdon was chosen in part due to his friendly demeanor and his service during the Revolutionary War.[122] His successors would be elected for a variety of different reasons. The author of the leading work on the early Senate, Roy Swanstrom, writes that it is difficult to discern why certain senators were chosen as presidents pro tempore: "The observer who tries to follow the reasoning of these early Senators in their choice of Presidents *pro tempore* must confess himself baffled, because men of such widely divergent experience, prestige, seniority, and political orientation were named—during a period when the same party [the Federalists] never failed to command a Senate majority."[123] Fourteen presidents pro tempore were chosen from 1789 to 1801.[124] Some were luminaries of the dominant Federalist Party, while others were mediocrities.[125] Preeminent Federalists in the Senate—such as Oliver Ellsworth of Connecticut and Rufus King of New York—never held the position.[126] Indeed, two senators turned down the office.[127]

The position occupied by Brown and other early presidents pro tempore was far different from the office today. First, early senators elected a president pro tempore only when the vice president was actually out of the Senate chamber. Senators interpreted the relevant constitutional provision strictly, meaning that the president pro tempore was needed only "in the Absence of the Vice President."[128] This explains why Brown (and John Pope, as discussed below) served such a brief time in office.[129] It also helps explain why the president pro tempore never developed into a de facto leadership position.[130]

This narrow interpretation of the president pro tempore's tenure, combined with the order of presidential succession, led to problems from time to time. The Presidential Succession Act of 1792, which governed until 1886, placed the president pro tempore immediately after the vice president in the line of succession.[131] During this period, prior to a congressional recess, it became common practice for the vice president to vacate the presiding officer's chair to permit the Senate to choose a president pro tempore.[132] That way, if both the president and vice president died during the recess, a president pro tempore would be in place to assume the position of chief executive.[133]

On occasion, however, vice presidents refused to vacate the chair at the end of a session, leaving open the possibility of succession problems. This occurred with Vice Presidents Elbridge Gerry, George Dallas, Chester Arthur, and Thomas Hendricks.[134] Hendricks actually died during a congressional recess, leaving the country without a presidential successor for weeks because no president pro tempore and no Speaker had been chosen, and the statute listed no other officer as a potential successor.[135]

In one case in which a vice president decided not to absent himself, it caused serious tension in the chamber. In 1835, Senator George Poindexter (Nat. Rep.–MS)—whose term as president pro tempore had expired scarcely a month before—wanted his job back and sent a menacing letter to Vice President Martin Van Buren.[136] In it, Poindexter accused Van Buren of attending the Senate session with the intent of precluding him from being chosen president pro tempore; at the same time, he claimed the vice president was discrediting him through the newspapers.[137] Ominously, the senator's letter also appeared to challenge Van Buren to a duel.[138]

Van Buren brushed aside Poindexter's allegations in a written response, but he felt sufficiently threatened by the senator that, "to prevent . . . any hostile attempt that might be made upon my person . . . I . . . , for the first and only time in my life, placed about my person, a pair of loaded pistols, of a size which I could carry without danger of exposure, and wore them in the chair and out of it, until I became fully satisfied that my adversary had made up his mind to drop the whole matter where my answer had left it."[139] The matter eventually resolved itself, with the vice president ultimately concluding that Henry Clay had inter- ceded and convinced Poindexter to desist with his threats.[140]

In 1876, by resolution, the Senate extended the president pro tempore's term of office to include recess periods and the beginning of the following congressio- nal session, pending the arrival of the vice president.[141] Moreover, the resolution clarified that the president pro tempore could be removed by the Senate.[142] In 1890, in what likely constitutes the most notable development in the position's history, the Senate abruptly changed its election procedure, determining that henceforth, the president pro tempore would be elected for an entire Congress, not simply when the vice president was not in the Senate.[143] This sensible change did not take place without dissent. Senator James Z. George (D-MS) was critical of the Republican majority's reversal of what had been a long-standing interpre- tation. He thundered: "this great constitutional question, which has been settled by the practice of a hundred years, has recently undergone revision in the high court of the Republican caucus."[144]

The 1890 decision affected the office in a number of ways. Not surprisingly, it immediately led to senators holding the position for much longer periods.[145] In 1896, Senator William Frye (R-ME) was elected president pro tempore and served fifteen years in the position.[146] As will be seen, this change also led to a fifty-year period marked by highly contentious elections for the office.[147] In addi- tion, the 1890 decision may have had the unintended effect of encouraging the vice president to absent himself from the Senate more often, permitting him to increase his executive branch role over time.[148]

A second difference between Brown's era and the modern day is that, during the Kentuckian's tenure, the president pro tempore—like the vice president he replaced—was expected to actually preside over Senate proceedings. Today, the president pro tempore typically takes the chair each morning at the beginning of Senate deliberations but then surrenders the gavel to junior members of the Senate majority party for the rest of the day.[149]

From 1969 to 1975, senators of the minority party sometimes presided in place of the president pro tempore.[150] However, on July 18, 1975, this practice was abruptly terminated when Senator Jesse Helms (R-NC) refused to recog- nize majority leader Mike Mansfield (D-MT), who, under Senate precedent and practice, had the right to the floor.[151] This enraged the normally unflappable

Mansfield, who promptly put a stop to minority party senators presiding over the body.[152]

A third difference is that, in Brown's day, election of the president pro tempore often involved a heated contest. In recent decades, the member of the majority party with the most seniority is designated the president pro tempore, but in previous eras, senators sometimes pursued the office quite vigorously, especially in the early twentieth century.[153] For instance, in 1911, the Senate needed to choose a successor to the long-serving Senator Frye, which set off a donnybrook that lasted for three months.[154] Senate tradition held that for a senator to be elected president pro tempore, he needed to secure a majority of votes, not a simple plurality.[155] A handful of wayward Republican senators diverted enough support to prevent the presumptive GOP candidate from getting a majority.[156] It was finally agreed that one Democrat and four Republicans would take turns serving as president pro tempore.[157]

A lengthy clash also ensued in 1923.[158] That year, progressive Republicans broke party ranks by opposing Albert Cummins (R-IA), who sought to retain both the position of president pro tempore and a coveted committee chairmanship.[159] The Senate deadlocked, and ultimately, Cummins stayed on as president pro tempore through inertia but failed to keep his committee gavel.[160] In 1931–1932, there was yet another protracted struggle over the position.[161]

A fourth difference between Brown's time and the present is that early officeholders were not chosen based on seniority. In 1795, Senator Henry Tazewell (Dem.-Rep.-VA) was chosen president pro tempore after having served in the chamber for a grand total of two months.[162] Furthermore, he was a member of the minority party at the time.[163] Perhaps with the debilitating 1911, 1923, and 1931–1932 contests in mind, the tradition of choosing the senator of the majority party with the greatest seniority as president pro tempore began to take hold after World War II.[164] This ended the era of contested elections for the post. Today, this tradition is almost inviolate. For instance, when unrepentant segregationist James Eastland (D-MS) was slated to become president pro tempore in 1972, only one Democrat opposed his elevation.[165]

A fifth and final difference is that, in Brown's era, there was no distinction in salary between the president pro tempore and other senators. Beginning in 1816, presidents pro tempore have been paid more than almost all their Senate colleagues.[166]

John Pope

Like Brown, John Pope was originally from Virginia.[167] He was born in 1770 into a distinguished family.[168] His parents were Colonel William Pope and Penelope

Edwards.[169] William served in the Revolutionary War, and in 1779, he moved his wife and children to western Virginia (today Kentucky); he soon became one of the early city fathers of Louisville.[170]

Regrettably, as with Brown, the historical record is largely silent on Pope's childhood.[171] What is known is that, as a youth, he had an accident while assisting his father with chores on the farm.[172] Young John was working with a cornstalk mill when his right arm became entangled in the device and was horribly mutilated.[173] The lad would have perished but for his father's quick thinking, which prevented him from bleeding to death, but the arm had to be amputated.[174] For the rest of his life, he would be known by the unfortunate nickname "One-Arm Pope."[175] Despite his disability, Pope found a way to defend himself in the rough-and-tumble early nineteenth century. One Kentucky author noted that Pope had a reputation as "a dangerous adversary in personal conflict. A rock was his favorite weapon, which he could throw with great force and accuracy."[176]

Sadly for Pope, his childhood injury would be the first of many hardships. The Kentuckian would be widowed three times, lose a daughter, and endure the death of a nephew with whom he was very close.[177] In 1795, Pope married Anne Henry Christian, who came from a prominent family; her uncle was Patrick Henry.[178] The marriage lasted until her passing in 1806 and produced no children.[179] Pope remarried four years later to Elizabeth Janet Dorcas Johnson (known as Eliza), whose sister was married to John Quincy Adams.[180] The couple would have two daughters.[181] Born in Britain, Eliza was used to the finer things in life, and to meet her expectations, Pope arranged for the great architect Benjamin Henry Latrobe to build them a home in Lexington, Kentucky.[182] Latrobe, of course, played a major role in designing and building the US Capitol.[183] Their home, called the "Pope Villa," stands to this day as a rare example of a Latrobe-built residence.[184] Sadly, Eliza did not enjoy it for long, as she passed away in 1818, leaving Pope on his own again.[185] He wed a third time in 1820 to a well-to-do widow, Frances Watkins Walton, and the couple had no children.[186] Frances predeceased Pope by two years.[187]

Pope's Political Ascent

Pope's drive and talent permitted him to overcome the trauma of losing an arm. In due course, he attended Dr. James Priestley's academy in Bardstown, Kentucky.[188] Under Priestley's direction, Pope was exposed to the classics.[189] Not long afterward, Pope appears to have come under the tutelage of George Nicholas of Lexington and read law.[190] Upon completing his legal studies, he worked as an attorney in Shelbyville, not far from Louisville.[191] He became an accomplished criminal defense attorney and soon took an interest in local politics.[192]

Pope's initial foray into public life was a run for the state senate in the late 1790s.[193] In pursuing elective office, Pope was aided by his debating skills. He was highly persuasive as an advocate, although at times he could be acerbic.[194] One nineteenth-century author summed up contemporary opinion: "when in debate and fully roused," Pope "was unapproachable."[195]

During this period, the commonwealth was energized by John Breckinridge's efforts to support the Kentucky Resolutions, which purported to nullify the congressionally enacted Alien and Sedition Acts.[196] Not Pope. As he would demonstrate throughout his career, he was not one to be pigeonholed politically. His biographer aptly described Pope as "a free lance politician."[197] He defied Democratic-Republican orthodoxy in the state and became a vigorous supporter of the Federalist Party.[198] As such, he took the lead in trying to soften the Kentucky Resolutions by removing the word "nullification," coming within a single vote of prevailing.[199] Pope's stance would later come back to haunt him.

In 1800, perhaps recognizing political reality, Pope pivoted sharply and switched from the Federalist camp to the Democratic-Republican Party.[200] That year, he represented the state in the Electoral College, supporting Thomas Jefferson's candidacy.[201] Pope briefly stepped away from political life not long thereafter, moving to Lexington in 1803 and resuming the practice of law.[202]

Pope's rise in politics was fueled by many factors, including his prominent family.[203] In the early 1830s, one newspaper opined, "in Kentucky the divine right of Popes is . . . indisputable."[204] He was wealthy and, at least in his early life, was apparently a slaveholder.[205]

His personal qualities also contributed to his success. He was an outstanding public speaker.[206] One nineteenth-century authority concluded that Pope rivaled Clay in forensic skill: "Clay possessed the higher art of oratory," but Pope enjoyed "the greater depth . . . the sharper wit, and at times a [more] polished irony."[207] Moreover, Pope was independent minded and displayed great intelligence and self-assurance.[208] Sometimes, however, people's strengths can also be their undoing. This was true of Pope in some ways. His self-belief often gave way to arrogance; his zealous advocacy to rigid inflexibility.[209] His peers often snickered about the "Pope ego."[210] These traits would repeatedly undermine an otherwise promising public career.

Though Pope was fickle with regard to party affiliation, he could be a loyal friend.[211] He had an enduring bond with another dyspeptic Kentucky lawmaker, Federalist Humphrey Marshall.[212] Finally, Pope's personal habits were exemplary.[213] He drank little and swore less.[214] Despite his wealth, he was not profligate in his tastes.[215]

Pope in the Senate and Beyond

In 1806, Pope returned to the state house, this time representing the Lexington area.[216] Henry Clay, future Tennessee senator Felix Grundy, and Pope formed a triumvirate that set the agenda for the legislature.[217] That same year, in a reflection of his stature, Pope ran successfully for US Senate against John Adair.[218] Not long after his election to the upper chamber, Pope emerged as one of the leading voices calling for an inquiry into the actions of a state judge.[219] The judge, Benjamin Sebastian, had allegedly maintained an improper and potentially seditious relationship with Spain.[220] Pope chaired the panel that uncovered the wrongdoing by Sebastian and his cohorts.[221] Interestingly, one of the witnesses called was John Brown.[222] Pope's central role in this investigation raised his profile and helped send him to the US Senate on a high note.[223]

When he arrived in Washington, Pope was not overawed. Early in his tenure, he commented: "I occupy much higher ground here both on the scale of talents and republicanism than . . . expected; except Breckinridge no man from the west ever had more popularity in Congress."[224] If his self-assessment is accurate, it might account for his election as president pro tempore.[225] Pope served as president pro tempore from February 23 to November 3, 1811.[226] He was also chosen for membership on a select committee on foreign affairs, the forerunner of today's Foreign Relations Committee.[227] Finally, the Kentuckian secured adoption of legislation ensuring that the US Navy give preference to American-made goods in its procurement process.[228]

In 1808, Pope proved to be a vigorous supporter of James Madison for president.[229] In fact, to advocate for Madison's election, Pope served on the Democratic-Republican Committee on Correspondence, an early effort at national political organizing.[230] Nonetheless, as he had demonstrated in the state house, Senator Pope was not a knee-jerk partisan. Unlike many of his Democratic-Republican brethren, Pope supported reauthorization of the Bank of the United States.[231] More seriously still—from a political perspective—he opposed the War of 1812.[232]

At the time, war fever gripped the nation. Great Britain was abducting American seamen and impressing them into naval service. Moreover, the British were encouraging Indian tribes to serve as a counterweight to American settlements in what was then considered the Northwest.[233] Outrage was especially high among those in the Democratic-Republican Party, and this was particularly true in Kentucky, where Indian raids were not a distant memory.[234] The state legislature sent instructions to the Kentucky national delegation, exhorting members to support hostilities against Britain.[235] Pope ignored the directive.[236] At a time when state legislatures elected US senators, this was a high-risk move. Undeterred, Pope sided with his former party, the Federalists, and actively opposed the war, working to delay and dilute the relevant legislation.[237]

Pope's posture was met with outrage in Kentucky.[238] Images of Pope were publicly burned.[239] Indeed, this stance cost him his Senate career. Given the overwhelmingly negative response to his opposition to the war, Pope decided not to stand for reelection in 1813.[240] He returned to Lexington and to legal work for the next three years.[241] He also found time to teach law at Transylvania University and would later serve on its Board of Trustees.[242]

Pope was not done with politics, however. In 1816, he saw an opportunity and returned to the public arena with a vengeance.[243] That year, Speaker of the House Henry Clay made one of his periodic political blunders.[244] Clay supported a modification of the congressional compensation system from a per diem basis to an annual wage, effectively legislating a pay increase for lawmakers.[245] This was quickly portrayed as a congressional "salary grab," and it provoked a popular outcry.[246] One Frankfort newspaper wrote of the vote, "In Kentucky, particularly, it has excited much controversy, and produced an opposition to some men whose popularity might have been supposed invulnerable."[247] Pope seized on this discontent and launched a spirited race for Clay's "supposed[ly] invulnerable" House seat.[248] Pope's candidacy would prove to be the greatest challenge Clay ever encountered in a Kentucky campaign.[249]

Prince Hal was nothing if not deft, however. Like Richard Mentor Johnson—the salary bill's primary advocate—Clay reversed himself and pledged to try to repeal the measure.[250] This took Pope's biggest campaign issue largely off the table.[251] Moreover, Clay quickly went on the offensive and savaged Pope's opposition to the Kentucky Resolutions and his support for a national bank.[252] In heavily Jeffersonian Kentucky, Clay landed a political haymaker by effectively labeling Pope a Federalist.[253]

Moreover, "Harry of the West" lashed Pope for disregarding instructions from the state legislature to oppose the bank.[254] Pope compounded his problems by lamely responding that the instructions had arrived only ninety minutes before he was scheduled to speak on the matter.[255] At the same time, Pope asserted that the legislature lacked the authority to tell him how to vote.[256] Clay piled on by highlighting Pope's unpopular stance against the War of 1812.[257]

Clay survived the close race, but Pope's strong campaign heralded his return to public life. And Clay clearly saw Pope as a threat. John Quincy Adams compared the two men, believing that Pope (his brother-in-law) was less talented than Clay but more upright. He shrewdly assessed Clay's persistent efforts to undermine Pope: "[Kentucky] is divided between two parties, with Clay the head of one of them, and Pope of the other. Clay, by the superiority of his talents, by a more artful management of popular feelings, and by the chances of good fortune, notwithstanding the more correct moral character of his antagonist, has acquired a great ascendency over him, and not only keeps him depressed in public estimation, but uses every possible means of the most rancorous and malignant enmity to ruin him."[258]

In 1816, despite Clay's efforts, Pope was named Kentucky's secretary of state, but the Democratic-Republicans in the state let it be known that they had not forgiven his heretical posture during the War of 1812.[259] Pope continued to be vilified, and he ultimately stepped down from the post in 1819.[260] At that point, he became involved again with the Federalist Party, which was on its last legs.[261]

Pope returned to the state legislature in the 1820s, where he waded into the middle of the "old court–new court" controversy that convulsed the state during this period.[262] This profound divide stemmed from major economic dislocations that resulted in competing state judicial bodies handing down conflicting rulings, sowing further discord and confusion.[263] Demonstrating yet again his unwillingness to be pigeonholed, Pope attempted with little success to bridge the gap between the two sides of the controversy, making himself less popular in the process.[264] His posture may have played a role in preventing his return to the Senate later in the decade.[265]

Pope's maverick ways manifested themselves once again in 1824. Not surprisingly, that year Pope came out in favor of his brother-in-law, John Quincy Adams, for president.[266] Yet, after the Electoral College failed to produce a victor and Clay backed Adams for president, Pope promptly cut ties with his brother-in-law.[267] Whether Pope's decision reflected his own moral rectitude, his enduring enmity toward Clay, or both is unclear.[268] What is clear is that four years later, Pope openly backed Adams's challenger, Andrew Jackson, who was elected president.[269] As a nod to Pope's support in the 1828 campaign, Jackson named him territorial governor of Arkansas the next year.[270]

As governor, Pope introduced a number of reforms in Arkansas. He converted many appointed positions into elected posts and helped create a regular postal route to the territory.[271] In addition, Pope encouraged greater settlement into what was then a wild and wooly region.[272] In this effort, he led by example; he was the first territorial governor to bring his family to Arkansas.[273] However, Pope's propensity to antagonize people materialized yet again, hampering his ability to govern. He and John Crittenden's younger brother, Robert, who had also moved to the territory, became embroiled in a vicious feud.[274] Given Robert's political following in Arkansas, the personal dispute distracted from important public business, such as the construction of the territorial capitol building.[275] Nor was this Pope's last vendetta in Arkansas.[276]

Pope's lack of political finesse manifested itself in other ways. He proved to be just as unreliable an ally to Jackson as he had been to Adams. In fact, Pope went so far as to write to Jackson and reprimand him for his actions as president.[277] Pope maintained that Old Hickory had collapsed the "wall of partition placed by the Constitution between the Legislative and Executive departments, [and as a result] the equilibrium of power established by that instrument [has been] overthrown."[278] As one might expect, such an opinion was not well received, and relations between the two men cooled rapidly.[279] Indeed, it is likely that Jackson would have cashiered Pope immediately but for the president's concern over the potential political fallout and its effect on his own reelection efforts.[280]

However, after being safely returned to the White House, Jackson relieved Pope of his duties as territorial governor. Despite the break with Jackson and his battles with numerous Arkansans, Pope's legacy lives on in the Natural State, as the Old State House still sits on the site chosen by the Kentuckian.[281] Furthermore, Pope County, Arkansas, is named after the former governor.[282] Following his termination, Pope returned to the commonwealth, where he became openly critical of the president.[283]

In 1837, Pope began a second tenure in Congress, this time as a member of the Whig Party.[284] He would serve three terms in the US House.[285] As one might expect, Pope was an unreliable Whig.[286] This became evident when Pope attempted to run for US Senate.[287] Toward this end, Pope unwisely wrote to former vice president and loyal Democrat Richard Mentor Johnson, proposing an alliance and indicating his willingness to leave the Whig Party.[288] The letter soon became public and ended Pope's political career.[289]

Yet, even when he was sailing into the political headwinds caused by his own poor judgment, Pope remained unbowed. He ran for reelection to the House, despite the damaging revelation of the Johnson letter.[290] A contemporary drew a poignant picture of the old war horse still fighting the good fight at a debate of the congressional candidates:

> [Pope] entered the crowded . . . room—venerable and very striking in appearance—swinging his armless sleeve. His speech was the most remarkable to which I ever listened. In the outset it was halting, his words came with difficulty, his sentences were not rounded, his gesticulation was unimpressive, his voice husky, and there was a painful impression that he was disabled by age. As he warmed up, however, all defects disappeared— his voice grew musical and his speech flowed in full and impassioned volume. The youthful fire of intellect transfigured the furrowed face and grey locks—and the old man was lost in the orator. He defended the integrity of his political course forcibly, earnestly, and eloquently. When, in his per-

oration, he begged that he should not be deserted and turned off in his old age, there was scarce a dry eye in the audience. The effect of the speech was wonderful. It converted almost every one who heard him.[291]

While Pope carried the county where he gave this dramatic speech, it was not enough.[292] In 1843, he failed to secure the Whig nomination as a candidate for the House and never again held public office.[293]

Pope died two years later in Springfield, Kentucky.[294] He left behind a legacy of unfulfilled potential, his obstinacy and independence hampering his ability to serve the public more effectively.

The President Pro Tempore and Senate Leadership

Given the talents of men such as Brown and Pope, the question remains: why did the office of president pro tempore never develop into a position of genuine leadership in the Senate? The one reason that is typically cited involves the office's relationship to the vice presidency. Until midway through the twentieth century, vice presidents spent considerable time presiding over the Senate.[295] Also, for the first century under the Constitution, the Senate elected a president pro tempore to serve only when the vice president was actually absent from the presiding officer's chair.[296] As a result, presidents pro tempore served at irregular intervals.[297] Thus, despite the dignity and esteem attached to the position as a constitutional office, it did not develop into an independent power center in the Senate in large part because, for extended periods, there was no such officeholder.[298] And even when there *was* a president pro tempore in place, he often served for only a short time.[299]

Senators who have independent prestige can sometimes lend stature to the positions they hold and, in the process, elevate the offices' standings.[300] With the president pro tempore's short, erratic tenure, this phenomenon had a hard time taking root. It is likely that during the first decades of the Senate—with the vice president regularly sitting in the chair—the Senate simply became accustomed to leadership coming from the floor instead of from the presiding officer.[301] When a president pro tempore did take the gavel on occasion, the Senate was already in the habit of looking elsewhere for direction.[302] Thus, neither of the two constitutional presiding officers of the Senate evolved into positions of enduring institutional leadership.[303]

That said, the president pro tempore has sometimes been delegated important functions. In 1823, the Senate deputized the "president of the Senate" to assign senators to committees.[304] At the time, it was generally expected that the vice president would absent himself at the beginning of a Congress and allow the president pro tempore to perform this duty.[305] In 1825, however, Vice President John C. Calhoun appeared in the chamber and peremptorily named committee members.[306] He also did so in a manner designed to frustrate President John Quincy Adams.[307] This prompted the Senate to tinker with its rules for determining which senators should sit on which committees, and on several occasions, the chamber granted this authority expressly to the president pro tempore.[308] By the mid-1840s, the presiding officer's ostensible power in this regard had become a mere formality; real authority over committee assignments had gravitated to the party caucuses.[309]

Like the modern vice president, the president pro tempore of today retains a number of ceremonial trappings of power. He signs and thereby authenticates official Senate actions, such as measures that have received bicameral approval and are on their way to the president's desk.[310] Into the twentieth century, the president pro tempore exercised some authority in assigning patronage posts within the Senate.[311] To this day, the president pro tempore maintains authority to name individuals to various national commissions, which is usually done in consultation with the floor leaders.[312]

* * *

Typically, every Monday that the Senate is in session, I convene the Republican leadership team. During this meeting, we map out the week ahead and strategize about upcoming matters confronting the Senate. This group includes, among others, majority whip John Cornyn (R-TX) and Republican Conference chairman John Thune (R-SD). Another key invitee is Orrin Hatch (R-UT), the current president pro tempore. Senator Hatch's participation in these leadership meetings reflects that, at least during my tenure as majority leader, the president pro tempore plays a real role in the leadership of the chamber. In the case of Senator Hatch, his influence extends beyond having a voice in leadership councils; he is also chair of the Finance Committee, one of the most powerful panels in the Senate.

* * *

The President Pro Tempore as the "Acting Vice President"

President pro tempore is a position of prestige as well as one of historical curiosity. Given its kinship to the vice presidency, one oddity associated with the office has occurred during a number of vice-presidential vacancies. In the absence of a sitting vice president, the president pro tempore has often been said to become the "acting vice president," even though no such position is mentioned anywhere in the Constitution or in federal statute.[313] For whatever reason, this unofficial designation of the president pro tempore has long been overlooked by scholars.[314]

From 1792 to 1886, federal law placed the president pro tempore directly after the vice president in the line of presidential succession.[315] Nonetheless, there was some question about whether the president pro tempore assumed a new status when there was no vice president. Did the president pro tempore become the vice president or the acting vice president? This question is not as farfetched as it might seem at first. Congress muddied the waters by taking action that tacitly supported the notion of the president pro tempore serving as the acting vice president. Following the death of Vice President George Clinton in 1812, which created the first vice-presidential vacancy, the Senate awarded double pay to president pro tempore William Crawford (Dem.-Rep.–GA).[316] Presumably, this was done to compensate him for his two new jobs: presiding over the Senate full time and assuming the vice president's administrative responsibilities. However, Crawford was apparently never referred to as the vice president or acting vice president.[317]

When President William Henry Harrison died in 1841—the first chief executive not to complete his term—Vice President John Tyler successfully asserted that he had become the president in fact, not the acting president.[318] Related questions flowed from Tyler's constitutional interpretation.[319] If the vice president left office prematurely, did the president pro tempore—as the vice president's constitutional substitute in the Senate and as the next in line to the presidency at the time—actually become vice president or merely acting vice president?[320]

After Tyler assumed the presidency, former president pro tempore George Poindexter (D-MS) urged Senator Samuel Southard (W-NJ), the current president pro tempore, to assume the title of acting vice president.[321] Southard did not claim the title, but like Crawford before him, he was apparently compensated at the vice-presidential level.[322] In 1856, Congress formalized the practice of increasing the president pro tempore's compensation when there is no vice president.[323]

Even though Southard declined the title of acting vice president, during subsequent vice-presidential vacancies, the media and others have referred to the president pro tempore as acting vice president or as the actual vice president.[324] For instance, following the 1865 assassination of President Abraham Lincoln and the elevation of Vice President Andrew Johnson to the presidency, it was variously reported in the press that president pro tempore Lafayette Sabine Foster (R-CT) was either vice president or acting vice president.[325]

In 1869, the cover of *Harper's Weekly* referred to Foster's successor as president pro tempore, Ben Wade (R-OH), as "Vice-President" when he swore in incoming vice president Schuyler Colfax (R-IN).[326] Similarly, Wade was characterized as acting vice president on both the Senate and House floor.[327] Former senator James G. Blaine (R-ME) made a comparable reference to Wade in his memoirs.[328]

During the period when the president pro tempore was immediately behind the vice president in the line of presidential succession, other officeholders were termed acting vice president within the halls of Congress and in numerous publications. They included David Atchison (D-MO),[329] David Davis (Ind.-IL),[330] Thomas Ferry (R-MI),[331] John J. Ingalls (R-KS),[332] Joseph Varnum (Dem.-Rep.–MA),[333] and John Sherman (R-OH).[334] In fact, during the vice-presidential vacancy following Chester Arthur's accession to the presidency in 1881, Senator George Edmunds (R-VT), who was president pro tempore from 1883 to 1885, used letterhead emblazoned with the words "Office of the Vice President" across the top.[335]

Theoretically, the uneven practice of tacitly considering the president pro tempore to be the acting vice president should have been extinguished in 1886, when the presidential succession statute was modified to remove the president pro tempore from the line of succession. However, from time to time afterward, the president pro tempore would still be treated as if he were acting vice president when a vice-presidential vacancy occurred.[336] Following Vice President Calvin Coolidge's ascension to the Oval Office after Warren Harding's death, president pro tempore Albert Cummins (R-IA) became the recipient of vice-presidential perquisites, including a higher salary, a car, and enhanced pay for his staff.[337] This followed a ruling from the comptroller general.[338] After President Franklin D. Roosevelt's passing, Harry Truman requested that president pro tempore Kenneth McKellar (D-TN) join cabinet meetings, filling the gap created by Truman's elevation.[339] During this period, lawmakers sometimes referred to the president pro tempore as the acting vice president.[340] This included allusions to past presidents pro tempore having served as such.[341]

A 1947 statute returned the president pro tempore to the line of succession.[342] However, this time, the officeholder was made third in line behind the Speaker of the House.[343] Nonetheless, lawmakers and the press continued to refer to presidents pro tempore as acting vice presidents. When former president pro tempore Carl Hayden (D-AZ) passed away in 1972, he was characterized on the floors of both houses as having been the acting vice president following President John F. Kennedy's assassination.[344] In late 1973, following the resignation of Vice President Spiro Agnew, news stories called president pro tempore James Eastland (D-MS) the acting vice president.[345] Several years later, Senator Robert Byrd (D-WV) described Eastland in the same manner.[346] Congressional opinion remained divided as to the legitimacy of the acting vice president "position." Legislation was proposed in 1963, 1964, 1973, and 1975 that would have expressly established such an office.[347] None of the bills was ever enacted.

Nevertheless, acknowledgment of the president pro tempore serving as the acting vice president has occurred throughout the history of the Senate, regardless of whether the office was included in the line of succession at the time. Although there has been support for the notion of an acting vice president in historical practice, floor debate, and the media, the "position" has never been formally recognized in law.

Other Historical Curiosities

In recent decades, the Senate has created variations of the president pro tempore position.[348] In 1964, with the Senate poised to consider civil rights legislation, majority leader Mike Mansfield worried about the health of the elderly president pro tempore, Senator Carl Hayden.[349] Mansfield believed that Hayden might not hold up under what promised to be a grueling and extended filibuster.[350] As a result, Lee Metcalf (D-MT) was named permanent acting president pro tempore.[351] Metcalf, the only senator to hold such a position, kept it until his passing fourteen years later.[352]

Similarly, following the failed attempt of former vice president and sitting senator Hubert Humphrey (D-MN) to be elected majority leader in late 1976, the Senate bestowed an honorific on the well-regarded Minnesotan, naming him deputy president pro tempore.[353] By Senate resolution, that title and modest perquisites are available to any senator who is so honored.[354] Senator George Mitchell (D-ME) was granted the title in 1987, when he substituted for president pro tempore John Stennis (D-MS), who had become ill.[355] In 2001, former president pro tempore Strom Thurmond (R-SC) became the Senate's first president pro tempore emeritus after his party lost the majority in 2001.[356]

Another oddity involving the position surrounds the legend of "President David Atchison." It has long been lore that president pro tempore Atchison (D-MO) served as president of the United States for one day: Sunday, March 4, 1849.[357] The circumstances were as follows: President James K. Polk's term ended at noon on Sunday, March 4, 1849.[358] It was decided that the inauguration of President-elect Zachary Taylor and Vice President–elect Millard Fillmore should not take place on the Sabbath but should be held instead on Monday, March 5.[359] Thus, even though Polk's term had expired, Taylor and Fillmore had not yet been sworn in, supposedly creating a brief executive "vacancy."[360] At the time, the president pro tempore was next in the line of succession, so it has been said that president pro tempore Atchison served as president of the United States on March 4.[361] Indeed, on occasion, Atchison would humorously reflect on his time as "president."[362] He was known to remark that his "was the honestest administration this country ever had."[363] Despite the persistence of the legend of the Atchison "presidency," scholars have not accepted it.[364]

A final curiosity about the president pro tempore position is that the office has its own seal. The upper chamber authorized the insignia in 1954 by resolution.[365] The vice president's office also has a seal, but it was adopted by the executive branch, not the Senate.[366]

The tenures of John Brown and John Pope as president pro tempore reflect one of the central shortcomings of the position in its early years: brevity of tenure. By the time the Senate took steps to ensure lengthier service in 1890, expectations about the office had crystallized, and other modes of leadership—be they formal or informal—had filled the void.

3

Senator as Presidential Spokesman

John Breckinridge

The president of the United States has always played a formal role in the law-making process. Under the Constitution, he submits his State of the Union message, which lays out his policy priorities for the nation. He is empowered to make recommendations to Congress on measures he believes the legislature should pursue. He can also call Congress into an extraordinary session. And, of course, the president has the authority to sign into law or veto bills that Congress has passed.[1]

Despite the president's significant legislative powers, he is hindered from more direct, formal involvement in the legislative process by the doctrine of separation of powers. As a result, he may not introduce legislation himself, engage in congressional debate, or exercise a line-item veto.[2] Moreover, for generations, informal presidential involvement with the legislative branch was looked upon with disfavor.[3] So the question remains, how did these early presidents secure adoption of their legislative priorities? One approach for chief executives was to work discreetly through trusted legislative lieutenants.[4] In the Senate, this was particularly true in the period before the emergence of formal party leadership positions.

If a lawmaker is seen as speaking on behalf of the president—the only person who can sign bills into law—that member will wield at least some influence in the chamber.[5] If this lawmaker possesses legislative skills of his own, he is likely to be a force to be reckoned with.[6] John Breckinridge was one such senator during the presidency of Thomas Jefferson.[7]

The Federalist Approach to Presidential-Congressional Relations

In the early years under the Constitution, presidents interpreted their legislative powers strictly and had little personal involvement with the lawmaking process.[8] When President George Washington brought issues to the attention of Congress, they usually involved foreign or military affairs or technical concerns within the departments.[9] In these cases, the president typically expressed the end result he wanted but left the legislative means to Congress.[10] Rare was the occasion when Washington raised legislative matters directly with lawmakers.[11]

That said, his secretary of the treasury, Alexander Hamilton, felt no such compunction.[12] He sought and was granted access to Congress that was unique among the early cabinet secretaries.[13] Because of his ties to Congress, Hamilton routinely submitted funding requests to lawmakers, appeared in person before congressional panels, and actively lobbied in support of his fiscal agenda.[14] In his legislative efforts, Hamilton was highly effective.

In 1791, one Hamilton opponent, Senator William Maclay (Anti-Admin.–PA), ruefully observed, "Congress may go home. Mr. Hamilton is all-powerful, and fails in nothing he attempts."[15] At another juncture, he complained, "Everything even . . . the naming of a committee is prearranged by Hamilton and his group of speculators."[16] Maclay derisively referred to the secretary's followers in the upper chamber as "the crew of the Hamilton galley" or Hamilton's "Senatorial Gladiators."[17] Historian Roy Swanstrom likened Hamilton to an "absentee floor leader."[18]

One of Hamilton's foremost allies was Oliver Ellsworth (Fed.-CT), an early Senate leader and Federalist Party spokesman.[19] John Adams dubbed him "the firmest pillar of [the Washington] administration in the Senate."[20] Ellsworth coupled party loyalty with great diligence and legislative acumen.[21] Yet, because of Washington's decision to remain aloof from Congress, Ellsworth and his Federalist cohorts, such as Rufus King of New York and George Cabot of Massachusetts, were Federalist Party or Hamiltonian advocates, not presidential advocates.[22] They received little if any informal legislative guidance from the president himself.

This era of executive-legislative cooperation began to unravel on three fronts as the 1790s progressed. First, Hamilton left government service. Second, Democratic-Republicans, under the sway of Jefferson, began to challenge the Federalists' legislative dominance in the mid-1790s.[23] Third, major divides emerged among the Federalists themselves during the presidency of John Adams.[24] Even as this polarization increased, Adams followed Washington's model of remaining largely detached from congressional actions.[25]

The election of 1800 ushered in a new era, as Jefferson was elected president and the Democratic-Republicans won majorities in both houses of Congress. One of the many ways Jefferson differed from his Federalist predecessors was in his approach to working with lawmakers. According to historian Ralph Harlow:

> In one important particular Jefferson improved upon Federalist legislative methods. Hamilton had his followers in Congress, and there was usually some one leader of prominence in charge of the party forces, but this floor

leader was not looked upon as the personal representative of the president himself. . . . From 1801 to 1808 the floor leader was distinctly the lieutenant of the executive. . . . The status of these men was different from that of the floor leader of to-day. . . . They were presidential agents, appointed by the executive. . . . Leadership was not the prerogative of seniority nor a privilege conferred by [Congress]; it was distinctly the gift of the president.[26]

John Breckinridge

John Breckinridge, who would become one of Jefferson's key lieutenants in the Senate, was born in 1760 near Staunton, Virginia, one of six children.[27] His father, Robert Breckinridge, was a planter and a leading member of the community.[28] John's mother was Lettice Preston, who came from a distinguished Virginia family and was the aunt of future senator John Brown.[29] Robert was elected trustee of Staunton and served as a justice of the peace, sheriff, and militia officer.[30] One suspects that Robert instilled in his son some appreciation of public affairs.

When John was only eleven, his father passed away, which almost assuredly had a profound impact on him.[31] His biographer, Professor Lowell Harrison, surmised: "If John Breckinridge in later life was to display a quiet reserve and an aloofness which sometimes seemed strange to his more gregarious associates, an explanation may be found in the sudden responsibility that was forced upon him at an unseasonable age. It almost seemed as if he were never young, so suddenly did he mature."[32] Harrison's views have the ring of truth, but unfortunately, the historical record from this period of Breckinridge's life is essentially barren, so it is difficult to draw any conclusions with complete confidence.[33]

John's prospects improved thanks to assistance from his maternal uncle, William Preston, who ensured that Breckinridge received what amounted to a high school education and facilitated his nephew's efforts to attend college.[34] Like his cousin John Brown, Breckinridge matriculated at the College of William and Mary.[35] Brown, who would later serve with Breckinridge in the US Senate, remarked: "[I] am happy to hear that cousin J. Breckinridge is determined to become a student of this University . . . his genius is such that if assisted by the Advantages this place affords I am well convinced he would not only become an important member of society but he would do honor to his connections."[36]

Despite help from his uncle, Breckinridge continued to experience financial woes, due in part to the economic problems wrought by the Revolutionary War.[37] His mother wrote to him: "I am sorry that it is out of my power to send you one farthing of money."[38] Breckinridge replied in despair: "When I look forward and see the many difficulties I have to encounter, in executing my present design, I am almost tempted to desist from it, as being too great for one of my expectations to look for."[39] In 1783, he endured another personal blow when his beloved Uncle William passed away.[40]

Yet, despite these hardships, Breckinridge made important contacts with fellow students at William and Mary that would later serve him well, including future senators William Giles (Dem.-Rep.–VA) and Stevens T. Mason (Dem.-Rep.–VA).[41] Like other prominent Virginians who attended the college (including Jefferson), Breckinridge apparently took legal instruction from the esteemed George Wythe.[42]

Breckinridge did more than study in Williamsburg; he also secured election to the Virginia House of Delegates.[43] In the state legislature, Breckinridge made a name for himself and befriended other lawmakers, including James Madison.[44] Indeed, Breckinridge supported Madison's efforts to ensure that Virginia did not establish a state-supported church.[45]

In 1784, Breckinridge departed from William and Mary and began to practice law.[46] He quickly proved to be a capable lawyer, and, on occasion, future chief justice John Marshall referred cases to him and provided welcome professional advice.[47] But competition for legal business in Virginia was fierce, as the state bar was highly distinguished.[48] Competition in the courtroom was equally daunting. As a young lawyer, Breckinridge found himself on several occasions standing before a judge and squaring off against the great orator Patrick Henry.[49]

If his law practice was professionally challenging, Breckinridge's service in the state house was downright hazardous to his well-being. Part of Breckinridge's tenure took place during the Revolutionary War; once, he and his colleagues had to flee from the invading British redcoats, barely escaping.[50] His colleague Daniel Boone was not so fortunate; he was taken prisoner by the British while trying to transport state records to safety.[51]

Breckinridge was described by his biographer as "a tall, slender man . . . with brown hair that held reddish tints brushed straight back and falling to his shoulders, and clear, grey eyes that could harden like steel. A long chin marred the symmetry of his face but reflected the determination contained in his sparse, muscular frame. His speech was easy but dignified, sometimes almost stern."[52] This is how Breckinridge must have looked when he met his future wife, the formidable Mary Hopkins Cabell, known as Polly.[53] The two were wed in 1785 and would raise a sizable family.[54] Their son Joseph Cabell Breckinridge, in turn, would father John C. Breckinridge, the future senator and vice president.[55] John and Mary would know not only great success together but also tremendous sorrow, losing two children at a young age.[56]

In the meantime, Breckinridge's political star began to rise. He befriended Jefferson following the latter's tenure as minister to France.[57] Breckinridge was elected to Congress as a representative from Virginia, but in 1793, prior to actually serving in Philadelphia, he moved his young family to the vicinity of Lexington, Kentucky.[58] Financial reasons apparently drove his decision to leave the Old Dominion.[59] Breckinridge evidently concluded that he could not adequately support himself in Virginia and decided to make his fortune in Kentucky.[60] His siblings had already moved to the Lexington area, making the decision a less difficult one.[61]

Political Rise in Kentucky

Once in the commonwealth, Breckinridge acquired substantial farmland and a number of slaves.[62] He also established a law practice devoted largely to property disputes.[63] Murky land titles drove the demand for able attorneys, and Breckinridge was soon recognized as one of Kentucky's leading lawyers.[64] His work reflected his disciplined mind, which was given to precision in legal argument.[65] In the words of his biographer, Breckinridge's legal arguments were marked not by "floral passages filled with overdrawn [al]lusions [like] . . . most of his colleagues,"[66] but rather by "clarity of thought and expression."[67]

The young lawyer's gradual ascent in public life was more the result of a sharp mind than a backslapping personality.[68] Breckinridge was not a glad-hander.[69] He was bookish and prone to withering sarcasm.[70] He was once gently chided by a colleague: "the People . . . like you well Enough—But they think you ought to ride through the country & be known to them, it is what they look for & what they say will operate most powerfully in your Favour—I think so too."[71] A eulogist described Breckinridge as "simple in his manners, grave and lofty in his carriage, self-denied in his personal habits . . . almost austere."[72]

This lack of a "hail fellow well met" personality may have contributed to Breckinridge's early failure to win a Senate seat.[73] In 1794, Breckinridge faced off against Federalist Humphrey Marshall and was defeated.[74] Marshall's victory, however, would prove to be one of the last gasps of the Federalist Party in Kentucky. Until the emergence of the Whigs, Democratic-Republicans would hold almost complete sway in the state.[75]

As political parties began to emerge in the 1790s, Breckinridge became a stalwart Jeffersonian.[76] Indeed, he would give his son Robert the middle name of Jefferson.[77] Further reflecting his commitment to the principles espoused by the Sage of Monticello, Breckinridge became president of the Lexington Democratic Society.[78] In addition to supporting Jeffersonian views, the group advocated vigorously for Kentucky to gain access to the Mississippi River.[79]

Philosophically, Breckinridge believed very strongly that the states should have wide latitude to govern themselves. Unlike his cousin John Brown, he had been slow to embrace the new US Constitution.[80] Like many Jeffersonians, he was dubious of the Senate, believing that the legislature should be based solely on population.[81] Breckinridge also questioned the wisdom of the Constitution's creation of a national judiciary.[82]

In 1795, Governor Isaac Shelby recognized Breckinridge's legal acumen and named him state attorney general.[83] Two years later, Breckinridge stepped down from that post and stood for the state house.[84] He was promptly elected and served for three eventful years, ultimately rising to become speaker.[85]

During the late 1790s, while Breckinridge was serving in the state legislature, war fever gripped the nation when the French government took a series of provocative actions against the United States. In response, the Federalist Party in Congress passed, and President John Adams signed into law, the notorious Alien and Sedition Acts, which restricted civil liberties. To his credit, Breckinridge opposed these measures.[86] In response, he worked closely with Vice President Jefferson on what came to be known as the Kentucky Resolutions.[87]

Breckinridge introduced one such measure in the state legislature in 1798 and another in 1799.[88] Both were adopted. Taken together, these two resolutions reasoned that the Union represented a mere compact of the states and that, should a state disagree with the lawfulness of a federal action, the state could simply void that act within its own boundaries.[89] These resolutions were intended to oppose an imprudent set of legislative measures, but unfortunately, they planted the seeds for John C. Calhoun's theory of "nullification," which would later be amplified by others prior to the Civil War to justify a state's "right" to secede from the Union.[90] The immediate result, however, was that Breckinridge's work with Jefferson on the resolutions began a partnership that would continue for the better part of a decade. It also catapulted Breckinridge to the forefront of the Jeffersonian Party in the commonwealth.[91]

In the state house, Breckinridge became a strong supporter of modernizing the state's criminal justice system.[92] At the time, the death penalty could be imposed for a host of minor offenses.[93] Breckinridge served on the legislative panel that drafted a new state criminal code that reformed many of these harsh penalties, and he subsequently fought to secure its adoption.[94]

In 1799, Breckinridge's stature was such that he was elected to the state convention charged with drafting a new constitution for the commonwealth.[95] Though he was initially skeptical of the need for a new state charter because of his concerns that it might undermine slavery (he was a major slaveholder himself), Breckinridge was chosen as a delegate to the convention.[96] He apparently played a major role in the drafting of the document.[97] Noted Kentucky historian

Thomas D. Clark concluded that Breckinridge "was perhaps the chief personal force in the new [constitutional] convention."[98]

Breckinridge also remained active in causes outside of the political context. In the 1790s, he lent his support to Transylvania University.[99] For four years, he was a trustee of the school, which helped earn Lexington the title "The Athens of the West."[100]

By the end of the eighteenth century, Breckinridge was seen as politically unassailable in Kentucky. A state lawmaker at the time noted: "none thwarted his plans, none attacked his position, or dared to enter with him [in] the arena of debate."[101] He was, therefore, ideally situated for another Senate run, and in 1800, Breckinridge was part of the pro-Jefferson tide that swept the Federalists from power. The state legislature sent him to Washington to join what has been called the "Revolution of 1800."[102] Before departing Kentucky, Breckinridge handed over much of his law practice to a promising young lawyer by the name of Henry Clay.[103]

In the Senate

As a newly elected president, with both houses of Congress soon to be filled with fellow partisans, Thomas Jefferson looked forward to pursuing an ambitious legislative agenda. Yet the political mores established by Washington and Adams dictated that, other than the president's formal constitutional responsibilities, the executive should involve himself in little legislative business.[104] Jefferson decided to take a different approach, concluding that presidential-legislative cooperation should be covert rather than overt.[105]

As a result, Jefferson took public steps that made it seem as if he were drawing a bright line between the presidency and Congress. For instance, he ended the custom of the president presenting his annual message to Congress in person—creating a new tradition that would remain in place until the Woodrow Wilson administration.[106] While symbolically removing himself from interaction with Congress, Jefferson broke new ground by personally working behind the scenes with friendly legislators.[107] He often hosted dinners for key members of Congress.[108] This allowed him to discreetly express his views, receive political intelligence, and cultivate allies.[109] Senator John Quincy Adams (Fed.-MA) described the Jeffersonian legislative approach as consisting of *Presidential* votes [whereby] the [Democratic-Republican] men . . . get in whispers his secret wishes, and vote accordingly."[110]

The president and his cabinet secretaries proved highly skilled at drafting legislative language for Congress to consider and persuading lawmakers of the merits of their position.[111] Jefferson's active direction of the cabinet to encourage legislative outcomes was a departure from the approach of President Washington, who had permitted Hamilton to exercise a fair amount of autonomy on legislative matters. According to scholar James Sterling Young, Jefferson's method of working through the cabinet permitted the "President to maintain . . . the outward appearance of conformity to community norms which decreed social distance between the President and Congress."[112]

To pursue this strategy successfully, Jefferson needed to find members of Congress who were both willing to work with him and his cabinet and sufficiently loyal and effective to secure the adoption of his agenda.[113] Given the pro-Jeffersonian majorities in both houses, his legislative liaisons became de facto floor leaders. In Jefferson's words, the ideal congressional floor leader would:

> consider the business of the nation as his own business, . . . take it up as if he were singly charged with it, and carry it through. I do not mean that any gentleman, relinquishing his own judgment, should implicitly support all of the measures of the administration; but that, where he does not disapprove of them, he should not suffer them to go off in sleep, but bring them to the attention of the House, and give them a fair chance. Where he disapproves, he will of course leave them to be brought forward by those who concur in the sentiment.[114]

One student of presidential-congressional relations during this period described how this informal leadership operated: "It was the special job of the floor leader . . . in the Senate to manage the Executive's program as it passed through the legislative mill. . . . [Leaders] planned the schedule, directed reference of matters to committees and controlled those committees with a firm hand, kept party members in line, defended the Administration on the floor, and served as a communications center between the Executive and the Republicans in Congress."[115] In the upper chamber, Jefferson needed able lieutenants, given that the Democratic-Republicans held a razor-thin seventeen-to-fifteen majority early in his tenure, and the Federalists were, by and large, the more seasoned legislators.[116] Initially, Jefferson looked to Virginian (and former Breckinridge college classmate) Stevens T. Mason (Dem.-Rep.) for Senate leadership.[117] Mason served as the primary presidential lieutenant in the early part of Jefferson's presidency, and Breckinridge was seen as second in command.[118] When Mason was not on the floor, Senator Adams characterized Breckinridge as being "at the wheel at helm."[119]

Given their long-standing personal bond and past collaboration on the Kentucky Resolutions, it is not surprising that Breckinridge emerged as one of Jefferson's main spokesmen in the Senate.[120] But Breckinridge's leadership in the chamber also stemmed from his keen analytical mind and skill in debate, which reinforced his high standing in Congress.[121] These factors were underscored by an important, informal network of which Breckinridge was a key part.[122] Like many legislators at the time, the Kentuckian belonged to a dining club.[123] This group of seventeen men regularly ate together, and a half dozen of them were senators, which accounted for more than one-sixth of the Senate at the time.[124] These informal gatherings presented an opportunity for Breckinridge to plot strategy with other lawmakers.

In his advocacy for Jefferson, Breckinridge proved highly capable.[125] Senator William Plumer (Fed.-NH) made this point indirectly when he compared Kentucky senator Buckner Thruston to Breckinridge. Plumer noted that Thruston "is not like his [former] colleague, Brackenridge [*sic*], or his present fellow Clay, [an] *effective man*. He very seldom takes an active part in the Senate—& when he does come forward in debate, he does not appear to advantage."[126]

One legislative item at the top of Jefferson's agenda was repealing the Judiciary Act of 1801, which had permitted the outgoing Federalist administration to pack the courts with like-minded judges.[127] On this issue, Breckinridge leaped to the forefront, putting forward a resolution concluding that the statute should be repealed.[128] This measure was clearly an assault on the independence of the judiciary and appears highly dubious to modern eyes.[129] However, Breckinridge believed in what he was doing, and he had home-state reasons for being so vocal.[130] Kentuckians were concerned that Federalist judges would overturn state court decisions regarding property disputes.[131]

In this context, Breckinridge did not wait for Jefferson or his cabinet to provide him with background material. The Kentuckian took the initiative, reaching out to other prominent Democratic-Republicans and requesting potential debating points he could use on the Senate floor.[132] Following a number of days of debate over repeal of the Judiciary Act, during which Breckinridge took the lead for the Jeffersonians, the resolution passed.[133] A three-person ad hoc committee was established to consider the measure.[134] Not surprisingly, Breckinridge was named to the panel.[135]

The committee promptly produced a repeal bill.[136] Later, a procedural setback prompted by Vice President Aaron Burr's defection from the Democratic-Republican ranks sent the measure to a new panel and jeopardized its adoption.[137] When it became clear that the party had reestablished a majority on the issue, it was Breckinridge who moved to discharge the bill from committee and secured Senate passage.[138] The measure constituted, in the words of one authority, "the first major triumph [for the Jeffersonians] as the majority party," and it paved the way for a highly productive legislative stretch for the president.[139]

Adoption of the bill cemented Breckinridge's status as an effective presidential spokesman and lawmaker.[140] Breckinridge would represent the "tip of the spear" for Jefferson on numerous legislative matters. In 1802, Spain restricted American access to the port of New Orleans, which threatened to have a devastating economic effect on western states such as Kentucky.[141] Federalists tried to pass a measure that essentially would have directed Jefferson to take military action against Spain.[142] This put Breckinridge in a tough political position. His constituents wanted immediate and decisive action, and he himself had been vocal about the need for Kentuckians to gain access to the Mississippi.[143] But Jefferson wanted the flexibility to try to resolve the matter peacefully.[144]

Breckinridge would not be the only Senate floor leader—de facto or otherwise—to be caught between the competing demands of his constituents and his fellow party members. Ultimately, Breckinridge secured the adoption of a measure that authorized, but did not require, Jefferson to raise troops.[145] Breckinridge also sent a public letter urging his constituents to keep their powder dry and to have faith in the administration.[146] Events would soon show the wisdom of this course of action, and a military solution proved unnecessary. In this regard, Breckinridge helped cool the passions of the moment.[147]

He remained active in the Senate on other matters. Breckinridge helped secure legislation granting Ohio statehood.[148] He fought successfully for James Monroe's confirmation as minister to France.[149] In addition, he played an indirect role in the famous litigation that would culminate in *Marbury v. Madison*. As part of this epic legal clash, Federalist William Marbury tried to gain access to Senate records.[150] Democratic-Republicans saw this litigation as a Federalist effort to move against the president, who had denied the frustrated Marbury the position of justice of the peace.[151] The Senate debated whether to provide Marbury with the evidence he needed for his lawsuit.[152] Breckinridge forcefully argued against handing the materials over to Marbury,[153] and ultimately, his advocacy helped persuade the Senate to deny the request.[154]

The Louisiana Purchase

In 1803, Jefferson took the most consequential action of his presidency. He committed the nation to buying the Louisiana Territory from France, which had taken over the colony from Spain. Adding the Louisiana Territory to the United States would double the size of the nation and resolve a pivotal security and economic problem by ensuring Americans unfettered access to the Mississippi River and the Gulf of Mexico (an issue that had flared up just months before).

At the time, however, it created a dilemma for Jefferson's followers.[155] The Democratic-Republican Party believed passionately in small government and in construing the Constitution strictly.[156] Yet the Constitution said nothing about the acquisition of territory and its incorporation into the Union, placing Jeffersonians in a quandary.[157] Should the Democratic-Republican Party abandon its principles (at least temporarily) and acquire the new territory through regular legislative means, or should the party stay true to its beliefs, try to amend the Constitution, and potentially risk losing this extraordinary opportunity to protect the nation's security and enhance its prosperity?[158] In the end, Jefferson chose the former.[159] But the president needed the Senate to approve the proposed treaty with France, and he needed the help of Congress as a whole to govern the territory. For this, Jefferson required an adept spokesman in the Senate. In May 1803, his primary Senate ally, Stevens T. Mason, passed away, leaving the president in need of a new lieutenant in the Senate.[160] Jefferson sought the assistance of Breckinridge.[161]

Almost immediately after learning of the potential acquisition of the Louisiana Territory, Jefferson reached out to the Kentuckian to build support for the legislative effort this would require.[162] On August 12, 1803, Jefferson wrote to Breckinridge, who was at home in Kentucky during a congressional recess.[163] In a mark of trust between the two men, the president openly acknowledged the constitutional difficulties involved with the proposed purchase and expressed the opinion that a constitutional amendment would likely be needed.[164] To that end, the president urged that all Jeffersonian lawmakers be on time for the start of the congressional session. Jefferson expressed to Breckinridge:

> This treaty must of course be laid before both houses, because both have important functions to exercise respecting it. [T]hey I presume will see their duty to their country in ratifying & paying for it, so as to secure a good which would otherwise probably be never again in their power. [B]ut I suppose they must then appeal to *the nation* for an additional article to the constitution, approving & confirming an act which the nation had not previously authorized. The constitution has made no provision for our holding foreign territory, still less for incorporating foreign nations into our Union. [T]he Executive in seising the fugitive occurrence which so much advanced the good of their country, have done an act beyond the constitution. [T]he legislature in casting behind them Metaphysical subtleties, and risking themselves like faithful servants, must ratify & pay for it, and throw themselves on their country for doing for them unauthorised what we know they would have done for themselves had they been in a situation to do it. . . .
>
> I hope yourself & all the Western members will make a sacred point of being at the first day of the meeting of Congress.[165]

Before Breckinridge could reply, a letter from the American minister to France made Jefferson think twice about encouraging Congress to begin deliberations over a constitutional amendment.[166] Jefferson dashed off another letter to Breckinridge six days after his first one:

> I wrote you on the 12th . . . on the subject of Louisiana, and the constitutional provision which might be necessary for it. [A] letter received yesterday shews that nothing must be said on that subject which may give a pretext for retracting; but that we should do sub silentio what shall be found necessary. [B]e so good therefore as to consider that part of my letter as confidential. [I]t strengthens the reasons for desiring the presence of every friend to the treaty on the first day of the session. [P]erhaps you can impress this necessity on the Senators of the Western states by private letter.[167]

In his reply to Jefferson, Breckinridge seemed untroubled by the "Metaphysical subtleties" of the constitutional matters involved, making no mention of them.[168] Instead, he focused on his own efforts to ensure that Jeffersonian lawmakers returned to the nation's capital in a timely fashion to debate and vote on the Louisiana Purchase.[169] Indeed, Breckinridge urged his fellow partisans to arrive early so that they could hold a caucus on the issue.[170]

With respect to securing the new territory, Breckinridge needed little encouragement; he enthusiastically carried the president's standard. After all, the purchase was pivotal to Kentucky's development because it ensured, once and for all, that the commonwealth's farmers and merchants would have access to the Mississippi River and, in turn, access to markets on the Eastern Seaboard and abroad.[171] This would have an immeasurable impact on the state's economic life.[172]

Jefferson called Congress back into session in October, earlier than planned.[173] Breckinridge performed his duties well, ensuring the attendance of all but one western senator at the opening of the session.[174] With Breckinridge's leadership and advocacy on the floor, the Senate approved the treaty on October 20, 1803.[175]

Once the Senate approved the treaty acquiring the Louisiana Territory, the United States had to take possession of the territory and govern it on an interim basis.[176] This required legislation.[177] Again, the Jefferson administration sought Breckinridge's assistance.[178] In this regard, Breckinridge worked closely with the president's "right-hand man," Secretary of the Treasury Albert Gallatin.[179] The secretary submitted a draft bill to Breckinridge to provide for the incorporation and governance of the newly acquired Louisiana Territory.[180] The Kentuckian introduced the Gallatin-drafted legislation, and it was referred to a three-person ad hoc panel.[181] Naturally, Breckinridge was made a member of the committee.[182] A day later, the panel reported out the measure, and it was quickly adopted by the Senate.[183] The bill was subsequently enacted with one modification by the House.[184]

Jefferson and Breckinridge still had one more item to address: an instrument to govern the territory on a long-term basis—that is, a territorial constitution.[185] Once again, the administration took the lead.[186] In November, the president and Breckinridge met—perhaps with others—to discuss the territorial constitution.[187] Afterward, Jefferson wrote to Breckinridge:

> I thought I perceived in you the other day a dread of the job of preparing a constitution for the new acquisition. [W]ith more boldness than wisdom I therefore determined to prepare a canvass, give it a few daubs of outline, and send it to you to fill up. I yesterday morning took up the subject, & scribbled off the inclosed. [I]n communicating it to you I must do it in confidence that you will never let any person know that I have put pen to paper on the subject, & that if you think the inclosed can be of any aid to you, you will take the trouble to copy it & return me the original. I am thus particular, because you know with what bloody teeth & fangs the federalists will attack any sentiment or principle known to come from me.[188]

This letter reflects once again Jefferson's trust in Breckinridge and the perceived need to avoid the appearance of presidential "meddling" in legislative affairs.

Breckinridge dutifully introduced legislation patterned after Jefferson's draft charter.[189] On the floor, he made sure that an ad hoc committee partial to the president was established to finalize the legislation related to governance of the newly acquired territory.[190] Once again, Breckinridge was named to the panel, and this time, he was made its chairman.[191] Following a lengthy debate and a handful of legislative modifications, the measure passed.[192]

Through these actions, Breckinridge—as an informal presidential spokesman—played a central role in the most important achievement of the Jefferson presidency and one of the most significant acts in American history: acquisition of the Louisiana Territory.[193] At this point, with the possible exception of William Cary Nicholas (Dem.-Rep.–VA), Breckinridge stood unrivaled in the Senate.[194] Also apparent was that Jefferson's method of working through informal floor leaders (in both houses) had borne fruit.

Subsequent Senate Career

In 1804, when Breckinridge's former classmate William Giles became a Democratic-Republican senator from Virginia, the latter quickly stepped into the role of primary presidential spokesman.[195] The Kentuckian remained a trusted lieutenant, however, as the Jefferson administration continued to quietly funnel him draft legislative language to try to get enacted.[196]

That same year, Breckinridge was active in the impeachment trial of Supreme Court justice Samuel Chase, part of the Jeffersonians' strategic assault against the Federalist-controlled judiciary.[197] Breckinridge, Giles, and three others served on the ad hoc committee that drew up the rules for conducting the trial.[198] To this end, Breckinridge and Giles worked together on the Senate floor to pave the way for Chase's removal.[199] The Kentuckian was one of only four senators who voted to remove Chase on seven of the eight counts brought against him.[200] Ultimately, Chase was acquitted by the Senate.

Despite his loyalty to Jefferson, it bears noting that Breckinridge did not always follow the president's lead. In 1805, for instance, the Kentuckian opposed a Jefferson-negotiated treaty with the Creek Indians.[201]

The 1804 Campaign and the Jefferson Cabinet

Going into the presidential election of 1804, the Democratic-Republican high command knew two things: they would be renominating Jefferson for president, and they would *not* be renominating Burr for vice president, as the latter had demonstrated party disloyalty. When the party convened its nominating caucus in the US Capitol in February, Breckinridge was seriously considered for the vice presidency.[202] Although George Clinton of New York ultimately got the nod, Breckinridge garnered the second most votes.[203]

He did not become vice president, but Breckinridge soon gained recognition for himself and for the region he represented: the West.[204] In August 1805, he accepted an appointment from President Jefferson to serve as the nation's fifth attorney general, making him the first cabinet officer from west of the Appalachian Mountains.[205] At the time, the position of attorney general was unique in the cabinet, since it had no bureaucracy or staff to support the officeholder.[206] The Department of Justice would not be created until after the Civil War.[207] Thus, in the early nineteenth century, the attorney general was largely on his own. Indeed, it was understood that officeholders would continue to practice law in a private capacity in order to support themselves.[208]

The Kentuckian continued his efforts at executive-legislative cooperation during his term as attorney general, only this time, the roles were reversed.[209] Breckinridge was now the one providing Congress with advice and draft legislative language, rather than being on the receiving end.[210] Nonetheless, Breckinridge's stint as attorney general was not a smashing success.[211] Of the six cases he argued before the Supreme Court, he won only one outright.[212] Moreover, there were rumors that the relationship between Jefferson and Breckinridge had grown more distant.[213]

In any case, Breckinridge's tenure in the cabinet was not a long one. Throughout his adult life, the Kentuckian had been plagued by ill health.[214] In the summer of 1806, he apparently contracted tuberculosis.[215] In late October, he complained to Jefferson of ill health and "severe indisposition" and informed the president that he would not be in the capital in November as he had hoped.[216] He never made it back. Breckinridge died before the end of the year at age forty-six.

The Jeffersonian legislative approach depended largely on three factors: the president's immense stature and political finesse, Democratic-Republican majorities in Congress, and talented congressional lieutenants.[217] Once Mason, Breckinridge, and Giles left the Senate, Jefferson's legislative achievements diminished accordingly.[218] Similarly, after Jefferson departed the White House, his example of providing effective legislative direction largely disappeared as well, leaving Senate leadership in a state of flux.[219]

Aside from the Kentucky Resolutions, Breckinridge's political legacy includes reform of the commonwealth's criminal code, his role in cooling the passions stirred by the Spanish restrictions on the port of New Orleans, and his crucial support for the Jeffersonian legislative agenda—most notably, effectuating the Louisiana Purchase.[220] In recognition of these achievements, Breckinridge County in midwestern Kentucky is named after him.[221]

More broadly, the Breckinridge family dynasty, which John Breckinridge founded, has left an indelible mark on Kentucky and the nation.[222] His grandson, John C. Breckinridge, represented the state in the Senate and became vice president. Five more Breckinridges would later serve in Congress.[223] Other family members were active in public affairs in other ways.[224] Even though Breckinridge's life was not a long one, he established a family whose contributions would be enduring.

* * *

The Jeffersonian approach of discreetly recruiting senators to serve as unofficial legislative spokesmen is largely obsolete. In the modern era, presidents typically make their legislative priorities clear; the reticence displayed by Jefferson was abandoned long ago. Moreover, if the Senate leader is from the same party as the president, he often—but not always—serves as the president's champion. That said, on occasion, individual members who are not part of the formal Senate leadership may enjoy close relations with the president. During my first two years in the chamber, for example, it was widely known that Senator Paul Laxalt (R-NV) was a good friend of Presi-

dent Ronald Reagan. It certainly did not hurt Senator Laxalt's stature in the Senate to be on intimate terms with the president.[225]

* * *

Legislative Lieutenants

Breckinridge is one of the first well-known presidential spokesmen in the Senate. Others would follow intermittently. Presidential lieutenants in the Breckinridge mode—actively working with the chief executive to enact his legislative agenda—were not the norm for most of the nineteenth century because most presidents did not actively pursue legislative programs.[226] Moreover, to a great extent, both the president and Congress accepted the idea that the executive should not "meddle" in legislative affairs. The ethos of nineteenth-century presidential-congressional relations was captured, with perhaps some exaggeration, by Senator George Hoar (R-MA), who wrote of the post–Civil War period: "The most eminent Senators . . . would have received as a personal affront a private message from the White House expressing a desire that they should adopt any course in the discharge of their legislative duties that they did not approve. If they visited the White House, it was to give, not to receive advice."[227]

Nonetheless, from time to time, presidents would work through Senate surrogates. Examples include Thomas Hart Benton (Jack./D-MO), Kentucky native Felix Grundy (Jack./D-TN), and Silas Wright (D-NY) during the Jackson and Van Buren presidencies; Oliver Morton (R-IN) during Ulysses Grant's time in office; and Senator Henry Cabot Lodge (R-MA) during the Theodore Roosevelt administration.[228] As noted, to a great extent, this informal role has been subsumed by floor leaders of the president's party.

4

Senator as National Political Leader

Henry Clay

The first two chapters of this book examined two formal Senate positions—the vice presidency and the office of president pro tempore. As demonstrated earlier, those institutions never succeeded in becoming effective agents of leadership in the Senate, and to fill that gap, informal means of guiding the Senate sprouted, such as the presidential lieutenant, discussed in chapter 3. Yet another means was through the leadership of a senator with a national political following.[1] Achieving national stature and leading the Senate in this way has been a rarity because it requires an extraordinary individual and a unique set of circumstances.[2] This chapter examines this approach to Senate leadership through the career of the consummate legislator: Henry Clay.

Early Life

Clay was born in Virginia in 1777, amidst the clash of arms of the American Revolution. Indeed, one of Clay's first recollections was of British soldiers plundering his childhood home.[3] He was one of nine children.[4] His father, John, was a minister who passed away when Henry was only four years old.[5] His mother, Elizabeth, remarried when Clay was still a young boy, and shortly thereafter, she and Clay's stepfather moved to Kentucky without him.[6] It was determined that the lad would stay behind in Virginia to learn a trade, so at fourteen years of age, Clay began to work as a store clerk in Richmond.[7] Nevertheless, Clay's origins were not quite as modest as he would later suggest.[8] With some exaggeration, he claimed to be "an orphan boy; who had never recognized a father's smile, nor felt his warm caresses; poor, penniless, without the favor of the great, with an imperfect and neglected education."[9]

Young Clay did, however, earn "the favor of the great" when the esteemed Virginia jurist George Wythe hired him to be his private secretary.[10] This proved to be a major opportunity, as Wythe had taught Thomas Jefferson, James Monroe, John Marshall, John Brown, and, in all likelihood, John Breckinridge.[11] Of Wythe, Clay would later say, "To no man was I more indebted by his instructions, his advice, and his example."[12] Clay learned much from the venerable jurist, which fueled his ambition and exposed him to the most elite bar in eighteenth-century America.[13] After working under Wythe in Virginia for five years, Clay became an attorney in his own right and decided it was time to make his own way in the world.[14] In 1797, he departed for the five-year-old commonwealth of Kentucky.

Clay settled near his relatives in Lexington and soon married into the prominent Hart family.[15] He and his wife, Lucretia, were married for more than half a century. During that time, the couple was no stranger to tragedy; seven of their eleven children predeceased them.[16]

Upon his arrival in Lexington, Clay began to practice law in earnest and proved himself a highly capable attorney. He was handsomely paid for his efforts, prompting Clay to quip, "I am not at all unwilling to receive liberal fees."[17] Despite his gratification at receiving "liberal fees," Clay sometimes represented clients without pay. One such instance involved his serving as pro bono defense counsel to Aaron Burr during the initial proceedings of the former vice president's treason trial.[18]

Clay's legal acumen extended to his performance before appellate courts as well.[19] He won nine of the eleven cases he argued before what is now the Kentucky Supreme Court and thirteen of the twenty-three cases he argued before the US Supreme Court.[20] Clay earned such a sterling reputation as an attorney that President John Quincy Adams proposed to nominate him to the Supreme Court.[21] Clay politely declined, as he had other plans.[22] Politics was always his true calling.[23]

Personal Attributes

By his early twenties, Clay had begun his meteoric rise in American politics. The question arises: what permitted this young man to reach such heights? To a great extent, his success was attributable to a rare combination of talents.

For one, he was a spellbinding orator. This was an essential skill in the era long before radio and television. Seeing a politician give an address in person might be the only contact a voter had with a candidate. It was therefore important to be well spoken. Of Clay's voice, a contemporary said: "Whoever heard one more melodious? There was a depth of tone in it, a volume, a compass, a rich and tender harmony, which invested all he said with majesty."[24] He could calibrate his delivery to great effect, raising his voice for emphasis one moment and then lowering it until his words were barely audible.[25]

It was not just the timbre of his voice but also his manner and delivery that made his speeches so memorable. His gestures, his facial expressions, and the modulation of his delivery all contributed to his ability to captivate an audience.[26] Watching Clay deliver a speech was like attending a theatrical production.[27] One onlooker painted a vivid portrait of Clay on the Senate floor:

> You are struck at once with his appearance. He is tall and slender of shape, his arms, defectively, too long for his size. In dress he is plain—yet adhering to the now antiquated blue coat and gilt buttons. When he commences his remarks, he appears rather awkward and ungainly—which appearance is heightened by a pronunciation of some words with marked peculiarity and impropriety. These defects, however are lost sight of, as he proceeds. . . . His form . . . becomes lofty and erect—his countenance beams with life. He looks, thinks, and feels every word he utters. His action is, at times, violent in the extreme, yet not overstrained or unnatural. His voice is indescribably fine, and constitutes one of the greatest charms of his oratory. Indeed no man can witness an effort of Mr. Clay's, without assenting to the trust of the remark of . . . [Demosthenes], who being asked wherein consisted eloquence, replied "action, action, action."
>
> Of Mr. Clay, as an orator, you can have no kind of idea, by reading his speeches. You are amazed when you peruse coolly in the papers, a day or two afterwards, what enchained your attention, and feasted your soul and your senses, midst the crowd and beauty at the capitol.[28]

Furthermore, Clay utilized props masterfully as he spoke.[29] Another observer described how Clay's "arms, hands, fingers, feet, and even his spectacles, his snuff-box, and his pocket-handkerchief, aided him in debate."[30]

Indeed, Clay's speaking ability was thought to be on a par with that of Daniel Webster (W-MA), although the two men had markedly different styles.[31] One fellow lawmaker provided a "tale of the tape" in comparing these two heavyweights of declamation:

> Compared to Clay, Webster has greater power of reasoning, and less native eloquence than the great Western orator. Webster acts directly on the understanding; Clay on the understanding through the passions. In acquired knowledge, in taste, in professional attainments and political science, Webster has the advantage; but in popular address, in the skillful adaption of means to ends, in the contagious enthusiasm which leaves no time for hesitation or doubt, in promptness, in confidence of power or success Clay possesses advantages over every person I ever saw, in the management of a popular assembly, Webster is generally grave, earnest, and argumentative.[32]

A closely related trait was Clay's great skill in marshaling arguments. One contemporary said of the Kentuckian's abilities, "hundreds, perhaps thousands, of men in the United States . . . exceed Henry Clay, in information on all subjects, but his superiority consists in the power and adroitness with which he brings his information to bear."[33]

Clay had a powerful intellect. The wife of one senator asserted that, of all the people she had ever encountered, "Prince Hal" was the most brilliant—and this woman had known both Thomas Jefferson and James Madison.[34] Clay also had a wonderfully creative and imaginative mind. He could, in today's parlance, "think outside the box." Yet, despite his innate ability, Clay was in many ways less "a reader of books [than] . . . a reader of men."[35]

In addition, he had a great sense of humor.[36] With this trait, he could charm his listeners and disarm his foes or cut them to ribbons.[37] On one occasion, Alexander Smyth (Dem.-Rep.–VA) was in the midst of an interminable oration.[38] Smyth suddenly pivoted, looked directly at Clay, and remarked disdainfully: "You, sir, speak for the present generation; but I speak for posterity."[39] Without batting an eye, Clay retorted, "Yes, and you seem resolved to speak until the arrival of *your* audience."[40]

In both small groups and one-on-one, Clay was extraordinarily affable.[41] He had great personal magnetism and an almost irresistible charm. Even one of his longtime rivals, John C. Calhoun (D-SC), said of him: "I don't like Henry Clay. He is a bad man, an imposter, a creator of wicked schemes. I wouldn't speak to him, but, by God, I love him."[42] (Clay's personal warmth and effervescence stood in marked contrast to the coldly logical Calhoun. It was remarked about the South Carolinian that he would be unable to pen a love poem since he would start each stanza with "whereas.")[43]

The Kentuckian's empathy extended to his interactions with everyday citizens.[44] A reporter said of Clay: "Whenever he saw a blacksmith forge, or a carpenter shop, or a mill, or a factory, or a stone quarry, or a steam engine, or a printing press, or a mart of commerce his heart thrilled with interest and went out in patriotic affection for the people who were at work in those places."[45]

Over time, Clay developed a vision regarding where he wanted to take the nation.[46] This became known as the "American System."[47] It was a nationalist agenda: protective tariffs to encourage fledgling US industry and economic development; infrastructure improvements to facilitate trade and more closely bind the Union; a reliable financial system guided by a Bank of the United States; a reaffirmation of the primacy of the legislative branch; and, above all, maintenance of the Union.[48] One political opponent complained that aspects of Clay's agenda "out-Hamilton[ed] Alexander Hamilton."[49]

Moreover, Clay saw potential ways to exercise power that others overlooked.[50] This led him to assert authority in novel ways.[51] Many talented public figures have come and gone who failed to understand how to harness either their own political prestige or the powers of their office to achieve their goals. Clay had no such difficulty.[52]

He understood the context in which he operated as a legislator. He knew that to get things done, he often had to give up a little. Clay utterly repudiated the view that a lawmaker should stand aloof and never make concessions. He stated: "All legislation, all government, all society, is founded upon the principle of mutual concession, politeness, comity, courtesy; upon these everything is based. . . . Compromise is peculiarly appropriate among the members of a republic, as of one common family. Let him who elevates himself above humanity, above its weaknesses, its infirmities, its wants, its necessities, say, if he pleases, I never will compromise; but let no one who is not above the frailties of our common nature disdain compromises."[53]

Not surprisingly, Clay's rare combination of gifts left an impression. Abraham Lincoln's law partner and longtime friend William Herndon recalled that in their substantial time together, the future president spoke favorably of only two past political figures.[54] One was Jefferson, and the other was Clay.[55]

Yet, despite his remarkable array of talents, Clay had a penchant for making stunningly bad political decisions. In part, this was because he was a risk taker by nature.[56] As one newspaper observed, "Mr. Clay is a gamester in politics but not a cool one."[57] This poor judgment ultimately cost him the great ambition of his life: the presidency.[58]

Moreover, Clay had a tendency to be domineering, high-handed, and cutting in debate.[59] These traits led him to litter the political landscape with lifelong enemies.[60] Among them would be the formidable Andrew Jackson.[61]

Early Political Career

After several successful years practicing law in the commonwealth, Clay decided to embark on a political career. He was elected to the Kentucky General Assembly in 1803 and quickly rose through the ranks, becoming speaker of the state house.[62] Three years later, Clay purchased Ashland, his home in Lexington, which today is a famed historical site.[63] That same year, he was first elected to the US Senate and arrived on the Washington scene.[64] Clay, just short of the minimum age of thirty, thus launched a congressional career that, despite a good many interruptions, would span more than forty-five years. In spite of his youth, Clay made an impression on the Senate. John Quincy Adams (Fed.-MA) took notice. He wrote, "Mr. Clay, the new member from Kentucky . . . is quite a young man [and] an orator—and a republican of the first fire."[65]

In the early nineteenth century, a seat in the Senate was generally thought to be less desirable than a seat in the House. Today, the usual career path is to start in the House and move to the Senate, not the other way around. But in the first few decades under the Constitution, the House was generally where the action was.[66] And Clay always wanted to be at the center of the action. The "turbulence" of the House of Representatives, he commented, was more to his liking than "the solemn stillness of the Senate Chamber."[67] His first two Senate terms, which he served as a Democratic-Republican, were brief—just a few months each. Then, in 1810, Clay was elected to the US House of Representatives.[68] He would not return to the Senate for more than two decades.

Clay arrived in the House with a policy agenda of his own.[69] Like many in what was then considered the West, he was angered by the indignities visited on the United States by Great Britain.[70] Allegations of British support for Indian raids on the western frontier, for instance, were commonplace.[71] The boarding of American ships by the Royal Navy and the seizing of US sailors were unacceptable to Clay and to major segments of the newly independent nation.[72] The Kentuckian and his allies believed that American pride and sovereignty demanded a bold response against the British.

Before his swearing in, Clay moved into a boardinghouse in Washington where several other newly elected lawmakers lived, one of whom was Calhoun.[73] Clay quickly won over his fellow boarders, which helped him take charge of the large, boisterous, nationalistic freshman class later known as the "War Hawks."[74] In 1811, with the help of these colleagues, Clay was chosen Speaker on his first day in the chamber.[75] Upon his elevation, Clay became the first of four Kentuckians to serve as House Speaker; the others—John White, Linn Boyd, and John G. Carlisle—also served in the nineteenth century.[76]

At the time of Clay's arrival in the House, the speakership was a position of little influence. It was more akin to the office of Speaker in the British House of Commons than a focus of real leadership.[77] The fact that the speakership today is a significant office is in large part due to the work of Clay.[78] The Kentuckian transformed the speakership from a position that merely maintained order to one that actually leads the majority party and sets legislative priorities.[79]

With his energy, creativity, charisma, and oratorical brilliance, Clay took the reins of the House and drove the chamber. In his new position, he saw the opportunity to exercise power that others had not recognized or perhaps had not dared to try. Prior to Clay, Speakers had enjoyed the authority to choose committee members, but this had been done in a nonpartisan, nonideological way.[80] Not so with Clay. He immediately filled the key committees with freshman War Hawks who shared his views.[81] Nor was he afraid to interpret the rules liberally if it helped his cause.[82]

In a departure from earlier practice, Clay would often leap into the middle of debate, something he had done as presiding officer in the state house.[83] Even today, this is an unusual action for the Speaker.[84] Clay's dramatic oratory and effectiveness as a debater, coupled with his creative use of power, all raised the profile of the speakership.[85] In this manner, Clay directed the flow of legislative business in the House for almost a decade.[86] Mary Follett, author of an early treatise on the office, termed Clay "the boldest of Speakers."[87]

During this era, members of Congress participated in congressional caucuses that helped select presidential candidates for their parties.[88] With the Federalist Party largely moribund, the Democratic-Republican Party—of which Clay was a prominent member—was essentially the only game in town. With his enhanced power as Speaker, and with the support of his fellow War Hawks, Clay played a significant role in leveraging the congressional caucus to persuade President James Madison—who desired a second term—to pursue hostilities against the British in what would become known as the War of 1812.[89] Again, Clay envisioned and executed groundbreaking use of power.

Once both the United States and the United Kingdom recognized the need to cease hostilities, efforts were initiated to formally end the war. This meant a negotiated settlement. In 1814, Clay stepped down as Speaker to serve as one of the five US diplomats sent to Europe to negotiate a peace treaty with Great Britain to end the war he had helped bring about.[90] Other negotiators included John Quincy Adams and former treasury secretary Albert Gallatin.

Once the delegation arrived in Ghent (in what is today Belgium), the American diplomats all lived together, which quickly developed into something reminiscent of an episode of the *Odd Couple*.[91] While serving in Congress, Clay was never averse to kicking up his heels.[92] Senator William Plumer (Fed.-NH) observed that Clay was "a great favorite with the ladies [and attended] all parties of pleasure—out almost every night—gambles much here—reads but little."[93] Clay was no different as a diplomat.

In contrast, Adams was a serious-minded man who followed a highly disciplined daily regimen. He often woke at 4:30 a.m. to begin an intense schedule of work and study.[94] Adams often started his day just as the others, led by Clay, were going to bed.[95] In his diary, Adams sniffed, "I hear Mr. Clay's company retiring from his chamber. . . . [Clay's group was playing] cards [and] they parted as I was about to rise."[96]

Despite these personal tensions, on Christmas Eve 1814, the American negotiators and their British counterparts agreed to the Treaty of Ghent, ending the conflict that has been likened to a "Second War of Independence."[97] Clay returned to the House the next year and was promptly elected Speaker again.[98]

Upon his return to the House, Clay helped secure the first of three monumental legislative measures that would preserve the Union and win him national acclaim. This stature later permitted him to achieve and maintain dominance in the Senate. With the expansion of the United States following the Louisiana Purchase, new territories became part of the Union. This led to the question of whether these territories would join as free states or slave states. As the North gained in population, the slave states in the South worried that they were losing influence in the House, where representation is based on population.[99] The slave states thus looked to the Senate, where each state has equal representation, to preserve what was euphemistically called the "peculiar institution."[100] At the time, the upper chamber was evenly divided between free states and slave states.[101]

The territory of Missouri brought the issue of slavery squarely before Congress in 1819 when it formally requested statehood as a prospective slave state.[102] This led to one of the most momentous debates in the nation's history. It was widely thought that the admission of new states would decide the future of slavery, as adding new states would jeopardize the delicate free-state–slave-state equilibrium in the Senate.[103] Southerners spoke openly of disunion in an effort to preserve slavery.[104] The aging Thomas Jefferson described the stakes in the controversy: "This momentous question, like a fire bell in the night, awakened and filled me with terror. I considered it at once as the knell of the Union."[105] Clay confided to Adams his deep concern "that within five years from this time the Union would be divided into three distinct confederacies."[106]

Throughout this controversy, President James Monroe exercised little leadership.[107] This was customary at a time when presidents generally interpreted their powers modestly.[108] Sensing opportunity, Clay stepped into the breach.[109]

The Kentuckian was only partly responsible for what is now called the First Missouri Compromise.[110] Many pieces of this legislative package, which helped defuse the crisis, were put in place without Clay's active involvement.[111] But he did propose tying the introduction of Maine as a free state to the introduction of Missouri as a slave state.[112] The other key element—a prohibition against slavery in territories above the 36° 30' parallel—was the work of Senator Jesse Thomas (Dem.-Rep.–IL).[113] In any case, Clay's novel use of the Speaker's power as presiding officer ensured that the agreement was not unraveled by opponents of the measure.[114] This compromise calmed frayed nerves, at least temporarily.

However, following this grand legislative effort, there remained the question of whether Missouri was in fact a state.[115] Congress had yet to approve Missouri's proposed constitution, and this led to more problems. Some northern congressmen were upset over a clause in the charter that restricted the entrance of free African Americans and people of mixed race into Missouri.[116] In response, Clay spearheaded the drafting of legislative language to the effect that Missouri would gain statehood under the condition that the controversial clause could never be interpreted to deny "privileges and immunities" to "any citizen."[117] The final language, which was eventually agreed on, made no reference to any racial category.

* * *

When drafting legislation, purposeful ambiguity—which allows both sides to claim victory or at least not to feel aggrieved—can sometimes be important to achieving success. So it was in the case of the Second Missouri Compromise. By avoiding any express reference to free African Americans, the wording papered over the cracks of sectional discord and ultimately allowed Missouri to achieve statehood in August 1821 without prompting violence or disunion.[118]

* * *

Prince Hal also played an important role in a coda to the two Missouri Compromises. The issue was whether Missouri's electoral votes should be counted in the 1820 presidential race.[119] The question was largely academic, as Monroe would have been elected easily either way, but the issue promised to reopen wounds that had only recently begun to heal.[120] Clay's solution was simple: tabulate the electoral votes with Missouri's total included, and then count them again and exclude the state's votes.[121] Once more, this commonsense approach reflected Clay's ingenuity.[122]

The Jackson Era and Clay's Senate Leadership

Winning the presidential election of 1824 was soon at the forefront of Clay's thinking. Yet, despite his best efforts, the Kentuckian finished fourth in the balloting behind Andrew Jackson, John Quincy Adams, and William Crawford. Since no candidate received a majority of electoral votes, the presidential race had to be decided by the House of Representatives for only the second time in history.[123]

As the powerful Speaker of the House, Clay was well positioned to be the "king maker."[124] Yet he never gave any serious thought to supporting Jackson, even though the former general had won the popular vote. Clay viewed Jackson as erratic and heedless of the Constitution.[125] The Kentuckian had also denounced him on the House floor in the late 1810s, ensuring the lifelong enmity of Old Hickory.[126] Near the end of his life, a friend asked Jackson whether he had any regrets.[127] Jackson said he had only two, and one of them was that he "didn't shoot Henry Clay."[128]

In the presidential contest of 1824, Clay ultimately threw his support to Adams, who was duly elected president by the House. Jackson, despite leading in electoral votes, was defeated. A few days after Adams's election, the president-elect approached Clay about becoming secretary of state.[129] Clay thought it over for a few days and then accepted.[130] Undoubtedly, he calculated that becoming secretary of state would advance his efforts to become president. After all, the previous four presidents—Jefferson, Madison, Monroe, and Adams—had all held the position, and the last three had been elected president as the sitting secretary. Yet this decision would prove to be one of the major strategic blunders of his political career and, indeed, in all of American history.

Predictably, Clay's elevation to secretary of state led to howls of protest from the Jacksonians. They dubbed his appointment the "corrupt bargain," contending that Clay had cast aside the will of the people, elevated Adams to the presidency, and in turn been made secretary.[131] Although there is little evidence of an explicit quid pro quo, Clay could not escape the "corrupt bargain" charge, and it placed a cloud over his tenure as secretary and ultimately over his presidential aspirations.[132] It also marked the end of a remarkable period in his career. As Mary Follett wrote in her treatise on the speakership, "It is not too much to say . . . that Clay was the most powerful man in the nation from 1811 to 1825."[133]

The next four years would prove less successful for Clay. The pro-Jackson Congress thwarted many of his diplomatic initiatives as secretary of state, such as participation in the Panama Congress, a major international gathering.[134] His tenure was not without some modest achievements, however. For instance, Clay inked more commercial treaties for the United States than any prior secretary.[135] His efforts to promote independence and autonomy for the newly liberated nations of Central and South America and proclaim American solidarity with them were farsighted if unfulfilled in the immediate term.[136] Nonetheless, Clay's time as chief diplomat was not his finest hour.[137]

During the 1824 campaign, the Democratic-Republican Party, which had been the only viable national political party for several years, began to splinter. Supporters of Adams and Clay came to be called National Republicans, while Jackson partisans continued to refer to themselves as Democratic-Republicans.[138] These two groups would square off in earnest four years later.

In the 1828 contest, Jackson was determined not to be denied the White House. He routed Adams in a rematch for the presidency, and Clay's term as secretary of state drew to a close. For the time being, he returned to private life in Kentucky.[139] With Adams's loss, however, Clay emerged as the acknowledged leader of the National Republicans and their presidential front-runner.[140]

In his quest for the White House, Clay believed he needed a platform.[141] Thus, in 1831, he returned to the Senate after an absence of twenty years, defeating Richard Mentor Johnson for the seat.[142] As his party's presumptive presidential nominee, Clay enjoyed a status in the chamber that could be likened to that of Senator Jackson after Adams's election. But, whereas Jackson had displayed little aptitude as a legislator and soon left the upper chamber, Clay remained in the Senate and excelled. One observer commented that the Kentuckian was "eminently calculated to head and lead a party—feeling enthusiasm and imparting it."[143]

"Harry of the West" excelled in the upper chamber not only because he brought a nationwide political following with him but also because he could draw on the prestige he had earned from nearly a quarter century of public life.[144] Moreover, the Senate had no effective formal leadership organs at the time.[145] As discussed earlier, vice presidents and presidents pro tempore did not direct the Senate's fortunes, and there was no majority leader who was expected to lead the body.[146] As a result, when Clay returned to Congress, he had the immediate opportunity to become, in essence, the preeminent senator.[147] Even though his party—the anti-Jacksonian National Republicans—did not constitute a majority in the Senate when he first returned to the body, Clay still managed to play an outsized legislative role.[148]

By and large, the House was where most of the legislative action occurred during the first few decades under the Constitution.[149] This dynamic began to shift in the 1820s.[150] During this period, slave states gradually lost representation in the House, and the Senate assumed a more prominent role as slave states and free states existed in equal numbers and hence enjoyed equal representation.[151] The Senate acquired greater importance in national affairs and, consequently, attracted the major political figures of the day, including John C. Calhoun, Daniel Webster, and Thomas Hart Benton (Jack.-MO).[152]

Clay's plan to use his de facto leadership perch in the Senate as a platform to pursue the presidency in 1832 proved a daunting task, however. Indeed, only three men have ever succeeded in securing the presidency directly from the upper chamber.[153] Moreover, Clay's opponent was a popular incumbent—his archrival Jackson. The Kentuckian profoundly misread the political climate, and Old Hickory thrashed him handily in the election.[154]

Despite his poor showing in the presidential race, Clay decided to remain in the Senate, where important work remained to be done. It had taken less than a decade for the wounds sutured by the two Missouri Compromises to reopen. The nation needed someone to broker another accord, or it faced potential ruin. This time, the issue involved the tariff, which had emerged as a political flashpoint in the late 1820s. Alexis de Tocqueville wrote at the time, "the Union has never shown so much weakness as on the celebrated question of the tariff."[155] Congress had increased tariff duties in 1828 and again in 1832.[156] Indeed, higher tariffs were part of Clay's American System. But the tariff issue highlighted the growing differences between North and South. The North wanted protection for its fledgling industries, and the South wanted free trade for its crops, especially cotton.

The state of South Carolina, under the sway of Calhoun, went so far as to declare its "right" to nullify federal laws, including the recent tariff measures.[157] This concept drew intellectual nourishment from John Breckinridge's Kentucky Resolutions from the late 1790s.[158] As had been the case a dozen years earlier, talk of disunion became commonplace.

President Jackson vigorously opposed the notion that a state could simply nullify laws it did not agree with, and he promised to use the military to compel state compliance with the statute.[159] Federal action against South Carolina had the potential to inflame the rest of the South, however, as federal troops would have had to cross through other southern territory to reach the Palmetto State, upsetting notions of states' rights and sovereignty. As one South Carolinian observed, "To reach us, the dagger must pass through others."[160] Representative John Randolph (D-VA)—a longtime Clay rival—recognized where the hopes of the nation resided: "There is one man, and only one man, who can save the Union. That man is Henry Clay."[161] While the rest of the body politic seemed to be stuck in a rut, Clay once again stepped forward, assumed leadership, and formulated a creative solution.

* * *

It has been my experience that unless the political winds are fully in your favor and will eventually force your opposition to bend, the best way to pass legislation is to convince members that the measure in question is in the best interests of their states and consistent with their policies and political goals. The legislative process ultimately runs on persuasion. Clay's bargain took this approach.

* * *

The Compromise Tariff of 1833 provided for a gradual reduction of the protectionist duties, as advocated by the South.[162] In this way, northern enterprises would still gain from the tariff and have a date certain on which to plan for its eventual phaseout.[163] With the end of the high tariff in sight, South Carolina did not feel the need to rebel over the issue.[164] Each side got some of what it wanted.[165] When Clay secured the bill's adoption, he called it "the most proud and triumphant day of [his] life."[166]

Even as the controversy over the tariff was being resolved, Jackson—emboldened by his overwhelming reelection victory—started another uproar by dismantling the Bank of the United States, a pillar of Clay's American System and an essential element of the nation's financial stability.[167] Clay fiercely opposed Jackson's actions.[168] After his party gained a majority in the Senate, Clay broke new ground by spearheading an effort in 1834 to censure the chief executive.[169]

Once again, Clay made creative use of the tools available to him. Unfortunately for Clay, when Jackson's allies regained control of the Senate three years later, the censure was expunged—also an unprecedented act.[170]

In response to Jackson's assertive executive actions, Clay branded the president's opposition—himself included—patriotic "Whigs," likening them to the British party that had taken issue with excessive royal authority.[171] Clay not only popularized the name but also was the Whig Party's unofficial national leader.[172] Representative Benjamin Bidlack (D-PA) characterized Clay on the House floor "as the great leader of the Whig party."[173]

Despite Clay's exalted status in Congress, Whig political bosses did not want a reprise of 1832, when Clay had been steamrolled by Jackson. Accordingly, the party declined to nominate Clay for president in 1836.[174] The result remained the same, however: the Democrats prevailed, this time with Jackson's vice president, Martin Van Buren, as the standard bearer. The first successful Whig presidential candidate would have to wait until 1840, but it would not be Clay. It would be William Henry Harrison of Indiana and his running mate, former Democratic senator John Tyler of Virginia.

Harrison's victory provided Clay with a great opportunity.[175] The Whigs now had majorities in both the Senate and the House, giving Clay even greater standing on Capitol Hill.[176] The Kentuckian's prestige translated into legislative clout.[177] Senator William Allen (D-OH) described the procedural manifestations of Clay's standing in the Senate, which resembled the prerogatives of a modern majority leader: "The announcement by the Senator from Kentucky of his July adjournment, and his laying down to us the measures which are to receive our action, is a form of legislative despotism."[178] Allen further stated, "When that Senator shakes his head and says, 'I hope not,' we know how the yeas and nays will stand as well as if they had been taken and counted."[179]

Given Harrison's political inexperience and Clay's high standing, the Kentuckian decided that he would set the policy agenda for the Whigs from Congress and advise the president on appointments.[180] However, Clay's hauteur quickly jeopardized this experiment.[181] Harrison made it clear that he—not Clay—would exercise the power to nominate officials.[182] But before matters could come fully to a head, the president died only weeks after his inauguration.[183] This left Vice President John Tyler—a man of uncertain Whig principles—as president.

Clay remained determined to drive the national policy agenda himself.[184] However, his presumption once again crashed up against the rocks of presidential power—in this case, repeated vetoes by Tyler.[185] For instance, the president vetoed Whig-prized legislation, such as a bill to reinstate a national bank. Tyler, a former Democrat, maintained sufficient support from his old party in

Congress to sustain his position. Clay's dilemma reflects the limits of legislative leadership in the American system of government. A willful president can thwart even the most accomplished lawmaker through the veto power.[186] Legislators need the support of two-thirds of the membership of both chambers to overturn a veto, while the president needs only one-third plus one in a single house of Congress to prevail.

Prince Hal soon grew exasperated at Tyler's obstinance and resolved to leave the Senate and resume his quest for the White House from outside the chamber. Following his valedictory address—one of the most famous and moving speeches in congressional history—Clay left the chamber for what was seemingly the final time in 1842.[187] His longtime friend John Crittenden compared his departure from the Senate to "the soul's quitting the body."[188]

Later Political Career

Unlike in 1836 and 1840, Clay secured the Whig Party's nomination in 1844. The race that year was a rough one. One piece of campaign literature termed Clay "that notorious, *Sabbath-breaker, Profane Swearer, Gambler, Common Drunkard, Perjurer, Duelist, Thief, Robber, Adulterer, Man-stealer, Slave-holder, and Murderer!*"[189] Today's campaigns seem mild by comparison.

It was in this race that Clay made another crucial political blunder. The major concerns of the day involved the interrelated issues of Texas annexation, slavery, and expansion.[190] Manifest Destiny was in the air.[191] Even so, Clay continued to push his American System, much of which had lost favor with voters.[192]

* * *

In politics, it is important for a candidate to have a platform of ideas to run on; however, one must be ever mindful of the priorities of the electorate. To me, campaigning and governing are a two-way street; they involve reciprocal communication between voters and those running for and holding public office. Clay was sometimes tone deaf to the wishes of the electorate, and in the 1844 election, he completely misread the temper of the time.

* * *

On the question of the annexation of Texas, Clay was initially hesitant to make a statement, and then he objected to immediate annexation; later, he refined and revised his position in ways that both bewildered and alienated many voters.[193] His opponent, Democrat James K. Polk, advocated for annexation and rode the issue to victory.[194] Despite Clay's poor campaign, fewer than 40,000 popular votes separated the two candidates, although the margin in the

Electoral College was decidedly in Polk's favor.[195] Again, poor political judgment had cost Clay dearly.[196]

The late 1840s brought open talk of disunion again. After the 1844 election, the lame-duck Tyler administration and Congress authorized the annexation of Texas. And, in the Mexican War that followed under President Polk, the United States gained additional territory. As had happened after the Louisiana Purchase, many of the new territories sought to join the Union as states. Again, the fragile balance between slave states and free states in the Senate was imperiled, which threatened to push the nation into civil war.

After several years' absence from the Senate and yet another unsuccessful attempt to obtain the Whig Party nomination for the presidency, Clay was elected for a final time to the upper chamber, where he took his seat in 1849.[197] Many of his countrymen looked to the venerable statesman to save the Union for a third time through his legislative and political acumen.[198] Once again, he was seen as a national political leader, even though fellow Whig Zachary Taylor occupied the White House.[199] Once again, Clay was not about to defer to a president, even one from his own party.[200] Despite his poor health, Clay took on the impending crisis with his usual zeal and assembled a bipartisan group of senators that met virtually every day to try to arrive at a legislative solution.[201]

* * *

My tenure in the Senate has taught me that navigating controversial legislation entails a number of factors. It requires an understanding of the political and policy constraints of fellow lawmakers and the president. It calls for persuasiveness and timing. It involves not only reading public opinion but also harnessing it and, if possible, driving it. It requires the discernment to see opportunities where obstacles abound. And at times, it can come down to something as seemingly mundane as packaging. In the case of what became known as the Compromise of 1850, Clay basically satisfied all these elements except for packaging.[202]

* * *

An "omnibus" was originally a horse-drawn coach that could carry several passengers at once.[203] In legislative terms, it has come to describe a bill that includes a number of unrelated measures. Clay introduced this expression into the legislative vernacular during the debate over the compromise.[204] In this respect, he attempted to solve all the outstanding sectional issues in one fell swoop by putting each of them into an omnibus bill.[205]

There were a number of elements in the eventual compromise, including California's acceptance as a free state into the Union, clarification of the border between Texas and New Mexico, authorization of territorial governments for New Mexico and Utah, prohibition of the slave trade (but not slavery itself) in the nation's capital, and a more draconian fugitive slave law.[206] Under Clay's proposal, both the North and the South would have gotten some of what they wanted: for the North, California's addition to the Union as a free state and a prohibition against the buying and selling of slaves in Washington, DC; for the South, a more aggressive fugitive slave law and preservation of slavery in the District.[207]

Debate over the compromise, first proposed by Clay in January 1850, was grueling and lasted for months.[208] Despite his failing health, Clay managed to summon some of the talents of his youth. One woman commented that his oratory still had the "old beguiling music."[209] He helped mobilize the public behind the compromise effort.[210]

President Taylor passed away in July, elevating Vice President Millard Fillmore, who was supportive of Clay's efforts, to the White House.[211] Notwithstanding Clay's valiant labors and Fillmore's support, in the end, the omnibus measure was defeated in the Senate. Clay, exhausted, disheartened, and apparently suffering from tuberculosis, left the Capitol for Newport, Rhode Island, to regain his strength.[212] Despite the failure of his omnibus bill, massive numbers of admirers cheered his coach as he headed north.[213] In Philadelphia, the crowds were so large that a multipassenger carriage on an adjacent street was blocked; Clay wryly noted that the "omnibus is like the omnibus I left at Washington, it didn't get through."[214]

Back in Washington, Senator Stephen Douglas (D-IL) correctly identified Clay's tactical error. Although Clay had been able to define the parameters of the legislative solution and its constituent parts, he had inadvertently constructed a bill that united opponents rather than proponents.[215] Douglas rescued Clay's compromise and shrewdly divided the measures into six separate pieces of legislation.[216] Thanks to shifting majorities, this proved vital, as only four senators voted for each of the individual bills.[217] In fact, all but one of the bills constituting the Compromise of 1850 passed before Clay returned from Rhode Island.[218] Much like the coach in Philadelphia, the Compromise of 1850 finally got through—but not in the form the Kentuckian had envisioned. Despite the failure of the omnibus approach, for the third time, Clay had played a fundamental role in saving the Union through legislation.[219]

Citing its importance, Professor Robert Remini argued that the "Compromise of 1850 delayed the . . . civil war for ten years, and those ten years were absolutely essential for preserving the American nation under the Constitution. Had secession occurred in 1850 . . . the country might well have split permanently into two nations."[220] Many other historians have echoed this view.[221] In the 1850s, the North made great advances in its industrial output, which helped it prevail in the war.[222] During this period, the North's population boomed.[223] The 1850s also witnessed the emergence of Abraham Lincoln.[224] Nonetheless, there is no gainsaying that the compromise came at a grave human cost: the continuation of slavery for more than a decade.

The compromise may have temporarily saved the Union, but it proved to be Clay's last gasp. He never fully regained his health and passed away in 1852. His body lay in state in the rotunda of the US Capitol, the first individual to be so honored.[225] Following a long procession through a number of major cities, Clay's remains were transported to Lexington, where thousands turned out to welcome Kentucky's favorite son.

Legacy

In the 1950s, Senator John F. Kennedy (D-MA) chaired a committee to determine which five senators deserved to be honored with portraits in the Senate Reception Room.[226] The committee polled a number of historians and political scientists, who ranked Clay second, and he was ultimately chosen as one of the five senators to be honored.[227] The others were his colleagues Daniel Webster and John C. Calhoun and twentieth-century senators Robert Taft (R-OH) and Robert La Follette Sr. (R-WI). A 1986 survey of professors conducted by Siena College reached a similar conclusion, ranking Clay as the greatest senator ever.[228] Another survey of twenty-six historians from the 1980s placed Clay in a tie as the nation's foremost senator, alongside La Follette.[229] In its 2006 listing of the 100 most influential Americans from all walks of life, the *Atlantic* placed Clay thirty-first, the highest ranked senator on the list.[230]

Since 1789, more than 650 legislators have served in both the Senate and the House, and no one has dominated both chambers to the degree Clay did. Moreover, while some lawmakers can claim authorship of important legislation, the Kentuckian can take credit for three legislative packages that quite possibly saved the nation from dissolution. The stakes could not have been higher, and each time he succeeded. Had he not, the nation could have fractured into two or more separate countries, with slavery likely enduring well past the 1860s in one or more of these breakaway nations.[231]

Clay also profoundly shaped American political institutions. He revolutionized the Speaker's office.[232] He played a major role in making the upper chamber the center of national debate and decision-making during the second quarter of the nineteenth century.[233] And Clay was central to the creation of a major political party—the Whigs—that for nearly two decades played a significant role in American public life.

Today, we rightfully view individuals as enduring public figures if they remain at or near the top of American politics for two or three decades. One thinks of George Washington, John Adams, Thomas Jefferson, and James Madison. Yet Henry Clay was at or near the top of American political life, with little interruption, for *four* decades, from his speakership to the end of his life.[234] Few American political figures can claim such a lengthy, prominent career.

On the other side of the ledger, Clay's record on slavery is disappointing.[235] As a newcomer to Kentucky in the late 1790s, he advocated that the commonwealth permit the gradual freeing of slaves, and he essentially maintained this position throughout his life.[236] He termed slavery the "deepest stain" on the "character of our country."[237] Yet, despite those noble sentiments, Clay was a slave owner until the day he died. To his discredit, he did not translate his apparent ideals into action by manumitting his slaves during his lifetime, although he did free those remaining in bondage in his will.[238] The best solution he could offer was to assist the transfer of freed slaves to West Africa.[239]

Another disappointment involves the American System. In spite of the prescience of much of Clay's vision, and in spite of his boundless legislative skill, he failed to get much of it enacted during his lifetime. However, a fair portion of it would be adopted by succeeding generations.[240]

In brief, there is much to consider in weighing the towering legacy of Henry Clay. He was a man of immense talents, a man of grand ambitions, a man who achieved dizzying heights and experienced epic defeats. Although he never assumed a formal leadership role in the Senate as he did in the House, Clay's de facto stewardship of the Senate left a deep and abiding imprint on the nation. The fact that Americans are living today in a single country, instead of two or three competing nation-states, is a testament to his life's great work: preservation of the Union.

For all his gifts, Clay's achievements owe much to context. First, he operated at a time when the Senate had no official floor leadership. As a result, Clay did not have to be elected to a specific position or vie with existing party leadership for control of the chamber. Second, there were many fewer senators during Clay's tenure, likely making the Senate a more fluid institution than at present. Third, seniority was generally less of a consideration during Clay's career.[241] These factors meant that power in the Senate was in many ways less settled and less formalized than today. As a result, even though Clay served in the Senate on four separate occasions, he did not start as low man on the totem pole each time he returned to the body.[242]

More broadly, as a general matter, the presidency was a much more modest institution at that time. In the nineteenth century, presidents were by and large content to let Congress take the lead on domestic matters.[243] In addition, from the 1830s to the 1850s, the House of Representatives lost some of the standing it had previously enjoyed.[244] These two considerations permitted the Senate to assume perhaps *the* preeminent role in American politics and governance at the time.[245] The political landscape therefore permitted Clay—as the informal Senate leader for much of his time in the chamber—to play a major role in influencing the destiny of the nation.

5

Senator as Committee Chairman

John J. Crittenden

The inability of the Senate's constitutional officers to set its agenda prompted other forms of institutional leadership to move to the forefront. The presidential lieutenant and the occasional senator with great national or regional prestige are two such examples, but over time, another platform for Senate leadership emerged: the committee chairmanship. During his career, John J. Crittenden chaired four different standing committees—Judiciary, Military Affairs, Engrossed Bills, and Revolutionary Claims—leading more panels than any other Kentuckian.[1]

The Origins of Senate Committees

Senate committees embody two related truths: (1) there must be a division of labor in the chamber, and (2) although senators need to be familiar with every major public policy issue, to be effective, they must specialize.[2] These principles are reflected in the fact that committees have been around in some form since the First Congress. As early as 1816, the Senate saw the need for permanent standing committees, and they have been a feature of the Senate ever since.

With committees, of course, come committee chairmen. If these chairmen are sufficiently skilled, they can exercise leadership in the areas that fall under their panels' jurisdiction. In the Senate, members typically defer to the chairman and ranking member on issues within a committee's jurisdiction because they are presumed to be experts.[3] A prestigious committee and a talented chairman can be a powerful combination. Indeed, most of the nitty-gritty of policy making in the Senate takes place in committee.[4]

For the first quarter century of its history, the Senate delegated substantive matters to ad hoc committees.[5] Upon completion of their tasks, the panels simply dissolved.[6] For example, the chamber regularly created ad hoc panels to analyze and respond to segments of the president's annual message (now known as the State of the Union address).[7] Typically, these ad hoc committees comprised three to five senators.[8] Although this committee size seems small to modern eyes, it must be remembered that the early Senate itself was a much smaller institution.[9] In the first half of 1789, there were only twenty senators in the nation's capital; by contrast, in the 115th Congress (2017–2019), the Senate Appropriations Committee alone had thirty-one members.[10]

One way that leadership manifested itself in the early Senate was through placement on and chairmanship of these ad hoc panels.[11] In the first few years of the Senate's existence, the number of committee assignments was seen in many ways as a barometer of the chamber's respect for a lawmaker.[12] Senator John Quincy Adams (Fed.-MA) observed, "As our committees are all chosen by ballot, the influence and weight of a member can be very well measured by the number and importance of those upon which he is placed."[13]

The Senate's first great chairman was Oliver Ellsworth (Fed.-CT), who was chosen to lead the first two panels.[14] One of these committees helped create the federal judiciary, while the other drafted the initial rules for the Senate.[15] In the first session of the Senate, Ellsworth sat on more than half of the forty panels created.[16] During the second session, Ellsworth was appointed to thirty-six ad hoc committees, more than three times the average.[17] Clearly, he was a Senate leader, and that status was reflected by his chairmanships.[18] In contrast, in the modern era, many senators become leaders *because* of their chairmanships.[19]

One reason that permanent standing committees did not sprout up immediately in the Senate was the Jeffersonian concern about too much power being placed in the hands of too few legislators.[20] Democratic-Republican doctrine put a premium on all members participating in the lawmaking process on an equal footing.[21] Permanent committees, it was thought, undermined that principle.[22] At the same time, Federalists seemed more content to let cabinet secretaries, such as Alexander Hamilton, take the initiative on policy matters.[23]

Gradually, however, ad hoc committees began to operate for longer stretches.[24] To some degree, they began to take on the appearance of standing or permanent committees.[25] Finally, in 1816, the Senate established eleven substantive standing committees.[26] This development was the work of Senator James Barbour (Dem.-Rep.–VA).[27] The initial standing committees were Foreign Relations, Judiciary, Finance, Commerce and Manufactures, Military Affairs, Militia, Naval Affairs, Claims, Public Lands, Pensions, and Post Offices and Post Roads.[28]

Congressional scholar Walter Kravitz described how the creation of standing committees altered the dynamics between panels and the parent chamber: "Whereas [ad hoc] select committees had been subordinate creatures of the Senate, the standing panels acquired prerogatives which almost completely reversed this relationship. . . . Measures [w]ould be referred to committees before the Senate considers them [not vice versa]. Instead of the Senate telling its committees what to put in legislation, the committees assumed the prerogatives of determining which substantive provisions the Senate should consider. Thus, the standing committees became policy-making bodies instead of merely technical aids to the chamber."[29]

Like other Senate innovations that seem groundbreaking in retrospect but occasioned little notice at the time (e.g., prior recognition, discussed in chapter 7), the establishment of Senate standing committees attracted hardly any contemporary attention or debate.[30] Perhaps this is because ad hoc Senate panels were sitting for longer periods and in some ways already resembled permanent panels.[31]

Once standing committees had been established, the question became how to choose members to serve on them.[32] In 1823, Senator Barbour suggested that the presiding officer be assigned this responsibility.[33] The wording of the proposal was somewhat ambiguous, but presumably it was intended for the president pro tempore to carry out this task.[34] This lack of clarity was not a concern at the time, as the incumbent vice president, Daniel Tompkins, rarely sat in the presiding officer's chair.[35] Matters came to a head, however, when his successor, Vice President John C. Calhoun, arrived in the Senate and not only made committee assignments but did so in a highly partisan way.[36] The Barbour approach, therefore, had to be revisited.[37] For nearly two decades, the Senate experimented with a variety of methods of determining committee assignments, with little success.[38] These approaches included selection by ballot and assignment by either the president pro tempore or the vice president.[39] In 1846, it was finally determined that each party caucus would submit its own slate of committee assignments to the chamber, and the entire Senate would approve the lists.[40] Determining committee slots remains largely a party matter to this day.[41]

Once committee membership was decided, the issue of selecting a chairman arose. Until the mid-1820s, it seems that the chairmen of Senate committees (ad hoc panels or otherwise) were the senators who had received the most votes to serve on the panels in question, and their names were therefore listed first.[42] In time, seniority would play a vital role in determining committee chairmanships, but that development was several decades away.[43] Indeed, it was not until 1921 that seniority on the actual committee became a more important consideration than seniority in the Senate itself.[44] Today, many of the rules governing the selection of committee chairmen and ranking members are put forth by each party's conference.[45]

John J. Crittenden's Early Life and Career

Since the mid-nineteenth century, all senators from Kentucky have toiled in the shadow of Henry Clay. This is particularly true with respect to John Jordan Crittenden, even though he was a remarkably able and highly accomplished figure in his own right.[46] Yet, to a great extent, when Crittenden is remembered at all, it is often as a protégé of Clay or as the author of a failed compromise proposal prior to the Civil War.[47] This is a misleading and unfair way to view Crittenden's legacy.

He was born in 1786, not far from Lexington.[48] As was the case with untold numbers of early Kentuckians, Crittenden's parents hailed from Virginia.[49] His family was not without distinction; Crittenden's father served in the Virginia legislature, and his mother's second cousin was Thomas Jefferson.[50]

Unfortunately, not much is recorded about Crittenden's childhood.[51] He began his legal education under the tutelage of George Bibb, who would represent Kentucky on two occasions in the US Senate.[52] Crittenden later attended William and Mary College and received his degree in 1807.[53] There, he studied law under the esteemed St. George Tucker and met a young Virginian named John Tyler.[54] After returning to Kentucky, Crittenden established himself as one of the premier attorneys in the commonwealth.[55] His legal acumen and affability won him prominent friends in the community and attracted some noteworthy clients.[56] James Madison, James Monroe, and Richard Mentor Johnson each enlisted Crittenden's services at one time or another.[57]

In 1811, Crittenden wed Sarah O. Lee.[58] He would be married twice more, as both Sarah and his second wife, Maria Innes Todd, predeceased him.[59] That same year, he began a long career in public office when voters elected him to the state legislature.[60] Within four years, he would become speaker of the state house.[61] In addition to the valuable contacts Crittenden made with notable Kentucky families, his considerable talents as an orator contributed greatly to his political ascent.[62] One onlooker praised his ability to sway an audience: "[Crittenden] poured forth like the mighty cataract of Niagara bearing down everything that seemed to impede his progress. Then again [at other points he was] like the smooth and majestic Hudson [as] he seemed to glide . . . along convincing and converting all the *fence men*."[63]

Crittenden was also exceedingly personable. Contemporaries noted that he was often too kindhearted to tell people no.[64] Just as important, by all accounts, he was a man of his word. He seemed to radiate integrity.[65]

A significant factor in Crittenden's rise was his military service during the War of 1812.[66] Not long after hostilities broke out, Crittenden volunteered for service as an aide to Governor Isaac Shelby.[67] Crittenden performed ably at the Battle of the Thames in 1813, where American forces decimated the British and their Indian allies in an encounter in present-day Ontario, Canada.[68] As a result, British and Indian forces were unable to coordinate with each other, quieting what was then the western frontier of the United States.[69] This great victory, widely celebrated in Kentucky, lent prestige to all involved, including Crittenden.[70]

Clay and Crittenden

During this period, Crittenden's career received a boost from another quarter: his budding friendship with Henry Clay.[71] The two men had many similarities, including a deep and abiding love for politics and a talent for public speaking.[72] And, when it came to political values, both men placed the Union ahead of all other considerations.[73] They would do everything they could to ensure that sectional strife did not destroy the nation.[74]

Like Clay, Crittenden had a disappointing record on slavery. Crittenden viewed the institution as morally repugnant but—to his discredit—he did not free those he held in bondage.[75] During the Civil War, Crittenden doggedly advocated that Kentucky should remain in the Union, but he did not alter his stance on slavery.[76] Indeed, he opposed the Emancipation Proclamation.[77]

On a personal level, Clay and Crittenden were skilled raconteurs and were engaging in small groups.[78] Both men enjoyed a good time.[79] Crittenden could usually be found enjoying a hefty plug of chewing tobacco.[80] In the words of his biographer Albert Kirwan, "Crittenden was no Puritan."[81] And, of course, neither was Clay. One contemporary who witnessed Crittenden and Clay together at a Kentucky racetrack in 1837 noted that they made a lively pair; the two men were "apparently . . . much excited, talking as loudly, betting as freely, drinking as deeply, and swearing as excessively as the jockeys themselves."[82] Both exhibited tremendous empathy for others.[83] Both were enduring public figures with long careers.[84]

Despite these similarities, there were important differences between the two men. On the one hand, Clay was not content to sit in anyone's political shadow for long.[85] He liked top billing.[86] Crittenden, on the other hand, did not crave the political spotlight.[87] He was content to work behind the scenes, to play second fiddle to the better-known Clay.[88] Moreover, unlike Clay, Crittenden was not entranced by the prospect of becoming president.[89]

Both men were skilled attorneys, but unlike Clay, Crittenden enjoyed the practice of law.[90] Clay saw it largely as a means to a political career.[91] Both men were offered seats on the Supreme Court. Clay was not interested, but Crittenden certainly was.[92]

Finally, Clay could be harsh and combative in debate.[93] He was not afraid to use sharp rhetoric or withering sarcasm.[94] As a result, and much to his own detriment, Clay left innumerable adversaries in his wake.[95] Although Crittenden could also be cutting in debate, he was typically more genteel and less willing to alienate others.[96] Thus, he lacked Clay's penchant for making enemies.[97]

Crittenden's First Term in the Senate

At the time of Crittenden's elevation to speaker of the state house, state legislatures elected US senators.[98] Given his high standing in state government, it is not surprising that Crittenden was soon sent to the US Senate as a member of the Democratic-Republican Party.[99] This would be the first of four terms in the Senate for Crittenden, covering a span of more than four decades from 1817 to 1861.[100]

Crittenden was chosen chairman of the Committee on Engrossed Bills in 1817, a minor post he held until 1819.[101] Also in 1817, Crittenden became chairman of the Senate Judiciary Committee, making him only the second chairman in the panel's history.[102] Even during this early period, the Judiciary Committee was considered one of the most prominent committees, along with Foreign Relations, Military Affairs, Finance, and Commerce and Manufactures.[103] This, in turn, often made these committee chairmen major players in the Senate.[104] Today, of course, a lawmaker with such little Senate experience would never chair such a prestigious committee.

The Senate Committee on the Judiciary

Today, the Judiciary Committee is one of the most visible Senate panels, handling matters such as revisions to the criminal code, immigration issues, and antitrust matters.[105] It is perhaps best known, however, for its consideration of federal judicial nominations, particularly Supreme Court nominees. During Crittenden's chairmanship, no Supreme Court vacancies occurred.[106] But even if there had been such an opening, it is uncertain whether Crittenden or his committee would have played a major role in reviewing the nomination. In the first half century of the committee's existence, one-third of Supreme Court nominations were never referred to the Judiciary Committee.[107] Instead, the nominees' names were often sent straight to the Senate floor a day after the paperwork arrived in the chamber.[108] Only in 1835 did the Senate begin to send Supreme Court nominations to the Judiciary Committee as a matter of course.[109]

For the first few decades of their existence, Senate standing committees played an uneven role in the review of nominations.[110] Over time, however, nominations of lower-level officials—largely patronage positions at the time—were increasingly sent to the committees of jurisdiction for consideration.[111] In 1868, the Senate changed its rules to comprehensively address how committees evaluated potential executive and judicial officials.[112] The new rule required them to be referred to the relevant panel.[113] This ensured that committee chairmen would play a key role regarding nominations.[114]

After adoption of the 1868 rule, panels started to evaluate nominees more carefully.[115] Gradually, in the latter half of the nineteenth century, committee practices in this regard became more recognizable to the modern eye.[116] For instance, Senate hearings regarding nominations seem to have been initiated during this period, although they were not open to the public as they are today.[117] The Judiciary Committee's handling of Supreme Court nominees is instructive. In 1873, President Ulysses Grant nominated George Williams to be chief justice.[118] Soon afterward, allegations surfaced that the nominee had spent government funds for personal purposes, and the Judiciary Committee conducted closed-door hearings to determine whether the claims were valid.[119] This represents the first time a Supreme Court nomination was the subject of a hearing.[120] As part of these proceedings, members reviewed documents and heard from witnesses, though not from the nominee himself.[121] Ultimately, Grant withdrew Williams's name from consideration.[122]

It would be more than forty years before another hearing on a Supreme Court nomination took place. In 1916, Kentucky's own Louis Brandeis was put forward by President Woodrow Wilson to serve on the Supreme Court. His nomination prompted strong opposition from many quarters.[123] To air these concerns, the committee broke new ground and held public hearings on the nominee, although Brandeis did not make an appearance.[124]

The nomination of Pierce Butler to the high court in 1922 occasioned a return to closed-door hearings.[125] Three years later, when Harlan Stone was nominated, controversy swirled around his efforts to bring to justice those implicated in the Teapot Dome scandal.[126] Stone set a precedent by appearing in person to defend himself at the Judiciary Committee hearing, albeit in closed session.[127]

Three of the next six Supreme Court nominations involved hearings, but no nominee appeared in person.[128] In 1937, however, the Judiciary Committee was roundly criticized for its failure to publicly examine Supreme Court nominee Hugo Black's ties to the Ku Klux Klan.[129] Thus, when the next controversial Supreme Court nominee—Felix Frankfurter—was put forward, for the first time the panel held public hearings in which the nominee himself appeared.[130] Within twenty years, open hearings at which Supreme Court nominees appeared would be the norm.[131]

The evolutionary path taken by the Judiciary Committee, which Crittenden chaired during its formative years, is emblematic of that taken by Senate committees in general in their consideration of nominations.[132] Today, the power of committee chairmen looms large over the fate of individual nominees.

The Role of Committee Chairmen

My own experience chairing Senate committees reflects how different they are in mission, in culture, and in output. I have had the privilege of serving as chairman of two Senate committees: the Committee on Rules and Administration, which I chaired for two and a half years, and the Committee on Ethics, which I chaired for two.

The Rules Committee is a standing committee that has legislative responsibility. In this regard, it is an authorizing committee and is responsible for providing policy direction on matters within its jurisdiction. To give an example of the work involved, while I was chairman and ranking member of the panel, my colleague Christopher Dodd (D-CT) and I worked to pass the Help America Vote Act, an effort to reform election procedures following the 2000 presidential election.

The Ethics Committee, however, is not a legislative committee. Its mission is to ensure that Senate personnel observe certain prescribed ethical standards. As such, the panel often investigates allegations of wrongdoing. While I was chairman of this committee, vice chairman Richard Bryan (D-NV) and I had to look into reports that Senator Bob Packwood (R-OR) had sexually harassed a number of female staffers and lobbyists. These allegations were demonstrated to be true, and the panel, at my urging, recommended his expulsion.[133]

In addition to these full committee chairmanships, I held the gavel of the Appropriations Subcommittee on Foreign Operations (since reconstituted as the State, Foreign Operations Subcommittee) for almost a dozen years. Unlike authorizing committees, the Appropriations Committee—through its subcommittees—is responsible for bills that fund the government.[134] These subcommittees have to enact measures every year to fund government operations. The State, Foreign Operations Subcommittee, among other things, allocates monies for foreign aid programs.

These chairmanships reflect not only different types of Senate panels—authorizing, investigative, and appropriations—but also their unique cultures and different responsibilities. Given the sensitive nature of its work, the Ethics Committee functions discreetly, whereas the Rules Committee and the State, Foreign Operations Subcommittee often hold high-profile public hearings. The secretary of state, for example, testifies every year in front of the State, Foreign Operations Subcommittee. That said, no matter what type of committee is involved, I have found that being a good chairman comes down to two things: what you know and how persuasive you are.

* * *

If, as has been said, Senate committees are like "little legislatures," then committee chairmen are like "little majority leaders."[135] Much as the majority leader largely decides what the full Senate considers, committee chairmen largely determine what transpires in their own panels (what legislation, nominations, oversight, and hearings they undertake).[136] As Professor Lawrence Evans rightly noted, "scheduling decisions are the central prerogative of [committee] leadership: They determine the set of issues actively considered in committee."[137]

In addition to whatever personal talents the chairman may possess, along with the formal procedural power to set the panel's agenda, the chairman typically has authority over committee staff and therefore enjoys an informational advantage within both the committee and the Senate as a whole in terms of the committee's policy areas.[138] Even in the increasingly individualized Senate, there still remains a fair amount of deference to the chairman and the ranking member of committees in their issue areas, and as a result, chairmen are typically Senate leaders in these areas.[139] While the autonomy of committees and their chairmen has fluctuated over time, given their expertise and resources, the legislative work of committees is often accepted by the Senate with only minor alterations.[140]

Once chairmen decide what they want to do, they need to secure their committees' approval of the legislation they want to enact, the nominees they want to confirm, or the investigations they want to undertake. With regard to legislation, for example, once the chairman has secured majority support on the committee, the committee "reports out" the bill to the full Senate, and it goes on the Senate calendar (the list of items available for Senate floor consideration). If the bill has the support of the majority leader, it is poised to potentially go to the Senate floor (typically, the Senate must adopt a motion to proceed beforehand). To be successful, the chairman must convince the majority leader to grant floor time for the committee's bill. (If the bill is relatively noncontroversial, it can be passed through unanimous consent, which requires minimal floor time.)

Before legislation is adopted, it must clear a number of hurdles: some amount of Senate floor time (however minimal), approval by the Senate (often at a 60-vote threshold), some amount of House floor time (however minimal), approval by the House, and, in most cases, a presidential signature.[141] That is not the case, however, with committee investigations.[142] When it comes to oversight, committee chairmen typically encounter fewer obstacles than in lawmaking, and such efforts can sometimes have an equally important impact on public policy.[143] This is accomplished through informal means—for example, by persuading agencies or outside entities to change their ways by shining an unwelcome spotlight on certain practices.[144]

* * *

As majority leader, I have now been on both sides of this interaction: seeking floor time and granting it. In the Senate, floor time is the coin of the realm. As majority leader, I must parcel out limited floor time in a strategic way that reflects my par-

ty's priorities for the nation. Before the beginning of each session, I put together a tentative schedule, and every week, to ensure that we are following that agenda, I meet with committee chairmen to keep close tabs on the progress of the various bills and nominations in committee. For this same reason, I consult regularly with the minority leader, individual senators, and the leadership of the House.

However, as the saying goes, "the best laid plans of mice and men often go awry."[145] Quite often, bills require more committee or floor time than planned, or unforeseen events cause certain items—bills or nominations—to be set aside either permanently or temporarily. A majority leader needs to be nimble and have the ability to adjust the schedule accordingly. At the same time, scheduling changes often frustrate committee chairmen whose bills were slotted for floor time and then are suddenly moved to the back burner.

I also learn a great deal from these weekly meetings with committee chairmen. As majority leader, I need to know a little bit about all the major issues. Senator Hubert Humphrey (D-MN), who served as whip, gave an apt description of the need to be knowledgeable about a broad range of issues: "I used to be an expert on disarmament. Now, as Senate Whip, I conduct a sort of political smorgasbord. A leader in this nation cannot confine his interest to just one or two subjects."[146] Although I need to be familiar with all high-profile matters, I typically look to the chairmen of the relevant committees for in-depth policy guidance. For instance, on education policy, I consult closely with Lamar Alexander (R-TN), who is chairman of the Health, Education, Labor, and Pensions Committee. Similarly, on energy policy, I listen with great interest to the views of Lisa Murkowski (R-AK), who chairs the Energy and Natural Resources Committee. The same is true for other chairmen in our conference. Ultimately, every issue of any importance runs through the majority leader's office, so it is vital to have some understanding of the substantive policy issues, as well as the potential political minefields, involved with measures as they wend their way through the system.

Even though I am majority leader, I am respectful of the authority of committee chairmen.[147] Several years ago, one senator described the status of chairmen during Mike Mansfield's (D-MT) tenure as majority leader: "Around here, committee chairmen are tribal chiefs to be bargained with, not lieutenants to be commanded."[148] That is not far off the mark. The majority leader must persuade committee chairmen to take certain actions; he cannot order them around.

Being a party leader is challenging because senators are exposed to many incentives that do not favor being a team player, such as enhanced media attention. If a senator wants to be noticed, a surefire way is to buck his own party's leadership. On occasion, being majority leader can feel like being a groundskeeper at a cemetery: everyone is below you, but no one is listening!

To make matters worse, a party leader has few carrots and even fewer sticks. Moreover, the use of sticks can be counterproductive. In the Senate, the most import- ant vote is the next one, and burning bridges by disciplining a recalcitrant member can come back to haunt a party leader.

* * *

Crittenden's Return to Kentucky

When Crittenden served as Judiciary Committee chairman, he did not have to contend with a majority leader. But he did have to deal with mounting personal expenses, which forced him to resign from the Senate in 1819.[149] He returned to the commonwealth, where he could better support his family through his grow- ing and increasingly lucrative law practice.[150]

Crittenden set up his household in Frankfort. His daughter fondly remem- bered life during this period: "[Our] house in Frankfort was a straggling, old-fashioned house on the corner of Main Street. The front door opened imme- diately on the street. . . . In fair summer evenings, the custom of the family was to take tea some time before night, and then assemble at the front door [and sit outside on the steps]. . . . The neighbors and friends would soon gather in and join the group at the front door. . . . Stragglers taking their evening walk would pause for awhile, and take part in the conversation." She continued: "There is no feature of the family life, as connected with [my father] more indelibly impressed upon my mind than these evening gatherings. [My father's] cordial and kindly greeting, his warm sympathy and interest in all that concerned the welfare of his friends and neighbors; his inimitable style of telling an anecdote and detailing the news of the day could not be surpassed; his quick appreciation of even an attempt at wit encouraged the timid to do their best, and sent every one home between ten and eleven satisfied with himself."[151] This passage reflects not only the rhythms of life in Frankfort at the time but also Crittenden's warm, friendly demeanor.

The "Corrupt Bargain" and Its Aftermath

During this same period, Crittenden did what he could to promote Clay's polit- ical fortunes. As detailed in chapter 4, Clay ran for president in 1824 in a four- way race against John Quincy Adams, Andrew Jackson, and William Crawford. Though Jackson won a plurality of electoral votes, none of the four candidates secured the majority, as required by the Constitution. The election was therefore sent to the House of Representatives for resolution. Clay, who finished fourth, was out of the running for chief executive, but he still enjoyed strong support in the House of Representatives as Speaker. Prince Hal threw his support to Adams, which helped the man from Massachusetts become president. Just days after his election, Adams offered to make Clay secretary of state.[152]

Crittenden imprudently encouraged Clay to accept the cabinet appointment.[153] After thinking it over for a few days, Clay followed Crittenden's recommendation and accepted—making one of the major strategic blunders of his political career.[154] Jackson's supporters howled in protest and almost immediately began to mobilize to defeat Adams (and Clay) in 1828. The memory of the so-called corrupt bargain was searing not only for Clay but also for Crittenden, and it would influence his own later career decisions.[155]

During the Adams presidency, Crittenden was rewarded for his support by being named US district attorney in 1827.[156] The next year, after Justice Robert Trimble died, Adams—recognizing Crittenden's legal talents—nominated him to serve on the US Supreme Court.[157] The Senate was firmly in Jackson's camp, however, and his allies refused to consider the nomination by the lame-duck president.[158] This would be the first of two near misses for Crittenden serving on the high court.

Following Jackson's victory over Adams at the polls in 1828, Crittenden lost his job as district attorney.[159] Yet, three years later, he stood poised to return to the Senate. Clay's supporters, however, believed that Clay needed a platform from which to challenge Jackson for the presidency in 1832.[160] As a result, Crittenden graciously removed himself from consideration and permitted Clay to be elected to the Senate as a National Republican.[161] Subsequently, however, Prince Hal lost the presidential race.

Crittenden's Reelection to the Senate and Elevation to the Cabinet

In 1835, Crittenden was elected to the Senate again, succeeding his mentor George Bibb (Jack.). This time, Crittenden joined as a member of the newly formed Whig Party, which stood in opposition to Jackson. Crittenden remained in the upper chamber until 1841, when the first Whig president and fellow veteran of the Battle of the Thames, William Henry Harrison, named him attorney general.[162] Crittenden did not hold that post for long, however.[163] President Harrison died only weeks after assuming office and was replaced by Crittenden's fellow William and Mary alumnus Vice President John Tyler, who did not embrace Whig principles. Crittenden and all but one of his colleagues left the cabinet not long thereafter.[164] The Kentuckian soon returned to the Senate, after defeating former vice president Richard Mentor Johnson for the post.[165]

In 1844, Clay mounted yet another attempt at the presidency. Once again, Crittenden assumed the role of loyal lieutenant in his friend's campaign.[166] For a third time, Clay went down to defeat, this time losing to Democrat James K. Polk.[167]

The Military Affairs Committee

After Clay's departure from the upper chamber, Crittenden came into his own as a senator, emerging as the de facto leader of the Whigs in the body.[168] From 1841 to 1845, Crittenden chaired the Committee on Military Affairs, the forerunner to today's Armed Services Committee.[169] To this day, Crittenden remains the only Kentuckian to lead that committee or its successor.

Today, the Armed Services Committee holds high-profile public hearings with cabinet secretaries and high-ranking military personnel, reviews nominations, and produces the annual National Defense Authorization Act (NDAA), which sets national security policy for the land. That, however, is not what its predecessor did in Crittenden's day. First, public hearings would not become a regular feature of committee activity until well into the twentieth century.[170] Second, Senate investigations during this time were typically undertaken by select committees, not by standing committees.[171] Third, as noted earlier, Senate panels did not secure clear authority to review nominees until after the Civil War.[172] And finally, the Armed Services Committee would not begin regular enactment of the NDAA until 1961.[173]

The Oregon Border Dispute

The Senate is sometimes portrayed as a stone in the shoe of the president with regard to foreign affairs. But a shrewd president can often use the Senate's role in a constructive fashion to help extricate himself from difficult spots. In the case of the Oregon Territory, President Polk took an overly aggressive posture with respect to the boundary between American and British territory (now Canada).[174] At the same time, the Senate was considering termination of the treaty with Britain that governed the area in question.[175] Polk's approach had the unintentional effect of emboldening the chairman of the Foreign Relations Committee, William Allen (D-OH), to take an even more confrontational stance.[176] The result was a committee-approved bill that threatened war with Britain.[177]

Even though he was the de facto head of the Senate party opposed to Polk, Crittenden was instrumental in resolving this bitter foreign policy dispute.[178] At a crucial moment, the Kentuckian stepped forward with a legislative alternative that played an important role in reshaping the final legislative measure, permitting Polk to save face and move away from his own initial imprudent position.[179]

Ultimately, the United States reached a satisfactory agreement with Britain,[180] and Crittenden has been credited with helping to keep the peace.[181] Although the Foreign Relations Committee had formal jurisdiction over the matter, Crittenden wrested control of the issue away from the chairman, Senator Allen.[182] Crittenden's actions demonstrate that although committee chairmen typically receive deference from their colleagues, they can still be defeated on the floor by a determined and skillful member.

In many respects, Crittenden's efforts regarding the border dispute reflect the best traditions of the Senate—letting passions cool and rendering balanced judgments. The Senate can not only act as a check on the president but also guide him in a constructive fashion.[183] These attributes were displayed by Crittenden.

Crittenden and Taylor

Following Clay's defeat in 1844, many in the Whig Party believed that the time had come for a new presidential candidate to be found. Crittenden saw potential in General Zachary Taylor.[184] Old Rough and Ready was a hero of the Mexican War and had few known political views, but the Whigs thought he could be a strong candidate.[185] Crittenden helped persuade Taylor to run and became his de facto campaign manager.[186] At the same time, Crittenden ran for governor of Kentucky.[187]

Crittenden's role in Taylor's campaign deeply stung Clay, who was considering yet another run for the presidency in 1848.[188] This severely damaged the long friendship between the two.[189] Crittenden's daughter later confessed that nothing had ever "distressed [her father] so much as his alienation from Mr. Clay."[190]

Despite playing an active role in getting Taylor elected president, Crittenden resisted any formal participation in Taylor's administration.[191] He feared charges of making his own "corrupt bargain."[192] Instead, he spent the next two years in the governor's mansion, tending to Kentucky business and calling for the commonwealth to establish a system of public education.[193]

Although he did not take a position with the Taylor administration, Crittenden still advised the president-elect.[194] For instance, he persuaded Old Rough and Ready not to include Vice President Millard Fillmore in cabinet deliberations.[195] This decision would maintain a custom that had begun during the tenure of Vice President John Adams and that would essentially endure until after World War I.[196]

Crittenden's self-imposed exile from national politics did not last long, however. Taylor died in office in July 1850 and was replaced by Fillmore.[197] The former vice president succeeded where his predecessor had failed, luring Crittenden back to Washington and naming him attorney general for a second time.[198] (Crittenden is the only individual to serve as attorney general on separate occasions.)[199] Upon taking his place in Fillmore's cabinet, the attorney general wasted little time in voicing his commitment to the Union and becoming a strong advocate for the Compromise of 1850—the legislative effort championed by Clay to settle sectional disputes and stave off civil war.[200]

Even as his final great legislative achievement was being enacted, Clay's health was failing. Crittenden was well aware of his condition, and the two men reconciled prior to Clay's death in 1852.[201]

Crittenden's Final Term in the Senate

Crittenden's departure from Washington at the conclusion of the Fillmore administration in 1853 was short-lived. He returned to the Capitol two years later for a final term in the Senate. By the mid-1850s, with the passing of Clay, Daniel Webster (W-MA), and John C. Calhoun (D-SC) and the reelection defeat of Thomas Hart Benton (D-MO), Crittenden had become one of the Senate's most distinguished and venerable members.[202] One onlooker detailed Crittenden's physical appearance: "His face is strongly marked, years and thoughtful experience completing the original outlines of nature. . . . His form is erect and spare, well formed and vigorous, his dark grey eyes gleam vividly beneath heavy grey eyebrows, and are canopied by long lashes; his nose is aquiline; his mouth, and all his features are large; lips, firmly set; chin, square; forehead, broad, high, and massive; head, long, splendidly developed, covered with grey, but not white, and his complexion is dark."[203]

During his last stint as senator—from 1855 to 1861—Crittenden was involved in responding to one of the most infamous acts that ever occurred on the floor of the Senate: the caning of Charles Sumner (R-MA).[204] Sumner was an acerbic senator and an implacable foe of slavery.[205] One day in May 1856, Sumner took to the Senate floor to direct a venomous attack on pro-slavery forces. He aimed particular scorn toward those who had supported the controversial Kansas-Nebraska Act in 1854, including Senator Andrew Butler (D-SC).[206] Butler was not present during this ad hominem attack, but word spread quickly of Sumner's reference to Butler's consorting with "the harlot slavery."[207] A few days afterward, following Senate adjournment, Butler's nephew, Congressman Preston Brooks (D-SC), strode onto the floor of the upper chamber with fellow House member Laurence Keitt (D-SC); there, Brooks approached Sumner as he sat at his desk, and started beating him senseless with a gold-headed cane.[208]

Shocked bystanders came to Sumner's rescue.[209] Upon hearing the clamor behind him, Crittenden attempted to intervene, but by then, the damage had been done.[210] After seizing what was left of Brooks's cane, Crittenden assisted the battered Sumner out of the chamber.[211]

This outrageous incident is worth noting for two reasons. First, it illustrates the bitter sectional divide that had developed between North and South by the mid-1850s. From the perspective of hindsight, it presaged the Civil War. Second, this event teaches a lot about Crittenden. It personified his commitment to keep the North and South from each other's throats.

The Constitutional Union Party

The increasingly bitter sectional split that consumed the nation prior to the Civil War shook the existing political structure to its very foundation. The Whig Party, which Crittenden had so long championed, fell apart over slavery and the North-South divide.[212] In this respect, passage of the Kansas-Nebraska Act in 1854 played a major role in this reordering of political parties.[213] The measure rescinded the Missouri Compromise of 1820, which had forbidden slavery in the western territories above 36° 30′ latitude.[214] The 1854 statute, which permitted the expansion of slavery into the territories, was based on the principle that people living in the territories could decide for themselves whether to permit slavery—an approach euphemistically called "popular sovereignty."[215] This upending of the Missouri Compromise prompted outrage among antislavery advocates.[216] Opposition to the expansion of slavery culminated in the creation of the Republican Party not long afterward.[217] For its part, the Democratic Party, like the rest of the nation, was divided between northern and southern camps.[218]

Crittenden did not fit neatly into either category and followed an independent course.[219] He opposed the Kansas-Nebraska Act but was concerned about the rise of the Republican Party, which he viewed as destabilizing to the country.[220] Instead, he joined a number of like-minded individuals to create the Constitutional Union Party to try to repair the cracks between North and South.[221] Again, Crittenden played the role of conciliator. As its name suggests, the new party was established to preserve the Union.[222] In fact, party members wanted to nominate Crittenden for president, but he declined.[223]

In 1860, Crittenden's party claimed thirty-nine electoral votes and carried Kentucky, but another native Kentuckian, Abraham Lincoln, was elected president. The South recoiled at Lincoln's election. Within days, South Carolina seceded from the Union, precipitating the breakup of the country.

The Crittenden Compromise

Devoted as he was to the preservation of the Union, Crittenden was aghast at these developments. His independent stature; his widely recognized role as a conciliator; his evenhanded demeanor; his close ties with Clay, the Great Compromiser; and his representation of a border state convinced many that Crittenden was the only person who could devise a legislative solution and save the country.[224] With constructive leadership not forthcoming from lame-duck president James Buchanan, people turned to Crittenden as perhaps the last hope for national reconciliation.[225]

At the time, Crittenden's party—the Constitutional Union Party—commanded a grand total of two Senate seats out of sixty-six.[226] Nonetheless, as Crittenden's biographer Albert Kirwan has written: "The country was . . . prepared for reconciliation, and with the convening of Congress, all eyes turned to Crittenden to work out the details of compromise."[227] A fellow senator said to Crittenden: "The best services of your best day will be needed as pacificator."[228]

The Kentuckian desperately tried to bridge the sectional divide through a series of constitutional amendments—a package of proposals known today as the Crittenden Compromise.[229] The main elements included reinstitution of the Missouri Compromise boundary of 36° 30′ and its expansion to the Pacific Ocean; continuation of slavery in the territories south of 36° 30′ and its prohibition to the north, with the caveat that once territories became states, they could decide matters for themselves; and adoption of constitutional amendments ensuring that Congress could never tamper with slavery in the existing states.[230]

Crittenden believed the compromise largely addressed the specific concerns of both North and South. For northerners, the measure would have repealed the loathsome Kansas-Nebraska Act, which was the animating principle behind the newly ascendant Republican Party.[231] Under Crittenden's proposal, territories north of the 36° 30′ boundary could not permit slavery.[232] And, as a practical matter, even after the northern territories became states, many believed that human bondage would not expand into those regions because the climate was not conducive to slave-based agriculture.[233] For southerners, the proposed compromise would have ensured that Congress could not interfere with slavery in the states, and it allowed for the possible expansion of slavery into the northern territories after they achieved statehood.[234] To modern eyes, these proposals are obviously abhorrent, but at the time, they held out some promise of preserving the Union.[235]

Vice President John C. Breckinridge named the Committee of Thirteen to consider Crittenden's proposal.[236] Crittenden worked diligently for its acceptance, but in the end, the panel did not support the compromise.[237] He then took the fight to the Senate floor, where it was defeated again.[238] Other iterations of Crittenden's proposal would be revived in different settings in the months that followed, but to no avail.[239] Republicans refused to countenance even the theoretical expansion of slavery.[240] And, behind the scenes, President-elect Lincoln strenuously opposed Crittenden's efforts.[241] At the same time, southern Democratic senators complained that matters were already past the point of no return, even though the package would have preserved the "peculiar institution."[242] Southern Democratic faith in northern intentions had simply evaporated.[243] For southerners, mere words on a page were not sufficient to protect slavery.[244]

* * *

Crittenden's unsuccessful efforts to get his compromise adopted reflect an important reality about the role of committees in the Senate. If a bill does not receive the support of the committee of jurisdiction, it does not augur well for floor consideration of the matter.[245]

The same principle holds true for nominations. I recall this dynamic in 1987, during the Senate's consideration of the nomination of Judge Robert Bork to serve on the Supreme Court. The Judiciary Committee, chaired by Democrat Joe Biden, voted 9 to 5 to report out Bork's nomination unfavorably. That vote presaged the defeat of Bork's nomination by the full Senate. Committees are indeed "legislatures in miniature," and they often serve as proxies for the larger chamber.[246]

* * *

Though Crittenden's prestige was immense and his attempt to save the Union heartfelt, at that point, no one could have saved the Union through legislation.[247] The clock simply could not be turned back to 1820 or even 1850.[248] At the end of the day, some issues in some settings are simply not susceptible to legislative solution, and the situation in early 1861 was one of them.[249]

Sinecure Committees

During his work on the compromise effort, Crittenden also chaired the Committee on Revolutionary Claims.[250] This vestigial panel reflects some of the realities of Senate committees during this period. By the 1860s, presumably all Revolutionary War claims had long since been addressed, but "sinecure committees" like this one served purposes that went well beyond their jurisdiction.[251] Efforts to abolish these panels encountered stiff resistance from senators. In 1857, a proposal to streamline committees by abolishing sinecure panels, such as the Committee on Revolutionary Claims, was put forward.[252] Crittenden himself deftly moved to defeat the effort on the Senate floor.[253] Why did he do so?

The answer appears to be that, as the federal government's responsibilities expanded in the nineteenth century, senators—particularly committee chairmen—needed office space and administrative assistance.[254] Starting in 1856, senators who chaired committees—even moribund ones—were given some clerical support.[255]

Once each senator was granted a staff member in 1884 and the first Senate office building was opened in 1909, the need for extraneous committees was eliminated.[256] As a result, in 1921, the Senate abolished forty-one inert committees.[257] In 1946, the Senate merged several existing viable committees, decreasing the number of panels yet again.[258] For instance, the Military Affairs Committee, which Crittenden had chaired a century before, combined with the Naval Affairs Committee to create the Armed Services Committee. Currently, there are sixteen standing committees in the Senate, four select or special Senate committees, and four joint panels with the House.[259]

Committee Chairmen from the Civil War to World War I

Taken as a whole, the power and prestige of Senate committee chairmen seem to have reached their zenith in the years between the Civil War and World War I.[260] During this period, the Senate lacked formal floor leaders, the result being that prominent committee chairmen often stepped into the breach.[261] Gerald Gamm and Steven S. Smith observe that, in the years following the Civil War, "standing committee leaders often led caucus discussion, and the leaders of the most important committees served as the de facto leaders of the party."[262] These distinguished scholars note that, "until the rise of party leadership, the Senate's agenda was set by debate on the floor and by closed-door meetings of committee chairs."[263]

During this era, powerful committee chairmen often went to the Senate floor on their own accord and moved that the chamber take up and consider measures that their panels had approved.[264] In 1878, the *New York Times* observed, "Congress . . . is without distinctly recognized leaders. Business is left to the initiative of individuals or of numerous unconnected committees."[265] Woodrow Wilson went so far as to write in 1885 that "Congressional government is Committee government."[266] With regard to the Senate, Wilson concluded, "Its proceedings bear most of the characteristic features of committee rule."[267]

Indeed, even as power began to centralize in the Senate toward the end of the nineteenth century, many of the de facto floor leaders drew much of their power from their committee gavels.[268] For example, one of the most influential senators in the late nineteenth and early twentieth centuries was Nelson Aldrich (R-RI).[269] A key to his influence was his chairmanship of the Senate Finance Committee at a time when currency and tariff matters were among the most salient issues of the day.[270] Similarly, an Aldrich contemporary, William Allison (R-IA), chaired the Appropriations Committee for more than two decades, greatly enhancing his prestige in the Senate.[271]

Senate Committees in the Modern Era

In the years following World War I, committee chairmen seem to have lost some ground within the Senate chamber relative to party floor leaders. The time when a committee chairman could decide on his own to come to the Senate floor and move to proceed with his pet legislation was gradually coming to an end.[272] Moreover, unlike informal party leaders in earlier decades, who drew much of their authority from their committee chairmanships, by the late 1920s and early 1930s, it became much less common for floor leaders to chair major committees; their influence would increasingly be traced to other sources.[273]

The Legislative Reorganization Act of 1946 not only lowered the number of panels; it also reduced the authority of chairmen within their committees.[274] More stringent committee quorum requirements were established, committee meetings were made more routine, hearings and committee reports were made more accessible to the public, and other reforms were instituted to better supply rank-and-file committee members with information.[275]

Nevertheless, even a decade after enactment of that measure, congressional correspondent William S. White could still write: "A Senate committee is an imperious force; its chairman, unless he be a weak and irresolute man, is emperor. It makes in its field in ninety-nine cases out of a hundred the real decisions of the Institution itself. What bills it approves are approved by the Senate; what bills it rejects are rejected, with rare exceptions."[276] With adoption of the Legislature Reorganization Act of 1970, additional reforms were instituted that further diminished the authority of chairmen vis-à-vis their fellow committee members.[277] These changes included greater public transparency of proceedings and empowering a committee majority to convene the panel if the chairman refuses to do so.[278]

Even with these limits on chairmen's authority, they remain a potent force in the Senate and on the national stage. To this day, when legislation is up for debate and amendment on the Senate floor, it is typically the chief responsibility of the chairman and ranking member of the committee of jurisdiction to "manage" the bill.[279] In this setting, the chairman and ranking member lead debate on the Senate floor involving measures within their panel's jurisdiction, and they are granted prior recognition over all other senators except the majority and minority leaders.[280] For example, when the National Defense Authorization Act is on the Senate floor, if no other senator is speaking, the chairman and ranking member of the Armed Services Committee are recognized to speak ahead of all other senators except for the two floor leaders.[281] In a sense, in this capacity, bill managers step into the shoes of party leaders on the floor, even speaking from the center-aisle seats otherwise reserved for the majority and minority leaders.[282]

* * *

Responsibility for managing a bill includes helping determine which amendments should be adopted without a recorded vote, which amendments should be voted on, and which amendments do not merit consideration at all. In this regard, bill managers typically coordinate closely with their respective parties' leaders, who have overall responsibility for ensuring that the membership's interests are protected as the bill is debated. I can say from firsthand experience that sometimes the interests of the chairman or ranking member collide with those of the party leader or those of party colleagues. These differences must be somehow reconciled, or they may imperil the underlying bill.

Managing a bill can be a major challenge, as Senate rules can make floor consideration of legislation seem like the Wild West. Under Senate rules, discussion is generally not limited to the subject matter of the bill at hand, so members may offer amendments that are not germane (i.e., they are basically unrelated to the underlying measure).[283] Or senators may go to the floor and advocate voting on legislation that has never even been considered by the relevant committee.[284]

As one writer put it more than a century ago, when a chairman's bill comes to the Senate floor, "peculiar enemies lie in wait for a committee; the chairmen of other committees, the speech-makers, the amenders, the filibusters."[285] Those same challenges vex Senate committee chairmen to this very day.

* * *

Keeping Kentucky in the Union

In 1861, after the collapse of his compromise, Crittenden slowly prepared to leave Washington for what seemed like the last time.[286] It was then that Lincoln gave serious consideration to nominating Crittenden to fill an anticipated vacancy on the Supreme Court.[287] The justice in question, however, ultimately decided not to retire.[288]

Although Crittenden thought his service to the country had drawn to a close, that same year, at the age of seventy-five, he stood for election to the US House of Representatives as a Unionist.[289] Crittenden prevailed in what was in many ways a political proxy battle between those loyal to the Union and secessionists.[290] During his tenure in the House, Crittenden's greatest contribution took place outside the lower chamber.[291] As a congressman and elder statesman,

Crittenden labored tirelessly to convince his fellow Kentuckians not to secede.[292] In countless speeches, letters, and conversations throughout the commonwealth, Crittenden used all his stature and persuasiveness to help convince Kentuckians to stay loyal to the Union.[293] As future Speaker of the House and Senator James G. Blaine (R-ME) later wrote, "But for [Crittenden's] strong hold upon the sympathy and pride of Kentucky . . . [the state might have been] forced . . . into the Confederacy."[294]

Kentucky remained loyal to the Union. This was pivotal to the North's success in this gravest of national challenges.[295] After all, Kentucky was a strategic bridge between North and South and between East and West. Abolitionist William Henry Furness wrote of Lincoln's posture: he "would like to have God on his side, but he must have Kentucky."[296]

For Crittenden, the Civil War was destroying not only his country but also his family. He had sons who served as generals on each side of the conflict.[297] In fact, his son George led the southern forces that met defeat at the Battle of Mill Springs in 1862 in Kentucky.[298] Alas, Crittenden would not live long enough to see his beloved country reunited. He died in 1863 in Frankfort, with the Civil War raging and the fate of the Union still very much in doubt.[299]

Crittenden's Legacy

John J. Crittenden's experience as a four-time standing committee chairman helps inform discussion of this leadership perch in the decades following the creation of permanent panels in 1816. Although their power would not truly emerge until after Crittenden's departure, the foundation for their enduring importance was laid during this period.

As to Crittenden's individual legacy, he is sometimes seen as a "poor man's Henry Clay."[300] Whereas Clay helped create the Whig Party, which was a major political force for two decades, Crittenden's Constitutional Union Party lasted barely one election. Three times, Clay helped save the Union through his legislative efforts; Crittenden's compromise plan for the Union failed.[301] These comparisons heighten the sense that Crittenden does not quite measure up to Clay.[302] But that is a profoundly unfair comparison. It is like saying that a president is no George Washington or a Supreme Court justice is no John Marshall. Likewise, precious few lawmakers can be compared with Clay.[303] Crittenden performed great public service, and his long career marks him among the most prominent men of his age. Crittenden played an important role in avoiding an unnecessary war with Britain. And he did all he could to preserve the Union prior to the Civil War and to help ensure that Kentucky remained loyal during the greatest crisis the nation has ever endured.[304] These are serious achievements that deserve great respect.

6

Senate Caucus Chairman

John W. Stevenson, James B. Beck, and Joseph C. S. Blackburn

enry Clay and Alben Barkley are well known to Americans. By contrast, the names John W. Stevenson, James B. Beck, and Joseph C. S. Blackburn are rarely heard on the lips of university faculty members, let alone average citizens. Similarly, the post that each of these men held—party caucus chairman—is nearly as obscure as they are. This chapter discusses these long-forgotten senators and this largely unknown position. All three individuals were significant figures in the Senate, and the caucus chairmanship slowly morphed into the post of formal Senate floor leader (i.e., majority and minority leaders).[1] The Senate careers of these three Kentuckians provide important touchstones regarding the caucus chairman position as it moved along this evolutionary path.

John W. Stevenson

In May 1812, a young, well-off couple in Richmond, Virginia—Andrew and Mary White Stevenson—welcomed a son into the world.[2] They named the infant John White Stevenson. The boy's birth was marred by tragedy, however, as Mary died shortly thereafter.[3] She hailed from an elite Virginia family; her ancestors included Carter Braxton, who had signed the Declaration of Independence.[4] Without a mother, young John was entrusted to his aunt and grandmother, who raised him until he was eleven.[5] After his father remarried, the lad returned to Richmond.[6]

John, an only child, gained wide exposure to politics as a youth. His father was a member of the US House of Representatives (Dem.-Rep.–VA) from 1821 to 1834, serving as Speaker during the last seven years.[7] Afterward, he served as minister to Great Britain in the Jackson and Van Buren administrations.[8] His father's status opened many doors for young John; he became acquainted with both Thomas Jefferson and James Madison.[9] In fact, Stevenson would later receive career advice from the latter. He benefited not only from his father's example and contacts but also from an education by private tutors.[10] This background prepared the boy for his studies at Hampden-Sidney College before he continued his academic career at the University of Virginia, where he earned a degree in 1832.[11] As a collegian in Charlottesville, Stevenson was a firebrand, supporting South Carolina's asserted "right" to nullify any federal law with which it disagreed.[12] In so doing, he took a position "directly opposed to . . . [that of his] father."[13]

Beginning in 1832, Stevenson read law under the tutelage of future Virginia congressman Willoughby Newton (W-VA).[14] It was during this time that an aging Madison suggested that Stevenson move out of the Old Dominion and seek his fortune elsewhere, preferably in one of the more recently admitted states.[15] Stevenson did just that and headed to Vicksburg, Mississippi.[16] With him he carried a number of volumes, gifts from the fourth president.[17] By 1840, however, Stevenson had had enough of Mississippi, finding insufficient legal work to support himself.[18] He decided to settle in Covington, Kentucky.[19] There, Stevenson would make his home and pursue his profession, practicing law with prominent local attorney Jefferson Phelps.[20] In 1843, Stevenson wed Sibella Winston.[21] The couple would have five children.[22]

Sources reveal little of what Stevenson was like as a person. What seems clear is that he was not especially charismatic. His speaking style was dry and intellectual; one contemporary account described him as "not an orator in the technical sense, [though] he was impressive by the command he manifested of the principles of law he invoked and applied."[23] Some thought him "haughty" and aloof.[24] However, in later life, Stevenson became something of a raconteur, recounting old political and legal "war stories" with relish.[25]

One authority described him as "somewhat reserved in demeanor . . . a great lover of the law . . . and . . . strongly religious."[26] Stevenson was indeed a devout Episcopalian and very active in the church, regularly participating in conferences.[27] Apparently, he happened upon an Episcopal church one night, walked in, and was deeply moved by the words of the bishop, who was speaking to a group about to be confirmed.[28] Stevenson requested that he be permitted to participate in the class and was accepted into the church.[29] From that moment forward, religion would play a vital role in Stevenson's life.[30]

Although he was not a "hail fellow well met" type, Stevenson seems to have made a good impression on people. "We hear from every quarter 'golden opinions' of him," commented his stepmother, "as to talents, standing, and general worth of character."[31]

Stevenson's Rise in Politics

With such a background, it is perhaps not surprising that Stevenson was drawn to public life. He won election to the state house three times in the 1840s, participated in the state constitutional convention of 1849, and regularly attended the Democratic National Convention.[32] At the same time, his stature within the state bar continued to grow. In 1854, he assisted in compiling the *Code of Practice in Civil and Criminal Cases* for the commonwealth.[33]

Within three years, he was poised to follow in his father's footsteps and was duly elected to the US House of Representatives as a Democrat.[34] Upon reaching the capital, he made some important alliances, including his Washington housemate, Vice President John C. Breckinridge.[35] Once in Congress, Stevenson advocated on behalf of the controversial pro-slavery Lecompton Constitution for Kansas.[36] He also favored the Crittenden Compromise, which attempted to prevent the Civil War.[37] In 1860, however, Stevenson suffered two professional setbacks: he lost his House seat, and his friend and fellow Kentuckian Breckinridge failed in his bid for the presidency.[38]

As the Civil War raged, Kentucky remained loyal to the Union, but the commonwealth was badly divided internally. There is little question, however, where Stevenson's sympathies lay.[39] At one point, he was incarcerated for attempting to recruit a Confederate military unit.[40] For the rest of the war, it seems that Stevenson kept a low profile.[41]

During Reconstruction, Stevenson supported Andrew Johnson, who had succeeded to the presidency after Lincoln's assassination.[42] At the same time, his own political star began to rise again as he was elected lieutenant governor.[43] Like Johnson, Stevenson quickly found himself elevated to higher office when Governor John L. Helm passed away less than a week after his swearing in.[44] In 1868, Stevenson ran for governor in his own right in a special election.[45] During the campaign, Stevenson did not impress and spoke infrequently.[46] Nonetheless, as would be the case for decades after the Civil War, Republicans fared poorly in Kentucky, and the Democrat Stevenson was elected by a huge margin.[47] He would serve as governor of the commonwealth until 1871, when he began his tenure in the US Senate.[48]

Stevenson as Governor

Governor Stevenson was a firm believer that the states—not the federal government—should take the lead in managing race relations and reintegrating former Confederate officials into public life.[49] He was an open advocate of the position that ex-rebels should not be saddled with political disabilities.[50] Moreover, his opposition to the Fifteenth Amendment to the Constitution, granting voting rights to African Americans, led to its defeat in the state legislature.[51]

As the commonwealth's chief executive, one of Stevenson's challenges was rampant vigilantism, a legacy of the Civil War.[52] In 1867 and 1869, Stevenson took steps to combat this lawlessness, deploying the Kentucky militia to a number of counties.[53] However, Stevenson displayed less alacrity in using state resources to protect African Americans from violence—such as when they tried to vote.[54] Furthermore, he did little to discourage the legislature from gerrymandering districts to make voting more difficult for African Americans; nor did he hinder efforts to keep freedmen from testifying in court against white Kentuckians.[55]

To his credit, Governor Stevenson was a strong proponent of improving public schools in the state.[56] Many of the reforms he implemented continued to be felt decades later.[57] In addition, his administration made strides toward putting the commonwealth's financial house in order and improving the Kentucky prison system.[58] Stevenson also established a state agency for immigration in an effort to draw more people to the commonwealth.[59]

As governor, Stevenson did not shy away from the nitty-gritty of politics. With an eye toward securing his own election to the Senate, he stoked the embers of the recently concluded Civil War by condemning two members of Kentucky's federal delegation for allegedly supporting a deeply unpopular office seeker.[60] It was no coincidence that both of them happened to be potential opponents in Stevenson's race for the Senate; in fact, one was the incumbent—Democrat Thomas Clay McCreery.[61] Stevenson's other opponent became so incensed at Stevenson that he demanded a duel.[62] Stevenson demurred, and the gambit ended successfully for him.[63] He defeated both rival candidates in the election and secured the Senate seat.[64]

Stevenson in the Senate

Stevenson remained in the upper chamber until 1877, during which time he held the gavel as chairman of the Committee on Revolutionary Claims, the same panel led by John J. Crittenden two decades before.[65] In keeping with his record as governor and his Jeffersonian philosophy, Stevenson was a fiscally conservative senator, coming out against federal infrastructure projects and arguing that the Constitution should be strictly construed.[66] Moreover, as a well-regarded attorney, Stevenson was assigned to the Judiciary Committee, where he served from 1873 to 1877.[67]

On that panel, Stevenson played a role in crafting the Judiciary Act of 1875.[68] In the long run, this measure greatly enhanced the federal courts and helped position them to become, in the words of two authorities, "the primary and powerful reliances for vindicating every right given by the Constitution, the laws, and treaties of the United States."[69] Years later, Supreme Court justice Felix Frankfurter paid tribute to Stevenson in an opinion for the Court, terming him and his committee colleagues "accomplished lawyers" and "men with outstanding professional experience."[70]

Stevenson as Caucus Chairman

For a number of years following the Civil War, Senate Democrats were in the political wilderness. By the opening of Congress in 1871, however, the party's fortunes had sufficiently revived to the point where one of their own was permitted to chair a Senate committee.[71] Senator Garrett Davis (D-KY) was named to head the Committee on Private Land Claims.[72] As noted earlier, one of the perquisites associated with chairmanship of a committee was that it came with office space and administrative assistance.[73] Davis's gavel ensured that, for the first time since before the Civil War, a Democrat would have control over a room in the Capitol.[74] As a result, Senate Democrats soon began to hold party meetings or caucuses in the committee office.[75]

Davis died in September 1872, but fourteen months later, an important step in caucus development centered around another Kentuckian: John W. Stevenson.[76] Groundbreaking research by Gerald Gamm and Steven S. Smith discovered that in late 1873, Stevenson was chosen as the first permanent head of the Democratic caucus, apparently at a meeting held in the same room that Davis's committee chairmanship had secured for the party.[77] Underscoring the work of Gamm and Smith is long-overlooked floor debate. For instance, the very first reference on the Senate floor to a Democratic caucus chairman was to Stevenson.[78]

Historical materials do not reveal why Democrats chose this moment to make the position permanent or why they chose Stevenson to fill the slot.[79] By all accounts, Stevenson was quite able. A sketch penned two decades after his passing commented, "We have heard it said, that [Stevenson] was regarded in Washington, as one of the most talented and scholarly men of the South."[80] Either because of his new position or because of his independent standing among Senate Democrats (or both), Stevenson was quickly seen as a Senate leader. A Democratic Party loyalist wrote to Stevenson just a few weeks after his election as caucus chairman, referring to Stevenson as one of "the leaders of the Dem[ocratic] Senators."[81] Stevenson would remain caucus chairman until the end of his term in 1877.[82]

As the first Democratic caucus chairman, Stevenson set an important precedent in 1875 by heading the panel that determined Democratic committee assignments.[83] This meant that, not long after the position's creation, the Democratic caucus chairman was displaying the potential to exercise significant authority within the caucus.[84] Thus, Stevenson did more than merely schedule Senate Democratic conclaves and wield the gavel during these proceedings.[85] Yet, as Gamm and Smith caution, not until the chairmanship of "[James] Beck . . . is [there] evidence that [chairmen] assumed any responsibility for managing [party] business."[86]

Stevenson Returns to Kentucky

Despite achieving high stature in the Senate in a relatively short time, Stevenson apparently declined to seek reelection.[87] Northern Kentucky beckoned, and Stevenson once again focused on his law practice.[88] This he did with his customary skill, arguing at least one case before the US Supreme Court.[89] In private life, Stevenson advised the Kentucky Central Railroad and gained a significant stake in the company.[90] At around the same time, he became a professor of law at Cincinnati Law School, providing instruction on contracts and criminal law.[91] Interestingly, Stevenson seems to have been teaching at the institution while William Howard Taft was a law student there.[92] Given the small size of the faculty at the time, there is reason to believe that the future president and chief justice may have studied under Stevenson.

The Kentuckian's commitment to the law was enduring. In 1884, Stevenson left Cincinnati Law School to become president of the American Bar Association, a position he held until 1885.[93] His commitment to the history of the commonwealth was equally evident. Stevenson was active in the revitalization of the Kentucky Historical Society in the late 1870s.[94]

Stevenson's success in politics and law attracted talented protégés, and he obligingly mentored others, as he himself had been tutored as a younger man.[95] His understudies included John G. Carlisle—future Speaker of the US House, US senator, and secretary of the treasury—and future governor William Goebel.[96] Stevenson made Goebel a partner in his firm and named him executor of his will.[97]

Following his return to Covington, Stevenson did not completely abandon politics, however. In 1880, he served as chairman of the Democratic National Convention.[98] Once again, he was following in his father's footsteps: Andrew had chaired the convention in 1848.[99] Stevenson seems to have spent his last years contentedly, living on a $1 million nest egg he had amassed, presumably from his railroad holdings.[100] In 1886, Stevenson was at a religious gathering in Sewanee, Tennessee, when his health took a sudden turn for the worse.[101] He was rushed home and died in Covington just days later at age seventy-four.[102]

Senate Caucus Chairman

The origins of Senate party caucuses are murky. American political parties began to form in the early 1790s, although they were far less formalized than they are today. The presence of these nascent organizations was soon manifested in the US Senate.[103] Party members would meet privately, away from the Senate floor, to deliberate about political and policy concerns.[104] There are a number of examples of these early conclaves. For instance, they were convened to determine party policy with respect to President George Washington's diplomatic nominations.[105] As early as 1797, party caucuses were informally determining which senators should sit on which ad hoc committees.[106] The next year, in the wake of France's actions in the XYZ affair, a joint Senate-House caucus of Federalists considered whether a declaration of war was warranted.[107] In 1799, "at a meeting of the federal members [of the Senate], it was agreed to reject the nomination" of William Vans Murray to undertake a diplomatic mission to France.[108] It was reported around the same time that Senator William Bingham (Fed.-PA) hosted a number of Federalist caucuses at his house, including one that attempted to bind all members to whatever the party majority decided.[109] Another Federalist caucus supposedly met in 1800 to determine how to analyze the validity of any disputed electoral votes in the upcoming presidential election.[110]

Caucuses continued during the Jefferson administration. John Taylor (Dem.-Rep.–VA) discussed a caucus gathering in 1803: "there was a general meeting of the friends [of the legislation] an evening or two before its passage, to consider a proposition for enabling a vice president to act as president, in every case of no existing president. I speak from memory, but this I believe was the object. The meeting was made no secret of, and the subject was discussed with great talents."[111] One can detect a note of defensiveness about the non-public aspect of the meeting. Because of concerns over the secretive nature of caucuses and their supposed undermining of formal Senate deliberations, until the last few decades of the nineteenth century, they were seldom acknowledged publicly.[112]

Also in 1803, William Plumer (Fed.-NH), who kept a diary during his Senate tenure, noted, "The last evening, the democratic senators met in caucus, to determine who should succeed [Samuel] Otis as Secretary [of the Senate]."[113] The next year, Plumer noted two more conclaves. About one of them, he observed, "The democratic senators held a Caucus last evening in which they settled the principles of the bill—& agreed to the same in the Senate without any debate."[114]

Even though these early caucuses tried to formulate unified policy positions, they ran into what would prove to be an enduring limitation on party leadership: they could not compel members to vote the party line. Senator Plumer gave an example of one unsuccessful party caucus meeting: "That at this caucus the question of removing [Secretary of the Senate Samuel] Otis from office was long debated—And that if a majority were in favor of removal, each individual member of the caucus in the Senate, whatever his private opinion might be, should support their resolution."[115] After heated debate and no clear decision, the gathering "broke up divided & irritated."[116]

* * *

I can confirm that this early-nineteenth-century caucus would not be the last in Senate history to conclude with members "divided & irritated." Many a Senate party gathering ends in this fashion. Just as disconcerting for a party leader, however, can be when a way forward is proposed at a party conference lunch and it is greeted by silence from the membership. Does this silence reflect assent, befuddlement, a wait-and-see approach, smoldering opposition? In these situations, the party leadership must somehow decipher the mood of the conference and find a way forward.

* * *

In the early nineteenth century, caucuses served not only legislative purposes but also political ends. They played a significant role in choosing party presidential and vice-presidential candidates.[117] Party caucuses would participate in national candidate selection until the 1820s.[118] On the whole, and despite some notable successes (e.g., during the Jefferson presidency), for the first few decades of the nineteenth century, formal party organization was rudimentary and party discipline generally lacking. Scholar James Sterling Young writes that during the early nineteenth century, "Parties on the Hill were largely unorganized groups. They were without an openly recorded membership, much less with differentiated leadership roles."[119]

As the nineteenth century continued, party caucuses began to play more of an institutional role. By the 1830s and 1840s, lawmakers were sitting in the Senate chamber in party blocs, although that remained only an informal tradition for many years.[120] In the middle of the 1840s, parties had assumed responsibility for assigning senators to committees.[121] Toward the end of the 1840s and continuing well into the next decade, Democratic members employed party caucuses to sanction dissident members as well as to pursue policy matters.[122] Republican caucuses would do the same in the 1860s and 1870s.[123] Party organization gradually grew more sophisticated as caucuses started to meet more regularly, and eventually, caucuses began to elect permanent chairmen.[124] Republicans were the first to do so.[125] John P. Hale (R-NH) is the first Republican caucus chairman on record, serving from 1857 to 1862.[126] Republican senators would come to choose party caucus chairmen based on seniority, although that was not true of the Democrats, as demonstrated by Stevenson.[127] The Kentuckian had been a senator for all of two years prior to his elevation.[128]

Early Republican caucus chairmen appear to have wielded less authority than their Democratic counterparts.[129] An example of this limited authority is illustrated by an event that took place in December 1862. At the time, Republican senators were deeply frustrated with Union military failures in the Civil War.[130] A GOP caucus was called to discuss how members' concerns could best be conveyed to President Abraham Lincoln.[131] As recorded by one of the senators at the gathering, the caucus chairman, Henry Anthony (R-RI), had not been told why the caucus had been called, and he "requested that the object of the meeting might be stated."[132] Moreover, when it was determined that a delegation from the caucus should meet with Lincoln, Anthony was not selected to be part of that group.[133] Today, under comparable circumstances, a floor leader would likely either speak with or meet with a president on his own to convey the conference's views, or he would lead a delegation on behalf of his members to formally meet with the chief executive.

Eventually, the Senate floor leader positions would grow out of these caucus chairman posts. As was the case with Stevenson, some of the steps along the way are demonstrated by the careers of James Beck and Joseph Blackburn.

James B. Beck

James Burnie Beck's path to the Senate followed an improbable course. He was born in 1822 in Dumfriesshire, Scotland.[134] As a youth, he was raised with an eye toward becoming a merchant in the family business headed by his mother's father, John Burnie.[135] James was educated by the Reverend Henry Duncan, one of the pioneers in the creation of savings banks.[136] As such, Duncan imbued the young Beck with a solid grounding in economics.[137]

For reasons that are unclear, Beck's father, Ebenezer, moved across the Atlantic in 1833, leaving young James behind.[138] Ebenezer settled first in Canada and then in New York State.[139] There, he established himself as a prosperous farmer and breeder of livestock.[140] In time, he also became active in local politics.[141] During this period, James's father entrusted him to the care of his uncles, who were to teach the young man about their overseas trading business.[142] Beck had other plans, however.[143]

The young man immigrated to the United States in 1838 at the age of sixteen, settling in New York.[144] For a time, Beck worked for his father, but he soon recognized that agriculture was no more his calling than international trade had been.[145] After an unsuccessful foray in land speculation, Beck headed to Lexington, Kentucky, where a family friend had recommended that he attend Transylvania University and study law.[146]

Good fortune smiled on Beck when he came to the attention of a notable local figure, W. Drummond Hunt.[147] Hunt hired Beck to run his farm and encouraged him to make use of his library for self-improvement.[148] Beck was thrifty, read voraciously, and saved sufficient funds to study law at Transylvania.[149] After completing his course of study, Beck read law for a time under the tutelage of Leslie Combs, a well-regarded political figure.[150]

With some financial assistance from his father, Beck became an attorney in his own right and gained some measure of esteem in Lexington.[151] A journalist described the arc of Beck's early legal career: "Beck's rise at the bar was not rapid. He was ever of slow growth—the oak, not the vine. . . . His rise was slow, but it was certain. . . . his ceaseless industry, his indefatigable energy, made him a successful lawyer. . . . He was a dangerous adversary in a common law trial. As a cross examiner he had no superior, and while he was no orator he was a powerful debater, and juries seemed to love to give him verdicts."[152]

While Beck's workmanlike approach to his profession gradually gained him a reputation in central Kentucky, two personal relationships he formed during this period propelled him to public prominence. The first was his marriage in 1848 to Jane Washington Thornton.[153] She came from a distinguished Virginia family and could claim the nation's first president as a relative.[154] Jane was characterized as "well educated and a woman of strong intellect and good judgment."[155] She also brought with her a significant dowry, which, through shrewd investments, Beck multiplied many times over.[156] He acquired vast swaths of property and a number of slaves.[157] Jane's family connections would greatly assist Beck's rise in political circles.[158] The marriage produced five children.[159]

In addition to marrying well, Beck became a protégé of John C. Breckinridge.[160] Indeed, the two soon became law partners and the best of friends.[161] They shared several common interests, including property speculation and Democratic Party politics.[162] Their loyalty to each other was unqualified and enduring. Beck campaigned vigorously for Breckinridge when he ran for president in 1860.[163] And after the Civil War, Beck advocated doggedly for a pardon for the former Confederate Breckinridge, meeting with President Andrew Johnson personally on the subject.[164] Later, Breckinridge entrusted his will to Beck, and Beck was a pallbearer at Breckinridge's funeral, where he spoke about his deceased friend.[165] His bond with the popular Breckinridge was well known throughout the Bluegrass State and would prove to be a major political asset for Beck in the future.[166]

Beck's Early Public Life

In 1861, Beck made his initial foray into elective politics, running for state senate.[167] His views, however, seemed to favor secession for Kentucky, sentiments that were deemed too extreme for his district.[168] As a result, his opponent— James Robinson, the future governor of the state—won handily.[169] Following his defeat and the onset of the Civil War, Beck softened his rhetoric and claimed to be neutral in the conflict, but his actions seemed to belie that assertion.[170] He lent covert assistance to Confederate soldiers.[171]

Beck's first political affiliation had been as a Whig, and he remained a

Whig until the party collapsed, whereupon he joined the Democrats. Proving the adage that there is no zeal like a convert's, Beck threw his heart and soul into the Democratic Party.[172] His efforts paid off handsomely. In 1866, after assisting in the restructuring of the state party, Beck was elected to the US House of Representatives, where he served four terms.[173] His election proved a turning point. Thereafter, in the words of a Kentucky congressman, Beck was "the recognized leader of the Democra[tic] [Party] of Kentucky."[174]

Much to his surprise, upon becoming a House member, Beck was assigned to the Committee on Reconstruction.[175] This set the stage for Beck's advocacy of the southern cause, leading to repeated clashes with committee chairman Thaddeus Stevens (R-PA).[176] Throughout his tenure in the House, Beck was a vocal and unapologetic opponent of civil rights for recently freed African Americans.[177] For this reason, Beck was regularly referred to as an "ex-Confederate," bringing him widespread fame and notoriety.[178] At the time, the *Louisville Courier-Journal* observed: "In less than one Congressional term, Beck has achieved a national reputation. He now stands confessedly in the front rank of the public men in the country."[179] Beck was dubbed "the Representative from the Ashland district and the eleven seceded States of the late Confederacy."[180] Despite his battles with Republicans over Reconstruction and civil rights, Beck demonstrated an ability to befriend and work constructively with those across the aisle, such as future House Speaker James G. Blaine (R-ME) and future senator William Allison (R-IA).[181]

Beck soon tired of the House and considered not pursuing a fourth term.[182] Although he wound up running and winning again, he declined to run a fifth time. Indeed, some of Beck's motivation may have been to avoid a bruising intraparty contest with an impatient young upstart by the name of Joseph C. S. Blackburn.[183] Nonetheless, following Beck's tenure in the House, he remained active in public life, serving on a commission established to resolve a border dispute between Virginia and Maryland.[184]

Beck in the Senate

His absence from Congress did not last long. In 1876, the state legislature elected Beck to the US Senate to replace Stevenson.[185] He would serve there for the rest of his life. In the Senate, it took little time for Beck to establish a record of regular support for Democratic Party positions.

With the education he received as a young man, Beck soon became an acknowledged Senate expert on financial matters.[186] Senator William Evarts (R-NY) opined that Beck "was regarded as in some sense at least the leader of the Democratic party in the important topics [trade and currency issues] which divide them from the Republican party."[187] With his extensive knowledge of tariff matters, it is small wonder that Beck was a member of the powerful Senate Finance Committee.[188] Indeed, he served simultaneously on both the Finance and the Appropriations Committees.[189]

Unlike his experience in the House, Beck thoroughly enjoyed working in the Senate. He developed a firm attachment to the upper chamber and believed the position of senator was the most prestigious in the land.[190] As such, he threw himself completely into his work. Perhaps because Beck was so focused on politics, he did not devote much time to his appearance. One journalist observed: "Mr. Beck . . . is noted for . . . his slovenly attire, the worst visible."[191]

Beck wasted little time rising through the Democratic ranks. In 1879, he was chosen Democratic caucus secretary.[192] Six years later, he became chairman of the Senate's Democratic caucus, a position he held until his death.[193] His tenure as caucus chairman broke new ground for the post.[194] Prior to Beck, caucus chairmen had not been expected to provide policy direction for their fellow partisans.[195] But as noted earlier, when Beck became caucus chairman, currency and tariff policy were among the biggest issues facing the nation.[196] The Kentuckian was already recognized as the Democratic caucus's expert on these subjects, and he sat on the relevant committees.[197] His policy knowledge and membership on key Senate panels on the one hand and his caucus chairmanship on the other proved to be mutually reinforcing.[198] This began to lead to the expectation that the caucus chairman should also be a party policy leader.[199]

With this in mind, it is perhaps not surprising that Beck was the first caucus chairman to be called the "Democratic leader" on the Senate floor.[200] His tenure was also noteworthy since he was the first caucus chairman of either party to be cited on multiple occasions in major newspapers as his party's leader in the Senate.[201] This reflects that, at some level within the Senate and the media, the caucus chairmanship was starting to be seen differently, more as a position of party leadership and less as a ministerial post.[202] Gamm and Smith conclude that Beck "began to enhance the value of the caucus chairmanship."[203] Yet Beck's role as Democratic caucus chairman did not deter him from spearheading the opposition to a president of his own party.[204] In Beck's case, notable examples include his resistance to President Grover Cleveland's civil service reform efforts and his policy on silver currency.[205]

Thus, Beck raised both the profile and the expectations of the caucus chairman position.[206] In many ways, Beck prepared the way for the groundbreaking tenure of his successor as caucus chairman, Arthur Pue Gorman (D-MD).[207]

Beck's Character

By all accounts, Beck was high strung and a man of great passion. His colleague, Senator Blackburn, described him as "pertinacious and aggressive in his nature, prompt to grapple with man or measure when his convictions were assailed."[208] In addition, he had tremendous energy. Fellow senator John James Ingalls (R-KS) said of Beck, he was "rugged, robust, and indomitable, the incarnation of physical force and intellectual energy [he] seemed a part of nature, inseparable from life and exempt from infirmity."[209] Beck's great vitality powered a tremendous work ethic. One contemporary concluded that Beck's "capacity for labor . . . was unexcelled, I might almost say unequaled, by that of any man whom I have ever known. . . . [He] approach[ed] work with a zest which resembled positive pleasure, his iron frame seemed incapable of fatigue."[210]

Even though he could appear gruff, Beck's manner betrayed an inner kindness that was regularly remarked upon by his peers. To Congressman W. C. P. Breckinridge (D-KY), Beck "had certain elements of sternness about [him] . . . a certain indisposition to promiscuous friendships; like the rough burr, the outside of which sometimes pricks the fingers, but the inside was absolutely smooth and tender."[211] Another House member, Asher Caruth (D-KY), confirmed that Beck had a "rough exterior" but a "kind . . . heart."[212]

His exterior could take a while to penetrate, however. Senator George Frisbie Hoar (R-MA) entered the Senate with Beck in 1877. Hoar did "not think any two men ever disliked each other more than we did for our first few years of our service."[213] Yet, over time, the two developed a mutual respect and fondness.[214] Tellingly, Senator Hoar discussed Beck in a book chapter titled "Leaders of the Senate in 1877."[215]

Beck had a particular soft spot for young people.[216] One lad shared fond memories of Beck: "I recall his appearance with interest because he was so affable, of a sunny disposition and very cordial in his greetings. I was fifteen years old at the time of his death and took considerable pride in the fact that he [had] always greeted me as if I was much older."[217]

He enjoyed humor and, in the words of a colleague, was "full of marvelous stores of anecdotes."[218] Given Beck's Scottish birth, which disqualified him from the White House, he often ribbed his Senate colleagues that he alone among them did not harbor presidential ambitions.[219]

For all his attributes, Beck was not a great orator. A reporter detailed his manner of speaking: "He was not a fluent talker, and frequently stopped and hesitated for a word. He was a rapid but jerky speaker, and when excited would emphasize his remarks with vigorous gestures. At such times his place of birth became plainly evident in his enunciation."[220] Congressman James B. McCreary (D-KY)—who would later serve in the Senate and as governor of the state— described Beck's speaking style when addressing the Senate: "[Beck's] mighty arms swing like hammers. His Scotch tongue thunders out the shortest and simplest Anglo-Saxon words that can be found to compose his terse sentences.

Now and then the clenched fist comes down on his desk with telling force. The whole speech is made up of facts and statistics. . . . he is a man of figures, and . . . he speaks like a problem in mathematics."[221] The result was that Beck's speaking style was often underwhelming, and as one newspaper drily remarked, "his speeches gain when read in print."[222]

Beck's Final Decade

Early in his Senate term, Beck found himself a stone's throw away from one of the tragedies of American political history. In 1881, the Kentuckian was near the Baltimore and Potomac Railroad Station in Washington when President James Garfield—his former House colleague—was shot by Charles Guiteau.[223] Beck hurried to the station, where he witnessed "men fleeing in every direction."[224] He arrived to find a score of people around the wounded president.[225] According to Beck, the crowd wished to lynch Guiteau on the spot, but the Kentuckian "remonstrated [against] . . . this sentiment."[226] The assassin was spared, but it is unclear whether Beck's words played any role in halting the mob. Either way, the image of a prominent public figure lying in extremis on the platform of the Baltimore and Potomac Railroad Station, surrounded by a crowd of concerned onlookers, would be replayed not long afterward in Beck's own life.[227]

Beck's intensity and work ethic came at a cost. By the late 1880s, his customary vigor had begun to desert him.[228] His attendance in the Senate became less consistent, and in early May 1890, after continued ill health, Beck traveled to New York with his daughter to be examined by a physician.[229] Following the appointment, the two returned to Washington.[230] Upon their arrival at the train station, the senator and his daughter were met by Beck's private secretary, Rogers Clay, who asked about Beck's health.[231] The senator casually replied, "Oh, Dr. Lomis has examined me and he says I am all right."[232] Beck's daughter then introduced him to a well-wisher, and as the senator reached out to shake the man's hand, he suddenly exclaimed, "How dizzy I am; I never felt this way before."[233] Beck's legs gave way, and he slowly sank to the ground, expiring within a few moments.[234]

In a poignant tableau, a crowd gathered as Beck was frantically being attended to, much as they had with Garfield nine years earlier.[235] Vice President Levi Morton and his family and several other lawmakers hurried past the scene, unaware of the identity of the victim at the center of the commotion.[236]

Following Beck's passing, his body was escorted from Washington to the Southern Presbyterian Church in Lexington by, among others, Senator Blackburn, whose "eyes [were] bedimmed with tears."[237] Beck's funeral was thought to be the biggest in Lexington since the passing of Henry Clay.[238] In a testament to the fading memory of this once prominent senator, the US Post Office authorized a plate for a stamp in Beck's honor in 1894, but for some reason, it was never issued.[239]

Joseph C. S. Blackburn

Even in a state that can boast such colorful lawmakers as Alben Barkley and A. B. "Happy" Chandler, Joseph Clay Stiles Blackburn stands out. As Kentucky native and former vice president Adlai Stevenson wrote of him: "he was . . . the hero of more interesting narratives than any member who ever crossed the Blue Ridge Mountains."[240] Given Blackburn's vivid personality, it is both unfortunate and surprising that he is largely forgotten today.[241]

Little is known of Blackburn's childhood. He was born in 1838, not far from Spring Station in central Kentucky.[242] His father, Edward Mitchell (Ned) Blackburn, was a local political figure of some renown and a noted breeder of horses.[243] Ned married Lavina St. Clair Bell.[244] Joseph (known as Jo) was the younger brother of Luke Pryor Blackburn, a physician and later governor of Kentucky from 1879 to 1883.[245] Luke himself was a notable figure, though mostly for negative reasons. He was, among other things, a pioneer in germ warfare, having attempted to infect Union forces and the North as a whole with yellow fever during the Civil War.[246] Luke also had a Hall of Fame racehorse named after him (presumably for unrelated reasons).[247] Another brother, James, served as Kentucky's secretary of state.[248]

Even at a young age, Jo Blackburn displayed a pleasing manner. A classmate recollected an occasion when Blackburn and a handful of others had played hooky and gone fishing.[249] When Blackburn and his cohorts discovered, to their dismay, that one of their fellow truants had disclosed their adventure to the headmaster, they naturally feared that "the teacher's hickory would make the fur fly."[250] Thinking quickly, the boys bought their instructor a pipe and deputized Blackburn to deliver the peace offering.[251] The combination of the gift and Blackburn's affability saved the day; the boys escaped punishment, and the teacher even complimented young Jo, predicting that he would in time assume "a high place in the nation's future."[252]

Blackburn matriculated at Sayre Institute in Frankfort.[253] From there, he went on to Centre College, earning his degree in 1857.[254] After moving to Lexington, he set out to learn the law under the tutelage of George Kinkead, an antislavery advocate and sometime attorney for Abraham Lincoln.[255] Blackburn was called to the bar in 1858.[256] That year would be an important one for Blackburn not only professionally but also personally, as he wed Therese Graham, a native of Danville, Kentucky.[257] The couple would have four children.[258]

For reasons that are unclear, not long after his marriage, Blackburn left the commonwealth for Chicago, where he worked as an attorney with his brother-in-law until 1860.[259] Later in life, Blackburn liked to regale listeners with a story about his days as a young lawyer in the Windy City:

> I was a very young man, beginning the practice of law, and for the first time was appearing in a United States Court in Chicago. The opposing counsel was Isaac N. Arnold, one of the most distinguished men of Chicago. When the case was reached I was so nervous that I became bewildered and made only a feeble effort. I was about to sit down and let the case go by default, as it were, when a tall, homely, loose-jointed man sitting in the bar, whom I had noticed giving close attention to the case, arose and addressed the court in behalf of the position I had assumed in my feeble argument, making the point so clear that, when he closed, the court sustained my demurrer.
>
> I didn't know who my volunteer friend was, but Mr. Arnold got up and attempted to rebuke him for interfering in the matter, when I for the first time heard that he was Abraham Lincoln of Springfield.
>
> Mr. Lincoln, in his good-natured reply to Mr. Arnold's strictures on his interference, said that he claimed the privilege of giving a young Kentucky lawyer from the State of his birth a boost when struggling with his first case, especially if he was pitted against an experienced practitioner.
>
> Of course, I thanked him, and departed the court as proud as a young field marshal. I never saw Mr. Lincoln again, and he probably never recalled the young struggling lawyer that he so kindly assisted and rescued from defeat in his maiden effort before a United States tribunal.[260]

This anecdote, at a minimum, reflects Blackburn's ability to spin a good yarn. It may also demonstrate his overall dissatisfaction with practicing law in Chicago.

Either way, in 1860, Blackburn moved back to central Kentucky and got his feet wet in politics.[261] That year, he campaigned for Breckinridge for president and served as a presidential elector for him.[262] Following Lincoln's election and the onset of the Civil War, Blackburn joined the Confederate army and became an aide to General William Preston.[263] By the end of the conflagration, Blackburn was commanding forces in Mississippi.[264] About Blackburn's unit, it was later said that "its activities were such as to make it equally obnoxious to friend and foe" alike.[265] Whatever the effectiveness of his military efforts, Blackburn's service in the Confederate army certainly aided him politically in later years.[266]

Following Appomattox, Blackburn moved to Arkansas, where he practiced law and farmed for a time.[267] Then, in 1868, he returned to the commonwealth for good and hung his shingle in Versailles.[268] Of his law practice, it was said that

Blackburn "was not overly profound . . . but as an advocate he was superb. His magnetism fix[at]ed the jury and his eloquence secured the verdict. . . . When on circuit, instead of burning the midnight oil poring over pleadings and precedents, he was sitting at the tavern cracking jokes . . . cussing the Republican party [and assessing] the coming event on the turf at Lexington."[269] The Kentuckian "knew something of books, but more of mankind."[270]

Blackburn's Political Rise and Personal Attributes

His affability, family ties, and war record helped Blackburn win election as a state representative in 1871.[271] Blackburn apparently "went to Frankfort talking. . . . All the time his tongue was a-going, and he never heard anybody else."[272] All told, he spent four years in the state house, where he established a reputation as a spirited partisan. A reporter noted that Blackburn "goes after his opponents in hammer-and-tongs fashion, asking no quarter, giving none."[273] Yet Blackburn was more than just a rhetorical brawler. As a state legislator, he regularly broke into fisticuffs with his nemesis, Republican lawmaker John D. White.[274] Rather than harm his political prospects, Blackburn's fights with the unpopular White seemed only to raise his standing among the voters.[275]

White was not the only one who prompted Blackburn's ire. When Blackburn ran for the US House of Representatives, he and his opponent, former Confederate general Humphrey Marshall, "frequently [had to be] separated by friends."[276] Nor did becoming a US senator mellow Blackburn, at least not immediately.[277] On one occasion, during a committee meeting, he reportedly grabbed Senator William Chandler (R-NH) by the ear following a heated exchange.[278] Despite or perhaps in part because of his violent temper, Blackburn defeated Marshall and was elected to the US House in 1874, taking the place of James B. Beck.[279]

Aside from being a devoted partisan, Blackburn's rise was aided greatly by his public speaking ability.[280] He seldom missed an opportunity to display this skill. For example, during Blackburn's first race for the House of Representatives, he happened across a public hanging.[281] Noting Blackburn's prominence in the community, the sheriff asked the candidate if he would like to sit next to the prisoner and his chaplain.[282] As related by Adlai Stevenson:

At the near approach of the fatal hour, the sheriff, with watch in hand, amid a sea of upturned faces, stated to the prisoner that he had yet five minutes to live, and it was his privilege if he so desired to address the audience. The prisoner meekly replied that he did not wish to speak. Whereupon, Mr. Blackburn, stepping promptly to the front of the scaffold, said: "As the gentleman does not wish to speak, if he will kindly yield me his time, I will take this occasion to remark that I am a candidate for Congress, regularly nominated by the Democratic Convention," etc.[283]

Blackburn was just getting under way when the exasperated prisoner cried out: "Please hang me first, *and let him speak afterwards!*"[284]

With the possible exception of this hapless prisoner, people found Blackburn spellbinding. This was so even when his mastery of the issue at hand was less than comprehensive. One journalist wrote, "The less intimately he is acquainted with the subject the more effectively he can expatiate upon it."[285]

Stevenson recalled another incident involving Blackburn's oratory in the Senate. After he had finished addressing the chamber, "the scene that followed his closing words had never been witnessed in legislative assembly. All were in tears. It was even said that venerable Senators, who had never shed a tear since the ratification of the treaty of Ghent, actually sobbed aloud, and refused to be comforted."[286] A Kentucky reporter provided a vivid portrait of Blackburn on the stump:

> His gestures are inimitable, and his sentences are unsurpassed as far as sound goes. Like the Roman orator, his periods are so well rounded they could be danced to very easily. He throws in a dozen unnecessary words to fill out the metre. . . . No man in Kentucky has a better voice. . . . He has an odd habit of shutting one eye while speaking and looking wildly around with the other. . . . His sentences all contain over 50 words, and he ends them all with the rising inflection. When the sense won't allow the sentence to be rounded, he throws sense to the dogs and rams and jams in words to fill up space and get the rhythmical one, two, three.[287]

Blackburn was as compelling in small groups as he was when addressing a large crowd.[288] However, from time to time, Blackburn had difficulty determining what the occasion called for. One day, he joined a gathering of some of his closest companions along a creek by the Kentucky River.[289] The food and drink flowed freely, yet Blackburn appeared dissatisfied.[290] A friend, observing that Blackburn was somewhat out of sorts, inquired what was wrong, to which Blackburn replied, "I don't like this crowd."[291] Incredulous, his companion countered, "Why, Joe, there's not a man here who wouldn't die for you."[292] Blackburn responded, "I know that. It's not the quality I'm objecting to, but the quantity. The d[amne]d crowd is too big for an anecdote and not big enough for a speech."[293]

His winning ways in small groups might have had something to do with, in the words of one journalist, "his loyal appreciation of the liquid products of his native State."[294] A story circulated that on one occasion, when Blackburn was visiting a friend, his host greeted him at the train station and inquired good-naturedly, "How are you, Joe?"[295] Blackburn responded: "I'm up against it. I lost the best part of my baggage en route."[296] His friend queried: "Did you misplace it, or was it stolen?"[297] "Neither," came the reply.[298] "The cork came out."[299] When questioned later about this anecdote, Blackburn categorically denied it.[300] He replied, "Not a word of truth in it. You know I would be more careful of the cork."[301]

Contemporary accounts of Blackburn at social events paint a picture of a lively man with an outsized personality. Blackburn was described at a political gathering in the early 1880s as a "dashing-looking gentleman with his broad-brimmed hat turned up on one side like a Spanish bull-fighter, and his mustachios twirled out to a most prodigious length. In spite of his fierce air he is the hero of the hour, and no toast is drank that Jo must not come in for his share. . . . Just now he is laughing till his face is red and bursting with good humor."[302] Blackburn was also an avid poker player and enjoyed attending horse races, a passion that ran in his blood.[303] It was remarked that Blackburn "was the life of every [social gathering], had the best mount in every fox chase, and was stationed at the best stand in every deer drive. Carpe diem was the order wherever he appeared."[304]

He won over people from all walks of life.[305] In the 1870s, a Sioux chief named White Cloud visited Washington, where he met a host of prominent government officials but took an immediate liking to Blackburn.[306] White Cloud was so impressed with the Kentucky orator that he made him an honorary member of the tribe and gave him the Sioux name "Roaring Wind of the Bluegrass."[307]

Blackburn had a memorable appearance. His full mustache alone caught people's attention. With respect to his bearing and appearance, Blackburn's "movements are quick, but full of a subtle grace and elasticity. His hair is a rich brown, his eyes are of a glinting blue in color, and wearing usually an expression which indicates great firmness of opinion and steadfastness of purpose in whatever cause he espouses."[308] Another observer described him as "tall, sinewy, and muscular with a fine head, square forehead, and eyes that are by turns humorous and stern. A heavy dark mustache shades a finely cut mouth."[309] Unlike Beck, Blackburn put effort into his wardrobe. Whether it was his signature red cravat or the formal cutaway jacket he wore whenever giving a speech on the Senate floor, Blackburn wanted to leave an impression.[310]

Particularly as a younger man, Blackburn was easily riled, which led to potentially dangerous situations. Never was his combustible side on greater display than when he almost got into a duel with another lawmaker over who should receive credit for a pork-barrel project in Kentucky.

* * *

Lawmakers often vie for credit for work they undertake for their states or districts. After all, lawmakers want their constituents to know they are achieving results for them. Disputes over credit can often lead to grumbling or even a public spat between elected officials, but that is typically the end of it. Not so with Blackburn.

* * *

The disagreement centered around whether Blackburn (then a member of the House) or Senator John S. "Cerro Gordo" Williams (D-KY) should receive credit for earmarking $100,000 for a federal building in the state capital.[311] When a newspaper sympathetic to Blackburn attributed the earmark to him, it infuriated Williams.[312] The senator fired off a letter to one of Blackburn's archrivals, claiming that he—not Blackburn—had secured the provision.[313] This got back to Blackburn, who began corresponding directly with Williams, the temperature rising with each exchange.[314]

Soon-to-be Speaker of the House John G. Carlisle did his best to persuade Blackburn not to accuse Williams of having "deliberately lied," which almost certainly would have prompted an affair of honor.[315] Three additional senators, including James B. Beck, were ultimately enlisted to help resolve the dispute and prevent a duel.[316] Finally, a formal meeting with liaisons was called, and the matter was smoothed over.[317] Afterward, a *New York Times* headline noted with relief: "Duel Averted."[318]

Nor was Blackburn's conflict with Williams unique.[319] In 1883, he almost fought a duel with state lawmaker Ben Robbins, stemming from the congressional race the year before.[320] It was also widely reported that Blackburn and Senator (and former Union general) Ambrose Burnside (R-RI) came close to fighting a duel of their own.[321]

Despite his quick temper, Blackburn could be pragmatic and "bury the hatchet" when need be. He and future governor William Goebel developed a fierce dislike for each other after Goebel killed one of Blackburn's friends.[322] At the funeral, Blackburn thundered, "I shall make it my life's mission to avenge him by burying his slayer in the depths of merited execration."[323] Yet, in time, mutual self-interest brought the two together: Blackburn needed Goebel to regain his Senate seat, and Goebel needed Blackburn to become governor.[324] Ultimately, each supported the other politically.[325] Following Goebel's assassination, Blackburn spoke movingly at his funeral. Goebel, in Blackburn's words, "lived an honest life and gave his life for your deliverance. . . . 'Earth never pillowed upon her bosom a truer son, nor heaven opened wide her portals to receive a manlier spirit.'"[326]

Blackburn in the House

Upon his arrival in the US House in 1875, Blackburn quickly distinguished himself.[327] Due to the declining health of Speaker Michael Kerr (D-IN) during the Forty-Fourth Congress (1875–1877), Democrats needed someone to preside over the chamber.[328] They selected the freshman Blackburn to act as Speaker pro tempore.[329] In addition, Blackburn played a key role on the committee that uncovered financial wrongdoing in the Grant administration's Department of War.[330] This led to the impeachment of Secretary of War William Belknap and his subsequent resignation.[331] Blackburn's role in this inquiry catapulted him into the limelight and advanced his career immeasurably.[332]

He gained further notice for his attack on the Electoral Commission of 1877, which was impaneled to determine the outcome of the disputed presidential election between Republican Rutherford B. Hayes and Democrat Samuel Tilden.[333] By one vote, the commission sided with Hayes. Blackburn's strong opposition to the commission elevated his standing even higher among his House Democratic colleagues.[334]

After narrowly securing reelection, Blackburn continued his efforts to climb the ladder in the House.[335] In 1879, he became a candidate for Speaker against incumbent Samuel Randall (D-PA).[336] Blackburn was able to draw significant support from southern Democrats, but in the end, he fell just short.[337] That same year, the House of Representatives adopted a Blackburn resolution calling for a major overhaul of the House's rules of procedure.[338] The body named a five-person panel to draft the new rules, which included future president James Garfield (R-OH), Speaker Randall, former vice president of the Confederacy Alexander Stephens (D-GA), and Blackburn.[339] The panel worked throughout the congressional recess in Long Branch, New Jersey.[340] When the House returned to session, the proposed changes were debated on and off for two months before the chamber agreed to the reforms, with some minor modifications.[341] That Blackburn was able to work so closely and effectively with his erstwhile rival Randall shows once again Blackburn's pragmatic streak.

After his impressive showing in the Speaker's race in 1879, it was clear that Blackburn had a significant following in the House. Following the 1882 elections, which returned the House to Democratic control after a two-year hiatus, it appeared that another opportunity to run for Speaker might present itself for Blackburn.[342] However, standing in his way was not only former Speaker Randall but also his Kentucky colleague, Congressman John Carlisle.[343] The two Kentuckians circled each other warily before Blackburn finally opted to run for the Senate.[344]

In so doing, Blackburn took on his old nemesis, the incumbent senator

"Cerro Gordo" Williams.[345] From the start, it was a slugfest, with two other candidates complicating the equation.[346] The state legislature was convulsed by the contest.[347] One authority writes: "The fight lasted for nearly a month, with some legislating going on between times; balloting of the joint democratic caucus during long evening sessions, and constant conferences, secret gatherings, wire-pulling and log rolling day and night."[348]

Blackburn's campaign headquarters was vividly described in the press: "Here there was always a crowd drinking, talking, planning. A barrel of whiskey—rarely full, however—occupied one corner of the room, and a half dozen white china pitchers were always available. There was an ever-spoken 'Help yourself, boys,' and of course they respond cheerfully to this invitation. . . . The crowd was never too large to prevent Capt. Blackburn from relating an experience, telling . . . jokes. . . . He was always cheerful, bright, called everybody by his first name, and, inspired by the confidence of hope and the surroundings, made friends slowly but surely."[349] Ballot after ballot produced the same results.[350] Finally, the third and fourth candidates withdrew from the race, and the election turned in Blackburn's favor.[351] In what must have been a most satisfying victory, Blackburn defeated Williams for the Senate seat in February 1884.[352] He would be reelected six years later.

Blackburn in the Senate

Given his prominence in the House, it is no surprise that Blackburn came to the Senate with a national reputation. Indeed, the year he entered the body, one of Alaska's great peaks was named Mount Blackburn.[353] The Kentuckian soon became a notable member of the upper chamber and sat at various times on the Committees on Appropriations, Finance, Judiciary, and Military Affairs.[354] Given his landmark work in the House on procedure, Blackburn later chaired the Senate Committee on Rules from 1893 to 1895, the first of three Kentuckians to hold the gavel.[355] Yet, for all his talents, Blackburn was not viewed as an accomplished legislator while in the Senate.[356] In many ways, he was a show horse, not a work horse. Blackburn rarely bothered to read newspapers, the primary means of keeping abreast of current events at the time.[357]

In an era when many senators lacked office space, members spent much of their time on the Senate floor.[358] Blackburn, however, could often be found in the Democratic cloakroom adjacent to the Senate chamber, where he would hold court and "swap yarns."[359] A fellow Democratic senator described the scene: "There are [those] who may be called cloakroom habitués, these are there almost every morning for ten, 15 or 30 minutes before 12, and leave the Senate chamber many times during the day to linger in the cloakroom. These constitute a class almost to themselves, and such men as [James] Berry, [John] Morgan, [George]

Vest, [Donelson] Caffery, [and] Blackburn belonged to it. They enjoy the humor of social interchange more than they do listening to speeches."[360] A reporter similarly noted, "In the cloakroom of the Senate he [Blackburn] is always the center of the group and he most agreeably dominates."[361] Yet, even though "it has been his custom to spend much more time in the Democratic cloakroom than upon the floor [Blackburn's] alertness as to what may be going on in the chamber is evidenced by the promptness with which he pushes through the cloakroom doors and appears in the chamber when a vote is being taken or anything else of importance is suddenly brought to the front."[362]

By mid-decade, the Democratic Party nationwide had become sharply divided over the currency issue: should the country's currency be supported solely by the gold standard, or should silver coins be widely issued as well? Blackburn was at the vanguard of the silver movement in his party, and he championed the cause at the 1896 Democratic National Convention in Chicago.[363] Indeed, Blackburn's stature was sufficiently high that he polled fourth in delegate votes for the presidential nomination that year.[364] Despite Blackburn's impressive showing at the convention, the currency issue caused serious problems for his reelection efforts in Kentucky.

Although Democrats controlled the state legislature, the party was hopelessly divided over the currency issue.[365] As a consequence, when Blackburn sought reelection, he could not muster sufficient support. The body was deadlocked and could not choose a senator. The impasse in the state legislature went on and on and finally grew so tense that the governor at one point ringed the capitol with state militia.[366] Ultimately, after more than a year, Blackburn was defeated on the 112th ballot by an alliance of Republicans and Democrats who supported the gold standard. Republican William Joseph Deboe was sent to the Senate in his place, the first GOP senator from the commonwealth.[367] Within two years, however, Blackburn was already taking steps to return to the upper chamber.[368]

Blackburn's Family Tragedies

Blackburn's marriage to Therese produced four children.[369] One of them, Corrine, inherited her father's zest for politics and displayed many of his traits, including a friendly demeanor and a great ability to remember people's names.[370] In 1896, she played a major role in Blackburn's reelection effort.[371] It was reported at the time that she "managed her father's correspondence almost entirely during the recent campaign, and it was largely owing to her adroitness in this work that the Senator received the [Democratic] nomination."[372]

Despite Corrine's efforts, her father was defeated, and the years following that loss were exceedingly difficult for Blackburn. In 1898, another of his daughters, Lucille, was involved in a horrible accident.[373] One night, while reaching for a garment in her dresser drawer—which also contained a pistol her father had given her—the article of clothing got enmeshed with the trigger and the gun discharged, almost killing her.[374]

Blackburn had his own frightening brush with mortality less than three months later. After witnessing the unveiling of several battleships, Blackburn collapsed and was unconscious for several hours.[375] Then, the very next year, Therese passed away from heart problems after more than forty years of marriage.[376]

In 1900, Blackburn's son-in-law Thomas Lane, who was married to Lucille, was diagnosed with Bright's disease.[377] He promptly shot himself in front of their four-year-old daughter at their home in Washington.[378] Lucille, who had almost been killed two years before in a gun accident, was in the very next room at the time.[379] According to news reports, upon hearing the tragic news over the telephone, Blackburn "reeled for a moment and, calling to a friend to take the receiver, sat down almost prostrated."[380] In 1902, Lucille developed a fever and died at the age of thirty-two.[381] Another tragedy struck that same year when Blackburn's son Jo Jr., who had been his father's private secretary when he was a senator, passed away at the age of thirty-five.[382]

Despite these repeated, heavy personal blows, the early twentieth century offered some solace for Blackburn. He married again, to Mary E. Blackburn.[383] The Kentucky legislature also elected Blackburn to the Senate, and in 1901, he returned to the chamber and quickly reestablished himself as a prominent member.[384]

Blackburn as Caucus Chairman and Beyond

One of the reasons party members meet in a caucus is to set policy for themselves. Often, senators of the same party unanimously agree on a course of action, but what happens when they do not? This problem dates back at least to the Federalist caucus hosted by Senator Bingham.[385] In December 1903, Blackburn put forward a plan to solve this age-old problem.[386] He proposed that if two-thirds of Senate Democrats agreed in a formal caucus to pursue a certain policy, all were bound to vote that way on the Senate floor.[387] The only exceptions were for matters of constitutional interpretation, a senator's earlier commitment to his home state, or a senator's having been directed by his state legislature to vote otherwise.[388] After three days of heated discussion within the Democratic ranks, the rule was approved.[389] A decade later, Blackburn's initiative helped the Senate's Democratic leadership as they worked to adopt President Woodrow Wilson's legislative agenda; the party, however, abandoned the policy near the end of World War I upon losing control of the chamber.[390] As the twentieth century progressed, the term "conference" would replace "caucus" to reflect the parties' inability to bind their membership.[391] For their part, Republicans never embraced a "Blackburn rule."[392]

In 1890, following the death of Senator Beck, the Senate Democratic caucus chose Arthur Pue Gorman to succeed him.[393] During his tenure, Gorman elevated the Democratic caucus chairmanship to new heights, to the extent that the position closely resembled that of a modern-day floor leader.[394] Along with Senator Joseph Bailey (D-TX), Blackburn was one of Gorman's main lieutenants.[395] In the early twentieth century, the Kentuckian was chosen as the caucus vice chairman—the first such officeholder.[396] When Gorman fell ill, Blackburn substituted for him and presided over gatherings of Democratic senators.[397]

Following Gorman's death in 1906, there was some question about who would take his place as chairman. By this time, Blackburn had been defeated a second time for reelection.[398] Not unlike his miscalculation of the political benefits of embracing "free silver" in the mid-1890s, Blackburn made another major misstep when he decided to run against the "Frankfort machine" of Democratic governor J. C. W. Beckham.[399] The result was that the governor's handpicked candidate, Thomas Paynter, triumphed over Blackburn in the state legislature.[400]

Blackburn's loss meant that he was now a "short timer in the Senate," but even so, the Kentuckian became caucus chairman.[401] Blackburn's elevation reflected to a great extent his popularity among his colleagues.[402] Senator Alexander Clay (D-GA) characterized Blackburn as "the most universally beloved man in the United States Senate."[403] Blackburn's skill in debate certainly did not hurt his cause either.[404]

Thus, in 1906, Blackburn was elected Democratic caucus chairman. His elevation marks another guidepost in the position's transition to that of formal Senate floor leader, since Blackburn was the first such officeholder of either party to be hailed as party "leader" in official party caucus records.[405] The resolution, which was offered and adopted, stated as follows: "The Democratic Senators in electing as their Chairman of the Conference Senator Blackburn of Kentucky, congratulate themselves and their several constituencies upon the fact that they have among their number one so well fitted by his marked capacity, his great acquirements, and his large experience in Congressional work, and especially by his power as an orator and as a debater, to render to his party associates the most signal and valuable services as their chosen *official leader* in the great forum of the Senate of the United States."[406] Coming on the heels of Gorman's groundbreaking tenure as caucus chairman, during which time he came to be seen as the party's de facto leader in the chamber, Blackburn was widely proclaimed in the press as the "minority leader" and "leader" of Senate Democrats.[407] The *Washington Post* reported that "Senator J. C. S. Blackburn will be elected to succeed the late Senator Gorman as chairman of the Senate Democratic caucus, which carries with it the floor leadership of the minority."[408] Indeed, fellow senator Lee Overman (D-NC) described Blackburn to the press as "the Democrats['] titular floor leader."[409] Nonetheless, despite the labeling of Blackburn as Senate Democratic "leader" in many circles, the caucus chairman position was still not fully on a par with a modern-day floor leader.[410] Most significantly, the modern function of the floor leader serving as presidential liaison or primary presidential opponent had not yet emerged.[411]

Following his brief tenure as caucus chairman, Blackburn left the Senate but remained active in public life. In 1907, President Theodore Roosevelt—a Republican—appointed him governor of the Panama Canal Zone.[412] In this role, Blackburn served under Secretary of War William Howard Taft and was in charge of the civil governmental functions of the Panama Canal Zone, as well as diplomatic relations with the Panamanian government.[413] Given the affable personalities of both Blackburn and Taft, it is not surprising that the two soon became good friends.[414] The Kentuckian served in this capacity until 1909.[415] In 1914, President Wilson chose him to serve on the commission to build the Lincoln Memorial.[416] Blackburn laid the cornerstone for the site honoring the man who had helped him as a young lawyer in Chicago decades before.[417]

Age, however, began to take its toll on Blackburn, and he suffered from a chronic heart condition.[418] In 1918, he passed away in Washington due to an apparent cardiac arrest.[419] One columnist wrote that "a Senate of Joe Blackburns would not be a body of wise lawgivers, and yet a Senate without its Joe Blackburns would be wanting in some of the qualities that have made the United States Senate so illustrious."[420]

The Continued Rise of the Caucus Chairman Position

The gradual transition of the caucus chairman position to that of formal floor leader occurred due to important external and internal factors affecting the Senate.[421] The predominant external factor was the rise of the activist presidency.[422] That is to say that the office of floor leader developed because of the Senate's need to work with, respond to, or oppose the president's agenda.[423] This new role for caucus chairmen would eventually lead to the formal recognition of new titles: majority leader and minority leader.

With few exceptions, presidents in the nineteenth century did not play outsized legislative roles.[424] For generations following Jefferson's presidency, the State of the Union was merely a written document sent to Capitol Hill, with no grand speech or spectacle.[425] There was no annual presidential budget to comprehensively capture the chief executive's spending and policy priorities.[426] The president largely managed the nation's foreign affairs and signed or vetoed whatever legislation Congress chose to send to him.[427]

Beginning with William McKinley and accelerating dramatically with Theodore Roosevelt and Woodrow Wilson, presidents began to initiate and pursue their own legislative agendas.[428] This structural change in the operation of the presidency had ripple effects on Congress as an institution.[429] This led to the question: who would the president regularly liaise with in the Senate if the chamber were controlled by the president's party?[430] The House has a Speaker, but the upper chamber has no equivalent formal officer; the vice president, after all, is not a senator and is not accountable to the body.[431] Moreover, presidents cannot realistically consult with all senators, although some have developed personal and political bonds with individual lawmakers. Such relationships have periodically led to certain senators becoming influential in their roles as informal liaisons with the White House (see chapter 3). Thus, during the late nineteenth and early twentieth centuries, the caucus chairman's responsibilities began to expand to meet the need for a presidential go-between (if the White House and Senate were controlled by the same party) or an opposition leader (if the two institutions were controlled by different parties).[432]

Another external factor likely affecting the evolution of Senate leadership was institutional change within the House of Representatives.[433] During the 1890s, the House began to centralize power in its leadership.[434] In 1899, the lower chamber formally created the position of House majority leader to help manage legislation.[435] It seems likely that this House innovation informed public perceptions (or misperceptions) of party leadership in the Senate, leading many commentators to refer to the caucus chairman as the "majority leader" or "minority leader" of the Senate.[436] These media characterizations likely enhanced expectations within both the Senate and the greater Washington political community about the caucus chairmen's roles and responsibilities.

Another school of thought focuses on the impact of internal dynamics on the creation of formal party leadership posts in the Senate.[437] This view, developed by Gamm and Smith, holds that the majority leader office evolved out of the caucus chairmanship due in part to increased interparty competition.[438] They argue that, when parties are closely matched for control of the chamber, they tend to innovate to try to achieve party goals and gain electoral advantage.[439] Formalizing party leadership may have reflected such an innovation.[440]

A second internal factor is that, beginning in the 1890s, the position of caucus chairman benefited considerably from the prestige of two senators who were powerful for reasons other than their caucus chairmanships.[441] They were Senators William Allison and Arthur Gorman.[442] Allison, who was elected Republican caucus chairman based on seniority, served in the position from 1897 to

1908 and was one of the most influential senators of his time.[443] In addition to chairing the caucus, Allison served as chairman of the powerful Appropriations Committee longer than any other senator, and he was part of a quartet of lawmakers known as the "Senate Four," which included the formidable Nelson Aldrich (R-RI), John Spooner (R-WI), and Oliver Platt (R-CT).[444] These senators and their allies exercised oligarchic control over the Senate in the late 1890s and early 1900s in large measure through a collective leadership panel called the Republican Committee on the Order of Business, also known as the Republican Steering Committee.[445] Thus, for the Iowan, the position of caucus chairman was only one of many overlapping and interlocking aspects of influence.[446]

For his part, Gorman chaired his party's caucus for two periods: 1890 to 1897 and 1903 to 1906.[447] As was the case with Allison, Gorman chaired the Senate Democratic Steering Committee.[448] Due to his personal dynamism and political acumen, Gorman played an outsized role as his party's caucus chairman.[449] Unlike Allison, who was part of a ruling clique headed largely by Aldrich, Gorman had no peer among Senate Democrats. He was undeniably their de facto leader.[450] Gorman was actually called the "Democratic leader" on the floor of the House as early as 1890.[451] Other allusions to him conveyed the same principle, but in somewhat more vivid language. In the Senate chamber in 1893, Henry Clay Hansbrough (R-ND) quoted with approval a reporter who had referred to Gorman as the "biggest toad in the Democratic puddle."[452]

In the latter half of the nineteenth century, caucus chairmen exercised some rudimentary leadership functions, but they were not initially responsible for setting the Senate's legislative agenda, scheduling items to be brought up for consideration, enforcing party discipline, managing legislation on the floor, driving policy outcomes, speaking for Senate party colleagues, or coordinating with (or opposing) the president or the House—all attributes of modern Senate floor leaders.[453] That changed over time, beginning with Beck's tenure and then accelerating rapidly under Gorman.[454]

Immediately after Gorman's first term as caucus chairman, one contemporary authority likened the position's power to that of Speaker of the House in one important respect: "the caucus chieftains['] power over the Senate committee system is of the same character as the power of the Speaker over the House committees."[455] He further noted that the caucus chairman "was the leadership which the Senate has evolved to supply the defects in its original endowment."[456]

By the time Gorman and, to a lesser extent, Allison had completed their service as caucus chairmen, there was an expectation that the position carried some leadership responsibility.[457] The view that the caucus chairman was a position of true leadership was much more pronounced on the Democratic side, however.[458] This gradual reconceptualization of the caucus chairman's role was reinforced by the press, which, as noted earlier, began to refer to caucus chairmen as either "minority leaders" or "floor leaders."[459]

Woodrow Wilson's words reflect this change in perception. In 1885—Beck's first year as caucus chairman—Wilson observed:

> Some Senators are, indeed, seen to be of larger mental stature and built of stauncher moral stuff than their fellow members, and it is not uncommon for individual members to become conspicuous figures in every great event in the Senate's deliberations. The public now and again picks out here and there a Senator who seems to act and speak with true instinct of states-manship and who unmistakably merits the confidence of colleagues and of people. But such a man, however eminent, is never more than *a* Senator. No one is *the* Senator. No one may speak for his party as well as for him-self; no one exercises the special trust of acknowledged leadership.[460]

By contrast, Wilson wrote in 1908, two years after Gorman's passing: "The leader of the Senate is the chairman of the majority caucus. Each party in the Senate finds its real, its permanent, its effective organization in its caucus, and follows the leadership, in all important parliamentary battles, of the chairman of that caucus. . . . The chairman of the majority caucus is much more nearly the counterpart of the Speaker of the House than is the president *pro tempore*."[461]

Thus, on the eve of the second decade of the twentieth century, the Senate was on the verge of a new era in terms of how it formally governed itself.

On the whole, Senate Democrats in the late nineteenth and early twentieth centuries assigned greater responsibility to caucus chairmen than did their Republican counterparts. Moreover, that authority increased markedly during this period, as Democrats came to treat caucus chairmen as party leaders. The careers of Democratic caucus chairmen John W. Stevenson, James B. Beck, and Joseph C. S. Blackburn reflect this evolving institution. Stevenson was the first Democratic caucus chairman, and even at this early stage, his tenure reflects the weightier duties that the Democrats granted their chairmen compared with their Republican peers. Beck infused the position with the expectation of policy lead-ership and paved the way for Gorman's dramatic expansion of the position in the 1890s. Blackburn was the first caucus chairman to be acknowledged as floor leader in official records, and he took steps to bind his fellow partisans on cer-tain policy matters. The tenures of these Kentuckians reflect notable touchstones in the development of the caucus chairman position in the decades between Reconstruction and the First World War, leading ultimately to the establish-ment of formal Senate floor leadership.

7

Senate Majority Leader

Alben Barkley

Alben Barkley is one of the most highly regarded Kentucky statesmen. At the same time, his eventful career offers insight into a frequently misunderstood institution: floor leadership in the US Senate.[1] Barkley was the leader of Senate Democrats from 1937 until 1949, and he was majority leader for all but the last two years.[2] In fact, only five lawmakers have exceeded Barkley's tenure as Senate floor leader: Mike Mansfield (D-MT), Joe Robinson (D-AR), Robert Byrd (D-WV), Harry Reid (D-NV), and the lead author.[3] Importantly, Barkley was majority leader when the position was enhanced by a consequential Senate precedent: prior recognition.

Barkley's Early Years

The story of Alben Barkley begins—literally—in a log cabin.[4] He would later drolly claim that this fact alone ensured that he would "one day enter politics."[5] The log cabin in question was on a tobacco farm in western Kentucky.[6] It was there that the future senator was born in 1877, the first child of John and Electra Barkley.[7] The boy inherited his affability from his father—described as "the laughin'est man you ever saw."[8] Young Alben inherited his assiduousness and determination in great measure from his mother.[9]

The Barkleys were not a family of means, and Alben grew up chopping wood, harvesting tobacco, and plowing fields.[10] This hardscrabble upbringing instilled in him the importance of diligence, and it stoked his ambition.[11] Exchanging anecdotes with his father's hired hands, Barkley developed the fun-loving, storytelling persona for which he would later become famous.[12]

As he matured, Barkley worked odd jobs to make ends meet. Although he did not graduate from high school, Barkley studied at tiny Marvin College, located in Clinton, Kentucky, while working as a janitor to pay for his school expenses.[13] Marvin College no longer exists, but one of its campus buildings reportedly had a sign boasting, "BARKLEY SWEPT HERE."[14] Subsequently, Barkley matriculated at Emory College, where he studied for a year, but he had insufficient funds to continue.[15] Soon thereafter Barkley took up the study of law. He learned at the knee of two prominent local attorneys and would later enroll in a summer program at the University of Virginia to round out his formal legal education.[16]

Barkley began his own law practice in 1901.[17] Around this time, he met Dorothy Brower, a native of Paducah, Kentucky, and the two wed in 1903.[18] During their marriage, Alben and Dorothy would raise three children—David, Marian, and Laura—in a lively household.[19] One of the homes where Barkley lived from 1937 to 1956, called "Angles," still stands as a historical landmark in Paducah.[20]

Barkley's First Steps toward a Political Career

The law led Barkley to discover his true passion—politics. Barkley's public career started with a long-shot race in 1905 for county attorney.[21] He bought "a one-eyed horse named Dick" that transported the candidate across the county.[22] The secret to Barkley's success lay less in his mode of transportation than in his personality. His ability to spin a yarn was rivaled only by his deep empathy for his fellow man.[23] Barkley truly enjoyed and related to people and their concerns.[24] As Lyndon Johnson recalled, he had "a genuine and unaffected interest in the problems of others."[25] The Texan observed that "people rejoiced with [Barkley] when he was happy, mourned with him when he was sad. And at all times they reposed in him the trust and confidence that are accorded only to very close and very dear friends."[26]

In addition to his personal warmth, Barkley was a compelling public speaker.[27] As one contemporary analyst concluded: "Barkley's chief forte as a political leader [was] his oratorical ability."[28] Barkley joked about his "natural inclination to stop whatever [he] was doing and start making a speech any time [he] saw as many as six persons assembled together."[29] About speechmaking, Barkley later reflected: "I like to do it. I like people and I enjoy the thrill of crowds."[30]

Another key trait was Barkley's diligence.[31] He would simply not be outworked on the hustings, earning him the sobriquet "Iron Man."[32] This combination of attributes helped the twenty-eight-year-old defeat the incumbent county attorney in the Democratic primary and easily win the general election.[33] Barkley was on his way.

Once in office, Barkley established himself as a reformer.[34] This reputation soon helped him win election as county judge.[35] He continued his rapid ascent and was elected to the US House of Representatives in 1912.[36] In the House, Barkley was an avid progressive and devotee of Democratic president Woodrow Wilson; he also befriended a young Texas lawmaker by the name of Sam Rayburn (D).[37]

Reelected six times to the House, Barkley rose quickly in national and state political circles. He emerged as one of the country's leading advocates for Prohibition.[38] Yet he grew impatient in the House and wanted more. As a result, in 1923, Barkley ran for governor of Kentucky.

On the hustings, Barkley drove himself relentlessly, campaigning up to sixteen hours a day and often sleeping less than four hours a night.[39] He lost in the Democratic primary, but it would be the only statewide campaign he ever lost.[40] Despite the defeat, he had acquitted himself well, and as is sometimes the case in politics, one can gain by losing.[41] This was true of Barkley.[42] The Paducah native had succeeded in raising his profile among state voters, and Kentuckians liked what they saw.[43] That good impression came in handy when Barkley ran for the Senate in 1926 and he was easily elected by Kentuckians.[44] (Since adoption of the Seventeenth Amendment in 1913, senators had been directly elected.) Notably, his campaign manager for that race was Fred Vinson, who would later become secretary of the treasury and then chief justice of the United States.[45]

Barkley the Storyteller

It was in the Senate where Barkley came into his own. It was also there that he became widely acclaimed as a first-rate storyteller. Many recall Senator Barkley saying, "A good story is like fine Kentucky bourbon, it improves with age and, if you don't use it too much, it will never hurt anyone."[46] Having a gift for storytelling was vitally important for politicians in the days before television and the Internet.[47] Barkley's storytelling added humor and texture to his engaging style of public speaking.[48]

One contemporary gave a vivid sense of Barkley as a raconteur: "His restrained postures, the finesse with which he takes tricks with his moderate Southern accent, his facility in coining a word if the immediately essential one is not in the dictionary, the eloquence of his eyebrows, his honest grin, [and] his basic bearing as a gentleman and scholar" all contributed to his captivating storytelling style.[49] His tendency to create words to suit his needs was evident in an address to the National Press Club.[50] In his remarks, Barkley described lawmakers in the upper chamber as "prima donnas" but noted that those in the press corps were "even more primadonn*ical*."[51]

Barkley's Election as Senate Majority Leader

In 1932, the landslide victory of Franklin D. Roosevelt ushered in a new Democratic majority in the Senate, and Barkley became the first Kentuckian reelected to the Senate in the twentieth century.[52] From the beginning, Barkley was a strong supporter of Roosevelt and a loyal lieutenant of Senate majority leader Joe Robinson (D-AR).[53] He helped the Arkansan pass much of the progressive legislation of this era.[54] It was written in the 1930s that Barkley's votes were "as regular as a metronome, supporting the party leader, Mr. Roosevelt, early, late and between times."[55] For his efforts, Robinson named Barkley assistant majority leader in 1935.[56] In addition, the Kentuckian raised his national profile through numerous radio addresses defending FDR's New Deal agenda.[57]

Barkley even supported the president's controversial Court-packing plan—a scheme to expand the membership of the Supreme Court so that Roosevelt could tilt its ideological balance in a direction that was more to his liking.[58] This was a centerpiece of Roosevelt's agenda after his landslide reelection in 1936, and its boldness reflected the huge Democratic majorities returned in both houses of Congress.

When the Seventy-Fifth Congress began in 1937, the Democrats held a whopping seventy-six of the ninety-six seats in the Senate.[59] But the Democratic Party was badly divided. As one columnist wrote at the time, "overwhelming majorities, like oversize amoebas tend to split," and that is just what occurred.[60] About half the Democratic caucus supported Roosevelt's New Deal policies, while the other half frequently opposed or undermined them.[61] The divisions within the caucus became fully exposed during consideration of FDR's Court-packing plan.[62]

In mid-July 1937, likely due to the strain of managing the divisive Court-packing legislation, Robinson died of a heart attack, providing the opportunity for Barkley to take over as majority leader.[63] But the manner of Barkley's ultimate election to the top spot would prove controversial and hamper his effectiveness as leader for years to come.[64]

In the race for majority leader, one faction of the Democratic caucus lined up behind Barkley, and the other supported the more conservative Pat Harrison (D-MS).[65] For several years, Harrison had been widely considered Robinson's heir apparent.[66] But Roosevelt preferred Barkley because the Kentuckian was more sympathetic to FDR's New Deal policies, particularly on tax matters.[67] In fact, the day after Robinson's death, Roosevelt sent Barkley a letter that began "Dear Alben" and made prominent mention of his status as the "acting majority leader."[68] The letter, which soon became public, left the impression that FDR was supporting Barkley's candidacy.[69] If there was any doubt as to his intentions, the president made them clear when he dispatched surrogates to exert pressure on wavering senators to vote for the Kentuckian.[70]

One week after Robinson's death, in a dramatic tableau, all seventy-five Senate Democrats assembled in the Senate Caucus Room to vote for the next majority leader.[71] They voted by dropping their ballots into an old Panama hat belonging to Senator Carter Glass (D-VA).[72] This prompted a quip that Senate Democrats were trying to ensure the confidentiality of the ballots by using a "glass" hat.[73]

The race was tight, and as the balloting progressed, Barkley became so tense that he bit off the end of his pipe.[74] The Kentuckian described the scene surrounding the opening of the last ballot: "When the teller reached in and pulled out the last folded slip [of paper], it looked as big as a bedquilt."[75] Barkley won the election by a single vote: 38 to 37.[76] But he lost the loyalty contest in the eyes of a good number of his Senate Democratic colleagues.[77] Many of them took umbrage at the president's interference in Barkley's election, and as a result, the Kentuckian began his tenure as majority leader at a serious disadvantage.[78] Although his colleagues granted him the title, they did not accord him the accompanying respect, viewing him to a great extent as FDR's man rather than the Senate's leader.[79]

Typically, if the majority leader's party controls the White House, the leader tries to secure adoption of the president's program and protect the president's priorities. This is much harder to do in a president's second term than in his first, when the incoming president usually has a full head of steam and strong popular support from his electoral mandate. In other words, a newly elected president ordinarily has a fair amount of clout. In mid-1937, Roosevelt's political clout was at an all-time low.[80] He was in his second term, and he was politically damaged from the bruising and unsuccessful Court-packing fight.[81] These difficulties were magnified by the ideological divisions among Democrats in the Senate. A majority leader's success is influenced to no small degree by context, and the circumstances surrounding Barkley's elevation to the position were highly challenging.[82]

Development of the Position of Senate Majority Leader

Senator John Worth Kern (D-IN), who served as Democratic caucus chairman at the beginning of the Wilson administration, is often credited as being the first Senate majority leader.[83] In 1912, Wilson was elected president, and the Democrats captured the Senate.[84] In addition, the Democrats had taken control of the

House after the 1910 midterms, giving them control of both the executive and legislative branches for the first time in nearly two decades.[85] The party did not want to squander this opportunity.[86]

Kern's caucus chairmanship is notable in part because of the manner in which he was elected to the post. In 1913, Kern, who had served only two years in the Senate, was chosen to head the Senate Democrats, largely because he shared Wilson's progressive views and was thought capable of shepherding the president's legislative agenda through the upper chamber.[87] Previously, the ability to work closely with an administration of the same party had not been seen as part of the caucus chairman's job description.[88] By becoming the legislative champion of a president of the same party, Kern's tenure broke new ground.[89] In addition, Kern inherited the enhanced prestige and responsibilities enjoyed by earlier Democratic caucus chairmen, who by this time were widely seen as de facto Senate floor leaders.[90] Despite carrying the official title of "caucus chairman," Kern was mentioned as "majority leader" in the press much more frequently than his predecessors had been.[91]

Similarly, Kern's caucus chairmanship marks the first time the term "majority leader" was used with any frequency to describe an individual senator on the Senate floor.[92] Indeed, during Kern's first year as caucus chairman, the "majority leader" position was mentioned in proposed legislation for the first time.[93] Further demonstrating the lasting impact of Kern's caucus chairmanship, use of the term "majority leader" on the Senate floor continued unabated after his tenure ended in 1917.[94] Besides repeated references on the floor to Kern as "majority leader," he was also called "Democratic leader."[95] The expression "floor leader" began to be used more regularly immediately following Kern's incumbency.[96] These floor references to Kern's position have long been overlooked in the literature, yet they mark a clear change from the way previous caucus chairmen were formally viewed by their peers. It is one thing to proclaim someone a party leader in a confidential caucus, but quite another to do so publicly in the solemn formality of the Senate floor. These indicia dovetail with other departures from past practice that took place during Kern's tenure; for instance, he played a bigger scheduling role—making more schedule-related procedural motions and floor statements—than earlier caucus chairmen.[97] This suggests that Senate leadership had made the transition from being largely informal and party based to being more formal and institutional.[98] For these reasons, Kern's time in office was groundbreaking.[99]

As noted earlier, some scholars view the Senate majority and minority leader positions as originating from developments that took place outside the Senate, while others argue that factors inside the chamber were paramount.[100] Kern's election reflects the influence of both considerations.[101] Among the relevant external developments, clearly President Wilson had an activist agenda and needed a champion in the Senate to guide his progressive policies to enactment.[102] The president needed a "dance partner," and he found one in Kern.[103] The Hoosier's role as a more formal, active, and regularized liaison with the president gave him added cachet and set him apart from his predecessors as caucus chairman.[104]

At the same time, developments within the Senate that fostered the rise of the majority leader position included the very small and vulnerable Democratic majority, which gave the party every reason to try to innovate to achieve positive outcomes.[105] A commentator in 1918 wrote: "It is not an exaggeration to say that when Woodrow Wilson took the oath of office the fate of the Democratic party for at least a generation rested with the small majority in the Senate."[106] This situation suggests that external and internal factors were not competing but actually complementary in explaining the creation of the office of Senate majority leader.[107]

By the end of World War I, Republicans—who had long operated under a collegial leadership arrangement—to a significant degree adopted the Democratic model and began to recognize a single floor leader.[108] This reflects, yet again, that the development of Senate party leadership was not uniform. Parties often innovate and adapt to gain advantage, and if an experiment is deemed successful, the other party tends to follow suit.[109]

In 1918, Henry Cabot Lodge of Massachusetts became the Republican caucus chairman, a post he held until his death in 1924.[110] Lodge's status as floor leader was frequently recognized in Senate debate. He was the first Republican to be referred to as "majority leader" with any regularity in debate, and he was called "Republican leader" much more than any other senator had been.[111] The Boston Brahmin became the Republican voice of opposition to Wilson's campaign for Senate approval of the Treaty of Versailles.[112] His prominence in the public debate over the proposed international agreement demonstrated a floor leader's potential role in opposing—instead of supporting—the president's agenda; in a sense, Lodge's tenure was a counterpoint to Kern's.[113]

At the time of Barkley's arrival in the Senate in 1927, the positions of Senate majority leader and minority leader had only recently been established. They did not, however, resemble the offices the public knows today. The majority leader in the mid-1920s exercised less control over the Senate schedule. Republicans, who had regained control of the Senate in 1919, had not completely abandoned their earlier collegial approach to floor leadership.[114] Senate debate from the 1920s and early 1930s indicates that, despite the emergence of a clear floor leader in Lodge, the venerable, collective leadership body—the Republican Committee on the Order of Business, or the Republican Steering Committee—continued to play an important role in scheduling floor activity; at times, perhaps, it was even more influential in this regard than the majority leader himself.[115]

In the contemporary Senate, the two floor leaders work from the center aisle seats on the Senate floor. Initially, these favorable seating assignments were not one of the perquisites of being party leader, however. Senate minority leader Oscar Underwood (D-AL) sat on the center aisle from 1921 to 1923.[116] He then kept the seat even after he stepped down from his leadership position.[117] The Senate Democratic leader (the Senate minority leader at the time) did not *permanently* occupy the center aisle desk until Joe Robinson secured it in 1927.[118] The Senate Republican leader did not stake a similar claim until Charles McNary (R-OR) took the other center aisle seat in 1937.[119] Before then, the front desks of the Senate had generally been assigned based on seniority.[120] Securing these choice seats carried the practical advantage of making it easier for the two leaders to seek recognition from the presiding officer and to be heard in the cacophonous chamber.[121] It added prestige to the positions as well.[122]

Today, both the majority leader and the minority leader occupy office space in the US Capitol Building adjacent to the Senate floor.[123] Again, this was not the case at the time of Barkley's arrival in the Senate. Underwood secured such a spot in 1921, but Republican floor leaders (who were also majority leaders at the time) would not do so until 1929.[124] This practical step of giving floor leaders easier access to the Senate floor no doubt enhanced their efficiency in executing their duties. Moreover, it added another measure of prestige to the nascent positions of majority leader and minority leader.

As the 1920s and 1930s progressed, floor leaders increasingly came to be seen as national party spokesmen, adding further luster to their offices.[125] In fact, in 1928 both the majority leader and the minority leader were selected as vice-presidential candidates for their respective parties. Majority leader Charles Curtis (R-KS) was elected vice president alongside President Herbert Hoover. Minority leader Robinson ran alongside the Democratic standard-bearer, New York governor Al Smith.[126]

During the New Deal, with activist President Roosevelt in the White House, certain expectations of the Senate floor leader position began to take firmer hold.[127] Increasingly, the leader of the president's party in the Senate came to be seen as the executive's champion in the chamber.[128] In this regard, Robinson's tenure heightened the visibility and prestige of the position.[129] The Arkansan built on the foundation Kern had helped establish in other ways: speaking more frequently on the Senate floor, garnering more media attention than most of his Senate colleagues, and assuming greater personal control over setting the Senate's agenda.[130] The majority leader began to regularly use unanimous consent agreements to accelerate the pace of Senate business.[131] (These procedural instruments are used to define the parameters for debate and amendment of certain measures, but they require that no senator object to them.)[132] This perception of the Senate majority leader as the president's legislative lieutenant would be tested mightily in the years to come, especially during Barkley's tenure.

The Origins and Development of Prior Recognition

Today, the main formal power enjoyed by the Senate majority leader is the right of "prior recognition."[133] Under Senate Rule XIX, the presiding officer must recognize the first senator who is on his or her feet seeking the floor.[134] But what happens when multiple senators want to be recognized at the same time? Prior recognition means that, if no senator holds the floor and if the majority leader is on his feet wanting to address the chamber, he will be recognized to speak before any other senator.[135] It also means that the minority leader will be recognized after the majority leader, followed by the senators who are actively managing the Senate business under consideration at the time—that is, the bill managers—first the majority bill manager and then his or her minority counterpart.[136]

As a practical matter, the recognition prerogative means that floor leaders are well positioned to try to offer whatever bills, motions, amendments, resolutions, nominations, or treaties they want to put forward.[137] In this respect, the right of prior recognition is vital to the majority leader's ability to set the Senate's schedule.[138] Former Senate majority leader Robert Byrd (D-WV) once wrote that prior recognition "is, by far, the most potent weapon in the majority leader's arsenal. . . . Without it, he would be like the emperor without clothes."[139] While this prerogative permits the majority leader to propose the next item for the Senate to consider, it is by no means a certainty that the Senate will in fact proceed to that measure.[140] With the exception of nominations and a small subclass of bills and resolutions, if the majority leader cannot muster 60 votes in favor of considering his preferred agenda item, the leader will be thwarted.[141] He will then have to negotiate with the minority or move on to other business.

Managing the floor schedule may seem somewhat mundane, but it is of cardinal importance.[142] No measure can be adopted by the Senate without receiving some amount of floor consideration, and the authority to allot floor time is largely in the hands of the majority leader. This means that the majority leader, to some degree, has a hand in everything the Senate as a whole considers. It also means that, to a great extent, he has the power to try to set the chamber's policy agenda.[143] As one authority on the Senate has written, "the act of scheduling is itself, under many circumstances, a kind of policy decision."[144] Given the importance of prior recognition, it is surprising that so little has been written about its origins and development.[145]

After the Democrats took control of the chamber in 1913, it became more common for the majority leader to attempt to lay out the Senate's schedule on the floor.[146] During this same period, a new rule was passed making it easier for the body to operate by unanimous consent.[147] These two developments proved to be mutually reinforcing and enhanced the standing of the nascent majority leader position.[148]

Data from floor proceedings demonstrate that, as a matter of practice, by the early 1920s, the majority leader was being granted what amounted to *informal* prior recognition.[149] Indeed, in 1922, William Tyler Page, the clerk of the House of Representatives, wrote of the upper chamber: "the [Senate] Majority and Minority floor leaders . . . are usually accorded prior recognition by the Chair."[150] The next year, Charles Curtis (R-KS), chairman of the Senate Rules Committee, majority whip, and soon-to-be majority leader, publicly agreed with this formulation.[151]

In March 1933, John Nance Garner, a former Speaker of the House, was sworn in as FDR's vice president. It took little time for him to leave his imprint on the upper chamber. In May, as Senate presiding officer, Garner recognized an early variant of prior recognition. He ruled "that when two Senators rise on the floor of the Senate and ask for recognition, one being in charge of the legislation pending before the Senate, it is [the vice president's] duty to recognize the Senator in charge of that legislation [the bill manager]."[152] Garner's ruling prompted some grousing at the time, and the vice president, as a former Speaker, was chided for allegedly importing House practices into the Senate.[153] The interpretation stood, however, and was reaffirmed two years later by the president pro tempore, Key Pittman (D-NV), who was in the chair at the time.[154] The 1933 and 1935 rulings would serve as building blocks for the future formal acknowledgment of the majority leader's right to be recognized before all others.[155]

Majority Leader Barkley and Prior Recognition

On August 11, 1937, Barkley had been majority leader for only a few weeks when a significant Senate dustup occurred.[156] This debacle prompted Garner's historic parliamentary pronouncement about prior recognition for the majority leader. The circumstances surrounding the establishment of this notable precedent require some elaboration.

In an attempt to manage the floor, Barkley would frequently provide Vice President Garner—as the presiding officer—with a document laying out the desired order of business and which senators were to be recognized in what sequence.[157] This "recognition list" was a purely informal means of coordinating floor activity; it was not sanctioned by Senate rules. On August 11, Senator William H. King (D-UT) was on Barkley's recognition list and was slated to be the next senator recognized to speak.[158] The plan was for Senator King to call up legislation involving aviation policy; however, for whatever reason, he was delayed in standing up and seeking the floor.[159] Into the void stepped Senator Robert Wagner (D-NY), who immediately moved that the Senate consider antilynching legislation, a highly contentious measure at the time.[160] This left Barkley scrambling to regain control of the Senate floor, arguing that King should have been recognized instead of Wagner.[161] Garner replied that Rule XIX required the chair to recognize the first senator on his feet: King had not been on his feet, and Wagner had been.[162] Bedlam ensued.[163]

Later that day, Barkley tried to adjourn the Senate, which would have removed Wagner's controversial motion from the floor.[164] But he was voted down by a combination of liberals from his own party and Republicans.[165] The minority leader, Senator McNary, then successfully moved that the Senate recess for the day, which preserved the right of Wagner to have his motion debated.[166] Barkley was utterly humiliated.[167] Senator Josh Lee (D-OK) queried the majority leader as to his vote recommendation on McNary's motion.[168] Barkley bellowed: "I don't know! Ask McNary! He's the only real leader round here."[169] Even though Democrats controlled the vast majority of Senate seats, the minority leader won this high-profile vote.

Typically, Barkley would meet with Garner before the Senate opened each day to coordinate how to manage the floor.[170] The recognition list had been part of that effort. But after the failure of the recognition list approach and the ensuing brouhaha over the Wagner motion, Barkley and Garner almost certainly discussed how to avoid future mishaps at their next morning meeting. What emerged was an unconventional approach to floor management that would take advantage of the decade-and-a-half-old custom of the majority leader being accorded informal prior recognition.

For the next day and a half, Barkley—with Garner's approval—sought recognition and then, upon gaining the floor, yielded to another senator who would bring up leadership-approved bills for consideration.[171] By "farming out . . . the Senate floor" in this fashion, Barkley prevented opponents from speaking and offering their own legislation.[172] This drew the ire of senators, who rightly claimed that this "farming out" approach was inconsistent with Senate rules and practice and, if continued, could permit the majority leader and his allies to dominate floor proceedings.[173] Senator Robert La Follette Jr. (R-WI), who was an expert on parliamentary procedure, took to the floor to criticize this method of managing legislation.[174] He also linked this approach to the fallout from the Wagner motion.[175] This prompted debate over appropriate recognition practices.[176]

Senator La Follette specifically questioned the propriety of the majority leader being recognized and then farming out his recognition to favored senators.[177] Vice President Garner explained why he chose to recognize the majority leader first if no one else held the floor:

> We are going to have a little order in the Senate. The chair recognized the Senator from Kentucky because he is the leader of the Democrats in the Senate. . . . The Chair thinks it is his duty to recognize the Senator from Kentucky when he is on his feet, or to recognize the Senator from Vermont . . . who is acting as leader of the minority at the present time, if he should be on his feet. . . . The Chair recognized the Senator from Kentucky because he is the leader on the Democratic side of the Chamber. He would recognize the . . . acting Republican leader . . . in the same way.[178]

Garner further reasoned that, once Barkley had been recognized, the Kentuckian could yield the floor to whomever he wished.[179] It is noteworthy that in Garner's pronouncement regarding prior recognition, he gave no indication that he was breaking new ground.[180] While he criticized the farming-out process, Senator La Follette notably did not contest the majority leader's customary right to prior recognition.[181] Garner and La Follette seemed to agree on this point.

The vice president's explanation of his recognition policy can be traced to several factors, all related to the Wagner incident. First, in the immediate context, Garner needed to clarify Barkley's authority to bolster his shaky case for permitting the farming-out practice, which was coming in for criticism. If the majority leader did not enjoy prior recognition, Barkley could not command the floor in the first place, let alone yield it to favored senators.[182] By formally acknowledging what had only recently become customary—that the majority leader is first among equals in commanding the floor—Garner partially addressed Senator La Follette's concerns.

However, the vice president gave an inconsistent and unpersuasive defense of the key aspect of La Follette's inquiry: whether the majority leader could, in effect, *transfer* his recognition to senators of his choosing.[183] At one point, Garner conceded that the majority leader could not in fact farm out his recognition, but at the same time, he asserted that if Barkley had indicated which senator he wanted to recognize, Garner would have simply recognized that senator.[184] Therefore, Garner asserted, there was no practical difference between Barkley yielding the floor to a favored senator and Garner recognizing that senator at the majority leader's request.[185] La Follette did not agree.[186]

Second, clarifying prior recognition was consistent with Garner's broader approach to being the Senate's presiding officer. The former House Speaker generally wanted to expedite Senate business.[187] In this case, it was more than merely the vice president's abstract preference for faster proceedings; the end of the Senate session was fast approaching, and work on several measures had to be completed.[188] Instituting a more orderly recognition process by formally acknowledging the majority leader's prerogative served this end.[189]

Third, Garner was a vigorous partisan who likely wanted to unify his divided party.[190] The vice president could not have relished the spectacle from two days before: his party's conservative and liberal wings at each other's throats on the Senate floor. Formalizing recognition policy and using the farming-out process reduced the likelihood of open displays of party divisiveness.[191]

A fourth and closely related point is that, at some level, Garner wanted to shore up Barkley's standing as majority leader. The Kentuckian was coming off a bruising leadership battle with Harrison; the Democratic conference was badly split after the Court-packing effort, and Barkley was widely seen, to his detriment, as the "president's man." On top of that, Barkley had just experienced the embarrassment of the Wagner episode. Seizing the opportunity to clarify and support Barkley's recognition authority helped the Kentuckian find his footing as floor leader.[192]

On two occasions the following year, Garner would refine and reiterate his rationale for granting prior recognition to floor leaders. Both took place in the context of Wagner's antilynching bill.[193] In January 1938, Garner essentially synthesized the 1933 and 1935 rulings—which confirmed prior recognition for bill managers—with the 1937 ruling, which recognized the same for floor leaders. The vice president opined: "the Chair feels that he ought to recognize in the order of precedence, first the Senator from Kentucky [Mr. Barkley] when he desires recognition, next the Senator from Oregon [Mr. McNary], and then the Senator in charge of the bill."[194]

In Garner's second ruling of 1938, he stated to Senator Wagner: "when the Senator from Kentucky is on his feet it is the custom of the Chair to recognize him first, since he is the leader of the Senate on the Democratic side. The Senator from Oregon [Mr. McNary], the leader on the Republican side, likewise has the preference when a number of the Senators are standing."[195] Wagner replied: "I make no complaint about that; and I recognize and understand what the Chair has said. I take it that even if I should make a request, and a request for recognition should also be made by the distinguished leader of the majority, my request would be considered after that of the distinguished Senator from Kentucky. I am a realist about these matters."[196] Thus, Wagner—like La Follette before him—agreed with the principle of prior recognition for floor leaders, even though it worked against his own immediate interests.

Like so many historical precedents in American governance, the importance of prior recognition became evident only with the passage of time.[197] In fact, even Barkley himself—the immediate beneficiary of the ruling—seemed oblivious to the precedent on at least one occasion many years later. In 1952, Vice President Barkley, as presiding officer, seemed unwilling to automatically accord the majority leader prior recognition.[198] He did mention the principle—though not the specific precedent—in his oral history the next year, however. Barkley noted, "The rules don't require it, but it is a moral obligation and the custom for the chair to recognize a majority leader, because he is the leader of the Senate and he maps the program."[199]

Despite its modest origins, it is largely on this precedent that a great deal of the modern floor leader's formal power rests.[200] For decades, committee chairmen went to the Senate floor to call up their own bills for consideration—a custom that continued until the 1930s.[201] Prior recognition eventually contributed to the end of that practice, and subsequent majority leaders, such as Lyndon Johnson, would assert the prerogative vigorously.[202]

Interestingly, the 1937 ruling turned out to be more important for minority leaders than majority leaders. From 1921 to 1937, in situations in which a majority leader and another senator (or senators) sought the floor, majority leaders were recognized just under 83 percent of the time.[203] Thus, for about a decade and a half, the informal practice was to favor the majority leader when he sought recognition. During this same period, in the same types of situations, minority leaders succeeded in gaining the floor less than 48 percent of the time.[204] From 1937 to 1961, majority leaders secured the floor more than 83 percent of the time when they competed for recognition with other lawmakers, virtually the same rate as before the Garner ruling.[205] However, during this same period, minority leaders secured recognition more than 81 percent of the time, a significant increase over the earlier rate.[206] The data therefore suggest that majority leaders enjoyed a customary right of prior recognition beginning in the early 1920s, but their minority counterparts did not truly gain this prerogative until the 1937 ruling.

The episode involving Barkley and prior recognition is one of the lesser known and lesser appreciated events of his tenure as leader; indeed, it was largely overlooked at the time. Yet it stands as a watershed in the history and development of Senate floor leadership.[207]

* * *

Despite the establishment of this crucial precedent, Barkley's early days as majority leader, particularly in 1937, were not easy ones.[208] He kept finding himself on the losing end of votes.[209] At the end of the day, a Senate party leader is just that: the leader of his party. Be he majority leader or minority leader, his power depends to a great extent on how unified his members are. If his members are divided, the leader has much less leverage to accomplish his goals. It is a simple matter of arithmetic: the majority leader needs at least a majority of the Senate to adopt any measure, and frequently he needs a supermajority under Senate rules.[210]

* * *

Early in his tenure as majority leader, Barkley's members were divided between those who wholeheartedly embraced the New Deal and those who did not.[211] Moreover, Senator Harrison, Barkley's opponent in the 1937 leadership race, was seen by many as the de facto majority leader.[212] Following the Court-packing controversy, a coalition between conservative Democrats disillusioned with Roosevelt and conservative Republicans began to coalesce in earnest; this grouping would hold the balance of power in the Senate on a number of issues for a generation.[213] Harrison was at the vanguard of this conservative coalition, which included other Senate powerhouses such as Jimmy Byrnes (D-SC).[214]

Equally troubling for Barkley was that Washington journalists, witnessing that the majority leader was unable to corral his colleagues, dubbed him "Bumbling" Barkley.[215] This sobriquet further undermined his prestige.[216] Some of this was Barkley's own doing, as he repeatedly advocated for FDR-supported initiatives even when their adoption was highly unlikely.[217] Perhaps the low point for Barkley's reputation was when *Life* magazine surveyed Washington journalists, asking them which members of Congress were the most skilled.[218] Senate minority leader McNary, Senators Harrison and Byrnes, the Speaker of the House, the House majority leader, and the House minority leader were all included, but not Barkley.[219] A *Washington Evening Star* political cartoon from around this time showed Harrison typing his own "Dear Alben" letter, asking "How does it feel to be Leader[?]"[220]

Gradually, however, Barkley gained respect and stature. In contrast to Robinson's "heavy-handed" leadership style, Barkley often sat down with fellow senators, disarming them with humor, and then made his case.[221] As reporter William S. White observed, Barkley "was convivial, garrulous, cheerfully ready to take his lumps from day to day."[222]

* * *

Many in Barkley's time and today misunderstand the nature of the majority leader position and the nature of the Senate. They grow frustrated and ask with exasperation: "Why can't the leader just jam this measure through?" There are several reasons. First, Senate rules simply do not permit it. Senate rules generally ensure that the minority party and individual lawmakers are not steamrolled in the legislative process. While the rights of the minority can often test the patience of the majority, as one authority well expressed, "legislation without a settled procedure is an example of a government of men without laws, which the constitution-framers of the 1780's viewed with such disfavor."[223] Because of the power given to the minority party and individual members, there is a gulf between what the public believes the majority leader can do and what he actually has the authority to do.[224] Like many before and after him, Barkley suffered from this gap.

Second, legislative leadership, particularly in the Senate, is far different from executive branch leadership. Decision-making in the executive branch is, by its very nature, top-down. When the president makes a decision, that decision is essentially final. If a cabinet secretary disagrees with the president, the president can simply remove him or her from office. In the legislative branch, decision-making is collegial. When the Senate majority leader makes a decision, that decision may or may not stick, as senators decide for themselves what to do. Unlike the president, the majority leader has little authority with which to discipline a recalcitrant member, and such action could easily backfire. That is why so many of my predecessors have rightly stressed that one of the keys to success as majority leader is being persuasive.[225]

And much of the ability to persuade stems from the ability to listen. A leader needs to know what the priorities and concerns of his members are. As leader, Lyndon Johnson was reputed to speak with each member of his caucus each day the Senate was in session.[226] I also keep in close touch with my members. That is vitally important. Only by keeping in regular contact with one's members can a Senate party leader truly lead.

* * *

Barkley's Reelection to the Senate

The year after Barkley's close election to Senate leadership, he faced another tough contest, this time in Kentucky. It involved a true clash of the titans in the Democratic primary, where Barkley was challenged by the popular incumbent governor, A. B. "Happy" Chandler.

To reward the majority leader for his loyal support, President Roosevelt visited Kentucky to back Barkley's reelection bid.[227] One of the planned events involved a presidential motorcade to a racetrack in northern Kentucky, culminating in an FDR address to a huge crowd.[228] Chandler, being the state's chief executive, was also asked to attend, and the plan was for the president, the majority leader, and the governor to ride together in a convertible.[229] Following the usual practice, FDR climbed into the automobile first.[230] According to Barkley, he was supposed to enter second and sit in the middle with Roosevelt and Chandler on either side of him.[231] Instead, as Barkley recalled, Chandler "literally leaped over" Roosevelt to ensure that he would be sitting next to the popular president, causing some anxiety for the Secret Service detail.[232] The Paducah native viewed the governor's actions as "pure unadulterated nerve."[233]

Once at the racetrack, Roosevelt joined Barkley and Chandler on stage in front of 50,000 bystanders.[234] FDR embraced Barkley publicly: "I have no doubt that Governor Chandler would make a good senator from Kentucky—but I think he would be the first to acknowledge that as a very junior member of the Senate it would take him many, many years to match the national knowledge, the experience and the acknowledged leadership in the affairs of our nation of that son of Kentucky of whom the whole nation is proud—Alben Barkley."[235] This was not altruism on Roosevelt's part. After endorsing Barkley in the majority leader's race, FDR could ill afford to see him defeated for reelection; such an outcome would have greatly embarrassed the president.[236]

That year's Senate race took many odd twists and turns, including Chandler's accusation that Barkley partisans poisoned him with tainted drinking water.[237] Barkley ultimately prevailed over the charismatic governor in the primary, winning by more than 70,000 votes; from there, he easily won the general election.[238] The "Iron Man" avoided becoming only the third majority leader up to that time to lose reelection: Democrat John Worth Kern in 1916 and Republican James Watson in 1932, both from Indiana.[239]

Barkley as Wartime Majority Leader

Not long after Barkley's reelection in 1938, war clouds darkened over Europe and the Pacific. It was in this setting that Barkley came into his own as Senate majority leader.[240] Historians rightly note the vital role the Kentuckian played in enacting the first peacetime military draft, passing the Lend-Lease Act, repealing the Arms Embargo Act, and removing the Neutrality Act from the books.[241] All were critical steps in putting the United States on a war footing. These efforts were possible because, in the realm of foreign policy (unlike in domestic affairs), conservative Democrats and Republicans largely supported Roosevelt's policies, especially as actions by the Axis powers began to directly threaten the United States.[242]

The year 1941 in many ways marked a watershed in Barkley's tenure as majority leader.[243] Harrison died that year, and Byrnes left the Senate for the Supreme Court; thus, Barkley's two main rivals for control of the Democratic caucus were gone.[244] Moreover, with the president's attention focused more on the war and less on politically divisive New Deal programs, the adoption of administration-supported measures became less challenging.[245]

Being an effective senator or an effective majority leader is measured not just in legislative output. It can be gauged in other ways, such as by bringing important matters to the public's attention, exercising what Woodrow Wilson called "the informing function of Congress."[246] That was just what Barkley did when he suggested that Winston Churchill speak before a joint meeting of Congress just a few weeks after Pearl Harbor.[247] The British prime minister delivered a famous, rousing address that went a long way toward solidifying the vital American relationship with Great Britain during the war.[248]

Effectiveness can also be exhibited through the exercise of congressional oversight, another key component of the "informing function." Following the Pearl Harbor bombing, there were wild rumors that FDR and other senior officials had been aware of the raid beforehand and had chosen to do nothing to prevent Japan from attacking Hawaii, in the hope of drawing America into the conflict.[249] Barkley helped secure adoption of a resolution to look into the events surrounding the Pearl Harbor attack and selected himself as chairman of the investigative committee.[250]

The committee report, approved by Barkley and several Republican members on the panel, determined that the senior civilian leadership "did not trick, provoke, incite, cajole, or coerce Japan into attacking this Nation in order that a declaration of war might be more easily obtained from Congress."[251] Barkley's actions helped to set the record straight about an event that understandably triggered strong emotions from the public.[252] In this regard, Barkley reflected the ideals of the Senate as he helped cool momentary passions.

Barkley's Relationship with Roosevelt

For a Senate floor leader to be effective, he must not only keep his caucus unified whenever possible but also have a good working relationship with the president if his party controls the White House. That is not always a given. Californian William Knowland, Republican floor leader in the 1950s, had a cool relationship with President Dwight Eisenhower, for example.[253] Knowland regularly and publicly opposed Eisenhower on foreign policy, believing the administration should have pursued a stronger anticommunist posture in Asia.[254] In recognition of his position as party leader, whenever he criticized the president, Knowland would leave the leader's desk and address the Senate as a backbencher.[255] In 1954, to express his concern over the possible extension of United Nations membership to the People's Republic of China, Knowland openly warned President Eisenhower that if this gambit were seriously considered, he would step down as leader and dedicate himself full time to combating this policy.[256] Knowland's threat succeeded in boxing in the president politically and preventing him from seriously pursuing this potential course of action.[257]

By contrast, Barkley got along well with fellow Democrat Franklin Roosevelt; the senator's humor often brought welcome relief to a president burdened by the pressures of war.[258] On one occasion, when Barkley was consulting with

Roosevelt in the White House, he told the president an anecdote about a minister who had just delivered a remarkable sermon.[259] One parishioner approached the minister afterward and exclaimed: "Reverend, that was a damn good sermon you preached this morning!"[260] The reverend, somewhat taken aback, responded: "I appreciate your compliment, but not your language."[261] The parishioner, undeterred, continued: "it was such a damn good sermon that I put $100 in the collection plate."[262] The reverend blurted out: "The *hell* you did!"[263] Roosevelt's laughter was so loud that it was apparently heard by a Secret Service agent on duty all the way down the hall.[264]

In addition to enjoying an easy friendship with the president, Barkley eagerly embraced the responsibility of leading the charge to adopt the administration's priorities.[265] But over time, the president haughtily came to expect that the majority leader would support him all the time, no matter what.[266] That ended when Senator Barkley dramatically broke with the president on a matter of principle.

In February 1944, with America in the midst of its great struggle against the Axis powers, President Roosevelt proposed a significant tax hike—more than $10 billion—to defray the costs of the war effort.[267] Barkley soon realized that Congress would not be enthusiastic about higher taxes.[268] The Kentuckian participated in the bill's development, which would have raised revenues by only $2.3 billion.[269] He also helped steer it across the Senate floor; Barkley well knew the views of his members.[270] Barkley pleaded with Roosevelt to accept the bill and sign it, but the president ignored that advice and vetoed the measure.[271]

Roosevelt's veto message was the coup de grace. It was petty and personal, and it stung Barkley.[272] The president stated imperiously that, having asked Congress "for a loaf of bread," the final bill was but "a small piece of crust."[273] His next words struck hardest of all.[274] He declared that the legislation was "not a tax bill but a tax relief bill, providing relief not for the needy, but for the greedy."[275]

After years of support for the president—often at the cost of the respect of a number of his own colleagues—this insult to Barkley's integrity as a legislator, as a leader, and as a disciple of the New Deal was too much.[276] The next day, still seething with indignation, Barkley dictated a speech to his secretary and marched out to the Senate floor before she could even finish typing it.[277] As rumors of what was coming leaked out, journalists rushed into the galleries, and senators clamored to their seats to hear what Barkley had to say.[278]

The Kentuckian's voice was filled with emotion as he relayed his history of steadfast support for the Roosevelt administration:[279]

> I dare say that during the past 7 years of my tenure as majority leader I have carried that flag over rougher terrain than was ever traversed by any previous majority leader. . . .

> But . . . there is something more precious to me than any honor that can be conferred upon me by the Senate of the United States or by the people of Kentucky or by the President of this Republic, and that is the approval of my own conscience and my own self-respect. That self-respect and the rectitude of that conscience I propose on this occasion to maintain.[280]

And with that, Alben Barkley announced his resignation as majority leader.[281] Barkley had always believed that, as Senate party leader, it was his job to support a president of his own party.[282] Unable to do that, he believed that stepping down was his only choice.[283] Because he had stood up to the president, who had become increasingly aloof toward Congress, and because he had defended the Senate as an institution, nearly every lawmaker in the chamber scrambled to his feet to cheer Barkley.[284] Those in the galleries followed suit.[285] Vice President Henry Wallace called it "the most dramatic occasion in the U.S. Senate over which I ever presided."[286] Floyd Riddick, a keen observer of the Senate and later the chamber's parliamentarian, wrote that the "speech was one of the most daring acts in the recent history of the Congress."[287]

Roosevelt immediately recognized that he was beaten and wrote a letter urging Barkley not to resign.[288] It was unnecessary. The next day, Senate Democrats unanimously reelected Barkley majority leader.[289] The Senate then easily overturned Roosevelt's veto by a vote of 72 to 14, with Barkley leading the effort.[290] Senator Elbert Thomas (D-UT) summed up the newfound power and prestige of the majority leader: "By his one-vote margin in the 1937 contest when he was first elected leader the impression was given, and it has been the impression ever since, that he spoke to us *for* the President," Thomas said. "Now . . . he speaks for us *to* the President."[291] As majority leader, Barkley had at last earned the unqualified respect and trust of his Senate colleagues.[292]

* * *

Barkley's dilemma reflects a reality of Senate party leadership: getting pulled in multiple directions at once. My experience has been that a party leader feels obligations to the president, particularly if he is from the same party; to his Senate party colleagues who elected him; to institutional considerations affecting the Senate as a whole; to his state; to his fellow party members in the House; to his party writ large; and, of course, to his own views of public policy. But the crucial point regarding Senate party leadership is that, at the end of the day, a Senate majority or minority leader is accountable first and foremost to the state that elected him and to his fellow senators, and only then to the president.[293]

* * *

Barkley's principled stance did not come without a cost, however. Dating back to 1928, the Kentuckian had regularly been on the short list of potential Democratic candidates for vice president.[294] Following the break with Roosevelt, a coolness emerged between the two men.[295] The result was that, when FDR was weighing vice-presidential candidates in 1944, Barkley was not given serious consideration.[296] Barkley's junior colleague, Senator Harry Truman (D-MO), was chosen instead. And of course, Truman became president when FDR died in 1945. Given Roosevelt's ill health, Barkley's stance in defense of the Senate may have ultimately cost him the presidency.[297]

Despite his disappointment at not receiving the vice-presidential nod, Barkley faithfully backed Truman's agenda.[298] As had been the case during the Roosevelt administration, the internal liberal-conservative split among Senate Democrats ensured that Barkley was more successful when it came to foreign affairs than domestic matters.[299] In that regard, Barkley facilitated the adoption of measures supporting the Bretton Woods agreement, providing an emergency loan to Great Britain, creating the United Nations, appropriating foreign aid to Greece and Turkey, and authorizing the Marshall Plan.[300]

Throughout all these challenges, few people knew that Barkley was also dealing with personal tragedy: his wife Dorothy's failing health.[301] During the war, Dorothy suffered a heart attack and soon needed constant medical care.[302] Mounting medical bills put the Barkleys in difficult financial straits.[303] In addition to his onerous duties as Senate majority leader, Barkley was forced to accept numerous speaking engagements across the nation to earn sufficient income to cover his wife's medical expenses.[304] Once again, Barkley's great endurance manifested itself.[305] Despite her medical treatment, Dorothy passed away in 1947, dealing a heavy blow to Barkley.[306]

Barkley as Vice President

In 1948, after giving a rousing speech at the Democratic National Convention, the delegates selected Barkley to be President Truman's vice-presidential running mate.[307] That fall, Truman and the Kentuckian squared off against Republican governors Tom Dewey and Earl Warren. Barkley hit the campaign trail with typical gusto, crisscrossing the country and logging more than 150,000 miles.[308] The result was a shocking upset victory for the Democratic ticket. Two months after the surprise Truman-Barkley electoral triumph, Barkley took the oath of office as the thirty-fifth vice president of the United States, sworn in by fellow Kentuckian, Supreme Court Justice Stanley Reed.[309]

Today, the term "veep" has newfound prominence due to the popular HBO series of the same name. Interestingly, Barkley was the first recipient of this nickname, which he attributed to his ten-year-old grandson, Stephen Truitt.[310]

As the story goes, Barkley's family was discussing how his official title, "Mr. Vice President," was too convoluted when young Stephen interjected: "Gramps, V.P. stands for Vice President. Why not stick in a couple of little *e's* and call it 'Veep'?"[311] The name stuck and has been used ever since.

Despite the title change from senator to vice president, Barkley remained close to his beloved Senate. In fact, Barkley's career in some ways marks the evolutionary crossroads of both the vice presidency and the majority leadership. In 1937, he was majority leader when the right of prior recognition was formally acknowledged. And in the late 1940s and early 1950s, as vice president, Barkley was the last officeholder to spend a significant amount of his workday as Senate presiding officer.[312]

Barkley—like Garner—was one of the few vice presidents up to that time to use the presidency of the Senate to successfully exercise some measure of legislative leadership. Barkley served as an important advocate for Truman's legislative agenda, regularly conferring with his successors as majority leader, Scott Lucas (D-IL) and Ernest McFarland (D-AZ).[313]

Even as vice president, Barkley retained his sense of humor. Once while Barkley was presiding over the Senate, Kenneth McKellar (D-TN) protested vigorously against the actions of majority leader Lucas, who had committed the unpardonable sin of yawning during McKellar's remarks.[314] Barkley deftly defused the tension, ruling from the chair: "The yawn of the Senator of Illinois will be stricken from the record."[315]

Some notable personal developments also took place during his vice presidency. In 1949, the widowed vice president had occasion to meet Jane Hadley.[316] The two hit it off, and after five months of courtship, the couple wed.[317] Barkley was undeterred by Jane's political inclinations, including her active support of the 1940 GOP presidential nominee, Wendell Willkie.[318] As the story goes, Jane's milkman had at one point expressed his support for President Roosevelt, and she countered by leaving a note that read: "No Willkie, no milkie."[319]

Despite their initial political differences, Jane saw a side of Barkley that the public did not. She recognized that his humor and "hail fellow well met" persona masked an exceedingly diligent and driven individual. "You are not quite the happy-go-lucky fellow you pretend to be," she commented. "You're so much more serious than most people realize."[320]

After four years as vice president and an unsuccessful effort to secure the 1952 Democratic nomination for president, Barkley retired from politics, seemingly forever. But he soon found himself drawn again to the Senate chamber.[321] Senator Earle Clements (D-KY) and Governor Lawrence Wetherby hit upon the idea of Barkley running for the Senate again; with the former vice president in the race, they believed the Democrats had an excellent chance to retake the seat.[322] So Barkley won reelection to the Senate in 1954, ousting the popular incumbent, Republican John Sherman Cooper.[323] Barkley returned to Washington as the junior senator from Kentucky.

Two years after his return to the Senate, Barkley was doing what he loved most: public speaking. He was addressing a crowd of students at a mock convention at Washington and Lee University.[324] He was explaining to the students why he had declined a seat in the front row of the Senate chamber, despite his earlier decades of service there. "I am glad to sit on the back row," the seventy-eight-year-old Barkley said. "For I would rather be a servant in the house of the Lord, than to sit in the seats of the mighty."[325] Those were Senator Barkley's last words before he suffered a cardiac arrest and collapsed.[326] The roar of the crowd was the last thing he would ever hear.[327]

Barkley's Legacy

Barkley's effectiveness as Senate floor leader was partly a result of his winning personality. He did not let temporary disagreements hamper long-term relationships. A patient, hardworking senator, Barkley used humor, charm, and political acumen to help push through much of Roosevelt's New Deal legislation and, later as majority leader, to adopt critical wartime and postwar measures.[328]

What Barkley lacked in legislative initiative and intellectual finesse, he more than made up for in his ability to get measures through the Senate.[329] As Senator Paul Douglas (D-IL) said of Barkley, "No one was better versed than he in how to get legislation enacted with a minimum of friction."[330]

The Office of Senate Floor Leader since Barkley

The position of Senate floor leader continued to evolve following Barkley's twelve-year tenure.[331] Starting in the mid-1940s and lasting into the beginning of the next decade, the office of Senate floor leader entered a period of decline.[332] Many leading senators simply did not want the aggravation of the job; two Senate party leaders during this period were rejected by the voters of their home states.[333] Few have heard of Senate party leaders Scott Lucas (D-IL), Wallace White (R-ME), or Kenneth Wherry (R-NE). Powerful senators such as Richard Russell (D-GA) wanted nothing to do with the position.[334]

However, the 1953 decision of Robert Taft (R-OH)—long a Senate powerhouse and de facto leader of Senate Republicans—to agree to become Senate majority leader added luster to the position.[335] He did so following the 1952 election of Republican Dwight Eisenhower to the presidency. In some ways, Taft's decision recalls how Senators William Allison (R-IA) and Arthur Pue Gorman

(D-MD) lent their own independent prestige and power to the caucus chairman position.[336] Taft brought cachet back to the majority leader slot.[337] His decision is also reminiscent of Senator Kern's elevation in 1913, in that it reflected both external dynamics—the need to work closely with a newly elected president of the same party—and internal dynamics—the need for a new Republican majority in the Senate to respond productively after being granted a rare opportunity to control the chamber.[338]

Lyndon Johnson's tenure as majority leader (1955–1961) reinforced the prominence of the office in American political life.[339] As noted earlier, Johnson made aggressive use of prior recognition.[340] In addition, he helped establish the norm whereby only the majority leader may move to proceed to the next item of Senate business.[341] Had it been customary for the majority leader to make this motion in 1937, the parliamentary controversy stemming from Senator Wagner's efforts to take up antilynching legislation would not have transpired. Barkley would not have had to use the dubious farming-out process to ensure that friendly senators called up the measures he wanted considered. He simply would have done so himself.

Johnson not only ruthlessly and efficiently ran the Senate but also sought and gained a great deal of media attention in the process.[342] He and Speaker of the House Sam Rayburn were seen in the press as representing the national Democratic Party vis-à-vis the Republican Eisenhower administration.[343] Johnson's later election to the presidency only heightened the stature of the office.

The changing media landscape played an increasingly important role with respect to Senate party leadership in the 1960s and beyond. In 1961, Senate minority leader Everett Dirksen (R-IL) inaugurated weekly joint press conferences with his counterpart, House minority leader Charles Halleck (R-IN).[344] Given Dirksen's colorful persona, these gatherings soon became major press events and were well covered on television and in print, bringing great public attention to the two Republican leaders and underscoring their roles as national spokesmen for their party.[345]

In 1971, another important step was taken with regard to the public aspect of the position. That year, the Senate adopted a measure calling for each floor leader to be granted time at the beginning of each day to speak to the Senate.[346] In keeping with the evolutionary nature of the office, "leader time" began as a three-minute opportunity for each side to dispose of routine procedural matters and inform the Senate of pending business.[347] But this practice morphed over time. By 1975, the length of time had been extended to ten minutes per side.[348] Leader time also evolved from an essentially "housekeeping" exercise to a political platform that allowed each leader to put forward his party's public message, in addition to discussing procedural matters.[349] The importance of leader time grew even more with the introduction of televised floor proceedings in 1986, giving the two lawmakers a much larger audience and wider communications platform.

* * *

This heightened press attention can be a double-edged sword, as it can lead to unreasonable expectations of the office's capacity to produce outcomes. The Senate majority leader's ability to deliver legislation is often in tension with the Senate's traditions of unlimited debate, protection of the rights of individual senators, and preservation of the rights of the minority party. For this reason, one of the things I have tried to do as majority leader is to define success by what is achievable. By the same token, it is important to avoid the opposite trap: defining success by what is not achievable. Success or failure in the Senate is often defined in the public consciousness by individuals other than the majority leader. The majority leader should not contribute to his own difficulties, however, by inordinately raising expectations himself.

* * *

Greater media attention has not only raised expectations of floor leaders' capacity to get things done but also enhanced the importance of party leaders being effective media spokesmen. In this respect, Senator Byrd's tenure as Senate Democratic leader (1977–1989) is a cautionary tale. An expert on Senate procedure and institutional history who was known for his florid oratory, Byrd was out of place in the era of the twenty-four-hour news cycle.[350] He was thought to be pressured to step down as Senate majority leader in 1989 in part to make way for a younger, more telegenic leader, who turned out to be George Mitchell (D-ME).[351]

Over the past several decades, senators have come to exercise greater individualism.[352] As Senator Bob Dole (R-KS) once commented in the 1980s, "We have a lot of self-starters up here. The last time I counted, there were a hundred."[353] This heightened individualism has placed greater pressure on the leadership, which is tasked with producing legislative outcomes.[354] Floor leaders must find a way to assemble a majority or supermajority in order to govern while attempting to satisfy the individual concerns of fellow members.

* * *

Like voters from the party leader's home state, his fellow Senate party members are also his constituents. Similarly, they want and expect the leader to be their advocate. For instance, they want the party leader to try to get their bills passed or secure votes on amendments they favor. Or they may want the party leader to protect them from the other side's perceived partisan mischief. This requires that a leader keep his conference as unified as possible. If a party leader can maintain conference unity, that will give him maximum leverage when negotiating on behalf of his individual members with the other party's leader. If the leader's conference is splintered, it will be very difficult for him to be a successful advocate for individual senators of his party.

As a party leader, I remind members of this unity principle when they are seeking conference support for a particular bill or amendment they favor. Not infrequently, however, the pursuit of one member's priorities pits fellow partisans against one another—one senator may wish for an amendment to be offered, and another of the same party may not. That puts the leader in the middle, and he must try to resolve the impasse.

* * *

Along with rising individualism, Senate rules and practices have been modified to provide modest enhancements to the majority leader's authority as he tries to manage the Senate floor.[355] Although it is difficult to quantify, many observers believe that in recent decades, Senate floor leaders have come to play an increasingly prominent role in policy formulation.[356] Whereas earlier leaders, such as Barkley, focused on scheduling and the "nuts and bolts" of legislative management, today's majority and minority leaders have become policy initiators and promoters of specific legislative outcomes, sometimes sidelining or bypassing committee chairmen altogether.[357] Indeed, Byrd's failure to successfully develop policy initiatives is thought to have eroded his support among Democratic senators in the 1980s.[358]

Over time, Senate floor leaders began to undertake greater responsibility for assembling coalitions to try to achieve the party's legislative goals.[359] Traditionally, this task had been more closely associated with committee chairmen as they managed their legislation on the floor, but it too has gravitated to some degree toward the leadership.[360]

One vital component of every modern floor leader's schedule is the weekly party lunch, held every Tuesday.[361] The exact origin of this practice is unclear; the only thing scholars seem to agree on is that the Republicans adopted the tradition before the Democrats.[362] The GOP started the practice as early as the 1940s, while the Democrats seem to have begun their own Tuesday lunches as early as the 1960s.[363] At these lunches, each party conference meets to strategize on how to proceed with its legislative and messaging agenda.[364] It offers an invaluable way for leaders to propose a path forward and get feedback from their membership.

* * *

At member lunches, I am often in "sales mode," trying to persuade my colleagues of the wisdom of a certain course of action. US senators are talented people with strong views, and it is by no means a given that I will succeed in convincing my colleagues.

* * *

Today's majority and minority leaders evolved from the party caucus chairman positions, which in turn evolved from the caucus system, which was established to deal with the reality of partisan affiliation inside the chamber. The creation of the majority and minority leader posts reflects an institutional change to meet the needs of the time. One suspects that Alben Barkley would still recognize the office he once held, but it has clearly come a long way since his tenure.

In the end, it is difficult not to agree with former historian of the Senate Richard Baker and Professor Roger Davidson, who wrote that the emergence of the formal position of Senate floor leader "can safely be judged as the most significant institutional development of the Senate's history."[365]

8

Senate Majority Whip

Wendell Ford

In the modern Senate, the second most important position in each party is the whip, which typically entails the additional title of assistant majority leader or assistant minority leader.[1] The whip—either majority or minority—is responsible for counting votes, helping the floor leader develop strategy and tactics, convincing members to support measures promoted by the party, filling in for the floor leader when he is away from the Senate, speaking publicly for the party, and notifying fellow partisans of the Senate schedule.[2] Three individuals from Kentucky have served in this capacity, more than from any other state. This chapter examines the career of Wendell Ford and the whip position.[3]

Origins of the Whip Position

Both the whip function and the expression "whip" are borrowed from Great Britain.[4] Efforts to secure the attendance of legislative allies in the House of Commons date back at least to the 1620s.[5] The genesis of the term itself stems from the "whipper in," who, as part of an English hunting party, had responsibility for ensuring the dogs were focused on the quarry, occasionally applying a whip to keep them in line.[6] In a Senate context, the whip is similarly responsible for keeping party members in line and focused on the legislative quarry, which is the adoption or rejection of the measure in question.

Edmund Burke, the renowned British member of Parliament and conservative philosopher, was apparently the first to apply the term "whipper in" in a lawmaking context in 1769.[7] "There was a great debate in the house of commons on [a matter]. . . . The king's Ministers made great efforts to bring their followers together from all quarters for this debate. Burke, who took part in the debate, referred to these efforts, and described how Ministers had sent for their friends to the north and to Paris, *whipping them in* . . . which he said . . . could not be a better phrase."[8] The term "whip" began to denote a parliamentary position not long afterward.[9]

In the nineteenth century, the expression was used from time to time on the Senate floor either to describe a lawmaker acting as a de facto party whip or to reflect a broader party effort to persuade fellow senators to vote a certain way.[10] Yet, for the first century and a quarter, the Senate operated without formal whips (and indeed, without any formal floor leaders).[11] As noted authority Walter Oleszek concluded: "It is likely that certain legislators performed tasks similar to those of contemporary whips, but the institutionalization of the office . . . did not occur until the twentieth century."[12] Indeed, in 1874, Senator Justin Morrill (R-VT) was scandalized by the mere notion of there being a whip in the Senate.[13] He proclaimed: "I do not propose to act as 'the whip' of the Senate. I think the [senators] are quite competent to express their own judgment without any whip. We have never had what is called a whip in the American Senate."[14]

In 1881, Senator James B. Beck (D-KY) noted the exercise of the whip function decades before the office's formal establishment. He commented that another senator "seemed to be the 'whip' of the other side."[15] Indeed, during this period, "whip" was often used as a term of derision. The next year, Senator Beck engaged in a testy exchange with Senator Morrill. The latter chided Beck for acting as if he were, in fact, a whip and stated, "The Senator from Kentucky . . . set himself up as the tariff instructor, the self-appointed whip and leader of his present party."[16] In 1888, British member of Parliament and author James Bryce wrote, "An English politician's first question when he sees Congress is, 'Where are the whips?'"[17]

As with the position of majority leader, the House of Representatives formally created the position of whip before the Senate did.[18] In 1897, House Republicans, who were in the majority at the time, named James Albertus Tawney (MN) as whip.[19] The House Democrats followed suit and named their own whip four years later.[20] It is not far-fetched to think that this innovation made some impression on the Senate.[21]

As will be recalled, in 1913, Senate Democrats elected John Worth Kern (IN) as their caucus chairman. In so doing, they gave him new responsibilities, making him, in effect, the first majority leader.[22] These duties proved daunting, as Kern faced attendance problems and dissent within the ranks.[23] To give Kern the help he needed, Senate Democrats named J. Hamilton Lewis (IL) the majority whip in 1913.[24] Like Kern, Lewis was a newcomer to the Senate, having been in office barely two months.[25] Lewis reflected later, "So far as I have been able to learn, I was the first Democratic whip appointed in the history of the United States Senate."[26] Interestingly, Lewis served two separate tenures as Democratic whip: from 1913 until 1919, when his term ended following electoral defeat, and from 1933 to 1939, after his return to the upper chamber.[27]

Often in the evolution of the Senate's party-based leadership institutions, imitation is the highest form of flattery. Just two years after Lewis's elevation, Senate Republicans named their own party whip: James Wadsworth (NY), who was also chosen to be the party's conference secretary.[28] Perhaps owing to the challenges of the newly created position, the New Yorker lasted only one week in the dual role of Republican whip and conference secretary.[29] He was soon replaced as whip by Charles Curtis (R-KS).[30] Wadsworth was given the consolation, however, of retaining the position of conference secretary.[31]

From Lewis's tenure forward, there has always been a Senate Democratic whip. The same, however, cannot be said of Senate Republicans. From 1935 to 1944, Republican ranks were so depleted by the Democrats' popularity under President Franklin D. Roosevelt that, at one point, the GOP could claim only seventeen senators.[32] With so few Republican senators, a formal full-time whip was deemed unnecessary.[33] Senate minority leader Charles McNary (R-OR) simply assigned Republican senators to act as whip on an ad hoc basis.[34] Despite the hiatus on the Republican side, in the ensuing decades, the office of whip would grow in prestige.

The Early Years of Wendell Ford

Wendell Ford, the second of four children, was born to Ernest and Irene Ford on September 8, 1924, just outside of Owensboro, in western Kentucky.[35] Irene was a devoutly religious woman from whom Wendell would inherit his compassionate nature.[36] His brother Reyburn described their mother as "saintly."[37] Ford inherited his zest for hard work from both parents, especially his mother, and his love of politics from his father, who farmed, started the family insurance business, and later became active in Democratic Party politics, serving in both houses of the state legislature.[38] While in the legislature, Ernest worked closely with Earle Clements, who would later become a friend of his son's as well.[39] Wendell would call Clements his "political father."[40] He would follow in Clements's footsteps as governor, US senator, and Senate majority whip.

Ford experienced politics firsthand. He frequently accompanied his father on public business in the district. He saw the importance of listening closely to constituents even when they were discontented.[41] Ford learned not only at his father's knee but also on the floor of the state house, where he served as a page.[42] Ernest taught his son about more than just politics. He also taught him how to farm.[43] As a boy, Wendell was expected to pitch in and do chores. He routinely milked thirty cows two times a day, to which he later attributed his firm handshake.[44] Working on the farm ingrained in Ford a number of enduring habits, one of which was being an early riser. His grandsons recalled spending several weeks with Ford when their own family home was being remodeled.[45] The boys never had to worry about being late for school while staying with their grandfather. He was up early and expected the same from them.[46]

Ford attended Daviess County High School, where he was popular and was named "most talkative."[47] He was an able student and later showed great skill in arithmetic—indeed, he would prove an adept vote counter.[48] However, Ford struggled with geometry, recalling that the subject made him feel "like that fella that said . . . 'pie are squared,'" to which "his daddy [replied] . . . '[We need to take] you out of [that] school; pie are round.'"[49]

During the summer following his high school graduation, Ford took a job at J. C. Penney's in downtown Owensboro.[50] There, he met a coworker named Jean Neal and asked her out.[51] As Ford reminisced, "She said she'd let me know."[52] Fortunately for him, a friend interceded and persuaded Jean to go out on a date with Wendell.[53] Ford stated, "I never dated any other woman after that."[54] Not long after high school graduation, on September 18, 1943, the two were wed.[55] Ford raised the money to purchase her wedding ring by selling a cow and its young offspring.[56] As he recalled, "I told [Jean] you got a Guernsey and a calf on [your] . . . finger there."[57] Almost without fail, he referred to her as "Mrs. Ford."[58] The couple would have two children: Shirley and Steven.[59] Jean loyally supported Ford through all his campaigns. She had her own way of handling the stress of public life: knitting.[60] Ford reflected that it was Jean's "therapy for being married to a politician."[61] In fact, she produced afghan blankets for three First Ladies.[62]

After high school, Ford began course work at the University of Kentucky, but family responsibilities and World War II interrupted his studies.[63] From 1944 to 1946, he served in the army as an instructor.[64] Ford was stationed at Fort Hood, Texas, and Jean joined him there.[65] On a weekly basis, Ford's father mailed him five dollars.[66] One night, at Jean's urging, Ford took the five-dollar bill and bought steaks for the two of them, receiving a silver dollar in change.[67] "I almost spent it two or three times," Ford recalled, "but I kept it . . . to remind me of that [evening]."[68] For the rest of his life, Ford would periodically take the coin out of his pocket and rub the keepsake, sometimes telling people of its origin.[69] Over time, the surface of the coin became completely smooth, but it would always remain a cherished memento.[70]

After the war, Ford returned to Kentucky and went into the family insurance business in Owensboro. He maintained his link to the military by joining the Kentucky National Guard in 1949, serving until 1962.[71] He became a major advocate for the reserve component of the armed forces once he became a senator.[72] Indeed, the Kentucky National Guard Regional Training Center was later named for him.[73]

One day in 1947, while on his lunch break, Ford decided to pick up an electric razor.[74] That minor errand would be a major turning point for Ford. During his stroll, he happened across Paul Ganoway, a member of the Junior Chamber of Commerce (the Jaycees).[75] The two men struck up a conversation, and Ganoway persuaded Ford to join the group.[76] Before long, Ford was heading the Owensboro chapter of the Jaycees and moving up the chain of command; he soon became its state president.[77]

By 1956, Ford was positioned to lead the Kentucky delegation to the National Jaycees Convention. Behind the motto and song "Shake, Rattle with Ford," he was elected the group's president.[78] As leader of the organization, it was Ford's responsibility to stay in touch with chapters throughout the country.[79] One memorable visit was to a small community in Washington State, where one member briefed him on the latest Jaycee fund-raising effort.[80] Anxious to impress the national president, the man excitedly told Ford: "We just raised enough money [to buy] a fire truck for our . . . fire department."[81] Ford asked: "Well, how'd you raise the money?" The Washington native replied: "Well, the dealer let us have a . . . convertible at cost and we raffled that sucker off . . . and raised enough money to buy this fire truck."[82] Ford was suitably impressed. He inquired, "What's your next project?" The man replied, "Raising enough money to pay off the . . . car."[83]

Ford's tenure in the Jaycees not only exposed him to unorthodox promotional efforts but also catapulted him into the upper reaches of Kentucky civic life.[84] In 1955, Ford was chosen one of the most promising young people in the state.[85] From the Jaycees, Ford went on to work as youth director for Democratic gubernatorial candidate Bert T. Combs.[86] After Combs's victory, Ford became one of the governor's top staffers in 1959.[87] Following his mother's passing in 1961, Ford left Combs's employ to return to the family insurance business.[88] This proved a short respite from politics, however; in less than a decade, Ford would be governor himself.

Ford's Ascent

The question arises: what factors accounted for Ford's rapid advancement in the Jaycees and later in state and national politics? First, Ford was tenacious. When he set his mind to do something, he would not quit. On the campaign trail, Ford simply would not be outworked. Twenty-hour days were not out of the ordinary.[89] And Ford left nothing to chance. As he once said, "One time when

I ran [for reelection] without opposition . . . in November, I worried there'd be a write-in [candidate]."[90]

Even health problems sidelined the relentless Ford only briefly. In 1972, Ford—an avid smoker—had to undergo an operation for an aneurysm.[91] Nonetheless, he attended the Democratic National Convention the very next month.[92] Ford worked doggedly and took few vacations. He liked to say, "I guess vacation for me is not shaving and not wearing a suit."[93]

A second attribute was Ford's skill as a negotiator. This made him very effective at the various jobs he undertook. *Congressional Quarterly* observed that Ford "is one of the best horse-traders in the Senate[;] he does not get everything he goes after, but almost always comes away with something."[94] One of his Senate colleagues, Dale Bumpers (D-AR), remarked that opposing Ford on an issue reminded him of wrangling "with [his] wife. . . . [The arguments] I win just ain't over [yet]."[95] Indeed, Ford's tenacity occasionally ruffled some feathers. One senator said of Ford's defense of Kentucky industries: "Sometimes he gets too abusive. He doesn't know when to quit."[96]

A third key ingredient to Ford's success was his genuine affinity for people. This came through to Kentuckians, as Ford would warmly greet people by name even if he had not seen them for years.[97] As a Republican county chairman acknowledged, Ford "absolutely had the ability to relate to the common man and . . . you had the feeling that when he talked to you, he was listening to you."[98] Senator Carl Levin (D-MI) relayed a telling anecdote about Senator Ford's kindness:

> A member of my staff had brought his 5-year-old son to work for the day. The staff member, needing to attend an important meeting, left his son to play with paper, crayons and [a] stapler, under the supervision of several co-workers. He returned to find his son no longer at the desk where he had been left. A quick search followed. The young boy was found just outside of the office in the Senate hallway where he had stopped Senator . . . Ford and attempted to sell him a book [of] artful pages of crayon scribbles, stapled together . . . for a nickel. Senator Ford was in the act of earnestly requesting two and trying to convince the young man to accept a dime as superior to the requested nickel.[99]

Ford cared about people, and it showed.

Fourth, Ford had a keen political mind. He called himself just a "dumb country boy with dirt between his toes," but no one believed anything of the kind.[100] He had learned at the knee of both his father and Clements, and he had learned his lessons well. Ford never lost a Kentucky election.

Fifth, Ford had a folksy sense of humor that endeared him to many and often disarmed his foes.[101] Once, at a gathering of the American Heart Association, the chain-smoking Ford spoke to the group and alluded to his earlier heart procedure. He commented that he was "living, breathing, smoking proof of the need for health research."[102]

Finally, Ford never forgot his roots. Senator Daniel Inouye (D-HI) described Ford's demeanor even after the man from Owensboro had become a prominent senator: "There were no ribbons, no frills, no bells. What you saw, you got."[103] Inouye said that Ford "was 'truth in packaging' personified."[104] Senator Phil Gramm (R-TX) concurred. To Gramm, his Democratic colleague was not a "cellophane politician"; the Kentuckian had "texture."[105]

Ford's Early Elections

From the 1930s until the 1960s, Democratic Party politics in Kentucky had been torn asunder by two warring groups: the A. B. "Happy" Chandler–led faction that tended to be more conservative, and the Clements-Combs faction that tended to be more liberal.[106] Ford emerged from the Clements-Combs bloc but benefited from an overall decline in Democratic divisiveness in the 1960s.[107] In the words of Kentucky state historian James Klotter, Ford "represented a new wave of leadership in Kentucky politics."[108]

Not long after leaving his position with Governor Combs, Ford took the job of managing Ned Breathitt's successful race for governor against Chandler in 1963.[109] Once Breathitt was in office, he grew frustrated with state senate majority leader Casper Gardner, who had blocked much of the governor's agenda.[110] Breathitt recruited Ford to challenge Gardner for his seat in the legislature.[111]

After a hard-fought primary campaign in 1965, local Democrats went to the polls. On Election Day, Ford anxiously awaited the results.[112] After bringing doughnuts and coffee to campaign volunteers, Ford found himself with nothing to do, so he journeyed to Ivan Paine's barbershop in Owensboro.[113] That prompted two Election Day traditions that would mark Ford's political career: getting a haircut and winning his campaign.[114] Ford won the primary over Gardner by a mere 305 votes and later prevailed in the general election.[115] He would serve only two years in the state senate, but it was a productive two years. During his tenure, Ford introduced twenty-two bills, each of which was enacted.[116]

As he was rapidly ascending the political ladder, Ford suffered a major personal blow in 1967 when his father died. Ernest had been more than Ford's devoted father; he was also his closest political adviser.[117] Following Ernest's passing, Ford came to rely even more heavily on former senator Clements.[118]

That same year, Ford ran for his first statewide office: lieutenant gover-nor. Yet again, he faced a formidable opponent in the Democratic primary. This time, it was state attorney general Robert Matthews.[119] Ford prevailed by a 631-vote margin.[120] That year, Ford won the general election, even though the Democratic candidate for governor lost. This meant that Ford would serve as lieutenant governor during the tenure of Republican governor Louie B. Nunn.[121]

Four years later, in 1971, Ford decided to run for governor himself, but there was a problem: his rival for the Democratic nomination was none other than his former boss, Bert Combs. In what must have been an uncomfortable conversa-tion, the two met in Combs's office to discuss matters, but neither man would budge.[122] As in his earlier races for state senate and lieutenant governor, Ford was thought to be the underdog.[123] Nonetheless, he defeated his former boss in the Democratic gubernatorial primary.

That was not the end of the battle, however. Ford was opposed in the general election by two candidates. On one end of the political spectrum was Republi-can Tom Emberton, Governor Nunn's anointed successor; on the other end was the old warhorse himself, Happy Chandler, who was campaigning as an inde-pendent.[124] Ford campaigned tirelessly, highlighting outgoing Governor Nunn's unpopular five-cent sales tax.[125] The lieutenant governor ridiculed "Nunn's nickel" and pledged to eliminate the sales tax on food and farm equipment.[126] Ford won the election, aided by a capable campaign team that included future US senator Walter "Dee" Huddleston and future governor Martha Layne Collins.[127]

Once in office, Governor Ford was productive. Like his mentor Earle Cle-ments, Ford tamed the state legislature.[128] He worked to repeal the sales tax on food, medication, and agricultural equipment.[129] He helped reform insurance practices, created the commonwealth's first program to provide impoverished defendants with legal counsel, and assisted coal miners afflicted with black lung disease.[130] He took steps against strip mining and set up clinics to combat drug and alcohol abuse.[131]

Ford also restructured state government, which had evolved into a mot-ley assortment of seemingly independent principalities.[132] Upon taking office, he was confronted with nearly seventy bureaucracies, which he consolidated into nine entities during his tenure.[133] He and many others considered this his finest accomplishment as governor.[134] In addition, Ford devoted much-needed resources to the University of Louisville and Northern Kentucky University when the two became part of the state university system.[135] Moreover, Martin Luther King Jr.'s birthday was made a state holiday nearly a decade before it was adopted nationwide.[136] With these achievements, it is not surprising that Gov-ernor Ford gained a national profile. He was chosen chairman of the National Democratic Governors' Caucus in 1973.[137]

Although he worked intensely during his time as governor, Ford also embraced some of the ceremonial trappings of the office. One of the perks of being the state's chief executive is presenting the garland and trophy to the owner of the winning horse in the Kentucky Derby.[138] Ford witnessed some historic winners. He had the good fortune to be on hand to honor the great Secretariat in 1973 and the next year's winner of the 100th "Run for the Roses": Cannonade.[139]

Ford was a big fan of the Derby and told an anecdote that reflected the commonwealth's deep attachment to the event: One year a gentleman spotted a vacant chair in a luxury box at the Kentucky Derby.[140] An elderly lady was sitting in the adjacent seat.[141] The passerby exclaimed, "This is the first empty seat I've seen today."[142] The lady replied, "Well, it belonged to my husband, but he died."[143] Incredulous, the man inquired, "Why didn't you give it to one of your relatives?"[144] "I would have," the lady responded, "but they're all at the funeral."[145]

Ford enjoyed being the state's chief executive. But like many before him, he was frustrated by the state constitutional provision that prevented governors from running for reelection. Like Chandler and Clements, Ford thought joining the US Senate would be the best way to continue his public service, so he decided to run for a Senate seat in 1974.[146] Standing in his way was Republican senator Marlow Cook of Louisville. Cook had served one term and was running for reelection, but incumbency was not an advantage for the GOP in 1974. The Watergate scandal was the major national issue at the time. Ford campaigned with his usual gusto and was elected to the first of his four terms in the Senate. In so doing, he became the first Kentuckian elected lieutenant governor, governor, and senator in succession.[147] Ford resigned as governor on December 28, 1974, and Lieutenant Governor Julian Carroll succeeded him.

Ford in the Senate

In the Senate, there are thought to be two types of members: show horses and work horses. The former strive for headlines; the latter strive for results. Wendell Ford was every bit the work horse. He saw himself as a "constituent senator" who had been elected to serve Kentucky.[148] As Ford recalled, "I wasn't interested in national issues. I was interested in Kentucky issues."[149] The man from Owensboro advocated doggedly for state interests, despite their unpopularity in many quarters of the nation's capital. Ford remarked: "I always say, We [in Kentucky] have beautiful women, fast horses, bourbon, cigarettes, and coal. And most of it [is] . . . habit forming."[150]

Examples of Ford's home-state advocacy abound. He helped ensure that cigarettes were exempted from the Consumer Product Safety Act and opposed efforts to tax tobacco to pay for President Bill Clinton's health care plan.[151] When one initiative harmful to the Kentucky coal industry was proposed, Ford warned that if the measure were pursued, there would be "blood on the floor of the Senate."[152] He voted against the 1990 bipartisan budget agreement because it increased taxes on tobacco and spirits.[153]

Ford did not shrink from political combat in Washington, DC. This is not surprising, as he was once described as "an almost compulsive campaigner."[154] When the opportunity arose for Ford to run for the chairmanship of the Democratic Senatorial Campaign Committee (DSCC) in late 1976, he jumped at it. In fact, Ford is one of only three senators to chair his party's campaign committee three times. The others are George Smathers (D-FL) and Barry Goldwater (R-AZ).[155]

During Ford's time as campaign chairman, Democratic electoral fortunes were not good.[156] In 1978, the party lost three seats. Two years later, Republicans reclaimed control of the upper chamber after a quarter century in the minority.[157] The trend continued in 1982, as Democrats lost two more partisans.[158] Even though Ford chaired the DSCC during a Republican groundswell, he managed to rack up chits with Democratic colleagues by fighting for their Senate seats.

Following his tenure at the DSCC, Ford chaired the Senate Rules and Administration Committee from 1986 to 1994.[159] As Rules Committee chairman, Ford was involved in helping to plan and convene the inaugural ceremonies of two incoming presidents: George H. W. Bush and Bill Clinton.[160] He also earned credit for something he did *not* do. He resisted pressure to establish a Senate bank akin to the scandal-plagued House of Representatives bank, which created a furor in the early 1990s.[161]

By 1988, Ford had gained sufficient stature to make a run for party whip. That year, he took on the incumbent, Senator Alan Cranston (D-CA).[162] The Californian beat back Ford's challenge, but the man from Owensboro made it clear that he was not going away.[163] Two years later, Cranston was ill and mired in controversy over the "Keating Five" savings-and-loan scandal.[164] He decided not to run for reelection as whip, and Ford had already cornered the market.[165]

The Kentuckian had been hard at work persuading colleagues that, with liberal George Mitchell (D-ME) as majority leader, they should choose a more moderate Democrat for the second leadership post.[166] In his quest for the position, Ford was meticulous in his preparation. He kept a small piece of paper on the left side of his desk with the names of senators who supported him and those who were undecided.[167] Once a senator promised to vote for him, Ford would write his colleague a thank-you note and request a signed proxy card, a tactic he had learned from Senator Robert Byrd (D-WV).[168] In other words, Ford shrewdly got his commitments in writing.[169]

One of Ford's predecessors as majority whip was Senator Edward Kennedy (D-MA), who had failed to take such precautions. In 1971, Kennedy was running for reelection as whip against Senator Byrd. Kennedy went into the election believing he had enough votes to be reelected, but it turned out he did not. The West Virginian beat him in a nail-biter.[170] Later that year, Kennedy gave a speech drolly describing his failed attempt to remain whip:

> I want to take this opportunity to thank the 28 Democratic senators who pledged to vote for me—and especially the 24 who actually did. According to a story in the *Washington Post,* the Secret Service says I receive more anonymous threatening letters than anyone else on Capitol Hill. It wasn't until [the] January [whip election] that I realized most of them came from my colleagues in the Senate. Since I lost the whip fight, many people have asked me when I realized I was in trouble. Frankly, it was the morning of the vote, when my staff told me that we had nailed down Joe Tydings, Ralph Yarborough, Albert Gore—and Senator Sorensen of New York.[171]

Tydings, Yarborough, Gore, and Sorensen had all been defeated a few weeks earlier and could not vote.[172]

* * *

While Kennedy's speech was humorous, it reflects a broader truth about the challenges involved in leadership elections. In congressional leadership races, it can be hard to pin down your colleagues and get them to state whether they are for you or against you. Politicians, I am told, can be coy. Ford learned his lessons well from Senator Byrd. He was unanimously elected majority whip in 1990.

* * *

Development of the Whip Position

The position Ford assumed had grown in stature over the past few decades.[173] In the late 1940s, whips began to participate in party Policy Committee meetings, which, at the time, were very select gatherings.[174] In 1957, majority leader Lyndon Johnson (D-TX) assigned the seat next to him on the Senate floor to majority whip Mike Mansfield (D-MT).[175] This added prestige to the position, publicly signaling that the whip was indeed the number-two person in the Senate party. Republicans followed suit, moving the minority whip to the front of the chamber three years later.[176] These developments were reinforced in the 1960s and early 1970s, when whips began to be more regularly designated "assis-

188 THE US SENATE AND THE COMMONWEALTH

tant majority leader" and "assistant minority leader."[177] With a few exceptions, whips have carried both titles ever since.[178]

One way the whip position has not changed is that the officeholder must work well with the party's floor leader.[179] Indeed, some leaders have assigned highly important and visible legislative tasks to their whips. As majority leader, Senator Mansfield assigned majority whip Hubert Humphrey (D-MN) the job of floor-managing what became the Civil Rights Act of 1964.[180]

* * *

In the early 2000s, the relationship between Republican leader Trent Lott (R-MS) and Republican whip Don Nickles (R-OK) was strained. Indeed, Nickles, in essence, publicly called for Lott to step down after the majority leader made controversial comments about Strom Thurmond's 1948 presidential candidacy.[181] When I started work as majority whip in what turned out to be the last few days of Lott's leadership tenure, I was committed to ensuring a positive and productive relationship with our party leader. I defended Lott to Republican senators and in public, though ultimately in vain. As the number-two member of the Republican conference, I also had to break the news to Lott that he had insufficient support to continue as leader.[182] Afterward, I tried to ensure a positive relationship with majority leader Bill Frist (R-TN). I was fortunate that Frist took me into his confidence and assigned me meaningful tasks. I have tried to emulate that model with Jon Kyl (R-AZ) and John Cornyn (R-TX), both of whom are very able senators who have served alongside me as whip.

* * *

It is by no means a given, however, that the two party leaders will have a close relationship.[183] In this vein, the modern whip has been likened to the vice president.[184] To a considerable degree, the tasks undertaken by the whip are contingent on what the floor leader is willing to delegate.[185] That is similar to the vice president's reliance on the president for meaningful assignments.[186] Senator John Worth Kern—generally seen as the first majority leader—had a cool relationship with the first whip, J. Hamilton Lewis.[187] Likewise, majority leader Mike Mansfield had a poor relationship with majority whip Russell Long (D-LA) and made little use of him.[188] Mansfield delegated authority instead to Senator Byrd, the Democratic conference secretary, who monitored the floor in place of Long.[189] When the West Virginian became whip, Mansfield continued to entrust him with the responsibilities of being the Democratic "point man" on the Senate floor.[190]

Another similarity with the presidential–vice-presidential relationship is that the whip sometimes adds balance to the party leadership team, which can be manifested ideologically, geographically, or both.[191] An example is Ford himself. As a moderate Democrat, he provided a counterpoint to the more liberal majority leaders George Mitchell (D-ME) and Tom Daschle (D-SD). Perhaps because of this regional and ideological divergence, Ford did not enjoy a close working relationship with either man.[192]

Comparison with the vice presidency yields a third commonality: the opportunity for career advancement.[193] Like vice presidents, who often have a leg up on becoming their party's presidential nominee, many whips are well positioned to become floor leader.[194] Yet many have been unsuccessful in this endeavor. Leverett Saltonstall (R-MA) was passed over on more than one occasion in the 1950s when the Republican leader was absent for an extended period or the position was vacant.[195] Neither Ted Stevens (R-AK) in 1984 nor Robert Griffin (R-MI) in 1977 succeeded in their efforts to become Republican leader.[196] In 2016, Democratic whip Richard Durbin (D-IL) did not secure election as floor leader, despite his long-standing interest in the position.[197]

In 1994, when majority leader Mitchell decided not to run for another term, his heir apparent Jim Sasser (D-TN) was defeated for reelection by Bill Frist. This provided an opportunity for Ford to run for Democratic floor leader, but he opted against doing so, explaining that he did not want to distract attention from his home-state priorities.[198] Other unspoken factors may have been at play as well. Given Ford's centrist views and advocacy for causes such as tobacco, he was increasingly out of step with the Senate Democratic conference, which was becoming more liberal.[199] Moreover, Ford may have concluded that he lacked the polished media skills to be an effective party spokesman, a problem encountered by his mentor Senator Byrd.[200]

Like the majority leader and minority leader positions, the job of whip comes with a heightened public profile.[201] Whips attract media attention because of their responsibilities and the presumption that they—like the floor leaders—speak for their party.[202] Given that whips are number two in the Senate party hierarchy, it is assumed that they—like other party leaders—will support the president's agenda if the president is a fellow partisan.[203] On occasion, however, whips—like floor leaders—have broken publicly with presidents of the same party.[204] One significant split took place when Senator Long openly repudiated fellow Democrat President Lyndon Johnson.[205] Another high-profile break took place when Senator Griffin, the Republican whip, opposed President Richard Nixon's naming of Clement Haynsworth to serve on the Supreme Court.[206]

Despite the heightened prestige that accompanies the office, party whips do not enjoy procedural prerogatives. For example, they do not have a right of prior recognition.[207] Moreover, whips have been defeated for reelection from time to time. Senators Griffin, Thomas Kuchel (R-CA), Felix Hebert (R-RI), Clements, Francis Myers (D-PA), Sherman Minton (D-IN), Peter Gerry (D-RI), and Lewis all lost their bids to return to the Senate.[208]

* * *

Whips are responsible for completing tangible work products. The most critical item is the "whip card." This is a compilation that provides a breakdown of where the party's senators are likely to fall on a particular issue should it come up for a vote.[209] Once the leadership knows where its members stand on a particular issue, it can determine how to proceed.[210] Often, if the leadership is short of votes, it may reach out to undecided members and try to persuade them to join the party position.[211] If the votes are insufficient to carry a measure, the leadership may decide to change course.

Producing an accurate vote count is the most important function of the whip. Accordingly, the questions posed to members on the whip card must be phrased with precision, so as not to distort the accuracy of the tabulation. Moreover, the questions need to be presented in as fair and accurate a way as possible; otherwise, leadership could wind up repelling wavering senators by seeming to be heavy-handed. After the whip cards are distributed, the whip collects the data, and based on that information, the party leader determines how to proceed on a matter. For me, as party leader, it is crucial that the whip count be accurate. If it is not, our leadership team might be embarrassed, and precious floor time could be wasted on a failed measure.

Former Senate majority leader Howard Baker (R-TN) once said, "The education of a Senate leader ends in the third grade. When you learn how to count, you've completed the educational requirement."[212] Behind the humor in Baker's quip is the fact that most Senate party leaders place a high premium on tallying the votes correctly. That function begins with the whip count.

The importance of an accurate vote count and the anxiety that is sometimes involved are reflected in an experience I had as whip. In 2005, the Senate was considering a deficit-reduction package.[213] My whip count indicated a 50–50 tie, which would have defeated the measure. We therefore needed Vice President Dick Cheney to break the tie.[214] There was only one problem—Cheney was in Afghanistan at the time.[215] So, based on my whip count, I had to ask the vice president to cut his trip short, fly halfway around the world, and break the tie.[216] Needless to say, it was important that my whip count be accurate, and the vote was indeed 50–50.[217] Cheney broke the tie to push the measure through.[218]

* * *

For whatever reason, not all floor leaders rely heavily on whip counts. When he became majority leader, Senator Mansfield de-emphasized their importance.[219] The Johnson White House assumed this responsibility, and after the election of Richard Nixon, the Democratic Policy Committee took over the function.[220] Mansfield's whip, Senator Byrd, was not asked to perform whip counts, and when the West Virginian became majority leader, his whip, Senator Cranston, rarely polled members of the Democratic caucus.[221] For many years, majority leader Bob Dole (R-KS) had the secretary for the majority—a nonmember—do whip counts for him.[222] In fact, Senator Lott was able to unseat Alan Simpson (R-WY) as whip in part because he emphasized the need for a member-to-member whip operation.[223] Each leader takes the approach that best suits his needs and those of his party colleagues.

Another product put forward by the whip is the "whip notice," which informs members and staff of the upcoming floor schedule.[224] The notice typically includes specific information, such as when the Senate will open for business in the morning, when debate on measures will commence, and when votes will take place.[225] The practice of circulating such notices to fellow partisans apparently began in the early 1970s under Senator Byrd for the Democrats and Senator Griffin for the Republicans.[226]

* * *

Having held the position of whip myself, I can vouch that it is a difficult job. As former minority whip Everett Dirksen (R-IL) once said, "Votes don't flutter down like handbills from an airplane. They don't shake off a tree. Effort . . . counts around here."[227] That is absolutely true; party leaders and whips have to <u>work</u> to get the votes they need. Typically, the whip is responsible not only for providing accurate vote counts but also for persuading undecided members to vote with the party leadership. The challenge is that senators have strong opinions of their own, are very protective of their independence, and are often difficult to convince. As Senator Cranston, the longest-serving whip, remarked: it "isn't just counting votes, it's figuring out how to influence the outcome by finding out what Senators could go one way or another" on a measure.[228]

One of the Senate's most distinguished whips, Senator Humphrey, elaborated on the position's responsibilities: "As the Whip in the Senate . . . my task is primarily to cajole and to persuade, and to be a psychoanalyst of my colleagues in the hope that by understanding what is bothering them on a particular day, or what motivates them relating to a particular piece of legislation, I [can help bring] a consensus or majority to support a program."[229] Humphrey's view of the whip position remains accurate today. A good whip needs to know what makes his members tick, what motivates them, and what concerns them. Such a level of understanding is vital when trying to determine what might persuade a lawmaker. This is not always easy to achieve, however, as senators often choose not to reveal what animates them. As the chamber's first whip, Senator Lewis, said of the position, it requires "tact, patience, good humor, and unfailing courtesy."[230]

In this day and age, Senate Republicans have three party lunches a week, each hosted by a different aspect of the membership. During each of these lunches, I am in "sales mode." I am trying to sell Republican members on what my leadership team and I think is the best approach for the nation, for the Senate, and for our confer-ence. Usually, the whip follows up with colleagues to reinforce the party's message. These lunches are an important element of my workweek and an inviolate part of my schedule.

In managing the Senate Republican conference, I have found as both majority leader and majority whip that what I call the "80-20 rule" applies. The Senate vari-ation of the 80-20 rule is that, as party leader, you spend 80 percent of your time on 20 percent of your members. Attempting to get this 20 percent to remain in the fold without wearing out your welcome can be challenging.

As leader, I try to conserve my chits. This is where the whip comes in. Quite often, the whip makes an initial run at the member in question. If that gambit fails, the whip and I may reach out to a colleague who has a close relationship with the wavering senator. Only as a last resort do I weigh in. Sometimes, on an important measure, I vote early and then linger in the well of the Senate near the vote tally sheet. Members have to come down to the well of the Senate to vote, and through my presence, I try to underscore the vote's importance to our leadership team and to our conference.

* * *

Ford's Later Senate Career

Despite Ford's distant relations with Senators Mitchell and Daschle, the Ken-tuckian held the position of Democratic whip until he left the Senate in 1999, winning reelection to the post three times. Even though his position as whip was demanding, Ford always placed a premium on family. Senator John Glenn (D-OH) recalled talking with fellow senators one August about their upcoming vacation plans; many of the itineraries involved trips to exotic locales.[231] When Glenn inquired whether Ford had scheduled any travel, he replied, "Yep; I'm going to travel to Kentucky to go fishing with the grandchildren."[232]

Ford's Senate record is hard to pigeonhole ideologically.[233] On the one hand, he supported the 1994 ban on assault weapons and opposed the North American Free Trade Agreement and the 1991 Gulf War authorization, all largely liberal positions.[234] On the other hand, he opposed the Panama Canal Treaty nego-tiated by the Carter administration in 1977, a conservative stance.[235] He also took moderate positions on social issues and earned the wrath of consumer and environmental advocates for his unapologetic defense of Kentucky industries.[236]

Senator Ford championed motor-voter legislation and pro-energy mea-sures.[237] He contributed to the Family and Medical Leave Act.[238] He was an advocate of reforming the congressional budget process, and he helped eliminate waste by lowering printing costs for the federal government.[239] Aviation was one of his areas of expertise, and in many quarters, Ford was viewed as *the* authority in the chamber on that subject.[240] He served as chairman of the Committee on Aeronautical and Space Sciences.[241] He used to say that his legislative interest in the subject vindicated a childhood spent absorbed in Buck Rogers comic books.[242] Today, travelers at the Louisville airport are greeted by a bust of Senator Ford, honoring his efforts on behalf of Kentucky aviation.

Even during congressional recesses, Ford rarely stopped working. During one congressional break, he and the secretary of transportation hashed out the details of airline legislation while sitting in rocking chairs in Ford's den in Owensboro, eating peanuts and sipping on soft drinks.[243]

As his seniority grew, Ford passed several milestones. In 1992, he received more votes than any Senate candidate in Kentucky up to that time. In addition, he was the first to win all 120 counties in a contested race.[244] In March 1998, Ford passed Alben Barkley to become the longest-serving senator from the commonwealth, and he remains the state's longest-serving Democratic senator.[245] Ford's tenure was not without occasional hiccoughs, however. In the mid-1970s, a federal investigation was undertaken into the use of state insurance contracts as patronage tools while he was governor.[246] No charges were ever brought against him, however.[247]

Much like Happy Chandler—one of his opponents in the 1971 gubernatorial race—Ford preferred being governor to being senator. He once remarked: "When you're governor you can get things done. You could get it done, walk outside and put your hand on it."[248] This enjoyment of serving as governor led him to consider forsaking his Senate seat and seeking state executive office again.[249] Despite his longing to return to the governor's mansion, Ford decided to remain in the US Senate.

Late in his fourth term, Ford concluded that the time had come to retire to Owensboro, and he did not run for reelection in 1998.[250] In the years that followed, he devoted a great deal of time to his family.[251] He was also involved in the creation of the Wendell H. Ford Government Education Center.[252] On January 22, 2015, Ford passed away at the age of ninety in Owensboro.

9

Senate Party Campaign Chairman

Earle Clements and Thruston Morton

Like many of the senators profiled in this book, Earle Clements and Thruston Morton have been largely forgotten. Yet in their day, both were prominent figures. Clements was Senate majority whip and served briefly as acting majority leader. Morton was seen as a possible challenger or successor to minority leader Everett Dirksen (R-IL) and was regularly thought to be a potential candidate for national office. Both men held the post of Senate party campaign chairman.[1] Clements and Morton are two of the four Kentuckians who have held the office, giving the commonwealth more Senate party campaign chairmen than any other state. This position and their careers are chronicled in this chapter.

Clements and Morton are closely intertwined not only with each other but also with another major figure in Kentucky history: A. B. "Happy" Chandler. Clements and Chandler engaged in a bitter rivalry that shaped Kentucky politics for decades. Morton was a beneficiary of their feud.

Earle Clements

In 1896, just outside of Morganfield in western Kentucky, Earle Clements was born, the youngest of six children.[2] Earle's father, Aaron Waller Clements, farmed, practiced law, and was a county political leader.[3] Sallie Anna Tuley Clements, his mother, hailed from the same part of the state.[4]

Earle stood out as a youth.[5] In high school, he excelled at sports and was elected senior class president; his yearbook correctly forecast that Clements was apt to "someday be a Senator."[6] The young man from Morganfield enrolled at the University of Kentucky, where he lettered in football.[7] He would later become an accomplished high school coach, attending seminars held by Knute Rockne.[8] During World War I, Clements served Stateside in the National Guard, rising to the rank of captain.[9]

Even though his classmates foretold his rise in public life, Clements did not have the classic politician's personality. He was not a "hail fellow well met" type.[10] He was inscrutable.[11] He could be acerbic, and he had a temper.[12] Nevertheless, Clements rose to great heights due to his work ethic and his skill as a political organizer and strategist.[13] One longtime observer of the Kentucky political scene said of Clements: "He may well have been the greatest political intellect of [the twentieth] century in Kentucky. . . . Those who watched Earle Clements . . . commented frequently on his ability to foresee not only the result of each action but the results of that result."[14]

Clements's approach was subtle. He once reflected that he "always preferred the quiet style of doing things."[15] One GOP rival commented about Clements: "I think he's solved the riddle of politics. Most of us stand in front of the curtains so we can take the bows. Earle stands in back of the curtain so he never gets the blame."[16]

Unlike his nemesis Chandler, who enjoyed a meteoric rise in Kentucky politics, Clements's ascent was steady, gradual, and systematic.[17] Clements followed his father into public life and, in a twenty-year period beginning in 1921, served in turn as deputy sheriff, acting sheriff, clerk, and county judge—a position akin to county executive in other states.[18] Of his time as county judge, Clements observed that there was "no better practical schooling in government than in that office."[19]

In 1927, Clements wed Sara Blue, who worked at a local bank and was the daughter of a prominent county official.[20] The couple had one child, Elizabeth ("Bess"), who shared her father's love of politics.[21] Bess served as an aide to First Lady Lady Bird Johnson and as an executive assistant to Second Lady Joan Mondale when her husband, Walter, was vice president.[22]

Origins of the Clements-Chandler Rivalry

In 1935, an event occurred that would have a far-reaching effect on Clements and the commonwealth. That year, riding a wave of popular acclaim, Lieutenant Governor Chandler sought the Democratic nomination for governor.[23] The incumbent, a fellow Democrat who was ineligible to run because of term limits, had handpicked his successor: Tom Rhea.[24] And Rhea's campaign chairman was a young man named Earle Clements.[25]

Clements and Chandler shared some superficial similarities. Both were intensely ambitious, rising from modest origins. Both were Democrats born in western Kentucky. Both were accomplished athletes in their youth and fine coaches thereafter.[26] Both had a gift for remembering names and faces.[27] Yet, despite their shared backgrounds and attributes, in other ways, the two men could not have been more different.[28] Clements was reserved and methodical, leaving nothing to chance.[29] A reporter said of Clements, he was "as plain as an old shoe."[30] Chandler was the opposite: colorful, extroverted, larger than life. He won elections in large part due to his charisma and zest for campaigning.[31]

Clements was not a great public speaker. One journalist described his orations as "masterpieces of mediocrity."[32] Chandler was nothing if not a captivating orator.[33] By and large, Clements was liberal, Chandler conservative.[34] And, in true Kentucky style, the two carried on a feud that lasted for decades. The Clements-Chandler divide was significant because, for most of the twentieth century, Kentucky had far more registered Democrats than Republicans. That meant it was exceedingly difficult for Republicans to win statewide elections. For the GOP to prevail, the factions of the Democratic Party had to be at each other's throats.

The rivalry between Clements and Chandler would have a profound effect on Kentucky politics, crystalizing the existing factionalism within the state Democratic Party.[35] The result of the 1935 governor's race was that the thirty-seven-year-old Chandler won the Democratic primary over Rhea and was elected to the state's highest office.[36] Possessed of a long memory, Chandler also had a tendency to hold a grudge, and he remembered his opponent Rhea's campaign manager.

Clements's Political Path

After his long tenure in county government, Clements was elected to the state senate in 1941. Once in the legislature, he quickly rose to the position of majority leader. In this capacity, Clements befriended fellow state senator Ernest Ford, father of Wendell, who would later follow in Clements's footsteps. After a brief stint in the US House of Representatives—during which he demonstrated a pro–civil rights record and served alongside a promising young lawmaker from Louisville named Thruston Morton—Clements declared himself a candidate for governor in 1947.[37] For a while that year it looked as if his Republican gubernatorial opponent might in fact be Morton.[38] But Morton wisely decided against running.[39] Clements was overwhelmingly elected the commonwealth's fiftieth governor.[40]

As state chief executive, Clements racked up a number of achievements.[41] He succeeded in part because he drove the legislature relentlessly and was not afraid to play hardball.[42] For important votes, Clements would often go to the house or senate chamber, ominously point his pencil at any legislator voting against him, and make a mental note.[43] During Clements's tenure, the *Louisville Courier-Journal* characterized one legislative session as "the most ruthlessly operated in anyone's memory."[44] But the results were undeniable. Under Clements, New York was the only state to spend more on state parks, and only Texas was more active in road construction.[45] Clements created the modern state police force and the Kentucky park system.[46] He also took steps to help integrate the University of Kentucky.[47]

However, like his rival Chandler (and many other Kentucky governors prior to the mid-1990s), Clements felt confined by the state constitution, which at the time prevented governors from serving consecutive terms. Like Chandler, Clements decided to leave the governor's mansion prior to the end of his term to pursue a seat in the US Senate. In 1950, he was elected to succeed Garrett Withers (D), who had been appointed to fill the vacancy created when Alben Barkley was elected vice president. He easily outpolled Republican Charles I. Dawson in the general election.[48]

Unlike Chandler, who neither enjoyed nor thrived in the Senate, Clements excelled in the upper chamber. He was quickly named chairman of the Democratic Senatorial Campaign Committee (DSCC). The DSCC and its Republican counterpart, the National Republican Senatorial Committee (NRSC), are nongovernmental entities designed to help elect fellow party members to the Senate. (There are similar Republican and Democratic institutions on the House side as well.) Clements served two terms as head of the DSCC and was responsible for the 1952 and the 1954 campaign cycles.[49] The former proved to be a difficult one for Clements and the Democrats, as the Republicans rode Dwight Eisenhower's coattails to take control of both the White House and Congress.[50] The 1954 campaign cycle, however, was an electoral success for Clements and Senate Democrats, who regained control of the upper chamber.[51] Democrats would hold a majority in the Senate until after the 1980 election.

Clements in the Senate and Afterward

Not long after his arrival in the Senate, Clements became an ally of rising star Lyndon Johnson (D-TX).[52] Kentucky's other senator at this time, Virgil Chapman (D), brought Clements and Johnson together, and the two consummate political animals hit it off immediately.[53] The alliance paid dividends for both men. Clements was one of the first to endorse Johnson for Democratic leader.[54] Once the Texan became Democratic floor leader, he helped promote Clements to the number-two post. Clements's rapid elevation to whip was only partly attributable to Johnson's patronage, however. It occurred in large part because Clements maintained good relations with both conservative and liberal Democrats, a particularly important trait in such a closely divided Senate.[55] In the words of two contemporary observers, LBJ promoted the Kentuckian to whip in no small measure "because he . . . wanted to take advantage of Clements' proficiency at the back-room political arts."[56] Once Clements became whip, Johnson elevated the position by making the Kentuckian an ex officio member of the Democratic Steering Committee and providing him with additional staff and office space.[57]

When the Democrats regained control of the Senate majority in 1955, John-

Richard Mentor Johnson. Johnson was an advocate for the downtrodden, but his controversial personal life hampered his national political aspirations. He remains the only vice president chosen by the Senate under the provisions of the Twelfth Amendment. (Oil on canvas by John Neagle, 1843, courtesy of the National Gallery of Art)

Richard Mentor Johnson slaying Tecumseh at the Battle of the Thames, 1813. Whether warranted or not, Johnson was credited with killing the famed Indian chief, which catapulted the Kentuckian to national prominence. (*Battle of the Thames* by John Dorival and Edward Williams Clay, c. 1833, courtesy of the Library of Congress, Prints and Photographs Division, LC-DIG-pga-03613)

Richard Mentor Johnson and Henry Clay. Both men were strong advocates for the War of 1812, and four years later, both supported the controversial "salary grab" legislation benefiting members of Congress. After Clay's alleged "corrupt bargain" with John Quincy Adams, Johnson broke with his fellow Kentuckian. (Graphite on cream textured woven paper by John B. Neagle, 1842–1843, courtesy of the National Portrait Gallery, Smithsonian Institution)

Political cartoon depicting the four-way presidential race in 1860, which broke down largely along sectional lines. Left to right: Abraham Lincoln, Stephen Douglas, John C. Breckinridge, and John Bell. With Douglas and Breckinridge dividing the Democratic vote, the Republican Lincoln emerged victorious. ("Dividing the National Map," c. 1860, courtesy of the Library of Congress, Prints and Photographs Division, LC-DIG-ppmsca-33122)

John C. Breckinridge. After a term as vice president, an unsuccessful presidential run in 1860, and several months as a US senator, Breckinridge left the Union to fight for the South. By the end of the Civil War, he was secretary of war for the Confederacy. (Portrait by Jules Emile Saintin, c. 1860, courtesy of the Library of Congress, Prints and Photographs Division, LC-DIG-pga-03237)

John C. Breckinridge. The Kentuckian was generally regarded as one of the finest orators of his day. (Oil on canvas by Nicola Marschall, 1870–1881, courtesy of The Filson Historical Society)

John Brown. Considered a founding father of Kentucky, Brown was one of the commonwealth's first two senators. (Pastel on paper by James Sharples, c. 1796, courtesy of Liberty Hall Historic Site Collections, Frankfort, KY)

John Brown was twice elected to serve as president pro tempore of the Senate. (Oil on panel by Matthew Harris Jouett, c. 1826, courtesy of Liberty Hall Historic Site Collections, Frankfort, KY)

John Pope. Pope overcame a horrible childhood injury to become president pro tempore of the Senate. At various stages in his career, Pope was a Federalist, a Democratic-Republican, a Jacksonian, and a Whig. (Portrait by Matthew Harris Jouett, c. 1812–1816, courtesy of the Blue Grass Trust for Historic Preservation)

John Breckinridge, founder of Kentucky's greatest political dynasty. (Portrait by Alban Jasper Conant, c. 1863, courtesy of the Department of Justice)

John Breckinridge was a friend of Thomas Jefferson and helped push the controversial Kentucky Resolutions through the state legislature. In the US Senate, Breckinridge was one of Jefferson's chief lieutenants and led legislative efforts to approve the Louisiana Purchase. (Portrait, c. 1800, courtesy of the US Senate Historical Office)

Henry Clay. Clay was the master of high-stakes legislating and is widely con-
sidered one of the greatest senators in history. On three occasions, his efforts in
Congress helped prevent the Union from dissolving. (Oil on canvas by Henry F.
Darby, c. 1858, courtesy of the US Senate Collection)

Despite his tremendous gifts, Clay made a series of epic political blunders that ultimately cost him the presidency. (Oil on canvas by George Peter Alexander Healy, c. 1845, courtesy of the National Portrait Gallery, Smithsonian Institution; on loan in the US Senate Majority Leader's Office, US Capitol)

Political cartoon depicting Clay sewing President Andrew Jackson's mouth shut. A heated rivalry defined the relationship between the two men. ("Symptoms of a Locked Jaw" by David Claypoole Johnston, c. 1834, courtesy of the Library of Congress, Prints and Photographs Division, LC-DIG-ds-00856)

John Crittenden. Crittenden lived in the shadow of his longtime friend
Henry Clay. In later years, the two would have a falling out, but that did not
slow Crittenden's political rise. (Photograph by Mathew B. Brady, c. 1844–
1846, courtesy of the Library of Congress, Prints and Photographs Division,
LC-USZ62-110095)

Crittenden chaired more Senate standing committees than any other Kentuckian and is the only person to serve on two separate occasions as US attorney general. (Photograph by Julian Vannerson, c. 1859, courtesy of the Library of Congress, Prints and Photographs Division, LC-DIG-ppmsca-26755)

As a senator, Crittenden attempted to fashion a last-minute compromise to save the nation from civil war, but his efforts fell short. (Oil on canvas by George Peter Alexander Healy, 1857, courtesy of the National Portrait Gallery, Smithsonian Institution)

John W. Stevenson. As the son of a Speaker of the US House of Representatives, politics was in Stevenson's blood. He represented Kentucky as congressman, governor, and
senator. (Pastel, c. 1910, courtesy of the Kentucky Historical Society, Mary Colston
Collection)

In 1873, Stevenson was elected the first permanent Senate Democratic caucus chairman, an office that would evolve into the Senate floor leader position. (Brady-Handy Photograph Collection, c. 1860–1875, courtesy of the Library of Congress, Prints and Photographs Division, LC-DIG-cwpbh-00148)

James B. Beck. Born in Scotland, Beck immigrated to Kentucky and rose to become Senate Democratic caucus chairman. (Brady-Handy Photograph Collection, c. 1870–1880, courtesy of the Library of Congress, Prints and Photographs Division, LC-DIG-cwpbh-03687)

THE ILLUSTRATED AMERICAN.

VOL. I.   New York.   For the Week Ending MAY 24, 1890.   With Extra Colored Plate.   No. 14
         Chicago.

THE LATE SENATOR JAMES BURNIE BECK, OF KENTUCKY. (See page 515.)

Beck raised the profile of the Senate Democratic caucus chairman position through his policy leadership on tariff and currency issues. (Courtesy of the US Senate Collection)

This stamp was designed to honor Beck after his death in 1890. For reasons that are unclear, naval officer Oliver H. Perry appeared on the stamp instead. (Engraved by G. F. C. Smillie and George U. Rose Jr., 1894, courtesy of the Bureau of Engraving and Printing)

Joseph C. S. Blackburn. One of the most colorful figures of his day, Blackburn was a gifted public speaker and raconteur. His oratory so impressed a visiting Sioux Indian chief that he made Blackburn an honorary member of the tribe and gave him the name "Roaring Wind of the Bluegrass." (Brady-Handy Photograph Collection, c. 1865–1880, courtesy of the Library of Congress, Prints and Photographs Division, LC-DIG-cwpbh-05210)

Blackburn was fiercely protective of his honor and almost fought a duel over who should receive credit for a Kentucky pork-barrel project. He would later serve as Senate Democratic caucus chairman. (Harris & Ewing Collection, c. 1905–1918, courtesy of the Library of Congress, Prints and Photographs Division, LC-DIG-hec-14967)

This portrait of Blackburn was donated by famed political cartoonist and Kentucky native Clifford Berryman to the Kentucky Historical Society in 1939. Blackburn had helped Berryman get his start in Washington decades earlier. (Oil on canvas by Nicholas Richard Brewer, courtesy of the Kentucky Historical Society, Mrs. Clifford K. Berryman Collection)

Alben Barkley, c. 1952. Barkley is one of only two Kentuckians
to serve as Senate majority leader. He played a pivotal role in the
enactment of wartime legislation in the 1940s. (Courtesy of the US
Senate Historical Office)

Alben Barkley (left) and Vice President John Nance Garner. This photograph was taken in 1937, immediately after the Kentuckian had been chosen majority leader in a "nail-biter" election. Just weeks later, Garner would make an important parliamentary ruling that would bolster the power of Senate floor leaders. (Harris & Ewing Collection, courtesy of the Library of Congress, Prints and Photographs Division, LC-DIG-hec-23065)

The Senate chamber in 1939, before the morning prayer. Alben Barkley is standing at the center aisle seat, which twelve years earlier had become the Senate Democratic leader's desk. (Courtesy of the US Senate Historical Office)

Wendell Ford, c. 1974. A protégé of Earle Clements, Ford followed in his footsteps, becoming governor, US senator, and Senate majority whip. (Courtesy of the Ford family)

Three Kentucky icons, 1974. From left to right: University of Kentucky basketball coach Adolph Rupp, Wendell Ford, and Colonel Harland Sanders. (Courtesy of the Ford family)

Earle Clements (seen here riding in a parade in 1949) came to the Senate as an accomplished governor. He rose quickly as Senator Lyndon B. Johnson's lieutenant. (Courtesy of the Kentucky Digital Library, James Edwin "Ed" Weddle Photographic Collection)

Earle Clements, 1950. Unlike his rival A. B. "Happy" Chandler, Clements eschewed theatrics and was the consummate insider. Clements's feud with Chandler ultimately cost him his Senate seat. (Courtesy of the Kentucky Digital Library, James Edwin "Ed" Weddle Photographic Collection)

A. B. "Happy" Chandler. The Kentuckian was a successful governor and later commissioner of baseball when Jackie Robinson integrated the sport. Chandler's political standing in Kentucky allowed him to play a major role in several Senate races, including the 1956 contest when Thruston Morton defeated Earle Clements. (Courtesy of the National Baseball Hall of Fame and Museum)

Thruston Morton (left) conferring with his colleague and friend, Senate majority leader Lyndon Johnson, c. 1960. Morton was a prominent political figure in the 1950s and 1960s and was often mentioned as a potential Senate floor leader or vice-presidential candidate. (Courtesy of the US Senate Historical Office)

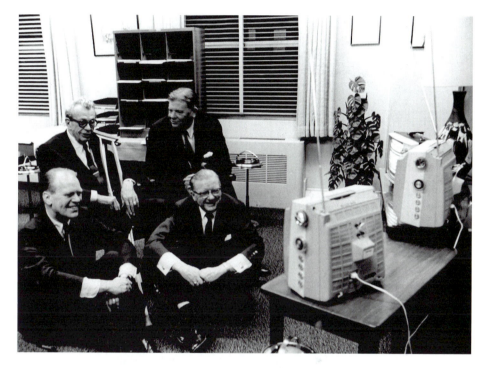

Thruston Morton (top right) with House minority leader Gerald Ford (bottom left); Morton's sometime rival, Senate minority leader Everett Dirksen (top left); and Republican National Committee chairman Ray Bliss (bottom right). They are watching the 1966 midterm election results, which made for a good night for the GOP. Morton was a savvy campaigner who served as head of the Republican National Committee and later as chairman of the National Republican Senatorial Committee. (Courtesy of the Gerald R. Ford Presidential Library)

John Sherman Cooper, c. 1950. His long and distinguished Senate career was interspersed with important diplomatic assignments. (Courtesy of the US Senate Historical Office)

The lead author (right), then a county judge executive, sitting next to his role model, John Sherman Cooper, at the 1979 announcement of Louie Nunn's candidacy for governor. (Courtesy of the McConnell Chao Archives)

John Sherman Cooper (center) with his Democratic cohort, Senator Frank Church of Idaho (right), c. 1971. Although he was neither chairman nor ranking member of the Senate Foreign Relations Committee, Cooper became a Senate leader in the bipartisan effort to restrict US military involvement in Southeast Asia. (Courtesy of the Boise State University Library)

The lead author in 2017, watching a Senate debate on television in his US Capitol office, flanked by portraits of Senators Alben Barkley and John Sherman Cooper. (Courtesy of the McConnell Chao Archives)

son became majority leader and Clements majority whip. They made an effective team, with Clements's low-key style serving as a welcome respite from LBJ's hard-charging approach. Lady Bird Johnson recalled that Clements "could appeal to members of the Senate that might be turned off by Lyndon sometimes."[58]

As whip, Clements was not a sentimentalist; he was clinical in his approach. In the mid-1950s, journalist William S. White wrote that Clements "looks at every political question with the aseptic objectivity of a surgeon's glance."[59] Former Johnson aide Harry McPherson sketched a vignette of Clements that reflected the same political realism: "[Clements was a] pol's pol. Back-room man, an embracer, an understander. I'm not sure whether he smoked or not, but I saw him as a George Bellows character in a room full of cigar haze and jousting laughter. He was aggressive and effective as Johnson's whip; not a 'modern' politician with an orientation toward issues and PR, but a professional who understood the play of traditional political forces—labor, farmers, and so on."[60]

Clements's tenure as whip under Johnson was sometimes difficult. The Kentuckian was called on to assist in a number of sensitive tasks, such as sanctioning fellow senator Joe McCarthy (R-WI).[61] Johnson's demanding nature did not make the whip job any easier. Clements's responsibilities grew even weightier in July 1955, when LBJ suffered a heart attack.[62] This left Senate Democrats without a true majority leader for the last few weeks of the session.[63] For the next twenty-nine days, Clements stepped into the breach and served as acting majority leader.[64] During this period, the Kentuckian had to lead the Senate without appearing to be a usurper in LBJ's absence—a difficult balance to strike. And even from his hospital bed at Bethesda Medical Center, Johnson remained an exacting taskmaster.[65] After visiting the Texan, Clements conveyed the majority leader's views on a particular piece of legislation, telling his fellow partisans, Johnson "would like the bill taken up yesterday and passed the day before yesterday."[66]

Interestingly, one of the tasks Clements performed for Johnson during his convalescence involved promoting an appreciation of the Senate as an institution. It had been Johnson's brainchild to establish a special panel to select the five greatest senators ever.[67] With the majority leader ailing, Clements and minority leader William Knowland (R-CA) put forward the resolution authorizing the committee.[68] Despite many challenges during Johnson's month-long absence, Clements held the fragile Democratic majority together until adjournment.[69] His efforts garnered favorable reviews.[70]

The year 1955 was an important one for Clements not only because of his work as acting majority leader but also because his old rival Happy Chandler was running for governor again, twenty years after first winning the office. Though he spent much of his time in Washington, Clements remained a power broker in Kentucky as head of one of the state Democratic Party's dueling factions. As such, Clements vigorously opposed Chandler's campaign.[71] Clements and his ally, incumbent Democratic governor Lawrence Wetherby, handpicked Bert Combs to oppose the popular former governor.[72] Chandler gleefully trained his fire on Combs's benefactors, derisively calling them "Clementine and Wetherbine."[73]

It was a vigorously contested race. Ultimately, Chandler prevailed behind the slogan "Be like your pappy and vote for Happy."[74] The next year, the shoe was on the other foot. Governor Chandler held the reins of state government, and Clements was before the voters.[75] Chandler was decidedly *un*happy about the prospect of Clements serving another term in the Senate. He was looking for payback.[76] He wanted to defeat Clements.[77]

As a key member of Senate leadership from an overwhelmingly Democratic state, many observers expected Clements to win reelection handily.[78] But they failed to account for a number of factors, even aside from Chandler. One was Republican president Dwight Eisenhower, who was also up for reelection in 1956 and carried Kentucky that year.[79] Another challenge was the caliber of Clements's opponent, his former House colleague Thruston Morton. To top it all off, Clements faced the bane of all legislators seeking reelection: a tough vote in the chamber.[80]

In 1956, Johnson was pressing the Senate to expand the Social Security program to include benefits for the disabled.[81] This was a difficult issue in Kentucky, given strong opposition from the state's doctors.[82] Clements had initially committed to opposing the legislation.[83] But when LBJ found himself one vote short of securing passage of the measure, Clements—ever the good soldier—reversed himself and cast the deciding vote in favor of the bill.[84]

Clements's predicament illustrates a dilemma for those in Senate leadership: they serve two constituencies—their home states and their fellow senators—and sometimes those interests collide. During an election year, such a Hobson's choice can be particularly difficult. The combination of Happy, Ike, Thruston, and the Social Security vote proved too much for Clements; he lost in a tight race, the only electoral defeat in his thirty-six-year public career. And considering Johnson's elevation to the vice presidency in 1960, Clements may have lost more than his Senate seat; he may have lost the opportunity to become majority leader.[85] Instead, Clements's successor as majority whip, Mike Mansfield (D-MT), assumed floor leadership following LBJ's departure from the Senate.[86] The man from Morganfield would not seek elective office again.[87]

Clements was far from done with politics, however. When his Senate term ended in 1957, Johnson promptly appointed him executive director of the DSCC, much to the irritation of Chandler.[88] As executive director of the organization he used to oversee, Clements enjoyed a measure of redemption. In the 1958 midterm elections, the Senate Democrats gained sixteen seats—going from forty-nine to sixty-five—representing the largest net gain for any party in the history of the Senate, outside of the unique circumstances of Reconstruction.[89] In addition, Clements assisted Johnson in his presidential run in 1959 and 1960.[90]

The next year, Clements got a measure of revenge in Kentucky when his favored candidate for governor, the previously defeated Bert Combs, bested Chandler's proxy in the Democratic primary.[91] The Clements-Chandler feud lived on. Following Combs's election, Clements returned to Kentucky, where he served as state highway commissioner, a powerful patronage position at the time. His tenure ended in controversy, however, related to irregularities stemming from the leasing of trucks to the state.[92]

Afterward, Clements embarked on a successful lobbying career in Washington on behalf of the maritime industry and tobacco interests.[93] In addition, he served as an unofficial political adviser to rising political star Wendell Ford. After a long period of ill health, Clements passed away in 1985 in Morganfield.[94]

The rivalry between Chandler and Clements is significant at the state level because it defined Kentucky politics for nearly thirty years.[95] The rivalry is also important because it reflected the turning point in the career of two men of national stature.[96] It ended the Senate career of Clements and marked the beginning of Thruston Morton's.

History of the Senate Party Campaign Committee

The history of party campaign committees dates to the nineteenth century, though the precise origins are murky.[97] An early form of national party organization—a Committee of Correspondence—was established for the Democratic-Republican Party when James Madison was president.[98] Kentucky's John Pope was active in this entity (see chapter 2). It was not until the 1840s that national parties as formal, permanent entities first came into being.[99] Their focus was on choosing and electing presidential candidates.[100] At the time, congressional races were seen as local affairs rather than national concerns.[101] Congressional candidates factored into the national party calculus only to the extent that the presidential nominee and the national party worked implicitly toward electing the full complement of party candidates.[102] Even so, the party's message was crafted and driven by its presidential nominee and national convention delegates, with generally little input from members of Congress and still less, one suspects, from congressional challengers.[103]

The exact date of origin of congressional campaign committees is uncertain. Nonetheless, it appears that new ground was broken in 1860,[104] when a Republican Party organization called the Executive Congressional Committee was established.[105] Senator Preston King (R-NY) was placed in charge of this entity, which circulated political material with an eye toward promoting the electoral fortunes of Republican House candidates.[106]

In 1864, Republican Abraham Lincoln and War Democrat Andrew Johnson were elected president and vice president on the Union Party ticket. Johnson succeeded to the presidency following Lincoln's assassination in 1865, and in short order, he and the Republican Congress clashed over Reconstruction policy for the defeated South.[107] This battle culminated in Johnson's impeachment and narrow acquittal in 1868.

By 1866, House Republicans had recognized that their political interests differed markedly from those of the president.[108] As a result, they decided to establish more clearly a national political arm to support candidates who reflected their own priorities.[109] Interestingly, this new campaign entity—called the Republican Congressional Committee—was located in Washington, even though the Republican National Committee (RNC) was centered in New York City, a situation that continued for decades after the Civil War.[110]

From the first, the chairmanship of the congressional campaign committee was seen as a position of party leadership.[111] Members assuming such responsibilities were looked upon with favor by their fellow partisans in Congress.[112] As illustrated by the establishment of other congressional leadership posts (e.g., floor leaders, whips), one party's successful innovation is often emulated by the other side.[113] Such was apparently the case when House Democrats established for themselves a national congressional campaign committee in the late 1860s.[114] Such an entity may have existed as early as 1866, but it was almost certainly in place by 1868.[115]

As Professor Robin Kolodny has observed, one of the benefits of congressional campaign committees is that they "provide important econom[ies] of scale for incumbents and challengers regarding Washington resources."[116] In the beginning, such assistance included the scheduling of speakers of major stature to aid candidates, the compilation of campaign materials with a nationwide focus, and assistance with media needs.[117]

It should be remembered that, until the Seventeenth Amendment was ratified in 1913, senators were chosen by state legislatures and not directly elected. In that regard, Senate races were different from House contests.[118] As a result, Senate-specific campaign committees did not come into being until around the time of World War I.[119] Nevertheless, senators frequently chaired the congressional campaign committees.[120] This was the case because senators were often political bosses in their home states and had great influence over who was nominated from their party to run for the House.[121] Seen in this light, it is not surprising that notable senators such as Arthur Pue Gorman (D-MD) and Zachariah Chandler (R-MI) filled the post of congressional campaign chairman in the first decades of these committees' operation.[122] Nonetheless, for reasons that are unclear, senatorial leadership of the Republican campaign committee ended abruptly in 1878.[123] The same occurred with respect to the Democratic campaign committee after 1890.[124]

Not long after the popular election of senators began in 1914, the need for separate Senate and House campaign entities became manifest.[125] The NRSC, largely the handiwork of future Senate minority leader Charles McNary (R-OR), was reportedly created in 1919.[126] The DSCC was apparently launched due to the efforts of Senator Key Pittman (D-NV).[127] The date of origin for the Democratic operation is uncertain, but it could have been as early as 1918.[128] As one might expect, in the early decades of the Senate campaign committees, they assembled background information on opposing candidates, drafted campaign literature for fellow partisans, and allocated monies to Senate aspirants.[129]

Almost from the start, heading the Senate campaign committee was considered an important post. A DSCC press statement from the 1930s referred to the position as part "of the Democratic high command."[130] The role, however, was not all consuming. Three chairmen—J. Hamilton Lewis (D-IL), Scott Lucas (D-IL), and Clements—served as DSCC chairman and party whip simultaneously.[131] Perhaps pulling double duty was possible because the DSCC's autonomy was limited, given that the Democratic National Committee (DNC) made the DSCC's funding decisions as late as 1950.[132]

It has been a long-standing tradition that lawmakers do not lead the Senate campaign committee when they are up for reelection themselves.[133] The rationale is twofold. First, senators who are running for reelection have enough on their plates campaign-wise. Second, the chairman needs to be viewed as dispassionate in terms of how resources are allocated. A senator could be put in an awkward position if his own campaign needs funding.[134] Yet, there have been exceptions to this informal rule. George Smathers (D-FL) was apparently the first to run for reelection and chair his party's campaign committee during the same cycle.[135] Kentucky's Wendell Ford was another.[136] In Ford's case, he was chosen because the Senate Democratic leadership opposed the other potential candidate, Howard Metzenbaum (D-OH).[137]

The Cross Pressures of Heading a Campaign Committee

Over the years, campaign chairmen have faced some recurring challenges. One involves the allocation of resources. Is the overriding goal of the chairman to reelect incumbents or to elect new members?[138] Incumbent lawmakers who are up for reelection never have enough resources, so they constantly seek assistance from the national campaign committee. At the same time, the committee chairman feels an overriding need to expand the party's membership. This sentiment is particularly acute if the party in question does not hold a majority in the Senate.[139] In this situation, focusing too much on protecting incumbents may prevent the party from gaining control of the chamber.

* * *

I faced these pressures during my tenure as head of the NRSC. One reform I instituted, which remains in place, was to eliminate what had become an entitlement for incumbents up for reelection. It had long been the custom for the NRSC to provide each incumbent with the maximum permissible amount from the committee. Given finite resources, I saw no need to invest in landslides or lost causes. Not surprisingly, many of my colleagues who were running for reelection were not happy with me.

The answer to the age-old incumbent-challenger dilemma is driven largely by the political context. One factor to consider is how many seats the party has to defend. Pursuant to Article I, section 3, of the Constitution, only about one-third of Senate seats are contested in any election cycle. Sometimes this means that one party has a disproportionately large number of incumbents up for reelection, in which case an "incumbent protection" approach might make the most sense. Conversely, if the opposite party is defending a large number of seats, it may be wiser to be more aggressive in trying to elect new members. I caution NRSC chairmen "not to fall in love with the map." In other words, our side should not get complacent; just because the other party is defending more seats than we are does not guarantee that our party will automatically make gains. Other key considerations include the following: What is the overall political climate? Are we the "in" party (in control of the White House and Congress) or the "out" party? Are the party's brand and policy initiatives viewed favorably by the electorate? Have we recruited good candidates? Have we raised sufficient funds? These concerns—as well as the number of seats the party is defending—factor into the overall equation.

* * *

As the political landscape has changed, the party campaign committees have evolved to meet new challenges. Technological advances are one example. For instance, in the 1950s and 1960s, the NRSC began to put together radio and television segments for Republican senators up for reelection.[140] Nonetheless, staff levels remained low throughout the period, often ranging between three and five full-time employees.[141] This reflected the committees' comparatively small workload at the time. Indeed, the DSCC did not begin to operate year-round until 1952.[142]

In the 1960s and early 1970s, two developments fundamentally changed the nature of Senate campaigns. The first was the rise of television advertising.[143] The need for candidates to buy airtime to advertise dramatically increased the cost of political campaigns. The second development was the adoption of campaign finance legislation.[144] These measures dramatically altered the role of the campaign committees.[145] Prior to adoption of these laws, the distribution of campaign funds was not one of the fundamental goals of the committees.[146] That soon changed. In addition, the campaign finance laws gave the Senate and House campaign committees greater independence from the RNC and DNC.[147]

* * *

With everything senators have going on, it seems reasonable to ask, why would a lawmaker want to be campaign chairman? There are several reasons. First, it places a senator within his party's leadership structure alongside the party leader and the whip. Second, it can be a good stepping-stone.[148] Assisting colleagues with their campaigns often means earning chits for the future for the chairman. Third, a senator serving as chairman has the opportunity to demonstrate his skill not only to those running for the Senate but also to the rest of his party conference.

In my case, I wanted to pursue Senate leadership. At the same time, I enjoy the thrust and parry of campaigning. Heading the NRSC seemed like a good fit for me. Other campaign chairmen before and after me have later become majority leader or minority leader. One example was George Mitchell (D-ME). The Washington Post *reported that Mitchell "became an overnight Democratic hero when he led the 1986 campaign that resulted in his party regaining Senate control."[149] By 1989, he was majority leader.[150] Others who have moved "up the ladder" to party leader after having served as party campaign chairman include Chuck Schumer (D-NY), Lucas, Everett Dirksen (R-IL), and McNary.[151] In addition, success as campaign chairman can help a senator move up to another leadership post or secure a powerful committee chairmanship.[152] In my case, I believe it helped me to become whip and, ultimately, party leader.*

It is my experience that being party campaign chairman is like being the quarterback on a football team. You get too much credit when you win (in good election cycles) and too much blame when you lose (in bad election cycles). While managing a successful election cycle can raise one's stock, a poor cycle can jeopardize it. When I led the NRSC in 2000, Republicans lost five Senate seats. I thought I had done the best job possible under the circumstances, but I remained apprehensive for some months afterward that this bad cycle might harm my prospects of becoming Senate Republican leader.

Perhaps I am biased in this regard, but judging a party campaign chairman's performance solely on wins and losses can be misleading. Each campaign cycle is different, and each campaign is different. Some campaigns may turn on national themes and some on local concerns. And, of course, the candidates themselves have a great deal to do with the outcome of their races.

In addition to aiding one's climb up the Senate leadership ladder, being campaign chairman can help a future presidential run by raising a senator's national profile and establishing important relationships with party loyalists and donors.[153] This was the case with Phil Gramm (R-TX), Barry Goldwater (R-AZ), Chuck Robb (D-VA), John Kerry (D-MA), Bob Kerrey (D-NE), and Ed Muskie (D-ME).[154]

One dynamic that seems to vary is party leader involvement in the campaign committee. When I chaired the NRSC, Trent Lott (R-MS), the majority leader at the time, basically left matters up to me. My impression is that majority leader Bill Frist (R-TN) took a similar, largely hands-off approach to the committee. By contrast, I have been closely involved in NRSC operations since becoming party leader. As noted, I enjoy the "give-and-take" of campaigning and the challenge of trying to elect more Republicans to the Senate. It is very much in my interest to take an active role in the NRSC. I do not view it as a burden.

Serving as campaign chairman is challenging. One particularly difficult aspect of the job is recruitment. Sometimes you get the candidate you want, but he or she goes bust. Sometimes you get a candidate who was not your first choice, but he or she turns out to be a very effective campaigner.

A large part of serving as party campaign chairman is fund-raising. A second reform I instituted at the NRSC that remains in place is urging senators to contribute their own campaign funds to the committee. This can be a tough sell. Fund-raising is arduous and time-consuming, so members tend to be protective of their own war chests. Giving away a big chunk of that money is not exactly the first thing that comes to mind for many lawmakers. Even if they are not in cycle, members do not want to donate large portions of their campaign funds only to wind up with shortfalls in their own races. One tactic I have used as leader is to assemble my party colleagues in a room at the NRSC, lock the door, make a big pledge myself, and then tell the group that we are not leaving until we meet our goal. Silence and peer pressure can sometimes work wonders.

Another aspect of the job of campaign chairman is dispensing advice to the various campaigns. Sometimes that advice is welcomed, and sometimes it is not. At the end of the day, each candidate runs his or her own campaign.

* * *

Another dynamic at play is the relationship between the White House and members of the president's party. On occasion, institutional tension flares up between the campaign chairman and the president, even though they are fellow partisans. Indeed, differing interests led to the creation of the congressional campaign committees in the first place. Once in a while, this friction has been aired publicly.

In the early 1980s, NRSC chairman Bob Packwood (R-OR) publicly criticized President Ronald Reagan.[155] He declared that Reagan's "idealized concept of America" made it more difficult for the GOP to garner support from women and minorities.[156] Immediately, Packwood was pressured to express regret, but the Oregonian never fully repudiated his remark, leading to the administration's effort to sack him.[157] In addition, the White House refused to permit the NRSC to go forward with a fund-raising appeal under the president's signature.[158] Senate majority leader Howard Baker (R-TN) refused to take steps against Packwood.[159] Baker and the White House agreed to a rapprochement of sorts, and Packwood completed the campaign cycle.[160] However, the White House urged Richard Lugar (R-IN) to challenge Packwood for NRSC chairman in the next election cycle, and Lugar prevailed in a tight race.[161] The Packwood episode reflects yet again that Senate leadership is *Senate* leadership. The views of a president of the same party are highly influential but not necessarily dispositive.

A similar incident happened on the House side in 1990. At the urging of adviser Ed Rollins, National Republican Congressional Committee chairman Guy Vander Jagt (R-MI) distributed a strategy document urging House Republicans to distance themselves from President George H. W. Bush's failure to uphold his promise not to raise taxes.[162] Bush called for Rollins to be dismissed, but Vander Jagt refused.[163] Unlike Packwood, Vander Jagt was reelected head of the campaign committee in the fall.[164]

Thruston Morton

Born in 1907, Thruston Ballard Morton was the scion of a wealthy Louisville family.[165] His father, David Cummins Morton, was a doctor.[166] The family of his mother, Mary Ballard, had made its fortune through flour milling.[167] The family emphasized public service.[168] Morton's maternal grandfather, S. Thruston Ballard, served as lieutenant governor of the commonwealth.[169] At age eleven, his grandfather appointed young Thruston to be a page in the state legislature.[170]

Morton was educated in public schools in the Louisville area before enrolling at an elite prep school in Virginia.[171] He then attended Yale, where he lettered in rowing before earning his diploma in 1929.[172] Morton was an intelligent, urbane young man with a sly sense of humor—traits that would mark his career.[173] After graduation, Morton returned to Kentucky and rose quickly in the family business, Ballard & Ballard Flour Milling, ultimately becoming its president.[174] In 1931, he wed Belle Clay Lyons, a union that would produce two children, Thruston B. Jr. and Clay Lyons Morton.[175]

Twelve years after Morton began working at Ballard & Ballard, the United States became engulfed in World War II following Japan's attack on Pearl Harbor.[176] Morton enlisted in the navy in 1941, ultimately rising to become a lieutenant commander.[177] During the war, most of Morton's duties were aboard minesweeper vessels.[178] Upon his return from the conflict, Morton was drawn to public life. After years of Democratic control of the White House and Congress, and with the Depression and the war behind them, the American people were in the mood for a change. Morton recognized that 1946 would be a good year for the GOP, and he ran for a seat in the US House of Representatives. Looking back, Morton remarked mordantly, "Anybody that had run on the Republican ticket without a jail record would have" won the race.[179] He had no jail record and was duly elected.

His first campaign was not without its mishaps, however. The year 1946 marked the implementation of voting machines in Kentucky, which were operated with hand-pulled levers.[180] There was some concern that this new technology might confuse voters, who were used to paper ballots.[181] At one rally, a Morton supporter who was explaining how to use the machines informed the crowd: "Pull the lever! Sending Mr. Morton to Congress is just as easy as flushing your own toilet."[182]

In 1947, Morton arrived in Washington to take his seat in the House. His maiden speech would be notable, but not for its subject matter.[183] Two journalists described the scene: "Attendance was low, interest lower. The subject was a bill on disposal of the government's surplus rubber plants. Fellow Republicans gossiped with each other. But [one lawmaker] carefully listened and then rose to commend Morton and pledge his support on the point at issue. It was a kindness Morton never forgot."[184] That fellow House member was a Texas Democrat by the name of Lyndon Baines Johnson.[185] Despite the partisan divide, the two men would become friends.[186]

As a House member, Morton supported President Harry Truman's foreign policy measures as well as antilynching legislation.[187] In 1952, after three terms, Morton decided he was through with the House but not with politics. He was the only Kentucky delegate to back General Dwight Eisenhower at the 1952 Republican National Convention.[188] That year, he also ran the successful Senate campaign of his friend and fellow Republican John Sherman Cooper.[189] After his election as president, Eisenhower acknowledged Morton's support by asking him to serve as assistant secretary of state for congressional relations.[190] Morton accepted and held that position from 1953 to 1956, advocating for the president's foreign policy agenda on Capitol Hill.[191]

Following Morton's tenure at the State Department, Eisenhower again reached out to him. This time, the president requested that Morton run against Senator Clements, in the hope that the Republicans could retake the majority after the 1956 election.[192] Morton agreed to throw his hat in the ring. Ike's strong support was vital to Morton's race. Throughout the campaign, Morton brandished an endorsement letter from the popular Eisenhower.[193] The president had written: "You have not only earned the profound respect of your colleagues throughout the Executive Branch, you have confirmed the high regard of those members of Congress with whom you served."[194]

Morton was the direct beneficiary of the Chandler-Clements feud, and he was aided by the political acumen of his campaign chairman, Louie Nunn, who would later serve as Kentucky's governor.[195] Perhaps most important of all, Morton was an effective campaigner. One-on-one and in small groups, he was engaging and often displayed disarming candor.[196] He was a good stump speaker.[197] In addition, he was bright and affable.[198] And he had a self-deprecating sense of humor. Years later, Morton—the sophisticated, East Coast–educated, former State Department official from Louisville—would tell audiences that he had plenty to learn about running for statewide office in 1956: "As a Member of the House I had represented a district which was strictly metropolitan. I had, for example, no problems with agriculture—my greatest agricultural problem as a Congressman was finding some flower seeds for the window boxes!"[199] Morton's use of humor, as well as his penchant for relating anecdotes, made him a lively candidate on the stump and contributed to his being dubbed "Alben Barkley in a Brooks Brothers suit."[200]

The race against Clements was tight—so tight, in fact, that around 6:00 on election night, Morton was heard to say, "I'm licked."[201] He went to bed at 2:30 a.m., not knowing the outcome.[202] The next morning, the *Louisville Courier-Journal*'s headline blared: "Clements Leads Morton."[203] However, thanks in large part to Chandler's support, Eisenhower's popularity, Clements's tough vote on Social Security, and his own skills out on the hustings, Morton defeated the Democratic incumbent—by fewer than 7,000 votes.[204]

Morton in the Senate

"Landslide Morton" arrived in the Senate enjoying the prestige of his much-publicized defeat of the influential Clements, his close bond with Eisenhower, and his prior relationship with many lawmakers from his days at the State Department.[205] The Louisvillian was placed on the Senate Post Office and Civil Service Committee, where, given his ties with the Eisenhower administration, it soon became clear that he would play a major role in distributing federal patronage in the state.[206] Morton also secured a seat on the prestigious Finance Committee.[207]

Like Clements, Morton rose quickly in stature in the Senate and transcended his party's conservative-liberal divide. Because of his ability to earn the respect and admiration of Republicans regardless of ideology, he was mentioned throughout the 1960s as a possible presidential or vice-presidential candidate or a potential Senate Republican leader.[208]

In the upper chamber, Morton's State Department background enabled him to be a forceful defender of Eisenhower's foreign policy.[209] For instance, he was an ardent supporter of the president's response to the Suez crisis.[210] In this instance, he publicly crossed swords with the future chairman of the Foreign Relations Committee, J. William Fulbright (D-AR).[211] Morton was not a rubber stamp for Eisenhower, however. For instance, he demonstrated independence by breaking with the president on budgetary matters during his first months in office, believing that the president's proposed plan did not sufficiently reduce federal spending.[212]

The Louisvillian established a commendable record on civil rights. At a time when vocal elements in the commonwealth were opposed to such measures, Morton voted in favor of both the 1957 and the 1960 Civil Rights Acts, which had been promoted by the Eisenhower administration.[213] Morton stated at the time: "Equality of rights and opportunities has not been fully achieved in the long period since the Fourteenth and Fifteenth Amendments to the Constitution were adopted and this inequality and lack of opportunity and the racial tensions which they engender are not of character with the spirit of a nation pledged to freedom and justice."[214] Later, he supported the 1964 Civil Rights Act, the 1965 Voting Rights Act, and the 1968 Civil Rights Act.[215] He was also a longtime board member of the Lincoln Institute, a Kentucky educational institution for African American students headed by Whitney Young Sr.[216]

For all his urbanity, Morton could display a quick temper. During the southern Democratic filibuster over what became the Civil Rights Act of 1960, Wayne Morse (D-OR) ostentatiously went to the Senate floor and tried to deposit a partisan cloture petition on the clerk's desk to end the filibuster.[217] Denied permission to do so, Morse made a show of leaving the petition with the clerk anyway, in violation of Senate rules.[218] This brazen action infuriated Morton, who grabbed the petition, ripped it up, and flung the remnants into a Senate spittoon.[219] He bellowed at Morse: "Censure me if you will! Do what you will. But if we're going to get this thing solved, we must leave partisan politics out of it."[220]

Morton and Party Politics

In 1959, Eisenhower approached Morton with yet another request: would he head the RNC?[221] Morton replied in jocular fashion: "Mr. President, you must be at the bottom of the barrel if you're asking me."[222] Eisenhower did Morton one better and retorted: "You're damn right I am."[223] All jesting aside, Ike thought very highly of Morton, confiding to his diary that the Kentuckian had "the qualifications" to one day be president.[224] In this instance, the former general chose Morton in the hopes of improving the relationship between the RNC and congressional Republicans.[225] Ike reasoned that if the RNC were headed by a member of Congress, this would help bridge the divide.[226] Morton accepted the position and headed the RNC from 1959 to 1961. A decade later, Rogers Morton, Thruston's younger brother, would hold the same position.

As head of the RNC, Morton was the public face of the party and one of its chief fund-raisers and organizers. It was a challenging period for Republicans, as they had been crushed in the 1958 midterm elections.[227] Nevertheless, Morton was hailed at the time as "the best rounded national chairman [the Republicans] have had in years."[228] In this role, Morton was a prodigious fund-raiser.[229] He also proved to be a hard-hitting partisan. The Kentuckian was known to say in the context of political campaigns: "In this game you've got to hit. I've made a lot of rough statements. But if [as a candidate] you don't say it strongly, you [will] wind up in the want ads. If you don't make the editor put it in the front page, hell, there's no use in saying it."[230]

Morton's performance in the Senate and at the RNC impressed party loyalists to such an extent that his name was floated as a vice-presidential nominee in 1960.[231] He would remain a potential candidate for national office for several years to come.[232] Despite garnering significant support, Morton was ultimately passed over by presidential nominee Richard Nixon, who selected former Massachusetts senator Henry Cabot Lodge Jr.

The 1962 Senate Race and the NRSC

Morton's take-no-prisoners approach to campaigning was on full display in 1962, when Kentucky Democrats nominated the liberal lieutenant governor Wilson Wyatt to challenge him.[233] Throughout the campaign, Morton hammered Wyatt on his left-of-center ties and won reelection to the Senate.[234] On the campaign trail, he was rightly termed a "gut fighter."[235] Wendell Ford later reflected, "Morton was just a better politician than" Wyatt.[236]

The race drew national attention. President John F. Kennedy made two stops in Kentucky that October to speak in favor of the Democratic candidate.[237] Former president Harry Truman did so as well.[238] Morton rolled out some heavy political artillery of his own. Eisenhower made two speeches in the commonwealth extolling him.[239]

* * *

A prominent Republican senator also made a few appearances in Kentucky that autumn, including one in which he expressed support for Morton.[240] That Republi-

can was Barry Goldwater, who was head of the NRSC at the time. I remember this well because I was president of the College Republicans at the University of Louisville, and I had invited Goldwater to speak at the university. The senator accepted my invitation, and I had the honor of introducing him at the official event that day.

As a twenty-year-old college student, I had naïvely assumed that Goldwater accepted simply because he wanted to speak at the University of Louisville. I am a bit older and wiser now. In retrospect, Goldwater's speech sounded suspiciously like he was laying the groundwork for a presidential run in 1964, which is exactly what he did.

In that 1962 Senate race, Morton's success was attributable to more than just his bare-knuckled political instincts and the assistance of Goldwater. Once again, he got a helping hand from "Happy" Chandler, who was positioning himself for yet another run for the governor's mansion in 1963.[241] Albert Benjamin Chandler chose as his motto "ABC in '63."[242] The two-time governor clearly believed he could aid his own cause by helping Morton.[243] I remember: the connection was not subtle. In some counties, the Chandler and Morton campaign offices were right next to each other. The irony is that Chandler helped get Morton elected but fell short in his own race the next year, losing in the Democratic primary to Ned Breathitt.

I can tell you from personal experience that the Clements-Chandler factionalism influenced all levels of Kentucky politics during this period, not just US Senate races. In the spring of 1966, I was a law student at the University of Kentucky and was running for president of the Student Bar Association. At the time, campaigning as a Louisville Republican on the campus of the University of Kentucky was not an enviable position to be in. I decided to emulate the approach taken by Morton and form a coalition of Republicans and pro-Chandler Democrats. Like Morton, I was able to win my election that way. How did I know who the Chandler Democrats were? It was not hard to figure out: I just approached all my Democratic classmates who did not have part-time jobs in the Breathitt administration.

Morton won reelection in 1962 by more than 43,000 votes, which eventually made him the first GOP senator from the commonwealth to complete back-to-back six-year terms.[244] The year after his reelection, Morton was tapped to succeed Goldwater as head of the NRSC. Under Morton's tenure, the Senate GOP lost two seats in 1964 but picked up four in 1966.[245]

The Kentuckian developed four criteria for evaluating what made a good Senate candidate. In his own words: "The first is the candidate—he must be articulate and obviously of Senate caliber. The second is issues—carefully selected and developed. The third is organization—the personal following supplemented by the regular party structure. Fourth is financing—and you start it early."[246] Morton's rules ring as true now as they did in 1969 when he wrote them.

* * *

Morton's Continued Rise in the Chamber and Subsequent Departure

Morton was not just a force in the Senate on the campaign side of things. As the 1960s wore on, he played an important policy role as well, especially in foreign affairs. He remained an advocate of foreign aid during the Kennedy administration.[247] He supported Kennedy's free-trade legislation and the nuclear test ban treaty.[248] At the same time, Morton faulted the president for other aspects of his overseas policy, such as the Bay of Pigs debacle and his posture regarding the turmoil in the Congo.[249]

His expertise in foreign affairs also provided an opening to challenge the standing of Senate minority leader Everett Dirksen.[250] By the middle of the decade, Morton had grown frustrated with the Republican position on the war in Southeast Asia, which he viewed as unimaginative.[251] In 1966, the Republican candidate for US Senate in Illinois, Charles Percy, proposed an "all-Asian peace conference" to attempt to resolve the conflict.[252] Dirksen opposed this idea at first, but Morton doggedly appealed to his fellow Republican senators to support the proposal.[253] Morton also persuaded former vice president Nixon to openly support the idea.[254] Having done the political legwork, Morton then presented Dirksen with a fait accompli at a gathering of Republican officeholders.[255] The GOP conference officially embraced the proposal, and Dirksen was forced to publicly unveil the party's decision.[256]

In 1967, Morton outmaneuvered Dirksen on two other occasions. First, the Kentuckian emerged as the key figure in getting the US-Soviet consular treaty approved by the Senate.[257] The Johnson administration had been hesitant to pursue the agreement due to the all-consuming nature of the Southeast Asian conflict.[258] Dirksen was publicly against the treaty.[259] But Morton thought the measure made sense; he believed it would help enhance American intelligence-gathering activities within the Soviet Union and improve security for US citizens traveling within the USSR.[260] Initially, he persuaded former president Eisenhower to embrace the treaty publicly, which removed a great deal of potential partisanship from the equation.[261] Then Morton used his knowledge of the subject matter and his reputation as a former senior State Department official to convince nearly two-thirds of his fellow Republican senators to favor the pact, forcing Dirksen to reverse course.[262] Once Morton had secured strong Republican support, he prodded his old friend President Johnson to weigh in with Senate Democrats.[263] LBJ obliged, and ultimately, the Senate gave its advice and consent to the treaty.[264]

* * *

Morton's success reflects how power in the Senate can fluctuate, depending on circumstances. Through a combination of timing, tenacity, policy expertise, political acumen, and individual standing within the chamber, an individual senator—even one in the minority party—can, on occasion, seize an issue and drive home an outcome.[265]

* * *

Morton's second victory over Dirksen in 1967 involved trade. That year, Dirksen had championed an effort to impose quotas on certain imports.[266] Morton, a free trader, opposed this policy and swung into action.[267] The Kentuckian reached out to International Harvester, a major employer in Dirksen's home state of Illinois with a significant export business, and persuaded the company to weigh in with the minority leader.[268] As Morton recalled, Dirksen "backed away from it. He said: 'I think we better put this over to next year.'"[269] In 1967, with these victories under his belt, the *New York Times* proclaimed Morton "one of the Senate's most influential Republicans."[270]

By the latter half of the 1960s, Morton's prestige led one congressional observer to conclude that he "had assumed a quasi-leadership [role] over the younger and more progressive Republican senators."[271] Owing to his standing within the Republican conference and the national party, coupled with his foreign policy credentials, his next move was highly publicized.[272] In August 1967, the previously hawkish Morton changed his position on the Vietnam War, breaking once again with Dirksen.[273] His change of heart, which had been presaged by his earlier efforts to encourage an all-Asia peace conference, sent shock waves throughout official Washington and further undermined support for President Johnson's handling of the conflict.[274] When asked about his change of heart, Morton replied with his usual disarming candor: "I was mistaken."[275]

By early 1968, Morton seemed to be at the summit of his career, and his political future had never looked brighter.[276] He was seen as a potential successor to Dirksen as Senate minority leader or even a possible Republican nominee for national office.[277] Yet Morton stunned the political world by announcing he would not run for reelection. He explained, "To use an old Kentucky expression, I suppose I am just plain track sore."[278] The factors behind this surprising decision were Morton's declining health; his disillusionment with the direction of the country, including the war in Southeast Asia, campus unrest, and urban riots; and, in Morton's view, the failure of the nation's political leadership to adequately address these matters.[279]

Morton remained active in his final year as a senator. He promoted New York governor Nelson Rockefeller's candidacy for president and was named campaign cochairman of that effort before it flamed out at the Republican National Convention.[280] Interestingly, this undertaking pitted Thruston against his brother Rogers, who served as a Nixon strategist at the convention.[281]

Despite ongoing health problems, Morton remained active in his retirement. He continued to advocate for Kentucky causes, serving as chairman of the board of Churchill Downs, president of the American Horse Council, vice chairman of Liberty National Bank in Louisville, and board member of several corporations, including Pillsbury.[282] Morton passed away in 1982.[283]

The careers of Earle Clements and Thruston Morton are forever linked by the election of 1956. Although these two Kentuckians had very different personalities and came from very different backgrounds, each proved adept at electoral politics, rising to chair his respective party's campaign committee for multiple cycles. As such, each man became a leader in the Senate: Clements serving as whip and as acting leader, and Morton as a powerful rival to minority leader Dirksen.

10

Senator as Informal Policy Leader

John Sherman Cooper

Much of this book has focused on formal aspects of Senate leadership, such as the floor leader and whip positions. But leadership in the US Senate can take many forms; it does not necessarily involve holding an official leadership post.[1] As discussed in chapter 3, senators have led the chamber as unofficial presidential spokesmen, and chapter 4 highlighted the leadership role of a senator with a national political following.

Informal leadership can also be displayed through personal attributes and expertise that, when coupled with the right political setting, can propel senators to the forefront of certain public policy areas. Indeed, the very nature of Senate floor proceedings encourages informal policy leadership. By contrast, floor activity in the House of Representatives is tightly controlled under the rules. As a result, House members' opportunities for policy-making take place largely in committee. This is less the case in the Senate, where permissive floor rules allow members a fair amount of leeway to pursue their agendas outside of the committee room; some members might even get "two bites at the apple." Lawmakers who do not sit on the committee of jurisdiction often have an opportunity to try to secure a vote on their legislation on the Senate floor. Senators who do, in fact, sit on the relevant committee can pursue their agenda in committee and, if they fail there, can try to relitigate the matter on the Senate floor.[2]

When senators arrive in the chamber for the first time, many of them are what political scientists call "policy entrepreneurs."[3] They are on the lookout for a few discrete policy areas to call their own.[4] Senators ought to have some knowledge about virtually every major policy issue, but they cannot be experts in everything.[5] To be effective, senators need to specialize.[6] But it takes a long time to develop substantive knowledge of an issue and a proper understanding of how the Senate and the Washington policy community operate in order to get things done.

* * *

Even the most successful senators may only be able to work at the margins of an issue. After all, to legislate a solution to a problem, there are 50 (or more) other senators and 218 House members who must be convinced. A number of these lawmakers may be committee or subcommittee chairmen with jurisdiction over the issue in question; they may have their own ideas about how the matter should be addressed. In addition, they may be anxious to protect their own turf, further complicating matters. Then, of course, there is the president, who wields the veto pen, to say nothing of the public, the bureaucracy, the media, and the relevant interest groups. Leading an effort to change policy in just one area can be exceedingly difficult, as inertia is a powerful force in government.

Moreover, being viewed as the Senate expert on a particular matter does not guarantee that a senator will enjoy that standing indefinitely. The higher profile an issue becomes, the greater the likelihood that new purported "leaders" will emerge, challenging the informal Senate policy leader and eroding the deference previously granted him or her by colleagues. Moreover, new senators with different backgrounds may join the chamber, staking their own claims to expertise in that area.

* * *

This chapter examines the life and career of a "leader without portfolio": a senator who developed the requisite policy knowledge and political standing within the Senate to lead on an issue, even though he was not a floor leader or a committee chairman or a ranking member.[7] John Sherman Cooper was a noted policy leader in the effort to reduce and ultimately end US military involvement in Southeast Asia.[8]

Cooper's Early Life

Cooper was born in Somerset, in south-central Kentucky, on August 23, 1901. He was one of six children and the oldest of three boys. His father, also named John Sherman, was an attorney, a county judge, a political appointee of President Theodore Roosevelt, and head of the county Republican Party.[9] He was among Somerset's most prominent citizens.[10]

Young John inherited much of his generous spirit from his father.[11] The elder Cooper was known to provide plates of food to a hungry neighbor at dinnertime.[12] Cooper's mother, Helen Tartar, was an educator.[13] According to his siblings, John was their mother's favorite. One of his brothers commented drolly that, to their mother, there were three sons in the family: "John, John, and John."[14] His mother's side of the family boasted a political pedigree of its own, with several relatives having also served as county judge.[15]

As a boy growing up, Cooper was an avid reader, reflecting the influence of both parents, and he was an outstanding student.[16] He attended Centre College and then, at his father's suggestion, transferred to Yale, where he compiled an exemplary academic record and captained the basketball team.[17] He graduated from Yale in 1923 and then began law school at Harvard.[18]

Everything seemed to be going Cooper's way until tragedy struck in 1924.[19] His father suffered a fatal stroke.[20] In addition to the personal loss, John Sr.'s passing revealed that the family was in dire financial straits.[21] As the eldest son, John assumed responsibility for the household. He dropped out of law school to help support his younger brothers and sisters.[22] However, John went even further, assuming his father's financial obligations as well. To John, it was a question of principle to repay his father's creditors.[23] It would take him a quarter century to do so, but he considered it a matter of honor.[24] This sense of duty would be a hallmark of Cooper's life and career.

Even though he had to leave Harvard, Cooper continued his legal studies on his own and was soon admitted to the Kentucky bar. Despite the interruption in his legal career, Cooper made rapid strides in politics. He was aided by his maternal uncle, Roscoe Conkling Tartar, who had been a county judge.[25] In 1927, Cooper was elected to the Kentucky state house.[26] Two years later, he was elected county judge, serving until 1938. He was sworn in by his uncle and became the seventh member of his family to hold this position.[27]

His tenure as county judge would have a significant impact on Cooper's outlook on public life.[28] Serving in this capacity during the depths of the Great Depression, Cooper regularly encountered impoverished constituents who desperately needed help and had nowhere else to turn.[29] Cooper's generosity of spirit was on full display. He made every effort to find lodging for the homeless and food for the hungry.[30] His sister described Cooper's operation as "functioning like a hotel and a café."[31] He would often write notes for his impoverished constituents to take to nearby diners, where they could exchange these chits for food that would later be paid for by Cooper.[32] His brother-in-law, who was a dentist, regularly treated penniless patients who arrived with only a piece of paper that read: "This man's broke. Pull his teeth. (signed) John."[33] The strain of trying to help so many in so much need was exhausting, and Cooper suffered an emotional breakdown.[34] Characteristically, he persevered, although it took many months to regain his health.[35]

After two terms as county judge, Cooper's standing in the state Republican Party had grown, and by 1939, he was positioned to pursue the GOP nomination for governor.[36] He mounted a spirited race in the primary against King Swope, a state judge, but in the end he came up short. Swope won the nomination but lost in the general election.[37]

Service in World War II

Fate soon intervened and took Cooper in a different direction. In December 1941, the Japanese attacked Pearl Harbor, drawing the United States into World War II. Cooper enlisted in the army as a private.[38] He was soon sent to Officer Candidate School and served much of his time with General George Patton's Third Army, first as part of a military police unit and later as a legal adviser.[39]

Cooper handled a variety of sensitive missions.[40] One of them took him to Buchenwald concentration camp.[41] There, he saw firsthand the unspeakable horrors of the Holocaust, witnessing scores of its emaciated victims as they left the camp.[42] It was a sight forever seared into Cooper's memory.[43]

After the war, Cooper stayed in Europe, working to establish a revamped judiciary for the German province of Bavaria.[44] He was also responsible for helping to carry out Allied treaty obligations by returning refugees to their countries of origin.[45] Families had been torn apart by the conflagration, and numerous refugees had married individuals from other countries.[46] As the Allies tried to repatriate displaced persons, the Soviet Union interpreted its treaty obligations narrowly, taking the position that only its own citizens could be accepted back into the USSR, meaning that scores of refugee families would be permanently divided.[47] Cooper was outraged and took the issue to senior army leadership.[48] The Kentuckian's determination helped get the policy changed in the area under the Third Army's control, saving scores of families from being broken apart.[49]

Cooper's service in Europe during and immediately after World War II had a profound impact on him.[50] His time in the army reinforced his innate humanitarian instincts and taught him the importance of active American involvement overseas and the folly of isolationism.[51]

Senate Career

At the end of World War II, Cooper's status was such that he was elected circuit judge while still serving overseas.[52] Upon returning Stateside, he took up his judicial duties with typical diligence. One issue soon became his top priority and was subsequently a defining aspect of his legacy: civil rights.[53] As a judge, Cooper insisted that African Americans be permitted to sit on juries.[54]

In 1946, not long into his judgeship, Cooper decided to run for the US Senate to complete the term of Kentucky legend A. B. "Happy" Chandler, who had left the Senate to become commissioner of Major League Baseball. Cooper—aided in the race by a dispute between Chandler and an opposing faction of the Democratic Party—was elected.[55] Thus began Cooper's memorable Senate career.

To say that Cooper's tenure in the Senate was unorthodox would be an understatement. Two years after completing Chandler's term, Cooper was defeated for reelection in 1948, a strong Democratic year. Never one to give up, Cooper was elected to another unexpired term in 1952, following the death of Democratic senator Virgil Chapman. Cooper's campaign was run by future senator Thruston Morton.[56] In 1954, when Cooper ran for reelection, it was a "clash of the Titans": Cooper squared off against former majority leader and former vice president Alben Barkley, and he lost again.[57] In 1956, however, Cooper won election to fill the vacancy caused by Barkley's death. His electoral prospects had been enhanced by President Dwight Eisenhower's popularity and yet another Chandler-inspired feud among Kentucky Democrats.[58]

In this, his third Senate term, Cooper finally found his footing. He even ran for Senate minority leader in 1958. Like Barkley's race for party leader in 1937, the president intervened. This time, however, the president was Eisenhower, and the intervention was much more subtle.[59] In a reversal of FDR's approach, Eisenhower went against the Kentucky candidate and supported his more conservative opponent.[60] As a result, Everett Dirksen (R-IL) was elected minority leader.[61]

Given the constraints imposed on Senate party leadership, one wonders how Cooper's career trajectory might have differed had he won this leadership election. Senator Clifford Case (R-NJ) suspected that Cooper might have had difficulty as minority leader, in that "his ability to be himself might have been somewhat compromised if he had taken on the responsibility of attempting to lead and draw together people on least common denominator propositions."[62] Cooper would certainly prove that he was not afraid to buck his own party.[63] Upon being asked about his independent streak, Cooper shrugged and said, "I reckon I'll vote as I see fit."[64]

Despite being rebuffed by his Senate Republican colleagues, the people of Kentucky reelected Cooper to a full term in 1960. He would be returned by a wide margin in 1966 and would retire six years later. In all, Cooper spent twenty years of interrupted service in the Senate representing Kentucky.

The Cooper "Magic"

Throughout his time in the Senate—on and off from 1947 until 1973—Cooper was a Republican in an overwhelmingly Democratic state.[65] There were several factors that permitted Cooper to perform this political high-wire act. He came from a prominent family and was highly intelligent.[66] Both factors were important to his electoral success. So were the Chandler-inspired splits among Democrats that weakened his opposition.[67] Cooper's regular support from Barry Bingham Sr., editor of the *Louisville Courier-Journal,* also played a role.[68]

Then there was Cooper's speaking style, which likely won over some wavering voters. He was not known for his booming oratory. His style on the stump was unconventional in part because it reflected another important and endearing Cooper trait: modesty. As Senator J. William Fulbright (D-AR) once said of him: "Seldom have I served [in the Senate] with one as modest and self-effacing. . . . And this is a body not noted for such characteristics."[69] One Senate observer noted that Cooper's "halting, sometimes plodding way of speaking plus his courtly appearance contributed to the impression of integrity and honesty held by his [Senate] colleagues."[70] Cooper's speeches were marked not by fire and brimstone but by candor and humility. One reporter described Cooper on the stump:

> Watching him in action, it is easy to sense but hard to explain why John Cooper is a formidable campaigner. He is not a dramatic speaker. His delivery is halting, low. He violates all the rules. He tells jokes on himself, and not very good jokes either, apologizes for not being able to please everyone, and even admits that he has made mistakes.
>
> Yet to all of this there is *agonizing sincerity*—in the sad, soft smile and the slow, soft speech—that enraptures audiences and infuriates his opponents. [One contemporary Democrat complained], "That [expletive] can tell people how wrong he's been and [then the voters] . . . run all over our [Democratic] men on their way to vote for him."[71]

If Cooper's unconventional style frustrated many Democrats, his voting record confounded many conservatives. But both sides still voted for him in droves. One constituent remarked: "I don't agree with one vote out of a hundred [of his] but I'm for that boy every time."[72] Another Kentuckian tried to explain Cooper's bond with his constituents: "Down here, they want a man they can revere, and depend on, and one who looks like a statesman. They also like someone who can't easily be criticized—and one who can whip the hell out of anyone if he has to. That's John Cooper."[73]

Despite this widespread sentiment, Cooper faced his share of challenges while campaigning in a predominantly Democratic state. On one occasion, he was out on the hustings in western Kentucky when he came upon an older constituent named, of all things, John Cooper.[74] Candidate Cooper warmly greeted the elderly constituent, who was a Democrat and was wary of the man from Somerset. The constituent asked the senator-to-be his religion and his party registration, to which the candidate responded "Baptist" and "Republican."[75] The old man slowly looked Cooper up and down and then remarked: "Well, young man, you have a good name, very little religion, and no politics at all."[76]

Noted political scientist Donald R. Matthews outlined the public's conflicting expectations about those who run for office: "[The candidate] should be above petty politics but he should bring home the bacon; he should run a clean and dignified campaign but he should be a fighter; he should bring his campaign to the voter but he should not spend money doing so; he should frankly state and act on his own convictions but represent his constituents."[77] For Kentucky voters, Cooper seemed to satisfy these apparently contradictory ideals.[78]

* * *

Above all else, Cooper realized that lawmakers need to work with others to get things done. Today's opponent might be tomorrow's ally, so holding grudges and burning bridges are counterproductive. To that end, Cooper was the consummate bridge builder in both the state and the Senate. At the time of Cooper's retirement, Senator James Buckley (Cons.-NY) remarked of him: "No Member of this body has more friends and fewer enemies."[79]

* * *

Cooper and the Kennedys

One of Cooper's close friends in the Senate was a young Democrat from Massachusetts, John F. Kennedy. Their wives enjoyed a friendship that predated theirs.[80] Despite partisan differences and a sixteen-year age gap, the relationship between the two senators proved enduring. According to JFK's brother, Senator Edward Kennedy (D-MA), "Cooper was one of President Kennedy's best friends."[81]

Jacqueline Kennedy recalled, "The first dinner party we went to after we were in the White House was at the Coopers'."[82] At Kennedy's first bill signing, Cooper was one of the invitees.[83] The incoming president had great faith in the Kentuckian's judgment and discernment.[84] At the beginning of his presidency, Kennedy asked Cooper to carry out a sensitive diplomatic assignment to the USSR.[85] The president wanted to get a better sense of Soviet impressions about his new administration, and he trusted Cooper to undertake this delicate mission.[86]

President Kennedy also urged others to seek Cooper's advice, including his own brother. As Senator Edward Kennedy recalled: "I arrived [in the Senate] at the ripe age of thirty years old. I was looking for counsel, looking for advice. And talking to my brother, then the President, one afternoon . . . he mentioned to me. He said, 'Someday Teddy, when you're in the United States Senate and some issue that comes up before that body and passions are aroused and voices are high, if you really want the unvarnished truth and you really want the facts on that issue, let me just say go to John Sherman Cooper and you will receive it.'"[87] Jacqueline Kennedy shared her husband's admiration for Cooper's judgment. She later served on a commission with him and marveled at "how often . . . there [would be] . . . a point that was being hotly argued, or a bind you couldn't see your way out of [and] how often his voice was listened to, and [how] usually [his view] was the path that turned out to be obviously the right one."[88]

Sadly, Cooper would have another link to Kennedy, one he would have gladly forgone. In 1963, President Lyndon Johnson named Cooper as one of the seven eminent Americans to serve on the Warren Commission to investigate the assassination of JFK.[89]

Colleagues' High Regard

During his time in the Senate, Cooper established an enduring legacy. In 1960, *Newsweek* surveyed fifty Washington correspondents to determine the most skilled senators of the day. Cooper ranked first among all Republicans, ahead of the man who had defeated him for the Senate minority leader post two years prior, Senator Dirksen.[90] The magazine wrote, "The Senator from Kentucky has long impressed unbiased onlookers with his quiet competence."[91] A dozen years later, his reputation remained undiminished. In 1972, the *Almanac of American Politics* concluded, "Cooper is one of the Senate's most respected men."[92]

Cooper's esteem did not end with his Senate career. Following Cooper's departure from the upper chamber in 1973, Senate majority leader Mike Mansfield (D-MT) mentioned him as a possible vice president after Spiro Agnew's resignation.[93] That same year, Cooper's name was floated as a possible special prosecutor in the Watergate investigation.[94]

Part of the reason that Cooper's colleagues in the Senate respected him was his intelligence. One staffer, who had followed a particular bill closely, recalled Cooper's remarks about the measure while it was being debated on the floor:

> Admitting almost apologetically that he had just read the bill for the first time, Cooper objected that it contained no guidelines, no "local control" provisions—nothing at all, in fact, to prevent the government from sending doctors into a community even if local physicians or the community itself objected. He was absolutely right, of course, for he had just discovered the accidental damage [an amendment in the committee markup] had caused. . . . Cooper's perceptiveness impressed me greatly; he had noticed the absence of [key] . . . criteria immediately, whereas the bill's cosponsors had not noticed the *presence* of those same criteria during the Committee meeting devoted to the bill.[95]

Furthermore, Cooper was affable. A fellow Senate Republican said of him: "I knew John Cooper the way I knew the palm of my right hand. John Cooper was a very easygoing, lovely sort of guy. You could disagree with John Cooper but, my God, you could never dislike him. . . . I mean there was something about John that was just sanctified; he was that kind of guy. He never raised his voice and he was very courteous to everyone."[96]

The man from Somerset was also highly regarded in the Senate in large part because of his principled stance on issues. "More than any of us," Senator John Stennis (D-MS) said, Cooper "has really made an extraordinary effort to cast every vote and every speech on the basis of what he believed to be right and just and the best thing for the country as he saw it."[97] For instance, Cooper opposed the heavy-handed tactics used by Senator Joe McCarthy (R-WI) in the 1950s.[98] In addition, Cooper was an early and vigorous supporter of civil rights legislation at a time when that was not a popular cause in many quarters.

* * *

I was an intern for Senator Cooper in 1964, and part of my job was to process his mail.[99] Even though polls showed that Kentuckians were in favor of civil rights overall, I saw that those who wrote to Senator Cooper were overwhelmingly opposed to the pending civil rights legislation.[100] But Senator Cooper was undeterred. He actively lobbied his colleagues to oppose the southern Democratic filibuster being carried out against the civil rights legislation.[101] I was exhilarated as I watched him take this courageous stance. But at the same time, I was apprehensive about Senator Cooper's political future, in light of the deep opposition he was facing.[102]

I could not resist asking Senator Cooper why he took such a stance, even though it was deeply unpopular with many of his constituents. His reply was something I have never forgotten. He said, "I not only represent Kentucky, I represent the nation, and there are times you follow, and times when you lead."[103] In this regard, Cooper took an Edmund Burke–like approach to his job.[104] Burke, the great eighteenth-century conservative thinker and member of Parliament, took the view that elected representatives owe it to their constituents to vote according to their best judgment, not simply to echo the voters' views.

* * *

Cooper the Diplomat

Cooper became a national leader on the reduction of US forces in Southeast Asia partly because of his experience in foreign affairs. Cooper was an accomplished diplomat, having advised Republicans and Democrats alike.[105] Between his first and second Senate terms, President Harry Truman named him to serve as a delegate to the General Assembly of the United Nations and as an adviser on NATO matters to Secretary of State Dean Acheson.[106]

He was also a US ambassador between his second and third Senate terms. Cooper was not the typical political appointee—a big campaign donor sent to London or Paris. He was sent to a challenging post at the height of the Cold War. In 1955, President Eisenhower tapped Cooper to become the US ambassador to India, establishing a rich tradition of esteemed individuals serving in that post, including John Kenneth Galbraith and Daniel Patrick Moynihan. Galbraith noted that Indian prime minister Jawaharlal Nehru "respected Cooper more than any other American."[107] He recalled that Nehru regularly began conversations with the phrase: "Ambassador Cooper once told me. . . ."[108]

Following his final Senate term, Cooper's diplomatic service began anew. In 1974, President Gerald Ford named Cooper the first American ambassador to East Germany.[109] Cooper was urged to consider becoming ambassador to Israel in 1982, but he declined.[110]

Cooper's Character Traits

Cooper was clearly a highly effective legislator and diplomat. But how did he become so successful? One key to Cooper's success was his wife, Lorraine, who was a cosmopolitan hostess in the Georgetown neighborhood of Washington.[111] Cooper had been married during World War II, but the couple divorced shortly thereafter.[112] In the years that followed, Cooper was married to his work, and few foresaw a second marriage for the man who routinely put in fourteen-hour days.[113]

John and Lorraine's first meeting was inauspicious. It took place at a dinner party in Washington. Lorraine, who was decidedly not from Kentucky, tried to make small talk with Cooper and asked, "How is the burley *cotton* crop doing in Kentucky this year?"[114] Lorraine may have confused cotton with tobacco, but it was a rare misstep for her. The two developed a deep and abiding bond and were wed in 1955. Lorraine proved to be a great help to Cooper's career. Her keen mind, charm, humor, and skills as a hostess helped Cooper develop and cement important friendships that contributed to his rise on the national and international scene.[115] Every year, Cooper and his wife hosted a gala at their home.[116] Often as many as fifty senators would be present at these occasions.[117]

Another important reason for Cooper's success in public life was his character.[118] He was fundamentally a decent, kind person who treated people with respect. W. R. Munday, a pastor at the African Methodist Episcopal Church in Somerset, said it best: "For [Senator] Cooper, everybody is somebody all the time."[119]

* * *

I can personally attest to Pastor Munday's sentiment. As noted earlier, I had been the senator's intern in 1964, and in the summer of 1965, I visited his office after finishing my first year as a law student.[120] I was waiting in Cooper's reception room, when all of a sudden the senator emerged from his office and beckoned me to follow him. I had no clue where we were going. We walked briskly to the Capitol Rotunda, where I was confronted with more security than I had ever seen before. It was only then that Senator Cooper revealed what was going on: President Johnson was holding a major ceremonial event prior to signing into law the landmark Voting Rights Act of 1965, which Senator Cooper had worked to pass.[121] I was awed to be attending such an event and deeply moved that the senator had invited me to witness this historic occasion.[122]

* * *

Another important character trait was Cooper's honesty. His colleague, Senator Morton, recalled that Cooper's earnestness seemed palpable. He described Cooper as having an "affidavit face."[123] The man from Somerset's integrity was reflected in the key role he played in creating the Senate Select Committee on Ethics, which works to ensure that Senate personnel observe prescribed ethical standards.[124]

Finally, Cooper brought a constructive, problem-solving approach to public policy. His "entrance into Senate debate, no matter how partisan or divisive it may have become," commented Senator Gordon Allott (R-CO), "meant that his fellow Senators lower[ed] their voices and listen[ed] instead of just attacking."[125] As Senator Edward Kennedy observed, "[he] always brought light to the problem rather than heat which was . . . a distinguishing characteristic."[126]

Senator Cooper, of course, was not infallible. He had his share of faults, which could be exasperating or amusing, depending on the context. For one, he was almost always late.[127] In fact, the only period in his life in which he carried a wristwatch was when he served in the army.[128] He did not drive an automobile.[129] People simply took care of him, whether that meant driving him around or assisting him with some other mundane task.[130]

* * *

In 1980, former senator Cooper decided to go to the Republican National Convention in Detroit. He flew to the Motor City, but once he arrived, he had no clue where to go or when to be there. As Jefferson County judge executive at the time, I just happened to bump into Cooper in the men's room. It was immediately apparent that he had no earthly idea where he was supposed to go. So I took him around and essentially helped staff him at the convention. Cooper just had an impossible-to-explain quality that virtually compelled people to assist him.[131]

* * *

Senator Cooper was notoriously absentminded. As one reporter observed: "He invariably looks like a man who has misplaced his train or plane ticket—which usually happens to be the case. He always seems to be vaguely hunting for something, and it might be anything from an elusive idea to a missing shoelace."[132] A cigarette smoker, Cooper was once riding in an automobile and asked to use someone's lighter; after taking a puff or two, without thinking, Cooper simply tossed the borrowed property out the window.[133]

Senator Morton recalled an incident of his own: He and Cooper had been campaigning in Fulton, Kentucky, which straddles the border with Tennessee.[134] The two men decided they could cover more ground if they split up.[135] But when they linked up again after a full day of campaigning, Morton discovered that Cooper had devoted the entire time to politicking on the Tennessee half of the border.[136]

In addition to these peccadilloes, Cooper often took a long time to make up his mind.[137] This trait could frustrate those who worked with him, and it sometimes made him look dithering to outsiders.[138] The Eisenhower administration became utterly exasperated with Cooper after he took half a year to decide on a nominee to fill a single federal judicial vacancy in Kentucky.[139] A contemporary remarked: "John likes to do one thing at a time. He won't decide on that judgeship until he's found a solution to Indochina."[140]

Foreign Affairs

Cooper was active in many public endeavors besides civil rights, including federal assistance to local schools, environmental protection, and creation of the Appalachian Regional Commission.[141] But of all the areas on which Cooper left an imprint, his work in the realm of foreign affairs is perhaps best known. Cooper's expert counsel on this subject was sought by senior members on both sides of the aisle.

* * *

The Senate plays, or is supposed to play, a significant role in foreign affairs. The Senate is authorized by the Constitution to provide its advice and consent to treaties as well as to the appointment of ambassadors. The Senate considers bills to set policy for and fund the Departments of State and Defense. The Senate plays a vital role in regulating foreign commerce and providing foreign aid. But these Senate powers are not self-executing. Senators must assert them, and they often have to do so against the executive branch's tendency to overstep its bounds. Cooper played a major role in defending the prerogatives of the Senate and of Congress.

* * *

Cooper's best-known Senate actions in the area of foreign affairs bear his name: the Cooper-Mansfield Amendment of 1969 and the Cooper-Church Amendment of 1970.[142] They are examples of a senator acting as a policy leader without portfolio.

Cooper had been skeptical of the 1964 Gulf of Tonkin Resolution, which authorized military involvement in Southeast Asia, but he ultimately supported the measure.[143] He soon came to doubt the wisdom of the conflict in Vietnam, however. These concerns manifested themselves in early 1966, when Cooper became one of the first senators to openly criticize the war effort.[144] His skepticism only grew thereafter. Following the 1968 election, Cooper huddled with other antiwar senators in majority leader Mike Mansfield's office to begin legislative efforts to limit the war.[145] In 1969, Senator Cooper crafted a groundbreaking amendment to restrict American military commitments in Thailand and Laos.[146] The amendment was adopted by the Senate but later dropped in a House-Senate conference. Yet Cooper and his allies were dogged. A subsequent version of the amendment was cosponsored by Senator Mansfield and became part of a defense spending bill.[147] In this undertaking, Cooper worked closely not only with Mansfield but also with Senator Frank Church (D-ID).[148] The amendment's success established Cooper as a pivotal player in congressional efforts to limit and ultimately end the American war effort in Indochina. Cooper's high-profile role that same year in opposing the Nixon administration's efforts to deploy an antiballistic missile system further burnished his reputation for working with Democrats on foreign policy matters.[149]

In 1970, President Nixon ordered a military incursion into Cambodia to combat sanctuaries and interdict supply routes used by the Vietcong to attack American forces in South Vietnam. Opposition to the war in Southeast Asia was already running high in the United States, but when Nixon's actions became public, they sparked a tremendous public outcry. Given his authorship of the Cooper-Mansfield Amendment, there was little question who would lead Republican efforts to curtail the president's actions in Cambodia.[150] This time, Senator Cooper worked in tandem with Senator Church. The two men attempted to use the "power of the purse" to cut off funding for US military operations in Cambodia.[151] Church's biographers paint a vivid portrait of this legislative "odd couple":

Age, party, and region separated Church and Cooper, [yet] they constituted a remarkably effective legislative team. Cooper [was] . . . tall and courtly . . . the model of a southern gentleman. With an expression that reminded some observers of a basset hound, he was thoroughly without pretension. Despite his good ol' boy mannerisms on the stump, he was thoughtful and learned. His judicious handling of legislation, as well as his [diplomatic and Senate] experience made him one of the most respected people on Capitol Hill.

In some respects, Cooper and Church were a study in contrast. Whereas Church was an orator, Cooper was a mumbler. According to one story, a young reporter had almost fallen from the press gallery while leaning over the edge in an effort to hear the Kentucky senator. And whereas Church had a very orderly mind, Cooper was notoriously absent-minded.

The two senators nevertheless had their similarities. Both were some-what anomalous in their home states. Church was a Democrat from largely Republican surroundings [in Idaho]; Cooper was a Republican from a [Democratic] state. . . . Cooper, like Church, had demonstrated a willingness to take issue with his party's leadership. . . . Temperamentally, Cooper and Church were skilled negotiators who disliked confrontation. And, although both had voted for the Tonkin Gulf resolution, they had [both] been early critics of the Vietnam war.[152]

The two senators were an effective pair, with the telegenic Church taking to the airwaves with gusto to promote the amendment.[153] In this regard, Church was an ideal complement to the more retiring Cooper, who was much less com-fortable and less effective in this context.[154] Cooper's contributions occurred outside of the limelight. As one authority on the amendment described the col-laboration: "Church, the orator and idea man, provided the active public force for the [effort]. Cooper, with his quiet unassuming manner, worked behind the scenes cajoling and compromising in order to bring about success."[155]

The resulting measure—known as the Cooper-Church Amendment—was vigorously opposed by the Nixon White House.[156] Despite the executive branch's objections, the measure had powerful patrons, including Mansfield and Senator George Aiken (R-VT), the ranking member of the Foreign Relations Commit-tee.[157] The Cambodian incursion and the Senate's legislative response seized the national spotlight for much of the summer of 1970.[158]

A foreign military sales bill that was under consideration by the Foreign Relations Committee provided Cooper and Church with an ideal legislative vehicle.[159] They offered their amendment, which carried in committee 9 to 5.[160] As modified, the bill then headed to the Senate floor for a fateful showdown.[161] Despite subsequently modifying the measure to address some of the adminis-tration's concerns and enhance the bill's prospects for adoption, Cooper and Church came in for some withering criticism.[162] They were accused of issuing a "declaration of surrender."[163]

The two senators were put through the paces.[164] The Cooper-Church Amendment prompted 288 Senate floor speeches and was debated for seven weeks.[165] Church's foreign affairs staffer recalled routinely putting in twenty-hour days during this stretch.[166] In his words, "It was tense and rugged."[167] Throughout the debate, Cooper was conflicted. Bryce Harlow, one of Nixon's senior aides, recalled that Cooper was "troubled over his own amendment" and did "not [wish to] *hurt* [the] P[resident]."[168] Ultimately, the Senate adopted a modified Cooper-Church Amendment by a vote of 58 to 37.[169] The ordeal was so trying for Cooper that he was hospitalized afterward for exhaustion.[170]

The amendment failed in the House, however. A six-month stalemate then ensued in the conference committee.[171] Ultimately, a revised version became law at the beginning of 1971, following the American withdrawal from Cambodia.[172] Senate passage of the amendment cutting off funds proved to be an important milestone in the war in Indochina.[173] Congress had demonstrated its political will to take the initiative in pushing for an end to the war.

How was Cooper—a member of a greatly outnumbered minority party and neither the chairman nor the ranking member of the Senate Foreign Relations Committee—able to become an informal Senate leader and, in fact, a national leader on the Vietnam War? There are several reasons. First, Cooper brought a unique prestige to the table. He was a respected senior member of the Senate, having served in the body—with two notable interruptions—since the late 1940s. One Senate staffer described Cooper's aura and its effectiveness: "One of the people they [the Democrats] most fear getting up and offering an amendment is John Sherman Cooper. . . . Cooper has [a quality] . . . that makes him almost a bipartisan-type character. If Cooper has a fairly decent amendment, even in this Senate [controlled by Democrats sixty-seven to thirty-three], he can go in and pick up forty to forty-five [votes] and sometimes carry it."[174]

Second, as a prominent former diplomat, Cooper was an acknowledged authority in the realm of foreign policy.[175] Above all, for a senator to become an informal leader on an issue, he or she must demonstrate expertise in the subject matter.[176] And Cooper knew the subject matter cold. In the Senate, there are formal and informal divisions of labor. Senators are willing to defer to other senators *if* they can show that they know what they are talking about.[177] Cooper studied the situation in Southeast Asia closely, and he was well known for his foreign policy expertise and experience; these factors played an important role in convincing other senators to go along with him. Cooper's widely recognized knowledge of foreign affairs both reassured fellow senators and shielded them from criticism that a funding cutoff would be imprudent from a policy standpoint.

Third, and equally important, was that Cooper was a Republican, and a Republican occupied the White House.[178] As one commentator put it: "Senator Cooper's sponsorship [of Cooper-Church] was vital because it lent an air of bipartisanship to the amendment and rendered less credible those charges from opponents that the amendment was a tool of the more extreme leftist elements of the Democratic Party. Cooper had a record as a moderate Republican and as a wise and able Senator. He had been a friend and supporter of President Nixon for years."[179] Church candidly noted that Cooper was "the strongest possible ally I could find on the Republican side of the aisle."[180] Thus, the Kentuckian provided political cover for Democrats, allowing them to support the amendment and, at the same time, deflect criticism that they were being partisan.

Fourth, Cooper was tactically savvy in crafting the amendment. He selected an issue around which a broad array of senators could coalesce.[181] The Cooper-Church Amendment was unlike more radical measures such as the Hatfield-McGovern Amendment, which would have eliminated funding for the entire Southeast Asian war and which went down to defeat.[182]

* * *

Finally, Cooper's self-effacing personality helped him in his efforts. In Congress, there is an old saying that it is amazing what you can accomplish if you let someone else take the credit. This is not as easy as it sounds. Recall that Senator Joseph C. S. Blackburn almost fought a duel over who received credit for securing a pork-barrel project for Kentucky. In contrast, Cooper was easy to work with because fellow senators did not have to battle him for public recognition. Not surprisingly, Cooper had little problem letting Church take the more public role in advocating for the amendment.

* * *

Cooper's efforts demonstrate the importance of contextual factors in becoming a Senate leader without portfolio, especially on an issue of such national and international significance.[183] Woodrow Wilson discussed the phenomenon of "lead[ing] without office."[184] He wrote:

> There must be something in the times or in the questions which are abroad to thrust great advocates or great masters of purpose into a non-official leadership, which is theirs because they represent . . . some principle at once vital and widely loved or hated, or because they possess . . . the ability to give voice to some living theme. There must be a cause to be advanced which is greater than the trammels of governmental forms, and which, by authority of its own imperative voice, constitutes its advocates the leaders of the nation, though without giving them official title—without need of official title.[185]

Cooper's prestige, experience, substantive knowledge, partisan affiliation, and willingness to let others take credit were all pivotal to his success. These factors all came together in the context of the war in Indochina. In other policy areas in which Cooper had less substantive knowledge, Democratic senators had less need for Republican support, and, most critically, the public was less concerned, Cooper likely would have been much less influential.

There is no doubt that Cooper deserves credit for recognizing and seizing the opportunity to assert informal leadership. He displayed great political courage in this regard; by becoming an informal leader on Southeast Asian policy, he pitted himself against a president of his own party on the most momentous issue of the day. Consequently, Cooper came in for tremendous criticism.

In many ways, the informal policy leader stands in contradistinction to the committee chairman. The power of committee chairmen is formal and jurisdictional. In the Senate, it is understood that the chairman and the ranking member generally take the lead (or should take the lead) on issues within their panel's remit. After all, that is why Senate committees exist in the first place: to divide up the workload and facilitate specialization (see chapter 5). Committee chairmen's status is magnified by the press attention they receive when high-profile developments take place within their panel's jurisdiction.[186] Chairmen draw additional support and expertise from the committee staff members who work under them.[187]

Informal policy leaders must work to overcome these disadvantages. In the case of Senator Cooper and the war in Southeast Asia, he was aided by the fact that the relevant committee chairman, Senator Fulbright, was sympathetic with Cooper's aims.[188]

With the Senate's consideration of the two Cooper amendments, the dam broke, and a tidal wave of antiwar bills and amendments hit the Senate floor.[189] In addition to being an important watershed in reflecting congressional opposition to the war in Southeast Asia, Cooper's amendments represented a historic reassertion of legislative branch prerogatives.[190] One authority wrote, "Cooper-Church provided the forum in which the Senate and the House began to reassess their role in foreign affairs [and] [w]hile no one event or piece of legislation ended the war in Vietnam, the Cooper-Church amendment of 1970 provided a necessary cog in the machinery that did."[191] The measure marked the first time Congress had restricted military funding during wartime, setting a precedent that would be used in other contexts in the future (e.g., Somalia in 1993).[192]

Legacy

After leaving the Senate and completing his diplomatic assignment in East Germany, John returned to Washington with Lorraine, where the couple lived until her passing in 1985.[193] Cooper followed her in 1991 and was buried in Arlington

National Cemetery.[194] Upon Cooper's death, former president Ronald Reagan called him "one of the most beloved and compassionate American statesmen of this or any century."[195] Scores of colleagues, friends, relatives, and others in the United States and abroad echoed Reagan's sentiments.

The life of John Sherman Cooper reflects many of the traits needed to become an informal policy leader in the Senate. He was acclaimed for his intelligence, work ethic, integrity, and distinguished foreign policy background. These traits all contributed to his earning a high degree of respect from his colleagues. This standing among his fellow senators elevated him to the status of a leader without portfolio in the chamber, even though he served in the minority party. Cooper's esteem, coupled with favorable circumstances, allowed him to transcend the Senate, propelling him to national leadership on an issue central to one of the most trying episodes in American history.

Conclusion

Woodrow Wilson wrote that government "is accountable to Darwin, not to Newton. It is modified by its environment, necessitated by its tasks, shaped to its functions by the sheer pressure of life."[1] These same principles are embodied in the evolutionary development of Senate leadership over more than two centuries. It began with the vice president, as president of the Senate, and the president pro tempore holding out the promise of legislative leadership through their constitutionally prescribed positions. In short order, it became apparent that neither office would perform a role akin to that of the Speaker of the House of Representatives. Instead, over time, Senate leadership developed in different ways to meet challenges from both within and without and, in so doing, attempted to address the needs of the nation.

Early on, some senators stepped into the initial leadership vacuum and helped direct the body through their close relationship with the president. Some would do so through a powerful national or regional following and the force of their own personality. Some would seize the initiative in certain policy areas by chairing important committees. Others, in the late nineteenth century, began to harness party positions in an attempt to lead the Senate; the position of caucus chairman is a prime example. However, only in the early decades of the twentieth century did Senate leadership begin to assume a fully recognizable form with the rise of formal Senate party positions such as floor leader, party whip, and campaign committee chairman.

Through it all, the experiences of Kentuckians have served as important touchstones along the way. The vice presidencies of Richard Mentor Johnson and John C. Breckinridge demonstrate that, even though premodern vice presidents spent most of their professional time presiding over the Senate, their ability to lead the upper chamber in a meaningful way was greatly limited. Their tenures also reflect more broadly the problems inherent in the vice presidency, concerns that were corrected only in the twentieth century as presidents started to make better use of their running mates.

John Brown and John Pope both served as president pro tempore. Like the vice presidency, the president pro tempore position offered the potential to lead the Senate—at least on paper. However, the abbreviated and oft-interrupted ten-ures of nineteenth-century presidents pro tempore made it difficult for them to exert authority from this perch. The brief incumbencies of Brown and Pope are emblematic of this shortcoming.

The career of John Breckinridge demonstrates how a senator can lead the chamber as a presidential spokesman. Breckinridge leveraged his close relation-ship with President Thomas Jefferson to help drive the Senate agenda, including the adoption of important measures such as legislative authorization to secure and govern the Louisiana Territory.

Henry Clay was a national leader in the Senate in a way that has seldom been replicated. His skill and stature helped elevate the upper chamber to per-haps its greatest period of influence. Twice, Senator Clay was the driving force behind legislation that helped prevent disunion (and still another time as a House member).

By contrast, Clay's good friend John J. Crittenden reflects the historic arc of Senate committee chairmen in the early to mid-nineteenth century. In 1816, the Senate established substantive standing committees for the first time. Critten-den was the second senator to chair the Judiciary Committee, beginning in 1817, and he later led the Military Affairs Committee from 1841 to 1845, meaning that he led two of the most highly regarded panels in the Senate. In addition, he chaired the Committee on Revolutionary Claims from 1859 to 1861, an entity whose very existence reflected the Senate's need for administrative assistance.

John W. Stevenson was the first senator to serve as Democratic caucus chairman. His successor as senator from Kentucky, James B. Beck, was the first caucus chairman to be termed "Democratic leader" on the Senate floor and the first to be regularly considered his party's leader by the media.[2] Beck's policy efforts with regard to some of the biggest issues of the day, such as monetary policy and the tariff, were groundbreaking for a caucus chairman and set an example that would be followed by his successors.[3] In the early twentieth cen-tury, Joseph C. S. Blackburn put forward a controversial initiative that involved trying to compel fellow partisans to follow caucus decisions. The result was the "binding caucus" rule, which proved a useful tool for Senate Democrats until the end of World War I. Moreover, Blackburn was the first caucus chairman to be referred to as "leader" in official caucus records, illustrating a notewor-thy point in the caucus chairmanship's gradual transformation into the formal position of floor leader.

Three decades later, Alben Barkley became Senate majority leader. Impor-tantly, he held that position when the parliamentary right of prior recogni-tion for floor leaders was first formalized. Prior recognition—the principle that permits the majority leader to command the floor before others who wish to speak—constitutes the primary formal power of the office. Barkley stands at the crossroads of two different leadership positions, as he was also the last vice president to devote a significant portion of his professional time to presiding over the Senate.

In the mid to late twentieth century, Wendell Ford, Earle Clements, and Thruston Morton each held important institutional leadership posts. Ford and Clements served as party whip, a position that came into being not long after the formalization of the floor leader post. All three held the post of Senate party campaign chairman.

Finally, John Sherman Cooper's career reflects the enduring power of informal Senate leadership and individualism. Despite the rise to prominence of formal leadership institutions in the past century, Senate rules and traditions still provide the opportunity for lawmakers to drive an outcome on an issue even if they do not hold a formal party or committee leadership post.

In all, sixty-six individuals have represented Kentucky in the US Senate. This volume has profiled fifteen of them. Some of these senators played key roles in the adoption of landmark measures: John Breckinridge and the legislative efforts to effectuate the Louisiana Purchase; Henry Clay and the Compromise Tariff of 1833 and the Compromise of 1850; John Sherman Cooper and the Cooper-Church Amendment. Others proved pivotal to the exercise of the Senate's "cooling" function, allowing momentary passions to dissipate and arriving at a reasoned outcome: John Breckinridge during the war fever that gripped the West following Spanish restrictions on the port of New Orleans; John J. Crittenden during the Oregon border dispute; Alben Barkley during the investigation of the Pearl Harbor attack. Yet these fifteen lawmakers were not demigods. In retrospect, they made poor decisions as well as wise ones. After all, many were slaveholders, some flirted with sedition, and some actually participated in it. As such, these Kentucky lawmakers reflect much that is good and much that is bad in American history. Nonetheless, each of these Kentuckians achieved some measure of de jure or de facto leadership in the Senate.

What their careers also illustrate is that there is no mathematical formula to becoming a Senate leader. Each of these individuals displayed unique traits and worked in unique circumstances. Each blazed his own path. Yet many of these influential senators shared certain attributes. All of them, almost by definition, had a high degree of political acumen. Clements and Morton, for example, were both highly regarded for their political sensibility and campaign savvy. But possessing political skill did not prevent some of them from making political errors. Clay, for instance, made some epic miscalculations. He agreed to serve as President John Quincy Adams's secretary of state after delivering the 1824 presidential election to Adams in the House of Representatives. In so doing, he tarred himself forever with the charge of having made a "corrupt bargain." Later, in the presidential race of 1844, Clay profoundly misread the public's sentiment about the annexation of Texas. It cost him the presidency.

Pope made a grave mistake when he wrote a letter to Richard Mentor Johnson, a prominent Democrat, suggesting that he would be willing to abandon the Whig Party. When this letter was made public, it ended Pope's congressional career. Similarly, Blackburn's decisions to become a silverite and to attack a sitting governor of the same party were major miscalculations; each misstep cost him an election.

Other senators took actions that reflected their personal convictions but cost them politically. Pope defied party expectations and prevailing sentiment in Kentucky by opposing the War of 1812. As a result, he served just one term in the Senate. John C. Breckinridge chose to join the Confederacy, even though Kentucky stayed loyal to the Union. This caused him to be expelled from the Senate and to flee the United States; moreover, it foreclosed any future national political ambitions he might have had. Barkley took the honorable step of resigning from Senate leadership after a public break with President Franklin Roosevelt over wartime tax legislation. However, the decision may have cost Barkley the vice presidency in 1944 and, ultimately, the White House when FDR died in office the next year.

Tenacity is an important attribute of a Senate leader, and most of the individuals outlined in this book possessed this trait in abundance. Barkley was termed the "Iron Man" for his indefatigable approach to campaigning and legislative work. Ford was reputed to put in twenty-hour days on the campaign trail. Contemporaries routinely marveled at Beck's diligence. Cooper was known to work every day of the week. By contrast, Johnson was not known to be a particularly hard worker—at least later in his career.

Another common characteristic is that many of these senators were good retail politicians—that is, they had a knack for making a positive impression one-on-one or in small settings. Clay certainly possessed this attribute, as did Johnson, Crittenden, John C. Breckinridge, Blackburn, Barkley, and Ford. Others succeeded without this particular skill. John Breckinridge was aloof and stiff, Brown was shy and withdrawn, and Beck had a gruff exterior. Clements was no back-slapper, and neither was Cooper.

Intellect is another important feature among many of these Kentucky leaders. Stevenson had a keen mind and was learned in the law. Clay was brilliant though not an intellectual per se. Cooper had great mental aptitude. Johnson, however, was not especially gifted.

Attendance at a prestigious university is another recurring theme. Brown attended Washington College, Princeton, and William and Mary and later studied under Thomas Jefferson. John Breckinridge and Crittenden also went to William and Mary. John C. Breckinridge attended Centre College and Princeton and studied law at Transylvania. Stevenson attended Hampton-Sydney and the University of Virginia. Blackburn graduated from Centre, and Beck studied law at Transylvania. Both Morton and Cooper graduated from Yale. However, Clay never even attended college. Indeed, he conceded that this gap in his experience "remained one of his weak points through life."[4] Johnson apparently did not attend college either. Ford did not complete a four-year degree.

Family connections were another important consideration in the rise of these public figures. John C. Breckinridge benefited from the reputation of his famed grandfather and other relatives. Stevenson's father had been Speaker of the US House of Representatives. Clements and Cooper both had blood relations who were active in local politics. Morton came from a wealthy family involved in public affairs. Blackburn had one brother who was a governor and another who was Kentucky secretary of state. Others come from less notable families. Clay, Barkley, and Beck all rose from unpromising circumstances.

As young men, many of these lawmakers were aided by notable patrons. Beck's association with John C. Breckinridge helped him overcome his modest origins and rise to prominence in public life. Brown and Clay (and possibly John Breckinridge) benefited from the assistance and tutelage of George Wythe, mentor to many of Virginia's legal elite. Crittenden profited politically from his friendship with Clay, and Ford was aided by Clements.

Success in a nonpolitical field can often propel a public career, especially if it involves the military. Johnson and Crittenden both fought in the War of 1812. Blackburn's tenure as a Confederate soldier aided him in post–Civil War Kentucky politics. Morton and Cooper helped their political careers by serving in the military during World War II. A successful career in law can also be an asset. This is not surprising, since the central task of being a lawmaker is making *law*. Clay, Crittenden, Pope, Stevenson, Beck, and John Breckinridge were accomplished lawyers. Morton and Ford were nonlawyers who were successful in private business and in politics as well.

Many used state executive office as a springboard to the Senate. Several Kentucky governors were frustrated by the commonwealth's long-standing prohibition against a governor succeeding himself and decided to run for the Senate. Clements and Ford are examples. Stevenson also used the governor's office to secure a Senate seat.

The lion's share of the individuals profiled in this study were compelling orators. One of Clay's many talents was his great ability as a public speaker. John C. Breckinridge was famed for his polished and persuasive declamation, which was said to rival that of Daniel Webster. Breckinridge's namesake was himself an outstanding debater. Barkley excelled as a stump speaker, his down-home style playing particularly well in rural communities. Blackburn was well regarded for his forensic ability. Pope was highly skilled in the art of disputation. Yet oratorical prowess is not an absolute necessity for success in the Senate. Cooper was decidedly not a compelling public speaker. Neither was Clements. Beck's skills as a public speaker were workmanlike at best, as were Johnson's.

Most of these Kentucky leaders were also "good party men." In the years before the twentieth century—when party affiliation was more fluid—being a loyal partisan was still important in establishing a leadership role in the Senate. Pope's career proves the rule. He went from being a Federalist to a Jeffersonian in the state house. Once he was in the US Senate, he opposed his party over the War of 1812 and promptly lost his seat. He later became essentially a Federalist again and then a Jacksonian, and then he clashed with Jackson. He became a Whig but was exposed for conspiring with Democrats to secure his reelection. As a result, Pope's public career was checkered, and he did not survive long enough in the Senate (or indeed, in any other public office) to leave a major legacy. Cooper, however, is an example to the contrary. He defied a president of his own party on the war in Southeast Asia, the biggest issue of the day. In Cooper's case, going against the grain of his party elevated his national and Senate standing, although it placed a great personal strain on him.

Some of these lawmakers placed great stock on their appearance. Blackburn, for example, "dressed to the nines" whenever he made a speech in the Senate. Others such as Johnson and Beck cared little how they looked.

Many of these individuals were effective senators for different reasons. Clay was an outstanding legislator due to a combination of factors. He commanded a major political following outside the Senate as well as in it. He was highly persuasive in debate. He was a creative thinker. He had a political vision—the American System—that he articulated and pursued.

Barkley's success was based on other considerations. He did not typically originate legislation on his own but was effective at getting bills enacted through his good relations with fellow lawmakers and the president. John Breckinridge—like Barkley—did not usually conceive of legislation by himself but received draft bills from friendly executive branch officials and successfully guided them through the legislative labyrinth. He was able to do this because he was known to speak for President Jefferson and because he was an effective debater. Furthermore, Breckinridge was shrewd in using parliamentary maneuvers to his advantage and was equally adept at committee work.

Finally, and perhaps most critically, the importance of steadfastly upholding political principles is manifested again and again in this volume. For Clay, preserving the Union was his lodestar. The same was true of Crittenden. For Brown, it was securing statehood and navigation rights on the Mississippi River for Kentucky. Johnson focused on helping the common laborer through his battle to end imprisonment for debt and to reform federal land policies in the territories. Barkley maintained a steadfast belief in the principles of the New Freedom and the New Deal. These lawmakers "stuck to their guns," but crucially, they were successful because they were willing to compromise, when necessary, to achieve their broader aims.

In sum, there is no uniform course to follow to become a successful senator. If the careers of these Kentucky senators serve as a guide, they demonstrate that there are any number of different paths to becoming a leader in the Senate.

A final question is, why have so many Kentuckians risen to leadership in the Senate? It could simply be an anomaly. However, we can cite several reasons for the commonwealth's prominent role in the upper chamber. First, Kentucky began as part of the Old Dominion and was heavily populated by former Virginians.[5] In the early years of statehood, Kentucky's political culture closely mimicked that of the mother commonwealth.[6] Virginia, of course, had an outsized influence on national politics in the first decades under the Constitution. Four of the first five presidents hailed from the Old Dominion, for instance. During the first quarter of the nineteenth century, Virginia was not only the birthplace of the dominant political party but also home to the leading political philosophy: Jeffersonianism. Both the party and the philosophy were embraced by Kentuckians.[7]

The early connection between Kentuckians and powerful Virginians is illustrated repeatedly in this volume. Brown and John Breckinridge both grew up in Virginia, and both befriended Jefferson. Breckinridge and Jefferson worked closely together on the Kentucky Resolutions.[8] They would later team up again when Breckinridge entered the Senate and Jefferson assumed the presidency. They cooperated on a host of matters, such as incorporating the Louisiana Territory into the United States.

Johnson and Pope were also born in Virginia. So was Clay, who—like Brown—was mentored by the Virginian Wythe. Stevenson grew up in Virginia, the son of a congressman from the Old Dominion. He regularly visited Jefferson and Madison in their later years. Crittenden's parents came from Virginia, and he graduated from William and Mary. These links to the most populous, powerful, and influential state in the early Union gave Kentucky lawmakers a leg up when they came to Washington, more so than if the state had been linked to, for example, Delaware or Georgia.[9]

Second, in the early nineteenth century, Kentucky was seen as the vanguard of a new region: the West. The commonwealth, in many ways, epitomized this new part of the country. Clay would become widely known as "Harry of the West." As the nineteenth century progressed and the concept of the West moved beyond the Mississippi River, Kentucky emerged as a bridge to yet another part of the country: the Midwest. Kentucky borders southern states such as Virginia and Tennessee as well as midwestern states such as Ohio, Indiana, Illinois, and Missouri.[10]

And, of course, Kentucky is a border state between North and South. The North-South divide has been one of the fundamental realities of the nation's political life, and Kentucky sits squarely astride the two regions. Reflecting these contrasts is that although much of Kentucky is culturally southern, the commonwealth did not secede from the Union. At the same time, the Democratic Party dominated the South for more than a century after the Civil War but often had little in common ideologically with Democrats from the North. Democratic senators from Kentucky helped bridge the North-South regional divide in the Senate because Kentucky itself bridged that gap.[11] To be elected, Kentucky senators had to overcome these same political fault lines (and they still do). Perhaps Kentucky's status as a border state helps explain the trio of Democratic caucus chairmen from the commonwealth immediately after the Civil War.

Because Kentucky sits at the dual intersection of North and South and East and Midwest, Kentucky lawmakers are not easily pigeonholed.[12] For instance, although it is often considered a southern state, both Kentucky senators—Cooper and Morton—voted for the 1964 Civil Rights Act.[13] No other state with a clear claim to the South can say the same.[14] Professor Thomas D. Clark rightly noted that Kentucky is indeed a "land of contrast."[15]

The Senate is a body of 100 individuals from every corner of the nation. To succeed in the upper chamber, one must have some appreciation of different viewpoints, and Kentucky's diverse citizenry provides its senators with a variety of perspectives.

In the late nineteenth century, Lauros McConachie wrote, "There has been a constant readjustment between the two prime functions which belong, as the supplements to each other, to every legislative body. . . . Deliberation *vs.* Action. The . . . test of success or failure for a Congress has ever been a wise balance between these two."[16] This tension between deliberation and action is perhaps more acute in the Senate than in any other national legislative assembly. It is the world's most powerful legislative body, but it also provides unparalleled power to the minority party and to individual senators.

Calibrating this fine balance and determining whether matters merit deliberation or action are ultimately the responsibility of leaders in the US Senate.

This enormous responsibility is heightened by the Senate's wide-ranging power. That Kentuckians have frequently led the chamber either formally or informally during the past two and a quarter centuries reflects the outsized role the commonwealth has played, through the legislative branch, in determining the fortunes of this nation.

Afterword
Mitch McConnell's Senate Leadership

Senator Lamar Alexander

The authors of this book about the history of Senate leadership and Kentucky lawmakers confronted a dilemma: how to include discussion of the longest serving Republican floor leader when that senator himself is an author of the book? Which is why I was asked to provide this afterword about Mitch McConnell's leadership.

In 1969, when I was twenty-nine and working in the Nixon White House, Senator Howard Baker Jr. (R-TN) said, "You might want to get to know that smart, young legislative assistant for Marlow Cook." Marlow Cook was Kentucky's newly elected Republican senator. "That smart, young legislative assistant" was twenty-seven-year-old Mitch McConnell.

If one has known him for a long time, the origins of Senator McConnell's Senate leadership style are not hard to trace. To begin with, when he was two years old, the doctor said, "Mitch has polio." It is hard to imagine today how terrifying those words were for parents then. McConnell remembers:

It was 1944. There was a serious epidemic that year all over the country. And the disease was very unpredictable. First, you'd think you had the flu and a couple of weeks later some people would be completely normal and some would be in an iron lung or dead.

In my case it affected my left quadriceps, the muscle between the knee and your thigh. And in one of the great good fortunes of my life, my mother was living with her sister in this little crossroads of Five Points, Alabama, where there was not even a stoplight—while my dad was overseas fighting the Germans—and it happened to be sixty miles from Warm Springs, where President Roosevelt had gone [to treat his own polio]. My mother took me to Warm Springs, they taught her a physical therapy regimen, and said do it four times a day and to keep me off my feet. She watched me every minute and prevented me from really walking. My first memory in life is when they told my mother I was going to be OK, that I'd be able to walk without a limp and we stopped at a shoe store in LaGrange, Georgia, on the way back to Alabama to get a pair of low-top shoes, which were a kind of symbol that I was going to have a normal childhood.

If one knows about the determination of Mitch McConnell's mother, it is not hard to imagine how her son determined as a college student to become a United States senator, and did. And how he determined to become Senate majority leader, and did.

Upon his reaching the Senate, the path to leadership was an arduous, two-decade-long journey: chairman of the National Republican Senatorial Committee (1997–2001), counselor to majority leader Trent Lott (2001–2003), majority whip (2003–2007), minority leader (2008–2014), and, finally, majority leader. As for his mother's example, McConnell says, "It sure had to have an effect on me, which was that if you stick to something, you keep working at it and giving it your best, the chances are that you may actually overcome whatever problem you're currently confronting."

A second leadership quality that Mitch McConnell learned early—in a fist-fight—was to not be pushed around. According to McConnell:

I was about seven, we lived in Athens, Alabama, and I had a friend across the street named Dicky McGrew, who was a year older than I was and considerably bigger. He was also a bully and he kept kind of pushing me around. And my dad called me over and said, "Son, I've been watching the way he's been pushing you around and I want you to go over there and I want you to beat him up." I went across the street and started swinging and I beat him up and bent his glasses, and it was an incredible lesson in standing up to bullies and I've thought about that throughout my life at critical moments when people are trying to push you around.

As a junior senator on the Senate Foreign Relations Committee, Mitch McConnell surprised colleagues when he sponsored sanctions against the apartheid regime in South Africa, and then in 1986 voted to override President Ronald Reagan's veto of those sanctions. But these colleagues would not have been surprised had they known McConnell twenty-five years earlier, when he was a student at the University of Louisville. He remembers:

The civil rights movement was the defining issue of our generation. Working as an intern in Congress during the summer of 1963, I got to see [Martin Luther King Jr.'s] "I Have a Dream" speech. Then, in 1964, I was an intern in [Kentucky] Senator John Sherman Cooper's office. Two important things happened in 1964. Cooper was in the middle of breaking the southern senators' filibuster on civil rights and we nominated Barry Goldwater, one of the few people who voted against the civil rights bill. Honestly, I was mad as hell about it. And I was so irritated about Goldwater voting against the civil rights bill and defining the Republican Party in a way that I thought would be unfortunate that I voted for Lyndon Johnson, which in retrospect was a huge mistake. But it was a protest vote.

That willingness as a college student to buck his own political party resurfaced forty years later in Senator McConnell's leadership on First Amendment free-speech issues. In 2006, he cast the deciding vote against adoption of a constitutional amendment to prohibit flag burning, when almost all of his Republican colleagues and almost all of his constituents had a different view. He argued that the First Amendment protects even personally offensive messages. McConnell also became the Senate's leading voice against restrictions on political speech under the guise of "campaign finance reform." Again, some in his own party disagreed, including President George W. Bush and Senator John McCain. But Senator McConnell remained undeterred, and on multiple occasions the Supreme Court has agreed with his view of protecting political speech under the First Amendment.

Two of the three US Senate Office Buildings in Washington, DC, are named for Philip A. Hart of Michigan and Richard B. Russell Jr. of Georgia, two senators who never were elected to formal party leadership positions by their colleagues. In this book, Senator McConnell discusses such "leaders without portfolio," describing occasions when a senator assumes a major policy role outside the confines of formal party or committee leadership. His favorite was Senator Cooper, whom McConnell has described as "my role model as a young man, a man of great conviction . . . [and] very smart." In his autobiography *The Long Game,* Senator McConnell tells of when Cooper took him to the ceremony preceding the signing of the Voting Rights Act of 1965 and, later on, of watching Cooper's principled questioning of the Vietnam War.[1]

Senator Cooper's example must have influenced his former intern's one-man crusade twenty years later against the repressive junta in far-away Burma. According to the *New York Times* in 2016, "[Senator McConnell] has been a lead sponsor of every major sanctions measure against the Burmese government over the last 20 years and has worked quietly and tirelessly with several administrations to try to bring democracy to the country."[2] As his former foreign policy adviser Robin Cleveland notes, unlike with the senator's efforts to oppose apartheid in South Africa, Burma in the early 1990s "was a totally unknown cause."[3] Senator McConnell tirelessly advocated for the release of Burma's pro-democracy leader Daw Aung San Suu Kyi, who for years had been under house arrest. In 2012, when Suu Kyi came to Washington, DC, as the new de facto head of government, she traveled to Kentucky "to thank [McConnell] for everything he did for us over, well, two decades. That's a long time."[4]

Of course, in order to become a Senate leader, one first has to be elected to the Senate. In Mitch McConnell's early career, one can find multiple clues that point to his fascination with political campaigns and the pugnacious style with which he wins them. An early signal was the fistfight with Dicky McGrew. Another: "I was probably the only fourteen-year-old in America watching political conventions from gavel to gavel. I began to practice the craft and see if I could get good at it." When he was elected president of his high school student body, "I was hooked," he remembers. At the University of Louisville, he was elected president of the student council of the College of Arts and Sciences, helped organize a civil rights march on the state capitol, and, as president of the College Republicans, persuaded Senator Barry Goldwater to speak on campus. In law school at the University of Kentucky, he ran successfully for president of the Student Bar Association.

McConnell did indeed learn the craft of politics and became good at it. He is undefeated in his own political campaigns, winning six Senate races in Kentucky, more than any other commonwealth senator. And he has been proficient in not just his own races. In 2010 and 2012, a political action committee called the Senate Conservative Fund helped nominate Republican candidates in five states who lost in the general election when more mainstream conservative nominees might have won, preventing Republicans from gaining control of the Senate. So, in 2014 and 2016, McConnell organized an effort to ensure that the most electable Republican Senate candidates were on the ballot and to defend incumbent Republicans who were challenged in primaries. He was successful in every case, including in his own primary. "We were not going to allow [what happened in 2010 and 2012] to happen anymore," he said. "And so, we got the most electable people nominated who basically took them on, because if you're dealing with a group of people who think compromise is a dirty word and who always want to make a point but never want to make a difference, the only thing to do if you want to win the election is to beat them."

Mostly, Mitch McConnell's political skills were born of necessity, growing up as he did in a state that was overwhelmingly Democratic. In July 1984, he was thirty-four points behind in his challenge to incumbent Democratic senator Walter "Dee" Huddleston. McConnell discovered that his opponent had been making speeches for money, which was legal then, but that he had been missing Senate votes to do it. He ran an ad featuring a Kentucky hunter with bloodhounds looking for Senator Huddleston to try to get him back to work. In another ad, the dog treed the senator right at the end of what became known as the "bloodhound campaign." McConnell defeated Huddleston by four-tenths of 1 percent of the vote.

I have searched in vain for early clues regarding one aspect of Mitch McConnell's leadership style: his parsimonious use of words. Sometimes he reverts to absolute silence. In his autobiography, he admits that he speaks to the press only when it is to his advantage. He also tells of when Microsoft founder Bill Gates visited him and the two of them just sat there waiting for the other to speak, making others in the room uncomfortable. He recounts that someone once told President George W. Bush that McConnell was excited over a certain vote and the president replied, "Really, how can you tell?"

Why so few words? McConnell's answer is: "I learn a lot more by listening. And so frequently I start out by listening and think about what I want to say before I do it. You typically don't get in trouble for what you don't say. There's nothing wrong with being cautious about your comments. I certainly don't mind talking but I usually like to know what I'm talking about before I venture down that path."

He is not the first Senate party leader to be frugal with words. According to columnist Bob Novak, former majority leader Mike Mansfield (D-MT) was the most difficult person for him to interview on *Meet the Press*. Novak recalled: "Mike Mansfield . . . had a different problem than most guests. . . . [H]is answers were too short, instead of too long. In fact, he really liked the yes or no answer. . . . I was warned that I would run out of questions with Senator Mansfield, and I did."[5] Former vice president Dick Cheney followed a similar approach. In his constitutional capacity as president of the Senate, Cheney would attend weekly luncheons of Republican senators, rarely saying a word. This made certain that when Cheney did rise to speak, senators listened. And silence, after all, was one of Benjamin Franklin's thirteen virtues and a tactic Franklin often employed in his own leadership style.

In July 2014, as minority leader, Senator McConnell spoke on the Senate floor about what kind of majority leader he would be if Republicans secured control of the chamber in the November elections. His model, he said, would be Senator Mansfield, the Democrat who was majority leader forty-five years earlier when McConnell was a Senate aide:

What I meant by that was . . . first of all you have to open the Senate up. The last year of the previous [Democratic] majority (2014) there were only fifteen roll-call votes on amendments the entire year. In the first year of our majority, in 2015, we had over 200. Open the Senate up, let people vote. Number two, we needed regular order, which means the bill is actually worked on together in committee, comes out to the floor with bipartisan support, and has a better chance of success. The best example I can think of was the bill to rewrite "No Child Left Behind." The law had proved to be unworkable and unpopular. And by the time it came out of committee, you had the Democrats and the Republicans lined up, it went to the floor, it was relatively open for amendments—not that absolutely everybody got everything they wanted—and in the end, it passed with a very large majority. President Obama called it a "Christmas miracle," and the *Wall Street Journal* said it was the "the largest devolution of federal control to the states in a quarter-century."

Senator McConnell is quick to list a series of achievements during his first two years as majority leader (2015 to 2016). Even with the Democrats controlling the White House, the senator helped secure what he regards as "concrete, bipartisan legislative results for the American people." In addition to the first major education reform since 2002, these accomplishments include the first significant reforms to Social Security since 1983, the first trade promotion authority bill since 2002, the first long-term highway bill since 2005, and the first major legislation to confront the nation's opioid crisis. And right before the end of 2016 came what many observers (including Senator McConnell himself) consider the biggest accomplishment of the 114th Congress: the "21st Century Cures Act." This legislation aims to ensure that medical breakthroughs get to patients more rapidly. It also reinvigorates the nation's efforts to combat cancer, helps ensure greater resources to combat opioid abuse, and provides a major overhaul of mental health treatment.

And don't forget, he says, measures to protect victims of human trafficking, to address Puerto Rico's fiscal crisis, to sanction North Korea, to strengthen the nation's cybersecurity defenses, to reform Medicaid, and to provide permanent tax relief for families and small businesses. These are serious accomplishments for a legislative body many had written off as irredeemably broken. "Now, what do all these things that we have done time after time under our majority have in common?" he asks. "In a time of divided government, we focused on the things that we can agree on, and do those. Because when people elect divided government, I think what they're saying is, 'I know you have big differences, but why don't you look for the things you agree on and do those.' And that's how this majority is totally different from the previous one."

No one should have been surprised at these legislative results. One only had to look to previous Congresses when Senator McConnell was minority leader and was at the center of four major bipartisan legislative efforts that helped keep the American economy from being seriously damaged. At the end of 2010, the country was facing a tax "cliff." Republicans controlled neither the White House nor Congress. With an economy still reeling from the "Great Recession," the expiration of tax relief threatened to further imperil the economy. Yet Senator McConnell led a bipartisan effort to ensure that taxes were not raised on any Americans.

The next year, the United States was on the verge of defaulting on its debt payments for the first time in history. With the clock ticking on the full faith and credit of the United States and calamitous economic consequences staring policy-makers in the face, Senator McConnell negotiated an eleventh-hour deal with Vice President Joe Biden. This measure avoided the devastating economic ramifications of default and resulted in the most significant spending reductions in recent memory.

In late 2012, the United States risked prolonging the Great Recession and increasing joblessness due to a series of expiring tax policies and indiscriminate spending cuts scheduled to take effect on January 1, 2013. Once again, Senator McConnell crafted a bipartisan compromise with Vice President Biden to avert this fiscal crisis by preventing a tax increase on a majority of Americans and ensuring that spending cuts were made in a more prudent manner.

Finally, in 2013, a standoff involving federal spending and the debt limit led to the second longest federal shutdown since 1980, threatening thousands of public- and private-sector jobs and putting the economic health of the country in jeopardy. Despite these challenges, Senator McConnell orchestrated an agreement with then–Senate majority leader Harry Reid (D-NV) that reopened the government and raised the debt ceiling, allowing the United States to continue making payments on its debt.

Despite his bipartisan work during times when the GOP did not control the White House, Senator McConnell's most enduring legacy as Senate party leader may ultimately involve working in tandem with a Republican administration. To date, a major part of that effort has involved the federal judiciary.[6] In early 2016, the esteemed conservative Supreme Court justice Antonin Scalia passed away. At the time, outgoing president Barack Obama was poised to replace Scalia with a liberal justice and swing the balance of the high court to the left. The Senate was in recess at the time, but Senator McConnell made it clear to the public that the next Supreme Court justice would be chosen by the incoming president, not by a lame duck. The American people would essentially decide the matter in the 2016 presidential campaign.

This step wound up making the filling of the Scalia vacancy a major issue in the race for the White House and helped rally conservatives around the Republican nominee. Despite taking slings and arrows from those on the left (who salivated at the chance to replace Scalia) and even some on the right (who were concerned that Hillary Clinton would name someone even more liberal than President Obama's choice), Senator McConnell stuck to his guns. The result was that in 2016 a Republican was elected president, and the next year, President Donald J. Trump chose—and the Senate confirmed—a distinguished conservative jurist, Neil Gorsuch, for the Supreme Court. Given that Gorsuch was only forty-nine upon his elevation, the senator's decision has the potential to affect the direction of the Court and the federal judiciary for decades. So too does the senator's work to ensure that federal circuit court vacancies are filled by conservative jurists. Under Senator McConnell's stewardship, more federal circuit court judges received advice and consent in 2017 than in the first year of any presidency dating back to the founding of the circuit courts in 1891.[7]

During the first year of the Trump presidency, Senator McConnell also vigorously pursued tax legislation. The result was the most far-reaching tax reform in over three decades. The senator also implemented the first widespread use of the long-dormant Congressional Review Act.[8] Revitalization of this arcane measure helped effectuate the most significant deregulation effort since the 1980s.[9]

The net result of Senator McConnell's first twelve months as majority leader with a Republican administration has been the most consequential year for conservatives since the Reagan era. In many ways, it served as a counterpoint to the Left's legislative victories in 2009 and 2010, when they enjoyed a 60-vote supermajority in the chamber.

Humorist Roy Blount Jr. has written, "You start getting in trouble when you stop sounding like where you grew up." The political corollary is that you start getting in trouble when you stop coming home. This is advice McConnell has not forgotten. He and his wife Elaine go home to Kentucky almost every weekend. He has kept his eye on Kentucky matters both large and small, including working toward the disposal of chemical weapons that have long been stored in the middle of the commonwealth, enacting a tobacco "buyout" to help local farmers, supporting the state's public universities, ensuring that Berea College will be able to continue to provide tuition-free education to low-income students, and advocating for workers at the Paducah Gaseous Diffusion Plant. Kentucky anglers and tourists appreciate his helping to enact a law to require the Army Corps of Engineers to allow fishing below dams on the Cumberland River. Twenty-five years ago, he created the McConnell Center at the University of Louisville, which provides academic scholarships at the university for promising young Kentuckians. The center also attracts a bipartisan parade of national and international leaders to visit with the McConnell scholars (e.g., six secretaries of state, including Colin Powell and Hillary Rodham Clinton).

His close bond with the state includes how he spends his leisure time. Each year, Mitch McConnell buys twelve season tickets to University of Louisville football games: "I have some regulars. We go to every home game and occasionally an away game. We make a day of it. We go out early. One of my friends has an RV in the parking lot, and we will talk about what will happen in the game and then go to the game, and then we talk about what did happen in the game and it's a complete, lengthy exercise. And one of the great joys of life."

Mitch McConnell's University of Louisville senior honors thesis on Henry Clay tempted him to pursue a doctorate in American history and a career as a professor, but those who know him doubt that he would have been satisfied interpreting the action rather than being in the middle of it. But his devotion to US history and his understanding of the importance of the Senate as a unique institution in American life have contributed a valuable extra dimension to his Senate leadership.

In a 2016 C-SPAN interview, he was asked: "What message would you like for us to take back to our students about the United States Senate and the future of our country?"[10] He replied: "That the Senate has been the indispensable legislative body. Because that's the place where things are sorted out, the place where only rarely does the majority get things exactly their own way, the place where stability can occur."[11]

And, at a time when many Americans are not optimistic about our country's future, he was asked: "What would you want those teachers to tell their students about their future in this country?"[12] "Because of our woeful ignorance of American history, we always think the current period we're in is tougher than others," Senator McConnell said. "[But] we have had nothing like the Civil War period. We haven't had a single incident where a Congressman from South Carolina came over and almost beat to death a Senator from Massachusetts. America's had plenty of tough challenges. World Wars. Depressions. This is a great country. We're going to deal with whatever our current problems are, and move on to another level. And I'm just as optimistic as I ever was that this generation is going to leave behind a better America than our parents left behind for us."[13]

Acknowledgments

This book is the outgrowth of a series of speeches Senator McConnell delivered at a number of Kentucky colleges and universities beginning in 2012. These talks benefited from the assistance of many people over the years, including the able research, editing, and proofreading skills of Phil Maxson, Nancy McKinstry, Hillary MacInnes, Ali Nepola, Hannah Hummelberg, Jacob Hart, Sydney Dooley, and James O'Brien. Drafts of these speeches benefited from the insightful reviews provided by Sharon Soderstrom, Brian McGuire, Josh Holmes, Rohit Kumar, Don Stewart, Justin Jones, Kevin Grout, and Brian Forest. Billy Piper, Terry Carmack, and Stefanie Muchow deserve special credit for making this series a reality.

Invaluable critiques were also provided by US Senate historian Betty Koed; Walter Oleszek of CRS; Kentucky state historian James Klotter of Georgetown College; former Eastern Kentucky University Foundation professor Tom Appleton; director of the University of Louisville's McConnell Center, Gary Gregg; and John Kleber, also of the University of Louisville. Individual speeches were greatly enhanced by the thoughtful comments of former historian of the US House of Representatives Robert Remini, former US representative Ben Chandler, associate US Senate historian Kate Scott, Professor Gerald Gamm of the University of Rochester, Professor Steven S. Smith of Washington University, Richard Beth of CRS, Chris Mosher (an expert on Senator Earle Clements), Fred Karem Sr., and the family of Senator Wendell Ford. Conversations with Ms. Soderstrom, Elizabeth MacDonough, Hazen Marshall, Laura Dove, Dr. Beth, Dr. Oleszek, Valerie Heitshusen, Christopher Davis, Elizabeth Rybicki, Dr. Gamm, Dr. Smith, and Mark Oleszek provided much-needed background information for these speeches.

In addition, the authors would like to express their appreciation to the staff of the US Senate Library, who were essential in tracking down countless documents. Particular recognition is due Nancy Kervin, the "Henry Clay of librarians," whose enthusiasm and extraordinary efficiency were indispensable. Staff at the Library of Congress and the libraries at the University of Kentucky, Princeton University, Georgetown University, the University of Wisconsin, the University of Texas, the University of Mississippi, Boise State University, and Duke University also secured essential materials.

The process of modifying and greatly expanding the speeches into book form prompts a separate round of acknowledgments, beginning with Dr. Gregg, whose idea it was to write and publish this volume. The authors would like to express their gratitude to Steve Wrinn and Ashley Runyon, two University Press of Kentucky (UPK) alumni, for their encouragement while this project was in its infancy. Thanks are due to UPK director Leila Salisbury for her unwavering support of the book and to Jackie Wilson for her marketing assistance. Patrick O'Dowd of UPK guided the project from book proposal through the review process and ultimately to completion, doing so with unfailing good humor, infinite patience, and wise counsel. He and the Editorial Board and staff of UPK, including David Cobb and Linda Lotz, could not have been more helpful.

Four anonymous readers provided incisive comments and critiques that sharpened the focus, and improved the content, of the book. Drs. Oleszek, Klotter, Appleton, and Kleber enhanced the manuscript immeasurably through their rigorous review. Similarly, US Senate historians emeriti Richard Baker and Donald Ritchie offered invaluable critiques. The authors are grateful for the efforts of the current Senate historian, Dr. Koed, who carefully reviewed chapters 1 through 6; Professor Joel K. Goldstein of St. Louis University Law School, who provided a searching review of chapters 1 and 2; and Kate Hesseldenz, curator and development assistant at Liberty Hall Historic Site, who read the pages on John Brown and helped secure images of the early senator. The book also benefited immensely from the generosity of Drs. Gamm and Smith, who shared a draft chapter from their forthcoming book on Senate party leadership.

For their aid in securing approval for the reproduction of images, the authors would like to acknowledge the efforts of US Senate curator Melinda Smith; assistant US Senate curator Amy Elizabeth Burton; Anum Mirza, executive assistant to the Senate curator; US Senate photo historian Heather Moore; retired curator of the McConnell Chao Archives at the University of Louisville, Deborah Skaggs; current curator of the McConnell Chao Archives, Nan Mosher; Kia Campbell, DeCarlos Boyd, and Tomeka Myers of the Library of Congress; Heather Potter and Jana Meyer of the Filson Historical Society; John Horne and Connie Robinson of the National Baseball Hall of Fame and Museum; Peter Huestis of the National Gallery of Art; Lydia Washington and Gwendolyn House of the Bureau of Engraving and Printing; Elizabeth Druga of the Gerald Ford Presidential Library and Museum; Jim Duran, Alex Meregaglia, and Cheryl Oestreicher of Boise State University; Holly Reed of the National Archives and Records Administration; Erin Beasley of the National Portrait Gallery at the Smithsonian Institution; Kent Whitworth, Cheri Daniels, and

Beth Carter of the Kentucky Historical Society; Peter Carr of the Department of Justice; Jack Brammer and Ron Garrison of the *Lexington Herald-Leader;* Sheila Omer Ferrell, Tom Moore, Tim Condo, and Jackson Osborne of the Blue Grass Trust for Historic Preservation; Jason Flahardy of the University of Kentucky Digital Library; and Clay Ford and the Ford family.

The authors would like to recognize Senator Lamar Alexander, who deserves particular thanks for contributing the book's afterword.

A tip of the cap is also due Sabina Beauchard and Sara Georgini of the Massachusetts Historical Society for their assistance securing documents. Deep appreciation is expressed to Kathy Reinke for her assistance with this project; to Elizabeth Dunn and the staff at the Rubenstein Library at Duke University for their help accessing the Floyd Millard Riddick Papers; and to Daniel Cameron, Tiffany Ge, Deborah Mayer, Lynn Tran, and Geoff Turley for their counsel.

Book writing is a time-consuming exercise, and as such, the authors would like to recognize their families above all for their steadfast support and sacrifice while this book was being written. Senator McConnell would like to thank his wife, Secretary Elaine L. Chao, and his daughters, Elly, Claire, and Porter. Mr. Brownell would like to express his profound appreciation to his wife, Sandra Adams, as well as to Eleanor Brownell, Ginanne Brownell, and Dr. Josiah Brownell.

With respect to all the individuals named above, the authors are, in the words of Alexis de Tocqueville, "glad to owe them a *debt* of *gratitude.*"

Any remaining errors are the authors' alone.

Senator Mitch McConnell
Roy E. Brownell II
2018

Notes

Abbreviations

AAAPSS	*Annals of the American Academy of Political and Social Science*
AAP	*Almanac of American Politics* (multiple editions)
AC	*Atlanta Constitution*
ADA	*American and Daily Advertiser*
AH	*American Heritage*
AHQ	*Arkansas Historical Quarterly*
AHR	*American Historical Review*
ALR	*Arkansas Law Review*
AMVB	*Autobiography of Martin Van Buren,* ed. John C. Fitzpatrick (Washington, DC: Government Printing Office, 1920)
AOC	*Annals of Congress*
APSA	American Political Science Association
APSR	*American Political Science Review*
BG	*Boston Globe*
BS	*Baltimore Sun*
CCG	*Cincinnati Commercial Gazette*
CD	*Congressional Digest*
CG	*Congressional Globe*
CGA	*Cincinnati Gazette*
CL	*Clarion-Ledger*
CQ	*Congressional Quarterly*
CR	*Congressional Record*
CRS	Congressional Research Service
CS	*Capitol Studies*
CSM	*Christian Science Monitor*
CT	*Chicago Tribune*
CWH	*Civil War History*
DNI	*Daily National Intelligencer*
FCHQ	*Filson Club History Quarterly*
FLR	*Fordham Law Review*
FMRP	Floyd Millard Riddick Papers, Duke University Libraries, Durham, NC
FSJ	*Frankfort State Journal*
GC	*Greenwood Commonwealth*
HC	*Hartford Courant*

HCP	Horace Chilton Papers, 1897, Dolph Briscoe Center for American History, University of Texas–Austin
HM	*Harper's Monthly*
HW	*Harper's Weekly*
IMH	*Indiana Magazine of History*
IY	*Idaho Yesterdays*
JOP	*Journal of Politics*
JQAM	*Memoirs of John Quincy Adams,* ed. Charles Francis Adams (Philadelphia: J. B. Lippincott, 1875)
JSCH	*Journal of Supreme Court History*
KF	*Knoxville Focus*
KJLPP	*Kansas Journal of Law and Public Policy*
KR	*Kentucky Review*
LAT	*Los Angeles Times*
LBF	*Louisville Business First*
LBNCOH	Louie B. Nunn Center for Oral History, University of Kentucky Libraries
LCJ	*Louisville Courier-Journal*
LDCN	*Lowell Daily Citizen and News*
LHL	*Lexington Herald-Leader*
LS	*Louisiana Studies*
LSI	*Law & Social Inquiry*
LSQ	*Legislative Studies Quarterly*
LT	*Louisville Times*
LVS	*Las Vegas Sun*
MHS	Massachusetts Historical Society
MVHR	*Mississippi Valley Historical Review*
MWPSA	Midwest Political Science Association
NA	*Norwich Aurora*
NAUSG	*North American and United States Gazette*
NDA	*Newark Daily Advertiser*
NHDP	*New Haven Daily Palladium*
NJD	*National Journal Daily*
NR	*National Review*
NYT	*New York Times*
NYUJLPP	*New York University Journal of Legislation and Public Policy*
NYW	*New York World*
OS	*Ohio Statesman*
PDT	*Portsmouth Daily Times*
PLR	*Pepperdine Law Review*
PLS	*Politics and the Life Sciences*
PLSQ	*Political Science Quarterly*
PSQ	*Presidential Studies Quarterly*
PTR	*Pittsburgh Tribune Review*
RB	*Ripley Bee*
RC	*Roll Call*
RKHS	*Register of Kentucky Historical Society*

RMSSJ	*Rocky Mountain Social Science Journal*
RODC	*Register of Debates in Congress*
SAQ	*South Atlantic Quarterly*
SCER	*Supreme Court Economic Review*
SDN	*Starkville Daily News*
SEJ	*Senate Executive Journal*
SEP	*Saturday Evening Post*
SJ	*Senate Journal*
SJLR	*St. John's Law Review*
SLGD	*St. Louis Globe-Democrat*
SLPD	*St. Louis Post-Dispatch*
SLR	*Stanford Law Review*
SLULJ	*St. Louis University Law Journal*
SWHQ	*Southwestern Historical Quarterly*
SWIJ	*Stanford, Kentucky, Semi-Weekly Interior Journal*
TA	*The Atlantic*
TH	*The Hill*
TJP	*Papers of Thomas Jefferson,* ed. James P. McClure and Barbara B. Oberg (Princeton, NJ: Princeton University Press, ongoing series)
TN	*The Nation*
TNR	*The New Republic*
TW	*The Whig*
UPI	*United Press International*
UPJCL	*University of Pennsylvania Journal of Constitutional Law*
VC	*Vermont Chronicle*
VLR	*Virginia Law Review*
WFLR	*Wake Forest Law Review*
WFMJ	*Woodberry Forest Magazine and Journal*
WJA	*Works of John Adams,* ed. Charles Francis Adams (Boston: Little, Brown, 1856)
WMJ	*Journal of William Maclay,* intro. by Charles A. Beard (New York: Albert & Charles Boni, 1927)
WP	*Washington Post*
WPM	*William Plumer's Memorandum of Proceedings in the United States Senate, 1803–1807,* ed. Everett Somerville Brown (New York: Macmillan, 1923)
WPQ	*Western Political Quarterly*
WS	*Washington Star*
WT	*Washington Times*
YCH	*Yazoo City Herald*

Introduction

1. Cf. A. C. Quisenberry, "Kentucky—Mother of United States Senators and Representatives," *RKHS* 18 (1920): 77; *Wendell Ford, United States Senator: Tributes in Congress* (Washington, DC: Government Printing Office, 1998), 6–7 (Sen. Byrd); Lee Lingo, "A Look at the State of Manufacturing in Kentucky," *LBF,* March 8, 2018.

2. Holmes Alexander, *The Famous Five* (New York: Bookmailer, 1958), 1, 4; David L. Porter, "America's Ten Greatest Senators," in *The Rating Game in American Politics: An Interdisciplinary Approach* (New York: Irvington Publishers, 1987), 112.

3. The other states are Indiana (John Worth Kern and James Watson), Tennessee (Howard Baker and Bill Frist), Maine (Wallace White and George Mitchell), and Kansas (Charles Curtis and Bob Dole). Most authorities date the beginning of the Senate majority leader office to 1913—the year Kern began his tenure as Democratic caucus chairman. Walter J. Oleszek, "John Worth Kern: Portrait of a Floor Leader," in *First among Equals: Outstanding Senate Leaders of the Twentieth Century,* ed. Richard A. Baker and Roger H. Davidson (Washington, DC: CQ Press, 1991), 7.

4. Cf. Lingo, "A Look."

5. "Leader J. C. S. Blackburn," *BS,* June 10, 1906.

6. As part of a broad compilation, H. Levin's *The Lawyers and Lawmakers of Kentucky* (Chicago: Lewis Publishing, 1897) included brief discussions of the lives of Kentucky senators up to that time. However, that work focused on distinguished attorneys, not senators per se, and it is more than a century old. For a helpful summary of events relating to Kentucky and the US Senate, see "States in the Senate: Kentucky Timeline," US Senate, accessed February 15, 2018, http://www.senate.gov/states/KY/timeline.htm.

7. The states are Texas, Tennessee, Georgia, Alabama, Illinois, and South Dakota.

8. Andrea Hatcher's *Majority Leadership in the U.S. Senate: Balancing Constraints* (Amherst, NY: Cambria Press, 2010) is one of only two books devoted entirely to the Senate majority leader position. The other is a work edited by noted scholar Colton Campbell, *Leadership in the U.S. Senate: Herding Cats in the Modern Era* (New York: Routledge, 2019). Baker and Davidson's classic *First among Equals* profiles a number of Senate majority *and* minority leaders. Two other esteemed scholars, Gerald Gamm and Steven S. Smith, are currently at work on a comprehensive treatment of the evolution of Senate party leadership.

9. Walter J. Oleszek, "Senate Leadership," in *The Encyclopedia of the United States Congress,* ed. Donald C. Bacon, Roger H. Davidson, and Morton Keller (New York: Simon & Schuster, 1995), 3:1261.

10. Donald A. Ritchie, *The U.S. Congress: A Very Short Introduction* (New York: Oxford University Press, 2010), 2–3, 13, 20–21, 74; Barbara Sinclair, "Coequal Partner: The U.S. Senate," in *Senates: Bicameralism in the Contemporary World,* ed. Samuel C. Patterson and Anthony Mughan (Columbus: Ohio State University Press, 1999), 32; Steven S. Smith and Gerald Gamm, "The Dynamics of Party Government in Congress," in *Congress Reconsidered,* 9th ed., ed. Lawrence C. Dodd and Bruce I. Oppenheimer (Washington, DC: CQ Press, 2009), 145.

11. George H. Haynes, *The Senate of the United States: Its History and Practice* (New York: Russell & Russell, 1960), 1:419.

12. "A Place of 'Sober Second Thought,'" US Senate, accessed February 15, 2018, http://www.senate.gov/artandhistory/history/idea_of_the_senate/1897Hoar.htm. For one prominent Framer's view of the anticipated deliberative qualities of the Senate, see *The Federalist* Nos. 62 and 63 (James Madison).

13. Nicol C. Rae, *Conservative Reformers: The Republican Freshmen and the Lessons of the 104th Congress* (Armonk, NY: M. E. Sharpe, 1998), 131–67; Ross K. Baker, *House and Senate,* 3d ed. (New York: W. W. Norton, 2001), 84.

14. Steven S. Smith, "Parties and Leadership in the Senate," in *The Legislative Branch,* ed. Paul J. Quick and Sarah A. Binder (New York: Oxford University Press, 2005), 274; Baker, *House and Senate,* 103–4.

15. Robert C. Byrd, *The Senate, 1789–1989: Addresses on the History of the United States Senate* (Washington, DC: Government Printing Office, 1991), 2:193; Smith and Gamm, "Dynamics," 145; Charles Tiefer, *Congressional Practice and Procedure: A Reference, Research, and Legislative Guide* (New York: Greenwood Press, 1989), 463–66; Ralph K. Huitt, "The Internal Distribution of Influence: The Senate," in *The Congress and America's Future,* ed. David B. Truman (Englewood Cliffs, NJ: Prentice-Hall, 1965), 80.

16. Vishnoo Bhagwan and Vidya Bhushan, *World Constitutions,* 8th ed. (New Delhi: Sterling Publishers, 2008), 219–21; cf. Haynes, *Senate,* vii. Because of its unique relationship to, and checks on, the House and the president, the Senate is often characterized as the most powerful legislative body within a separated system of government. Bhagwan and Bhushan, *World Constitutions,* 218–19, 223–26; Donald R. Matthews, *U.S. Senators and Their World* (Chapel Hill: University of North Carolina Press, 1960), 4–6; Ritchie, *Congress,* 15.

17. Elaine K. Swift, *The Making of an American Senate: Reconstitutive Change in Congress, 1787–1841* (Ann Arbor: University of Michigan Press, 2002), 51–52; Neil MacNeil and Richard A. Baker, *The American Senate: An Insider's History* (New York: Oxford University Press, 2013), 54; Matthews, *Senators and Their World,* 5; Roy Swanstrom, *The United States Senate, 1787–1801* (Washington, DC: Government Printing Office, 1988), 14; Katherine Scott and James Wyatt, "Robert C. Byrd: Tactician and Technician," in Campbell, *Leadership,* 83.

18. Robert C. Byrd, *The Senate—Great Forum of Constitutional Liberty* (Louisville, KY: McConnell Center for Political Leadership, 2000), 16; Haynes, *Senate,* vii; cf. Swanstrom, *Senate,* 143, 147.

19. James Madison to Thomas Jefferson, October 24, 1787, *The Founders' Constitution,* accessed February 15, 2018, http://press-pubs.uchicago.edu/founders/documents/v1ch17s22.html. James Bryce expressed a similar view: the Senate is "a centre of gravity in the government, an authority able to correct and check on the one hand the 'democratic recklessness' of the House, on the other the 'monarchical ambition' of the President. Placed between the two, it is necessarily the rival and generally the opponent of both." James Bryce, *The American Commonwealth* (London: Macmillan, 1888), 1:150.

20. "A Great Compromise," US Senate, accessed February 15, 2018, https://www.senate.gov/artandhistory/history/minute/A_Great_Compromise.htm.

21. Ibid.

22. Ritchie, *Congress,* 1.

23. Before the Seventeenth Amendment, senators were elected by state legislatures and not directly by the public, which made the Senate even more insulated from popular pressure.

24. George Rothwell Brown, *The Leadership of Congress* (Indianapolis: Bobbs-Merrill, 1922), 254.

25. Floyd M. Riddick, *Majority and Minority Leaders of the Senate* (Washington, DC: Government Printing Office, 1988), 2–3.

26. Haynes, *Senate,* 207–8; Michael Nelson, "Background Paper," in *Report of the Twentieth Century Fund Task Force on the Vice Presidency* (New York: Priority Press Publications, 1988), 62–63; Gerald Gamm and Steven S. Smith, "Last among Equals: The Senate's Presiding Officer," in *Esteemed Colleagues: Civility and Deliberation in the U.S. Senate,* ed. Burdett A. Loomis (Washington, DC: Brookings Institution, 2000), 105–6.

27. Gamm and Smith, "Last among Equals," 106; Haynes, *Senate,* 209–10, 473.

28. George Goodwin Jr., *The Little Legislatures: Committees in Congress* (Amherst: University of Massachusetts Press, 1970), 222. Indeed, as discussed in chapter 4, the Speaker did

not emerge as the true leader of the House until the second decade of the nineteenth century, after Henry Clay had been elevated to the position.

29. Kentucky's other two vice presidents were Adlai Stevenson and Alben Barkley. Stevenson is omitted because he never served as a senator and did not live in Kentucky during his public career. Barkley's life and career are examined in chapter 7.

30. Walter Kravitz, "The Presiding Officers," in "The United States Senate: A History" (unpublished manuscript on file with the authors), 49.

31. Ibid.

32. Walter Kravitz, "Leadership, Old Style: The Leading Men," in "The United States Senate: A History," 4–5, 10–11, 15–16, 37.

33. Riddick, *Majority and Minority Leaders,* 2.

34. Ibid.

35. Ibid.

36. Richard A. Baker and Roger H. Davidson, introduction to *First among Equals,* 1–2; Ritchie, *Congress,* 52; Swift, *Making of an American Senate,* 178; Claude G. Bowers, *The Life of John Worth Kern* (Indianapolis: Hollenbeck Press, 1918), 294–95; Kravitz, "Leadership, Old Style," 2, 22; Byrd, *Senate, 1789–1989,* 207.

37. MacNeil and Baker, *American Senate,* 16; Clara Hannah Kerr, *The Origin and Development of the United States Senate* (Ithaca, NY: Andrews & Church, 1895), 80.

38. Robert Luce, *Legislative Procedure: Parliamentary Practices and the Course of Business in the Framing of Statutes* (Boston: Houghton Mifflin, 1922), 508; Kerr, *Origin,* 81–82; M. Ostrogorski, "The Rise and Fall of the Nominating Caucus, Legislative and Congressional," *AHR* 5 (1899): 253, 259–62; Swift, *Making of an American Senate,* 71–72.

39. Gerald Gamm and Steven S. Smith, "Emergence of Senate Party Leadership," in *U.S. Senate Exceptionalism,* ed. Bruce I. Oppenheimer (Columbus: Ohio State University Press, 2002), 218–21. Caucuses chose chairmen in the early nineteenth century, but it appears that both the caucuses and the chairmanships were temporary. *WPM,* 597–98.

40. Gamm and Smith, "Emergence" (2002), 232.

41. Gerald Gamm and Steven Smith, "The Rise of Floor Leaders, 1890–1913" (draft book chapter), 10, 12–14. The first Democratic caucus chairman on record, John W. Stevenson of Kentucky, had been in the Senate only two years when he was chosen by his fellow partisans. Gerald Gamm and Steven S. Smith, "The Senate without Leaders: Senate Parties in the Mid-19th Century" (paper prepared for the APSA annual meeting, 2001), 12–13.

42. Gerald Gamm and Steven Smith, "The Emergence of Senate Party Leadership, 1913–1937: The Case of the Democrats" (paper delivered at the Congress and History Workshop, Vanderbilt University, May 21–23, 2015), 4–5.

43. Gamm and Smith, "Emergence" (2002), 219–20.

44. Margaret Rampton Munk, "Origin and Development of the Party Floor Leadership in the United States Senate" (PhD diss., Harvard University, 1970), 9–16, 81–160; Gamm and Smith, "Emergence" (2002), 18–33.

45. Hatcher, *Majority Leadership,* 98–99.

46. Munk, "Origin," 3–7, 116–29; Baker and Davidson, introduction to *First among Equals,* 1, 2; cf. Randall B. Ripley, *Majority Party Leadership in Congress* (Boston: Little, Brown, 1969), 4–5.

47. Ripley, *Majority Party Leadership,* 3.

48. Gamm and Smith, "Emergence" (2002), 229–36; Garrison Nelson, "Leadership Selection in the U.S. Senate, 1899–1985: Changing Patterns of Recruitment and Institu-

tional Interaction" (unpublished paper, 1985), 1; Richard E. Cohen, *Congressional Leadership: Seeking a New Role* (Beverly Hills, CA: Sage Publications, 1980), 23; cf. David W. Rohde, *Parties and Leaders in the Postreform House* (Chicago: University of Chicago Press, 1991), 31–34.

49. This prerogative is also referred to as the right of "priority recognition," "preferential recognition," and "first recognition."

50. For earlier discussion of the precedent, see chapter 7, note 145.

51. Walter J. Oleszek, "Party Whips in the United States Senate," *JOP* 33 (1971): 955, 958–60.

52. The others are Earle Clements, who is profiled in chapter 9, and this book's lead author.

53. Robin Kolodny, *Pursuing Majorities: Congressional Campaign Committees in American Politics* (Norman: University of Oklahoma Press, 1998), 54, 68, 70, 72.

54. Ibid., 63, 159–96.

55. The others are Wendell Ford, who is considered in chapter 8, and this book's lead author.

56. There are two unpublished PhD dissertations about Brown's life and a handful of articles, many of which focus on his alleged political intrigues with the Spanish. Only an unpublished master's thesis and a series of Senate memorial addresses discuss Beck's life at any length. One academic article describes Blackburn, but it centers around his service as governor of Panama; there are also a handful of contemporary journalistic character sketches. Finally, Morton is profiled in an unpublished PhD dissertation and a brief sketch in an alumni magazine.

57. Kentuckians have also contributed to the development of House leadership institutions. Chapter 4 describes Henry Clay's impact on the Speaker's office; see also Cohen, *Congressional Leadership*, 26 (discussing John G. Carlisle's influence on the Speaker's prerogatives).

1. President of the Senate

1. US Constitution, Article I, section 3, clause 4.

2. Roy E. Brownell II, "A Constitutional Chameleon: The Vice President's Place within the American System of Separation of Powers, Part II: Political Branch Interpretation and Counterarguments," *KJLPP* 24 (2015): 294, 297–374.

3. Ibid.

4. Joel K. Goldstein, "The New Constitutional Vice Presidency," *WFLR* 30 (1995): 505, 510–15. For incisive treatment of the origins of the vice presidency, see ibid.; Edward J. Larson, "A Constitutional Afterthought: The Origins of the Vice Presidency," *PLR* 44 (2017): 515.

5. *The Records of the Federal Convention of 1787* (Max Farrand ed., 1966), 1:292, 2:155, 158, 165, 172, 179, 186, 239, 367, 427 (hereafter *Farrand*).

6. *Farrand* 1:292, 2:172, 186, 427.

7. *Farrand* 2:537 (Hugh Williamson); see also Larson, "Constitutional Afterthought," 516–22; Joel K. Goldstein, "History and Constitutional Interpretation: Some Lessons from the Vice Presidency," *ALR* 69 (2016): 647, 659–60.

8. *Farrand* 2:536–37.

9. *The Federalist* No. 68 (Alexander Hamilton).

10. *Farrand* 2:537.

11. *The Federalist* No. 68.

12. US Constitution, Article II, section 1, clause 3 (superseded by the Twelfth Amendment).

13. Joel K. Goldstein, "An Overview of the Vice-Presidency," *FLR* 45 (1977): 786, 789; Arthur M. Schlesinger Jr., "On the Presidential Succession," *PLSQ* 89 (1974): 475, 489.

14. Michael Nelson, "Background Paper," in *A Heartbeat Away: Report of the Twentieth Century Fund Task Force on the Vice Presidency* (New York: Priority Press Publications, 1988), 28–29.

15. Ibid.

16. Brownell, "Constitutional Chameleon, Part II," 297–329.

17. Earl Leon Shoup, "The Vice-Presidency of the United States" (PhD diss., Harvard University, 1923), 151–52; Nelson, "Background Paper," 62.

18. George H. Haynes, *The Senate of the United States: Its History and Practice,* 2d ed. (New York: Russell & Russell, 1960), 1:44, 271 n. 1; Nelson, "Background Paper," 62.

19. John C. Calhoun broke thirty-one tie votes. Senate Historical Office, Compilation of Tie-Breaking Votes (on file with the authors). In 1794, Vice President Adams wrote to his wife: "I would gladly go home; but at a time so critical as this, it would not be justifiable to quit my post. . . . the senate is nearly divided in all great questions . . . my retirement would give an entire new complexion to the government." John Adams to Abigail Adams, March 15, 1794, *WJA,* 1:468; see also Shoup, "Vice-Presidency," 445.

20. *WMJ,* 301.

21. Ibid., 2–3, 16, 20–23, 26, 32, 37–38, 44, 63, 115, 153, 159, 186, 191, 237, 248, 271, 303, 322. On May 12, 1789, Maclay expressed surprise that Adams did *not* speak at length to the Senate that day. Ibid., 30. Today, vice presidents occasionally address the Senate briefly to explain rulings or by unanimous consent of the membership. Floyd M. Riddick and Alan Frumin, *Riddick's Senate Procedure: Precedents and Practice* (Washington, DC: Government Printing Office, 1992), 1390–92; Memorandum on Participation by Vice President in Debate, CRS, n.d. (on file with the authors).

22. *WMJ,* 26.

23. Ibid., 1.

24. Ibid., 318–19; see also Roy Swanstrom, *The United States Senate, 1787–1801: A Dissertation on the First Fourteen Years of the Upper Legislative Body* (Washington, DC: Government Printing Office, 1988), 204. In the days before formal floor leaders, the vice president often "took the initiative under the rules [and practices at the time] to move the Senate from one stage [of business] to the next without prompting from the floor." Gerald Gamm and Steven S. Smith, "The Emergence of Senate Leadership, 1881–1946" (paper presented at the MWPSA, April 10–12, 1997), 31. Today, this would be done by the majority leader with the subsequent concurrence of the Senate.

25. *WMJ,* 112–13, 163, 177. Adams had particular sway with senators from the Northeast. Ibid., 24.

26. 1 *SJ* 332 (1791); see also Haynes, *Senate,* 273 n. 3. With minor exceptions, committees were not permanent at the time and would not become permanent until 1816. For more on the development of Senate panels, see chapter 5.

27. Brownell, "Constitutional Chameleon, Part II," 301, 314.

28. Irving G. Williams, *The Rise of the Vice Presidency* (Washington, DC: Public Affairs Press, 1956), 23; see also Nelson, "Background Paper," 62; cf. Swanstrom, *Senate,* 253, 255.

Interestingly, Adams tasked his son, John Quincy, to research the ancient Roman position of *Princeps Senatus,* the "Prince of the Senate." John Adams to John Quincy Adams, July 9, 1789, Adams Papers, MHS, accessed February 15, 2018, https://www.masshist.org /publications/apde2/view?id=ADMS-04-08-02-0209. The *Princeps Senatus* enjoyed the privilege of addressing the Roman Senate before any other senator on any matter, roughly akin to prior recognition for the majority leader. Ibid., n. 4. It seems likely that Adams was looking for a historical parallel to bolster his standing in the early Senate.

29. Swanstrom, *Senate,* 254–57.

30. *WMJ,* 13; see also Walter Kravitz, "The Presiding Officers," in "The United States Senate: A History" (unpublished manuscript on file with the authors), 15. Adams's ally Congressman Fisher Ames (Fed.-MA) also expressed exasperation at the vice president's fixation on trying to persuade the Senate to adopt august titles. Swanstrom, *Senate,* 254.

31. John Trumbull urged Adams to involve himself less in debate, expressing concern that he was acting "too much like the leader of a party." Page Smith, *John Adams* (Garden City, NY: Doubleday, 1962), 2:788–89; Mark O. Hatfield with the US Senate Historical Office, *Vice Presidents of the United States, 1789–1993* (Washington, DC: Government Printing Office, 1997), 8.

32. 46 *CR* 473 (1910) (Sen. Bailey) ("We do not choose our Presiding Officer. He is chosen, as the President is chosen, by the electoral college, and we have no power ourselves to depose him."); *RODC* 282 (1828) (Sen. Benton) ("The Vice President . . . is in no way responsible to us. We do not elect him, and we cannot displace him, except by an impeachment, which must be instituted in the other House."); *CG* 20 (1845) (Sen. Mangum) ("The Vice President . . . is not responsible to this body for his course of action."). See also Gerald Gamm and Steven S. Smith, "Last among Equals: The Senate's Presiding Officer," in *Esteemed Colleagues: Civility and Deliberation in the U.S. Senate,* ed. Burdette A. Loomis (Washington, DC: Brookings Institution, 2000), 106; Garrison Nelson, "Leadership Selection in the U.S. Senate, 1899–1985: Changing Patterns of Recruitment and Institutional Interactions" (unpublished paper, 1985, on file with the authors), 4.

33. Cf. Swanstrom, *Senate,* 253.

34. Ibid., 253–57. Vice President Adams was delegated some modest executive branch assignments. Brownell, "Constitutional Chameleon, Part II," 303, 308–9.

35. Brownell, "Constitutional Chameleon, Part II," 302–13.

36. Ibid., 303.

37. Ibid., 303–4, 319–20; Henry Barrett Learned, *The President's Cabinet: Studies in the Origin, Formation and Structure of an American Institution* (New Haven, CT: Yale University Press, 1912), 384–90; H. B. Learned, "Some Aspects of the Vice-Presidency, *APSA Proceedings* 9 (1912): 162, 173–75. For more on the history of the vice presidency and the cabinet, see the citations in Brownell, "Constitutional Chameleon, Part II," 303–4, nn. 40–41.

38. Swanstrom, *Senate,* 256–57.

39. Ibid., 257.

40. Hatfield, *Vice Presidents,* 87–89; Elaine K. Swift, *The Making of an American Senate: Reconstitutive Change in Congress, 1787–1841* (Ann Arbor: University of Michigan Press, 2002), 134–35; Haynes, *Senate,* 273–74; Senate Historical Office, *Pro Tem: Presidents Pro Tempore of the United States Senate since 1789* (Washington, DC: Government Printing Office, 2008), 9–10. Calhoun took an exceedingly narrow view of his leeway as presiding officer to maintain order, prompting a major debate on the vice president's legislative branch authority. One scholar contends that Calhoun's position further diminished the powers of

the vice presidency. Shoup, "Vice-Presidency," 318. In the years since, vice presidents have periodically been delegated some modest authority to appoint senators to select committees, conference committees, and ceremonial panels. Owing largely to his personal standing in the Senate, Vice President John Nance Garner was one of the rare vice presidents who exercised this authority to some degree on his own accord. 79 *CR* 5296–97 (1935); see also note 398; Floyd M. Riddick, *The United States Congress: Organization and Procedure* (Manassas, VA: National Capitol Publishers, 1949), 81; Earl L. Shoup, *The Government of the American People* (Boston: Ginn, 1946), 452.

41. Hatfield, *Vice Presidents*, 94.

42. Ibid., 110–11. For instance, Vice President Van Buren requested that Senator Silas Wright (D-NY) speak out on behalf of the administration. *AMVB*, 728–30; see also George Lee Robinson, "The Development of the Senate Committee System" (PhD diss., New York University, 1954), 113.

43. Haynes, *Senate*, 209, 473; Swanstrom, *Senate*, 254–57; Brownell, "Constitutional Chameleon, Part II," 302–5. In the years following Washington's early discussions with Adams, vice-presidential advice was occasionally solicited and tendered on substantive matters. For example, in 1807, Vice President George Clinton huddled with Secretary of War Henry Dearborn on the best way to defend New York harbor (Clinton was the former governor of New York). Everett Lee Long, "Jefferson and Congress: A Study of the Jeffersonian Legislative System" (PhD diss., University of Missouri, 1966), 70–71. Jefferson also requested that Clinton advocate in the Senate for a piece of legislation of interest to Thomas Paine. Ibid., 229.

44. Hatfield, *Vice Presidents*, 75–78, 127–30.

45. Ibid., 87–92; Kravitz, "Presiding Officers," 21–23.

46. Haynes, *Senate*, 215–16; see also Kravitz, "Presiding Officers," 24–27; Riddick and Frumin, *Senate Procedure*, 739. Burr reprimanded senators for eating apples and cake on the floor and for other breaches of etiquette. *WPM*, 285; see also Kravitz, "Presiding Officers," 22.

47. Haynes, *Senate*, 240–47; Bruce Ackerman and David Fontana, "Thomas Jefferson Counts Himself into the Presidency," *VLR* 90 (2004): 551, 640–42; Irving Gregory Williams, "The Vice-Presidency of the United States in the Twentieth Century: History, Practices, and Problems" (PhD diss., New York University, 1953), 17–18.

48. Nelson, "Background Paper," 63; James Wallner, "Parliamentary Rule: The Origins, Development, and Role of the Senate Parliamentarian in the Legislative Process" (paper delivered at the Congress and History Conference, Providence, RI, June 8–10, 2011), 17–26, 31, 36–40; Michael S. Lynch and Anthony J. Madonna, "The Vice President in the U.S. Senate: Examining the Consequences of Institutional Design" (unpublished paper, September 3, 2010), 28, 36 n. 22; Anthony J. Madonna, "The Evolution of Frustration: Revisiting the Role of Inherited Institutions in the United States Senate" (PhD diss., Washington University, 2008), 143, 147–48, 154; "Office of the Parliamentarian," US Senate, accessed February 15, 2018, https://www.senate.gov/artandhistory/history/common/generic/People_Parliamentarian .htm. Vice presidents have, on occasion, gone against the advice of the parliamentarian. For example, Nelson Rockefeller did so in 1975, but the Senate essentially overturned his action. Hatfield, *Vice Presidents*, 510. Hubert Humphrey apparently went against the parliamentarian on more than one occasion. Niels Lesniewski, "The Ties that Bind: A 269–269 Deadlock Could Be Tricky for Senate," *CQ Weekly*, October 29, 2012, 2112. Alben Barkley also went against the parliamentarian's advice in 1949 and was overturned. Lynch and Madonna, "Vice President in the U.S. Senate," 19. Reportedly, Dick Cheney had no intention of seeking

the advice of the parliamentarian before ruling on whether the Senate could confirm judicial nominees by a strict majority vote; however, the matter never came to a head during his vice presidency. Madonna, "Evolution of Frustration," 148 n. 7.

49. Wallner, "Parliamentary Rule," 17–26, 31, 36–40. For a discussion of some nineteenth-century procedural rulings by vice presidents, see Shoup, "Vice-Presidency," 338–42.

50. Writing in 1923, Shoup, "Vice-Presidency," 454, states, "in *almost* all aspects of his duty as presiding officer the Vice-President has declined in power since the days of John Adams" (emphasis added).

51. Woodrow Wilson's vice president, Thomas Marshall, went so far as to pair his vote with that of a senator. 53 *CR* 8510 (1916); see also Charles M. Thomas, *Thomas Riley Marshall, Hoosier Statesman* (Oxford, OH: Mississippi Valley Press, 1939), 162–63; "Tie Vote in Senate Disposes of Rublee," *NYT,* May 24, 1916; Roy E. Brownell II, "A Constitutional Chameleon: The Vice President's Place within the American System of Separation of Powers, Part I: Text, Structure, Views of the Framers and the Courts," *KJLPP* 24 (2014): 1, 45. As a result, Marshall and the senator in question both absented themselves, knowing it would not affect the outcome.

52. For literature on Johnson, see Leland Winfield Meyer, *The Life and Times of Colonel Richard M. Johnson of Kentucky* (1942; reprint, New York: AMS Press, 1967); David Petriello, *The Days of Heroes Are Over: A Brief Biography of Vice President Richard Mentor Johnson* (Washington, DC: Westphalia Press, 2016); Christina Snyder, *Great Crossings: Indians, Settlers, and Slaves in the Age of Jackson* (New York: Oxford University Press, 2017); Hatfield, *Vice Presidents,* 120–34; Jonathan Milnor Jones, "The Making of a Vice President: The National Political Career of Richard M. Johnson of Kentucky" (PhD diss., University of Memphis, 1998). Johnson is thought to be the first state lawmaker, the first congressman, and the first vice president born in Kentucky. Meyer, *Life and Times of Johnson,* 20; Snyder, *Great Crossings,* 42.

53. Jones, "Making of a Vice President," 2.

54. Ibid.

55. Ibid., 3. His father also left Johnson a considerable estate. Ibid., 7; Petriello, *Days of Heroes,* 14.

56. Jones, "Making of a Vice President," 4; Petriello, *Days of Heroes,* 6–7; Meyer, *Life and Times of Johnson,* 21–24. According to family lore, during an Indian raid, a flaming arrow landed near Johnson's crib. His sister immediately put out the fire and saved her little brother. Robert Bolt, "Vice President Richard M. Johnson of Kentucky: Hero of the Thames—Or the Great Amalgamator?" *RKHS* 75 (1977): 191, 193.

57. Jones, "Making of a Vice President," 7.

58. Meyer, *Life and Times of Johnson,* 40. The Kentucky Resolutions are discussed in chapter 3.

59. Meyer, *Life and Times of Johnson,* 41.

60. Ibid., 325.

61. Ibid., 27.

62. Ibid.

63. Ibid., 290–292; Hatfield, *Vice Presidents,* 122.

64. Meyer, *Life and Times of Johnson,* 304; Snyder, *Great Crossings,* 64.

65. Meyer, *Life and Times of Johnson,* 290–92; Petriello, *Days of Heroes,* 13. Nicholas had been taught law by George Wythe, who had also mentored Henry Clay, John Brown, and likely John Breckinridge. Hatfield, *Vice Presidents,* 122.

66. Meyer, *Life and Times of Johnson*, 49.

67. Ibid., 58.

68. Betty Koed, "Richard Mentor Johnson and the Hollow Earth Proposal," *Unum,* Autumn 2011, 12.

69. Meyer, *Life and Times of Johnson*, 293–94.

70. Ibid., 336.

71. Ibid., 298.

72. Petriello, *Days of Heroes*, 13.

73. Meyer, *Life and Times of Johnson*, 309.

74. Ibid., 310.

75. Henry B. Stanton, *Random Recollections* (New York: Harper & Brothers, 1887), 61.

76. Jones, "Making of a Vice President," 17–18.

77. Ibid., 23–24; Petriello, *Days of Heroes*, 21.

78. Jones, "Making of a Vice President," 24.

79. Ibid., 39–41; Meyer, *Life and Times of Johnson*, 97, 129–32; Petriello, *Days of Heroes*, 45–47. Apparently, Johnson went to great lengths to become a good officer, going so far as to write Thomas Jefferson and ask his advice on which military science books to read. Jones, "Making of a Vice President," 32–33.

80. Jones, "Making of a Vice President," 41–42.

81. Stuart S. Sprague, "The Death of Tecumseh and the Rise of Rumpsey Dumpsey: The Making of a Vice President," *FCHQ* 59 (1989): 455–61.

82. Petriello, *Days of Heroes*, 49.

83. Jones, "Making of a Vice President," 45–46.

84. Ibid., 49 n. 2; Meyer, *Life and Times of Johnson*, 129–35; Petriello, *Days of Heroes*, 50–51.

85. Jones, "Making of a Vice President," 65–66.

86. Ibid., 66–70.

87. Petriello, *Days of Heroes*, 63.

88. Jones, "Making of a Vice President," 68–69.

89. Meyer, *Life and Times of Johnson*, 167–68.

90. Jones, "Making of a Vice President," 70.

91. Ibid.; Meyer, *Life and Times of Johnson*, 170.

92. Jones, "Making of a Vice President," 70–74, 88–90. In 1816, as a sign of Johnson's newfound stature, he was named secretary of the Democratic-Republican caucus that chose James Monroe to be the party's presidential nominee. Ibid., 89; Meyer, *Life and Times of Johnson*, 183.

93. Ida A. Brudnick, "Salaries of Members of Congress: Recent Actions and Historical Tables," *CRS Report for Congress,* April 11, 2018, 15.

94. Jones, "Making of a Vice President," 73; Meyer, *Life and Times of Johnson*, 156–57.

95. Jones, "Making of a Vice President," 72–74.

96. Petriello, *Days of Heroes*, 22.

97. Ibid., 66–67, 81; Jones, "Making of a Vice President," 74–83; Meyer, *Life and Times of Johnson*, 176–82.

98. Jones, "Making of a Vice President," 77, 84–91; Meyer, *Life and Times of Johnson*, 178–81.

99. Hatfield, *Vice Presidents*, 123–24; Jones, "Making of a Vice President," 102–3.

100. Meyer, *Life and Times of Johnson*, 193–206; Jones, "Making of a Vice President," 102–3.

101. Meyer, *Life and Times of Johnson,* 193–206; Jones, "Making of a Vice President," 102–3; Snyder, *Great Crossings,* 49.

102. Hatfield, *Vice Presidents,* 123–24.

103. Jones, "Making of a Vice President," 93–142; Meyer, *Life and Times of Johnson,* 193–206; Snyder, *Great Crossings,* 49.

104. Jones, "Making of a Vice President," 143; Petriello, *Days of Heroes,* 70–71; Snyder, *Great Crossings,* 48–50.

105. Ella Wells Drake, "Choctaw Academy: Richard M. Johnson and the Business of Indian Education," *RKHS* 91 (1993): 260, 265.

106. Koed, "Johnson and Hollow Earth," 12; see also Petriello, *Days of Heroes,* 73–74.

107. Koed, "Johnson and Hollow Earth," 12.

108. Ibid.

109. Ibid.

110. Ibid; see also Petriello, *Days of Heroes,* 73–74.

111. Koed, "Johnson and Hollow Earth," 12. The theory of a hollow earth was accepted in certain scientific circles at the time.

112. Johnson's brother, who was a congressman, pursued the idea in the House. This raises the question of whether the Johnsons saw this undertaking as a personal financial opportunity. Petriello, *Days of Heroes,* 73–74.

113. Jones, "Making of a Vice President," 157.

114. Ibid.; Drake, "Choctaw Academy," 265–71; Snyder, *Great Crossings,* 38–40.

115. Jones, "Making of a Vice President," 180, 371, 381–82; Drake, "Choctaw Academy," 270, 280, 294.

116. Jones, "Making of a Vice President," 378–81; Drake, "Choctaw Academy," 261, 265–66, 270, 279, 282, 286–87, 288, 293, 294; Snyder, *Great Crossings,* 162–64, 226–28, 259–60, 270.

117. Jones, "Making of a Vice President," 377. For discussion of the questionable aspects of Johnson's running of the academy, see Petriello, *Days of Heroes,* 108; Snyder, *Great Crossings,* 162–64, 226–28, 259–60, 270. Johnson favored President Andrew Jackson's tragic Indian removal efforts because he believed the policy could bolster attendance at his academy. Snyder, *Great Crossings,* 129, 163–64.

118. Meyer, *Life and Times of Johnson,* 209–15. Johnson also served on the select committee that had considered the measure earlier. Ibid., 210.

119. Ibid., 282; Petriello, *Days of Heroes,* 71; Jones, "Making of a Vice President," 191, 203–15, 266–67; see also Meyer, *Life and Times of Johnson,* 282–89.

120. Roy E. Brownell II, "Vice Presidential Secrecy: A Study in Comparative Constitutional Privilege and Historical Development," *SJLR* 84 (2010): 423, 506 n. 348.

121. Meyer, *Life and Times of Johnson,* 285; Petriello, *Days of Heroes,* 72–73.

122. Meyer, *Life and Times of Johnson,* 289; Hatfield, *Vice Presidents,* 124.

123. Hatfield, *Vice Presidents,* 124.

124. Meyer, *Life and Times of Johnson,* 263, 281–83, 432; Jones, "Making of a Vice President," 180, 392.

125. Meyer, *Life and Times of Johnson,* 244–45.

126. Ibid., 257; Jones, "Making of a Vice President," 223–24.

127. Jones, "Making of a Vice President," 222; Meyer, *Life and Times of Johnson,* 257–63.

128. Meyer, *Life and Times of Johnson,* 257; Jones, "Making of a Vice President," 223–24.

129. Jones, "Making of a Vice President," 224–27.

130. Petriello, *Days of Heroes*, 77–79; Hatfield, *Vice Presidents*, 124. Congressman and future president James Buchanan commended Johnson's report. Meyer, *Life and Times of Johnson*, 259.

131. Jones, "Making of a Vice President," 182–85; Meyer, *Life and Times of Johnson*, 240–44.

132. Jones, "Making of a Vice President," 194–202, 233; Meyer, *Life and Times of Johnson*, 232–37.

133. Meyer, *Life and Times of Johnson*, 220.

134. Robert V. Remini, *Henry Clay: Statesman for the Union* (New York: W. W. Norton, 1991), 268; Petriello, *Days of Heroes*, 76; see also Hatfield, *Vice Presidents*, 125.

135. Meyer, *Life and Times of Johnson*, 221–23; Jones, "Making of a Vice President," 218–21; Hatfield, *Vice Presidents*, 125.

136. Jones, "Making of a Vice President," 220–22.

137. Ibid.

138. Meyer, *Life and Times of Johnson*, 256.

139. Ibid., 261–63; Hatfield, *Vice Presidents*, 124.

140. Jones, "Making of a Vice President," 64.

141. Ibid., 253.

142. By 1830, Johnson was seen as a potential presidential candidate in some quarters. Meyer, *Life and Times of Johnson*, 395.

143. Jones, "Making of a Vice President," 46.

144. Both Richard Nixon in 1960 and Al Gore in 2000 came close to being elected president as sitting vice presidents. Prior to Van Buren, the only other incumbent vice presidents elected to the presidency were Adams and Jefferson.

145. Joel H. Silbey, "Election of 1836," in *History of American Presidential Elections, 1789–1968,* ed. Arthur M. Schlesinger Jr. (New York: Chelsea House Publishers, 1971), 1:584; Thomas Brown, "The Miscegenation of Richard Mentor Johnson as an Issue in the National Election Campaign of 1835–1836," *CWH* 39 (1993): 5, 7. Criticism of Johnson's liaisons continued while he was vice president. Brown, "Miscegenation," 27.

146. Meyer, *Life and Times of Johnson*, 311; Brown, "Miscegenation," 6.

147. Meyer, *Life and Times of Johnson*, 318–19; Hatfield, *Vice Presidents*, 125; Petriello, *Days of Heroes*, 85; cf. Snyder, *Great Crossings*, 53.

148. Hatfield, *Vice Presidents*, 125; Meyer, *Life and Times of Johnson*, 317; Brown, "Miscegenation," 6; Snyder, *Great Crossings*, 53–56, 61–63.

149. Hatfield, *Vice Presidents*, 125; Snyder, *Great Crossings*, 56–60.

150. Brown, "Miscegenation," 6; Hatfield, *Vice Presidents*, 125; Meyer, *Life and Times of Johnson*, 317; Snyder, *Great Crossings*, 62–64.

151. Brown, "Miscegenation," 6; Snyder, *Great Crossings*, 148; Petriello, *Days of Heroes*, 89. At one point in his career, Johnson professed to be somewhat in sympathy with emancipation. Snyder, *Great Crossings*, 7, 61. Nonetheless, he never liberated Julia Chinn, although he apparently freed others he held in bondage. Ibid., 62; Meyer, *Life and Times of Johnson*, 295–96.

152. Petriello, *Days of Heroes*, 89.

153. Ibid., 90.

154. Ibid.; Brown, "Miscegenation," 6; Snyder, *Great Crossings*, 194–218.

155. For a sampling of the racist invective directed against Johnson because of his relationship with Chinn and others, see Bolt, "Vice President Johnson," 199–202.

156. John Catron to Andrew Jackson, March 21, 1835, Library of Congress, accessed February 15, 2018, https://www.loc.gov/resource/maj.01089_0346_0349/?st=text; see also Hatfield, *Vice Presidents,* 121.

157. Hatfield, *Vice Presidents,* 126, 128.

158. Ibid.

159. Jones, "Making of a Vice President," 291–93, 309–11, 317; Brown, "Miscegenation," 27.

160. "The Senate Elects a Vice President," US Senate, accessed February 15, 2018, https://www.senate.gov/artandhistory/history/minute/The_Senate_Elects_A_Vice_President.htm.

161. Ibid.

162. *CG* 170 (1837); Meyer, *Life and Times of Johnson,* 429; "Senate Elects a Vice President"; Thomas H. Neale, "Contingent Election of the President and Vice President by Congress: Perspectives and Contemporary Analysis," *CRS Report for Congress,* November 3, 2016, 8–9. Clay and Crittenden—both Whigs—voted for Granger. *CG* 170 (1837).

163. Learned, "Some Aspects," 170.

164. Petriello, *Days of Heroes,* 103; Hatfield, *Vice Presidents,* 126–28.

165. Petriello, *Days of Heroes,* 108–9.

166. Ibid.

167. Meyer, *Life and Times of Johnson,* 340–41; Petriello, *Days of Heroes,* 108–9; Hatfield, *Vice Presidents,* 129.

168. Joel K. Goldstein, *The Modern American Vice Presidency: The Transformation of a Political Institution* (Princeton, NJ: Princeton University Press, 1982), 8.

169. Jones, "Making of a Vice President," 355.

170. 28 *SJ* 27–28 (1837); 29 *SJ* 27 (1837); see also Lauros G. McConachie, *Congressional Committees: A Study of the Origins and Development of Our National and Local Legislative Methods* (New York: Thomas Y. Crowell, 1898), 330.

171. For more on committee assignments, see chapter 5.

172. *CG* 128 (1850) (Sen. King); cf. 47 *CR* 1949–50 (1911) (Sen. Bacon); see also Shoup, "Vice-Presidency," 433–37; Henry Barrett Learned, "Casting Votes of the Vice-Presidents, 1789–1915," *AHR* 20 (1915): 571, 572.

173. US Constitution, Article I, section 3 ("The Vice President . . . shall have no Vote, unless they [the Senate] be equally divided"). Cf. Riddick and Frumin, *Senate Procedure,* 1395.

174. Cf. Riddick and Frumin, *Senate Procedure,* 1395. In addition to voting on traditional legislation stemming from the authority conferred by Article I, section 7, the Senate is authorized to vote on other matters based on a host of different constitutional provisions: providing advice and consent on nominations and treaties under Article II; voting on constitutional amendments under Article V; engaging in Senate rule making under Article I, section 5; voting to elect Senate officers under Article I, section 3; deciding vice-presidential elections under the Twelfth Amendment; voting on impeachment and removal under Articles I and II; deciding whether to seat potential senators or to discipline sitting senators under Article I, section 5; and deciding whether to expel sitting senators under Article I, section 5. Other matters the Senate votes on, such as actions related to Senate investigations, fall under the body's implicit constitutional authority.

175. Cf. Haynes, *Senate,* 23–24, 52–57.

176. 5 *SEJ* 274–75 (1840); see also Learned, "Casting Votes," 571.

177. 20 *SJ* 468–69 (1830); 20 *SJ* 457 (1830); 4 *SEJ* 199, 203 (1832); 1 *SEJ* 97–98 (1792); see also Riddick and Frumin, *Senate Procedure,* 1395. In 1925, Vice President Charles Dawes was napping at his residence and missed an opportunity to break a tie in favor of confirming attorney general nominee Charles Warren. Ryan Kelly, "40 Winks and 39 Votes: If Only Vice President Charles G. Dawes Had Woken up a Little Sooner," *RC,* February 8, 2017.

178. 132 *CR* 17360 (1986); cf. 2 *SEJ* 29 (1806); *JQAM,* 2:421.

179. 30 *SJ* 207, 258 (1839). Johnson broke these ties.

180. 22 *SJ* 138–39 (1832); 31 *SJ* 164 (1840). Johnson broke the latter tie.

181. 31 *SJ* 359 (1840); 46 *CR* 1825–26 (1911). Johnson broke the former tie. See also Williams, "Vice-Presidency," 131.

182. 6 *CR* 730, 737 (1877); see also Learned, "Casting Votes," 572–73; Riddick and Frumin, *Senate Procedure,* 1395.

183. *CG* 127–28 (1850); 20 *SJ* 28 (1829); Learned, "Casting Votes," 572; Riddick and Frumin, *Senate Procedure,* 1395.

184. 72 *CR* 9138, 9195 (1930); see also Riddick and Frumin, *Senate Procedure,* 1395.

185. 131 *CR* 11475 (1985); Riddick and Frumin, *Senate Procedure,* 1395.

186. 52 *CR* 3780–81 (1915); Henry H. Gilfry, *Precedents: Decisions on Points of Order in the United States Senate* (Washington, DC: Government Printing Office, 1915), 2:268, 292.

187. *CG* 1950 (1870); *CG* 2266 (1870).

188. 96 *CR* 6245 (1950); see also Margaret Conway, memorandum regarding "List of Questions Decided in the Senate by a Vote of the Vice-President since 1915," American Law Division, Legislative Reference Service, April 16, 1956, 3; see also Haynes, *Senate,* 510; *WPM,* 582.

189. 147 *CR* 8, 14–15, 71–72, 75–76, 78–90, 94, 144–45 (2001) (Sens. Dorgan, Lott, Stevens, Domenici, Bennett, Nickles, Conrad, Levin, and Kerry).

190. 30 *SJ* 197 (1839); 31 *SJ* 412 (1840). Johnson broke both ties.

191. 133 *CR* 24750 (1987); 123 *CR* 37138 (1977); 52 *CR* 3781 (1915); *CG* 1950 (1870); see also Riddick and Frumin, *Senate Procedure,* 1395.

192. 132 *CR* 17360 (1986).

193. 6 *CR* 650 (1877); *CG* 1083 (1861); see also Riddick and Frumin, *Senate Procedure,* 1395; Senate Historical Office, Compilation of Tie-Breaking Votes.

194. Riddick and Frumin, *Senate Procedure,* 1395. Several questions remain about the extent of the vice president's authority to break ties. For instance, it is unclear under the Twelfth Amendment whether an incumbent vice president could break a tie related to his own disputed reelection or a tie on procedural or preliminary matters related to his own impeachment trial (assuming he could even preside). Todd Garvey and Jack Maskell, "Legal Sidebar. Can the Vice President Elect Himself?" *CRS Reports and Analysis,* October 11, 2012; Lesniewski, "Ties that Bind," 2112; Joel K. Goldstein, "Can the Vice President Preside at His Own Impeachment Trial? A Critique of Bare Textualism," *SLULJ* 44 (2000): 849. Interestingly, when Senate Democrats were deadlocked in their party leadership election in 1920, there was apparently no suggestion that fellow partisan Vice President Thomas Marshall break the impasse. Thomas W. Ryley, *Gilbert Hitchcock of Nebraska—Wilson's Floor Leader in the Fight for the Versailles Treaty* (Lewiston, NY: Edwin Mellen Press, 1998), 261–62; "Hitchcock Quits Leadership Fight," *NYT,* April 24, 1920; "Democratic Leadership Deadlock," US Senate, accessed February 15, 2018, https://www.senate.gov/artandhistory/history/minute/Democratic_Leadership_Deadlock.htm.

Presumably, since the Senate changed its method of electing a president pro tempore in

1890, a vice president could vote to break a tie in the election of that officer. In 1931, Vice President Charles Curtis effectively decided a hotly contested race for president pro tempore, though not by breaking a tie. Haynes, *Senate,* 253–54; Nelson, "Leadership Selection," 20.

195. Asher C. Hinds, *Hinds' Precedents of the House of Representatives of the United States* (Washington, DC: Government Printing Office, 1907), 4:518; see also Irving G. Williams, *The American Vice-Presidency: New Look* (Garden City, NY: Doubleday, 1954), 40–41; Shoup, "Vice-Presidency," 439; Learned, "Casting Votes," 571; Garvey and Maskell, "Can the Vice President Elect Himself?"

196. Riddick and Frumin, *Senate Procedure,* 1395. If a vice president does not vote, under parliamentary law, the measure is defeated. Thus, a vice president voting in the negative to break a tie is legally gratuitous. Ibid., 1394–95.

197. 69 *CR* 8063 (1928); 62 *CR* 5168 (1922); see also Riddick and Frumin, *Senate Procedure,* 1395.

198. 61 *CR* 3962–63 (1921); 60 *CR* 2839 (1921); 59 *CR* 1866 (1920); 57 *CR* 2896 (1919); 55 *CR* 767 (1917); see also Riddick and Frumin, *Senate Procedure,* 1395.

199. 55 *CR* 767 (1917); see also Riddick and Frumin, *Senate Procedure,* 1395.

200. 1 *SJ* 42 (1789); *WMJ,* 116. Earl Shoup opined that the effect of this tiebreaking vote supported a constitutional interpretation that "ranks with the greatest of Supreme Court decisions in its importance." Shoup, "Vice-Presidency," 441; see also Learned, "Casting Votes," 574.

201. Learned, "Casting Votes," 574.

202. Ibid.

203. Louis Clinton Hatch and Earl L. Shoup, *A History of the Vice-Presidency of the United States* (Westport, CT: Greenwood Press, 1970), 35.

204. 12 *CR* 32–35 (1881); 147 *CR* 8, 14–15, 71–72, 75–76, 78–90, 94, 144–45 (2001) (Sens. Dorgan, Lott, Stevens, Domenici, Bennett, Nickles, Conrad, Levin, and Kerry); Shoup, "Vice-Presidency," 417–31; Learned, "Casting Votes," 573–74.

205. Karen Tumulty and William J. Eaton, "Gore Casts Tie-Breaking Vote as Senate OKs Clinton Budget," *LAT,* August 7, 1993.

206. "Cheney Breaks Ties on Senate Tax-Cut Bill," *Fox News,* May 15, 2003, accessed February 15, 2018, http://www.foxnews.com/story/2003/05/15/cheney-breaks-tie-on-senate-tax-cut-bill.html.

207. The legal reality is evinced by James F. Byrnes, who served as both a senator and a Supreme Court justice. He wrote that "participation by the Vice President in Senate voting [may be], either in support of his own views or the President's." James F. Byrnes, *All in One Lifetime* (New York: Harper & Brothers, 1958), 233. Professors Lynch and Madonna concur, noting that "the vice president does not always act as a reliable agent of the majority." Lynch and Madonna, "Vice President in the U.S. Senate," 14; see also ibid., 9, 17–19.

208. Roy E. Brownell II, "The Independence of the Vice Presidency," *NYUJLPP* 17 (2014): 297.

209. Ibid.; Nelson, "Background Paper," 64–69.

210. Brownell, "Independence," 323, 325, 326, 327, 329, 331, 340, 360. Other vice presidents have presided over the Senate in ways contrary to the president's views. Vice Presidents Levi Morton, Adlai Stevenson, Charles Fairbanks, Dawes, and Garner all acted independently from the president while in the chair. Ibid., 333–34, 336–40, 360.

211. Bill Clinton, *My Life* (New York: Alfred A. Knopf, 2004), 536. The authors would like to thank Professor Joel Goldstein for identifying this anecdote. Former president George

W. Bush made a similar remark about Cheney's tiebreaking votes in the Senate. Nora Kelly, "Dick Cheney Gets Busted," *TA*, December 4, 2015.

212. Bruce G. Peabody, "Dick Cheney, the 101st Senator," *NYT*, January 3, 2001.

213. Michael Tackett, "Pence Postpones Trip to Middle East, Citing Vote on Tax Bill This Week," *NYT*, December 18, 2017.

214. Meyer, *Life and Times of Johnson*, 434.

215. Jones, "Making of a Vice President," 336.

216. Meyer, *Life and Times of Johnson*, 436–37.

217. Ibid., 442–43.

218. Ibid., 446–47.

219. The political norm of the vice president being renominated by his party did not take hold until the twentieth century. From the vice presidency of John C. Calhoun (1825–1832) until that of James Sherman (1909–1912), no officeholder was renominated by his party. Nelson, "Background Paper," 42.

220. Jones, "Making of a Vice President," 356–58.

221. Ibid., 358.

222. Meyer, *Life and Times of Johnson*, 452.

223. Ibid., 454.

224. Petriello, *Days of Heroes*, 130.

225. Meyer, *Life and Times of Johnson*, 452–57.

226. Ibid., 457; Hatfield, *Vice Presidents*, 131.

227. Meyer, *Life and Times of Johnson*, 457; Hatfield, *Vice Presidents*, 131.

228. Meyer, *Life and Times of Johnson*, 458–61; Hatfield, *Vice Presidents*, 131.

229. Meyer, *Life and Times of Johnson*, 458–61; Hatfield, *Vice Presidents*, 131.

230. Meyer, *Life and Times of Johnson*, 470.

231. Ibid., 469–70.

232. Jones, "Making of a Vice President," 387–88.

233. Meyer, *Life and Times of Johnson*, 471–72.

234. Hatfield, *Vice Presidents*, 131.

235. Meyer, *Life and Times of Johnson*, 472–73; Jones, "Making of a Vice President," 387. President Zachary Taylor named Johnson to a commission to look into disputed California land claims after the Mexican War. Petriello, *Days of Heroes*, 135.

236. Petriello, *Days of Heroes*, 137.

237. Ibid.; Meyer, *Life and Times of Johnson*, 473.

238. Jones, "Making of a Vice President," 388.

239. Ibid.; Meyer, *Life and Times of Johnson*, 473.

240. Meyer, *Life and Times of Johnson*, 474.

241. John D. Feerick, *The Twenty-Fifth Amendment: Its Complete History and Applications*, 3d ed. (New York: Fordham University Press, 2014), 5–8.

242. Nelson, "Background Paper," 30–31.

243. Ibid., 31.

244. Ibid., 32.

245. See, generally, James C. Klotter, *The Breckinridges of Kentucky* (Lexington: University Press of Kentucky, 1986).

246. Ibid., ix.

247. Lucille Stillwell, *John Cabell Breckinridge* (Caldwell, ID: Caxton Printers, 1936), 15.

248. William C. Davis, *Breckinridge: Statesman, Soldier, Symbol,* 2d ed. (Lexington: University Press of Kentucky, 2010), 9.

249. Klotter, *Breckinridges,* 40.

250. Davis, *Breckinridge,* 10–11.

251. Ibid., 13.

252. Ibid., 12; Klotter, *Breckinridges,* 95–97.

253. Klotter, *Breckinridges,* 96.

254. Davis, *Breckinridge,* 13.

255. Ibid., 15.

256. Ibid.

257. Ibid., 15–16.

258. Ibid., 16–17; Klotter, *Breckinridges,* 98–99.

259. Davis, *Breckinridge,* 21; Klotter, *Breckinridges,* 99.

260. Davis, *Breckinridge,* 21–29.

261. Ibid., 29–30. An ugly side of Breckinridge's oratory was his condemnation of Catholics during the 1850s. Thomas D. Clark, *A History of Kentucky* (Lexington, KY: John Bradford Press, 1960), 311.

262. Davis, *Breckinridge,* 33.

263. Ibid.

264. Stillwell, *Breckinridge,* 23–24.

265. Davis, *Breckinridge,* 85 (quoting the *Erie Gazette*). His declamation proved so powerful that, it was said, he once nearly brought Clay to tears. Ibid., 50–51; see also Klotter, *Breckinridges,* 103.

266. Davis, *Breckinridge,* 54 (quoting the *Lexington Kentucky Statesman*).

267. Frank H. Heck, *Proud Kentuckian: John C. Breckinridge, 1821–1875* (Lexington: University Press of Kentucky, 1976), x.

268. Klotter, *Breckinridges,* 101.

269. Davis, *Breckinridge,* 95–96, 138, 170, 305, 383–84, 419; Klotter, *Breckinridges,* 99–101.

270. Davis, *Breckinridge,* 383–84; see also ibid., 96.

271. Ibid., 57.

272. Ibid., 34.

273. Ibid., 34–40.

274. Ibid., 48.

275. Ibid., 45.

276. Stillwell, *Breckinridge,* 144–45; Klotter, *Breckinridges,* 113.

277. Heck, *Proud Kentuckian,* 30.

278. Davis, *Breckinridge,* 56; Klotter, *Breckinridges,* 105; Heck, *Proud Kentuckian,* 25.

279. Davis, *Breckinridge,* 65, 114.

280. Ibid., 97–98.

281. Ibid., 98–99. Three decades later, two Kentuckians would again vie for the Speakership: John G. Carlisle and Joseph C. S. Blackburn (see chapter 6).

282. Davis, *Breckinridge,* 101–2; Klotter, *Breckinridges,* 108; Heck, *Proud Kentuckian,* 25, 41–42.

283. Davis, *Breckinridge,* 105–19, 131.

284. Ibid., 105–9, 131; Heck, *Proud Kentuckian,* 41–42.

285. Davis, *Breckinridge,* 119, 123.

286. Stillwell, *Breckinridge,* 63; Heck, *Proud Kentuckian,* 59.

287. David Herbert Donald, *Lincoln* (New York: Simon & Schuster, 1995), 192–93.

288. Davis, *Breckinridge,* 150, 164; Heck, *Proud Kentuckian,* 63; Lowell H. Harrison and James C. Klotter, *A New History of Kentucky* (Lexington: University Press of Kentucky, 1997), 183.

289. Davis, *Breckinridge,* 131.

290. Ibid., 157; Klotter, *Breckinridges,* 112.

291. Nelson, "Background Paper," 42–44.

292. Ibid., 43–44; Joel K. Goldstein, *The White House Vice Presidency: The Path to Significance; Mondale to Biden* (Lawrence: University Press of Kansas, 2016), 22–24. Andrew Jackson essentially selected Martin Van Buren as his running mate in 1832, but no president did so again until 1940. That said, Alben Barkley maintained that in 1924, Democratic presidential nominee John W. Davis played a role in the selection of the party's vice-presidential nominee Charles W. Bryan. Alben W. Barkley, "The Vice-Presidency," May 1952, 10–11, Papers of Alben Barkley, University of Kentucky.

293. Goldstein, *Modern American Vice Presidency,* 141; Nelson, "Background Paper," 42–44.

294. Brownell, "Independence," 319–58.

295. Davis, *Breckinridge,* 189.

296. Ibid., 190–92.

297. Ibid., 170–71.

298. Ibid.

299. Ibid.; see also Heck, *Proud Kentuckian,* 67.

300. David S. Barry, *Forty Years in Washington* (Boston: Little, Brown, 1924), 191–92.

301. Ibid. After telling this anecdote, Stevenson was asked whether he had had occasion to advise President Cleveland. He replied: "Not yet. But there are still a few weeks of my term remaining." Ibid. Buchanan made at least one other unusual request of Breckinridge. He inquired whether he would serve as minister to Spain, but Breckinridge declined. Davis, *Breckinridge,* 192.

302. Davis, *Breckinridge,* 169, 170–72.

303. Ibid., 252.

304. Ibid. A few decades later, President William McKinley would ask Vice President Garret Hobart to dismiss Secretary of War Russell Alger. David Magie, *Life of Garret August Hobart: Twenty-Fourth Vice President of the United States* (New York: G. P. Putnam's Sons, 1910), 208–11; Barry, *Forty Years,* 259.

305. Heck, *Proud Kentuckian,* 75. Early on, Adams spoke in debate with some regularity; see note 21 above. Aaron Burr questioned witnesses during the impeachment trial of Supreme Court justice Samuel Chase. 14 *AOC* 93 (1805); see also Brownell, "Constitutional Chameleon, Part II," 388. Burr also delivered a famous oration about the Senate on the occasion of his departure from office. 14 *AOC* 71 (1805). Until well into the twentieth century, vice presidents gave brief inaugural addresses to the Senate and encomia to the body at the end of their tenure. See, for example, 1 *AOC* 22–23 (1789) (Adams inaugural address); 6 *AOC* 1549–51 (1797) (Adams valedictory address); 6 *AOC* 1581–86 (1797) (Jefferson inaugural address); 10 *AOC* 753–54 (1801) (Jefferson valedictory address); see also Riddick and Frumin, *Senate Procedure,* 1390–92.

306. 51 *SJ* 93–100 (1859).

307. *CG* 1364 (1861); see also Riddick and Frumin, *Senate Procedure,* 1395.

308. 47 *CR* 1922–23 (1911); see also Learned, "Casting Votes," 575–76; Riddick and Frumin, *Senate Procedure,* 1395. Another of Breckinridge's votes opposed the Homestead Act. Davis, *Breckinridge,* 195–96.

309. This reality may have further antagonized Buchanan. Klotter, *Breckinridges,* 112.

310. Breckinridge owned slaves and publicly embraced the Supreme Court's *Dred Scott* decision. Stillwell, *Breckinridge,* 72–73; Harrison and Klotter, *New History,* 184.

311. Lincoln happened to be married to Breckinridge's cousin, Mary Todd.

312. Davis, *Breckinridge,* 248–52. The Crittenden Compromise is discussed in chapter 5.

313. Davis, *Breckinridge,* 248–51.

314. Albert D. Kirwan, *John J. Crittenden: The Struggle for Union* (Lexington: University of Kentucky Press, 1962), 378–79; Heck, *Proud Kentuckian,* 94. In 1861, following the mass resignation of senators from the seceding states, Breckinridge appointed lawmakers to fill the committee vacancies. McConachie, *Congressional Committees,* 331.

315. US Constitution, Twelfth Amendment.

316. Davis, *Breckinridge,* 257–58; Heck, *Proud Kentuckian,* 97.

317. Davis, *Breckinridge,* 257–58; Heck, *Proud Kentuckian,* 97.

318. Davis, *Breckinridge,* 257–58; Heck, *Proud Kentuckian,* 97.

319. Davis, *Breckinridge,* 258; Heck, *Proud Kentuckian,* 97.

320. Davis, *Breckinridge,* 258; Heck, *Proud Kentuckian,* 97.

321. A handful of others have returned to the Senate after presiding as vice president. They include John C. Calhoun, Andrew Johnson, Hannibal Hamlin, and Hubert Humphrey.

322. Davis, *Breckinridge,* 202–5; Klotter, *Breckinridges,* 112.

323. *CG* 1413 (1861); see also Heck, *Proud Kentuckian,* 97; Klotter, *Breckinridges,* 118.

324. 53 *SJ* 402 (1861); Klotter, *Breckinridges,* 118; Heck, *Proud Kentuckian,* 97.

325. Davis, *Breckinridge,* 268–78; Klotter, *Breckinridges,* 118–20.

326. Klotter, *Breckinridges,* 118–20.

327. Ibid.

328. Davis, *Breckinridge,* 268.

329. Ibid., 269–78; Stillwell, *Breckinridge,* 98–100.

330. Davis, *Breckinridge,* 275–76.

331. Ibid., 276.

332. "Senator Killed in Battle," US Senate, accessed February 15, 2018, https://www.senate.gov/artandhistory/history/minute/Senator_Killed_In_Battle.htm.

333. "Expulsion and Censure," US Senate, accessed February 15, 2018, https://www.senate.gov/artandhistory/history/common/briefing/Expulsion_Censure.htm.

334. Ibid; "Lazarus W. Powell Expulsion Case (1862)," US Senate, accessed February 15, 2018, https://www.senate.gov/artandhistory/history/common/expulsion_cases/042Lazarus-Powell_expulsion.htm.

335. Davis, *Breckinridge,* 432, 631–32.

336. Ibid., 313, 322, 375, 451; Heck, *Proud Kentuckian,* 130.

337. Davis, *Breckinridge,* 314, 377, 384–99, 437, 480.

338. Ibid., 443–49.

339. Klotter, *Breckinridges,* 127.

340. John B. Gordon, *Reminiscences of the Civil War* (Baton Rouge: Louisiana State University Press, 1993), 314–15.

341. Davis, *Breckinridge,* 496–98; Heck, *Proud Kentuckian,* 133–34.

342. Davis, *Breckinridge,* 525–40.

343. Ibid., 543–90.

344. Ibid., 587–88; Heck, *Proud Kentuckian,* 198. Breckinridge had been indicted for treason in Washington, DC, and Virginia during the war. Davis, *Breckinridge,* 530, 543, 548.

345. Heck, *Proud Kentuckian,* 151.

346. Davis, *Breckinridge,* 600–606.

347. Ibid., 612. Breckinridge also supported permitting African Americans to testify in court against white citizens, a public position that was not widely shared at the time in Kentucky. Ibid., 611.

348. Klotter, *Breckinridges,* 135.

349. Brownell, "Constitutional Chameleon, Part II," 319–22, 329–37; Learned, *President's Cabinet,* 384–90; Learned, "Some Aspects," 173–75; George Frederick Howe, *Chester A. Arthur: A Quarter-Century of Machine Politics* (New York: Dodd, Mead, 1934), 150; Ben Perley Poore, *Perley's Reminiscences of Sixty Years in the National Metropolis* (Philadelphia: Hubbard Brothers, 1886), 2:428; "Gen. Arthur in Washington," *NYT,* July 4, 1881; "Blaine and Arthur Closeted," *NYT,* July 7, 1881; Henry F. Graff, "A Heartbeat Away," *AH* 86 (1964). There is some uncorroborated evidence that Vice President James Sherman joined President William Howard Taft's cabinet meetings. Robert T. Small, "Harding Plans to Have Coolidge Sit with Cabinet in All Its Talks," *PDT,* December 18, 1920. Historian George Haynes expressed skepticism about the accuracy of this account, noting that Taft, among others, had conveyed to him that any Sherman visits to cabinet meetings had been haphazard and not official. Haynes, *Senate,* 225 n. 2.

350. Arthur M. Schlesinger Jr., *The Cycles of American History* (Boston: Houghton Mifflin, 1986), 347–50. For this chapter segment as a whole, see, generally, Roy E. Brownell II, "Vice Presidency," in *American Political Culture: An Encyclopedia* (Santa Barbara, CA: ABC-CLIO, 2015), 3:1130–35.

351. Schlesinger, *Cycles,* 347–49; Brownell, "Constitutional Chameleon, Part II," 329–30; Joel K. Goldstein, "Vice-Presidential Behavior in a Disability Crisis: The Case of Thomas R. Marshall," *PLS* 33 (2014): 37, 39.

352. Goldstein, "Vice-Presidential Behavior," 39.

353. Brownell, "Constitutional Chameleon, Part II," 331–74; Nelson, "Background Paper," 32; Schlesinger, *Cycles,* 347–50. Coolidge's vice president, Charles Dawes, declined to join cabinet meetings. Brownell, "Constitutional Chameleon, Part II," 334–35.

354. Schlesinger, *Cycles,* 347–50.

355. Nelson, "Background Paper," 35–37, 74–76; Goldstein, *Modern American Vice Presidency,* 135–42, 146–76, 305–6; Paul C. Light, *Vice-Presidential Power: Advice and Influence in the White House* (Baltimore: Johns Hopkins University Press, 1984), 28–52; Brownell, "Constitutional Chameleon, Part II," 329–73.

356. Shoup, "Vice-Presidency," 391–92; see also ibid., 431, 455.

357. Goldstein, *Modern American Vice Presidency,* 15–45, 135–42, 146–76, 305–6.

358. Goldstein, *White House Vice Presidency,* 16–34; Nelson, "Background Paper," 25–38, 61–69; Goldstein, *Modern American Vice Presidency,* 142–46, 151–76.

359. Goldstein, *White House Vice Presidency,* 21.

360. Williams "Vice-Presidency," 397–451; Nelson, "Background Paper," 33.

361. Nelson, "Background Paper," 29, 33, 42–44; Goldstein, *White House Vice Presidency,* 22–24.

362. Goldstein, *Modern American Vice Presidency,* 141, 302.

363. Ibid.; Nelson, "Background Paper," 42–45.

364. John D. Feerick, *From Failing Hands: The Story of Presidential Succession* (New York: Fordham University Press, 1965), 199–202; Nelson, "Background Paper," 25, 34, 44.

365. Feerick, *Failing Hands*, 202.

366. William R. Tansill, "Number of Days Certain Vice Presidents Actually Presided over the Senate," memorandum, June 27, 1955, Legislative Reference Service (on file with the authors); Goldstein, *White House Vice Presidency*, 22.

367. Goldstein, *White House Vice Presidency*, 25; Goldstein, *Modern American Vice Presidency*, 159.

368. Goldstein, *White House Vice Presidency*, 25–26; Feerick, *Twenty-Fifth Amendment*, 19–24.

369. Nelson, "Background Paper," 36. Hitherto, the vice president's only office space had been in the Senate.

370. Goldstein, "New Constitutional Vice Presidency," 508–10, 526–40.

371. US Constitution, Twenty-Fifth Amendment, section 4.

372. Light, *Vice-Presidential Power*, 63–75, 128; see also Brownell, "Constitutional Chameleon, Part II," 357–61.

373. Goldstein, *White House Vice Presidency*, 36–104; Light, *Vice-Presidential Power*, 75–99.

374. Goldstein, *White House Vice Presidency*, 63, 70–86; Light, *Vice-Presidential Power*, 75–99.

375. Goldstein, *White House Vice Presidency*, 105–72; cf. Light, *Vice-Presidential Power*, 268–69.

376. Goldstein, *White House Vice Presidency*, 133.

377. Additional informal aspects of presiding have developed over the years. For instance, if a vote is meaningful to the president—even if the vice president's tiebreaking vote is not needed—the vice president sometimes chairs the proceedings. This is seen in political circles as raising the profile of the vote. Jody C. Baumgartner and Thomas F. Crumblin, *The American Vice Presidency: From the Shadow to the Spotlight* (Lanham, MD: Rowman & Littlefield, 2015), 181. For instance, Vice President Joe Biden presided when the Senate voted on the Affordable Care Act, the New START Treaty, and Obama administration–backed tax, gun control, and immigration measures. Ibid.

A number of other oddities have taken place related to the vice president's role in the Senate. For instance, in 1949, Vice President Barkley gave the morning prayer when the Senate chaplain was absent. 29 *CR* 14333 (1949); see also Alben Barkley, *That Reminds Me—* (Garden City, NY: Doubleday, 1954), 209; Polly Ann Davis, *Alben W. Barkley: Senate Majority Leader and Vice President* (New York: Garland, 1979), 287–88.

378. Coolidge once commented, "the President of the Senate can and does exercise a good deal of influence over its deliberations." Williams, *American Vice-Presidency*, 31.

379. Emma Brown, "With Historic Tiebreaker from Pence, DeVos Confirmed as Education Secretary," *WP*, February 7, 2017.

380. 147 *CR* 8, 14–15, 71–72, 75–76, 78–90, 94, 144–45 (2001) (Sens. Dorgan, Lott, Stevens, Domenici, Bennett, Nickles, Conrad, Levin, and Kerry).

381. If no other senator holds the floor, the vice president must first recognize the majority leader if he is on his feet attempting to address the chamber, followed in order by the minority leader and then the bill managers. Riddick and Frumin, *Senate Procedure*, 1091, 1093–94, 1096, 1098. The House Speaker may inquire about the subject matter of the mem-

ber's intended remarks before recognizing him or her. Riddick, *Congress: Organization and Procedure*, 80. This is not within the vice president's authority. Ibid.; 129 *CR* S10159 (1983) (exchange between the presiding officer and Sen. Metzenbaum).

382. Gilfry, *Precedents*, 223; Riddick and Frumin, *Senate Procedure*, 1091; cf. Paul Rundquist, "A Senate without an Equal Party Division: Some Organizational and Procedural Issues," *CRS Memorandum*, December 12, 2000, 5; Riddick and Frumin, *Senate Procedure*, 769. Moreover, it has been asserted that the Senate may not remove the vice president's recognition power. 52 *CR* 3839 (1915) (quoting Vice President Marshall: "The Senate can not take away from the presiding officer the right to recognize a Senator"); see also 68 *CR* 5349 (1927); 83 *CR* 752 (1938); Gilfry, *Precedents*, 223; FMRP, boxes WS14–WS18, WS24.

383. Hatfield, *Vice Presidents*, 510–11.

384. Rockefeller ultimately felt the need to apologize to the senators involved. Hatfield, *Vice Presidents*, 510–11. For another controversial exercise of the vice president's recognition power, see Joseph A. Davis, "Energy Standards Bill Delayed: Byrd and Bush Clash in Senate Power Struggle," *CQ Weekly*, February 7, 1987.

385. Harry S. Truman, *Year of Decisions* (New York: Doubleday, 1955), 195; Hatfield, *Vice Presidents*, 416; Allen Drury, *A Senate Journal: 1943–1945* (New York: McGraw-Hill, 1963), 354–55.

386. Riddick, *Congress: Organization and Procedure*, 83; Kravitz, "Presiding Officers," 31–33. There have been several actual or potential vice-presidential parliamentary rulings of significance. In 1975, Vice President Nelson Rockefeller made efforts from the chair to water down the filibuster. Hatfield, *Vice Presidents*, 510. In 1977, Vice President Walter Mondale worked with Senate majority leader Robert Byrd to sidetrack post-cloture filibusters. Ibid., 523.

The filibuster, which permits an individual senator, a group of senators, or the minority party to block a measure unless sixty votes can be mustered, is a large part of what makes the Senate distinctive among legislative chambers. It permits individual senators and the minority party to play a key role in how the Senate operates. Before he left the vice presidency, Aaron Burr made recommendations for Senate rule changes, including what would become the progenitor of the filibuster. Sarah A. Binder and Steven S. Smith, *Politics or Principle? Filibustering in the United States Senate* (Washington, DC: Brookings Institution Press, 1997), 37–39.

387. Chapter 7 examines Garner's action in some detail.

388. Robert C. Byrd, *The Senate 1789–1989, Addresses on the History of the United States Senate* (Washington, DC: Government Printing Office, 1991), 2:190; 106 *CR* 13367 (1960) (Sen. Johnson).

389. Riddick, *Congress: Organization and Procedure*, 82.

390. Field v. Clark, 143 U.S. 649, 672 (1892); see also Gilfry, *Precedents*, 213.

391. *Field*, 143 U.S. at 672.

392. Riddick, *Congress: Organization and Procedure*, 84; see also 55 *CR* 5296 (1917); *CG* 631–33 (1850); Riddick and Frumin, *Senate Procedure*, 798; cf. 2 *AOC* 105–6 (1803).

393. Haynes, *Senate*, 230, 377 n. 1.

394. "Cliff Role Boosts Biden," *PTR*, January 9, 2013 ("Biden came away looming politically larger than Sen. Harry Reid, who should have been the Democrats' star negotiator. The Nevada Democrat is the majority leader, after all."). See also Noam Scheiber, "The Inside Story of How Obama Could Have Gotten a Better Tax Deal without Biden," *TNR*, January 9, 2013. As Malcolm Jewell and Samuel Patterson noted, "when the Vice-President

serves in a liaison capacity, he is duplicating the job of the floor leader." Malcolm Jewell and Samuel Patterson, *The Legislative Process in the United States* (New York: Random House, 1966), 151. For a firsthand account of the negotiations with the vice president, see Mitch McConnell, *The Long Game: A Memoir* (New York: Sentinel, 2016), 208–12.

Prior to his break with Roosevelt over the Court-packing proposal, Garner was an effective advocate for the president in the Senate. Carl Brent Swisher, *The Theory and Practice of American National Government* (Boston: Houghton Mifflin, 1951), 291–92 ("John N. Garner . . . exercise[d] highly effective party leadership in the Senate while at the same time maintaining liaison with the White House").

395. Jules Witcover, *The American Vice Presidency: From Irrelevance to Power* (Washington, DC: Smithsonian Books, 2014), 517.

396. Goldstein, *White House Vice Presidency,* 136.

397. Ibid.

398. Joseph Alsop and Turner Catledge, *The 168 Days* (New York: Doubleday, Doran, 1938), 238: "No man was more influential in the Senate than Garner. Almost as many men were beholden to him for help . . . as were beholden to [majority leader Joe] Robinson. Many more were personally devoted to him than to the majority leader." See also James T. Patterson, *Congressional Conservatism and the New Deal* (Lexington: University of Kentucky Press, 1967), 154, 232, 292, 295–96; Martha H. Swain, *Pat Harrison: The New Deal Years* (Jackson: University of Mississippi Press, 1978), 168, 170–71, 180; Lionel V. Patenaude, "Garner, Sumners, and Connally: The Defeat of the Roosevelt Court Bill in 1937," *SWHQ* 74 (1970): 36–37, 47–51. Vice President Charles Dawes briefly displayed similar standing when he hammered out an arrangement whereby the Senate would consider both high-profile banking and farm legislation. Joseph P. Chamberlain, *Legislative Processes: National and State* (New York: D. Appleton–Century, 1936), 138. As was the case with Garner in the late 1930s, Dawes's prestige was unrelated to his relationship with the president.

399. "Cactus Jack on Top," *LAT,* July 23, 1937.

400. Patterson, *Congressional Conservatism,* 154, 232, 292, 295–96; Swain, *Harrison,* 168, 170–71, 180.

401. Bascom N. Timmons, *Garner of Texas: A Personal History* (New York: Harper & Brothers, 1948), 225–26; see also note 40. Garner apparently acted in this vein with a fair amount of freedom vis-à-vis the Senate. Riddick, *Congress: Organization and Procedure,* 310.

402. Baumgartner and Crumblin, *American Vice Presidency,* 165.

403. Ibid; Jonathan Miller, "Pence's Hostile Office Takeover," *CQ,* February 27, 2017.

404. Baumgartner and Crumblin, *American Vice Presidency,* 185.

405. John T. Bennett and Rema Rahman, "Praise for Pence Persists," *RC,* October 2, 2017. Biden was not a regular participant in Senate Democratic lunches. Lisa Mascaro, "Biden Unwelcome in Senate Huddles, Where Cheney Wielded Power," *LVS,* December 7, 2008. Garner often attended Senate Democratic conference meetings. Hatfield, *Vice Presidents,* 394, n. 24. As vice president, Barkley joined gatherings of the Senate Democratic Policy Committee. Davis, *Barkley,* 293.

406. Nelson, "Background Paper," 63.

407. Ibid.

408. Ibid.

409. Timmons, *Garner,* 178; see also Barkley, "Vice-Presidency," 13; Truman, *Year of Decisions,* 197–98.

2. President Pro Tempore

1. US Constitution, Article II, section 3, clause 5. *Pro tempore* is a Latin expression the translation of which is "for the time being." Senate Historical Office, *Pro Tem: Presidents Pro Tempore of the United States Senate since 1789* (Washington, DC: Government Printing Office, 2008), 7.

2. George H. Haynes, *The Senate of the United States: Its History and Practice*, 2d ed. (New York: Russell & Russell, 1960), 1:254, 473–74; cf. Roy Swanstrom, *The United States Senate, 1787–1801: A Dissertation of the First Fourteen Years of the Upper Legislative Body* (Washington, DC: Government Printing Office, 1988), 257–58.

Over the years, a number of prominent senators have been elected president pro tempore. For example, several have served either before or after as Senate floor leader: Jacob Gallinger (R-NH), Charles Curtis (R-KS), Henry Cabot Lodge (R-MA), Styles Bridges (R-NH), and Robert Byrd (D-WV). Others served as de facto majority leaders: Pat Harrison (D-MS), Richard Russell (D-GA), and Arthur Vandenberg (R-MI). Still others achieved national elected office: John Tyler (D-VA) became vice president and then president, and William King (D-AL) and Curtis served as vice president.

3. Haynes, *Senate,* 254; Swanstrom, *Senate,* 257.

4. Walter Kravitz, "The Presiding Officers," in "The United States Senate: A History" (unpublished manuscript on file with the authors), 48. In theory, the president pro tempore can be any American citizen except the president or vice president, who are prohibited from presiding under the Constitution.

5. 3 *AOC* 126 (1792); 126 *CR* 11575 (1980) (Byrd); cf. 5 *AOC* 81, 83 (1796); see also Senate Historical Office, *Pro Tem,* 9; Haynes, *Senate,* 252 n. 1.

6. See chapter 7.

7. George P. Furber, *Precedents Relating to the Privileges of the Senate of the United States,* Senate Miscellaneous Document No. 68, 52d Congress (Washington, DC: Government Printing Office, 1893), 181; Kravitz, "Presiding Officers," 48.

8. Haynes, *Senate,* 254; Senate Historical Office, *Pro Tem,* 9.

9. Robert Byrd, preface to Senate Historical Office, *Pro Tem,* 5.

10. Haynes, *Senate,* 255 n. 3; Kravitz, "Presiding Officers," 63–64; Thomas H. Neale, "The President Pro Tempore of the U.S. Senate: The Historical Development of the Office and a Synopsis of Its Duties and Responsibilities," *CRS Report,* May 12, 1981, 9. John Crittenden, who is profiled in chapter 5, played a major role in contesting the vice president's attempt to claim the authority to assign a temporary successor to the chair. Earl Leon Shoup, "The Vice-Presidency of the United States" (PhD diss., Harvard University, 1923), 377–79.

It remains an open question whether a president pro tempore can preside over debate regarding his own expulsion. The Senate has never been confronted with this situation. Jesse Bright (D-IN) was expelled two years after his service as president pro tempore. He later moved to Covington, Kentucky, and was elected to the state house. A. C. Quisenberry, "Kentucky—Mother of United States Senators and Representatives," *RKHS* 18 (1920): 77, 83.

11. Senate Historical Office, *Pro Tem,* 7–9; Swanstrom, *Senate,* 257–58. Occasionally, in the early years, a president pro tempore would be considered a de facto Senate leader, but that owed to factors other than his service as the Senate's presiding officer. Elaine K. Swift, *The Making of an American Senate: Reconstitutive Change in Congress, 1787–1841* (Ann Arbor: University of Michigan Press, 2002), 77.

12. Stuart Seely Sprague, "Senator John Brown of Kentucky, 1757–1837: A Political Biography" (PhD diss., New York University, 1972), 15.

13. Ibid., 14–15; Elizabeth Warren, "John Brown and His Influence on Kentucky Politics, 1784–1805" (PhD diss., Northwestern University, 1937), 2, 6–7.

14. Sprague, "Brown," 13–14. Breckinridge is profiled in chapter 3.

15. Sprague, "Brown," 15.

16. Ibid.; email from Kate Hesseldenz, curator, Liberty Hall Historic Site.

17. Hesseldenz email.

18. Warren, "Brown," 9.

19. "James Brown," Congressional Biographical Directory, accessed February 15, 2018, http://bioguide.congress.gov/scripts/biodisplay.pl?index=b000921; William Elsey Connelley and E. M. Coulter, History of Kentucky, ed. Charles Kerr (Chicago: American Historical Society, 1922), 3:76.

20. Warren, "Brown," 10–11; Hesseldenz email.

21. Warren, "Brown," 11.

22. Sprague, "Brown," 15–16.

23. Ibid. (quoting Brown's son).

24. Ibid., 1.

25. Patricia Watlington, The Partisan Spirit: Kentucky Politics, 1779–1792 (New York: Atheneum, 1972), 81.

26. Alonzo Thomas Dill, George Wythe: Teacher of Liberty (Williamsburg: Virginia Independence Bicentennial Commission, 1979), 51.

27. Whether Brown left Princeton to serve in the Revolutionary War is a disputed question. Warren, "Brown," 14–15; Sprague, "Brown," 19–20.

28. "John Brown," Congressional Biographical Directory, accessed February 15, 2018, http://bioguide.congress.gov/scripts/biodisplay.pl?index=B000929.

29. Sprague, "Brown," 24–31.

30. Ibid., 24–31, 35; Warren, "Brown," 16–17, 20; Dill, Wythe, 2, 42, 44, 51.

31. Sprague, "Brown," 30; see also Warren, "Brown," 20.

32. Warren, "Brown," 21.

33. Ibid.; Sprague, "Brown," 31.

34. Sprague, "Brown," 34.

35. "Founding Father of Kentucky," Liberty Hall, accessed February 15, 2018, https://www.libertyhall.org/john-brown/founding-father-of-kentucky.

36. Warren, "Brown," 20.

37. James C. Klotter, The Breckinridges of Kentucky (Lexington: University Press of Kentucky, 1986), 5–6; see also Lowell H. Harrison and James C. Klotter, A New History of Kentucky (Lexington: University Press of Kentucky, 1997), 24–25.

38. Frederick A. Wallis and Hambleton Tapp, A Sequi-Centennial History of Kentucky (Hopkinsville, KY: Historical Record Association, 1945), 2:759, accessed February 15, 2018, https://ia800709.us.archive.org/4/items/sesquicentennia102wall/sesquicentennia102wall.pdf.

39. "John Brown," Congressional Biographical Directory.

40. "Founding Father," Liberty Hall.

41. Ibid.

42. Ibid.

43. Ibid.

44. Sprague, "Brown," 134–36; Warren, "Brown," 91–92; "Founding Father," Liberty Hall; Connelley and Coulter, *History of Kentucky,* 1:253–54.

45. "Founding Father," Liberty Hall.

46. Ibid.; Warren, "Brown," 91–92.

47. Warren, "Brown," 91–92, 94–95, 125–26.

48. Sprague, "Brown," 82; see also "Founding Father," Liberty Hall; Warren, "Brown," 92–93, 95–96.

49. Sprague, "Brown," 87–88; Warren, "Brown," 95–96.

50. "Founding Father," Liberty Hall.

51. Warren, "Brown," 91–101; Sprague, "Brown," 134.

52. Sprague, "Brown," 31.

53. Ibid., 88, 104, 114–15; Warren, "Brown," 90.

54. James Madison to Mann Butler, October 11, 1834, "Legacy," Liberty Hall, https://www.libertyhall.org/legacy.

55. Sprague, "Brown," 152.

56. 2 *AOC* 1452 (1790); Sprague, "Brown," 122–23; Warren, "Brown," 122.

57. "Slavery," Liberty Hall, https://www.libertyhall.org/slavery.

58. 2 *AOC* 1885 (1791); see also Warren, "Brown," 126.

59. "States in the Senate, Kentucky Timeline," US Senate, accessed February 15, 2018, http://www.senate.gov/states/KY/timeline.htm.

60. Ibid.; see also "John Brown," Congressional Biographical Directory.

61. Another Federalist, Martin Hardin, was appointed and served from 1816 to 1817.

62. Harrison and Klotter, *New History,* 49, 52, 70–71.

63. Thomas D. Clark, *A History of Kentucky* (Lexington, KY: John Bradford Press, 1960), 98; Warren, "Brown," 118–19.

64. Clark, *History of Kentucky,* 98; Warren, "Brown," 86, 123.

65. Clark, *History of Kentucky,* 98–99.

66. Warren, "Brown," 139; Sprague, "Brown," 153–54.

67. Sprague, "Brown," 197–99.

68. Ibid., 244; see also ibid., 71. He has been described as "a quiet, behind the scenes" politician. "Founding Father," Liberty Hall.

69. "President Pro Tempore," US Senate, accessed February 15, 2018, https://www.senate.gov/artandhistory/history/common/briefing/President_Pro_Tempore.htm; Sprague, "Brown," 244, 248.

70. Everett Lee Long, "Jefferson and Congress: A Study of the Jeffersonian Legislative System" (PhD diss., University of Missouri, 1966), 252. Though Taylor does not mention Brown by name, the Kentuckian's election as president pro tempore was the only such election that took place during Taylor's time in the Senate.

71. Party caucuses are discussed in chapter 6.

72. Sprague, "Brown," 245.

73. Ibid., 244–45, 247–49.

74. *WPM,* 110; see also Warren, "Brown," 153.

75. *WPM,* 173; see also Warren, "Brown," 152. Brown did vote to remove Supreme Court justice Samuel Chase on four counts during his impeachment trial. *WPM,* 309; Warren, "Brown," 152.

76. Cf. Sprague, "Brown," 71.

77. Lowell H. Harrison, *John Breckinridge: Jeffersonian Republican* (Louisville, KY: Filson Club, 1969), 145.

78. "President Pro Tempore," US Senate.

79. The law has since been amended, and the president pro tempore is now third in line to the presidency behind the vice president and the Speaker of the House. 3 U.S.C. §19.

80. Sprague, "Brown," 248.

81. Ibid., 221–22; "Family Life," Liberty Hall, https://www.libertyhall.org/family-life.

82. Sprague, "Brown," 234; "Family Life," Liberty Hall. One of their grandchildren, Benjamin Gratz Brown, a Unionist, would become a US senator in his own right, serving Missouri from 1863 to 1867, and he was the Democratic Party's nominee for vice president in 1872. Benjamin Gratz Brown was in fact the grandson of two Kentucky senators, the second being Jesse Bledsoe (Dem.-Rep.). Warren, "Brown," 180; "Benjamin Gratz Brown," Congressional Biographical Directory, accessed February 15, 2018, http://bioguide.congress. gov/scripts/biodisplay.pl?index=b000905.

83. "Family Life," Liberty Hall.

84. Warren, "Brown," 148; Hesseldenz email.

85. Sprague, "Brown," 233.

86. Ibid.

87. Ibid., 249–50.

88. Ibid., 244–45. Brown's questionable dealings with the Spanish and with Aaron Burr, which are touched on later, seemingly played no role in his defeat. Warren, "Brown," 155–63.

89. Warren, "Brown," 155.

90. Ibid., 155–63; Sprague, "Brown," 249–50.

91. "Legacy," Liberty Hall; Warren, "Brown," 175–76.

92. "Legacy," Liberty Hall.

93. Ibid.; Warren, "Brown," 176, 181.

94. "Legacy," Liberty Hall.

95. Ibid.

96. Warren, "Brown," 177–78.

97. "Site History," Liberty Hall, https://www.libertyhall.org/about/site-history.

98. Warren, "Brown," 178.

99. "Site History," Liberty Hall.

100. "Slavery," Liberty Hall.

101. Ibid.

102. Ibid.

103. Ibid.

104. "Founding Father," Liberty Hall.

105. Sprague, "Brown," 245.

106. "Founding Father," Liberty Hall.

107. Ibid.

108. Sprague, "Brown," i.

109. Sprague, "Brown," 89–112; Clark, *History of Kentucky,* 87–89; Warren, "Brown," 70–89.

110. Warren, "Brown," 70–89, 100–112, 187–92.

111. Cf. ibid., 182–90.

112. Ibid., 155–75; Sprague, "Brown," 257–66. Brown was subpoenaed in Burr's treason trial, but it is uncertain whether he appeared. Warren, "Brown," 173.
113. "Site History," Liberty Hall; see also "Liberty Hall," National Park Service,
accessed February 15, 2018, https://www.nps.gov/places/liberty-hall.htm.
114. "Site History," Liberty Hall; Warren, "Brown," 143; cf. Sprague, "Brown," 208–9.
115. "Site History," Liberty Hall.
116. Nancy Stearns Theiss, "Liberty Hall and Blue Wing: The Brown Family Legacy,
Part I," *LCJ*, October 3, 2017.
117. Sprague, "Brown," 233–34, 239, 244–45, 248.
118. Swanstrom, *Senate*, 254–57.
119. Haynes, *Senate*, 249; Richard C. Sachs, *The President Pro Tempore of the Senate:
History and Authority of the Office* (New York: Novinka Books, 2003), 39 n. 1.
120. Robert C. Byrd, *The Senate, 1789–1989: Addresses on the History of the United
States Senate* (Washington, DC: Government Printing Office, 1991), 2:168.
121. Ibid.
122. Swanstrom, *Senate*, 258.
123. Ibid., 259.
124. Ibid.
125. Ibid.
126. Ibid.
127. Ibid.
128. Kravitz, "Presiding Officers," 52.
129. Senate Historical Office, *Pro Tem*, 7.
130. Ibid.; Haynes, *Senate*, 473; Kravitz, "Presiding Officers," 49. Professors Steven S.
Smith and Gerald Gamm contend that the effect of interrupted tenure on the prestige of
the president pro tempore position may be somewhat overstated given the existence of what
they term "presumptive presidents pro tempore," lawmakers who were likely to fill the slot
the next time the vice president vacated the chair. Gerald Gamm and Steven S. Smith, "Last
among Equals: The Senate's Presiding Officer," in *Esteemed Colleagues: Civility and Deliberation in the U.S. Senate*, ed. Burdette A. Loomis (Washington, DC: Brookings Institution,
2000), 107.
131. 1 Stat. 239 (1792); 24 Stat. 1 (1886).
132. Henry H. Gilfry, "President of the Senate Pro Tempore," Senate Document No.
104, 62d Congress (1911), 7, 8, 11, 12, 15–16, 17, 18, 20, 34, 35, 47, 50; Vice President
Elbridge Gerry to Mrs. Gerry, April 17, 1814, *MHS Proceedings* 47 (1913): 480, 502; see also
Senate Historical Office, *Pro Tem*, 55.
133. Senate Historical Office, *Pro Tem*, 55.
134. Kravitz, "Presiding Officers," 54–55; Sachs, *President Pro Tempore*, 41 n.23.
135. Senate Historical Office, *Pro Tem*, 56–57.
136. *AMVB*, 2:759–60.
137. Ibid.
138. Ibid.
139. Ibid., 761–62. For other incidents involving threats to vice-presidential well-being, see Roy E. Brownell II, "Vice Presidential Inability: Historical Episodes that Highlight
a Significant Constitutional Problem," *PSQ* 46 (2016): 434–35, 438–52. The president pro
tempore clause is the closest the Constitution comes to expressly providing for vice-presidential incapacity. As such, in the eighteenth and nineteenth centuries, the president pro tem-

pore assumed the presiding officer's chair when the vice president was ill. Gilfry, "President of the Senate," 10, 11, 12, 14, 17, 26, 44; see also 2 *AOC* 1864 (1791) (Rep. Sherman); John F. Manning, "Not Proved: Some Lingering Questions about Legislative Succession to the Presidency," *SLR* 48 (1995): 141, 149 n. 46.

140. *AMVB,* 2:762.

141. 4 *CR* 316 (1876); see also Sachs, *President Pro Tempore,* 5.

142. 4 *CR* 316 (1876); see also Shoup, "Vice-Presidency, 385–88; Kravitz, "Presiding Officers," 53, Sachs, *President Pro Tempore,* 5. In 1861, Senator James Bayard (D-DE) contended that the Senate could remove the president pro tempore only by expelling him from the body. He maintained that, other than through expulsion, the power to remove the president pro tempore was essentially held by the vice president. *CG* 437 (1861).

A number of presidents pro tempore have resigned from the position. Gilfry, "President of the Senate," 37 (Sen. King), 167 (Sen. Davis), 212 (Sen. Ingalls), 213 (Sen. Manderson), 223 (Sen. Frye). Samuel Southard (W-NJ), Charles E. Stuart (D-MI), and John Sherman (R-OH) apparently did so as well. Furber, *Precedents,* 184–86.

143. Haynes, *Senate,* 251; Kravitz, "Presiding Officers," 53, 55–56; Sachs, *President Pro Tempore,* 1; 21 *CR* 2153 (1890). For debate surrounding the change, see Senate Historical Office, *Pro Tem,* 73–74. There had been earlier efforts to give the office some degree of permanence. *CG* 436–38 (1861).

144. Senate Historical Office, *Pro Tem,* 73–74.

145. Haynes, *Senate,* 251.

146. Byrd, *Senate,* 178.

147. Ibid., 178–80.

148. Shoup, "Vice-Presidency," 391–92. A handful of Senate rule changes also likely contributed to this dynamic. Ibid.

149. Senate Historical Office, *Pro Tem,* 96–97.

150. Ibid., 96.

151. Ibid.; Betty K. Koed, "Senate Historical Minute: When Minority Senators Presided" (document on file with the authors). The majority leader's right to prior recognition is discussed in chapter 7.

152. Senate Historical Office, *Pro Tem,* 96; Koed, "Minority Senators"; see also Charles Tiefer, *Congressional Practice and Procedure: A Reference, Research, and Legislative Guide* (New York: Greenwood Press, 1989), 494. As part of its power-sharing agreement in 2001, minority party senators briefly presided again. The authors would like to thank Walter Oleszek for his comments in this regard.

153. Haynes, *Senate,* 252–54; Byrd, preface, 5.

154. Byrd, preface, 5; Haynes, *Senate,* 251–52.

155. Sachs, *President Pro Tempore,* 7; Byrd, preface, 5; Senate Historical Office, *Pro Tem,* 74; Haynes, *Senate,* 252 n. 1.

156. Sachs, *President Pro Tempore,* 7; Senate Historical Office, *Pro Tem,* 74; Haynes, *Senate,* 252.

157. Sachs, *President Pro Tempore,* 7; Byrd, preface, 5; Senate Historical Office, *Pro Tem,* 74; Haynes, *Senate,* 252.

158. Senate Historical Office, *Pro Tem,* 74–75.

159. Ibid.

160. Ibid.

161. Ibid., 75; Haynes, *Senate,* 253.

162. Byrd, *Senate,* 170.

163. Ibid.

164. Byrd, preface, 5; Senate Historical Office, *Pro Tem,* 74–75; Sachs, *President Pro Tempore,* 7–8. Senator Arthur Vandenberg (R-MI) is the sole exception to this practice since World War II. He served from 1947 to 1949. Sachs, *President Pro Tempore,* 7–8, 29. Had the Senate followed a strict seniority rule, Senator Arthur Capper (R-KS) would have been chosen. Capper, however, suffered from ill health and was outside of the ideological mainstream of Senate Republicans at the time. Ibid., 41 n. 30.

165. J. Lee Annis Jr., *Big Jim Eastland: The Godfather of Mississippi* (Jackson: University Press of Mississippi, 2016), 274–75. The lone Democratic senator to oppose Eastland was Phil Hart (D-MI). Ibid.

166. "President Pro Tempore," US Senate; Ida A. Brudnick, "Congressional Salaries and Allowances: In Brief," *CRS Report for Congress,* April 11, 2018, 9.

167. Orval Walker Baylor, *John Pope, Kentuckian: His Life and Times, 1770–1845* (Cynthiana, KY: Hobson Press, 1943), 2; Orval W. Baylor, "The Life and Times of John Pope, 1770–1845," *FCHQ* 15 (April 1941): 59, 60.

168. Baylor, *Pope,* xii, 133–34.

169. Baylor, "Pope," 77 n. 1; "John Pope," Congressional Biographical Directory, accessed February 15, 2018, http://bioguide.Congress.gov/scripts/biodisplay.pl?index=P000431; Baylor, *Pope,* 2.

170. Baylor, *Pope,* 5; "Senator Pope House," Kentucky Trust for Historical Preservation, accessed February 15, 2018, http://www.thekentuckytrust.org/pope.htm.

171. Baylor, "Pope," 60.

172. Ibid.; Baylor, *Pope,* 11.

173. Baylor, "Pope," 60; Baylor, *Pope,* 11.

174. Baylor, *Pope,* 11; Baylor, "Pope," 60.

175. Baylor, *Pope,* 11.

176. Lucius P. Little, *Ben Hardin: His Times and Contemporaries* (Louisville, KY: Courier-Journal, 1887), 250.

177. Baylor, *Pope,* 324, 375–78.

178. Baylor, "Pope," 77 n. 1.

179. Baylor, *Pope,* 29.

180. Baylor, "Pope," 77 n. 1.

181. Ibid.

182. "Pope House," Kentucky Trust; Heather Vance, "Senator John Pope House," Tour of Historic Sites in Central Kentucky, May 5, 1997, accessed February 15, 2018, http://www.uky.edu/~dolph/sites/pope.html; "The Pope Villa," Blue Grass Trust for Historic Preservation, accessed February 15, 2018, https://www.bluegrasstrust.org/new-page-26/.

183. "History of the U.S. Capitol Building," Architect of the Capitol, accessed February 15, 2018, https://www.aoc.gov/history-us-capitol-building; "Pope House," Kentucky Trust; "Pope Villa," Blue Grass Trust.

184. "Pope House," Kentucky Trust; "The Pope Villa," Blue Grass Trust; Benjamin Forgey, "The Benjamin Latrobe Appreciation Society," *WP,* May 16, 2002; Vance, "Pope House."

185. "Pope House," Kentucky Trust.

186. Ibid.; Baylor, "Pope," 77 n. 1; Baylor, *Pope,* 18, 168–69, 325–26.

187. Baylor, "Pope," 77 n. 1.

188. Baylor, *Pope*, 11.

189. Ibid., 12.

190. Ibid.

191. Ibid., 15.

192. Ibid., xii, 17–18; Little, *Hardin*, 247.

193. Baylor, *Pope*, 18–19.

194. George T. Blakey, "Rendezvous with Republicanism: John T. Pope vs. Henry Clay in 1816," *IMH* 62 (September 1966): 233, 234; Baylor, *Pope*, 24; Little, *Hardin*, 250.

195. Little, *Hardin*, 250.

196. For more on Breckinridge and the Kentucky Resolutions, see chapter 3.

197. Baylor, *Pope*, xii.

198. Ibid., 22.

199. Ibid., 22, 115; Baylor, "Pope," 61; Connelley and Coulter, *History of Kentucky*, 1:421.

200. Baylor, "Pope," 61; Baylor, *Pope*, 22–23.

201. Baylor, "Pope," 61; Baylor, *Pope*, 22–23.

202. Baylor, *Pope*, 26–27.

203. Ibid., 133–34.

204. Ibid., 134 (quoting the *Louisville Journal and Focus*).

205. Ibid., 171.

206. Ibid., 15–16, 212, 418.

207. Ibid., 419 (quoting John Hallum).

208. Ibid., 86–87, 207, 317, 401; Blakey, "Rendezvous with Republicanism," 234.

209. Baylor, *Pope*, 16, 86–87; Blakey, "Rendezvous with Republicanism," 234–35.

210. Baylor, *Pope*, 16.

211. Ibid., 410.

212. A. C. Quisenberry, *The Life and Times of Hon. Humphrey Marshall* (Winchester, KY: Sun Publishing, 1892), 10, 50; see also Baylor, *Pope*, 46, 54. Among other things, the two shared a loathing of Henry Clay. "States in the Senate," US Senate; Baylor, *Pope*, 33.

213. Baylor, *Pope*, 18.

214. Ibid.

215. Ibid.

216. Ibid., 29–30.

217. Ibid., 30.

218. Ibid., 32–36; Baylor, "Pope," 62.

219. Baylor, *Pope*, 36, 41–47, 54–58.

220. Ibid., 39.

221. Ibid., 41–46, 54–58.

222. Warren, "Brown," 171; see also Baylor, *Pope*, 45–47.

223. Baylor, *Pope*, 41–46, 54–58.

224. Senate Historical Office, *Pro Tem*, 34 (quoting Pope).

225. Ibid.

226. Ibid. One authority on the period characterized Pope as a "Republican of national prominence." Ralston Hayden, *The Senate and Treaties, 1789–1817* (New York: Da Capo Press, 1970), 183.

227. James W. Gould, "The Origins of the Senate Committee on Foreign Relations," *WPQ* 12 (1959): 670, 675–76; Hayden, *Senate and Treaties*, 182–85.

228. Baylor, *Pope*, 67–68.

229. Ibid., 62–63.

230. Ibid., 88.

231. Blakey, "Rendezvous with Republicanism," 242.

232. Some believed that Pope opposed the war because of the views of his wife, who had been born in Britain and was thought to be sympathetic toward the land of her birth. Baylor, *Pope*, 87.

233. Harrison and Klotter, *New History*, 87–88.

234. Ibid., 87–88, 92–93.

235. Baylor, *Pope*, 83; Baylor, "Pope," 62.

236. Baylor, "Pope," 62.

237. Ibid.; Clark, *History of Kentucky*, 126; Blakey, "Rendezvous with Republicanism," 246.

238. Baylor, "Pope," 62; Blakey, "Rendezvous with Republicanism," 246; Baylor, *Pope*, 92–93.

239. Clark, *History of Kentucky*, 126; Blakey, "Rendezvous with Republicanism," 246.

240. Baylor, *Pope*, 98.

241. Ibid., 95; Baylor, "Pope," 62.

242. Baylor, "Pope," 62; Baylor, *Pope*, 95; Blakey, "Rendezvous with Republicanism," 238.

243. Blakey, "Rendezvous with Republicanism," 233, 236; Baylor, *Pope*, 96.

244. Blakey, "Rendezvous with Republicanism," 236; Baylor, *Pope*, 107. For more on Clay's career, see chapter 4.

245. Blakey, "Rendezvous with Republicanism," 236.

246. Ibid.

247. Ibid. (quoting the *Frankfort Argus of Western America*).

248. Ibid., 236–41.

249. Ibid., 234.

250. Ibid., 237, 241.

251. Ibid.

252. Ibid., 241–43, 246–48; Baylor, *Pope*, 114–17.

253. Blakey, "Rendezvous with Republicanism," 247, 250; Baylor, *Pope*, 116–17.

254. Blakey, "Rendezvous with Republicanism," 240–45.

255. Ibid., 244.

256. Ibid.; Baylor, *Pope*, 112–13.

257. Blakey, "Rendezvous with Republicanism," 245–47; Baylor, *Pope*, 114–18.

258. *JQAM*, 4:228.

259. Baylor, "Pope," 62–63.

260. Ibid.

261. Baylor, *Pope*, 155–59.

262. Ibid., 176–218.

263. Ibid., 176–218, 248–75; Baylor, "Pope," 63–66. Earlier in the decade, Pope had served on a state commission to determine how Kentucky could better educate its citizens. John Adams, Thomas Jefferson, and James Madison each submitted suggestions to the panel; however, the state failed to act on the entity's recommendations. Harrison and Klotter, *New History*, 149.

264. Baylor, *Pope*, 199–207, 217–18, 250.

265. Ibid., 319–21.

266. Ibid., 291–92; Baylor, "Pope," 67.

267. Baylor, "Pope," 67–68.

268. Baylor, *Pope,* 292, 295, 309–10. Pope was hoping to be named US attorney general, so he was at first ambivalent about the Arkansas appointment. Ibid., 329–30.

269. Ibid., 295; Baylor, "Pope," 68.

270. Baylor, *Pope,* 239; Baylor, "Pope," 68.

271. Robert Patrick Bender, "John Pope," *Encyclopedia of Arkansas History and Culture,* accessed February 15, 2018, http://www.encyclopediaofarkansas.net/encyclopedia/entry -detail.aspx?entryID=318; Baylor, *Pope,* 340–41, 344.

272. Bender, "Pope."

273. Ibid.

274. Ibid.; Baylor, *Pope,* 380–99.

275. Bender, "Pope."

276. Lonnie J. White, "The Fall of Governor John Pope," *AHQ* 23 (1964): 74, 83–84.

277. Baylor, *Pope,* 402–4, 408.

278. Baylor, "Pope," 71.

279. Ibid., 68.

280. Ibid.

281. Bender, "Pope."

282. Ibid.

283. Baylor, *Pope,* 407–9.

284. Ibid., 422–25. During his time as a Whig, Pope never fully made peace with Clay, who was the party's national leader. Ibid., 459.

285. Baylor, "Pope," 68.

286. Baylor, *Pope,* 446–47, 459–61.

287. Ibid., 458–61.

288. Ibid.

289. Ibid., 460–70.

290. Ibid., 462–70.

291. Little, *Hardin,* 251 (quoting Gerard D. L. Adair).

292. Ibid.

293. Ibid.; Baylor, "Pope," 68–70.

294. Baylor, "Pope," 70.

295. Roy E. Brownell II, "A Constitutional Chameleon: The Vice President's Place within the American System of Separation of Powers, Part II: Political Branch Interpretation and Counterarguments," *KJLPP* 24 (2015): 294, 295–343.

296. Sachs, *President Pro Tempore,* 1; Haynes, *Senate,* 254–55, 473–74; Senate Historical Office, *Pro Tem,* 73–74.

297. "President Pro Tempore," US Senate; Kravitz, "Presiding Officers," 49–53; Senate Historical Office, *Pro Tem,* 7.

298. Haynes, *Senate,* 255, 473–74; Kravitz, "Presiding Officers," 49–53; "President Pro Tempore," US Senate; Senate Historical Office, *Pro Tem,* 7–9.

299. "President Pro Tempore," US Senate; Senate Historical Office, *Pro Tem,* 7–9; Kravitz, "Presiding Officers," 49–53.

300. As will be seen in chapters 6 and 7, the evolution of the caucus chairman position into that of formal floor leader is an example of this phenomenon.

301. Swanstrom, *Senate*, 254–57; Senate Historical Office, *Pro Tem*, 7–9.

302. Senate Historical Office, *Pro Tem*, 7–9; cf. Kravitz, "Presiding Officers," 49; Swanstrom, *Senate*, 257.

303. Cf. Gamm and Smith, "Last among Equals," 105–34.

304. Senate Historical Office, *Pro Tem*, 9. During the 1820s and 1830s, when the president pro tempore was tasked with making committee assignments, the Senate would assign him a prestigious committee of his own to chair. Lauros G. McConachie, *Congressional Committees: A Study of the Origins and Development of Our National and Local Legislative Methods* (New York: Thomas Y. Crowell, 1898), 336.

305. Haynes, *Senate*, 273–74.

306. Senate Historical Office, *Pro Tem*, 9–10; Haynes, *Senate*, 273–74.

307. Mark O. Hatfield with the US Senate Historical Office, *Vice Presidents of the United States, 1789–1993* (Washington, DC: Government Printing Office, 1997), 87–89; Roy E. Brownell II, "The Independence of the Vice Presidency," *NYUJLPP* 17 (2014): 297, 326; Swift, *Making of an American Senate*, 134–35.

308. Senate Historical Office, *Pro Tem*, 9–10; Gamm and Smith, "Last among Equals," 112–17.

309. Gamm and Smith, "Last among Equals," 112–17; Senate Historical Office, *Pro Tem*, 10.

310. Shoup, "Vice-Presidency," 290; Floyd M. Riddick and Alan S. Frumin, *Riddick's Senate Procedure: Precedents and Practice* (Washington, DC: Government Printing Office, 1992), 1023. Courts assign some weight to authentication in certain settings. United States v. Miles, 244 Fed. Appx. 31, 33; 2007 U.S. App. Lexis 16142 (7th Cir. 2007); see also Public Citizen v. U.S. District Court, 486 F.3d 1342, 1343, 1350 (D.C. Cir. 2007); cf. Field v. Clark, 143 U.S. 649, 672 (1892).

311. Byrd, *Senate*, 182.

312. Ibid.; Riddick and Frumin, *Senate Procedure*, 1020.

313. Richard A. Posner, "The 2000 Presidential Election: A Statistical and Legal Analysis," *SCER* 12 (2004): 1, 29; see also Nona Brown, "Mystery No More: It Is Now Known Why Lafayette Foster's Bust Broods over Alben Barkley's Chambers," *NYT*, April 23, 1950.

314. The only exception appears to be Betty K. Koed, "Senate Historical Minute—The Acting Vice President" (on file with the authors). Ruth C. Silva touched on a closely related question in *Presidential Succession* (Ann Arbor: University of Michigan Press, 1951), 23–24.

315. 1 Stat. 239 (1792).

316. Koed, "Acting Vice President."

317. Ibid.

318. Silva, *Presidential Succession*, 14–24; John D. Feerick, *The Twenty-Fifth Amendment: Its Complete History and Application*, 3d ed. (New York: Fordham University Press, 2014), 5–8. Section 1 of the Twenty-Fifth Amendment has since resolved this question. Feerick, *Twenty-Fifth Amendment*, 108.

319. Silva, *Presidential Succession*, 23–24.

320. Ibid.; cf. Manning, "Not Proved," 149 n. 46. Distinctions among the relevant constitutional clauses governing the positions of vice president and president pro tempore—both at the time of Tyler's elevation and now—may call this parallelism into question. For example, does the "acting" in "acting president" mean the same thing as "pro tempore" in "president pro tempore"? Compare Article II, section 1, clause 6; section 3 of the Twentieth Amendment; and sections 3 and 4 of the Twenty-Fifth Amendment, with Article I, section

3, clause 5. Other reasons for skepticism are the fact that being president of the Senate is only a small part of the modern vice president's responsibilities. For more, see section 4 of the Twenty-Fifth Amendment; Silva, *Presidential Succession*, 23 n. 46; Joel K. Goldstein, *The White House Vice Presidency: The Path to Significance; Mondale to Biden* (Lawrence: University Press of Kansas, 2016), 21–22.

321. George Poindexter to Samuel L. Southard, April 21, 1841, in "President of the Senate of the United States," *DNI*, May 27, 1841; *CG* 4–5 (1841); cf. 34 *SJ* 64 (1842). For contemporary views about Southard's status, see "Acting Vice President," *CGA*, May 28, 1841 ("Some of our contemporaries speak of Mr. Southard, the President pro tem. of the Senate, as *acting Vice President*. We think this is incorrect. The Constitution makes no provision for an ACTING Vice President, in case of the death or disability of the Vice President, or of that office being otherwise vacant."); "The Opening of Congress," *NA*, June 9, 1841 (referring to Southard as "vice president pro tempore"); *OS*, July 14, 1841 (calling Southard "Vice President"); "Congressional Proceedings," *ADA*, April 27, 1842 (same); "The Princeton Catastrophe," *VC*, March 13, 1844 (same). See also Silva, *Presidential Succession*, 23–24; Oscar Doane Lambert, *Presidential Politics in the United States, 1841–1844* (Durham, NC: Duke University Press, 1936), 5–6. Senator Robert Byrd (D-WV) submitted a letter for inclusion in the *Congressional Record* from a Dr. R. Krasner that referred to Southard as acting vice president. 138 *CR* 19453 (1992). This segment on the acting vice president benefited from helpful exchanges with the Senate historian, Dr. Betty Koed.

322. Betty Koed, email, 2015.

323. 11 Stat. 48 (1856); see also Koed, "Acting Vice President."

324. Edmund Alton, *Among the Law-Makers* (New York: Charles Scribner's Sons, 1886), 128. Senators John Gaillard (Dem.-Rep.–SC) and Henry Anthony (R-RI) were also referred to as acting vice president in the press. "Presidents and Cabinets," *NYT*, August 18, 1903; "Senatorial Caucuses," *NYT*, March 4, 1875.

325. "Letter from President Johnson," *DNI*, August 30, 1865 ("At Philadelphia on Monday evening, on the occasion of the closing ceremonies of the Volunteer Refreshment Saloon, letters were received from President Johnson, Vice President Foster"); "Sundry Matters," *NHDP*, September 18, 1865 ("Acting Vice-President Foster and lady . . . are at the New Haven Hotel"); see also "The Connecticut Senatorship," *NYT*, May 11, 1872; "The Obsequies," *NYT*, April 22, 1865; "The Over and Stage Robbed—Fears for Vice President Foster," *NAUSG*, August 30, 1865; Charles Lanman, *Dictionary of the United States Congress*, 3d ed. (Washington, DC: Government Printing Office, 1866), 137.

326. "Vice-President Wade Administering the Oath to Schuyler Colfax," *HW*, March 20, 1869, accessed February 15, 2018, http://www.senate.gov/artandhistory/art/artifact/chamber/Ga_chamber_38_00394.htm; see also "Vice-President Wade," *RB*, March 27, 1867; Koed, "Acting Vice President."

327. *CG* 1416 (1868) (Sen. Dixon); *CG* 1699 (1868) (Sen. Dixon); 3 *CR* 632 (1875) (Sen. Thurman); *CG* 765 (1867) (Rep. Noell); *CG* 244 Appendix (1868) (Rep. Phelps); *CG* 1566 (1868) (Rep. Kerr); see also 4 *CR* 3007 (1876) (Rep. Hardenbergh); 99 *CR* A402 (1953) (Rep. Bolton). References in Congress to an "acting vice president" without regard to an individual officeholder include 4 *CR* 809 (1876) (Rep. McCrary); 89 *CR* 3286 (1943) (Speaker Rayburn); 91 *CR* 8495 (1945) (Rep. Sabath); 115 *CR* 1372 (1969) (Sen. Thurmond). For similar references in the press, see Richard Maney, "Lloyd Lewis' Colorful Grab-Bag of Americana," *NYT*, August 24, 1947; "Washington. Conflicting Interests in Union Pacific and Credit Mobilier—Senator Wilson's Successor—Mr. Colfax," *NYT*, February 3, 1873;

"Washington. Affairs at the National Capital," *NYT,* July 19, 1867; "Banquet to the Senatorial Excursion Party at St. Louis," *NYT,* June 16, 1867.

328. James G. Blaine, *Twenty Years of Congress from Lincoln to Garfield* (Norwich, CT: Henry Bill Publishing, 1886), 2:389. For a period, Blaine lived and worked in Kentucky. Harrison and Klotter, *New History,* 262.

329. *CG* 872 (1854) (Rep. Peckham); *CG* 250 (1855) (Rep. Yates); *CG* 2196 (1856) (Rep. Giddings); see also "The Nebraska Bill," *NYT,* May 30, 1854; "What 'Law and Order' Mean in Kansas," *NYT,* February 22, 1856.

330. 13 *CR* 268 (1882) (Rep. Rice); 18 *CR* 1836 (1887) (Rep. Cutcheon); see also "Death of Henry Swayne," *NYT,* November 26, 1893; "Ex-Senator Davis," *NYT,* July 31, 1883; "Mr. Edmunds Presiding: David Davis Resigns the Senate Presidency," *NYT,* March 4, 1883; "Death of David Davis," *NYT,* June 27, 1886.

331. 21 *CR* 6102 (1890) (Rep. O'Neill); 24 *CR* 667 (1893) (Rep. O'Neill); 106 *CR* 10597 (1960) (Rep Bentley); 147 *CR* 8513 (2001) (Rep. Norton); see also Ben Perley Poore, *CD,* 1st ed., 45th Congress, 1st session (Washington, DC: Government Printing Office, 1877), 33; Alton, *Among the Law-Makers,* 236. Ferry, himself a former "acting vice president," once mentioned the "position" on the floor. 13 *CR* 4451 (1882). For other references to Ferry's serving as "acting vice president," see *Hinds' Precedents of the House of Representatives* (Washington, DC: Government Printing Office, 1907), 3:131; "News of the Day," *LDCN,* November 27, 1875 ("Acting Vice-President Ferry denies being an inflationist"); see also "Two Points Settled," *NYT,* December 20, 1876; "Tilden's Investigation," *NYT,* June 7, 1878; "Potter's Fraud Machine," *NYT,* June 8, 1878; "The Matthews Committee. Its Members Announced by Acting Vice-President Ferry," *NYT,* June 9, 1878; "A Bit of Secret History," *NYT,* July 6, 1880; "The Electoral Court in 1876," *NYT,* January 5, 1883; "Thomas White Ferry Dead," *NYT,* October 15, 1896.

332. 19 *CR* 6146 (1888) (Rep. Weaver).

333. 19 *CR* 579–80 (1888) (Rep. Allen).

334. 18 *CR* 27 (1887) (Rep. Campbell).

335. George Frederick Howe, *Chester A. Arthur: A Quarter Century of Machine Politics* (New York: Dodd, Mead, 1934), 249–50; Silva, *Presidential Succession,* 24 n. 50.

336. 17 *CR* 5614 (1886) (debating a House member's effort to reduce the salary of the acting vice president several months after the president pro tempore had been removed from the line of succession).

337. "Cummins to Receive Vice President's Pay," *WP,* September 2, 1923; see also Koed, "Acting Vice President."

338. "Cummins to Receive"; see also Koed, "Acting Vice President."

339. Harry S. Truman, *Year of Decisions* (New York: Doubleday, 1955), 525–27; Margaret Truman, *Harry S. Truman* (Norwalk, CT: Easton Press, 1972), 248; Allen Drury, *A Senate Journal, 1943–1945* (New York: McGraw-Hill, 1963), 428; Earl L. Shoup, *The Government of the American People* (Boston: Ginn, 1946), 576; Cabinet Meeting Minutes, October 26, 1945, Matthew J. Connelly Papers, Harry Truman Library, accessed February 15, 2018, https://www.trumanlibrary.org/whistlestop/study_collections/mjc/index.php?documentid=hst-mjc_naid2839467-01; Cabinet Meeting Minutes, March 1, 1946, Connelly Papers, Truman Library, accessed February 15, 2018, https://www.trumanlibrary.org/whistlestop/study_collections/mjc/index.php?documentVersion=original&documentid=hst-mjc_naid2839481-01&pagenumber=1; "Sen. McKellar Invited to Sit with Cabinet," *AC,* April 22, 1945; "McKellar's Sitting in Cabinet Sessions Sets up Precedent," *CSM,* April 23, 1945.

340. 17 *CR* 5614 (1886); 89 *CR* 3286 (1943); 91 *CR* 8495 (1945).

341. 48 *CR* 3298 (1912) (Sen. Johnson); 108 *CR* 4101–2 (1962) (Sen. Murphy; submitting a document into the record); 93 *CR* A116 (1947) (Sen. Smith); see also 36 *CR* 318 (1902) (guest House pastor).

342. A recent manifestation of the president pro tempore's role in the line of succession was when Senator Orrin Hatch, the current president pro tempore, did not attend the inauguration of President Donald J. Trump. Alex Rogers, "The Perks of Being the Designated Survivor," *NJD,* April 4, 2017.

343. For an example of the press's allusion to the Speaker as acting vice president, see William Safire, "On the Give," *NYT,* October 14, 1974.

344. 118 *CR* 1299 (1972) (Sen. Talmadge); 118 *CR* 3363 (1972) (Sen. Moss); 118 *CR* 5234 (1972) (Rep. Eilberg); 118 *CR* 1918 (1972) (Sen. Fannin; material for the record); see also "Carl T. Hayden Is Dead at 94; Arizonian in Congress 56 Years," *NYT,* January 26, 1972.

345. These news items were apparently generated at least in part by Eastland's office. Larry Speakes [Eastland's press secretary], "Eastland Serves as Acting V.P.," *GC,* November 21, 1973; "A New Role for Sen. Eastland," *YCH,* December 6, 1973 ("Eastland is the acting Vice President of the United States"); "Eastland Gladly Forfeits Vice President's Benefits," *AC,* December 7, 1973 ("Eastland became acting vice president"); "Eastland Is Acting U.S. Vice-President," *CL,* November 21, 1973.

346. 126 *CR* S5675 (1980).

347. 109 *CR* 23027 (1963) (Rep. Ayres); 109 *CR* 24421 (1963) (Sen. Bayh); 110 *CR* 4037 (1964) (Rep. Lindsay); 110 *CR* 12121 (1964) (Sen. Clark); 119 *CR* 37219 (1973) (Sen. Pastore); 121 *CR* 2076 (1975) (Sen. Pastore); cf. 125 *CR* 3775 (1979) (Rep. Gonzalez); "Presidential Inability and Vacancies in the Office of Vice President," Hearings before the Subcommittee on Constitutional Amendments of the Committee on the Judiciary, US Senate, 88th Congress (1964), 230 (exchange between Mr. Leban and Mr. Rossiter); "Presidential Succession between the Popular Election and the Inauguration," Hearing before the Subcommittee on the Constitution of the Committee on the Judiciary, US Senate, 103d Congress (1994), 4 (Sen. Bayh).

The concept of an acting vice president—whether involving the president pro tempore or not—has been alluded to in different manifestations in a handful of articles and congressional hearings. Akhil Reed Amar and Vikram David Amar, "Is the Presidential Succession Law Constitutional?" *SLR* 48 (1995): 113, 138 n. 144; Joel K. Goldstein, "The New Constitutional Vice Presidency," *WFLR* 30 (1995): 505, 526 n. 118; Statement of John D. Feerick, "Examination of the First Implementation of Section Two of the Twenty-Fifth Amendment," Hearing before the Subcommittee on Constitutional Amendments of the Committee on the Judiciary, US Senate, 95th Congress (1975), 145–46.

348. Senate Historical Office, *Pro Tem,* 97.

349. Ibid.

350. Ibid.

351. Ibid.

352. Ibid.

353. Ibid.

354. Ibid.

355. Ibid., 98.

356. Ibid.

298 Notes to Pages 58–61

357. George H. Haynes, "President of the United States for a Single Day," *AHR* 30 (1925): 308–10; Richard A. Baker, *200 Notable Days: Senate Stories, 1787–2002* (Washington, DC: Government Printing Office, 2006), 52; Byrd, *Senate*, 177; Haynes, *Senate*, 256. Atchison was born in the commonwealth. Quisenberry, "Kentucky—Mother of Senators," 86.

358. Baker, *200 Notable Days,* 52.

359. Ibid.

360. Ibid.

361. Ibid.

362. Byrd, *Senate*, 177.

363. Ibid. (quoting Atchison).

364. Ibid.; Baker, *200 Notable Days,* 52. The arguments against Atchison's claim are: (1) under the terms of the Constitution, Zachary Taylor became president at the appointed time and date (March 4), irrespective of whether he took the oath of office (arguably, Taylor may have been unable to *execute* the office until he took the oath); (2) the historical record makes no mention of Atchison in a presidential capacity (and indeed, Atchison did not take the oath himself); and (3) Atchison's tenure as president pro tempore likely expired with the end of the previous Congress. Haynes, "President," 308–10; Baker, *200 Notable Days,* 52; Byrd, *Senate*, 177.

365. 110 *CR* 14472 (1954) (S. Res. 314); see also Riddick and Frumin, *Senate Procedure*, 1023.

366. "Coat of Arms, Seal, and Flag of the Vice President of the United States," Executive Order No. 10016, November 10, 1948; "Prescribing the Official Coat of Arms, Seal, and Flag of the Vice President of the United States," Executive Order No. 11884, October 7, 1975. In 1936, President Franklin D. Roosevelt had issued an official flag for the vice president but not a seal. "Prescribing the Official Flag of the Vice President of the United States," Executive Order No. 7285, February 7, 1936. The authors would like to thank the Senate Historical Office for its assistance on the subject of the two offices' coats of arms.

3. Senator as Presidential Spokesman

1. US Constitution, Article II, section 3, and Article I, section 7.

2. New York v. Clinton, 524 U.S. 417 (1998).

3. Wilfred Binkley, *President and Congress* (New York: Alfred A. Knopf, 1947), 26–186; Roy Swanstrom, *The Senate, 1787–1801: A Dissertation on the First Fourteen Years of the Upper Legislative Chamber* (Washington, DC: Government Printing Office, 1988), 79, 261; Walter Kravitz, "Leadership, Old Style: The Leading Men," in "The United States: A History" (unpublished manuscript on file with the authors), 4–5; cf. James Bryce, *The American Commonwealth* (New York: Macmillan, 1888), 1:280–81.

4. Donald A. Ritchie, *The U.S. Congress: A Very Short Introduction* (New York: Oxford University Press, 2010), 88; Kravitz, "Leadership, Old Style," 4–5, 15–16, 37.

5. Cf. Alex B. Lacy Jr., "Jefferson and Congress: Congressional Method and Politics, 1801–1809" (PhD diss., University of Virginia, 1963), 307–9.

6. Everett Lee Long, "Jefferson and Congress: A Study of the Jeffersonian Legislative System, 1801–1809" (PhD diss., University of Missouri, 1966), 156–57.

7. Scholars routinely refer to Breckinridge as a de facto Senate floor leader during Jefferson's presidency. Lowell H. Harrison, *John Breckinridge: Jeffersonian Republican* (Lou-

isville, KY: Filson Club Publications, 1969), ix, 140, 164, 167, 178, 194, 198–99; Elaine K. Swift, *The Making of an American Senate: Reconstitutive Change in Congress, 1787–1841* (Ann Arbor: University of Michigan Press, 2002), 70–71; James Albert Van Kirk, "The Public Career of John Breckinridge" (PhD diss., Northwestern University, 1937), 374; Kravitz, "Leadership, Old Style," 10–11; Long, "Jefferson and Congress," 145, 333, 338; Lacy, "Jefferson and Congress," 205–6, 213, 223–24; William C. Davis, *Breckinridge: Statesman, Soldier, Symbol,* 2d ed. (Lexington: University Press of Kentucky, 2010), 7; Lowell H. Harrison, "John Breckinridge and the Jefferson Administration," *RMSSJ* 4 (1967): 83–84; cf. James C. Klotter, *The Breckinridges of Kentucky* (Lexington: University Press of Kentucky, 2006), 32.

    8. Swanstrom, *Senate,* 261.

    9. Ibid.

    10. Ibid., 261–62; Stephen J. Wayne, *The Legislative Presidency* (New York: Harper & Row, 1978), 8; see also Jack D. Warren Jr., "'The Line of My Official Conduct': George Washington and Congress, 1789–1797," in *Neither Separate nor Equal: Congress in the 1790s,* ed. Kenneth R. Bowling and Donald R. Kennon (Athens: Ohio University Press, 2000), 238–68.

    11. Swanstrom, *Senate,* 262. In 1790, President Washington spoke with Senator Charles Carroll (Pro-Admin.–MD) and Ralph Izard (Pro-Admin.–SC), advocating that the Senate increase funding for the foreign service. That same year, Washington urged his attorney general to speak with lawmakers about the pending Judiciary Act. Ibid.; see also ibid., 265.

    12. Ibid., 269–71; see also Joanne B. Freeman, "'The Art and Address of Ministerial Management': Secretary of the Treasury Alexander Hamilton and Congress," in Bowling and Kennon, *Neither Separate nor Equal,* 269–93.

    13. Swanstrom, *Senate,* 269–70.

    14. Wayne, *Legislative Presidency,* 8–9.

    15. *WMJ,* 376.

    16. Ibid., 321.

    17. Ibid., 202–3, 228; see also Clinton Rossiter, *Alexander Hamilton and the Constitution* (New York: Harcourt, Brace & World, 1964), 75, 288 n. 30.

    18. Swanstrom, *Senate,* 271.

    19. Ibid., 268–69, 271; Kravitz, "Leadership, Old Style," 7–8.

    20. John Adams to James Lloyd, January 1815, in *WJA,* 10:112; see also Kravitz, "Leadership, Old Style," 8.

    21. Kravitz, "Leadership, Old Style," 7–8; Swanstrom, *Senate,* 268–70. Ellsworth's legislative skill is discussed in chapter 5.

    22. Swanstrom, *Senate,* 270–72.

    23. Ibid.

    24. Ibid., 301–4.

    25. Ibid., 263.

    26. Ralph Volney Harlow, *The History of Legislative Methods in the Period before 1825* (New Haven, CT: Yale University Press, 1917), 176–77. Harlow is referring to House leadership during this period, but the same principles apply to the Senate. For comparable observations, see Wayne, *Legislative Presidency,* 9; Leonard D. White, *The Jeffersonians: A Study in Administrative History, 1801–1829* (New York: Macmillan, 1956), 48; Binkley, *President and Congress,* 49–56; Noble E. Cunningham, *The Process of Government under Jefferson* (Princeton, NJ: Princeton University Press, 1978), 188–213; Long, "Jefferson and Congress," 2–3, 84.

27. Harrison, *Breckinridge, 3.*

28. Ibid.

29. Elizabeth Warren, "John Brown and His Influence on Kentucky Politics, 1784–1805" (PhD diss., Northwestern University, 1937), 2, 6–7; Stuart Seely Sprague, "Senator John Brown of Kentucky, 1757–1837: A Political Biography" (PhD diss., New York University, 1972), 13–15.

30. Harrison, *Breckinridge,* 2–3.

31. Ibid., 4.

32. Ibid.

33. Ibid.

34. Ibid., 5–6.

35. Ibid., 6–8.

36. Van Kirk, "Public Career of Breckinridge," 3; see also Harrison, *Breckinridge,* 6.

37. Van Kirk, "Public Career of Breckinridge," 3–4.

38. Ibid., 4.

39. Ibid.

40. Harrison, *Breckinridge,* 12–13; Van Kirk, "Public Career of Breckinridge," 5.

41. Harrison, *Breckinridge,* 7.

42. Ibid., 7–8, 35; Harrison, "Breckinridge and the Jefferson Administration," 83; Alonzo Thomas Dill, *George Wythe: Teacher of Liberty* (Williamsburg: Virginia Independence Bicentennial Commission, 1979), 51.

43. Harrison, *Breckinridge,* 8; Van Kirk, "Public Career of Breckinridge," 5.

44. Harrison, *Breckinridge,* 14–15.

45. Ibid., 15.

46. Ibid.

47. Ibid., 25–26.

48. Ibid., 24–26; Van Kirk, "Public Career of Breckinridge," 11–12.

49. Harrison, *Breckinridge,* 26.

50. Ibid., 10.

51. Ibid.

52. Ibid., 79; see also Van Kirk, "Public Career of Breckinridge," 372.

53. Harrison, *Breckinridge,* 23.

54. Ibid.

55. See chapter 1 for more on John C. Breckinridge.

56. Harrison, *Breckinridge,* 49.

57. Ibid., 90 n. 28; Van Kirk, "Public Career of Breckinridge," 12.

58. Harrison, *Breckinridge,* 36–41.

59. Ibid., 23–24.

60. Ibid.

61. Van Kirk, "Public Career of Breckinridge," 13–15, 20.

62. Harrison, *Breckinridge,* 114–15, 119, 122–24.

63. Ibid., 50.

64. Ibid., 50–51. Breckinridge also became one of the state's early horse breeders. Lowell H. Harrison and James C. Klotter, *A New History of Kentucky* (Lexington: University Press of Kentucky, 1997), 137.

65. Van Kirk, "Public Career of Breckinridge," 11.

66. Harrison, *Breckinridge,* 27.

67. Ibid., 51.

68. Ibid., 36–37. Albert Gallatin thought highly of Breckinridge's talents. He somewhat immodestly wrote to a friend: "During the twelve years I was in the Treasury, I was anxiously looking for some man that could fill my place there and in the general direction of national concerns, for one indeed that could replace Mr. Jefferson, Mr. Madison, and myself. Breckinridge, of Kentucky," was one such candidate, but he had no sooner "appeared . . . [than he] died." Henry Adams, *The Life of Albert Gallatin* (Philadelphia: J. B. Lippincott, 1879), 598.

69. Harrison, *Breckinridge,* 36.

70. Ibid., 33; Van Kirk, "Public Career of Breckinridge," 89–90, 374.

71. Harrison, *Breckinridge,* 36.

72. Ethelbert Dudley Warfield, *The Kentucky Resolutions of 1798: An Historical Study* (New York: G. P. Putnam's Sons, 1887), 72.

73. For other potential factors, see Harrison, *Breckinridge,* 63.

74. Ibid.

75. Harrison and Klotter, *New History,* 72–73, 81, 89.

76. Harrison, *Breckinridge,* 52–59.

77. Davis, *Breckinridge,* 7.

78. Harrison, *Breckinridge,* 52; Van Kirk, "Public Career of Breckinridge," 40.

79. Lowell H. Harrison, "John Breckinridge and the Acquisition of Louisiana," *LS* 7 (1968): 7, 8–17.

80. Harrison, *Breckinridge,* 37–38.

81. Ibid., 38; Klotter, *Breckinridges,* 28.

82. Van Kirk, "Public Career of Breckinridge," 12; Harrison, *Breckinridge,* 37–38; cf. Klotter, *Breckinridges,* 28–29.

83. Van Kirk, "Public Career of Breckinridge," 112.

84. Ibid., 121.

85. Ibid., 121–22.

86. Harrison, *Breckinridge,* 72–75.

87. Ibid., 75–77; Klotter, *Breckinridges,* 20–21; Van Kirk, "Public Career of Breckinridge," 131–59. The Virginia legislature adopted comparable resolutions. For a helpful discussion of the Kentucky and Virginia Resolutions, see *TJP,* 30:529–35.

88. Breckinridge softened some of Jefferson's proposed language. Klotter, *Breckinridges,* 20–21.

89. Harrison and Klotter, *New History,* 82. Interestingly, Breckinridge had taken an earlier position on the nature of the federal union that was seemingly at odds with his views of the late 1790s. Harrison, *Breckinridge,* 17.

90. Klotter, *Breckinridges,* 22; Ron Chernow, *Alexander Hamilton* (New York: Penguin Press, 2004), 573–74; Harrison and Klotter, *New History,* 82; Harrison, *Breckinridge,* 84.

91. Klotter, *Breckinridges,* 22; Harrison and Klotter, *New History,* 82; Harrison, *Breckinridge,* 81, 109.

92. Van Kirk, "Public Career of Breckinridge," 123–31.

93. Ibid., 123.

94. Ibid., 128, 131.

95. Ibid., 177.

96. Klotter, *Breckinridges,* 22–27; Harrison, *Breckinridge,* 24, 119–22. For more on Breckinridge and slavery, see Klotter, *Breckinridges,* 23–27; Harrison, *Breckinridge,* 24, 33, 119–20.

97. Van Kirk, "Public Career of Breckinridge," 191; cf. Harrison, *Breckinridge,* 106–9.

98. Thomas D. Clark, introduction to Harrison, *Breckinridge,* vi. Other authorities believe that Breckinridge's role has been overstated. Klotter, *Breckinridges,* 27.

99. Harrison, *Breckinridge,* 64–65; Klotter, *Breckinridges,* 14.

100. Klotter, *Breckinridges,* 14; Harrison, *Breckinridge,* 64.

101. Klotter, *Breckinridges,* 28.

102. Van Kirk, "Public Career of Breckinridge," 198.

103. Klotter, *Breckinridges,* 28.

104. Swanstrom, *Senate,* 260–64.

105. Wayne, *Legislative Presidency,* 9; Binkley, *President and Congress,* 26–48, 53–54; Long, "Jefferson and Congress," 138; cf. Swanstrom, *Senate,* 260–64.

106. Sidney M. Milkis and Michael Nelson, *The American Presidency: Origins and Development, 1776–1993* (Washington, DC: CQ Press, 1994), 241.

107. Wayne, *Legislative Presidency,* 9; Long, "Jefferson and Congress," xi–xii, 193–95; Binkley, *President and Congress,* 49–55.

108. *WPM,* 211–13, 543–47; James MacGregor Burns, *The Deadlock of Democracy: Four-Party Politics in America* (Englewood Cliffs, NJ: Prentice-Hall, 1963), 36; Wayne, *Legislative Presidency,* 10; Long, "Jefferson and Congress," 193–94, 248, 375.

109. Wayne, *Legislative Presidency,* 10; Long, "Jefferson and Congress," 193–94, 248.

110. *JQAM,* 1:431.

111. Wayne, *Legislative Presidency,* 9; see also George H. Haynes, *The Senate of the United States: Its History and Practice,* 2d ed. (New York: Russell & Russell, 1960), 1:475. In 1791, as secretary of state, Jefferson had drafted legislation for Congress to consider. Swanstrom, *Senate,* 270 n. 71.

112. James Sterling Young, *The Washington Community, 1800–1828* (New York: Columbia University Press, 1966), 167.

113. Long, "Jefferson and Congress," 135–39, 144–46.

114. Ibid., 136.

115. Lacy, "Jefferson and Congress," 122.

116. "Party Division," US Senate, accessed February 15, 2018, https://www.senate.gov/history/partydiv.htm; Harrison, "Breckinridge and the Jefferson Administration," 84, 90; Lacy, "Jefferson and Congress," 128.

117. Dumas Malone, *Jefferson: The President, First Term, 1801–1805* (Charlottesville: University of Virginia Press, 1970), 4:117–18; Kravitz, "Leadership, Old Style," 10; Lacy, "Jefferson and Congress," 204–6.

118. Lacy, "Jefferson and Congress," 205–6; cf. Malone, *Jefferson,* 117. Another authority on Congress contended that "John Breckinridge . . . was *the* leading Republican in the Senate" during his tenure. Long, "Jefferson and Congress," 145 (emphasis added).

119. *JQAM,* 1:346; see also Long, "Jefferson and Congress," 206.

120. Malone, *Jefferson,* 117; Long, "Jefferson and Congress," 150; Lacy, "Jefferson and Congress," 205.

121. Klotter, *Breckinridges,* 28; see also Long, "Jefferson and Congress," 46–47.

122. Noble E. Cunningham Jr., *The Jeffersonian Republicans in Power: Party Operations, 1801–1809* (Chapel Hill: University of North Carolina Press, 1963), 102–3.

123. Ibid.

124. Ibid.

125. Long, "Jefferson and Congress," 150.

126. *WPM,* 576.

127. Lacy, "Jefferson and Congress," 22.

128. Lacy, "Jefferson and Congress," 28, 41–43; Long, "Jefferson and Congress," 145; Harrison, *Breckinridge,* 141; see also Klotter, *Breckinridges,* 28–29. At the time, Senate procedure dictated that a resolution be adopted before a bill could be introduced. Lacy, "Jefferson and Congress," 42; Joseph Cooper and Elizabeth Rybicki, "Analyzing Institutional Change: Bill Introduction in the Nineteenth Century," in *U.S. Senate Exceptionalism,* ed. Bruce I. Oppenheimer (Columbus: Ohio State University Press, 2002), 183–84; see also Richard A. Baker, "The United States Senate in Philadelphia: An Institutional History of the 1790s," in *The House and Senate in the 1790s,* ed. Kenneth R. Bowling and Donald R. Kennon (Athens: Ohio University Press, 2002), 308.

129. Lacy, "Jefferson and Congress," 64. Breckinridge's views also reflected Democratic-Republican doctrine at the time, which opposed the concept of judicial review. Ibid., 66–68.

130. Malone, *Jefferson,* 117; Lacy, "Jefferson and Congress," 36, 42; Harrison, *Breckinridge,* 151.

131. Lacy, "Jefferson and Congress," 36; Harrison, *Breckinridge,* 141.

132. Long, "Jefferson and Congress," 145, 209–10.

133. Lacy, "Jefferson and Congress," 43–46; Harrison, *Breckinridge,* 141–46.

134. Lacy, "Jefferson and Congress," 46; Harrison, *Breckinridge,* 144. The development of the Senate's committee structure is discussed in chapter 5.

135. Lacy, "Jefferson and Congress," 46.

136. Ibid.

137. Ibid., 46–50; Harrison, *Breckinridge,* 144–46.

138. Lacy, "Jefferson and Congress," 51–53; Harrison, "Breckinridge and the Jefferson Administration," 84–85.

139. Lacy, "Jefferson and Congress," 72–73.

140. Harrison, *Breckinridge,* 146.

141. Ibid., 148–49; Stuart Seely Sprague, "Jefferson, Kentucky and the Closing of the Port of New Orleans, 1802–1803," *RKHS* 70 (1972): 312–17.

142. Long, "Jefferson and Congress," 146; Van Kirk, "Public Career of Breckinridge," 257–64.

143. Sprague, "Jefferson, Kentucky and Port of New Orleans," 312 (quoting a Lexington man who wrote, "Should this prohibition not be taken off very soon our citizens will kick *up a dust.* They already *talk of war.*"); ibid., 315 (quoting a letter that observed, "the Kentuckians are all in a Hubbub, all ready and waiting to step on board and sail down and take possession of New Orleans"); see also Harrison, "Breckinridge and the Acquisition of Louisiana," 18–19; Van Kirk, "Public Career of Breckinridge," 254–56.

144. *TJP,* 39:554n; Long, "Jefferson and Congress," 146; Klotter, *Breckinridges,* 29; Sprague, "Jefferson, Kentucky and Port of New Orleans," 314–15; Harrison, "Breckinridge and the Acquisition of Louisiana," 20–21.

145. Harrison, "Breckinridge and the Acquisition of Louisiana," 20–21; Harrison, "Breckinridge and the Jefferson Administration," 85–86; Harrison, *Breckinridge,* 151–53; Van Kirk, "Public Career of Breckinridge," 257–64. Breckinridge's stance during Jefferson's presidency was less hawkish than his earlier views when the Federalists held the reins of government. Klotter, *Breckinridges,* 29; Harrison, "Breckinridge and the Acquisition of Louisiana," 19.

146. Sprague, "Jefferson, Kentucky and Port of New Orleans," 317.

147. Ibid.; Klotter, *Breckinridges,* 29; Harrison, "Breckinridge and the Acquisition of Louisiana," 19–21; Van Kirk, "Public Career of Breckinridge," 260–68.

148. Harrison, *Breckinridge,* 154. For other legislative initiatives by Breckinridge, see ibid., 154, 173.

149. Harrison, "Breckinridge and the Jefferson Administration," 85.

150. 12 *AOC* 34–50 (1803); see also Lacy, "Jefferson and Congress," 230–34; Harrison, *Breckinridge,* 153.

151. Lacy, "Jefferson and Congress," 230–32.

152. 12 *AOC* 34–50 (1803); see also Lacy, "Jefferson and Congress," 231–34.

153. 12 *AOC* 40 (1803); see also Lacy, "Jefferson and Congress," 232.

154. 12 *AOC* 50 (1803); see also Lacy, "Jefferson and Congress," 233–34.

155. White, *Jeffersonians,* 32; Harrison and Klotter, *New History,* 84–85.

156. White, *Jeffersonians,* 32; Harrison and Klotter, *New History,* 84–85; Harrison, *Breckinridge,* 163–65.

157. Harrison and Klotter, *New History,* 84–85; Jeremy D. Bailey, *Thomas Jefferson and Executive Power* (Cambridge: Cambridge University Press, 2007), 176–94.

158. Harrison and Klotter, *New History,* 84–85; David P. Currie, *The Constitution in Congress: The Jeffersonians, 1801–1829* (Chicago: University of Chicago Press, 2001), 97–107; White, *Jeffersonians,* 32.

159. Harrison, *Breckinridge,* 163; Bailey, *Jefferson and Executive Power,* 178–83; White, *Jeffersonians,* 32; Harrison and Klotter, *New History,* 84–85; Lacy, "Jefferson and Congress," 222.

160. Lacy, "Jefferson and Congress," 206.

161. Harrison, *Breckinridge,* 162; Harrison and Klotter, *New History,* 84–85; cf. Long, "Jefferson and Congress," 145. Alex Lacy contends that at this point, Breckinridge shared top billing with Wilson Cary Nichols (Dem.-Rep.-VA). Lacy, "Jefferson and Congress," 206.

162. Harrison and Klotter, *New History,* 84–85.

163. Thomas Jefferson to John Breckinridge, August 12, 1803, in *TJP,* 41:184.

164. Ibid., 186.

165. Ibid. In an undated letter apparently sent to Breckinridge, Jefferson included a draft constitutional amendment. "Resolution for Introduction of Constitutional Amendment," in *TJP,* 41:305; see also Long, "Jefferson and Congress," 160.

166. Lacy, "Jefferson and Congress," 217–18; Bailey, *Jefferson and Executive Power,* 179–80; Currie, *Constitution in Congress,* 98. For a discussion of the legal issues involved, see Currie, *Constitution in Congress,* 95–114.

167. Thomas Jefferson to John Breckinridge, August 18, 1803, in *TJP,* 41:209.

168. John Breckinridge to Thomas Jefferson, September 10, 1803, in *TJP,* 41:357–58; see also Malone, *Jefferson,* 320; Lacy, "Jefferson and Congress," 217; Harrison, *Breckinridge,* 163. In December 1803, Breckinridge dismissed the need for a constitutional amendment on the Senate floor, cheerfully conceding that the amendment approval procedure was "long and tedious" and best avoided, giving clear priority to practical considerations. *WPM,* 76–77; see also Currie, *Constitution in Congress,* 104–5.

169. Breckinridge to Jefferson, September 10, 1803; see also Long, "Jefferson and Congress," 334–35; Bailey, *Jefferson and Executive Power,* 183; Lacy, "Jefferson and Congress," 219.

170. Breckinridge to Jefferson, September 10, 1803; see also Long, "Jefferson and Congress," 334–35. Senate caucuses are discussed in more detail in chapter 6.

171. Klotter, *Breckinridges,* 15–16.

172. Harrison and Klotter, *New History,* 102.

173. Long, "Jefferson and Congress," 332–33; Bailey, *Jefferson and Executive Power,* 183.

174. Lacy, "Jefferson and Congress," 219.

175. Harrison, *Breckinridge,* 164. Just a few months after becoming a senator in 1804, Giles was being called "the ministerial leader in the Senate" and the "Lord of the ascendant." *WPM,* 204; Lacy, "Jefferson and Congress," 207.

176. Lacy, "Jefferson and Congress," 219–20; Currie, *Constitution in Congress,* 98; Harrison, *Breckinridge,* 164; Long, "Jefferson and Congress," 146–47; Van Kirk, "Public Career of Breckinridge," 278–79.

177. Currie, *Constitution in Congress,* 98.

178. Long, "Jefferson and Congress," 146–47; Harrison, *Breckinridge,* 164; Van Kirk, "Public Career of Breckinridge," 278–79; Lacy, "Jefferson and Congress," 219–20.

179. Long, "Jefferson and Congress," 146–47; Van Kirk, "Public Career of Breckinridge," 279; Harrison, *Breckinridge,* 164.

180. Cunningham, *Jeffersonian Republicans,* 98; Long, "Jefferson and Congress," 146–47; Lacy, "Jefferson and Congress," 220.

181. Lacy, "Jefferson and Congress," 220; see also Long, "Jefferson and Congress," 146–47, 338; Harrison, *Breckinridge,* 164–70.

182. Lacy, "Jefferson and Congress," 220.

183. Ibid., 220–21.

184. Ibid., 221.

185. Ibid., 221–22; Long, "Jefferson and Congress," 338–43.

186. Lacy, "Jefferson and Congress," 221–22; Long "Jefferson and Congress," 147–49.

187. Harrison, "Breckinridge and the Jefferson Administration," 87; Harrison, *Breckinridge,* 167; Long, "Jefferson and Congress," 338–43.

188. Thomas Jefferson to John Breckinridge, November 24, 1803, in *TJP,* 42:37. Jefferson sent a follow-on letter the next day with express language about the slave trade. Thomas Jefferson to John Breckinridge, November 25, 1803, ibid., 40.

189. Lacy, "Jefferson and Congress," 222; Long, "Jefferson and Congress," 165, 338.

190. Long, "Jefferson and Congress," 149, 165, 338.

191. Ibid.; Harrison, *Breckinridge,* 167–68.

192. Long, "Jefferson and Congress," 149, 165, 338–43; Lacy, "Jefferson and Congress," 222; Harrison, "Breckinridge and the Jefferson Administration," 87; Harrison, *Breckinridge,* 167–70. For a full itemization of the legislation involved, see Currie, *Constitution in Congress,* 98.

193. Jefferson and Breckinridge also corresponded on appointments requiring Senate advice and consent. *TJP,* 42:54, 37:402, 40:60n; Lacy, "Jefferson and Congress," 100. On at least one other occasion, Jefferson forwarded proposed legislation to Breckinridge. In 1803, the president sent him language involving the judiciary, which had been sent to Jefferson by a friend. Thomas Jefferson to John Brackinridge [*sic*], February 17, 1803, in *TJP,* 39:543.

194. Lacy, "Jefferson and Congress," 206; see also ibid., 223.

195. Ibid., 223–24; Long, "Jefferson and Congress," 150–52.

196. Long, "Jefferson and Congress," 151.

197. Harrison, *Breckinridge,* 172–73, 179–80.

198. Lacy, "Jefferson and Congress," 253.

199. Ibid., 253–57.

200. Ibid., 262; Harrison, *Breckinridge,* 180. No senator voted to convict on all eight counts. Lacy, "Jefferson and Congress," 262.

201. *WPM,* 263.

202. Harrison, *Breckinridge,* 175–76; Klotter, *Breckinridges,* 31.

203. "Report on Meeting of Republican Caucus," in *TJP,* 42:546; see also Harrison, *Breckinridge,* 176.

204. Harrison, *Breckinridge,* 187–88.

205. Ibid.; Harrison, "Breckinridge and the Jefferson Administration," 88.

206. Henry Barrett Learned, *The President's Cabinet: Studies in the Origin, Formation and Structure of an American Institution* (New Haven, CT: Yale University Press, 1912), 105; Klotter, *Breckinridges,* 32; Harrison, *Breckinridge,* 189.

207. Learned, *President's Cabinet,* 105.

208. Harrison, "Breckinridge and the Jefferson Administration," 89; Harrison, *Breckinridge,* 189.

209. Harrison, "Breckinridge and the Jefferson Administration," 90; Harrison, *Breckinridge,* 193.

210. *WPM,* 475; Long, "Jefferson and Congress," 177; Klotter, *Breckinridges,* 32; Harrison, *Breckinridge,* 193–94.

211. Harrison, "Breckinridge and the Jefferson Administration," 89.

212. Harrison, *Breckinridge,* 191. He did render legal advice that presaged the Supreme Court's landmark decision in McCulloch v. Maryland, 17 U.S. 316 (1819). Harrison, "Breckinridge and the Jefferson Administration," 89; Harrison, *Breckinridge,* 190.

213. *WPM,* 478. For more on this question, see Harrison, *Breckinridge,* 192–93.

214. Harrison, *Breckinridge,* 42 nn. 12, 74.

215. Klotter, *Breckinridges,* 34.

216. John Breckinridge to Thomas Jefferson, October 21, 1806, Library of Congress, accessed February 15, 2018, https://www.loc.gov/resource/mtj1.036_1066_1067/?sp=1; see also Harrison, "Breckinridge and the Jefferson Administration," 91; Harrison, *Breckinridge,* 197–98.

217. Lacy, "Jefferson and Congress," 212–14.

218. Ibid., 212–13. Some of this decline in legislative influence is attributable to Jefferson being a lame duck in his second term. Long, "Jefferson and Congress," 239–40.

219. Binkley, *President and Congress,* 55–186.

220. Van Kirk, "Public Career of Breckinridge," 294–98; Clark, introduction, vi–vii. Of Breckinridge's performance in the Senate, Lowell Harrison wrote, "Without his legislative skills and tactful handling of temperamental colleagues, major portions of the Republican program would probably have been delayed in their passage." Harrison, "Breckinridge and the Jefferson Administration," 91.

221. Van Kirk, "Public Career of Breckinridge," 359.

222. Klotter, *Breckinridges,* ix, xv–xviii.

223. Ibid., xv–xviii, 290; Congressional Biographical Directory, accessed February 15, 2018, http://bioguide.congress.gov/biosearch/biosearch1.asp (search term: "Breckinridge").

224. Klotter, *Breckinridges,* xv–xviii.

225. Christopher J. Bailey, *The Republican Party in the U.S. Senate: 1974–1984; Party Change and Institutional Development* (New York: St. Martin's Press, 1988), 93; Charles Tiefer, *Congressional Practice and Procedure: A Reference, Research, and Legislative Guide* (New York: Greenwood Press, 1989), 489.

226. Binkley, *President and Congress,* 55–191; Wayne, *Legislative Presidency,* 10.

227. George F. Hoar, *Autobiography of Seventy Years* (New York: Charles Scribner's Sons, 1903), 2:46.

228. Kravitz, "Leadership, Old Style," 15–16, 37; John A. Garraty, *Henry Cabot Lodge: A Biography* (New York: Alfred A. Knopf, 1953), 222–24; Claude G. Bowers, *The Tragic Era: The Revolution after Lincoln* (Boston: Houghton Mifflin, 1929), 290, 336. The long-forgotten Morton, a vigorous partisan, was memorably described as follows: "In his more savage moments—and he was never gentle—he had no patience with a sword—he grasped a battle-axe. Given a cause of merit, his argument was devastating, and [even] in support of . . . [unworthy] causes . . . he was tremendous. A great giant, with flashing eyes and set jaws, smashing through the barbed-wire entanglements of logic and evidence, there was something in the spectacle to command respect." Bowers, *Tragic Era,* 289.

4. Senator as National Political Leader

1. Floyd M. Riddick, *Majority and Minority Leaders of the Senate* (Washington, DC: Government Printing Office, 1988), 2; Robert C. Byrd, *The Senate, 1789–1989: Addresses on the History of the United States Senate* (Washington, DC: Government Printing Office, 1991), 2:186; see also Neil MacNeil and Richard A. Baker, *The American Senate: An Insider's History* (New York: Oxford University Press, 2013), 63; George Rawlings Poage, *Henry Clay and the Whig Party* (Gloucester, MA: Peter Smith, 1965), 27.

2. Walter J. Oleszek, "Senate Leadership," in *The Encyclopedia of the United States Congress,* ed. Donald C. Bacon, Roger H. Davidson, and Morton Keller (New York: Simon & Schuster, 1995), 3:1262.

3. David S. Heidler and Jeanne T. Heidler, *Henry Clay: The Essential American* (New York: Random House, 2011), 9.

4. Robert V. Remini, *Henry Clay: Statesman for the Union* (New York: W. W. Norton, 1991), 3.

5. Merrill D. Peterson, *The Great Triumvirate: Webster, Clay, and Calhoun* (New York: Oxford University Press, 1987), 8–9; Remini, *Clay,* 4–5.

6. Remini, *Clay,* 5, 8.

7. Ibid., 8–9.

8. Ibid., 5; Peterson, *Great Triumvirate,* 8; Fergus M. Bordewich, *America's Great Debate: Henry Clay, Stephen A. Douglas, and the Compromise that Preserved the Union* (New York: Simon & Schuster, 2012), 74.

9. Bordewich, *America's Great Debate,* 74.

10. Ibid.; Remini, *Clay,* 9–12; Heidler and Heidler, *Clay,* 19–24, 30–31.

11. Remini, *Clay,* 9, 14; Heidler and Heidler, *Clay,* 19–20; Alonzo Thomas Dill, *George Wythe: Teacher of Liberty* (Williamsburg: Virginia Independence Bicentennial Commission, 1979), 51.

12. Remini, *Clay,* 10.

13. Ibid., 10–11, 13.

14. Ibid., 10–14.

15. Ibid., 14, 17, 29, 31; Harlow Giles Unger, *Henry Clay: America's Greatest Statesman* (Boston: DaCapo Press, 2015), 2; Heidler and Heidler, *Clay,* 38.

16. Remini, *Clay,* 31 nn. 45, 200.

17. Heidler and Heidler, *Clay,* 397.

18. Remini, *Clay,* 42–46; see also Heidler and Heidler, *Clay,* 54–64.

19. Jeremy M. McLaughlin, "Henry Clay and the Supreme Court," *JSCH* 34 (2009): 28, 36–49.

20. Maurice G. Baxter, *Henry Clay, the Lawyer* (Lexington: University Press of Kentucky, 2000), 111–12; see also McLaughlin, "Clay," 42–49. Clay filed the first ever amicus curiae (friend of the court) brief in the Supreme Court. McLaughlin, "Clay," 42.

21. McLaughlin, "Clay," 34; Remini, *Clay,* 339.

22. Remini, *Clay,* 339–40.

23. Ibid. Supreme Court Justice Joseph Story commented to a colleague: "Your friend Clay has argued before us with a good deal of ability and if he were not a candidate for higher offices, I should think he might attain great eminence at this Bar. But he prefers the fame of popular talents to the steady fame of the Bar." McLaughlin, "Clay," 43.

24. Remini, *Clay,* 21.

25. Ibid., 514; McLaughlin, "Clay," 40–41; Heidler and Heidler, *Clay,* 237.

26. Remini, *Clay,* 7, 19, 49–50, 181–82, 431–32, 514, 540–41, 596; McLaughlin, "Clay," 40–41.

27. Remini, *Clay,* 7, 19, 49–50, 181–82, 431–32, 514, 540–41, 596; Heidler and Heidler, *Clay,* 65.

28. *Sketches of United States' Senators of the Session of 1837-8* (Washington, DC: William M. Morrison, 1839), 13–14.

29. Heidler and Heidler, *Clay,* 237; Remini, *Clay,* 49.

30. Remini, *Clay,* 382; see also Heidler and Heidler, *Clay,* 237.

31. Webster was at various times an ally and an adversary of Clay not only in the political realm but also as a Supreme Court advocate. McLaughlin, "Clay," 45, 48.

32. Robert V. Remini, *Daniel Webster: The Man and His Time* (New York: W. W. Norton, 1997), 218–19 (quoting Rep. William Plumer Jr.).

33. Heidler and Heidler, *Clay,* 237.

34. Remini, *Clay,* 72, 338–39 (quoting Margaret Smith).

35. Robert A. Caro, *The Path to Power* (New York: Vintage Books, 1990), 287 (describing Lyndon Johnson); see also Remini, *Clay,* 6, 77; Holmes Alexander, *The Famous Five* (New York: Bookmailer, 1958), 17; Heidler and Heidler, *Clay,* 111; Lowell H. Harrison and James C. Klotter, *A New History of Kentucky* (Lexington: University Press of Kentucky, 1997), 89. This is not to say that Clay was unlettered. Heidler and Heidler, *Clay,* 293–94. John Quincy Adams described Clay as follows: "In politics, as in private life, Clay is essentially a gamester, and with a vigorous intellect, an ardent spirit, a handsome elocution, though with a mind very defective in elementary knowledge, and a very undigested system of ethics." Randall Strahan et al., "The Clay Speakership Revisited," *Polity* 32 (2000): 561, 567.

36. Remini, *Clay,* 24–25, 49, 431–32, 476–77, 539, 540–41, 565.

37. Ibid., 49, 431–32.

38. Ibid., 11.

39. Ibid.

40. Ibid.

41. Heidler and Heidler, *Clay,* 215.

42. Richard B. Cheney and Lynne V. Cheney, *Kings of the Hill: How Nine Powerful Men Changed the Course of American History* (New York: Touchstone Books, 1996), 5.

43. Peterson, *Great Triumvirate,* 27.

44. Alexander, *Famous Five,* 2; Remini, *Clay,* 25.

45. Bordewich, *America's Great Debate,* 73.

46. Harrison and Klotter, *New History,* 112; Remini, *Clay,* 59–61; Heidler and Heidler, *Clay,* 166.

47. Remini, *Clay,* 61; Heidler and Heidler, *Clay,* 166.

48. Remini, *Clay,* 633–34; Peterson, *Great Triumvirate,* 384.

49. Heidler and Heidler, *Clay,* 124.

50. Ibid., 153; Remini, *Clay,* 79–82, 151.

51. Heidler and Heidler, *Clay,* 153.

52. Ibid.

53. *CG* 662 (1850).

54. William H. Townsend, introduction to Edgar DeWitt Jones, *The Influence of Henry Clay upon Abraham Lincoln* (Lexington, KY: Henry Clay Memorial Foundation, 1952), 1.

55. Ibid.

56. Remini, *Clay,* 166.

57. Ibid., 1–2; see also Peterson, *Great Triumvirate,* 11.

58. Heidler and Heidler, *Clay,* 325; Remini, *Clay,* 167.

59. Bordewich, *America's Great Debate,* 73–74, 272–73, 284, 301; Poage, *Clay,* 22–23, 50–56.

60. Bordewich, *America's Great Debate,* 73–74; Remini, *Clay,* 11.

61. Bordewich, *America's Great Debate,* 73–74; Harrison and Klotter, *New History,* 120; Remini, *Clay,* 163–67.

62. Remini, *Clay,* xvii.

63. Ibid., 73.

64. Ibid., xvii; "Henry Clay," Congressional Biographical Directory, accessed February 15, 2018, http://bioguide.congress.gov/scripts/biodisplay.pl?index=c000482.

65. *JQAM,* 1:444; see also Unger, *Clay,* 36.

66. Ross Baker, *House and Senate,* 3d ed. (New York: Norton & Norton, 2001), 37–40; MacNeil and Baker, *American Senate,* 58; "Missouri Compromise Ushers in Senate's Golden Age," US Senate, accessed February 15, 2018, https://www.senate.gov/artandhistory/history/minute/Missouri_Compromise.htm.

67. Remini, *Clay,* 47.

68. Ibid., xviii.

69. Heidler and Heidler, *Clay,* 84.

70. Ibid.; Remini, *Clay,* 76.

71. Heidler and Heidler, *Clay,* 84; Judith Bentley, *Speakers of the House* (New York: Franklin Watts, 1994), 33–34; Remini, *Clay,* 75.

72. Heidler and Heidler, *Clay,* 84.

73. Remini, *Clay,* 76.

74. Ibid., 76–78.

75. Ibid., 78–79; see also *History of the United States House of Representatives, 1789–1994* (Washington, DC: Government Printing Office, 1994), 88. The only other members to become Speaker in their first terms were William Pennington (R-PA) in 1860 and Freder-

ick Muhlenberg (Pro-Admin.–PA) at the beginning of the government, when all lawmakers were freshmen. Valerie Heitshusen, "The Speaker of the House: House Officer, Party Leader, and Representative," *CRS Report to Congress,* May 16, 2017, 3.

76. "List of Speakers of the House," US House of Representatives, accessed February 15, 2018, http://history.house.gov/People/Office/Speakers-List/. After his speakership, Carlisle would serve as senator from Kentucky from 1890 to 1893. For more on Clay's speakership, see Strahan et al., "Clay Speakership."

77. Bentley, *Speakers*, 32; Remini, *Clay*, 80–82.

78. Cheney and Cheney, *Kings*, 2; Remini, *Clay*, 80–82; M. P. Follett, *The Speaker of the House of Representatives* (New York: Longmans, Green, 1896), 69–75; cf. Leonard D. White, *The Jeffersonians: A Study in Administrative History, 1801–1829* (New York: Macmillan, 1956), 55.

79. Remini, *Clay*, 80–82; Bentley, *Speakers*, 32; *History of the House*, 92–95; Cheney and Cheney, *Kings*, 2; Follett, *Speaker*, 71–77.

80. Cheney and Cheney, *Kings*, 8–9; Remini, *Clay*, 80; *History of the House*, 92–95.

81. Remini, *Clay*, 80–82; Cheney and Cheney, *Kings*, 9.

82. Remini, *Clay*, 151; Follett, *Speaker*, 72–73.

83. Cheney and Cheney, *Kings*, 15; Remini, *Clay*, 81–82; Heidler and Heidler, *Clay*, 86; *History of the House*, 93.

84. *History of the House*, 93.

85. Ibid.

86. Remini, *Clay*, 151.

87. Follett, *Speaker*, 72.

88. Cheney and Cheney, *Kings*, 18; Remini, *Clay*, 91. For more on caucuses, see chapter 6.

89. Cheney and Cheney, *Kings*, 18; Remini, *Clay*, 91.

90. "Clay," Congressional Biographical Directory.

91. Remini, *Clay*, 108–11, 113.

92. Ibid., 22–24, 47–48, 59, 251–52.

93. *WPM*, 608; see also Heidler and Heidler, *Clay*, 66.

94. Remini, *Clay*, 113.

95. Ibid.

96. Ibid. (quoting Adams).

97. How well the United States actually fared under the treaty is a matter of some dispute. Peterson, *Great Triumvirate*, 46.

98. "Clay," Congressional Biographical Directory.

99. Heidler and Heidler, *Clay*, 144.

100. Ibid.; Remini, *Clay*, 172.

101. Heidler and Heidler, *Clay*, 144–45; Remini, *Clay*, 172.

102. Heidler and Heidler, *Clay*, 143–46; Remini, *Clay*, 172.

103. Heidler and Heidler, *Clay*, 144; Remini, *Clay*, 172.

104. Heidler and Heidler, *Clay*, 144–45.

105. Thomas Jefferson to John Holmes, April 22, 1820, Monticello, accessed February 15, 2018, https://www.monticello.org/site/jefferson/fire-bell-night-quotation.

106. Remini, *Clay*, 182.

107. Ibid., 184.

108. Wilfred E. Binkley, *President and Congress* (New York: Alfred A. Knopf, 1947), 60–62; see also ibid., 51–191.

109. Remini, *Clay,* 184.

110. Heidler and Heidler, *Clay,* 147.

111. Ibid.

112. Ibid., 146–47.

113. Ibid., 147. Thomas lived and worked in Kentucky as a younger man. "Jesse Thomas," Congressional Biographical Directory, accessed February 15, 2018, http://bioguide.congress .gov/scripts/biodisplay.pl?index=t000171.

114. Heidler and Heidler, *Clay,* 148; Remini, *Clay,* 184.

115. Remini, *Clay,* 190.

116. "Constitution of Missouri—1820," in *The Federal and State Constitutions: Colonial Charters, and Other Organic Laws of the States, Territories, and Colonies,* ed. Francis Newton Thorpe (Washington, DC: Government Printing Office, 1909), 4:2150, 2154; see also Heidler and Heidler, *Clay,* 150–52.

117. 3 Stat. 645, March 2, 1821; see also Heidler and Heidler, *Clay,* 150–52; Remini, *Clay,* 191.

118. Remini, *Clay,* 191–92; Heidler and Heidler, *Clay,* 150–52.

119. Heidler and Heidler, *Clay,* 151.

120. Ibid.

121. Ibid., 151–52; Unger, *Clay,* 96.

122. Heider and Heidler, *Clay,* 151–52.

123. The first occasion was 1800.

124. Remini, *Clay,* 253.

125. Heidler and Heidler, *Clay,* 179, 206.

126. Ibid., 140–43; Remini, *Clay,* 163–67.

127. Remini, *Clay,* 1.

128. Ibid.

129. Peterson, *Great Triumvirate,* 129–30.

130. Ibid., 129.

131. Remini, *Clay,* 251–72.

132. Ibid., 253–58, 271–72.

133. Follett, *Speaker,* 79. His rival John Randolph called Clay "the second man in the nation." Unger, *Clay,* 55–56; see also Remini, *Clay,* 79.

134. Heidler and Heidler, *Clay,* 194–96.

135. Remini, *Clay,* 306.

136. Ibid., 276, 298–305. For his earlier advocacy of South American independence while Speaker, see ibid., 173–76; Peterson, *Great Triumvirate,* 52–58; Heidler and Heidler, *Clay,* 154.

137. Remini, *Clay,* 311.

138. "National Republican Party," *Encyclopedia Britannica,* accessed February 15, 2018, https://www.britannica.com/topic/National-Republican-Party.

139. Heidler and Heidler, *Clay,* 216–24.

140. Poage, *Clay,* 5.

141. Heidler and Heidler, *Clay,* 231.

142. Albert D. Kirwan, *John J. Crittenden: The Struggle for Union* (Lexington: University of Kentucky Press, 1962), 90–91.

143. *Sketches of US Senators,* 16.

144. Unger, *Clay,* 162.

145. James Sterling Young, *The Washington Community, 1800–1828* (New York: Columbia University Press, 1966), 126–30, 136–37, 147.

146. Cf. Unger, *Clay,* 162.

147. Ibid., 162–63.

148. "Party Division," US Senate, accessed February 15, 2018, www.senate.gov/history/partydiv.htm.

149. MacNeil and Baker, *American Senate,* 58; Baker, *House and Senate,* 37–40; "Missouri Compromise Ushers in Senate's Golden Age," US Senate.

150. MacNeil and Baker, *American Senate,* 58.

151. Ibid.; Betty K. Koed, "Senate Historical Minute—Missouri Compromise Ushers in Senate's Golden Age" (unpublished document on file with the authors).

152. MacNeil and Baker, *American Senate,* 58.

153. The three are Warren Harding, John Kennedy, and Barack Obama. "Senators Who Became President," accessed February 15, 2018, http://www.senate.gov/artandhistory/history/common/briefing/senators_became_president.htm.

154. Remini, *Clay,* 364, 402–3, 409–11.

155. Quoted in Louis P. Masur, *The Civil War: A Concise History* (New York: Oxford University Press, 2011), 8.

156. Remini, *Clay,* 329–30, 395–96.

157. Heidler and Heidler, *Clay,* 251.

158. Ibid., 227; Masur, *Civil War,* 4–5.

159. Heidler and Heidler, *Clay,* 251–52.

160. Ibid., 251.

161. Remini, *Clay,* 425; Peterson, *Great Triumvirate,* 217. Clay and Randolph fought a duel in 1826. Remini, *Clay,* 293–95.

162. Remini, *Clay,* 415–16.

163. Ibid.; Heidler and Heidler, *Clay,* 253.

164. Heidler and Heidler, *Clay,* 251–56; Remini, *Clay,* 415–16.

165. Remini, *Clay,* 415.

166. Ibid., 435. For further treatment of the crisis, see ibid., 412–35.

167. Ibid., 450.

168. Peterson, *Great Triumvirate,* 206–12, 236–52; Heidler and Heidler, *Clay,* 246–47. Clay had been against the bank at the dawn of his political career. Heidler and Heidler, *Clay,* 125–26.

169. "Senate Censures President," US Senate, accessed February 15, 2018, http://www.senate.gov/artandhistory/history/minute/Senate_Censures_President.htm.

170. Ibid.

171. Heidler and Heidler, *Clay,* xiii–xiv, 266; Remini, *Clay,* 458; Unger, *Clay,* 177–78.

172. Heidler and Heidler, *Clay,* 27, 266–67, 284; Riddick, *Majority and Minority Leaders,* 2; Unger, *Clay,* 162–63, 214–15; Alexander, *Famous Five,* 7, 10, 38, 80.

173. *CG* ii, Appendix (1841); see also *CG* 66 (1841) (Rep. Dawson). George Rawlings Poage, author of a study on Clay and the Whig Party, repeatedly refers to Clay's informal Senate party leadership during this period. Poage, *Clay,* 25, 29, 37, 41–42, 55, 59. Indeed, Clay set the chamber's policy agenda and schedule, two hallmarks of modern Senate leadership. Ibid., 89–90. He also played an important role in committee assignments. Ibid., 41.

174. Remini, *Clay*, 525.

175. Unger, *Clay*, 214–15.

176. Poage, *Clay*, 13, 19; Unger, *Clay*, 214–15. One Clay biographer described him as "de facto majority leader" during the early 1840s. Unger, *Clay*, 215, 217. Clay's legislative clout transcended the Senate, however; he apparently played a role in the selection of House Speaker and some House committee chairmen. Poage, *Clay*, 42–43.

177. Remini, *Clay*, 584–85. For Clay's Senate leadership in the 1830s, see Peterson, *Great Triumvirate*, 239–40.

178. *CG* 47 (1841).

179. Ibid.

180. Unger, *Clay*, 215–17; Poage, *Clay*, 15–21; MacNeil and Baker, *American Senate*, 170. Clay's approach to President Harrison was not unlike that of Senate majority leader Robert Taft (R-OH) to the incoming administration of fellow Republican Dwight D. Eisenhower. Taft purported to lead the politically inexperienced Eisenhower on domestic policy matters, but he died before the efficacy of this approach could be determined. William S. White, *Citadel: The Story of the U.S. Senate*, 2d ed. (New York: Harper & Brothers, 1957), 101.

181. Poage, *Clay*, 20–21, 26–27, 29–31; MacNeil and Baker, *American Senate*, 63.

182. Poage, *Clay*, 19–21, 28–31.

183. Ibid., 29–32; MacNeil and Baker, *American Senate*, 63.

184. Poage, *Clay*, 37.

185. Ibid., 49–91; Remini, *Clay*, 587–94.

186. Clay was not the last congressional leader whose efforts to direct national policy from Capitol Hill were thwarted by the veto. Majority leader Lyndon Johnson experienced the same difficulties in 1959 when he attempted to steamroll Republican president Dwight Eisenhower after a Democratic landslide in the previous year's elections. Rowland Evans and Robert Novak, *Lyndon Johnson: The Exercise of Power* (New York: New American Library, 1966), 205–8, 220. Congressional Republican leadership faced the same challenge in 1995 and 1996 with respect to President Bill Clinton. Nicol C. Rae, *Conservative Reformers: The Republican Freshmen and the Lessons of the 104th Congress* (Armonk, NY: M. E. Sharpe, 1998), 216.

187. Bob Dole, *Historical Almanac of the United States Senate* (Washington, DC: Government Printing Office, 1989), 87.

188. Remini, *Clay*, 609.

189. Ibid., 648.

190. Ibid., 633–34, 658; Heidler and Heidler, *Clay*, 380.

191. Remini, *Clay*, 633.

192. Ibid., 633–34.

193. Heidler and Heidler, *Clay*, 380–83, 386, 389–91.

194. Ibid., 392; Remini, *Clay*, 655.

195. Heidler and Heidler, *Clay*, 392.

196. Poage, *Clay*, 151.

197. "Clay," Congressional Biographical Directory.

198. Remini, *Clay*, 737–38.

199. Poage, *Clay*, 199–204, 232–34; Holman Hamilton, *Prologue to Conflict: The Crisis and Compromise of 1850* (Lexington: University Press of Kentucky, 2005), 82.

200. Poage, *Clay*, 190, 232–34; Hamilton, *Prologue*, 98; Remini, *Clay*, 742.

201. Robert V. Remini, *At the Edge of the Precipice: Henry Clay and the Compromise that Saved the Union* (New York: Basic Books, 2010), 82–83, 148; Poage, *Clay,* 218.

202. Remini, *Edge of the Precipice,* 139–42, 148; Remini, *Clay,* 756–57.

203. Remini, *Edge of the Precipice,* 88.

204. Ibid.

205. Remini, *Clay,* 747. Clay originally resisted the omnibus approach but was persuaded to pursue it by Senator Henry Foote (D-MS). Poage, *Clay,* 210–17, 263; Peterson, *Great Triumvirate,* 460. Once convinced of the wisdom of this approach, Clay pursued it vigorously.

206. Remini, *Clay,* 747; Michael F. Holt, introduction to Hamilton, *Prologue,* xii.

207. Remini, *Edge of the Precipice,* 137.

208. Ibid., 70–73, 147.

209. Remini, *Clay,* 754 (quoting Grace Greenwood).

210. Ibid., 749, 761; Heidler and Heidler, *Clay,* 477.

211. Clay was seen as representing President Fillmore's views in Congress during the compromise debates. Hamilton, *Prologue,* 108; Remini, *Clay,* 753.

212. Bordewich, *America's Great Debate,* 301.

213. Remini, *Edge of the Precipice,* 143.

214. Ibid.

215. Ibid., 141, 148, 152; Remini, *Clay,* 733, 759–61; Heidler and Heidler, *Clay,* 477; Hamilton, *Prologue,* 117.

216. Remini, *Edge of the Precipice,* 144–47; Hamilton, *Prologue,* 133–50. Following the defeat of the omnibus, Clay signaled his openness to moving the bills seriatim. Remini, *Edge of the Precipice,* 141.

217. Remini, *Edge of the Precipice,* 147.

218. Ibid.

219. Ibid., 148, 152; Remini, *Clay,* 761. Some scholars have downplayed Clay's contributions to the compromise. Hamilton, *Prologue,* 117, 149.

220. Remini, *Edge of the Precipice,* 157; cf. Hamilton, *Prologue,* 184–88.

221. Jones, *Influence of Clay,* 27 n. 10 (quoting Carl Schurz); Bordewich, *America's Great Debate,* 395–97. Others have been more critical of the compromise itself. Hamilton, *Prologue,* 166–90.

222. Remini, *Edge of the Precipice,* 158.

223. Bordewich, *America's Great Debate,* 395.

224. Remini, *Edge of the Precipice,* 158.

225. Heidler and Heidler, *Clay,* xvii; Remini, *Clay,* 783.

226. For more about this undertaking, see chapter 8. See also, generally, Alexander, *Famous Five.*

227. George Norris (R-NE) was ranked first among outside experts but was not chosen by the committee. "The 'Famous Five' Now the 'Famous Nine,'" US Senate, accessed February 15, 2018, https://www.senate.gov/artandhistory/history/common/briefing/Famous_Five_Seven.htm; see also Alexander, *Famous Five.* Since then, the portraits of Arthur Vandenberg (R-MI) and Robert Wagner (D-NY) have been added. The images of Roger Sherman (Pro-Admin.–CT) and Oliver Ellsworth (Fed.-CT) also adorn the room, symbolizing the Great Compromise that created Congress at the Philadelphia Convention in 1787.

228. Thomas O. Kelly II, codirector, Siena Research Institute, to Richard A. Baker, historian of the US Senate, June 19, 1986 (on file with the authors).

229. David L. Porter, "America's Ten Greatest Senators," in *The Rating Game in American Politics: An Interdisciplinary Approach* (New York: Irvington Publishers, 1987), 110–12.

230. Ross Douthat, "They Made America," *TA*, December 2006, 64. Harry Truman and Andrew Jackson were ranked above Clay, and although they both served in the Senate, they were recognized for their accomplishments as president. Three former House members also appear ahead of Clay: Abraham Lincoln, John Marshall, and James Madison. With the exception of Madison, who was recognized in part for his work on the Bill of Rights, these statesmen were not chosen for their congressional tenure either.

231. Remini, *Edge of the Precipice*, 157–58; Remini, *Clay*, 182, 192.

232. Follett, *Speaker*, 69–82; Remini, *Clay*, 80–82; Cheney and Cheney, *Kings*, 2.

233. Koed, "Missouri Compromise."

234. Cf. Harrison and Klotter, *New History*, 119.

235. Heidler and Heidler, *Clay*, 445–51.

236. Ibid., 35, 446; Remini, *Clay*, 718; Peterson, *Great Triumvirate*, 12.

237. McLaughlin, "Clay," 33; see also Heidler and Heidler, *Clay*, 446–52; Remini, *Clay*, 51.

238. Heidler and Heidler, *Clay*, 131, 446, 450–52; Harrison and Klotter, *New History*, 121; cf. Remini, *Clay*, 179–80.

239. Heidler and Heidler, *Clay*, 131–32, 217–18, 450–52; Remini, *Clay*, 179–80.

240. Remini, *Clay*, 596; see also ibid., 297–300.

241. Eric Schickler, "The Development of the Congressional Committee System," in *The Oxford Handbook of the American Congress*, ed. Eric Schickler and Frances E. Lee (New York: Oxford University Press, 2011), 729; Walter Kravitz, "Evolution of the Senate's Committee System," *AAAPSS* 411 (1974): 28, 32–33; Richard A. Baker, *Traditions of the United States Senate* (Washington, DC: Government Printing Office, n.d.), 7–8, accessed February 15, 2018, https://www.senate.gov/reference/resources/pdf/Traditions.pdf. One example of the greater emphasis on seniority in the modern day than in Clay's era is the election of the president pro tempore. The position used to involve heated elections and was sometimes filled by junior members. Since World War II—with only one exception—the most senior member of the majority party has automatically been chosen. See chapter 2.

242. Cf. Unger, *Clay*, 162.

243. Binkley, *President and Congress*, 51–191. Andrew Jackson's efforts to terminate the Bank of the United States are a notable exception.

244. Baker, *House and Senate*, 37–40; MacNeil and Baker, *American Senate*, 58; "Missouri Compromise Ushers in Senate's Golden Age," US Senate.

245. Richard A. Baker, "The United States Senate in Philadelphia: An Institutional History of the 1790s," in *The House and Senate in the 1790s*, ed. Kenneth R. Bowling and Donald R. Kennon (Athens: Ohio University Press, 2002), 319.

5. Senator as Committee Chairman

1. "Chairmen of Senate Standing Committees, 1789–Present," 19, 41, 47, 63, US Senate, accessed February 15, 2018, https://www.senate.gov/artandhistory/history/resources/pdf/CommitteeChairs.pdf.

2. Elaine K. Swift, *The Making of an American Senate: Reconstitutive Change in Congress, 1787–1841* (Ann Arbor: University of Michigan Press, 2002), 73, 178; Roland Young, *This Is Congress* (New York: Alfred A. Knopf, 1943), 99–100; Richard F. Fenno Jr., *The*

United States Senate: A Bicameral Perspective (Washington, DC: American Enterprise Institute, 1982), 18; Eric Schickler, "The Development of the Congressional Committee System," in *The Oxford Handbook of the American Congress,* ed. Eric Schickler and Frances E. Lee (New York: Oxford University Press, 2011), 713; Ross K. Baker, *House and Senate,* 3d ed. (New York: W. W. Norton, 2001), 215; Donald R. Matthews, *U.S. Senators and Their World* (Chapel Hill: University of North Carolina Press, 1960), 97; C. Lawrence Evans, *Leadership in Committee: A Comparative Analysis of Leadership Behavior in the U.S. Senate* (Ann Arbor: University of Michigan Press, 1991), 75.

3. Randall B. Ripley, *Power in the Senate* (New York: St. Martin's Press, 1969), 123, 149, 171; David E. Price, *Who Makes the Laws? Creativity and Power in Senate Committees* (Cambridge, MA: Schenkman, 1972), 9–10; Donald A. Ritchie, *The U.S. Congress: A Very Short Introduction* (New York: Oxford University Press, 2010), 50.

4. Evans, *Leadership,* 2–3; Ritchie, *Congress,* 44–45; see also Kate Scott, "Senate Standing Committees Celebrate 200 Years," *Unum* 20 (2016): 1.

5. For examples of ad hoc committees, see Ralston Hayden, *The Senate and Treaties, 1789–1817* (New York: Da Capo Press, 1970). For more administrative matters, a handful of early standing committees had been created: the Joint Standing Committee on Enrolled Bills, created in 1789; the Committee on Engrossed Bills, established in 1806; the Joint Standing Committee for the Library, also established in 1806; and the Committee to Audit and Control the Contingent Expenses of the Senate, created in 1807. George Haynes, *The Senate of the United States: Its History and Practice* (New York: Russell & Russell, 1960), 1:271.

6. Walter Kravitz, "Evolution of the Senate's Committee System," *AAAPSS* 411 (1974): 28.

7. Hayden, *Senate and Treaties,* 170, 173–74, 181, 185–86; Scott, "Senate Standing Committees," 1.

8. Haynes, *Senate,* 271–72, 277–78; Scott, "Senate Standing Committees," 1; Lauros G. McConachie, *Congressional Committees: A Study of the Origins and Development of Our National and Local Legislative Methods* (New York: Thomas Y. Crowell, 1898), 267.

9. Haynes, *Senate,* 271.

10. Ibid.; "Committee on Appropriations," US Senate, accessed February 15, 2018, https://www.senate.gov/general/committee_membership/committee_memberships_SSAP.htm.

11. Swift, *Making of an American Senate,* 70, 76–77; Hayden, *Senate and Treaties,* 180.

12. Swift, *Making of an American Senate,* 76–77, 217 n. 121; Hayden, *Senate and Treaties,* 171–72. Before 1816, typically the senator proposing the legislation would be chosen to chair the ad hoc committee. George Lee Robinson, "The Development of the Senate Committee System" (PhD diss., New York University, 1954), 22. For additional discussion of early ad hoc committee chairmanships, see ibid., 22–23, 40–41; see also Hayden, *Senate and Treaties,* 189–92, Haynes, *Senate,* 271–74.

13. *JQAM,* 1:329.

14. Roy Swanstrom, *The United States Senate, 1787–1801: A Dissertation of the First Fourteen Years of the Upper Legislative Body* (Washington, DC: Government Printing Office, 1988), 268–69.

15. Ibid.; see also Kravitz, "Evolution," 28.

16. Swanstrom, *Senate,* 231; Kravitz, "Evolution," 28 n. 1.

17. Swanstrom, *Senate,* 231, 269.

18. Ibid., 121, 133, 180, 226, 230–31, 234, 268–69, 277.

19. Ibid., 224; cf. Kravitz, "Evolution," 27, 30.

20. Schickler, "Development," 714; Gerald Gamm and Kenneth Shepsle, "Emergence of Legislative Institutions: Standing Committees in the House and Senate, 1810–1825," *LSQ* 14 (1989): 39, 44; David T. Canon and Charles Stewart III, "The Evolution of the Committee System in Congress," in *Congress Reconsidered*, 7th ed., ed. Lawrence C. Dodd and Bruce I. Oppenheimer (Washington, DC: CQ Press, 2001), 164, 166, 170, 182.

21. Schickler, "Development," 714; Canon and Stewart, "Evolution," 166.

22. Schickler, "Development," 714; Canon and Stewart, "Evolution," 166, 182.

23. Canon and Stewart, "Evolution," 166; Wilfred E. Binkley, *President and Congress* (New York: Alfred A. Knopf, 1947), 31–38; Swanstrom, *Senate*, 269–71.

24. Hayden, *Senate and Treaties*, 180–93.

25. Ibid.

26. Robinson, "Development," 52–54. Some have speculated that standing committees were formalized to address the Senate's increased workload stemming from the War of 1812 and its aftermath and the accompanying need for specialization. Hayden, *Senate and Treaties*, 194–95; Robinson, "Development," 51–52.

27. "Creation of the Senate's Permanent Standing Committees," US Senate, accessed February 15, 2018, https://www.senate.gov/artandhistory/history/common/generic/CreationStandingCommittees.htm. Although he represented Virginia, Barbour had ties to Kentucky through his landholdings in the commonwealth. Charles D. Lowery, *James Barbour, a Jeffersonian Republican* (Tuscaloosa: University of Alabama Press, 1984), 15.

28. "Senate Committees," US Senate, accessed February 15, 2018, https://www.senate.gov/artandhistory/history/common/briefing/Committees.htm.

29. Kravitz, "Evolution," 27, 30.

30. Ibid., 30; Swift, *Making of an American Senate*, 132–33; Gamm and Shepsle, "Emergence," 53–54; Hayden, *Senate and Treaties*, 181.

31. Hayden, *Senate and Treaties*, 180–94; Kravitz, "Evolution," 29. Creation of standing committees may well reflect the Senate emulating the House. McConachie, *Congressional Committees*, 253–54, 315; Gamm and Shepsle, "Emergence," 56–57; Kravitz, "Evolution," 29. Many scholars believe that the 1820s marked a rapid elevation of the Senate's status vis-à-vis the House. Baker, *House and Senate*, 37–40; Neil MacNeil and Richard A. Baker, *The American Senate: An Insider's History* (New York: Oxford University Press, 2013), 58; "Missouri Compromise Ushers in Senate's Golden Age," US Senate, accessed February 15, 2018, https://www.senate.gov/artandhistory/history/minute/Missouri_Compromise.htm. This rise was likely helped at least to some degree by the Senate's creation of permanent counterparts to the House's standing committees.

32. Before the advent of standing committees, party caucuses often decided which senators were assigned to ad hoc panels. Everett Lee Long, "Jefferson and Congress: A Study of the Jeffersonian Legislative System, 1801–1809" (PhD diss., University of Missouri, 1966), 111, 250–51.

33. McConachie, *Congressional Committees*, 279–80.

34. Haynes, *Senate*, 273–74; Senate Historical Office, *Pro Tem: Presidents Pro Tempore of the United States Senate since 1789* (Washington, DC: Government Printing Office, 2008), 9.

35. Haynes, *Senate*, 273; Swift, *Making of an American Senate*, 134.

36. Swift, *Making of an American Senate*, 134–35; Mark O. Hatfield with the US Senate Historical Office, *Vice Presidents of the United States, 1789–1993* (Washington, DC: Gov-

ernment Printing Office, 1997), 87–89; Roy E. Brownell II, "The Independence of the Vice Presidency," *NYUJLPP* 17 (2014): 297, 326.

37. Swift, *Making of an American Senate,* 135.

38. Ibid., 135–37; Haynes, *Senate,* 273–77.

39. Haynes, *Senate,* 273–77.

40. Ibid., 277; McConachie, *Congressional Committees,* 283–84.

41. McConachie, *Congressional Committees,* 289–90; Judy Schneider, "Committee Assignment Process in the U.S. Senate: Democratic and Republican Party Procedure," *CRS Report for Congress,* November 3, 2006.

42. McConachie, *Congressional Committees,* 274.

43. Kravitz, "Evolution," 32–33; see also Schickler, "Development," 729. For more on the historical development of the selection of chairmen, see McConachie, *Congressional Committees,* 274–78; Haynes, *Senate,* 273–77. The role of seniority in choosing standing committee chairmen accelerated after party caucuses began determining committee membership in 1846. Kravitz, "Evolution," 32, 33.

44. Robert C. Byrd, *The Senate, 1789–1989: Addresses on the History of the United States Senate* (Washington, DC: Government Printing Office, 1991), 2:244; Kravitz, "Evolution," 35; Schickler, "Development," 729.

45. Judy Schneider, "Senate Committees: Categories and Rules for Committee Assignments," *CRS Report for Congress,* December 19, 2014, 2.

46. Albert D. Kirwan, *John J. Crittenden: The Struggle for Union* (Lexington: University of Kentucky Press, 1962), v–vii; cf. Allen E. Ragan, "John J. Crittenden, 1787–1863," *FCHQ* 18 (1944): 3.

47. Kirwan, *Crittenden,* v–vii; cf. Ragan, "Crittenden," 3.

48. "John Jordan Crittenden," Congressional Biographical Directory, accessed February 15, 2018, http://bioguide.congress.gov/scripts/biodisplay.pl?index=c000912.

49. Kirwan, *Crittenden,* 3–4; Ragan, "Crittenden," 3–4.

50. Ragan, "Crittenden," 4; Kirwan, *Crittenden,* 14.

51. Ragan, "Crittenden," 4; Kirwan, *Crittenden,* 3.

52. Ragan, "Crittenden," 4; Kirwan, *Crittenden,* 9–10. Crittenden lived with Bibb for a period of time and named his oldest son after him. Kirwan, *Crittenden,* 30.

53. Ragan, "Crittenden," 4; Kirwan, *Crittenden,* 10–14.

54. Kirwan, *Crittenden,* 12, 14. Tucker took over as the school's professor of law following the retirement of George Wythe, who played a vital role in the professional development of John Brown, Henry Clay, and perhaps John Breckinridge. A. E. Dick Howard, *The Road from Runnymede: Magna Carta and Constitutionalism in America* (Charlottesville: University of Virginia Press, 1968), 269; Alonzo Thomas Dill, *George Wythe: Teacher of Liberty* (Williamsburg: Virginia Independence Bicentennial Commission, 1979), 44, 51; see also chapters 2, 3, and 4.

55. Kirwan, *Crittenden,* 14, 30, 37–40.

56. Ragan, "Crittenden," 4.

57. Kirwan, *Crittenden,* 39.

58. Ibid., 16; Ragan, "Crittenden," 5.

59. Kirwan, *Crittenden,* 16, 45, 64–65, 269, 283; see also Ragan, "Crittenden," 5.

60. Ragan, "Crittenden," 4–5.

61. Jennie C. Morton, "Governor John J. Crittenden," *RKHS* 3 (1905): 11; Kirwan, *Crittenden,* 30–31.

62. Ragan, "Crittenden," 7.

63. Kirwan, *Crittenden,* 134.

64. Ibid., 30, 85–86, 247, 263–64.

65. Ibid., vii; Patsy S. Ledbetter, "John J. Crittenden and the Compromise Debacle," *FCHQ* 51 (1977): 125, 126.

66. Kirwan, *Crittenden,* 18–26.

67. Ibid., 21; Ragan, "Crittenden," 5.

68. Kirwan, *Crittenden,* 21–26. Richard Mentor Johnson fought with distinction in this battle as well; see chapter 1.

69. Kirwan, *Crittenden,* 22.

70. Ibid., 25–26.

71. Ibid., vi, 33, 88.

72. Ibid., 33–34, 104, 107, 112, 117, 184; Randall Capps, "Some Historic Kentucky Orators," *RKHS* 73 (1975): 356, 367, 374.

73. Kirwan, *Crittenden,* vii–viii.

74. Ibid.

75. Ibid., 268, 344, 462, 470–71, 475; Leonard L. Richards, *Who Freed the Slaves? The Fight over the Thirteenth Amendment* (Chicago: University of Chicago Press, 2015), 17. Unlike Clay, Crittenden did not make arrangements to free his slaves at his death. Kirwan, *Crittenden,* 475; David S. Heidler and Jeanne T. Heidler, *Henry Clay: The Essential American* (New York: Random House, 2011), 451–52.

76. Richards, *Who Freed,* 17–20, 24–25, 31, 55, 59, 91.

77. Kirwan, *Crittenden,* 462; see also Ragan, "Crittenden," 25–26.

78. Ragan, "Crittenden," 7.

79. Ibid., 8.

80. Capps, "Kentucky Orators," 371; Richards, *Who Freed,* 16.

81. Kirwan, *Crittenden,* 102.

82. Ibid.

83. Ibid., 264.

84. Ibid., 477.

85. George Rawlings Poage, *Henry Clay and the Whig Party* (Gloucester, MA: Peter Smith, 1965), 27, 233.

86. Ibid.

87. Ragan, "Crittenden," 3, 9; Kirwan, *Crittenden,* vi–vii, 201–2, 218, 353.

88. Kirwan, *Crittenden,* vi–vii, 90–91, 94, 201–2; Ragan, "Crittenden," 9. Indeed, Crittenden ran a number of Clay's campaigns. Kirwan, *Crittenden,* 93, 130–31, 167, 178.

89. Kirwan, *Crittenden,* vii–viii, 201–2, 218, 314, 352–53. Crittenden turned down a chance to be a vice-presidential nominee as well. Ibid., 281.

90. Ibid., 84, 426.

91. Robert V. Remini, *Henry Clay: Statesman for the Union* (New York: W. W. Norton, 1991), 209, 339–40; Maurice G. Baxter, *Henry Clay: The Lawyer* (Lexington: University Press of Kentucky, 2000), 32, 37.

92. Remini, *Clay,* 339–40; Kirwan, *Crittenden,* 84, 426; Ragan, "Crittenden," 8.

93. Remini, *Clay,* 163–67; Poage, *Clay,* 22–23, 50–56.

94. Remini, *Clay,* 11.

95. Ibid., 11, 163–67; Kirwan, *Crittenden,* 129–30; Fergus M. Bordewich, *America's Great Debate: Henry Clay, Stephen A. Douglas, and the Compromise that Preserved the Union*

(New York: Simon & Schuster, 2012), 73–74; Lowell H. Harrison and James C. Klotter, *A New History of Kentucky* (Lexington: University Press of Kentucky, 1997), 120.

96. Kirwan, *Crittenden,* 107, 112.

97. Ibid., 107, 112, 129–30; Bordewich, *America's Great Debate,* 73–74; Remini, *Clay,* 11, 163–67; Harrison and Klotter, *New History,* 120.

98. "Crittenden," Congressional Biographical Directory.

99. In fact, Crittenden was initially chosen by the state legislature in 1811 to serve in the Senate, but he was three years under the constitutional minimum age of thirty. "The Crittenden Compromise," US Senate, accessed February 15, 2018, http://www.senate.gov/artandhistory/history/minute/Crittenden_Compromise.htm.

100. "Crittenden," Congressional Biographical Directory.

101. "Chairmen of Senate Standing Committees," 19.

102. Ibid., 41. Dudley Chase (Dem.-Rep.–VT) was the first chairman. Only one other Kentuckian, John Rowan, has chaired the panel. *History of the Committee on the Judiciary, United States Senate, 1816–1976* (Washington, DC: Government Printing Office, 1976), 18–19.

103. Swift, *Making of an American Senate,* 137, 174, 232–33; see also 41 *AOC* 25–26 (1823) (Sen. Eaton; putting forward a proposal involving "the five most important committees"—Foreign Relations, Finance, Commerce and Manufactures, Military Affairs, and Judiciary); "Patrick Henry" to "Onslow," No. 5, August 8, 1826, in *Patrick Henry–Onslow Debate: Liberty and Republicanism in American Political Thought,* ed. H. Lee Cheek Jr. et al. (Lanham, MD: Lexington Books, 2013), 74 (referencing "four highly important standing committees . . . Foreign Relations, Finance, Indian Affairs, and the Judiciary"); Robert W. Packwood, "The Senate Seniority System," in *Congress in Change: Evolution and Reform,* ed. Norman J. Ornstein (New York: Praeger, 1975), 66; cf. David T. Canon and Charles Stewart III, "Parties and Hierarchies in Senate Committees, 1789–1946," in *U.S. Senate Exceptionalism,* ed. Bruce I. Oppenheimer (Columbus: Ohio State University Press, 2002), 172–75. Many prominent past senators have chaired the Judiciary Committee, including Martin Van Buren (D-NY), Lyman Trumbull (R-IL), George Frisbie Hoar (R-MA), Orville Platt (R-CT), George Norris (R-NE), Edward Kennedy (D-MA), and Joe Biden (D-DE). *History of Judiciary Committee,* 5–73.

104. Swift, *Making of an American Senate,* 137, 174, 232–33.

105. "Senate Committee on the Judiciary: Jurisdiction," accessed February 15, 2018, https://www.judiciary.senate.gov/about/jurisdiction.

106. "Supreme Court Nominations, Present–1789," US Senate, accessed February 15, 2018, https://www.senate.gov/pagelayout/reference/nominations/Nominations.htm.

107. Paul M. Collins Jr. and Lori Ringhand, "The Institutionalization of Supreme Court Confirmation Hearings," *LSI* 41 (2016): 126, 129.

108. Email from Kate Scott, associate Senate historian.

109. Richard S. Beth and Betsy Palmer, "Supreme Court Nominations: Senate Floor Procedure and Practice, 1789–2011," *CRS Report for Congress,* March 11, 2011, 5.

110. Hayden, *Senate and Treaties,* 189; Scott email. Prior to 1816, select committees occasionally considered nominations. Kravitz, "Evolution," 28; Joseph P. Harris, *The Advice and Consent of the Senate: A Study of the Confirmation of Appointments by the United States Senate* (Berkeley: University of California Press, 1953), 45–46, 49–50, 58–59, 241, 244–45; Byrd, *Senate,* 213; Clara Hannah Kerr, *The Origin and Development of the United States Senate* (Ithaca, NY: Andrus & Church, 1895), 106; Scott email. In 1822, an effort to require

that all nominations be reviewed by the relevant standing committee was defeated. Kerr, *Origin and Development of Senate,* 106. Before 1816, treaties were not uniformly referred to select committees. Hayden, *Senate and Treaties,* 105–6, 136, 170–72, 198.

111. Scott email; Robinson, "Development," 250–51.

112. Robinson, "Development," 251–52.

113. Ibid.; Scott email; *CG* 848 (1867).

114. Harris, *Advice and Consent,* 248.

115. Robinson, "Development," 254–56; see also Harris, *Advice and Consent,* 81, 83, 84.

116. Robinson, "Development," 255–57; see also Harris, *Advice and Consent,* 81.

117. Robinson, "Development," 254–57; see also McConachie, *Congressional Committees,* 61, 260.

118. Collins and Ringhand, "Institutionalization," 129–30.

119. Ibid.

120. Ibid.

121. Ibid. Before 1816, Senate select committees would sometimes have witnesses other than the nominee himself appear. As secretary of state, Thomas Jefferson came before a Senate panel to discuss names put forward for various diplomatic posts. Byrd, *Senate,* 213–14.

122. Collins and Ringhand, "Institutionalization," 129–30.

123. Ibid., 130.

124. Ibid.

125. Ibid.

126. Ibid.

127. Ibid.

128. Ibid., 130–31.

129. Ibid., 131.

130. Ibid., 131–32.

131. Ibid., 132.

132. During Crittenden's chairmanship, the committee's tasks were somewhat more mundane than those in the modern day. See 8 *SJ* (1817), 90, 118, 119, 124, 135, 152, 154, 174, 225, 317. The committee was, however, charged with considering whether the number of Supreme Court justices could be allowed to decrease due to attrition. Ibid., 122. No legislation was adopted.

133. For more on the lead author's experience with the Packwood investigation, see Mitch McConnell, *The Long Game: A Memoir* (New York: Sentinel, 2016), 99–101.

134. "Committee Jurisdiction," US Senate Committee on Appropriations, accessed February 15, 2018, https://www.appropriations.senate.gov/about/jurisdiction.

135. McConachie, *Congressional Committees,* 64; see also ibid., 6 ("Congress, a miniature of the nation, is in turn miniatured in each of its committees"). It is not unheard of for chairmen to compete for autonomy and influence with their own subcommittee chairmen. Richard E. Cohen, *Congressional Leadership: Seeking a New Role* (Beverly Hills, CA: Sage, 1980), 50.

136. Evans, *Leadership,* 3.

137. Ibid., 70.

138. Ibid., 3, 27–28.

139. In the modern era, one Democratic senator noted the link between formal floor leadership and committee chairmen: "Chairmen are . . . sort of [a] rump part of the leadership. They go in and out, depending on their interests." Ripley, *Power,* 123.

140. Kravitz, "Evolution," 30; Ritchie, *Congress,* 50; Price, *Who Makes Laws,* 9–10.

141. Schickler, "Development," 731. Congress may override the president's veto with a two-thirds majority in each house. A bill can also become law if the president does not sign the measure and Congress is in session.

142. Ibid.

143. Ibid.

144. Cf. ibid.

145. Robert Burns, "To a Mouse," Poetry Foundation, accessed February 15, 2018, https://www.poetryfoundation.org/poems/43816/to-a-mouse-56d222ab36e33.

146. Winthrop Griffith, *Humphrey: A Candid Biography* (New York: William Morrow, 1965), 268.

147. The power dynamics between party leaders and committee chairmen have been important historically. One scholar has argued that seniority practices related to committee chairmanships ensured that party leadership in the Senate did not become as powerful as in the House. Ripley, *Power,* 49.

148. John F. Manley, *American Government and Public Policy* (New York: Macmillan, 1976), 272; see also Malcolm E. Jewell and Samuel C. Patterson, *The Legislative Process in the United States* (New York: Random House, 1966), 166.

149. Kirwan, *Crittenden,* 35–36; Ragan, "Crittenden," 6.

150. Capps, "Kentucky Orators," 367; Ragan, "Crittenden," 6; Kirwan, *Crittenden,* 35–36.

151. *The Life of John J. Crittenden: With Selections from His Correspondence and Speeches,* ed. Mrs. Chapman Coleman [Ann Mary Crittenden Coleman] (Philadelphia: J. B. Lippincott, 1871), 1:42 (quoting Crittenden's daughter); see also Kirwan, *Crittenden,* 43–45.

152. Kirwan, *Crittenden,* 70.

153. Ibid., 70, 238.

154. Merrill D. Peterson, *The Great Triumvirate: Webster, Clay, and Calhoun* (New York: Oxford University Press, 1987), 129; Kirwan, *Crittenden,* 70–71.

155. Kirwan, *Crittenden,* 66, 79, 238, 265.

156. Ibid., 84.

157. Ibid.

158. Ibid.; see also J. Myron Jacobstein and Roy M. Mersky, *The Rejected: Sketches of the 26 Men Nominated for the Supreme Court but Not Confirmed by the Senate* (Milpitas, CA: Toucan Valley Publications, 1993), 19–23; Henry J. Abraham, *Justices, Presidents, and Senators: A History of the U.S. Supreme Court Appointments from Washington to Clinton* (Lanham, MD: Rowman & Littlefield, 1999), 28–29; Beth and Palmer, "Supreme Court Nominations," 4–5. About the Senate's treatment of Crittenden's nomination, two experts wrote: "the early Senate declined to endorse the principle that proper practice required it to consider and proceed to a final vote on every [Supreme Court] nomination." Beth and Palmer, "Supreme Court Nominations," 5.

159. Kirwan, *Crittenden,* 84.

160. Heidler and Heidler, *Clay,* 231.

161. Kirwan, *Crittenden,* 90–91.

162. Ibid., 138; Capps, "Kentucky Orators," 368–69.

163. For Crittenden's tenure, see Kirwan, *Crittenden,* 143–55.

164. Ibid., 151–55; Ragan, "Crittenden," 12.

165. Kirwan, *Crittenden,* 167.

166. Ibid., 170, 173–75, 178–80.

167. Ibid., 170–80.

168. Walter Kravitz, "Leadership, Old Style: The Leading Men," in "The United States Senate: A History" (unpublished manuscript on file with the authors), 22–23; Kirwan, *Crittenden,* 192. For more on Crittenden's stature in the Senate at the time, see Kirwan, *Crittenden,* 184–85, 187–92, 197.

169. In addition to Crittenden, the Senate Committee on Military Affairs had a number of prominent figures serve as chairman: Andrew Jackson (Dem.-Rep.–TN), William Henry Harrison (Pro-Adams–OH), Thomas Hart Benton (D/Jack.-MO), Lewis Cass (D-MI), Jefferson Davis (D-MS), and Henry Wilson (R-MA). Its successor panel has also had some distinguished past chairmen: Chan Gurney (D-SD), Richard Russell (D-GA), John Stennis (D-MS), Barry Goldwater (R-AZ), Sam Nunn (D-GA), and John McCain (R-AZ).

170. US Senate Historical Office, "Draft US Senate Committee History Timeline, 1789–Present" (on file with the authors), 11–13.

171. Marshall Edward Dimock, *Congressional Investigating Committees* (Baltimore: Johns Hopkins Press, 1929), 58. As was the case in other areas (e.g., initial legislative output, creation of standing committees, openness to the public), the Senate trailed the House in exercising the investigative function. For many years after the Senate's creation, its committees engaged in far fewer investigations than did House panels. Ibid., 30; Robinson, "Development," 208–16. The date of the first Senate investigation is a matter of some dispute, ranging from the 1810s to the 1830s. Dimock, *Congressional Investigating Committees,* 30; Robinson, "Development," 83–107, 215–16.

172. "Draft US Senate Committee History Timeline," 4.

173. Pat Towell, "Presidential Vetoes of Annual Defense Authorization bills," *CRS Insight,* October 1, 2015.

174. Kirwan, *Crittenden,* 186–87.

175. Ibid., 187.

176. Ibid., 186–88; cf. Frederick Merk, "Presidential Fevers," *MVHR* 47 (1960): 3, 9–27; Robert W. Merry, *A Country of Vast Designs: James K. Polk, the Mexican War, and the Conquest of the American Continent* (New York: Simon & Schuster, 2009), 225–27.

177. Kirwan, *Crittenden,* 187–92.

178. Merk, "Presidential Fevers," 26–31; Kirwan, *Crittenden,* 187–92.

179. Merk, "Presidential Fevers," 30; Kirwan, *Crittenden,* 187–92; Merry, *Country of Vast Designs,* 235–37.

180. Merk, "Presidential Fevers," 26–27, 30–33; Kirwan, *Crittenden,* 192.

181. Kirwan, *Crittenden,* 186–88, 192; cf. Merk, "Presidential Fevers," 26–27, 30–33.

182. Merk, "Presidential Fevers," 26–27; Kirwan, *Crittenden,* 187–92.

183. Swift, *Making of an American Senate,* 51–52.

184. Kirwan, *Crittenden,* 225–26.

185. Ibid., 226.

186. Ibid., 225, 231–32.

187. Ibid., 230–31.

188. Ibid., 225–29.

189. Ibid., 225–29, 237.

190. Ibid., 227.

191. Ibid., 237–38, 240.

192. Ibid.

193. Ibid., 243–44; Capps, "Kentucky Orators," 370.

194. Kirwan, *Crittenden*, 239, 247; Ragan, "Crittenden," 16.

195. Kirwan, *Crittenden*, 249.

196. Roy E. Brownell II, "A Constitutional Chameleon: The Vice President's Place within the American System of Separation of Powers: Part II: Political Branch Interpretation and Counterarguments," *KJLPP* 24 (2015): 294, 297–337; Henry Barrett Learned, *The President's Cabinet: Studies in the Origin, Formation and Structure of an American Institution* (New Haven, CT: Yale University Press, 1912), 384–90; H. B. Learned, "Some Aspects of the Vice-Presidency," *APSA Proceedings* 9 (1912): 162, 173–75. There were a handful of cabinet appearances by vice presidents prior to World War I. See chapter 1, page 31, note 349.

197. Taylor is buried in Louisville. Kirwan, *Crittenden*, 264.

198. Ibid., 265.

199. "Attorneys General of the United States," Department of Justice, accessed February 15, 2018, https://www.justice.gov/ag/historical-bios?page=3.

200. Kirwan, *Crittenden*, 266–67. For more on his tenure, see ibid., 265–84; Ragan, "Crittenden," 18–19.

201. Kirwan, *Crittenden*, 284.

202. Ibid., 322–23, 378; Kravitz, "Leadership, Old Style," 26.

203. Ragan, "Crittenden," 20 (quoting a contemporary).

204. "The Caning of Senator Charles Sumner," US Senate, accessed February 15, 2018, https://www.senate.gov/artandhistory/history/minute/The_Caning_of_Senator_Charles_Sumner.htm.

205. Kirwan, *Crittenden*, 315.

206. Ibid., 315–16.

207. Ibid., 316.

208. Ibid.

209. Ibid.

210. Ibid.

211. Ibid.

212. Ibid., 291.

213. Ibid.

214. Ibid.; "Kansas-Nebraska Act," US Senate, accessed February 15, 2018, https://www.senate.gov/artandhistory/history/minute/Kansas_Nebraska_Act.htm.

215. "Kansas-Nebraska Act," US Senate.

216. Ibid.

217. Kirwan, *Crittenden*, 291.

218. Walter Ray Fisher, "An Analysis of the Arguments in the Senate Debate on the Crittenden Compromise Resolutions, 1860–61" (PhD diss., University of Iowa, 1960), 13, 70–71.

219. Kirwan, *Crittenden*, 346–49.

220. Ibid., 314, 346–48. Not long thereafter, Crittenden opposed the pro-slavery Lecompton Constitution for Kansas. Ibid., 321–32.

221. Ragan, "Crittenden," 21–23; Kirwan, *Crittenden*, 349–53. After the implosion of the Whig Party, Crittenden was a member of the nativist Know-Nothing Party for a time, although he distanced himself from its anti-Catholic rhetoric. Kirwan, *Crittenden*, 298–308; "Crittenden," Congressional Biographical Directory.

222. Kirwan, *Crittenden*, 346–51.

223. Ibid., 351–52.

224. Ibid., vii, 373; Fisher, "Analysis of Arguments," 49–51; Ledbetter, "Crittenden and the Compromise," 126.

225. Ledbetter, "Crittenden and the Compromise," 127.

226. "Party Division," US Senate, accessed February 15, 2018, http://www.senate.gov/history/partydiv.htm; cf. Kirwan, *Crittenden,* 378.

227. Kirwan, *Crittenden,* 373.

228. "Crittenden Compromise," US Senate.

229. Kirwan, *Crittenden,* 375–76.

230. Ibid.; Ledbetter, "Crittenden and the Compromise," 129.

231. Kirwan, *Crittenden,* 383.

232. Ibid., 375.

233. Ibid., 383, 400–401; Ledbetter, "Crittenden and the Compromise," 134–135; Fisher, "Analysis of Arguments," 139–40.

234. Kirwan, *Crittenden,* 375. For a full discussion of Crittenden's compromise efforts, see ibid., 366–421.

235. Ibid., 379–80. Many believed there was widespread public support for Crittenden's efforts. Ibid., 404.

236. Ibid., 378.

237. Ibid., 382.

238. Ibid., 392–421.

239. Ibid., 406–20.

240. William C. Harris, *Lincoln and Congress* (Carbondale: Southern Illinois University Press, 2017), 8–9; Ledbetter, "Crittenden and the Compromise," 135; Kirwan, *Crittenden,* 380–84.

241. Harris, *Lincoln and Congress,* 8–9; Kirwan, *Crittenden,* 380–81, 386.

242. Fisher, "Analysis of Arguments," 18, 20, 22–24, 35; Ledbetter, "Crittenden and the Compromise," 127.

243. Ledbetter, "Crittenden and the Compromise," 127, 130, 137, 142.

244. Ibid., 142.

245. H. Paul Jeffers, *How the U.S. Senate Works: The ABM Debate* (New York: McGraw-Hill, 1970), 64.

246. Robert Luce, *Legislative Problems* (Boston: Houghton & Mifflin, 1935), 335; see also "Committee Jurisdiction," US Senate Committee on Appropriations.

247. Ledbetter, "Crittenden and the Compromise," 141–42; Fisher, "Analysis of Arguments," 57–58, 168–69; Bordewich, *America's Great Debate,* 394.

248. Bordewich, *America's Great Debate,* 370–85, 394–95.

249. Ledbetter, "Crittenden and the Compromise," 142.

250. "Chairmen of Senate Standing Committees," 62–63.

251. Haynes, *Senate,* 282; "Meeting Places and Quarters," US Senate, accessed February 15, 2018, https://www.senate.gov/artandhistory/history/common/briefing/Meeting_Places_Quarters.htm.

252. *CG* 848 (1857).

253. Ibid.; Robinson, "Development," 157–58.

254. "Meeting Places," US Senate; Haynes, *Senate,* 283–84; McConachie, *Congressional Committees,* 293–95; Kravitz, "Evolution," 33–34; 17 *CR* 88 (1885) (Sen. Frye).

255. "Staffing: Senate Committees," US Senate, accessed February 15, 2018, https://www.senate.gov/artandhistory/history/common/briefing/Committees.htm; Haynes, *Sen-*

ate, 283–84; McConachie, *Congressional Committees,* 293–95; "Meeting Places," US Senate; Kravitz, "Evolution," 34; 17 *CR* 88 (1885) (Sen. Frye).

256. Kravitz, "Evolution," 34; Haynes, *Senate,* 282–84; see also "Senate Committees," US Senate.

257. Kravitz, "Evolution," 35; cf. Haynes, *Senate,* 284.

258. Kravitz, "Evolution," 35.

259. "Committees," US Senate, accessed February 15, 2018, https://www.senate.gov/pagelayout/committees/d_three_sections_with_teasers/committees_home.htm.

260. Richard A. Baker and Roger H. Davidson, introduction to *First among Equals: Outstanding Senate Leaders of the Twentieth Century,* ed. Richard A. Baker and Roger H. Davidson (Washington, DC: CQ, 1991), 1–2; Ritchie, *Congress,* 52; Swift, *Making of an American Senate,* 178; Claude G. Bowers, *The Life of John Worth Kern* (Indianapolis: Hollenbeck Press, 1918), 294–95; Kravitz, "Leadership, Old Style," 2, 22; Byrd, *Senate,* 207; cf. David J. Rothman, *Politics and Power: The United States Senate, 1869–1901* (Cambridge, MA: Harvard University Press, 1966), 58.

261. "Congressional Debates and Public Opinion," *NYT,* December 15, 1878; Swift, *Making of an American Senate,* 178; Byrd, *Senate,* 207, 222–23; Allan G. Bogue, *The Earnest Men: Republicans of the Civil War Senate* (Ithaca, NY: Cornell University Press, 1981), 78–85; see also Rothman, *Politics and Power,* 30, 292; cf. Byrd, *Senate,* 230–31.

262. Gerald Gamm and Steven S. Smith, "The Senate without Leaders: Senate Parties in the Mid-19th Century" (paper delivered at the APSA annual meeting, August 30–September 2, 2001), 8; cf. Swift, *Making of an American Senate,* 174–75.

263. Gerald Gamm and Steven S. Smith, "Policy Leadership and the Development of the Modern Senate," in *Party, Process, and Political Change in Congress: New Perspectives on the History of Congress,* ed. David W. Brady and Mathew D. McCubbins (Stanford, CA: Stanford University Press, 2002), 295; see also Steven S. Smith and Gerald Gamm, "The Evolution of Senate Party Organization: An Overview" (paper presented for the Congress Project, Woodrow Wilson Center for Scholars, September 14, 2001), 6; cf. Rothman, *Politics and Power,* 58; David Brady, Richard Brody, and David Epstein, "Heterogeneous Parties and Political Organization: The U.S. Senate, 1880–1920," *LSQ* 14 (1989): 205, 209.

264. Floyd M. Riddick, *Majority and Minority Leaders of the Senate: History and Development of the Offices of the Floor Leaders* (Washington, DC: Government Printing Office, 1988), 3–4; Gerald Gamm and Steven S. Smith, "The Emergence of Senate Leadership, 1881–1946" (paper presented at the MWPSA annual meeting, April 10–12, 1997), 31–32.

265. "Congressional Debates and Public Opinion"; see also Rothman, *Politics and Power,* 30, 292.

266. Woodrow Wilson, *Congressional Government* (New York: Meridian Books, 1956), 24.

267. Ibid., 146; see also James Bryce, *The American Commonwealth* (New York: Macmillan, 1888), 1:274, 401.

268. As Gerald Gamm and Steven S. Smith have observed, during this period, "caucus chairmen and other prominent leaders were visible on the [Senate] floor primarily in their capacity as committee chairmen and bill managers." Gamm and Smith, "Emergence of Senate Leadership," 32. They note that, as late as 1899 to 1900, "bill management remained entirely in the hands of committee chairmen and bill sponsors." Gamm and Smith, "Policy Leadership," 14.

269. Byrd, *Senate,* 240–42.

270. Ibid., 240; cf. 42 *CR* 7173 (1908) (Sen. La Follette).

271. Rothman, *Politics and Power,* 58–59, 107–8.

272. Riddick, *Majority and Minority Leaders,* 3–4. That is not to say that Senate committee chairmen were not still powerful within their own domain. Their ability to block legislation, for example, remained largely undiminished.

273. Gamm and Smith, "Policy Leadership," 303; Walter Kravitz, "Leadership, New Style: The Floor Leaders," in "The United States Senate: A History" (unpublished manuscript on file with the authors), 35, 41.

274. Byrd, *Senate,* 252. At the same time, reducing the number of committees broadened the jurisdiction of the remaining chairmen, likely raising the cachet of wielding a gavel. Kravitz, "Evolution," 36.

275. Byrd, *Senate,* 252.

276. William S. White, *Citadel: The Story of the U.S. Senate* (New York: Harper & Brothers, 1957), 180.

277. Byrd, *Senate,* 258–59; Kravitz, "Evolution," 36–38.

278. Byrd, *Senate,* 259–60; Kravitz, "Evolution," 36–38.

279. This, of course, assumes that the ranking member supports the legislation, which is not always the case.

280. Floyd M. Riddick and Alan S. Frumin, *Riddick's Senate Procedure: Precedents and Practice* (Washington, DC: Government Printing Office, 1992), 1091, 1093–94, 1098–99.

281. Formal acknowledgment of priority recognition for bill managers actually predates that for party leaders. 77 *CR* 4148 (1933); 79 *CR* 3609 (1935); Riddick and Frumin, *Senate Procedure,* 1094, 1096.

282. Cf. George Rothwell Brown, *The Leadership of Congress* (Indianapolis: Bobbs-Merrill, 1922), 258; Thomas Claude Donnelly, "Party Leadership in the United States Senate" (PhD diss., New York University, 1930), 120.

283. Martin B. Gold, *Senate Procedure and Practice* (Lanham, MD: Rowman & Littlefield, 2004), 104; Schickler, "Development," 716.

284. Ibid.

285. McConachie, *Congressional Committees,* 118.

286. Kirwan, *Crittenden,* 425–26.

287. Ibid.

288. Ibid., 425–26.

289. Capps, "Kentucky Orators," 373.

290. Kirwan, *Crittenden,* 438–39; Ragan, "Crittenden," 25.

291. Ragan, "Crittenden," 25. In 1861, Crittenden succeeded in getting the House to adopt a resolution that, while blaming southern secessionists for the conflict, tried to limit the aims of the Civil War to reunification of the country. Harris, *Lincoln and Congress,* 22–25. Had such a measure been implemented, it would have continued the existence of slavery. Ibid., 22–25, 37, 75.

292. Kirwan, *Crittenden,* 445, 480; Donald W. Zacharias, "John J. Crittenden Crusades for the Union and Neutrality in Kentucky," *FCHQ* 38 (1964): 193, 205; see also Kirwan, *Crittenden,* 432–35, 439.

293. Zacharias, "Crittenden Crusades," 194–203; Ragan, "Crittenden," 3, 25.

294. Kirwan, *Crittenden,* 445 (quoting Blaine); see also Zacharias, "Crittenden Crusades," 203 (quoting others who credit Crittenden with helping to keep Kentucky loyal).

295. Kirwan, *Crittenden,* 480.

296. William D. Kelley, *Lincoln and Stanton: A Study of the War Administration of 1861 and 1862* (New York: G. P. Putnam's Sons, 1885), 83; see also Zacharias, "Crittenden Crusades," 203 n. 1 (noting in a different context the premium Lincoln placed on keeping Kentucky in the Union). For more on Kentucky's strategic importance in the war, see William C. Davis, *Breckinridge: Statesman, Soldier, Symbol,* 2d ed. (Lexington: University Press of Kentucky, 2010), 285, 298, 325.

297. Kirwan, *Crittenden,* 446–48.

298. Ibid., 447.

299. Ragan, "Crittenden," 26.

300. Kirwan, *Crittenden,* v–vi.

301. Cf. Ragan, "Crittenden," 3.

302. Remini, *Clay,* 701.

303. For more on Clay's historical legacy, see chapter 4.

304. Kirwan, *Crittenden,* 480; Zacharias, "Crittenden Crusades," 203.

6. Senate Caucus Chairman

1. Blackburn was well known in his day and was hailed as "one of the giants of the Democratic party." O. O. Stealey, *130 Pen Pictures of Live Men* (New York: Publishers Printing Co., 1910), 61, 62. The lack of scholarly attention devoted to Beck may have been anticipated at the time of his passing, as reflected by the remarks of Senator William Allison (R-IA): "Whoever shall write the annals of our time will fail to make a faithful portraiture if the name of JAMES B. BECK does not conspicuously appear on many of its pages." *Memorial Addresses on the Life and Character of James B. Beck,* US Senate and House of Representatives, August 23 and September 13, 1890 (Washington, DC: Government Printing Office, 1891), 81.

2. Tom Owen, "John White Stevenson," in *Kentucky's Governors, 1792–1985,* ed. Lowell H. Harrison (Lexington: University Press of Kentucky, 1985), 81. For more on Stevenson, see Jennie C. Morton, "Governor John W. Stephenson [*sic*]," *RKHS* 5 (1907): 13–15; Ellis Merton Coulter, "John White Stevenson," in *Dictionary of American Biography,* ed. Dumas Malone (New York: Charles Scribner's Sons, 1946), 17:633–34; "John White Stevenson," *Annual Report of the American Bar Association* 9 (1886): 528 (hereafter *ABA Report*); Lowell H. Harrison, "John White Stevenson," in *The Kentucky Encyclopedia,* ed. John E. Kleber (Lexington: University Press of Kentucky, 1992), 854.

3. Coulter, "Stevenson," 633.

4. "John W. Stevenson: Death of a Distinguished Public Man," *CCG,* August 11, 1886.

5. Francis Fry Wayland, *Andrew Stevenson: Democrat and Diplomat, 1785–1857* (Philadelphia: University of Pennsylvania Press, 1949), 23.

6. Ibid., 57.

7. Hambleton Tapp and James C. Klotter, *Kentucky: Decades of Discord, 1865–1900* (Frankfort: Kentucky Historical Society, 1977), 460.

8. Wayland, *Stevenson,* 112.

9. Ibid., 208.

10. Ibid., 57.

11. Ibid.; Tapp and Klotter, *Kentucky,* 460.

12. Wayland, *Stevenson,* 94.

13. Ibid.

14. Ibid., 207.

15. Ibid.

16. Ibid.

17. "Stevenson," *ABA Report,* 529–30.

18. William Horatio Barnes, *The American Government* (Washington, DC: W. H. Barnes, 1875), 1:228.

19. Ibid.

20. Morton, "Stephenson," 13; "Stevenson," *ABA Report,* 529.

21. Morton, "Stephenson," 13.

22. Owen, "Stevenson," 182.

23. "Stevenson," *ABA Report,* 535.

24. "Stevenson: Death of a Distinguished Public Man."

25. Ibid.

26. Coulter, "Stevenson," 634.

27. Ibid.

28. E. Polk Johnson, *A History of Kentucky and Kentuckians: The Leaders and Representative Men in Commerce, Industry and Modern Activities* (Chicago: Lewis Publishing Company, 1912), 2:1073–74. It has been maintained that Stevenson's stepmother encouraged his religiosity at a young age. "Stevenson," *ABA Report,* 528.

29. Johnson, *History of Kentucky,* 2:1073–74.

30. Ibid.

31. Wayland, *Stevenson,* 207.

32. Tapp and Klotter, *Kentucky,* 461; Owen, "Stevenson," 98. In the early 1840s, Stevenson also served as county attorney. William Elsey Connelley and E. M. Coulter, *History of Kentucky,* ed. Charles Kerr (Chicago: American Historical Society, 1922), 2:1096; Morton, "Stephenson," 13.

33. Ron D. Bryant, "John White Stevenson," in *American National Biography,* ed. John A. Garraty and Mark C. Carnes (New York: Oxford University Press, 1999), 20:729.

34. Ibid.

35. William C. Davis, *Breckinridge: Statesman, Soldier, Symbol,* 2d ed. (Lexington: University Press of Kentucky, 2010), 192.

36. Owen, "Stevenson," 82.

37. Ibid.

38. Ibid.

39. Coulter, "Stevenson," 633–34; Lowell H. Harrison and James C. Klotter, *A New History of Kentucky* (Lexington: University Press of Kentucky, 1997), 242.

40. Anne E. Marshall, *Creating a Confederate Kentucky: The Lost Cause and Civil War Memory in a Border State* (Chapel Hill: University of North Carolina Press, 2010), 43.

41. Coulter, "Stevenson," 633–34.

42. Ibid., 634.

43. Owen, "Stevenson," 82.

44. Ibid.; Ross A. Webb, *Kentucky in the Reconstruction Era* (Lexington: University Press of Kentucky, 2009), 29–30.

45. "John White Stevenson," Congressional Biographical Directory, accessed February 15, 2018, http://bioguide.congress.gov/scripts/biodisplay.pl?index=s000894.

46. Tapp and Klotter, *Kentucky,* 25.

47. Ibid.; Morton, "Stephenson," 13; Harrison and Klotter, *New History*, 242.

48. "Stevenson," Congressional Biographical Directory.

49. Owen, "Stevenson," 82–83.

50. Ibid., 83.

51. Tapp and Klotter, *Kentucky*, 26.

52. Owen, "Stevenson," 82.

53. Ibid.; Marshall, *Creating a Confederate Kentucky*, 68; Tapp and Klotter, *Kentucky*, 380–82.

54. Owen, "Stevenson," 83; Bryant, "Stevenson," 729; cf. Kentucky Commission on Human Rights, *Kentucky's Black Heritage* (Frankfort: Kentucky Commission on Human Rights, 1971), 51–53.

55. Owen, "Stevenson," 83; cf. Bryant, "Stevenson," 730.

56. Owen, "Stevenson," 83. Stevenson's plan provided much less funding for African American students, however. Ibid.

57. Z. F. Smith, *The History of Kentucky* (Louisville, KY: Prentice Press, 1895), 764; Bryant, "Stevenson," 730.

58. Owen, "Stevenson," 83; Bryant, "Stevenson," 730.

59. Bryant, "Stevenson," 730.

60. Tapp and Klotter, *Kentucky*, 27; Owen, "Stevenson," 83; Coulter, "Stevenson," 634.

61. Tapp and Klotter, *Kentucky*, 27.

62. Ibid.

63. Ibid.

64. Ibid. Stevenson's seating in the Senate was delayed by Republican efforts to question the Kentuckian's loyalty during the Civil War. Ultimately, legislation was passed removing Stevenson's legal disability and that of a number of others. Ironically, Senator McCreery was instrumental in its adoption. Webb, *Kentucky*, 66.

65. "Stevenson," Congressional Biographical Directory.

66. Coulter, "Stevenson," 634; Owen, "Stevenson," 83; "Stevenson," *ABA Report*, 531; cf. "Stevenson: Death of a Distinguished Public Man."

67. *History of the Committee on the Judiciary, United States Senate, 1816–1876*, Senate Doc. No. 94-227 (Washington, DC: Government Printing Office, 1976), 122. Stevenson was also a member of the Committees on Appropriations, Indian Affairs, and Revolutionary Claims. Johnson, *History of Kentucky*, 2:1074; "Stevenson," Congressional Biographical Directory.

68. Romero v. International Terminal Operating Company, 358 U.S. 354, 366 n. 22 (1959); see also 2 *CR* 4987 (1874) (roll-call vote).

69. Felix Frankfurter and James M. Landis, *The Business of the Supreme Court: A Study in the Federal Judicial System* (New York: Macmillan, 1928), 65; see also Russell R. Wheeler and Cynthia Harrison, *Creating the Federal Judicial System*, 2d ed. (Washington, DC: Federal Judicial Center, 1994), 12. Whether Stevenson—as a strict Jeffersonian—recognized the legislation's full potential for enhancing the federal courts is unclear.

70. *Romero*, 358 U.S. at 366, 366 n. 22.

71. Gerald Gamm and Steven S. Smith, "Senate without Leaders: Senate Parties in the Mid-19th Century" (paper delivered at APSA annual meeting, 2001), 12.

72. Ibid.

73. Ibid.

74. Ibid.

75. Ibid.

76. Ibid. Early press mentions of Stevenson as caucus chairman include "Democratic Caucus of Senators," *NYT,* December 10, 1873; "Washington. The Republican and Democratic Caucuses," *NYT,* March 7, 1875; "Democratic Senatorial Caucus," *NYT,* February 4, 1876. The authors would like to thank Professors Gerald Gamm and Steven S. Smith for directing them to these articles.

77. Gamm and Smith, "Senate without Leaders," 12. There is evidence that prior to the mid-nineteenth century, ad hoc party caucus gatherings chose chairmen, but those positions apparently did not endure beyond the particular caucus meeting. *WPM,* 597–98; Gamm and Smith, "Senate without Leaders," 6.

Democrat Allen Thurman (OH)—not Stevenson—was Davis's successor as chairman of the Private Land Claims Committee. Stevenson would not lead a committee himself until two years later, when he chaired the Revolutionary Claims panel. "Chairmen of Senate Standing Committees, 1789–present," 63, US Senate, accessed February 15, 2018, https://www.senate.gov/artandhistory/history/resources/pdf/CommitteeChairs.pdf.

78. A HeinOnline search of the *Annals of Congress,* the *Register of Debates,* the *Congressional Globe,* and the *Congressional Record* using the terms "caucus chair," "caucus chairman," "caucus chairperson," "chairman of the caucus," "chairman of the Democratic caucus," "chairman of the Republican caucus," "chairman of the Democratic conference," and "chairman of the Republican conference" reveals that Stevenson was the first Democrat referred to in this capacity. 4 *CR* 144–45 (1875). The first reference ever to a caucus chairman on the floor was in 1866 to the Republican caucus chairman, although the identity of the officeholder is unclear. *CG* 3039 (1866). Other early references to caucus chairmen include *CG* 1752 (1873) (referring to Henry Anthony, R-RI); 4 *CR* 144 (1875) (referring to Anthony); 9 *CR* 136 (1879) (apparently referring to William Wallace, D-PA); 9 *CR* 538 (1879) (apparently referring to Wallace); 9 *CR* 798–800 (1879) (referring to Anthony and John Hale, R-NH); 9 *CR* 1243 (1879) (referring to George Pendleton, D-OH); 10 *CR* 748, 3748 (1880) (referring to Wallace); 12 *CR* 12 (1881) (referring to Wallace); 12 *CR* 58 (1881) (referring to Anthony); 12 *CR* 101 (1881) (referring to Anthony); 12 *CR* 265 (1881) (referring to John Sherman, R-OH); 14 *CR* 636 (1882) (referring to Joseph Hawley, R-CT). Given the nonpublic nature of caucus proceedings, references to caucus chairmen of the opposite party were sometimes incorrect. Senator Beck mistakenly referred to Senator Hawley as Republican caucus chairman, and this was corrected by Hawley himself. 14 *CR* 636 (1882).

79. Stevenson enjoyed some national standing at the time. In 1872, he was the only person other than eventual vice-presidential nominee B. Gratz Brown to receive support for the second slot on the national Democratic ticket. *Official Proceedings of the National Democratic Convention* (Boston: Rockwell & Churchill, 1872), 71–72. Brown was born in Kentucky but later moved to and represented Missouri in the Senate. A. C. Quisenberry, "Kentucky—Mother of United States Senators and Representatives," *RKHS* 18 (1920): 77, 86.

80. Morton, "Stephenson," 14.

81. Richard Vaux to John W. Stevenson, January 13, 1874, Andrew Stevenson and J. W. Stevenson Papers, Library of Congress. The two other lawmakers viewed in the letter as Senate Democratic "leaders" were Thomas Bayard (DE) and Allen Thurman. Ibid.

82. Gerald Gamm and Steven S. Smith, "Emergence of Senate Party Leadership," in *U.S. Senate Exceptionalism,* ed. Bruce I. Oppenheimer (Columbus: Ohio State University Press, 2002), 219.

83. Gerald Gamm and Steven Smith, "The Rise of Floor Leaders, 1890–1913" (draft

book chapter), 14. For whatever reason, Republicans did not grant their chairmen such authority. Ibid.

84. Ibid.

85. Ibid., 14, 60, 61.

86. Ibid., 17.

87. Bryant, "Stevenson," 730.

88. Ibid.; Coulter, "Stevenson," 634.

89. Bryant, "Stevenson," 730; Coulter, "Stevenson," 634; "Stevenson: Death of a Distinguished Public Man"; Grigsby v. Purcell, 99 U.S. 505 (1879).

90. Bryant, "Stevenson," 730.

91. Ibid.; Coulter, "Stevenson," 634.

92. "History," Cincinnati College of Law, accessed February 15, 2018, https://law.uc.edu/about/history.html.

93. "Stevenson," Congressional Biographical Directory; Bryant, "Stevenson," 730.

94. Thomas E. Stephens, "'A Glorious Birthright to Guard': A History of the Kentucky Historical Society," *RKHS* 101 (2003): 7, 12.

95. "Stevenson: Death of a Distinguished Public Man," 5.

96. Morton, "Stephenson," 14; James C. Klotter, *William Goebel: The Politics of Wrath* (Lexington: University Press of Kentucky, 1977), 7–8.

97. Morton, "Stephenson," 14; Klotter, *Goebel,* 7–8.

98. Tapp and Klotter, *Kentucky,* 461.

99. Wayland, *Stevenson,* 227.

100. *SWIJ,* August 13, 1886.

101. "Obituary," *SLGD,* August 11, 1886; *SWIJ,* August 13, 1886.

102. "Obituary."

103. Elaine K. Swift, *The Making of an American Senate: Reconstitutive Change in Congress, 1787–1841* (Ann Arbor: University of Michigan Press, 2002), 71–72; Robert Luce, *Legislative Procedure: Parliamentary Practices and the Course of Business in the Framing of Statutes* (Boston: Houghton Mifflin, 1922), 508; Lauros G. McConachie, *Congressional Committees: A Study of the Origins and Development of Our National and Local Legislative Methods* (New York: Thomas Y. Crowell, 1898), 265; Roy Swanstrom, *The United States Senate, 1787–1801: A Dissertation on the First Fourteen Years of the Upper Legislative Body* (Washington, DC: Government Printing Office, 1988), 297; Everett Lee Long, "Jefferson and Congress: A Study of the Jeffersonian Legislative System, 1801–1809" (PhD diss., University of Missouri, 1966), 263. For further references to early Senate party caucuses, see Long, "Jefferson and Congress," 246–53, 335, 364, 381–82; Alex B. Lacy Jr., "Jefferson and Congress: Congressional Method and Politics, 1801–1809" (PhD diss., University of Virginia, 1964), 116.

104. *Minutes of the Senate Democratic Conference, 1903–1964,* ed. Donald A. Ritchie (Washington, DC: Government Printing Office, 1998), xvii. Early party caucuses sometimes involved both senators and representatives. *Memoirs of Aaron Burr,* ed. Matthew L. Davis (Freeport, NY: Books for Libraries Press, 1970), 1:408; Long, "Jefferson and Congress," 246; Leonard D. White, *The Jeffersonians: A Study in Administrative History, 1801–1829* (New York: Macmillan, 1961), 49–50.

105. Clara Hannah Kerr, *The Origin and Development of the United States Senate* (Ithaca, NY: Andrus & Church, 1895), 81.

106. Luce, *Legislative Procedure,* 508; Swanstrom, *Senate,* 229.

107. Swanstrom, *Senate,* 297; Luce, *Legislative Procedure,* 508.

108. Alexander Hamilton to Theodore Sedgwick, February 25, 1799, in *The Works of Alexander Hamilton,* ed. John C. Hamilton (New York: John F. Trow, 1851), 6:399–400. For another caucus during this period, see Thomas Claude Donnelly, "Party Leadership in the United States Senate" (PhD diss., New York University, 1930), 38 (describing a Democratic-Republican caucus that recommended a nominee as minister to France).

109. Swanstrom, *Senate,* 297–98, 307.

110. Ibid., 304.

111. Swift, *Making of an American Senate,* 72.

112. Gamm and Smith, "Senate without Leaders," 12–13.

113. *WPM,* 28.

114. Ibid., 141; see also Long, "Jefferson and Congress," 246–53; *JQAM,* 1:300, 384–85. For other caucuses during the period, see *WPM,* 220–21.

115. *WPM,* 597.

116. Ibid., 598.

117. Moisei Ostrogorski, *Democracy and the Party System in the United States: A Study in Extra-Constitutional Government* (New York: Macmillan, 1926), 7–15, 283.

118. Ibid., 11–15.

119. James Sterling Young, *The Washington Community: 1800–1828* (New York: Columbia University Press, 1966), 147.

120. Richard A. Baker, *Traditions of the United States Senate* (Washington, DC: Government Printing Office, n.d.), 7, accessed February 15, 2018, https://www.senate.gov/reference/resources/pdf/Traditions.pdf; email from Betty K. Koed, Senate historian. By the mid-1870s, in the words of Senate historian emeritus Richard Baker, "the center aisle [had become] a clear boundary." Baker, *Traditions,* 7.

121. Randall B. Ripley, *Power in the Senate* (New York: St. Martin's, 1969), 25, 38; Gerald Gamm and Steven S. Smith, "Last among Equals: The Senate's Presiding Officer," in *Esteemed Colleagues: Civility and Deliberation in the U.S. Senate,* ed. Burdette A. Loomis (Washington, DC: Brookings Institution, 2000), 117.

122. Gamm and Smith, "Senate without Leaders," 6; Walter Kravitz, "Party Organization," in "The United States Senate: A History" (unpublished manuscript on file with the authors), 13–14.

123. Gamm and Smith, "Senate without Leaders," 10; Kravitz, "Party Organization," 14.

124. Gamm and Smith, "Senate without Leaders," 6, 9, 12–13.

125. Ibid., 9.

126. Ibid.

127. Ibid.; Gamm and Smith, "Rise of Floor Leaders," 10–14.

128. Gamm and Smith, "Senate without Leaders," 9, 12; Gamm and Smith, "Rise of Floor Leaders," 78, 83.

129. Gamm and Smith, "Rise of Floor Leaders," 14.

130. William C. Harris, *Lincoln and Congress* (Carbondale: Southern Illinois Press, 2017), 61.

131. Francis Fessenden, *Life and Public Services of William Pitt Fessenden* (Boston: Houghton, Mifflin, 1907), 1:231 (quoting an account from Sen. Fessenden); see also *The Diary of Orville Hickman Browning, 1850–1864,* ed. Theodore Calvin Pease and James G. Randall (Springfield: Illinois State Historical Library, 1925), 1:596–99, 603–4; Harris, *Lincoln and Congress,* 61–63; Allan G. Bogue, *The Earnest Men: Republicans of the Civil War Senate* (Ithaca, NY: Cornell University Press, 1981), 76.

132. Fessenden, *Life,* 231.

133. Ibid., 237–38.

134. "James Burnie Beck," Congressional Biographical Directory, accessed February 15, 2018, http://bioguide.congress.gov/scripts/biodisplay.pl?index=b000289.

135. T. Ross Moore, "The Congressional Career of James B. Beck, 1867–1875" (MA thesis, University of Kentucky, 1950), 2–3.

136. Ibid., 2; *Memorial Addresses,* 24 (Sen. Blackburn).

137. *Memorial Addresses,* 24; Moore, "Congressional Career of Beck," 2.

138. Moore, "Congressional Career of Beck," 3.

139. Ibid.

140. Ibid., 3–4.

141. Ibid., 4.

142. Ibid., 95.

143. Ibid.

144. Ibid.

145. Ibid., 5.

146. Ibid., 5–7.

147. Savoyard, "James Burnie Beck," *WP,* July 23, 1905; Moore, "Congressional Career of Beck," 6.

148. Moore, "Congressional Career of Beck," 6–7.

149. Ibid., 7; Savoyard, "Beck."

150. Moore, "Congressional Career of Beck," 9. Combs, a Whig, would later lose a congressional race to Beck's friend John C. Breckinridge. Ibid., 20.

151. Ibid., 9–10.

152. Savoyard, "Beck."

153. Moore, "Congressional Career of Beck," 11–12.

154. *Memorial Addresses,* 100.

155. Moore, "Congressional Career of Beck," 11.

156. Ibid. Beck invested in real property, real estate, and a manufacturing concern. Ibid., 18.

157. "James Burnie Beck," in Kleber, *Kentucky Encyclopedia,* 64.

158. Moore, "Congressional Career of Beck," 11–12.

159. Ibid.

160. Davis, *Breckinridge,* 131; *Memorial Addresses,* 100–101 (Rep. Breckinridge).

161. Moore, "Congressional Career of Beck," 10, 14–15; *Memorial Addresses,* 100–101 (Rep. Breckinridge).

162. Davis, *Breckinridge,* 131. One area of disagreement between the two friends concerned the rise of the Ku Klux Klan in Kentucky. Breckinridge, who was out of office at the time, condemned the group; Beck did not and even opposed efforts to bring the Klan to heel. Ibid., 612; "Beck," in Kleber, *Kentucky Encyclopedia,* 65.

163. Moore, "Congressional Career of Beck," 27–28.

164. Davis, *Breckinridge,* 568, 583, 587, 588.

165. Ibid., 623; Lucille Stillwell, *John Cabell Breckinridge* (Caldwell, ID: Caxton Printers, 1936), 170, 175. When Beck drew up his own will in 1856, he indicated that he wished Breckinridge to counsel his wife. "Written Many Years Ago. Senator Beck's Will, Filed Yesterday, was Drawn in 1856," *WP,* May 18, 1890. Obviously, Beck survived Breckinridge by many years, so this provision in Beck's will was moot.

166. *Memorial Addresses*, 101 (Rep. Breckinridge): "The constant esteem shown to Mr. Beck in parts of Kentucky where his person was unknown was in part due to the transmitted friendship which these people had borne for Breckinridge and which in his retirement and on his death they conferred on Mr. Beck."

167. Moore, "Congressional Career of Beck," 37.

168. Ibid., 38–40.

169. *Memorial Addresses*, 103 (Rep. Breckinridge); Moore, "Congressional Career of Beck," 40.

170. Moore, "Congressional Career of Beck," 41–43.

171. Ibid.

172. Savoyard, "Beck."

173. Ibid.; *Memorial Addresses*, 103–4 (Rep. Breckinridge).

174. *Memorial Addresses*, 105 (Rep. Breckinridge).

175. Ibid.; Moore, "Congressional Career of Beck," 55.

176. Moore, "Congressional Career of Beck," 55–56, 126.

177. Ibid., 45, 63, 65, 66, 73–74, 127. Beck was also among the most vocal opponents of women's suffrage in Congress. Allison L. Sneider, *Suffragists in an Imperial Age: U.S. Expansion and the Woman Question, 1870–1929* (New York: Oxford University Press, 2008), 81–83; *The Selected Papers of Elizabeth Cady Stanton and Susan B. Anthony*, ed. Ann D. Gordon (New Brunswick, NJ: Rutgers University Press, 1997), 4:128–29 n. 1.

178. Moore, "Congressional Career of Beck," 67–68, 126–27.

179. Ibid., 67–68.

180. Savoyard, "Beck."

181. Ibid. Allison was one of the honorary pallbearers at his memorial service at the US Capitol. *Memorial Addresses*, 4.

182. Moore, "Congressional Career of Beck," 85.

183. Savoyard, "Joseph C. S. Blackburn," *WP*, November 19, 1905.

184. "Beck," Congressional Biographical Directory. Ultimately, the Kentuckian dissented from his colleagues' decision. "Maryland and Virginia Boundary Commissions," *BS*, January 20, 1877; Kenneth Lasson, "A History of Potomac River Conflicts" (paper presented at a conference hosted by the Maryland Department of National Resources, September 1, 1976).

185. "Beck," Congressional Biographical Directory.

186. *Memorial Addresses*, 46–47 (Sen. Vance).

187. Ibid., 42 (Sen. Evarts); see also "Senator Beck's Sudden Death in a Railroad Depot," *BS*, May 5, 1890 ("He . . . was the leader of his party in all matters relating to the tariff. On this question he was especially useful because of his familiarity with the details of our tariff laws, and the reasons for and against their continuance.").

188. "Beck's Sudden Death"; *Memorial Addresses*, 79–80.

189. "Beck's Sudden Death."

190. Savoyard, "Beck."

191. Fredirick S. Daniel, "The Senate and Its Leaders," *Frank Leslie's Popular Monthly*, April 4, 1890.

192. Kravitz, "Party Organization," 125.

193. Gamm and Smith, "Emergence," 219. Beck replaced George Hunt Pendleton (D-OH) as caucus chairman following Pendleton's defeat for renomination in Ohio. Ibid.; "George Hunt Pendleton," Congressional Biographical Directory, accessed February 15, 2018, http://bioguide.congress.gov/scripts/biodisplay.pl?index=p000203.

194. Gamm and Smith, "Rise of Floor Leaders," 14–18, 78.

195. Ibid.

196. Ibid., 14–15.

197. Ibid.; see also "Beck's Sudden Death."

198. Gamm and Smith, "Rise of Floor Leaders," 14–15.

199. Ibid.

200. A HeinOnline search demonstrates that Beck was only the third lawmaker and the first caucus chairman to be so termed. 2 *CR* 1355 (1874) (John W. Stevenson referring in retrospect to Sen. Thomas Hart Benton [MO]); 10 *CR* 2753 (1880) (referring to Sen. Allen Thurman); 17 *CR* 773 (1886) (referring to Beck); see also Gamm and Smith, "Emergence," 219 (listing caucus chairmen).

201. Gamm and Smith, "Rise of Floor Leaders," 15–16, 84.

202. Ibid., 10, 15–16, 84. This reality would become manifest under Beck's successor as caucus chairman. Ibid., 84.

203. Ibid., 15.

204. Harry Thurston Peck, *Twenty Years of the Republic, 1885–1905* (New York: Dodd, Mead, 1929), 147.

205. Ibid.; "Blackburn, Beck & Co. to Fight the President on the Silver Question," *NYT,* December 28, 1885; "The Politics of Silver," *NYT,* December 25, 1885.

206. Gamm and Smith, "Rise of Floor Leaders," 14–17, 78.

207. Ibid., 18.

208. *Memorial Addresses,* 28.

209. Ibid., 31. Another prominent Republican senator described Beck in similar terms: "Beck was a man of great mental as well as physical power. . . . He was aggressive, affirmative and dogmatic, and seemed to take special delight in opposing me on all financial questions. He and I . . . had many verbal contests, but always with good humor." *John Sherman's Recollections of Forty Years in the House, Senate and Cabinet: An Autobiography* (New York: Werner, 1895), 740.

210. *Memorial Addresses,* 47 (Sen. Vance).

211. Ibid., 112 (Rep. Breckinridge).

212. Ibid., 132 (Rep. Caruth).

213. George F. Hoar, *Autobiography of Seventy Years* (New York: Charles Scribner's Sons, 1903), 2:72. Hoar said of Beck: "When he died I think there was no other man in the Senate, on either side, whose loss would have occasioned . . . [such] profound sorrow." Ibid., 73.

214. Ibid., 72.

215. Ibid., 71–73.

216. John Carlisle, former House Speaker and Beck's successor in the Senate, said of him: "No young man struggling to rise at the bar or in politics was ever repressed or discouraged by him or by anyone else with his approval." *Memorial Addresses,* 87; see also ibid., 112 (Rep. Breckinridge).

217. Moore, "Congressional Career of Beck," 15 (quoting C. R. Staples).

218. Hoar, *Autobiography,* 72; see also "James Burnie Beck," *HC,* May 5, 1890.

219. "Senator Beck Dead," *WP,* May 4, 1890.

220. "Beck's Sudden Death."

221. *Memorial Addresses,* 120 (Rep. McCreary).

222. Gamm and Smith, "Rise of Floor Leaders," 64 (quoting the *Raleigh Register* from 1885).

223. "Senator Beck. An Interview," *CT,* July 12, 1881.

224. Ibid.

225. Ibid.

226. Ibid.

227. "Senator Beck Dead."

228. "Beck's Sudden Death." He was described in one paper as "an invalid." "Beck," *HC.*

229. "Beck's Sudden Death"; "Senator Beck Dead."

230. "Beck's Sudden Death"; "Senator Beck Dead." Beck's regular doctor had urged him to step down from the Senate, but he declined to do so. "Senator Beck Dead."

231. "Beck's Sudden Death"; "Senator Beck Dead."

232. "Beck's Sudden Death."

233. Ibid.

234. Ibid.; "Senator Beck Dead."

235. "Beck's Sudden Death"; "Senator Beck Dead."

236. "Senator Beck Dead"; "Beck's Sudden Death."

237. *Memorial Addresses,* 3, 6.

238. "Last Rites over Beck: Immense Gathering of Grief-Stricken Kentuckians Present," *WP,* May 9, 1890.

239. Bill McAllister, "Cabinet Unofficials," *WP,* October 1, 1993. See also Senator Allison's remarks in note 1.

240. Adlai E. Stevenson, *Something of Men I Have Known* (Chicago: A. L. McClurg, 1909), 36.

241. There has been only one academic article devoted to Blackburn, and it focuses almost exclusively on his career as it involved the Panama Canal. Leonard Schlup, "Joseph Blackburn of Kentucky and the Panama Question," *FCHQ* 51 (October 1977): 350–62.

242. "Joseph Clay Stiles Blackburn," Congressional Biographical Directory, accessed February 15, 2018, http://bioguide.congress.gov/scripts/biodisplay.pl?index=b000508.

243. Nancy Disher Baird, *Luke Pryor Blackburn: Physician, Governor, Reformer* (Lexington: University Press of Kentucky, 1979), 2. Blackburn's father hosted Henry Clay at his home, and his grandfather entertained the Marquis de Lafayette in 1825 and was acquainted with George Rogers Clark. Ibid.

244. Johnson, *History of Kentucky,* 2:778. Blackburn's father died in 1867 and his mother in 1863. Ibid.

245. Baird, *Blackburn,* vii; "Making History," Office of Kentucky Governor, accessed February 15, 2018, https://governor.ky.gov/about/gubernatorial-history/.

246. Edward Steers Jr., "A Rebel Plot and Germ Warfare," *WT,* November 10, 2001.

247. "Luke Blackburn," National Museum of Racing and Hall of Fame, accessed February 15, 2018, http://www.racingmuseum.org/hall-of-fame/luke-blackburn.

248. "Secretary of State James W. Blackburn," Office of Kentucky Secretary of State, accessed February 15, 2018, http://apps.sos.ky.gov/secdesk/sosinfo/default.aspx?id=45.

249. Hugh Ridenour, "John Orlando Scott," *RKHS* 97 (1999): 158, 163.

250. Ibid.

251. Ibid.

252. Ibid.

253. "'Jo' Blackburn Passes away in Sudden Attack," *FSJ,* September 13, 1918.

254. Ibid.

255. Ibid.; Tom Eblen, "Living Arts & Science Center Plans $5 Million Expansion Project," *LHL*, November 16, 2011.

256. "'Jo' Blackburn."

257. "Former Senator Blackburn Dead," *WP*, September 13, 1918.

258. Johnson, *History of Kentucky*, 2:779.

259. "'Jo' Blackburn."

260. James Tandy Ellis, "The Tang of the South," *LT*, March 9, 1932, 1; see also Elizabeth Rouse Fielder, "The George Blackburn Family of Leaders," accessed February 15, 2018, http://kentuckyancestors.org/the-george-blackburn-family-of-leaders/.

261. Thomas W. Herringshaw, *The Biographical Review of Prominent Men and Women of the Day* (Washington, DC: A. B. Gehman, 1888), 431.

262. Ibid.

263. "'Jo' Blackburn."

264. Ibid.

265. R. S. Cotterill, "Joseph Clay Styles [*sic*] Blackburn," in *Dictionary of American Biography*, ed. Allen Johnson (New York: Charles Scribner's Sons, 1946), 1:316; see also *The War of the Rebellion: A Compilation of the Official Records of the Union and Confederate Armies*, ser. 1, ed. Daniel S. LaMont (Washington, DC: Government Printing Office, 1897), 49(1):1009–11; G. A. Mellander, *The United States in Panamanian Politics: The Intriguing Formative Years* (Danville, IL: Interstate Printers & Publishers, 1971), 134.

266. George Lee Willis Sr., *Kentucky Democracy: A History of the Party and Its Representative Members—Past and Present* (Louisville, KY: Democratic Historical Society, 1935), 1:271; Cotterill, "Blackburn," 1:316. It was reported that Blackburn was seriously wounded at the Battle of Shiloh. "Little Joe Blackburn Hall," *WP*, January 21, 1894.

267. Cotterill, "Blackburn," 1:316; "'Jo' Blackburn."

268. "'Jo' Blackburn."

269. Savoyard, "Blackburn."

270. O. O. Stealey, *Twenty Years in the Press Gallery* (New York: Publishers Printing Company, 1906), 213.

271. John J. McAfee, *Kentucky Politicians: Sketches of Representative Corn-Crackers* (Louisville, KY: Courier-Journal, 1886), 19; Cotterill, "Blackburn," 1:316.

272. Savoyard, "Blackburn."

273. Stealey, *Twenty Years*, 214; see also "A Wordy Duel," *NYT*, January 15, 1882: "Mr. Blackburn is a master of the English language, and when he ascends to the greater altitudes of vituperation, the air of the blue-grass region becomes sulphorous."

274. "Joe Blackburn's Fists," *HC*, May 29, 1903.

275. Ibid.

276. Ibid.

277. Later in life, Blackburn apparently became less violent. Ibid.

278. Ibid.; "Chandler Saved His Ear: Words which Angered a Kentucky Senator," *NYT*, February 24, 1889.

279. "Joe Blackburn's Fists"; "'Jo' Blackburn."

280. Stealey, *Twenty Years*, 214; Savoyard, "Blackburn."

281. Stevenson, *Something of Men*, 37.

282. Ibid.

283. Ibid., 38.

284. Ibid.

285. "Tales of 'Joe' Blackburn: One of the Most Picturesque Figures in Washington Life," *BS,* January 15, 1906.

286. Stevenson, *Something of Men,* 37.

287. "Kentucky People Elated," *NYT,* April 25, 1882.

288. Stealey, *130 Pen Pictures,* 63.

289. "Tales of 'Joe' Blackburn."

290. Ibid.

291. Ibid.

292. Ibid.

293. Ibid.

294. Ibid.

295. Ibid.

296. Ibid.

297. Ibid.

298. Ibid.

299. Ibid.

300. "Small Talk of Washington," *NYT,* March 14, 1906.

301. Ibid. While he was chairman of the Rules Committee, it was common knowledge that Blackburn kept a discreet bar in his Senate office. "Finest Club in the World," *NYT,* December 17, 1893. Blackburn apparently gave up drinking later in life. "Tales of 'Joe' Blackburn"; "Guesses Whisky Is All Gone," *WP,* December 9, 1907.

302. "A Kentucky Bird Dinner: Annual Frolic of Her Statesmen in the Woods," *NYT,* November 20, 1882.

303. "Poker Players among Senators," *NYT,* March 23, 1884; "Senator Blackburn Injured. Thrown from His Carriage while Driving to His Home," *NYT,* October 24, 1890.

304. Savoyard, "Blackburn."

305. Blackburn could be very generous. He helped famed political cartoonist and fellow Kentuckian Clifford Berryman get his start in Washington. Nelson Shepard, "Berryman to Give Portrait of Blackburn to Kentucky," *WS,* June 23, 1939.

306. "Kentucky Playfulness," *NYT,* March 27, 1876.

307. Ibid.

308. McAfee, *Kentucky Politicians,* 19.

309. Herringshaw, *Biographical Review,* 432.

310. "An Eloquent Kentuckian," *AC,* October 14, 1893.

311. "Another Duel Averted: The Troubles of Senator Williams and Representative Blackburn," *NYT,* May 20, 1882; see also "Kentucky 2014—Are You One of Us? Kentucky Constituent & Partisan Roots Firmly Plant across Time, Electing the Senate," Brown University, November 10, 2014, accessed February 15, 2018, https://www.brown.edu/research/projects/electing-the-senate/news/2014–11/kentucky-2014-are-you-one-us-kentucky-constituent-partisan-roots-firmly-planted-across-. Senator Williams was given the "Cerro Gordo" moniker after he participated in the Battle of Cerro Gordo during the Mexican-American War.

312. "Another Duel Averted."

313. Ibid.

314. Ibid.

315. Ibid.

316. Ibid.

317. Ibid.

318. Ibid.

319. "Two Irate Kentuckians," *NYT,* December 31, 1881.

320. "Another Duel Averted."

321. Herringshaw, *Biographical Review,* 432.

322. Klotter, *Goebel,* 34–35.

323. Ibid., 35; see also "Tales of 'Joe' Blackburn."

324. Klotter, *Goebel,* 38–41, 62–63, 84–85, 93, 96.

325. For instance, in 1899, Blackburn campaigned for Goebel until a bout of bad health caused him to stop. "Blackburn Drops Campaign. Compelled by Illness to Cease Work in Kentucky for Goebel," *NYT,* September 3, 1899; "The Kentucky Campaign," *NYT,* August 13, 1899; "Blackburn and the Senate," *NYT,* December 19, 1898.

326. Klotter, *Goebel,* 2 (quoting Blackburn).

327. Savoyard, "Blackburn." "In a tumultuous body like the House Joe Blackburn was a commanding figure." Ibid.

328. "'Jo' Blackburn."

329. Ibid.; "Jos. C. S. Blackburn, Ex-Senator, Is Dead," *NYT,* September 13, 1918.

330. Champ Clark, *My Quarter Century of American Politics* (New York: Harper & Brothers, 1920), 1:207.

331. "'Jo' Blackburn."

332. Clark, *My Quarter Century,* 207.

333. Michael Bellesiles, *1877: America's Year of Living Violently* (New York: New Press, 2010), 41; "Mr. Blackburn on the Commission," *NYT,* February 20, 1877; Cotterill, "Blackburn," 1:316.

334. Bellesiles, *1877,* 41.

335. Thomas D. Clark, *A History of Kentucky* (Lexington, KY: John Bradford Press, 1960), 416.

336. Albert Virgil House Jr., "The Political Career of Samuel Jackson Randall" (PhD diss., University of Wisconsin, 1934), 113–18; "Affairs at Washington," *NYT,* March 8, 1879.

337. House, "Political Career of Randall," 115–18. A columnist familiar with Blackburn speculated that "he would have secured the caucus nomination against Randall but for the conservatism of some Southern members, who did not think the Kentuckian discreet enough for the position." Savoyard, "Blackburn."

338. House, "Political Career of Randall," 145.

339. McConachie, *Congressional Committees,* 38; Albert V. House Jr., "The Contributions of Samuel J. Randall to the Rules of the National House of Representatives," *APSR* 29 (1935): 837, 839. Congressional scholar Lauros McConachie wrote of the committee's efforts (with a fair amount of exaggeration): "This was a labor brilliant and far-reaching. It was in direct line of succession to the work of the convention which framed the Federal Constitution in 1787." McConachie, *Congressional Committees,* 38–39.

340. House, "Contributions of Randall," 839.

341. McConachie, *Congressional Committees,* 38; House, "Contributions of Randall," 839.

342. "Events at Washington: The Rival Kentucky Candidates for the Speakership," *NYT,* January 10, 1883; see also "Washington Gossip," *NYW,* December 17, 1882 (regarding the speakership, "Mr. Blackburn is dying for it, Mr. Carlisle is hankering for it, Mr. Randall is determined to have it. . . . Mr. Blackburn and Mr. Randall are not on good terms at all. Mr. Blackburn thinks that Mr. Randall was discourteous to him after their previous contest for

the Speakership."). Blackburn and Carlisle would be rivals for many years to come. "Events at Washington"; "Carlisle Not a Candidate: Will Not Enter the Senatorial Contest in Kentucky, nor Is He Likely to Support Blackburn," *NYT,* January 15, 1895; "Carlisle Will Not Interfere," *NYT,* February 20, 1896; "Kentuckians Are Bitter: Aroused by the Political Fight in Their State," *NYT,* October 4, 1896.

343. "Events at Washington."

344. "Blackburn out of the Contest: Not to Run for Speaker but Bound to Go to the Senate," *NYT,* August 30, 1883.

345. Stealey, *Twenty Years,* 214–15.

346. Willis, *Kentucky Democracy,* 1:273–74.

347. Ibid., 273.

348. Ibid. Allegations of bribery were later made and led to a resolution calling for an inquiry. "Did Blackburn Use Money? A Question which the Kentucky Legislature Intends to Have Answered," *NYT,* March 6, 1884: "That money was freely used by the Blackburn and Williams people nobody seems to deny."

349. "Whiskey Free to All Comers: How J. S. C. [*sic*] Blackburn Secured the United States Senatorship," *NYT,* August 15, 1885.

350. Willis, *Kentucky Democracy,* 1:273.

351. Ibid., 274.

352. "A Surprise from Kentucky," *NYT,* February 6, 1884.

353. Donald J. Orth, *Dictionary of Alaska Place Names* (Washington, DC: Government Printing Office, 1967), 139. Blackburn also had a cargo ship named after him during World War II. "Joe C. S. Blackburn," Maritime Administration, accessed February 15, 2018, https://www.marad.dot.gov/sh/ShipHistory/Detail/2506. In addition, he had a town in Oklahoma named in his honor. Fittingly, in its early years, the Oklahoma settlement was known as a "whisky town," as it abutted a "dry" jurisdiction. Linda D. Wilson, "Blackburn," *The Encyclopedia of Oklahoma History and Culture,* accessed February 15, 2018, http://www.okhistory.org/publications/enc/entry.php?entry=BL006.

354. "'Jo' Blackburn."

355. The others are Wendell Ford and the lead author.

356. "Blackburn's Gloomy Future," *NYT,* July 1, 1895 (noting his "settled indifference to legislative work"); "Democracy Not on Trial," *NYT,* November 8, 1895 (commenting that Blackburn's "lack of capacity as a legislator is thoroughly appreciated" in Washington).

357. "Eloquent Kentuckian."

358. Neil MacNeil and Richard A. Baker, *The American Senate: An Insider's History* (New York: Oxford University Press, 2013), 290.

359. *HCP,* 34–35, 38, 44–45, 47–48, 69.

360. Ibid., 48. Senator George Vest was born in Kentucky but represented Missouri. Quisenberry, "Kentucky—Mother of Senators," 86.

361. "Leader J. C. S. Blackburn," *BS,* June 10, 1906.

362. Ibid.

363. "Blackburn Issues a Challenge: Says He Is Running for Re-election to the Senate as a Silver Man," *NYT,* April 22, 1895. Blackburn's interest in the silver issue was sudden, and his immediate conversion was thought to reflect his intent to catch the populist wave. "At the National Capital," *NYT,* June 28, 1895; "Blackburn's Balderdash," *NYT,* October 5, 1895; "'Jo' Blackburn"; "Now a Blackburn Boom," *NYT,* June 5, 1896; "Big Field of Starters," *NYT,* July 3, 1896; "Many Booms Floated," *NYT,* July 4, 1896.

364. "Presidential Campaigns & Elections, an American History Reference Source, 1896," accessed February 15, 2018, https://presidentialcampaignselectionsreference .wordpress.com/overviews/19th-century/1896-overview/; see also Willis, *Kentucky Democracy,* 1:358.

365. "Blackburn's Promising Threat," *NYT,* July 17, 1895; "Kentucky Is in Doubt," *NYT,* August 20, 1895.

366. "Troops in the Capitol," *NYT,* March 17, 1896; "The Troops Called Out," *NYT,* March 16, 1896.

367. "Deboe Is Chosen Senator," *NYT,* April 29, 1897; Harrison and Klotter, *New History,* 268; see also Willis, *Kentucky Democracy,* 1:355.

368. "Blackburn and the Senate: The Kentucky Politician Eager to Get Back into Congress," *NYT,* December 19, 1898.

369. Another of Blackburn's daughters, Therese, married General William Preble Hall, winner of the Congressional Medal of Honor. "Gen. William P. Hall, Indian Fighter, Dies," *NYT,* December 15, 1927.

370. "Miss Corinne Blackburn: A Brilliant Young Kentucky Politician," *CT,* January 26, 1896; cf. "Some Southern Women," *CT,* January 27, 1887.

371. "A Fair Kentucky Campaigner: Miss Corrine Blackburn's Splendid Service in Her Father's Behalf," *SLPD,* February 9, 1896; "Corinne Blackburn."

372. "Fair Kentucky Campaigner"; "Corinne Blackburn."

373. "Shot Near the Heart," *WP,* January 17, 1898.

374. Ibid.

375. "Ex-Senator Blackburn Ill," *NYT,* March 26, 1898.

376. "Death of Mrs. Blackburn," *WP,* September 18, 1899.

377. "Thomas F. Lane Commits Suicide," *BG,* October 17, 1900.

378. Ibid.

379. Ibid.

380. "Bullet in His Brain," *BS,* October 17, 1900.

381. "Mrs. Thomas F. Lane Dead. Senator Blackburn's Daughter Succumbs after Short Illness," *WP,* July 19, 1902.

382. "Jo Blackburn, Jr., Dead. Son of Kentucky Senator Passes away at Frankfort," *WP,* February 13, 1902.

383. "In the Public Eye," *AC,* August 16, 1901; "Senator Blackburn Married in Washington," *CT,* December 12, 1901. Her earlier married name was Blackburn; her maiden name was McHenry. "In the Public Eye." Blackburn's second wife passed away just before him in 1918. "Ex-Senator Sues for Title to Home," *WP,* May 9, 1918.

384. "Blackburn," Congressional Biographical Directory.

385. Swanstrom, *Senate,* 297–98, 307.

386. Randall B. Ripley, *Majority Party Leadership in Congress* (Boston: Little, Brown, 1969), 65. Gorman appears to have played some role in this effort. Jos. Ohl, "Gorman Tired of Leadership," *AC,* December 13, 1903; Kravitz, "Party Organization," 64. For more on the history of attempts to bind party caucuses, see Kravitz, "Party Organization," 52–69.

387. Ripley, *Majority Party,* 65.

388. 52 *CR* 3841–42 (1915) (Sen. Cummins); Ripley, *Majority Party,* 65.

389. John R. Lambert, *Arthur Pue Gorman* (Baton Rouge: Louisiana State University Press, 1953), 303–4.

390. Donald A. Ritchie, *The U.S. Congress: A Very Short Introduction* (New York:

Oxford University Press, 2010), 88; Donnelly, "Party Leadership," 45–48; Steven S. Smith and Gerald Gamm, "The Dynamics of Party Government in Congress," in *Congress Reconsidered*, 9th ed., ed. Bruce I. Oppenheimer (Washington, DC: CQ Press, 2009), 156; Donald A. Ritchie, "Historical Minute, December 15, 1903: Senate Democrats Adopt a Binding Caucus Rule" (on file with the authors); cf. Ripley, *Majority Party,* 65–66. In the early 1930s, Senate Democrats adopted a resolution comparable to Blackburn's, although with bigger loopholes; it seems to have been invoked rarely, if at all. Kravitz, "Party Organization," 68–69; George H. Haynes, *The Senate of the United States: Its History and Practice* (New York: Russell & Russell, 1960), 1:478 n. 1; Ripley, *Power,* 36–37.

391. Ripley, *Power,* 35; Charles Tiefer, *Congressional Practice and Procedure: A Reference, Research, and Legislative Guide* (New York: Greenwood Press, 1989), 485; Kravitz, "Party Organization," 50–52.

392. Haynes, *Senate,* 476–78; Ripley, *Power,* 37. Indeed, in 1913, Senate Republicans changed the name of their gatherings from "caucuses" to "conferences" to connote their tacit rejection of the notion of binding their members. Ripley, *Power,* 37. Senate Republican Party caucus or conference meetings—with apparently one exception in 1919—have always been closed to the public to ensure candid deliberation. John Thune, "History, Rules and Precedents of the Senate Republican Conference," December 2014, 1, https://www .republican.senate.gov/public/_cache/files/65589e31-c184-4c95-9947-770f1b3998c1/ A669DDFC6A0CAF777199282DC623467F.conference-rules-2015.pdf. Democratic conferences are also confidential; it is unclear whether any Democratic meetings have ever been open to the public.

393. Gamm and Smith, "Emergence," 219.

394. Gamm and Smith, "Rise of Floor Leaders," 48, 57, 58, 63, 72, 76. A fellow Democratic senator perceptively described the way the Marylander operated:

> Gorman rarely ever announced a position until after he had conferred with his Democratic associates sufficiently to know that the view he espoused, was endorsed to the extent that it would command a large support. In other words Gorman took no chances on standing alone or with two or three, on a roll-call. He always made sure that his view expressed met [with] sufficient approval among the other senators, to make his announcement a view more or less representative or authoritative. . . . [As a result,] Gorman . . . vote[d] nearly always as a leader . . . [though] his opinion was not simply his, but a composite which he had gathered from consultation.

HCP, 67–68.

395. "Gorman Still Leader," *BS,* December 9, 1905. Blackburn was also a member of the Democratic Steering Committee. Ibid.

396. Gerald Gamm and Steven S. Smith, "The Emergence of Senate Leadership, 1881–1946" (paper presented at the annual meeting of the MWPSA, 1997), 26.

397. "Blackburn Will Fill Chair Gorman Left," *WP,* June 8, 1906; Gamm and Smith, "Emergence, 1881–1946," 26.

398. "Blackburn," Congressional Biographical Directory.

399. "Is Booster in Blue Grass," *LAT,* November 25, 1906; "People Met in Hotel Lobbies," *WP,* September 12, 1905; Savoyard, "Kentucky Politics," *WP,* September 7, 1905; R. L. McClure, "Bitter Warfare Being Waged between Kentucky Democrats," *AC,* February 19, 1905.

400. "Kentucky Democrats Gain. Indications that Blackburn Will Be Defeated in Sen-

ate Race," *NYT,* November 8, 1905; "Senator Blackburn Beaten," *NYT,* January 3, 1906. As an indication of Blackburn's standing, the March 9, 1921, edition of the *New York Times* ran the following headline upon Paynter's death: "Ex-Senator Paynter Dead: Kentucky Judge Who Defeated Senator Blackburn Was 69." Given Blackburn's unquestioned popularity among Kentuckians, one suspects he might have been an even more formidable Senate candidate after ratification of the Seventeenth Amendment. "Blackburn for Governor?" *BS,* January 4, 1906.

401. "Blackburn to Lead," *BS,* June 9, 1906; "Bailey Will Not Be Leader," *NYT,* January 3, 1906; "The Senate's Minority Leadership," *WS,* May 3, 1907; see also Gamm and Smith, "Emergence, 1881–1946," 12; cf. "Blackburn Will Fill Chair."

402. "Blackburn to Lead"; Raymond, "Democrats at Sea without a Pilot," *CT,* February 19, 1907. In some respects, Bailey was the de facto leader of the Senate Democrats while Blackburn was caucus chairman. "Senate Democrats Look for a Leader," *NYT,* January 30, 1907. Yet Bailey was not selected as chairman the next year, and at least one Democratic senator bemoaned the lack of choices for caucus chairman after Blackburn's departure: "who is there? We ought to have a man like Joe Blackburn, but we just haven't got him. So what are we going to do?" Ibid.

403. "Blackburn to Lead." Even though Blackburn was a vigorous partisan, he had friends on the Republican side of the aisle. Joseph Benson Foraker, *Notes of a Busy Life* (Cincinnati: Stewart & Kidd, 1916), 2:13.

404. "Leader J. C. S. Blackburn"; Resolution by Senator Bacon, quoted in *Minutes of the Senate Democratic Conference, 1903–1964,* ed. Donald A. Ritchie (Washington, DC: Government Printing Office, 1998), 9.

405. Ritchie, *Minutes of Senate Democratic Conference,* 9; see also Walter J. Oleszek, "John Worth Kern," in *First among Equals*: *Outstanding Senate Leaders of the Twentieth Century,* ed. Richard A. Baker and Roger H. Davidson (Washington, DC: CQ, 1991), 34 n. 13. In March 1903, Gorman was elected caucus chairman, but there are no extant records of those proceedings. Therefore, it is unknown how he was formally characterized by his fellow senators within the caucus. Ritchie, *Minutes of Senate Democratic Conference,* 1. The press certainly saw him as the party leader. For example, the *Washington Post* announced that Gorman had been chosen "minority leader" by his colleagues. "Hon. Arthur P. Gorman," *WP,* March 7, 1903; see also Ritchie, *Minutes of Senate Democratic Conference,* 1.

406. Bacon resolution in Ritchie, *Minutes of Senate Democratic Conference,* 9. Reference to the Democratic caucus chairman as leader in this context would soon become the norm. Ibid., 43–44, 258, 278.

407. Gamm and Smith, "Rise of Floor Leaders," 67.

408. "Blackburn Will Fill Chair."

409. "Blackburn to Lead."

410. Gamm and Smith, "Rise of Floor Leaders," 71–73. The *New York Times* Washington correspondent wrote a book in 1906 about leaders in the nation's capital. Twelve senators were profiled, but Blackburn was not among them. Charles Willis Thompson, *Party Leaders of the Time* (New York: G. W. Dillingham, 1906), 25–145. Blackburn was dismissed as an "unimportant" senator by one leading publication several years after his tenure. McGregor, "The Converted Senate," *HW,* November 29, 1913, 20. However, in 1895, Joseph West Moore wrote, "From 1870 to 1885 . . . the list of prominent men [included] . . . James B. Beck [and] Joseph C. S. Blackburn." Joseph West Moore, *The American Congress: A History of National Legislation and Political Events, 1774–1895* (New York: Harper & Brothers, 1895),

450–51. Similarly, when discussing the Senate at the end of the 1880s, he wrote, "The prominent members of the Senate were . . . [among others] James B. Beck [and] Joseph S. C. [*sic*] Blackburn." Ibid., 491. Moreover, Blackburn was regularly included in group caricatures of high-profile senators and congressional leaders in contemporary publications such as *Puck, Frank Leslie's Weekly,* and *Judge.* See essays by Diane K. Skvarla and Donald A. Ritchie in Office of Senate Curator, *United States Senate Catalogue of Graphic Art* (Washington, DC: Government Printing Office, 2006), 271, 369, 379, 392, 396–97, 406, 408, 413, 418, 442.

411. Gamm and Smith, "Rise of Floor Leaders," 71–73.

412. Schlup, "Blackburn of Kentucky," 355. Ironically, Blackburn had not been a consistent supporter of the treaties governing the canal. Ibid., 352–54. For more on Blackburn's time in Panama, see ibid., 350–62; Mellander, *United States in Panamanian Politics,* 134–39, 143–48, 153–71, 181–86.

413. Schlup, "Blackburn of Kentucky," 356–357. The extent to which Blackburn's duties were truly meaningful is open to some question. David McCullough, *The Path between the Seas: The Creation of the Panama Canal, 1870–1914* (New York: Simon & Schuster, 1977), 568.

414. Schlup, "Blackburn of Kentucky," 360–61.

415. Ibid., 361.

416. Ibid.

417. Ibid.

418. "Ex-Senator Is Dead"; "'Jo' Blackburn."

419. "'Jo' Blackburn."

420. Savoyard, "Blackburn."

421. Margaret Rampton Munk, "Origin and Development of the Party Floor Leadership in the United States Senate" (PhD diss., Harvard University, 1970), 4–5, 245–46, 249–50, 289; Gamm and Smith, "Emergence," 229–36.

422. Munk, "Origin and Development," 4–5, 116–60, 249–50, 289; Richard A. Baker and Roger H. Davidson, introduction to *First among Equals,* 1, 2; cf. Ripley, *Majority Party,* 4–5.

423. Cf. Munk, "Origin and Development," 4–5, 116–60, 249–50, 289. This same phenomenon may explain the innovative use of de facto Senate floor leaders by President Jefferson. Long, "Jefferson and Congress," xii.

424. Thomas Jefferson, Andrew Jackson, James Polk, Abraham Lincoln, and William McKinley are the exceptions that prove the rule. Wilfred Binkley, *President and Congress* (New York: Alfred A. Knopf, 1947), 49–191; Stephen J. Wayne, *The Legislative Presidency* (New York: Harper & Row, 1978), 9–13; Leonard D. White, *The Jacksonians: A Study in Administrative History 1829–1861* (New York: Macmillan, 1954), 20, 47–48; Leonard D. White, *The Republican Era: A Study in Administrative History, 1869–1901* (New York: Macmillan, 1967), 24–26, 41–44; Munk, "Origin and Development," 234–35; Ripley, *Majority Party,* 4, 24.

425. Presidents George Washington and John Adams delivered their annual messages in person. Jefferson discontinued the custom, and it was not resuscitated until Woodrow Wilson's presidency. Sidney M. Milkis and Michael Nelson, *The American Presidency: Origins and Development, 1776–1993* (Washington, DC: CQ Press, 1994), 241.

426. The annual presidential budget would not begin until enactment of the Budget and Accounting Act of 1921. Prior to this statute, presidents had only sporadically supervised departmental budget requests before their submission to Congress. Louis Fisher, *Presidential Spending Power* (Princeton, NJ: Princeton University Press, 1975), 9–10.

427. "Congressional Debates and Public Opinion," *NYT,* December 15, 1878: "The executive . . . cannot openly and does not often secretly influence the course of Congress. It is expected simply to obey, and apart from the veto power, its opinions are of little consequence."

428. Wayne, *Legislative Presidency,* 13–16; Binkley, *President and Congress,* 187–215; Steven S. Smith, *Party Influence in Congress* (Cambridge: Cambridge University Press, 2007), 73.

429. Smith, *Party Influence,* 73. Changes in the executive branch have prompted other changes in Senate leadership institutions. For example, the vice presidency's gravitation toward the executive branch has essentially "cost" the Senate its full-time presiding officer. Joel K. Goldstein, "Constitutional Change, Originalism, and the Vice Presidency," *UPJCL* 16 (2013): 369, 390–92; Joel K. Goldstein, *The Modern American Vice Presidency: The Transformation of a Political Institution* (Princeton, NJ: Princeton University Press, 1982), 23–34, 140–42, 301.

430. Cf. Binkley, *President and Congress,* 195–98.

431. Cf. ibid.

432. Munk, "Origin and Development," 4, 5, 116–53, 249–50; Baker and Davidson, introduction to *First among Equals,* 2; cf. Smith, *Party Influence,* 73; Ripley, *Power,* 16. The modern majority leader represents the Senate and his party members not only to the president but also to the House and its leadership. Steven S. Smith and Gerald Gamm, "Emergence of the Modern Senate: Party Organization, 1937–2002" (paper prepared for the APSA annual meeting, August 29–September 1, 2002), 1, 3; cf. Roger H. Davidson, "Senate Leaders: Janitors for an Untidy Chamber?" in *Congress Reconsidered,* 3d ed., ed. Lawrence C. Dodd and Bruce I. Oppenheimer (Washington, DC: CQ Press, 1985), 248. The modern Senate majority leader also represents his party in discussions with the Senate minority leader, and vice versa.

Gamm and Smith rightly point out that some caucus chairmen (e.g., Gorman) began to act increasingly like floor leaders during the 1890s alongside presidents who did not actively pursue major legislative programs. Gamm and Smith, "Emergence, 1881–1946," 3–4. Moreover, some caucus chairmen took assertive action when the opposite party controlled the White House. Ibid. This indicates that an activist presidency of the same party was not the sole reason for the birth of the formal floor leader position. Ibid.

433. Cf. Garrison Nelson, "Leadership Selection in the U.S. Senate, 1899–1985: Changing Patterns of Recruitment and Institutional Interactions" (academic paper, 1985, on file with the authors), 3.

434. Gamm and Smith, "Rise of Floor Leaders," 5–6.

435. "Majority Leaders of the House," US House of Representatives, accessed February 15, 2018, http://history.house.gov/People/Office/Majority-Leaders/; Ripley, *Majority Party,* 3.

436. The Senate has emulated the House from time to time on structural and organizational matters. McConachie, *Congressional Committees,* 259, 315; chapter 5, note 171.

437. Over time, the Senate as a whole may have concluded that, as the size and workload of the chamber expanded, some type of formalized leadership was needed. 13 *CR* 675 (1882) (Sen. Edmunds) ("The business [of the Senate] has so increased and accumulated with the increasing number of Senators . . . that it has become a matter of more labor, difficulty, and time . . . to find out what bill we are willing to consider than to consider it and dispose of it. . . . We are in a continual struggle . . . that takes up time, to see what it is we will do rather than in spending our time doing it."). See also Gamm and Smith, "Last among Equals,"

121–23; Nelson, "Leadership Selection," 1; Gamm and Smith, "Emergence," 224; Steven S. Smith and Gerald Gamm, "The Evolution of Senate Party Organization and Leadership: An Overview" (paper prepared for the Congress Project, Woodrow Wilson Center for Scholars, Washington, DC, September 14, 2001), 7; MacNeil and Baker, *American Senate,* 174–75; McConachie, *Congressional Committees,* 313–21; David J. Rothman, *Politics and Power: The United States Senate, 1869–1901* (Cambridge, MA: Harvard University Press, 1966), 108; Ripley, *Power,* 50; cf. Nicol C. Rae, "Ambition and Achievement: The Senate Republican Leadership of Trent Lott," *in Leadership in the U.S. Senate,* ed. Colton C. Campbell (New York: Routledge, 2019), 189. In 1888, the Senate consisted of seventy-six senators. Twenty years later, there were ninety-two, and the body may have been seen as too unwieldy. Cf. McConachie, *Congressional Committees,* 312–14; Rae, "Ambition and Achievement," 189. As Herbert Spencer wrote, "In societies, as in living bodies, increase of mass is habitually accompanied by increase of structure." Quoted in McConachie, *Congressional Committees,* 2.

438. Gamm and Smith, "Emergence," 212–38; see also David W. Rohde, *Parties and Leaders in the Postreform House* (Chicago: University of Chicago Press, 1991), 31–34.

439. Gamm and Smith, "Emergence," 212–38.

440. Ibid.

441. Ripley, *Power,* 48; Gamm and Smith, "Emergence," 221; Rothman, *Politics and Power,* 44–50, 107–8; cf. Samuel C. Patterson, "Party Leadership in the U.S. Senate," in *Leading Congress: New Styles, New Strategies,* ed. John J. Kornacki (Washington, DC: Congressional Quarterly, 1990), 36.

442. Munk, "Origin and Development," 28; Patterson, "Party Leadership," 36; Mac-Neil and Baker, *American Senate,* 176–77; Ripley, *Power,* 48.

443. Rothman, *Politics and Power,* 44–45; Gamm and Smith, "Emergence," 219; see also McConachie, *Congressional Committees,* 341. This pattern of choosing Republican caucus chairmen based largely on seniority continued for some time. George Rothwell Brown, *The Leadership of Congress* (Indianapolis: Bobbs-Merrill, 1922), 255; Gamm and Smith, "Senate without Leaders," 9; Gamm and Smith, "Rise of Floor Leaders," 10, 12–13.

444. Robert C. Byrd, *The Senate 1789–1989: Addresses on the History of the United States Senate* (Washington, DC: Government Printing Office, 1991), 2:178, 186; *United States Senate Committee on Appropriations, 135th Anniversary, 1867–2002* (Washington, DC: Government Printing Office, 2002), 45; Munk, "Origin and Development," 12, 61–62; Ripley, *Power,* 27; see also MacNeil and Baker, *American Senate,* 176–80; Thompson, *Party Leaders,* 25–37.

445. Gerald Gamm and Steven S. Smith, "Policy Leadership and the Development of the Modern Senate," in *Party, Process, and Political Change in Congress: New Perspectives on the History of Congress,* ed. David W. Brady and Mathew D. McCubbins (Stanford, CA: Stanford University Press, 2002), 288; Rothman, *Politics and Power,* 48–49, 58–59; see also Ripley, *Power,* 26–28. The Republican Steering Committee was established on an ad hoc basis in 1874 to help schedule the order of business in the body. As such, it handled some of the responsibilities of a modern majority leader. Donald A. Ritchie, *A History of the United States Republican Policy Committee, 1947–1997* (Washington, DC: Government Printing Office, 1997), 4; Smith and Gamm, "Evolution," 3–7. The party steering committees generally began to atrophy with the rise of formal floor leadership in the 1910s, although the Republican Steering Committee would experience a brief renaissance in the 1920s and early 1930s when the GOP reclaimed control of the Senate and the White House. Gamm and Smith, "Emergence, 1881–1946," 25; William C. Widenor, "Henry Cabot Lodge: The

Astute Parliamentarian," in Baker and Davidson, *First among Equals,* 53–54; see also chapter 7. Fred Sackett (R-KY) chaired the Republican Steering Committee in the late 1920s during its brief resurgence. Kravitz, "Party Organization," 87.

446. Rothman, *Politics and Power,* 48–49, 58–59, 107–8.

447. Gamm and Smith, "Emergence," 219.

448. Rothman, *Politics and Power,* 63. The creation of enduring steering committees in 1892–1893 marked an important step in party governance. Prior to this time, steering committees had been ad hoc in nature. Smith and Gamm, "Dynamics of Party Government," 153–54; Rothman, *Politics and Power,* 48–49; Smith and Gamm, "Evolution," 3–7.

449. Gamm and Smith, "Rise of Floor Leaders," 18–34; MacNeil and Baker, *American Senate,* 176.

450. Ripley, *Power,* 28–29; Gamm and Smith, "Rise of Floor Leaders," 21–34; Rothman, *Politics and Power,* 61.

451. 21 *CR* 10631 (1890). Gorman was referred to in similar terms on subsequent occasions. 41 *CR* 2087 (1907) (called, in retrospect, the "minority leader" on the Senate floor); 41 *CR* 2175 (1907) (called, in retrospect, the "minority leader" on the House floor). For whatever reason, Gorman was never referred to as "caucus chairman" on the Senate floor.

452. 25 *CR* 153 (1893).

453. Gamm and Smith, "Emergence," 5; Smith and Gamm, "Evolution," 1, 3. One of the more visible aspects of the caucus chairman's responsibilities was to introduce housekeeping measures at the start of Senate sessions. Gamm and Smith, "Senate without Leaders," 9.

454. Gamm and Smith, "Rise of Floor Leaders," 14–48.

455. McConachie, *Congressional Committees,* 265.

456. Ibid., 338.

457. Gamm and Smith, "Rise of Floor Leaders," 33–34, 38–39; Rothman, *Politics and Power,* 44–46. By the beginning of the twentieth century, Gorman had already established this "leadership" expectation in the Democratic caucus chairman position. Gamm and Smith, "Rise of Floor Leaders," 33–34, 38–39; Andrea C. Hatcher, *Majority Leadership in the U.S. Senate: Balancing Constraints* (Amherst, NY: Cambria Press, 2010), 28–29; Ripley, *Power,* 41, 48. Senator Horace Chilton (D-TX) noted that Gorman's service as caucus chairman was one of the formal reasons why he exercised more authority than his Democratic colleagues. Chilton wrote: "On account of his [Gorman's] long service to the Senate—his occupancy of the place as Chairman of the Democratic Caucus and member of the Committee of Rules he had opportunity to employ individual methods which were not enjoyed by any other Senator on the Democratic side." *HCP,* 74. For Caucus Chairman Allison's status, see, e.g., 47 *CR* 3335 (1911) (Rep. Hull).

458. Gamm and Smith, "Emergence, 1881–1946," 13–14.

459. Gamm and Smith, "Emergence," 230–31; Hatcher, *Majority Leadership,* 28–29; Floyd M. Riddick, *Majority and Minority Leaders of the Senate* (Washington, DC: Government Printing Office, 1981), 6.

460. Woodrow Wilson, *Congressional Government* (New York: Meridian Books, 1956), 146–47. At the time, Wilson was not alone in this opinion. In 1878, just a few years before Wilson's book was published, the *New York Times* wrote that the upper chamber did not have "distinctly recognized leaders," noting that Senate "business is left to the initiative of individuals or of numerous unconnected committees." "Congressional Debates"; see also MacNeil and Baker, *American Senate,* 175. In 1888, James Bryce wrote that the Senate lacked "recognized leaders . . . [and had] no chieftains." He observed that "no senator can be said to

have any authority beyond that of exceptional talent and experience." James Bryce, *American Commonwealth* (New York: Macmillan, 1888), 1:270; see also ibid., 271, 274, 400; MacNeil and Baker, *American Senate,* 175.

461. Woodrow Wilson, *Constitutional Government in the United States* (New York: Columbia University Press, 1961), 133–34.

7. Senate Majority Leader

1. For the lead author's reflections on his own tenure as Senate party leader, see Mitch McConnell, *The Long Game: A Memoir* (New York: Sentinel, 2016), 158–250.

2. "Longest-Serving Party Leaders, Majority and Minority Leaders," US Senate, accessed December 20, 2018, https://www.senate.gov/artandhistory/history/common/briefing/Majority_Minority_Leaders.htm#4.

3. Ibid.

4. James K. Libbey, *Alben Barkley: A Life in Politics* (Lexington: University Press of Kentucky, 2016), 5.

5. Ibid.

6. James K. Libbey, *Dear Alben: Mr. Barkley of Kentucky* (Lexington: University Press of Kentucky, 1979), 2.

7. Libbey, *Barkley,* 8. Through his mother, Barkley was also distantly related to Vice President Adlai Stevenson. Ibid., 9.

8. Ibid., 11. Barkley indicated that he inherited his love of storytelling from his father. Interview with Alben W. Barkley, July 17, 1953, Alben W. Barkley Oral History Project, LBNCOH, accessed February 15, 2018, https://kentuckyoralhistory.org/catalog/xt7wdb7vnq3j (hereafter Barkley Oral History No. 3).

9. Libbey, *Barkley,* 8–9.

10. Ibid., 10; Libbey, *Dear Alben,* 3; Alben W. Barkley, *That Reminds Me—* (Garden City, NY: Doubleday, 1954), 37–38.

11. Libbey, *Barkley,* 9–10, 27; Barkley Oral History No. 3.

12. Barkley, *That Reminds Me,* 45; Libbey, *Dear Alben,* 3.

13. Libbey, *Dear Alben,* 4–5.

14. Ibid., 5.

15. Ibid., 7; Libbey, *Barkley,* 27–29.

16. Libbey, *Barkley,* 32–36; Barkley, *That Reminds Me,* 69–70.

17. Libbey, *Barkley,* 36; Barkley, *That Reminds Me,* 69–70.

18. Libbey, *Barkley,* 36–37; Libbey, *Dear Alben,* 10; Barkley, *That Reminds Me,* 70–71.

19. Barkley, *That Reminds Me,* 71, 73–74.

20. Libbey, *Barkley,* 194.

21. J. B. Shannon, "Alben W. Barkley: 'Reservoir of Energy,'" in *Public Men in and out of Office,* ed. J. T. Salter (Chapel Hill: University of North Carolina Press, 1946), 244.

22. Barkley, *That Reminds Me,* 77; Libbey, *Dear Alben,* 11.

23. Libbey, *Barkley,* 11, 15.

24. Ibid.

25. Donald A. Ritchie, "Alben Barkley: The President's Man," in *First among Equals: Outstanding Senate Leaders of the Twentieth Century,* ed. Richard A. Baker and Roger H. Davidson (Washington, DC: CQ Press, 1991), 156.

26. Ibid.; see also Libbey, *Barkley,* 43; Libbey, *Dear Alben,* 10.

27. Libbey, *Barkley*, 21, 26–27.

28. Shannon, "Barkley," 248.

29. Libbey, *Barkley*, 37.

30. Alben W. Barkley, "The Vice-Presidency" (1952), 14, Papers of Alben Barkley, University of Kentucky.

31. Libbey, *Barkley*, 1, 27, 42–43.

32. Ibid., 1; see also ibid., 10.

33. Ibid., 41–43.

34. Shannon, "Barkley," 244.

35. Ibid.

36. Libbey, *Barkley*, 52–55.

37. Ibid., 59; Barkley, *That Reminds Me*, 27, 99. For Barkley's support of Wilson's agenda, see Polly Ann Davis, *Alben W. Barkley: Senate Majority Leader and Vice President* (New York: Garland Publishing, 1979), 1–2.

38. Libbey, *Barkley*, 77–79, 84, 99–100. For Barkley's apparent reversal on the temperance question, a signature issue for him, see ibid., 161.

39. Shannon, "Barkley," 246–47.

40. Ibid.

41. Ibid.

42. Ibid.

43. Libbey, *Barkley*, 115–17, 121; Libbey, *Dear Alben*, 36–37, 42–43; interview with Alben W. Barkley, July 24, 1953, Alben W. Barkley Oral History Project, LBNCOH, accessed February 15, 2018, https://kentuckyoralhistory.org/catalog/xt7mw6694660.

44. Libbey, *Dear Alben*, 36–37, 42–43; Libbey, *Barkley*, 121–24.

45. Libbey, *Dear Alben*, 46.

46. "Senate Leaders: Alben Barkley: Congressional Voice of Liberty," US Senate, accessed February 15, 2018, https://www.senate.gov/artandhistory/history/common/generic/People_Leaders_Barkley.htm.

47. Libbey, *Barkley*, 43.

48. Ibid., 21.

49. Davis, *Barkley*, 171–72 (quoting Adolph Shelby Ochs).

50. Ibid., 172.

51. Ibid.

52. Libbey, *Dear Alben*, 61.

53. Ritchie, "Barkley," 131; Libbey, *Barkley*, 167, 174.

54. Walter Kravitz, "Leadership, New Style: The Floor Leaders," in "The United States Senate: A History" (unpublished manuscript on file with the authors), 36; Libbey, *Barkley*, 167, 174–75.

55. Margaret Rampton Munk, "Origin and Development of the Party Floor Leadership in the United States Senate" (PhD diss., Harvard University, 1970), 255, 293 (quoting *Literary Digest* from 1937); see also Libbey, *Dear Alben*, 67–68.

56. Libbey, *Barkley*, 174; see also ibid., 167.

57. Ibid., 170, 175; cf. Libbey, *Dear Alben*, 67.

58. Libbey, *Barkley*, 185–87; Libbey, *Dear Alben*, 72.

59. "Party Division," US Senate, accessed February 15, 2018, https://www.senate.gov/history/partydiv.htm.

60. Davis, *Barkley*, 38 (quoting *Time* magazine).

61. Ibid.; James T. Patterson, *Congressional Conservatism and the New Deal: The Growth of the Conservative Coalition in Congress, 1933–1939* (Lexington: University of Kentucky Press, 1967), 38–42, 77–127; Ritchie, "Barkley," 132–35; Libbey, *Barkley*, 188.

62. Patterson, *Congressional Conservatism*, 77–127.

63. Libbey, *Barkley*, 187–90.

64. Davis, *Barkley*, 23; Ritchie, "Barkley," 127–29.

65. Patterson, *Congressional Conservatism*, 145–48; Ritchie, "Barkley," 127–29.

66. Martha H. Swain, *Pat Harrison: The New Deal Years* (Jackson: University Press of Mississippi, 1978), 154; Patterson, *Congressional Conservatism*, 146. Apparently, Robinson had initially approached Harrison, who was "his closest friend," about becoming assistant majority leader, but the Mississippian demurred in part because of competing obligations as chairman of the Finance Committee. Swain, *Harrison*, 285 n. 25.

67. Swain, *Harrison*, 155–59; Ritchie, "Barkley," 128; Davis, *Barkley*, 32.

68. Swain, *Harrison*, 156–57; Libbey, *Barkley*, 188; Libbey, *Dear Alben*, 73; cf. Ritchie, "Barkley," 128.

69. Swain, *Harrison*, 156; Ritchie, "Barkley," 128–29; Patterson, *Congressional Conservatism*, 146–47; Libbey, *Barkley*, 188; Davis, *Barkley*, 23.

70. Ritchie, "Barkley," 128–29; Davis, *Barkley*, 31–32; Swain, *Harrison*, 158–59; Patterson, *Congressional Conservatism*, 147–48. In contrast with Roosevelt, Garner was scrupulously neutral in the Barkley-Harrison leadership race. Bascom N. Timmons, *Garner of Texas: A Personal History* (New York: Harper & Brothers, 1948), 222–24. Afterward, Garner expressed his belief that he could have swung the race in Harrison's favor. Garner had been asked his opinion by fellow Texan senator Morris Shepard, but he did not deem it appropriate to make a recommendation, given FDR's professed neutrality. Ibid., 224.

71. *Minutes of the Senate Democratic Conference, 1903–1964*, ed. Donald A. Ritchie (Washington, DC: Government Printing Office, 1998), 353–54.

72. Libbey, *Dear Alben*, 74.

73. Ibid.

74. Swain, *Harrison*, 160.

75. Barkley, *That Reminds Me*, 156.

76. Ibid. The leadership election, which occurred at the tail end of the Court-packing controversy, prompted a memorable constituent letter to the new majority leader: "I became excited when I read the '38 to 37' head-lines. I first thought the President had increased the Supreme [Court] membership to 75." Swain, *Harrison*, 286 n. 34.
Barkley's race is not the only tight leadership election to take place in the Senate. Tom Daschle (D-SD) defeated Christopher Dodd (D-CT) in another one-vote nail-biter at the end of 1994. Burdett Loomis, "Senate Leaders, Minority Voices: From Dirksen to Daschle," in *The Contentious Senate: Partisanship, Ideology, and the Myth of Cool Judgment*, ed. Colton C. Campbell and Nicol C. Rae (Lanham, MD: Rowman & Littlefield, 2001), 104. Similarly, Howard Baker (R-TN) defeated Robert Griffin (R-MI) by a single vote in 1977. Roger H. Davidson, "The Senate: If Everyone Leads, Who Follows?" in *Congress Reconsidered*, 4th ed., ed. Lawrence C. Dodd and Bruce I. Oppenheimer (Washington, DC: CQ Press, 1989), 284. In January 1920, Oscar Underwood (D-AL) and Gilbert Hitchcock (D-NE) deadlocked at 19 votes apiece in their race for party leader. Thomas W. Ryley, *Gilbert Hitchcock of Nebraska—Wilson's Floor Leader in the Fight for the Versailles Treaty* (Lewiston, NY: Edwin Mellen Press, 1998), 261–62; "Democratic Leadership Deadlock," US Senate, accessed February 15, 2018, https://www.senate.gov/artandhistory/history/minute/Democratic

_Leadership_Deadlock.htm. In April, Hitchcock withdrew from the protracted contest and permitted Underwood to be elected. "Hitchcock Quits Leadership Fight," *NYT,* April 24, 1920; "Democratic Leadership Deadlock."

77. Ritchie, "Barkley," 129; Patterson, *Congressional Conservatism,* 148; Libbey, *Dear Alben,* 75–76; Libbey, *Barkley,* 224.

78. Patterson, *Congressional Conservatism,* 148. Presidents have had mixed results when weighing in on the election of Senate floor leaders of the same party. President Dwight Eisenhower was quietly supportive of Everett Dirksen (R-IL) in his contest for Senate minority leader against John Sherman Cooper (R-KY). Dirksen prevailed. Neil MacNeil, *Dirksen: Portrait of a Public Man* (New York: World Publishing, 1970), 162–63; Kravitz, "Leadership, New Style," 101. President Richard Nixon was reportedly against the election of Hugh Scott (PA) as Senate Republican leader in both 1969 and 1971. Nonetheless, Scott won both times. Roger H. Davidson, "Senate Leaders: Janitors for an Untidy Chamber?" in *Congress Reconsidered,* 3d ed., ed. Lawrence C. Dodd and Bruce I. Oppenheimer (Washington, DC: CQ Press, 1985), 235. Bill Frist was President George W. Bush's preferred candidate to succeed Trent Lott as Senate majority leader in 2003 and was elected without opposition. None of these presidents was as heavy handed as Roosevelt, however. There were media stories that President Harry Truman preferred Joseph O'Mahoney (D-WY) over Ernest McFarland (D-AZ) in 1950, but McFarland discounted these reports, believing that Truman had been neutral. Ernest W. McFarland, *Mac: The Autobiography of Ernest W. McFarland* (self-published, 1979), 115. For President Wilson's apparent involvement in John Worth Kern's election, see note 87.

79. Patterson, *Congressional Conservatism,* 148; Ritchie, "Barkley," 129.

80. Patterson, *Congressional Conservatism,* 127, 148.

81. Ibid.

82. Walter J. Oleszek, "Senate Leadership," in *The Encyclopedia of the United States Congress,* ed. Donald C. Bacon, Roger H. Davidson, and Morton Keller (New York: Simon & Schuster, 1995), 3:1263, 1265; Ralph K. Huitt, "The Internal Distribution of Influence: The Senate," in *The Congress and America's Future,* ed. David B. Truman (Englewood Cliffs, NJ: Prentice-Hall, 1965), 79, 82–83; Mark J. Oleszek and Walter J. Oleszek, "Legislating in the Senate: From the 1950s into the 2000s," in *Leadership in the U.S. Senate,* ed. Colton C. Campbell (New York: Routledge, 2019), 2–32.

83. Andrea C. Hatcher, *Majority Leadership in the U.S. Senate*: *Balancing Constraints* (Amherst, NY: Cambria Press, 2010), 1; Walter J. Oleszek, "John Worth Kern: Portrait of a Floor Leader," in Baker and Davidson, *First among Equals,* 7; Richard A. Baker and Roger H. Davidson, introduction to *First among Equals,* 2; James Burnham, *Congress and the American Tradition* (Chicago: Henry Regnery, 1965), 153.

84. "Party Division," US Senate.

85. Ibid.

86. Munk, "Origin and Development" (1970), 120–21; Randall Ripley, *Power in the Senate* (New York: St. Martin's, 1969), 48.

87. Hatcher, *Majority Leadership,* 33, 102–4; Margaret Munk, "Origin and Development of Party Floor Leadership in the United States Senate," *CS* 2 (1974): 23, 31; Ripley, *Power,* 29–31; see also Kravitz, "Leadership, New Style," 26. The extent to which President Wilson was involved in Kern's selection is unclear. Walter Kravitz, "The Organization of the Senate in 1913" (History and Government Division, Legislative Reference Service, 1963), 5 n. 11 (on file with the authors); Claude G. Bowers, *The Life of John Worth Kern* (Indianapolis:

Hollenbeck Press, 1918), 289. Given Wilson's interest in lowering the walls separating the political branches—he was the first president in more than a century to give the State of the Union address in person—one suspects he was active behind the scenes in promoting the like-minded Kern. Baker and Davidson, introduction to *First among Equals,* 2; Woodrow Wilson, *Constitutional Government in the United States* (New York: Columbia University Press, 1961), 59–60, 70–74; Burnham, *Congress,* 153–54; Sidney M. Milkis and Michael Nelson, *The American Presidency: Origins and Development, 1776–1993* (Washington, DC: CQ Press, 1994), 241. Not everyone has lauded Kern's innovations. Some believe they heralded improper presidential dominance over the Senate. Henry Lee Myers, *The United States Senate: What Kind of Body?* (Philadelphia: Dorrance, 1939), 109–11; Burnham, *Congress,* 153–54.

For whatever reason (perhaps because of less presidential focus on the adoption of major legislative items), early Republican Senate majority leaders such as Henry Cabot Lodge (MA), Charles Curtis (KS), and James Watson (IN) were less apt to support presidents of their own party. Richard E. Cohen, *Congressional Leadership: Seeking a New Role* (Beverly Hills, CA: Sage Publications, 1980), 38.

88. Gerald Gamm and Steven S. Smith, "The Rise of Floor Leaders, 1890–1913" (draft book chapter), 31–33, 59, 71–73. In 1888, James Bryce observed, "by its exclusion from Congress the executive is deprived of the power of leading and guiding the legislature and of justifying in debate its administrative acts." James Bryce, *The American Commonwealth* (New York: Macmillan, 1888), 1:281. He believed that one of "the defects" in American government was "the want of opportunities for the executive to influence the legislature." Ibid., 400.

89. Gamm and Smith, "Rise of Floor Leaders," 31–33, 59, 71–73.

90. Ibid., 46–48.

91. Gerald Gamm and Steven S. Smith, "Emergence of Senate Party Leadership," in *U.S. Senate Exceptionalism,* ed. Bruce I. Oppenheimer (Columbus: Ohio State University Press, 2002), 230; Steven S. Smith, "Recent Senate Party Leaders in a Historical Perspective," in Campbell, *Leadership,* 273; Gerald Gamm and Steven S. Smith, "Policy Leadership and the Development of the Modern Senate," in *Party, Process, and Political Change in Congress: New Perspectives on the History of Congress,* ed. David W. Brady and Mathew D. McCubbins (Stanford, CA: Stanford University Press, 2002), 291. On the Senate floor, Kern never referred to himself as "majority leader," "Democratic leader," or "floor leader." He called himself "caucus chairman." 50 *CR* 5882 (1913); 51 *CR* 9849 (1914); 51 *CR* 16405 (1914); 53 *CR* 12945 (1916). For procedural and practical innovations during Kern's tenure, see Gamm and Smith, "Policy Leadership," 299–302.

92. A HeinOnline search of the *Annals of Congress,* the *Digest of Debates,* the *Congressional Globe,* and the *Congressional Record* for the term "majority leader" reveals that the first reference on the Senate floor occurred in 1896, but it was not directed toward a specific senator. 28 *CR* 553 (1896). The next reference occurred in 1908, when Robert La Follette (R-WI) called Nelson Aldrich (R-RI) the "majority leader." 42 *CR* 7173 (1908). There were no other references to the "position" on the Senate floor until Kern's tenure, when they became unexceptional. 50 *CR* 196 (1913); 51 *CR* 10196 (1914); 52 *CR* 906 (1915); 52 *CR* 2226 (1915); 52 *CR* 3266 (1915) (marking the first time the Senate's official reporter recognized a lawmaker as majority leader); 53 *CR* 4109 (1916) (constituent letter submitted for the record); 53 CR 6888 (1916) (constituent letter); 53 *CR* 7754 (1916) (constituent letter); 53 *CR* 8454 (1916) (constituent letter); 53 *CR* 12612 (1916); 54 *CR* 318 (1917); see also 55 *CR* 6266 (posthu-

mous reference to Kern). It was also during Kern's time in office that the Senate majority leader position was first mentioned on the House floor. 52 *CR* 225 (1914) (Rep. Underwood).

Use of the same HeinOnline methodology reveals that the first references to an individual as "minority leader" in the modern sense were retrospective mentions of Senator Arthur Pue Gorman (D-MD) following his passing in 1907. 41 *CR* 2083–84, 2087 (1907) (including, among other references, an article submitted for the record); 41 *CR* 2175 (1907); 50 *CR* 1598 (1913) (article submitted for the record). There is also a 1907 reference to Senator William Bate (D-TN) as "minority leader," but in this context, he is being referred to as the modern equivalent of a bill manager. 41 *CR* 1270 (1907). Senator Charles Culberson (D-TX) was the first senator to be referred to as Senate "minority leader" on the House floor. 42 *CR* 593 (1908). Senator Hernando Money (D-MS) was the first sitting senator to be referred to as "minority leader" on the Senate floor. 45 *CR* 7642 (1910); 47 *CR* 1668 (1911). Senator Jacob Gallinger (R-NH) was the first sitting lawmaker to be regularly referenced as "minority leader" on the Senate floor. 53 *CR* 8782 (1916) (constituent letter submitted for the record); 54 *CR* 4889 (1917) (article submitted for the record); 56 *CR* 59 (1917) (constituent letter submitted for the record); 56 *CR* 1405 (constituent letter); 56 *CR* 4182 (1918) (constituent letter); see also 56 CR 10004 (1918) (Sen. Lodge; first use of the title by the official reporter); cf. Smith, "Recent Senate Party Leaders," 273.

93. The measure was apparently never adopted. Senate Resolution No. 45, 50 *CR* 196 (1913), authorizing a research bureau in the Senate subject to rules "formulated by the majority leader," with "the confirmation of [personnel] appointments . . . [made] by the majority leader." The authors would like to thank Valerie Heitshusen, Michael Green, and Walter Oleszek for alerting them to this measure.

94. The term "majority leader" was used steadily with respect to Kern's successor, Thomas Martin (D-VA). 55 *CR* 684 (1917); 55 *CR* 2963 (1917) (submission of a document for the record); 55 *CR* 4800 (1917); 55 *CR* 7272 (1917); 56 *CR* 59 (1917) (constituent letter for the record); 56 *CR* 1405 (1918) (constituent letter); 56 *CR* 4182 (1918) (constituent letter); 56 *CR* 7280 (1918); 56 *CR* 8686 (1918); 56 *CR* 8745 (1918); 58 *CR* 8373 (1919) (posthumous reference); 59 *CR* 5491 (1920) (posthumous reference); 60 *CR* 3102 (1921) (posthumous reference).

The tenure of Martin's successor as majority leader, Henry Cabot Lodge, reflects the same steady use of the term "majority leader." 59 *CR* 542 (1920); 59 *CR* 538 (1920); 59 *CR* 5586 (1920) (letter for the record); 60 *CR* 3464–65 (1921); 61 *CR* 5596 (1921); 61 *CR* 6067 (1921); 61 *CR* 6277 (1922); 62 *CR* 997 (1922); 62 *CR* 4230 (1922); 62 *CR* 4250 (1922); 62 *CR* 8906 (1922) (article for the record); 65 *CR* 4021 (1924).

95. A HeinOnline search demonstrates that there were some references to senators as "Democratic leader" prior to Kern. 2 *CR* 1355 (1874) (John W. Stevenson referring, in retrospect, to Sen. Thomas Hart Benton [MO]); 10 *CR* 2753 (1880) (referring to Sen. Allen Thurman [OH]); 17 *CR* 773 (1886) (referring to Sen. James Beck [KY]); 20 *CR* 792 (1889) (unclear reference); 25 *CR* 153 (1893) (reference to Sen. Arthur Pue Gorman [MD] from a news article); 46 *CR* 1339 (1911) (referring to Sen. Charles Culberson [TX]); 46 *CR* 4293 (1911) (referring to Sen. Hernando Money [MS]); 47 *CR* 1667 (1911) (referring to Sen. Thomas Martin [VA]); cf. 25 *CR* 2947 (1893) (referring to leadership, although possibly in a non-Senate context). However, Kern is the first senator repeatedly referred to as "Democratic leader" on the Senate floor. 51 *CR* 15367 (1914); 52 *CR* 2932 (1915); 53 *CR* 11793 (1916); 53 *CR* 12947 (1916); 54 *CR* 1051 (1917) (article for the record); cf. 48 *CR* 8733 (1912) (quoting

a committee witness). The first reference to a Senate Democratic leader on the House floor was to Gorman. 21 *CR* 10631 (1890).

Also reflecting Kern's stature as formal leader of the Senate Democrats is that, from the end of the Civil War until the end of World War I, he was mentioned on the floor as "caucus chairman" far more often than any other senator. 50 *CR* 4478 (1913); 50 *CR* 5882 (1913); 51 *CR* 9849 (1914); 51 *CR* 16405 (1914) (Kern's first self-reference on the floor); 52 *CR* 2313 (1915); 52 *CR* 3100 (1915); 52 *CR* 3333 (1915); 53 *CR* 12940 (1916); 53 *CR* 12945 (1916) (Kern himself, repeating an earlier reference); 53 *CR* 12948 (1916); 53 *CR* 12965 (1916); 53 *CR* 13111 (1916); 53 *CR* 13904 (1916); see also 62 *CR* 10035 (1922) (posthumous reference).

96. 40 *CR* 6937 (1906) (Sen. Bailey mentioned in an article submitted for the record); 47 *CR* 1680 (1911) (Sen. Martin mentioned as "floor leader"); 47 *CR* 2856–57 (1911) (Sen. Gallinger mentioned as "floor leader," which, according to Gallinger, was incorrect); 53 *CR* 12066 (1916) (Sen. Gallinger); 54 *CR* 1385 (1917) (Sen. Kern); 55 *CR* 4585 (1917) (Sen. Martin mentioned in a letter from President Wilson submitted for the record); 55 *CR* 4748–49 (1917) (Sen. Martin in the same letter from Wilson); 55 *CR* 6266 (1917) (posthumous reference to Sen. Kern); 56 *CR* 882 (1918) (apparently Sen. Martin); 56 *CR* 912 (1918) (Sen. Martin): 56 *CR* 8491 (1918) (Sen. Martin); 56 *CR* 10395 (1918) (apparently Sen. Martin); 56 *CR* 10843 (1918) (Sen. Lodge mentioned in an article submitted for the record); 56 *CR* 11492 (1918) (Sen. Lodge); 57 *CR* 1813 (1919) (Sen. Lodge); 57 *CR* 2261 (1919) (Sen. Lodge); 58 *CR* 329–30 (1919) (Sen. Lodge mentioned in articles submitted for the record).

97. Gerald Gamm and Steven S. Smith, "The Emergence of Senate Party Leadership, 1913–1937: The Case of the Democrats" (paper presented at Congress and History Workshop, Vanderbilt University, May 21–23, 2015), 21–24, 36–37.

98. Cf. ibid.

99. Beginning with Kern, Senate leaders of both parties became more vocal on the Senate floor and more active in offering amendments. Gamm and Smith, "Policy Leadership," 305–8.

100. Hatcher, *Majority Leadership*, 98–99; cf. Lauros G. McConachie, *Congressional Committees: A Study of the Origins and Development of Our National and Local Legislative Methods* (New York: Thomas Y. Crowell, 1898), vii ("Legislative bodies are living, more or less rapidly changing political organisms. Each has its own external and internal conditions."). For another rationale, see Davidson, "Senate Leaders," 226–27.

101. Munk, "Origin and Development" (1970), 245–46, 249; Gamm and Smith, "Emergence," 230–36.

102. Munk, "Origin and Development" (1970), 245–46, 249; email from Walter Oleszek, CRS.

103. Munk, "Origin and Development" (1970), 245–46, 249.

104. Gamm and Smith, "Rise of Floor Leaders," 31–33, 59, 71–73.

105. Gamm and Smith, "Emergence," 232, 235–36; cf. David W. Rohde, *Parties and Leaders in the Postreform House* (Chicago: University of Chicago Press, 1991), 31–34.

106. Bowers, *Kern*, 283; see also ibid., 282.

107. Cf. Hatcher, *Majority Leadership*, 98–99; McConachie, *Congressional Committees*, vii.

108. Gamm and Smith, "Policy Leadership," 291; Gamm and Smith, "Emergence," 231.

109. Gamm and Smith, "Policy Leadership," 291–93; Gamm and Smith, "Emergence, 1913–1937," 52; Gamm and Smith, "Emergence," 215, 231–36.

110. Gamm and Smith, "Emergence," 231.

111. Regarding application of the title "majority leader" to Senator Lodge on the floor, see note 94. He was also referred to as "Republican leader" on the floor far more often than any of his predecessors. 56 *CR* 6763 (1918); 56 *CR* 9094 (1918); 56 *CR* 10902 (1918); 58 *CR* 2067 (1919); 58 *CR* 6401 (1919); 58 *CR* 8271 (1919) (referring to Sen. Penrose); 59 *CR* 2521 (1920); 61 *CR* 207 (1921) (posthumous reference to Sen. Aldrich); 61 *CR* 324 (1921); 61 *CR* 1528 (1921); 61 *CR* 6072 (1921) (article submitted for the record); 62 *CR* 2601 (1922); 62 *CR* 3042 (1922); 62 *CR* 3568 (1922); 62 *CR* 4551 (1922); 62 *CR* 4588 (1922); 62 *CR* 7087 (1922) (article submitted for the record); 62 *CR* 7631 (1922) (referring to Sen. McCumber); 62 *CR* 13081 (1922); 64 *CR* 1234 (1923). For the earliest references to "Republican leader" on the Senate floor, see 28 *CR* 5544 (1896) (referring to Sen. Sherman); 30 *CR* 2375 (1897) (referring to Sen. Sherman); 36 *CR* 96 (1903) (unclear); 44 *CR* 1379, 1387 (1909) (referring to Sen. Aldrich); 44 *CR* 1454 (1909) (referring to Sen. Aldrich); 44 *CR* 3126 (1909) (referring to Sen. Aldrich); 46 *CR* 3893 (1911) (referring to Sen. Aldrich); 49 *CR* 4697 (1913) (referring to Sen. Aldrich); 51 *CR* 8550 (1914) (referring to Sen. Gallinger); cf. 47 *CR* 2580 (1911). Lodge was also referred to as "floor leader" more than any other early Republican caucus chairman. See note 96.

112. John A. Garraty, *Henry Cabot Lodge: A Biography* (New York: Alfred A. Knopf, 1953), 391; William C. Widenor, "Henry Cabot Lodge: The Astute Parliamentarian," in Baker and Davidson, *First among Equals,* 43–50; email from Betty Koed, Senate historian.

113. Ibid.

114. Widenor, "Lodge," 53–54.

115. 62 *CR* 12388 (1922) (Sen. Borah) ("The steering committee determines what bills are to be passed at this session"); 62 *CR* 12394 (1922) (Sen. King) ("no reclamation measure before us . . . has the support of the Republican leaders or the Republican steering committee which determines what measures shall be brought before the Senate"); 67 *CR* 10400 (1926) (majority leader Curtis) ("The chairman of the steering committee is arranging the [legislative] program now and hopes to call the steering committee together within a day or two and arrange a program for the rest of the session. . . . I can not say, of course, what they will do."); 67 *CR* 9678 (1926) (Sen. Simmons) ("the steering committee . . . has charge of outlining legislation in this body"); 72 *CR* 7806 (1930) (majority leader Watson) ("The majority is responsible for the legislation that occurs here, in so far as the order in which it is taken up is concerned. To carry that out with some degree of system, some method of order, always a steering committee is appointed; always that committee makes a report; and in the absence of some special reason to the contrary, the report of that committee is adopted, and the order of procedure is carried out."); 72 *CR* 8652 (1930) (Sen. Vandenberg) ("It is the concentrated, unanimous judgment of the [steering] committee . . . in consultation with the Republican leader and the Republican assistant leader, as to the order of business"); see also 59 *CR* 7480 (1920) (Sen. McKellar); 59 *CR* 8087 (1920) (Sens. Wadsworth and Kenyon); 61 *CR* 2560 (1921) (Sens. Curtis, Kenyon, King, and Lodge); 62 *CR* 12319 (1922) (Sen. McNary); 64 *CR* 343 (1922) (Sen. Harrison); 66 *CR* 3717 (1925) (Sens. Watson and Howell); 66 *CR* 4310 (1925) (Sen. McLean); 66 *CR* 4521 (1925) (majority leader Curtis); 66 *CR* 4864 (1925) (Sen. Borah, majority leader Curtis, and Sen. McNary); 66 *CR* 5010 (1925) (Sen. Sterling); 67 *CR* 7970–71 (1926) (Sens. Watson and Harrison and majority leader Curtis); 67 *CR* 8292 (1926) (Sens. Watson, Robinson, Wadsworth, and Bruce); 67 *CR* 8492 (1926) (Sens. Bruce and Norbeck); 67 *CR* 9359 (1926) (majority leader Curtis); 67 *CR* 9589 (1926) (Sen. Robinson and majority leader Curtis); 67 *CR* 10400–401 (1926) (Sens. Bingham, Copeland,

and McNary and majority leader Curtis); 67 *CR* 10476 (1926) (majority leader Curtis and Sen. Simmons); 69 *CR* 4230 (1928) (Sen. Jones); 69 *CR* 4612 (1928) (Sen. Harrison); 69 *CR* 4972 (1928) (Sen. Jones and majority leader Curtis); 69 *CR* 5433 (1928) (Sens. Caraway and Sackett); 69 *CR* 5480 (1928) (majority leader Curtis); 69 *CR* 8968 (1928) (Sen. Metcalf); 69 *CR* 10090 (1928) (Sen. Johnson); 70 *CR* 4112 (1929) (Sens. Harris and Sackett); 70 *CR* 4228 (1929) (Sen. Dill); 70 *CR* 4537 (1929) (Sens. Vandenberg and Robinson); 72 *CR* 7805–6 (1930) (majority leader Watson and Sens. Wagner and Swanson); 74 *CR* 2964–2965 (1931) (Sens. Walsh and Howell and majority leader Watson). See also Arthur W. MacMahon, "First Session of the Sixty-Ninth Congress," *APSR* 20 (1926): 604, 611; Arthur W. MacMahon, "Second Session of the Sixty-Ninth Congress," *APSR* 21 (1926): 297, 299–300; Thomas Claude Donnelly, "Party Leadership in the United States Senate" (PhD diss., New York University, 1930), 90–98, 114; "When the Sixty-Eighth Congress Convenes: How a New Congress Is Organized," *CD* 3 (1923): 40; Walter Kravitz, "Party Organization," in "The United States Senate: A History" (unpublished manuscript on file with the authors), 75; George Rothwell Brown, *The Leadership of Congress* (Indianapolis: Bobbs-Merrill, 1922), 252–53, 258–59, 261–62; Widenor, "Lodge," 53–54; George H. Haynes, *The Senate of the United States: Its History and Practice* (New York: Russell & Russell, 1960), 1:483–87. For more on the evolution of the Senate scheduling function, see Kravitz, "Party Organization," 71–78; Gamm and Smith, "Policy Leadership," 298–300. For discussion of the Republican Steering Committee's authority and procedures, see 72 *CR* 7805–6 (1930); 72 *CR* 8651–57 (1930); 74 *CR* 3162–63 (1931).

116. Floyd M. Riddick, *Majority and Minority Leaders of the Senate* (Washington, DC: Government Printing Office, 1981), 16. Underwood's tenure provides another link between Kentucky and Senate leadership, as he was born in Louisville. "Oscar Wilder Underwood," Congressional Biographical Directory, accessed February 15, 2018, http://bioguide.congress.gov/scripts/biodisplay.pl?index=u000013. Underwood moved to Alabama, where he was elected to the Senate as a Democrat and was later chosen by his party colleagues to serve as Senate minority leader. Interestingly, this is the exact opposite path taken by the lead author, who was born in Alabama, moved to Louisville, was elected to the Senate as a Republican, and was later chosen by his party colleagues to be Senate minority leader (and later majority leader).

117. Riddick, *Majority and Minority Leaders*, 16. Underwood is one of four Senate party leaders to remain in the Senate after his leadership tenure. The others are Styles Bridges (R-NH), Robert Byrd (D-WV), and Trent Lott (R-MS).

118. Ibid.

119. Ibid. McNary may have claimed that seat as early as 1935. Gamm and Smith, "Emergence, 1913–1937," 26.

120. Munk, "Origin and Development" (1970), 361.

121. Ross K. Baker, *House and Senate*, 3d ed. (New York: W. W. Norton, 2001), 57; Steven V. Roberts, "Pick a Seat (But Not) Any Seat," *NYT,* December 1, 1986. Riddick, *Majority and Minority Leaders*, 16; Kravitz, "Leadership, New Style," 120; Richard A. Baker, *Traditions of the United States Senate* (Washington, DC: Government Printing Office), 8, accessed February 15, 2018, https://www.senate.gov/reference/resources/pdf/Traditions.pdf; email from Richard Baker, Senate historian emeritus. An exchange from 1950 is illustrative of the importance of the center aisle seat:

Mr. CAPEHART, Mr. HAYDEN, Mr. WHERRY, and Mr. CORDON rose.

Mr. CAPEHART. Mr. President—

The VICE PRESIDENT. The Chair recognizes the Senator from Nebraska.

Mr. CAPEHART. Mr. President, a point of order. I addressed the Chair, and the Senator from Nebraska [minority leader Kenneth Wherry] did not even open his mouth.

The VICE PRESIDENT. The Chair would suggest to the Senator from Indiana that he is behind the Senator from Nebraska while the Chair is in front of him. The Chair understood the Senator from Nebraska to address the Chair.

96 *CR* 11698 (1950).

122. Baker, *House and Senate,* 57; Baker, *Traditions,* 8; Roberts, "Pick a Seat." Recognition that serving as Senate party leader was becoming a full-time job can be seen in the decline in the number of party leaders who held major committee chairmanships in the 1920s and 1930s. Gamm and Smith, "Policy Leadership," 303; Kravitz, "Leadership, New Style," 35, 41.

123. On this subject, the authors benefited greatly from email exchanges and conversations with Betty Koed, Gerald Gamm, and Steven S. Smith.

124. Francis G. Matson, Joint Committee on Printing, *Official Congressional Directory* (Washington, DC: Government Printing Office, 1921), 254; Elmer C. Hess, Joint Committee on Printing, *Official Congressional Directory* (Washington, DC: Government Printing Office, 1925), 240; Elmer C. Hess, Joint Committee on Printing, *Official Congressional Directory* (Washington, DC: Government Printing Office, 1929), 276; Koed email.

125. Gamm and Smith, "Emergence, 1913–1937," 49–50; Kravitz, "Leadership, New Style," 35.

126. Bob Dole, *Historical Almanac of the United States Senate* (Washington, DC: Government Printing Office, 1989), 210–11. Other Senate majority and minority leaders have been their parties' vice-presidential nominees, including Charles McNary for the Republicans in 1940, Barkley for the Democrats in 1948, and Lyndon Johnson for the Democrats in 1960. In 1996, Bob Dole (R-KS) became the first (and, to date, the only) sitting majority leader to become his party's presumptive presidential nominee; however, Dole stepped down from the Senate before being officially nominated.

127. Barbara Sinclair, "Congressional Leadership: A Review Essay and a Research Agenda," in *Leading Congress: New Styles, New Strategies,* ed. John J. Kornacki (Washington, DC: CQ Press, 1990), 134; Ripley, *Power,* 16.

128. Sinclair, "Congressional Leadership," 134; Gamm and Smith, "Emergence, 1913–1937," 5, 49–52.

129. Gamm and Smith, "Emergence, 1913–1937," 5, 28–32, 49–52; Kravitz, "Leadership, New Style," 35–37. Some early de facto Senate party leaders, such as Arthur Pue Gorman (D-MD), had mastered the art of manipulating the media long before Robinson. A fellow senator wrote of Gorman:

He was also in close touch with the newspaper correspondents—especially the representatives of the Washington papers. His influence was very strong with those papers. And through his connection with the press representatives and his constant cultivation of that craft, he had at hand instrumentalities of information and methods of expressing his views which was [*sic*] beyond the reach of other Senators. Every morning the Senators from every state would peruse the great capitol daily—every evening they would glance at the Star or Times. And things that Gorman thought made an insuspectible headway as if they were the things that impressed disinterested observers.

HCP, 77–78.

130. Steven S. Smith, "Parties and Leadership in the Senate," in *The Legislative Branch*, ed. Paul J. Quirk and Sarah A. Binder (New York: Oxford University Press, 2005), 264; Gamm and Smith, "Emergence, 1913–1937," 5, 49–51; Kravitz, "Party Organization," 35.

131. Gamm and Smith, "Policy Leadership," 304. Prior to Joe Robinson's tenure, bill managers (usually committee chairmen and ranking members) put forward unanimous consent agreements to try to expedite Senate consideration of legislation. Robinson, as majority leader, assumed responsibility for unanimous consent agreements, which bolstered his authority and that of the office. Ibid.

132. Floyd M. Riddick and Alan S. Frumin, *Riddick's Senate Procedure: Precedents and Practice* (Washington, DC: Government Printing Office, 1992), 1311–69.

133. This prerogative is also referred to as the right of "priority recognition," "preferential recognition," and "first recognition." Discussions with Betty Koed, Elizabeth Mac-Donough, Walter Oleszek, Elizabeth Rybicki, Richard Beth, Christopher Davis, Mark Oleszek, Gerald Gamm, Steven S. Smith, and Nancy Kervin over the years have enhanced the authors' understanding of the history of prior recognition.

134. "Standing Rules of the Senate, Rule XIX (1)(a)," US Senate Committee on Rules and Administration, accessed February 15, 2018, https://www.rules.senate.gov/rules-of-the-senate: "When a Senator desires to speak, he shall rise and address the Presiding Officer, and shall not proceed until he is recognized, and the Presiding Officer shall recognize the Senator who shall first address him."

135. Riddick and Frumin, *Senate Procedure*, 1091, 1093–94, 1098–99.

136. Ibid.

137. Steven S. Smith, *Party Influence in Congress* (Cambridge: Cambridge University Press, 2007), 77.

138. Ibid., 68, 77–78. Majority leaders can also use the right of prior recognition to prevent amendments, a step called "filling the amendment tree," but this gambit may result in the minority blocking the underlying bill. Barbara Sinclair, "The Senate Leadership Dilemma: Passing Bills and Pursuing Partisan Advantage in a Nonmajoritarian Chamber," in Campbell and Rae, *Contentious Senate*, 86–88.

139. Robert C. Byrd, *The Senate 1789–1989: Addresses on the History of the United States Senate* (Washington, DC: Government Printing Office, 1991), 2:190; see also 106 *CR* 13367 (1960) (quoting Lyndon Johnson: "The majority leader has no real power except the power of recognition."); Tom Daschle and Charles Robbins, *The U.S. Senate* (New York: Thomas Dunne Books, 2013), 65; Trent Lott, *Leading the United States Senate: The Leader's Lecture Series* (Washington, DC: Government Printing Office, 2002), 36 (quoting Howard Baker).

140. Smith, "Parties and Leadership," 256–57; Smith, *Party Influence*, 77.

141. Smith, "Parties and Leadership," 256–57; Smith, *Party Influence*, 77.

142. For a time, even after the "prior recognition" precedent of 1937, the majority leader was thought to share the scheduling function with his party's policy or steering committee. Donald A. Ritchie, *A History of the United States Senate Republican Policy Committee 1947–1997* (Washington, DC: Government Printing Office, 1997), 22, 24–26, 38, 62–63, 68, 115; Kravitz, "Party Organization," 76–78; Smith, "Parties and Leadership," 263–64; Steven S. Smith, "Forces of Change in the Senate Party Leadership and Organization," in *Congress*

Reconsidered, 5th ed., ed. Lawrence C. Dodd and Bruce I. Oppenheimer (Washington, DC: CQ Press, 1993), 273; Steven S. Smith and Gerald Gamm, "Emergence of the Modern Senate: Party Organization, 1937–2002" (paper prepared for the APSA annual meeting, August 29–September 1, 2002), 8; Hugh A. Bone, "An Introduction to the Senate Policy Committees," *APSR* 50 (1956): 339, 349. On the GOP side, when Senator Robert Taft (D-OH) left the Republican Policy Committee to become majority leader in 1953, his vast authority went with him, with long-term negative repercussions for the committee. Malcolm E. Jewell and Samuel C. Patterson, *The Legislative Process in the United States* (New York: Random House, 1966), 150; cf. Ritchie, *History of Republican Policy Committee,* 36–39. The Democratic leader chaired that party's policy committee until 1995. Although it is often prudent for a majority leader to consult his leadership team and membership before acting, he is no longer seen as essentially being required to do so.

143. Smith, *Party Influence,* 68, 77.

144. Kravitz, "Party Organization," 78.

145. Smith, *Party Influence,* 68 (historical "developments [such as prior recognition] initiated the modern regime in which the majority leader assumed responsibility for the Senate's agenda, and had modest tools with which to attempt to do so"). The precedent has been discussed only briefly elsewhere. Neil MacNeil and Richard A. Baker, *The American Senate: An Insider's History* (New York: Oxford University Press, 2013), 198–99; "Floor Leaders Receive Priority Recognition," US Senate, accessed February 15, 2018, https://www.senate.gov/artandhistory/history/minute/Priority_Recognition_of_Floor_Leaders.htm; Michael S. Lynch and Tony Madonna, "The Vice President in the U.S. Senate: Examining the Consequences of Institutional Design" (paper, January 25, 2010), 16–18; Kravitz, "Leadership, New Style," 46–47, 119–20; Riddick and Frumin, *Senate Procedure,* 1091, 1093–94, 1098–99; Gamm and Smith, "Policy Leadership," 304; Smith, "Recent Senate Party Leaders," 274. In the late nineteenth and early twentieth centuries, there was no principle of prior recognition, and determining the order of business could devolve into anarchy, with various senators pursuing their own pet legislative projects. Steven S. Smith and Gerald Gamm, "The Dynamics of Party Government in Congress," in *Congress Reconsidered,* 9th ed., ed. Lawrence C. Dodd and Bruce I. Oppenheimer (Washington, DC: CQ Press, 2009), 154–55; Gerald Gamm and Steven S. Smith, "Steering the Senate: The Consolidation of Senate Party Leadership, 1879–1913," (paper presented at the Congress and History Conference, Massachusetts Institute of Technology, 2003), 13; Gerald Gamm and Steven S. Smith, "The Emergence of Senate Leadership, 1881–1946" (paper presented at the MWPSA annual meeting, April 10–12, 1997), 31–32; Gerald Gamm and Steven S. Smith, "Policy Leadership and the Development of the Modern Senate" (paper presented at the History of Congress Conference, Stanford University, January 15–16, 1999), 12–13.

146. Gamm and Smith, "Policy Leadership" (2002), 298.

147. Ibid., 299–300; see also "Unanimous Consent," US Senate, accessed February 15, 2018, https://www.senate.gov/reference/glossary_term/unanimous_consent.htm.

148. Gamm and Smith, "Policy Leadership" (2002), 298–303.

149. A HeinOnline search of the expression "addressed the chair" from March 1913 (the beginning of Kern's tenure) until August 1937 (the date of the formal prior recognition precedent), and subsequently pared down to instances involving either the majority or minority leader and another senator seeking the floor, provides a good cross section of these procedural "jump balls" for recognition. Some instances are clearer than others, but the overall trends seem clear. From 1913 until 1921, Senate majority leaders had a poor record of receiving rec-

ognition from the chair, succeeding only 20 percent of the time. 52 *CR* 622 (1915) (majority leader Kern not recognized); 53 *CR* 5732 (1916) (Kern not recognized); 53 *CR* 11963 (1916) (Kern not recognized); 56 *CR* 4186 (1918) (majority leader Martin recognized); 56 *CR* 8545 (1915) (Martin recognized); 58 *CR* 325 (1919) (majority leader Lodge not recognized); 58 *CR* 7499 (1919) (Lodge not recognized); 59 *CR* 291 (1920) (Lodge not recognized); 59 *CR* 1535 (1920) (Lodge not recognized); 59 *CR* 1816 (1920) (Lodge not recognized). Beginning in 1921 and lasting until the 1937 precedent, the majority leader was recognized much more regularly, just under 83 percent of the time. 61 *CR* 5722 (1921) (Lodge recognized); 61 *CR* 6526 (1921) (Lodge recognized); 61 *CR* 6653 (1921) (Lodge recognized); 62 *CR* 3413 (Lodge not recognized); 62 *CR* 10901 (1922) (Lodge recognized); 64 *CR* 2873 (1923) (Lodge recognized); 65 *CR* 453 (1923) (Lodge recognized); 65 *CR* 8888 (1924) (Lodge recognized); 66 *CR* 2561 (1925) (majority leader Curtis recognized); 66 *CR* 5131 (1925) (Curtis not recognized); 68 *CR* 5586 (1927) (Curtis recognized); 69 *CR* 1184 (1928) (Curtis recognized); 69 *CR* 2563 (1928) (Curtis recognized); 69 *CR* 5304 (Curtis recognized); 69 *CR* 5864 (1928) (Curtis recognized); 71 *CR* 592 (1929) (majority leader Watson recognized); 71 *CR* 698 (1929) (Watson recognized); 72 *CR* 3589 (1930) (Watson not recognized); 75 *CR* 14467–68 (1932) (Watson recognized); 79 *CR* 14526 (1935) (majority leader Robinson recognized); 80 *CR* 3759 (1936) (Robinson not recognized); 80 *CR* 5225 (1936) (Robinson recognized); 81 *CR* 8173 (1937) (majority leader Barkley recognized).

Unlike majority leaders, who saw a spike in their success rate after 1921, minority leaders' success in securing recognition decreased from 1913 to 1937. From 1913 to 1921, minority leaders gained the floor 50 percent of the time. 51 *CR* 13498 (1914) (minority leader Gallinger recognized); 53 *CR* 1139 (1916) (Gallinger not recognized); 53 *CR* 3462 (1916) (Gallinger not recognized); 53 *CR* 11612 (1916) (Gallinger recognized); 54 *CR* 1055 (1917) (Gallinger recognized); 54 *CR* 1109 (1917) (Gallinger recognized); 55 *CR* 1467 (1917) (Gallinger not recognized); 56 *CR* 1841 (1918) (Gallinger not recognized). The rate declined to slightly below 48 percent from 1921 to 1937. 60 *CR* 2433 (1921) (minority leader Underwood not recognized); 61 *CR* 902 (1921) (Underwood not recognized); 61 *CR* 2744 (1921) (Underwood recognized); 62 *CR* 3413 (1922) (Underwood recognized); 62 *CR* 8370 (1922) (Underwood recognized); 62 *CR* 11153 (1922) (Underwood recognized); 64 *CR* 34 (1922) (Underwood not recognized); 64 *CR* 2866 (1923) (Underwood not recognized); 65 *CR* 979 (1924) (minority leader Robinson not recognized); 66 *CR* 4404 (1925) (Robinson recognized); 68 *CR* 4453–54 (1927) (Robinson recognized); 68 *CR* 5168 (1927) (Robinson recognized); 68 *CR* 5476 (1927) (Robinson not recognized); 75 *CR* 5082 (1932) (Robinson recognized); 76 *CR* 3180 (1933) (Robinson not recognized); 79 *CR* 12727 (1935) (minority leader McNary not recognized); 79 *CR* 13770 (1935) (McNary recognized); 80 *CR* 8401 (1936) (McNary not recognized); 81 *CR* 7112 (1937) (McNary not recognized); 81 *CR* 7112 (1937) (McNary recognized); 81 *CR* 7361 (1937) (McNary not recognized).

One authority's description of the emergence of Senate standing committees seems equally relevant regarding prior recognition: "In this instance, as in many others to be found in the study of the procedure of legislative bodies, the fact preceded the form; the institution . . . was gradually coming into existence before it was formally recognized and named." Ralston Hayden, *The Senate and Treaties, 1789–1817* (New York: Da Capo Press, 1970), 181.

150. William Tyler Page, "Political Organization of Congress Explained," *CD* 1 (1922): 23. There was no Senate parliamentarian at the time. Some news stories from the 1920s support Page's observation that the majority leader received some deference in recognition. "Senate Ends Extra Session: Woodlock Nomination Falls," *WP*, March 19, 1925 ("Adjourn-

ment came late in the afternoon on the peremptory motion of the Republican leader, Senator Curtis, to adjourn sine die, while several senators were on their feet clamoring for recognition"); see also 67 *CR* 371 (1925); "Senate Session Ends in Squabble," *BS,* March 19, 1925; Charles S. Groves, "Heflin, Defeated, Halted in Tirade," *BG,* May 2, 1929; Kravitz, "Leadership, New Style," 46; Gamm and Smith, "Emergence, 1913–1937," 2 n. 1. The authors would like to thank Valerie Heitshusen, Michael Green, and Walter Oleszek for sharing their expertise in this area.

Senator Richard Russell (D-GA), one of the chamber's great authorities on rules and precedents, rightly noted that prior recognition constituted a "time-hallowed custom or tradition or practice" that began prior to Vice President John Nance Garner's tenure in 1933. 110 *CR* 6608 (1964) (Sen. Russell); Kravitz, "Leadership, New Style," 120; cf. Riddick and Frumin, *Senate Procedure,* 1094. However, in 1930, in perhaps the lengthiest treatment of Senate floor leadership up to that time, Thomas Donnelly made no reference to floor leaders enjoying prior recognition, even though he discussed Senate recognition practices in some detail. Donnelly, "Party Leadership," 23, 72–89, 171–72.

151. "When the Sixty-Eighth Congress Convenes," 39 (noting that "this article has been approved by Senator Charles Curtis, Chairman, Senate Committee on Rules, and by Hon. Wm. Tyler Page, Clerk of the House of Representative"). It stated that "the majority and minority floor leaders . . . are usually accorded prior recognition by the Chair." Ibid., 40.

152. 77 *CR* 4149 (1933); see also 77 *CR* 4148 (1933) (quoting Garner: "It is the policy of the Chair to recognize the Senator who is in charge of the legislation pending before the Senate. . . . [I]t is [the vice president's] duty to recognize the Senator in charge of legislation that is pending before the Senate as the unfinished business."). Senator Arthur Robinson (R-IN) maintained that Garner's ruling and recent manner of presiding constituted "in these latter days [a] departure" from traditional practice. 77 *CR* 4149; see also Riddick and Frumin, *Senate Procedure,* 1096. The pronouncement apparently received no academic attention at the time. E. Pendleton Herring, "American Government and Politics: First Session of the Seventy-Third Congress, March 9, 1933 to June 16, 1933," *APSR* 28 (1934): 65–83. For an abortive attempt to establish some sort of prior recognition practice for bill managers seventeen years earlier, see 53 *CR* 2264 (1916) (exchange between the presiding officer and Sen. Fletcher).

153. 77 *CR* 4148, 4149 (1933) (Sen. Robinson); see also Riddick and Frumin, *Senate Procedure,* 1096; MacNeil and Baker, *American Senate,* 198. Garner disputed that he was following House practice. He stated that the vice president "has the right of recognition, and he is going to exercise that right so long as he occupies this position." 77 *CR* 4148 (1933).

At the time of Garner's elevation to vice president, it was indeed House custom for the Speaker to recognize floor leaders and bill managers first if others were also seeking the floor. This was true even though, under House rules and practice at the time, the Speaker enjoyed (and indeed still enjoys) greater discretion in recognizing lawmakers than the vice president in the Senate. Barely a week before becoming vice president, and only three months before his first Senate pronouncement on prior recognition, Speaker Garner stated from the House chair, "The usual custom is that the Member who reports the legislation coming before the House is the one the Chair ordinarily recognizes. . . . The Speaker would recognize the gentleman who has been directed by the committee to report the bill. . . . The Chair will recognize the gentleman who reported [the bill]." 76 *CR* 4913 (1933); see also Clarence Cannon, *Cannon's Precedents of the House of Representatives of the United States* (Washington, DC: Government Printing Office, 1935), 6:445. For other related precedents, see 43 *CR* 583–584 (1909) (Rep. Olmsted):

The Speaker's eye is controlled and his vision directed, not merely by the written rules, but also by what may be termed the "common law" of the House. In very many matters he is by the unwritten rule bound to recognize the minority leader in preference to any other Member on that side of the House, although they may all be upon their feet clamoring to be heard. He would consider himself equally bound to recognize . . . the leader of the majority upon the floor. In the case of a bill coming from any committee he would recognize the chairman or other committee member reporting the bill before any other Member. . . . He would next recognize the ranking Member of the minority party upon that committee.

Cf. 38 *CR* 388–89 (1904) (Rep. Robinson); Asher C. Hinds, *Hinds' Precedents of the House of Representatives of the United States* (Washington, DC: Government Printing Office, 1907), 2:923–32; *Cannon's Precedents,* 6:441, 443, 444.

154. 79 *CR* 3609 (1935) (quoting Sen. Pittman): "[The senator] in charge of the joint resolution now before the Senate . . . is entitled to recognition by the Chair. It has been the practice for many years that the Senator in charge of the bill under consideration should be recognized when he asked for recognition." See also Riddick and Frumin, *Senate Procedure,* 1096; FMRP, boxes WS14–WS18, WS24.

155. Riddick and Frumin, *Senate Procedure,* 1096.

156. Kravitz, "Leadership, New Style," 46–47; Ritchie, "Barkley," 133–34.

157. Kravitz, "Leadership, New Style," 46–47; Patterson, *Congressional Conservatism,* 156–57; Ritchie, "Barkley," 133–34; Dewey L. Fleming, "Anti-Lynch Bill Further Jams Senate Wheels," *BS,* August 12, 1937, 1; "The Congress: Hell & Close Harmony," *Time,* August 23, 1937; "Congress: Home Calls Democrats, 'Must' Bills Die, and the Split Widens," *Newsweek,* August 21, 1937; Turner Catledge, "Legislation Tied Up," *NYT,* August 12, 1937. The presiding officer's use of recognition lists to schedule speakers was not new in 1937. 54 *CR* 5012–13 (1917) (remarks by Sen. La Follette Sr.). The practice continued for a considerable time thereafter. 110 *CR* 6608 (1964); see also Riddick and Frumin, *Senate Procedure,* 1094.

158. Davis, *Barkley,* 42–43.

159. Patterson, *Congressional Conservatism,* 156–57; Catledge, "Legislation Tied Up"; Fleming, "Anti-Lynch Bill."

160. Patterson, *Congressional Conservatism,* 156–57; Libbey, *Dear Alben,* 75; Davis, *Barkley,* 42–46; Ritchie, "Barkley," 133; Libbey, *Barkley,* 191.

161. 81 *CR* 8694 (1937); see also Patterson, *Congressional Conservatism,* 156–57; Ritchie, "Barkley," 133. For more on Barkley's civil rights record, see Libbey, *Barkley,* 256–57; Davis, *Barkley,* 317.

162. 81 *CR* 8694 (1937); see also Ritchie, "Barkley," 133; Davis, *Barkley,* 43.

163. Catledge, "Legislation Tied Up."

164. 81 *CR* 8695–8696; Ritchie, "Barkley," 133; Libbey, *Barkley,* 191.

165. 81 *CR* 8696 (1937); see also Ritchie, "Barkley," 133; Libbey, *Barkley,* 191.

166. 81 *CR* 8696–8697 (1937); see also Ritchie, "Barkley," 133; Libbey, *Barkley,* 191; Davis, *Barkley,* 44; Fleming, "Anti-Lynch Bill."

167. Ritchie, "Barkley," 133–34.

168. Libbey, *Barkley,* 191; Ritchie, "Barkley," 133–34; Davis, *Barkley,* 45–46.

169. Ritchie, "Barkley," 134; Davis, *Barkley,* 44; Libbey, *Barkley,* 191.

170. Libbey, *Barkley,* 191; Libbey, *Dear Alben,* 75. Barkley recalled: "When John Garner was vice president and I became majority leader, he insisted that I come to his office

every day at least a quarter of an hour before the Senate would meet to tell him what my program was so that he'd know when I rose for recognition what my object was. . . . [A]ll during Garner's eight years, he did that with Joe Robinson in the first place and with me. And we worked very harmoniously because he knew what my program was and I knew how he felt about it." Interview with Alben W. Barkley, July 22, 1953, Alben W. Barkley Oral History Project, LBNCOH, accessed February 15, 2018, https://kentuckyoralhistory.org/catalog/xt7vdn3ztj40 (hereafter Barkley Oral History No. 7); see also Libbey, *Barkley,* 191. He further recollected:

> When I became majority leader, the first thing John Garner said to me, he said, "Now, you're majority leader. . . . It's your job to help carry the program of the administration, and while my rulings will always be impartial on parliamentary questions and on any other question that is presented to me while I'm presiding over the Senate, you and I really constitute a team, the pitcher and the catcher. You're the pitcher and I'm the catcher. . . . I want to know what your program is each day before the session begins so that I will not be ignorant as to what your moves are and what your motions are to be, whether you want to be recognized and so on." Well, during the rest of his term he and I worked together in great harmony. . . . he didn't hesitate to make rulings, and he did them positively. . . . I always went into his office fifteen minutes before the Senate met, because he wanted me to do that, and I wanted to do it, so as to tell him what my program was as majority leader for the day so he'd know what it would be and he could cooperate.

Interview with Alben W. Barkley, July 25, 1953, Alben W. Barkley Oral History Project, LBNCOH, accessed February 15, 2018, https://kentuckyoralhistory.org/catalog/xt712j684361 (hereafter Barkley Oral History No. 13); see also Barkley, *That Reminds Me,* 158; Davis, *Barkley,* 40.

Barkley had less success in this regard with Henry Wallace, who did not regularly preside. The practice was revived when Harry Truman became vice president. Barkley, *That Reminds Me,* 196–97; Davis, *Barkley,* 168; interview with Alben Barkley, reel 5, side 2, p. 22, Alben Barkley Papers, Harry S. Truman Library.

171. 81 *CR* 8836 (1937); 81 *CR* 8838–39 (1937); Turner Catledge, "Cotton Loan Truce Speeds Congress," *NYT,* August 14, 1937. In modern practice, the Senate majority leader simply seeks recognition and then moves to proceed to bills on his own. See notes 201 and 355. The attempt by Garner and Barkley to use the illegitimate "farming out" process to indirectly proceed to leadership-approved measures seems like an evolutionary middle point between what had been the traditional practice of bill managers and committee chairmen moving to proceed to favored bills on their own accord and the modern-day practice whereby the majority leader moves to proceed on virtually all matters. This evolutionary process is perhaps reflected by the earlier occasional use of the term "floor leader" or "leader" to denote what would be considered a bill manager in today's parlance. Brown, *Leadership of Congress,* 258 (historically, "a Senator in charge of a bill was always the Floor Leader," and there existed "the power of any Member to call up a bill at any time"); see also 60 *CR* 2059 (1921) (referring to Sen. Simmons as "the minority leader on this particular legislation"); 60 *CR* 2433 (1921) (referring to Sen. Simmons as "the minority leader on this measure"); 61 *CR* 1018 (1921) (referring to Sen. Simmons as "the minority leader on this legislation"); 61 *CR* 5829 (1921) (referring to Sen. Simmons as "the minority leader in charge of the bill"); 41 *CR* 1270 (1907); cf. Donnelly, "Party Leadership," 74.

172. 81 *CR* 8839–40 (Sen. La Follette).

173. At the time, "farming out" the floor was not viewed as acceptable Senate practice. 45 *CR* 3271, 3274–75 (1910); 50 *CR* 1430 (1913); 51 *CR* 5175 (1914); see also Haynes, *Senate*, 384–85. Indeed, today this episode is cited to support the proposition that such a practice violates Senate rules. Riddick and Frumin, *Senate Procedure*, 1094.

174. 81 *CR* 8839–40 (1937) (Sen. La Follette); Charles Cooke, "The Man Who Tells Senators How to Behave," *WS*, May 25, 1952 ("'Young Bob [La Follette] was practically brought up in the Senate chamber,' said Charlie Watkins. Then he added the highest praise the parliamentarian of the United States Senate could possibly bestow: 'Young Bob' he said, 'knew Senate procedure.'").

175. 81 *CR* 8840 (1937).

176. Ibid., 8839–40.

177. Ibid.

178. Ibid.; see also Riddick and Frumin, *Senate Procedure*, 1094.

179. 81 *CR* 8839 (1937) (Garner).

180. 81 *CR* 8839–40 (1937). Barkley's defense of Garner's actions implied that prior recognition was already a tradition. He stated, "from time immemorial it has been the custom late in the afternoon for the Senator in charge of the program to obtain the floor and then yield to other Senators to call up bills which were not controversial." Ibid., 8840. Interestingly, the vice president's explanation did not indicate that floor leaders should necessarily be recognized before bill managers. Ibid., 8839–40; see also 83 *CR* 1062 (1938); FMRP, boxes WS14–WS18, WS24.

181. 81 *CR* 8839–40 (1937) (Sen. La Follette) ("Of course, I have no objection to the Vice President recognizing the Senator from Kentucky"). Rare contemporary press reports of Vice President Garner's pronouncement include Catledge, "Cotton Loan"; Robert C. Albright, "Farm 'Deal' by Roosevelt Paves Way to Adjournment," *WP*, August 14, 1937. This procedural ruling was overshadowed not only by the Wagner gambit and the backlog of legislation but also by Hugo Black's controversial nomination to the Supreme Court. Franklyn Waltman, "'Dark-Horse' Nomination of Alabaman Facing Study," *WP*, August 13, 1937.

182. 81 *CR* 8839–40 (1937); Catledge, "Cotton Loan," 6; see also 84 *CR* 10738 (1939) (Vice President Garner stating that he would recognize a senator to bring up a bill at the request of majority leader Barkley).

183. 81 *CR* 8840 (1937).

184. Ibid. (quoting Garner: "The Senator from Wisconsin is absolutely correct that the Senator from Kentucky cannot farm out his time. However, the Chair would have recognized the Senator from Nevada upon the suggestion of the Senator from Kentucky."). Barkley himself conceded that he had "no desire to farm out the right to be recognized on the floor." Ibid.

185. Ibid. (quoting Garner: through either approach, "the result is about the same").

186. Ibid. (quoting La Follette: "the result is not the same for all Senators are not given an equal opportunity to address the Chair and seek recognition from the Chair").

187. Barkley Oral History No. 13 ("By reason of his long experience in the House, his knowledge of parliamentary law, and his experience as speaker of the House of Representatives, he was a very efficient vice president. . . . [I]n the efficient conduct of the vice presidential office, as presiding officer [Garner] made as efficient and as valuable . . . a vice president as any man within my recollection."). See also Timmons, *Garner*, 185–87, 195; "Roosevelt's Plea Ignored on Sugar," *NYT*, August 13, 1937; "Senate in 59 Minutes Votes

Changes in Lower Courts; Session End by Aug 21 Seen: A Coup by Garner," *NYT,* August 8, 1937; Turner Catledge, "Balk Drive to Pass Tax Bill in a Hurry," *NYT,* August 19, 1937; Lynch and Madonna, "Vice President," 17; Catledge, "Cotton Loan." Garner described his efforts to expedite the Senate as a "buggy whip" approach. Betty K. Koed, "Senate Historical Minute, Cactus Jack Presides" (on file with the authors). In later years, Garner admitted that he was not completely impartial in using the presiding officer's power of recognition. Timmons, *Garner,* 186.

188. Turner Catledge, "Senate Is Startled," *NYT,* August 13, 1937.

189. Lynch and Madonna, "Vice President," 17.

190. Catledge, "Senate Startled"; Lionel V. Patenaude, "Garner, Sumners, and Connally: The Defeat of the Roosevelt Court Bill in 1937," *SWHQ* 74 (1970): 36, 50; Barkley Oral History, reel 4, side 2, p. 21, Barkley Papers, Truman Library.

191. As noted earlier, both Garner and Barkley ultimately conceded that farming out was not an appropriate process under the rules. 81 *CR* 8840 (1937).

192. The genuine friendship between the two men probably was not irrelevant either. Barkley Oral History No. 13 ("We [Garner and I] were great personal friends, and I think there was a mutual admiration between us which still exists. . . . [O]ur wives became great friends, and so forth. . . . [He is] a great personal friend.").

193. For example, 83 *CR* 1033–62 (1938).

194. Ibid., 1062; see also FMRP, boxes WS14–WS18, WS24. There is a logic to granting prior recognition only to floor leaders and bill managers, based on the linkage between the two sets of senators and their close relationship to the Senate's consideration of floor business. Floor leaders are responsible in a broad sense for the flow of legislative business, and bill managers are responsible for the matter immediately at hand.

195. 83 *CR* 2202 (1938); see also Riddick and Frumin, *Senate Procedure,* 1094.

196. 83 *CR* 2202 (1938).

197. One authority discussed the mishap that preceded Garner's ruling and commented about "procedural novel[ties]," but he made no specific mention of prior recognition. O. R. Altman, "First Session of the Seventy-Fifth Congress," *APSR* 31 (1937): 1071, 1078–80. Alternatively, he could have been referring to the "farming out" practice.

It took some time before this ruling and the proposition it embodies—that the majority leader enjoys prior recognition—were acknowledged in authoritative works on Senate procedure. George Haynes, in his magisterial history of the Senate, made no mention of the Garner-Barkley precedent, the custom of prior recognition that preceded it, or the 1933 and 1935 rulings about bill managers. This was the case even though his work was originally published a year after the 1937 precedent. Haynes, *Senate,* 383–85, 480–82. Neither the precedent nor the preexisting custom was included in a 1939 article on Senate procedure. Col. E. A. Halsey, "Procedure in the Senate," *CD* 18 (1939): 122–23. Likewise, the precedent was omitted from three books written in the 1940s and early 1950s by close Senate observer and future Senate parliamentarian Floyd Riddick. Floyd M. Riddick, *Congressional Procedure* (Boston: Chapman & Grimes, 1941), 308–9, 311; Floyd M. Riddick, *The United States Congress: Organization and Procedure* (Washington, DC: National Capitol Publishers, 1949), 80; George H. E. Smith and Floyd M. Riddick, *Congress in Action (How a Bill Becomes a Law),* 3d ed. (Washington, DC: National Capitol Publishers, 1953), 39. Indeed, two decades after the ruling, the Senate parliamentarians failed to mention the precedent, although, interestingly, they did refer to bill managers receiving prior recognition. Charles L. Watkins and Floyd M. Riddick, *Senate Procedure: Precedents and Practice* (Washington, DC: Government

Printing Office, 1958), 468–70. Not until the 1964 edition of the treatise was the majority leader's authority cited. Charles L. Watkins and Floyd M. Riddick, *Senate Procedure: Precedents and Practices* (Washington, DC: Government Printing Office, 1964), 536: "In 1937, the Vice President announced a policy of giving priority of recognition to the majority and minority leaders when they were on their feet seeking recognition." Subsequent editions have also acknowledged the precedent. Floyd M. Riddick, *Senate Procedure: Precedents and Practices* (Washington, DC: Government Printing Office, 1974), 674; Floyd M. Riddick, *Senate Procedure: Precedents and Practices* (Washington, DC: Government Printing Office, 1981), 878–83; Riddick and Frumin, *Senate Procedure,* 1091, 1093–94, 1098–99.

198. Barkley's comments as vice president are as follows:

THE VICE PRESIDENT. The Senator from Tennessee, who is in charge of the conference report, was on his feet earlier in the evening. The Chair thinks that if the Senator has recognition—
MR. MCFARLAND [the majority leader]. Mr. President—
MR. MCKELLAR. I yield to the Senator from Arizona.
MR. MCFARLAND. I was on my feet asking for recognition. The Chair does not have any right to say who is going to get the floor.
THE VICE PRESIDENT. The Senator from Arizona knows it is the custom for the Chair to recognize those who are in charge of a bill or a conference report.
MR. MCFARLAND. Yes; and it is also the custom to recognize the majority leader when he rises to ask recognition.
THE VICE PRESIDENT. The Chair recognizes the Senator from Arizona.
MR. MCFARLAND. Very well. I thank the Chair.
THE VICE PRESIDENT. The Senator from Arizona is welcome.

98 *CR* 9567 (1952). For a similar example of Barkley apparently ignoring the principle of prior recognition while vice president, see 96 *CR* 12872 (1950).

It is unclear whether this exchange indicates that the precedent regarding prior recognition for the majority leader was not yet firmly recognized, that Barkley was unaware of the precedent, or that he simply mishandled the situation. Barkley was known to make mistakes as presiding officer and to operate from time to time irrespective of precedent. Floyd M. Riddick, Senate parliamentarian, 1964–1974, Oral History Interview No. 3, July 12, 1978, 67, US Senate, accessed February 15, 2018, http://www.senate.gov/artandhistory/history/resources/pdf/Riddick_interview_3.pdf. There are examples from Barkley's time as majority leader when he was not assertive in claiming his own right of prior recognition. 91 *CR* 679 (1945); Harry S. Truman, *Memoirs of Harry S. Truman: Year of Decisions* (New York: Da Capo Press, 1986), 195.

199. Barkley Oral History No. 7. He omitted any reference to prior recognition in both his memoirs and a 1949 book chapter on the majority leader's office. Alben W. Barkley, "The Majority Leader in the Legislative Process," in *The Process of Government*, ed. Simeon S. Wells et al. (Lexington: Bureau of Government Research, University of Kentucky, 1949), 36–48. Garner's biographer does not discuss the ruling, and the Garner papers do not include any documentation on it; neither do Barkley's papers or Wagner's papers.

200. Smith, *Party Influence*, 77–78.

201. Riddick, *Majority and Minority Leaders,* 3–4, 19, 23; cf. Byrd, *Senate,* 187; Munk, "Origin and Development" (1970), 147, 332; Andrew J. Glass, "Mike Mansfield, Majority Leader," in *Change and Party Leadership,* ed. Norman J. Ornstein (New York: Praeger, 1975),

147. Today, the majority leader or his designee almost exclusively makes motions to proceed. Richard S. Beth and Mark J. Oleszek, "Motions to Proceed to Consider Measures in the Senate: Who Offers Them?" *CRS Report to Congress,* May 18, 2015; Senate Resolution No. 8, 107th Cong., 1st sess. (January 5, 2001); Robert A. Caro, *Master of the Senate* (New York: Alfred A. Knopf, 2002), 582–84.

The scheduling function exercised by Democratic majority leaders preceded prior recognition but was later reinforced by it. Gerald Gamm and Steven S. Smith, "The Rise of Floor Leaders in the United States Senate, 1890–1915" (paper prepared for the Conference on the US Senate, Oxford University, April 2–3, 2005), 22.

202. This exchange is illustrative:

Mr. Javits and Mr. Johnson of Texas addressed the chair.
The Presiding Officer. The Senator from New York.
Mr. Johnson of Texas. Mr. President, I addressed the Chair.
Mr. Javits. I yield, of course, to the majority leader.
Mr. Johnson of Texas. No, I do not want recognition under those circumstances.

106 *CR* 6955 (1960); see also 103 *CR* 11454 (1957). The authors would like to thank Elizabeth MacDonough for identifying this exchange.

203. See note 149.

204. See note 149.

205. Compare majority leader citations in note 149 with 83 *CR* 1213 (1938) (majority leader Barkley recognized); 84 *CR* 943 (1939) (Barkley recognized); 84 *CR* 6576 (1939) (Barkley recognized); 84 *CR* 8131 (1939) (Barkley recognized); 85 *CR* 924 (1939) (Barkley recognized); 86 *CR* 2441 (1940) (Barkley recognized); 87 *CR* 1971 (1941) (Barkley not recognized); 88 *CR* 4172 (1942) (Barkley recognized); 88 *CR* 8897–98 (1942) (Barkley recognized); 91 *CR* 679 (1945) (Barkley recognized); 91 *CR* 6918 (1945) (Barkley recognized); 91 *CR* 6926 (1945) (Barkley recognized); 91 *CR* 7053 (1945) (Barkley recognized); 92 *CR* 3550 (1946) (Barkley recognized); 92 *CR* 5522 (1946) (Barkley not recognized); 92 *CR* 5522 (1946) (Barkley not recognized); 92 *CR* 5522 (1946) (Barkley recognized); 92 *CR* 5723 (1946) (Barkley recognized); 92 *CR* 5813 (1946) (Barkley recognized); 95 *CR* 847 (1949) (majority leader Lucas recognized); 95 *CR* 864 (1949) (Lucas recognized); 95 *CR* 1569–70 (1949) (Lucas recognized); 95 *CR* 3596 (1949) (Lucas not recognized); 95 *CR* 3835 (1949) (Lucas recognized); 95 *CR* 13351 (1949) (Lucas not recognized); 95 *CR* 14081 (1949) (Lucas recognized); 96 *CR* 2066 (1950) (Lucas recognized); 96 *CR* 7197 (1950) (Lucas recognized); 96 *CR* 8731 (1950) (Lucas recognized); 96 *CR* 9750 (1950) (Lucas recognized); 96 *CR* 11782 (1950) (Lucas not recognized); 96 *CR* 11783 (1950) (Lucas recognized); 96 *CR* 12872 (1950) (Lucas not recognized); 96 *CR* 16059 (1950) (Lucas recognized); 97 *CR* 3104 (1951) (majority leader McFarland recognized); 97 *CR* 4175–76 (1951) (McFarland recognized); 98 *CR* 1574 (1952) (McFarland recognized); 98 *CR* 1726 (1952) (McFarland recognized); 98 *CR* 2512 (1952) (McFarland recognized); 98 *CR* 6439 (1952) (McFarland recognized); 98 *CR* 6606 (1952) (McFarland not recognized); 98 *CR* 6607 (1952) (McFarland recognized); 102 *CR* 14675 (1956) (majority leader Johnson recognized); 103 *CR* 2091 (1957) (Johnson recognized); 103 *CR* 7849 (1957) (Johnson recognized); 103 *CR* 11454 (1957) (Johnson recognized); 104 *CR* 4876 (1958) (Johnson recognized); 104 *CR* 4878 (1958) (Johnson recognized); 104 *CR* 18687 (1958) (Johnson not recognized); 104 *CR* 18750 (1958) (Johnson recognized); 104 *CR* 19163 (1958) (Johnson recognized); 105 *CR* 3583 (1959) (Johnson recognized); 105 *CR* 13995 (1959) (Johnson recognized); 105 *CR* 19325 (1959) (Johnson recognized); 106 *CR*

3412 (1960) (Johnson recognized); 106 *CR* 5994 (1960) (Johnson recognized); 106 *CR* 6814 (1960) (Johnson recognized); 106 *CR* 6955 (1960) (Johnson not recognized); 106 *CR* 8894 (1960) (Johnson recognized); 106 *CR* 17832 (1960) (Johnson recognized). As noted before, not all these instances are equally clear, but the trend is evident. These citations reflect a HeinOnline search of "addressed the chair" from August 1937 to January 1961 involving the majority leader.

206. Compare minority leader citations in note 149 with 83 *CR* 1062 (1938) (minority leader McNary recognized); 83 *CR* 1818 (1938) (McNary recognized); 84 *CR* 6576 (1939) (McNary not recognized because majority leader Barkley obtained the floor); 86 *CR* 1155 (1940) (McNary recognized); 87 *CR* 8700 (1941) (McNary recognized); 87 *CR* 9832 (1941) (McNary recognized); 89 *CR* 3689 (1943) (McNary not recognized); 89 *CR* 3767 (1943) (McNary recognized); 89 *CR* 6824–25 (1943) (McNary not recognized); 92 *CR* 81 (1946) (minority leader White not recognized); 92 *CR* 7438 (1946) (White not recognized); 93 *CR* 5939 (1947) (minority leader Barkley recognized); 94 *CR* 8071 (1948) (Barkley not recognized); 94 *CR* 8558 (1948) (Barkley recognized); 95 *CR* 2414 (1949) (minority leader Wherry recognized); 95 *CR* 11242 (1949) (Wherry recognized); 96 *CR* 1944 (1950) (Wherry recognized); 96 *CR* 15345 (1950) (Wherry recognized); 96 *CR* 10171 (1950) (Wherry recognized); 97 *CR* 867 (1951) (Wherry recognized); 97 *CR* 3104 (1951) (Wherry not recognized because majority leader McFarland obtained the floor); 97 *CR* 4175–76 (1951) (Wherry not recognized because majority leader McFarland obtained the floor); 97 *CR* 8920 (1951) (Wherry not recognized); 100 *CR* 14215 (1954) (minority leader Johnson recognized); 102 *CR* 8801 (1956) (minority leader Knowland recognized); 102 *CR* 10636 (1956) (Knowland recognized); 102 *CR* 13715 (1956) (Knowland recognized); 103 *CR* 9780 (1957) (Knowland recognized); 104 *CR* 3236 (1958) (Knowland recognized); 105 *CR* 17325 (1959) (minority leader Dirksen recognized); 105 *CR* 17329 (1959) (Dirksen recognized); 106 *CR* 994 (1960) (Dirksen recognized); 106 *CR* 5994 (1960) (Dirksen recognized); 106 *CR* 7435 (1960) (Dirksen recognized); 106 *CR* 12689 (1960) (Dirksen recognized). The HeinOnline methodology is the same as earlier, although the percentage figure omits instances when the minority leader did not secure the floor because the majority leader was recognized.

207. Smith, *Party Influence,* 68.

208. For examples of Barkley's difficulty controlling his conference, see David L. Porter, *Congress and the Waning of the New Deal* (Port Washington, NY: Kennikat Press, 1980), 84, 101; Ritchie, "Barkley," 129, 132–34.

209. Swain, *Harrison,* 178–80; Richie, "Barkley," 134–36; Libbey, *Barkley,* 191.

210. With the exception of nominations and certain types of legislation (e.g., budget matters), Senate rules and practice typically require 60 votes to proceed to consideration of a measure and 60 votes to pass it.

211. Libbey, *Dear Alben,* 75–76; Ritchie, "Barkley," 133.

212. Ritchie, "Barkley," 134–35; Swain, *Harrison,* 193; Patterson, *Congressional Conservatism,* 232.

213. Patterson, *Congressional Conservatism,* 146–48, 151, 154, 304.

214. Ibid., 304; Swain, *Harrison,* 162–94, 249; Davis, *Barkley,* 37, 46.

215. Davis, *Barkley,* 37; Ritchie, "Barkley," 129; Libbey, *Barkley,* 195.

216. Ritchie, "Barkley," 129, 132–34.

217. Ibid.

218. "Washington Correspondents Name Ablest Congressman in Life Poll," *Life,* March 20, 1939; see also Ritchie, "Barkley," 134–35.

219. "Washington Correspondents Name Ablest"; Ritchie, "Barkley," 134–35.

220. Swain, *Harrison*, 194.

221. Ritchie, "Barkley," 139.

222. Ibid., 140.

223. Earl L. Shoup, *The Government of the American People* (Boston: Ginn, 1946), 450.

224. Daschle and Robbins, *Senate*, 64–65.

225. Riddick, *Majority and Minority Leaders*, 15 (quoting Lyndon Johnson: "the only real power available to the leader is the power of persuasion"); Daschle and Robbins, *Senate*, 65–66 ("A Leader must employ a whole spectrum of persuasive options, from plain reason to politics, emotion, personal relationships, threats, to even using surrogates"); Walter J. Oleszek, Mark J. Oleszek, Elizabeth Rybicki, and Bill Heniff Jr., *Congressional Procedures and the Policy Process*, 10th ed. (Los Angeles: Sage/CQ Press, 2016), 19 (quoting George Mitchell: "What influence I have is based upon . . . respect and reasoned persuasion and some sensitivity to the political and other concerns of individual Senators"); Lott, *Leading*, 36 (quoting Howard Baker: "the right of prior recognition under the precedent of the Senate and the conceded right to schedule the Senate's business . . . together with the reliability of his commitment and whatever power of personal persuasion one brings to the job, are all the tools a Senate leader has"); Trent Lott, *Herding Cats: A Life in Politics* (New York: Harper-Collins, 2005), 78 ("The art of government . . . involve[s] equal parts patience, persistence, and persuasion"). It has been argued that the "power to persuade" is pivotal to the success of other high government officials as well. Richard E. Neustadt, *Presidential Power and the Modern Presidents* (New York: Free Press, 1990), 28–49.

226. Jewell and Patterson, *Legislative Process*, 171; MacNeil and Baker, *American Senate*, 203.

227. Walter L. Hixson, "The 1938 Kentucky Senate Election: Alben W. Barkley, 'Happy' Chandler, and the New Deal," *RKHS* 80 (1982): 309, 321–22.

228. Ibid., 321; Libbey, *Barkley*, 197–98.

229. Hixson, "1938 Kentucky Senate," 321; Libbey, *Barkley*, 197–98.

230. Hixson, "1938 Kentucky Senate," 321–22; Libbey, *Barkley*, 197–98.

231. Barkley, *That Reminds Me*, 166; Davis, *Barkley*, 67; Hixson, "1938 Kentucky Senate," 321–22; Libbey, *Barkley*, 197–98.

232. Hixson, "1938 Kentucky Senate," 321–22; Barkley, *That Reminds Me*, 166; Libbey, *Barkley*, 197–98; Davis, *Barkley*, 67. Chandler had a much different recollection of events. Happy Chandler with Vance Trimble, *Heroes, Plain Folks, and Skunks: The Life and Times of Happy Chandler* (Chicago: Bonus Books, 1989), 136–37.

233. Libbey, *Barkley*, 198.

234. Hixson, "1938 Kentucky Senate," 322.

235. Ibid.

236. Barkley, *That Reminds Me*, 162; Lowell H. Harrison and James C. Klotter, *A New History of Kentucky* (Lexington: University Press of Kentucky, 1997), 369; Libbey, *Dear Alben*, 80.

237. Libbey, *Dear Alben*, 80. The head of Louisville's police force dubbed the alleged poisoning "a political bedtime story." Libbey, *Barkley*, 199. At campaign stops, Barkley turned the tables on Chandler by making a big show of drinking a glass of water. Barkley, *That Reminds Me*, 164.

238. Libbey, *Dear Alben*, 80–81.

239. Electoral defeat of Senate floor leaders has been a relatively rare occurrence. The

only other Senate majority leaders to lose their bids for reelection are Scott Lucas in 1950, Ernest McFarland in 1952, and Tom Daschle in 2004. Barkley avoided becoming the first Senate majority leader to lose in a primary.

240. Ritchie, "Barkley," 140; Davis, *Barkley*, 120.

241. Ritchie, "Barkley," 140–41; Libbey, *Barkley*, 207–8, 213–17, 221; Davis, *Barkley*, 99–108.

242. Patterson, *Congressional Conservatism*, 337; Libby, *Barkley*, 212, 221–22.

243. Ritchie, "Barkley," 135.

244. Ibid.

245. Ibid., 141; Libbey, *Barkley*, 221–22.

246. Woodrow Wilson, *Congressional Government* (New York: Meridian Books, 1956), 198.

247. Davis, *Barkley*, 108–10.

248. Ibid., 109–10.

249. Ibid., 197–98, 204; Ritchie, "Barkley," 150–51; Libbey, *Barkley*, 242; Libbey, *Dear Alben*, 90–91.

250. "Alben Barkley," in *Current Biography: Who's News and Why*, ed. Anna Rothe (New York: H. W. Wilson, 1949), 28; "Joint Committee on the Investigation of the Pearl Harbor Attack," US Senate, accessed February 15, 2018, https://www.senate.gov /artandhistory/history/common/investigations/PearlHarbor.htm; Ritchie, "Barkley," 150–51; Davis, *Barkley*, 198; Barkley, *That Reminds Me*, 266; Libby, *Barkley*, 242–43.

251. Libbey, *Barkley*, 243; see also "Barkley," in *Current Biography*, 28; Davis, *Barkley*, 197–207.

252. Ritchie, "Barkley," 151; Davis, *Barkley*, 206; Barkley, *That Reminds Me*, 264–65. Barkley led another important oversight initiative related to the war. At the request of Generals George Marshall and Dwight Eisenhower, he headed a delegation of lawmakers that inspected Nazi concentration camps immediately following their liberation. Libbey, *Barkley*, 237–38; Barkley, *That Reminds Me*, 266. The Barkley-written Senate report helped document the horrors of the Holocaust. Libbey, *Barkley*, 237–38.

253. Ripley, *Power*, 75–76. Other examples of poor relationships between presidents and Senate leaders of the same party include Herbert Hoover and James Watson (R-IN), Richard Nixon and Hugh Scott (R-PA), Jimmy Carter and Robert Byrd (D-WV), and George W. Bush and Trent Lott (R-MS). Munk, "Origin and Development" (1970), 276–77; Smith, "Forces of Change," 278; MacNeil and Baker, *American Senate*, 214; Robert L. Peabody, "Senate Party Leadership from the 1950s to the 1980s," in *Understanding Congressional Leadership*, ed. Frank H. Mackaman (Washington, DC: CQ Press, 1981), 82, 94–95; Davidson, "Senate Leaders," 245; Norman J. Ornstein, Robert L. Peabody, and David W. Rohde, "Change in the Senate: Toward the 1990s," in *Congress Reconsidered*, 4th ed., ed. Lawrence C. Dodd and Bruce I. Oppenheimer (Washington, DC: CQ Press, 1989), 25. Majority leader Robert Byrd once famously said of President Jimmy Carter: "I am the president's friend; I am not the President's man." Janet Hook, "The Byrd Years: Surviving in a Media Age through Details and Diligence," *CQ Weekly*, April 16, 1988, 977.

254. Malcolm E. Jewell, *Senatorial Politics and Foreign Policy* (Lexington: University of Kentucky Press, 1962), 55, 59, 61, 63, 65, 81.

255. Ibid., 63–64; Don Oberdorfer, *Senator Mansfield: The Extraordinary Life of a Great American Statesman and Diplomat* (Washington, DC: Smithsonian Books, 2003), 266.

256. Jewell, *Senatorial Politics*, 64.

257. Ibid. Mike Mansfield opposed President Lyndon Johnson's foreign policy in Southeast Asia, but he did so privately. Oberdorfer, *Mansfield,* 266–347.

258. Barkley, *That Reminds Me,* 30; cf. Libbey, *Barkley,* 224–25.

259. Barkley, *That Reminds Me,* 30.

260. Ibid.

261. Ibid.

262. Ibid.

263. Ibid.

264. Ibid.

265. Ritchie, "Barkley," 129, 143; Libbey, *Barkley,* 224–25.

266. Ritchie, "Barkley," 143; Libbey, *Dear Alben,* 86.

267. Libbey, *Dear Alben,* 85; Libbey, *Barkley,* 229; Davis, *Barkley,* 138. For more on this episode, see Davis, *Barkley,* 137–55.

268. Ritchie, "Barkley," 145; Davis, *Barkley,* 138–40; Libbey, *Dear Alben,* 85–86.

269. Libbey, *Barkley,* 229; Libbey, *Dear Alben,* 85–86; Ritchie, "Barkley," 145; Davis, *Barkley,* 138.

270. Ritchie, "Barkley," 145; Davis, *Barkley,* 140; Libbey, *Barkley,* 229.

271. Libbey, *Barkley,* 229–30; Ritchie, "Barkley," 145; Davis, *Barkley,* 138–41; Libbey, *Dear Alben,* 85–86.

272. Allen Drury, *A Senate Journal: 1943–1945* (New York: McGraw-Hill, 1963), 86, 87; Libbey, *Barkley,* 230; Ritchie, "Barkley," 145–46; Barkley, *That Reminds Me,* 172–73.

273. Barkley, *That Reminds Me,* 172.

274. Ibid., 173.

275. Ibid. Sometime afterward, Kentuckian Ed Prichard claimed that he had coauthored the controversial statement. Ritchie, "Barkley," 147.

276. Ritchie, "Barkley," 129, 143, 145–46.

277. Ibid., 146; Barkley, *That Reminds Me,* 173–74; Libbey, *Dear Alben,* 86. Journalist Allen Drury described Barkley as being "in a cold fury." Drury, *Senate Journal,* 86; see also Barkley, *That Reminds Me,* 173.

278. Barkley, *That Reminds Me,* 174; Ritchie, "Barkley," 146.

279. Libbey, *Dear Alben,* 86.

280. 90 *CR* 1966 (1944).

281. Ibid.; see also Ritchie, "Barkley," 147. For a firsthand account of the dramatic events, see Drury, *Senate Journal,* 85–97.

282. Barkley, *That Reminds Me,* 173. Indeed, Barkley referred to himself in his memoirs as "the Administration's floor leader." Ibid. The conflict over the tax bill was not Barkley's only break with FDR. Barkley opposed the president on a veterans' bill in 1936, and he split with FDR on the need to reduce government relief funding in 1939. Kravitz, "Leadership, New Style," 48; Libbey, *Barkley,* 177, 202; Libbey, *Dear Alben,* 69; Ritchie, "Barkley," 146; Davis, *Barkley,* 79–81.

283. Barkley, *That Reminds Me,* 173.

284. Drury, *Senate Journal,* 90; Ritchie, "Barkley," 147; Libbey, *Barkley,* 229; Libbey, *Dear Alben,* 87.

285. Drury, *Senate Journal,* 90; Libbey, *Dear Alben,* 87.

286. Davis, *Barkley,* 147.

287. Floyd M. Riddick, "Congress versus the President in 1944," *SAQ* 44 (July 1945): 308, 311. For Barkley's recollection of the incident, see *That Reminds Me,* 169–82.

288. Drury, *Senate Journal,* 93; Ritchie, "Barkley," 147.

289. Drury, *Senate Journal,* 92–93.

290. Ibid., 95.

291. Ibid., 93 (emphasis added). Another Senate Democrat was less charitable: Barkley "will really be the Senate majority leader and not just the Administration's stooge." Ibid., 90. For one scholar's take on Barkley's Senate standing in the mid-1940s, see Jewell, *Senatorial Politics,* 56.

292. Shannon, "Barkley," 240–41; Drury, *Senate Journal,* 90, 96; Ritchie, "Barkley," 149; see also Roland Young, *Congressional Politics in the Second World War* (New York: Columbia University Press, 1956), 139–43. Journalist Allen Drury wrote at the time: "Looking back in hasty retrospect, three days after the event and its aftermath, the Barkley resignation still looks like what it did on the day it happened: a basically sincere protest by a man who just got fed up." Drury, *Senate Journal,* 95.

293. Cf. John Bernard Rogers, "Fifty Plus One: The Floor Leader in the United States Senate" (senior thesis, Harvard College, 1964), 56–57. For one majority leader's solution to this dilemma, see McFarland, *Mac,* 124, 128.

294. Libbey, *Barkley,* 135.

295. Ibid., 232; Ritchie, "Barkley," 150; Barkley, *That Reminds Me,* 170. Barkley believed the relationship improved after his electioneering for the national Democratic ticket in the fall of 1944. Barkley, *That Reminds Me,* 191.

296. Libbey, *Barkley,* 232–33; Ritchie, "Barkley," 150; Davis, *Barkley,* 154. Barkley maintained that some time before their break, FDR had hinted about the Kentuckian becoming his successor. Barkley, *That Reminds Me,* 170.

297. Barkley, *That Reminds Me,* 169–70; Libbey, *Barkley,* 233.

298. Richard S. Conley, "Triumphs, Tribulations, and Turnip Day Sessions in the 80th Congress: Harry Truman Copes with Divided Government," in *Congress and Harry Truman: A Conflicted Legacy,* ed. Donald A. Ritchie (Kirksville, MO: Truman State University Press, 2011), 40.

299. Davis, *Barkley,* 120, 163, 211–17, 219.

300. Ibid., 211–17, 241–42, 247, 317–18; Libbey, *Barkley,* 238–39, 246, 248; Libbey, *Dear Alben,* 91.

301. Libbey, *Barkley,* 222; Libbey, *Dear Alben,* 89–90.

302. Libbey, *Barkley,* 222; Libbey, *Dear Alben,* 89–90.

303. Libbey, *Barkley,* 222; Libbey, *Dear Alben,* 89–90; Ritchie, "Barkley," 153.

304. Libbey, *Dear Alben,* 89–90; Ritchie, "Barkley," 153; see also interview with Alben W. Barkley, July 18, 1953, Alben W. Barkley Oral History Project, LBNCOH, accessed February 15, 2018, https://kentuckyoralhistory.org/catalog/xt74tm71wb99.

305. Ritchie, "Barkley," 153.

306. Davis, *Barkley,* 239; Libbey, *Barkley,* 223.

307. Davis, *Barkley,* 259–61.

308. Ibid., 264; Libbey, *Barkley,* 253.

309. Libbey, *Barkley,* 254.

310. Barkley, *That Reminds Me,* 21–22.

311. Ibid.

312. William R. Tansill, Legislative Research Service, memorandum, "Number of Days Certain Vice Presidents Actually Presided over the Senate," July 17, 1955; Joel K. Goldstein, *The White House Vice Presidency: The Path to Significance, Mondale to Biden* (Lawrence: Uni-

versity Press of Kansas, 2016), 22, 320; "Alben W. Barkley, 35th Vice President," US Senate, accessed February 15, 2018, http://www.senate.gov/artandhistory/history/common/generic/VP_Alben_Barkley.htm; Barkley Oral History No. 3, 65. Barkley saw the vice presidency, at least to some extent, as being in the executive branch. Barkley Oral History No. 7 ("it had become customary for the vice president to sit in cabinet meetings, not by law, but by invitation of the president. He's part of the team, part of the administration.").

313. Libbey, *Barkley,* 256.

314. Davis, *Barkley,* 287.

315. Ibid.

316. Libbey, *Dear Alben,* 101.

317. Ibid.

318. Barkley, *That Reminds Me,* 220.

319. Ibid.

320. Jane R. Barkley (as told to Frances Spatz Leighton), *I Married the Veep* (New York: Vanguard Press, 1958), 48.

321. Libbey, *Barkley,* 274.

322. Ibid. For more on Clements, see chapter 9.

323. Davis, *Barkley,* 312. For more on Cooper, see chapter 10.

324. Libbey, *Barkley,* 114.

325. "Alben W. Barkley's Final Speech," audio recording, Washington and Lee University Library, accessed February 15, 2018, https://repository.wlu.edu/handle/11021/28570.

326. Libbey, *Dear Alben,* 115–16.

327. Ibid.

328. Ritchie, "Barkley," 139.

329. Libby, *Dear Alben,* 112; Ritchie, "Barkley," 137–39; Shannon, "Barkley," 256.

330. Davis, *Barkley,* 316–17.

331. For procedural evolution of the floor leader position, see Richard S. Beth, memorandum for Senator Mitch McConnell, "Selected Changes in Senate Procedure and Practice Affecting the Power of the Majority Leader, 1914–2013," Congressional Research Service, January 31, 2017 (on file with the authors).

332. Sinclair, "Congressional Leadership," 119–20; Peabody, "Senate Party Leadership," 57; Davidson, "Senate Leaders," 227; Kravitz, "Leadership, New Style," 68–72. One commentator voiced the prevailing view at the time: "The office is one that requires no gifts of a high order. . . . It has generally been held as a reward for enterprising mediocrity." Davidson, "Senate Leaders," 227 (quoting Richard Rovere).

333. MacNeil and Baker, *American Senate,* 197.

334. Byrd, *Senate,* 185; Peabody, "Senate Party Leadership," 57; cf. David B. Truman, *The Congressional Party: A Case Study* (New York: John Wiley & Sons, 1959), 97.

335. Munk, "Origin and Development" (1970), 189–202; Peabody, "Senate Party Leadership," 61; MacNeil and Baker, *American Senate,* 199; Davidson, "Senate Leaders," 227; Oleszek, "Senate Leadership," 1262.

336. Gamm and Smith, "Rise of Floor Leaders" (2005 paper), 18–34; Ripley, *Power,* 48; David J. Rothman, *Politics and Power: The United States Senate, 1869–1901* (Cambridge, MA: Harvard University Press, 1966), 44–50, 107–8.

337. MacNeil and Baker, *American Senate,* 199–200. Taft's tenure was a brief one, as he passed away six months after Eisenhower's inauguration.

338. Cf. ibid., 203–4; Munk, "Origin and Development" (1974), 31; Gamm and

Smith, "Emergence," 214–21, 229–36. In 1981, following the Reagan landslide in which the GOP gained control over the Senate for the first time in a quarter century, Senate Republicans under majority leader Howard Baker felt the same pressure to produce results. Wendy J. Schiller and Cory Manento, "Howard Baker and the Conditional Use of Parliamentary Procedure in the U.S. Senate," in Campbell, *Leadership,* 52.

339. MacNeil and Baker, *American Senate,* 203–4; see also Austin P. Sullivan Jr., "Lyndon Johnson and the Senate Majority Leadership" (senior thesis, Princeton University, 1964).

340. See note 202.

341. Caro, *Master,* 582–84; see also notes 171, 201, and 355.

342. Davidson, "Senate Leaders," 230; Steven S. Smith, "Congressional Party Leaders," in *The President, the Congress, and the Making of Foreign Policy,* ed. Paul E. Peterson (Norman: University of Oklahoma Press, 1994), 140–41.

343. Cf. Howard E. Shuman, "Lyndon B. Johnson: The Senate's Persuader," in Baker and Davidson, *First among Equals,* 219–20.

344. Betty K. Koed, "Senate Historical Minute—The Ev and Charlie Show" (on file with the authors).

345. Ibid. Dirksen employed a florid rhetorical style. On one occasion, instead of promising to publicly reprimand a fellow senator, he said he would "invoke upon him every condign imprecation." Kravitz, "Leadership, New Style," 101.

346. 117 *CR* 1073 (1971); 119 *CR* 10 (1973); Koed email; Glass, "Mansfield," 151. For background on this development, see Kravitz, "Leadership, New Style," 97–98.

347. Koed email.

348. 121 *CR* 15 (1975); 123 *CR* 22 (1977); 125 *CR* 3047 (1979).

349. 125 *CR* 3047–48 (1979); Cokie Roberts, "Leadership and the Media in the 101st Congress," in Kornacki, *Leading Congress,* 88.

350. Hatcher, *Majority Leadership,* 64–67; Smith, "Parties and Leadership," 264; Katherine Scott and James Wyatt, "Robert C. Byrd: Tactician and Technician," in Campbell, *Leadership,* 86–87, 91–93. For discussion of Byrd's procedural innovations as majority leader, see Beth memorandum, 12–17; Scott and Wyatt, "Byrd," 92–93.

351. John J. Kornacki, introduction to *Leading Congress,* 8; Smith, "Parties and Leadership," 264; Sinclair, "Senate Leadership Dilemma," 73; Smith, "Forces of Change," 281–82; Norman J. Ornstein, "Can Congress Be Led?" in Kornacki, *Leading Congress,* 23–24; Janet M. Martin, "George J. Mitchell: Majority Leader," in Campbell, *Leadership,* 137. Howard Baker may have been chosen Senate Republican leader for reasons similar to those that promoted Mitchell. Davidson, "Senate Leaders," 249; Ornstein et al., "Change in the Senate," 23.

352. Smith and Gamm, "Emergence of the Modern Senate," 3.

353. Burdett A. Loomis, "Bob Dole's Leadership: The Partisan as Dealmaker," in Campbell, *Leadership,* 111.

354. Smith and Gamm, "Emergence of the Modern Senate," 3.

355. Cf. Smith, "Recent Senate Party Leaders," 282. For instance, over time, it has generally been accepted that the majority leader will offer motions to proceed to legislative or executive business, negotiate unanimous consent agreements, circulate cloture petitions, and exercise some control over committee schedules (along with the minority leader). See notes 171 and 201; Beth memorandum, 2–3, 5, 7, 8, 9. This was not always so. 68 *CR* 1761 (1927) (majority leader Curtis); 69 *CR* 6380 (1928) (Sen. Sackett); cf. 150 *CR* 25797 (2004) (Sen. Byrd). Moreover, in the last few decades, statutes and rule interpretations have authorized

the Senate to consider nominations and certain types of legislation (e.g., the budget, Congressional Review Act resolutions) under a strict majority-rule standard. Beth memorandum, 10–11, 31.

356. Gamm and Smith, "Policy Leadership" (2002), 287–88; Smith, "Recent Senate Party Leaders," 278, 290.

357. Gamm and Smith, "Policy Leadership" (2002), 287–88; Smith, "Recent Senate Party Leaders," 278, 290.

358. Gamm and Smith, "Policy Leadership" (2002), 287–88.

359. Smith, "Parties and Leadership," 264–65; Steven S. Smith and Gerald Gamm, "The Evolution of Senate Party Organization and Leadership: An Overview" (paper prepared for the Congress Project, Woodrow Wilson Center for Scholars, Washington, DC, September 14, 2001), 14.

360. Smith and Gamm, "Evolution," 14.

361. Daschle and Robbins, *Senate*, 66. For more, see Emily Goodin, "Weekly Lunches Give Senators a Chance to Air Their Differences," *TH*, May 5, 2013.

362. Sinclair, "Senate Leadership Dilemma," 75; Smith, "Parties and Leadership," 270–71; Goodin, "Weekly Lunches."

363. Smith, "Parties and Leadership," 270–71; Scott and Wyatt, "Byrd," 92; Goodin, "Weekly Lunches"; Sinclair, "Senate Leadership Dilemma," 75.

364. Sinclair, "Senate Leadership Dilemma," 75.

365. Baker and Davidson, "Introduction," 2.

8. Senate Majority Whip

1. For the lead author's recollections of his own tenure as whip, see Mitch McConnell, *The Long Game: A Memoir* (New York: Sentinel, 2016), 132–34, 139, 147–48, 241.

2. Erin M. Bradbury, Ryan A. Davidson, and C. Lawrence Evans, "The Senate Whip System: An Exploration" (paper, 2007), 4; Robert C. Byrd, *The Senate 1789–1989: Addresses on the History of the United States Senate* (Washington, DC: Government Printing Office, 1991), 2:198–99; C. Lawrence Evans and Claire E. Grandy, "The Whip Systems of Congress" (paper prepared for the 9th edition of *Congress Reconsidered,* June 2008), 22; 80 *CR* 7045–46 (1936) (Sen. Guffey quoting Sen. Lewis).

3. Earle Clements was the first whip from Kentucky; see chapter 9. The lead author is the third Kentuckian to serve in this capacity.

4. Walter J. Oleszek, "Party Whips in the United States Senate," *JOP* 33 (1971): 955, 957–58; cf. 80 *CR* 7045 (1936).

5. Edward Porritt and Annie G. Porritt, *The Unreformed House of Commons: Parliamentary Representation before 1832* (Cambridge: Cambridge University Press, 1903), 1:509; Byrd, *Senate,* 195–96; "The Whips," Senate Historical Office document (on file with the authors).

6. Oleszek, "Party Whips," 957; Byrd, *Senate,* 195.

7. Oleszek, "Party Whips," 957.

8. Courtenay Ilbert, *Parliament: Its History, Constitution and Practice* (London: Williams & Norgate, 1911), 152 (emphasis added); see also Robert Luce, *Legislative Procedure: Parliamentary Practices and the Course of Business in the Framing of Statutes* (Boston: Houghton Mifflin, 1922), 501–2; see also Byrd, *Senate,* 195–96.

9. Porritt and Porritt, *Unreformed,* 509.

10. For example, *CG* 1132 (1850) (Sen. Turney); *CG* 2493 (1866) (Sen. Cowan); *CG* 1131 (1872) (Sen. Morton); 4 *CR* 132 (1875) (Sen. Withers); 13 *CR* 2003 (1882) (Sen. Morrill); 14 *CR* 3581 (1883) (Sen. Beck); 15 *CR* 3928 (1884) (Sen. Gorman); 18 *CR* 1724 (1887) (Sen. Riddleberger); 19 *CR* 6849 (1888) (Sen. Morgan); 21 *CR* 6129 (1890) (Sen. Vest); 23 *CR* 2982 (1892) (Sen. Wolcott); 23 *CR* 5656 (1892) (Sen. Morgan).

11. Oleszek, "Party Whips," 958; Byrd, *Senate,* 196.

12. Oleszek, "Party Whips," 959.

13. Ibid., 958; Byrd, *Senate,* 196.

14. 2 *CR* 2488 (1874).

15. 12 *CR* 282 (1881). One of the party whip's early functions was to coordinate pairs, which meant that if a senator on one side knew he would be absent for a vote, the whip of the opposite party would try to find a member on his own side to be absent in order to avoid changing the outcome of the vote. Ibid. This practice has almost fallen into desuetude. For recent, rare examples of pairing, see Niels Lesniewski, "Brett Kavanaugh to Be Rare Beneficiary of Senate Paired Voting," *RC*, October 6, 2018, accessed October 30, 2018, https://www.rollcall.com/news/politics/brett-kavanaugh-rare-beneficiary-senate-paired-voting; Niels Lesniewski, "After Coons Demonstrates Comity, Pompeo Avoids Dubious Distinction," *RC*, April 23, 2018, accessed October 30, 2018, https://www.rollcall.com/news/politics/coons-demonstrates-comity-pompeo-avoids-dubious-honor.

16. 13 *CR* 2003 (1882); cf. 15 *CR* 2997 (1884) (Sen. Morrill).

17. James Bryce, *The American Commonwealth* (New York: Macmillan, 1888), 1:272; see also ibid., 271.

18. Randall B. Ripley, *Majority Party Leadership in Congress* (Boston: Little, Brown, 1969), 3. In the 1890s, Senator Arthur Pue Gorman (D-MD), as Democratic caucus chairman, carried out whip functions, such as alerting fellow partisans to the floor schedule. Gerald Gamm and Steven S. Smith, "The Rise of Floor Leaders, 1890–1913" (draft book chapter), 69.

19. "Republican Whips (1897 to Present)," US House of Representatives, accessed February 15, 2018, http://history.house.gov/People/Office/Republican-Whips/.

20. "Democratic Whips (1901 to Present)," US House of Representatives, accessed February 15, 2018, http://history.house.gov/People/Office/Democratic-Whips/.

21. The Senate, for example, emulated the House in the creation of standing committees and may have done the same regarding the majority leader position. See chapters 5 and 7.

22. Richard A. Baker and Roger H. Davidson, introduction to *First among Equals: Outstanding Senate Leaders of the Twentieth Century,* ed. Richard A. Baker and Roger H. Davidson (Washington, DC: CQ Press, 1991), 2; Walter J. Oleszek, "John Worth Kern: Portrait of a Floor Leader," in Baker and Davidson, *First among Equals,* 10; Gerald Gamm and Steven S. Smith, "Policy Leadership and the Development of the Modern Senate," in *Party, Process, and Political Change in Congress: New Perspectives on the History of Congress,* ed. David W. Brady and Mathew D. McCubbins (Stanford, CA: Stanford University Press, 2002), 299–302; Gerald Gamm and Steven S. Smith, "The Emergence of Senate Party Leadership, 1913–1937: The Case of the Democrats" (paper presented at the Congress and History Workshop, Vanderbilt University, May 21–23, 2005), 21–24, 28–29.

23. Oleszek, "Party Whips," 958–59; Byrd, *Senate,* 196–97; Gamm and Smith, "Emergence, 1913–1937," 12–14; Steven S. Smith and Gerald Gamm, "The Evolution of Senate Party Organization and Leadership: An Overview" (paper prepared for the Congress Project, Woodrow Wilson Center for Scholars, September 14, 2001), 9.

24. "Democrats Agree to Lobby Inquiry," *NYT,* May 29, 1913; "Senator J. Ham. Lewis Elected Party Whip," *WS,* May 28, 1913; see also Smith and Gamm, "Evolution," 9.

25. Byrd, *Senate,* 196.

26. 80 *CR* 7046 (1936). For more on the context of the appointment, see "Democrats Agree to Lobby Inquiry"; Claude G. Bowers, *The Life of John Worth Kern* (Indianapolis: Hollenbeck Press, 1918), 350–51; *Minutes of the Senate Democratic Conference, 1903–1964,* ed. Donald A. Ritchie (Washington, DC: Government Printing Office, 1998), 79.

27. "James Hamilton Lewis," Congressional Biographical Directory, accessed February 15, 2018, http://bioguide.congress.gov/scripts/biodisplay.pl?index=L000284; Oleszek, "Party Whips," 965.

28. Oleszek, "Party Whips," 959; Byrd, *Senate,* 198. The conference secretary records the minutes for formal party conferences and provides strategic advice to the floor leader. "Conference Secretaries," US Senate, accessed February 15, 2018, http://www.senate.gov/artandhistory/history/common/briefing/Conference_Secretaries.htm. Like Lewis, Wadsworth was a first-term senator upon his elevation. Byrd, *Senate,* 198.

29. Byrd, *Senate,* 198.

30. Ibid.

31. Ibid.

32. Ibid.

33. Ibid.; Oleszek, "Party Whips," 964 n. 39.

34. John Thune, "History, Rules and Precedents of the Senate Republican Conference," December 2014, 1, https://www.republican.senate.gov/public/_cache/files/65589e31-c184-4c95-9947-770f1b3998c1/A669DDFC6A0CAF777199282DC623467F.conference-rules-2015.pdf. Until 1944, the whip was an appointed position for Senate Republicans. Gamm and Smith, "Emergence, 1913–1937," 13 n. 12.

35. "Wendell Hampton Ford," Congressional Biographical Directory, accessed February 15, 2018, http://bioguide.congress.gov/scripts/biodisplay.pl?index=f000268; *Wendell Ford: From Yellow Creek to the Potomac,* (documentary, Kentucky Educational Television, 1999), accessed February 15, 2018, https://www.ket.org/episode/KWFRD%20000000/ (hereafter Ford documentary).

36. "Ford," Congressional Biographical Directory; Ford documentary; oral history interview with Wendell H. Ford, February 17, 1994, LBNCOH, 2, 29; telephone interview with Reyburn Ford and Ford family members, April 22, 2016 (hereafter Ford family interview).

37. Ford family interview.

38. Ibid.; Ford oral history, February 17, 1994, 1–2, 14–19; oral history interview with Wendell H. Ford, March 28, 1994, LBNCOH, 14; Ford documentary; Al Cross, "Legacy Is Defined by Focus on Kentucky," *LCJ,* January 3, 1999.

39. Joseph Gerth, "Wendell Ford, Former U.S. Senator, Dies," *LCJ,* January 22, 2015.

40. Oral history interview with Wendell H. Ford, June 6, 2000, LBNCOH, 61.

41. Oral history interview with Wendell H. Ford, March 7, 2013, LBNCOH, accessed February 15, 2018, https://www.kentuckyoralhistory.org/catalog/xt79057cv82n.

42. Ford documentary. Four of Ford's grandchildren would follow in his footsteps and serve as legislative pages, though they would do so in the US Senate.

43. Ibid.

44. Ibid.; Ford oral history, February 17, 1994, 9; oral history interview with Wendell H. Ford, May 9, 2000, LBNCOH, 77.

45. Ford family interview.

46. Ibid.

47. Ford documentary.

48. Ford oral history, February 17, 1994, 26.

49. Ibid.

50. Ford oral history, March 28, 1994, 4.

51. Ibid., 7.

52. Ibid.

53. Ibid.

54. Ibid.

55. Ibid., 21.

56. Ibid.

57. Ford oral history, February 17, 1994, 27.

58. Ford documentary.

59. Ibid.

60. A. B. Stoddard, "Sen. Ford's Finger Is on Pulse of Bluegrass State," *TH,* May 29, 1996.

61. Ibid.

62. Ibid.

63. Ford oral history, March 28, 1994, 10–13. Although Ford never graduated from a four-year college, he noted that he was well schooled in the "Kentucky state government college of political knowledge." Mike King, "Wendell Ford: A Tough Foe to Know," *LCJ,* June 12, 1983. He did graduate in 1947 from the Maryland School of Insurance. "Ford," Congressional Biographical Directory.

64. Ford oral history, May 9, 2000, 1–2; Ford documentary.

65. Ford oral history, May 9, 2000, 3–4.

66. Ibid., 3.

67. Ibid., 3–4.

68. Ibid.

69. Ibid.

70. Ibid.

71. "Senator Wendell Hampton Ford," National Guard History eMuseum, accessed February 15, 2018, http://archive.li/rqSkC.

72. Ibid.

73. Ibid.

74. Ford documentary; Ford oral history, May 9, 2000, 45.

75. Ford oral history, May 9, 2000, 45; Ford documentary.

76. Ford documentary.

77. Ibid.; "Wendell Ford-1956–1957," United States Jaycees Foundation, accessed February 15, 2018, http://www.usjayceefoundation.org/history/1950/1956/index.htm; Ford oral history, May 9, 2000, 47.

78. Ford documentary.

79. For a brief description of Ford's tenure as the head of the Jaycees, see "Ford," Jaycees Foundation. After his tenure as president, Ford held high positions in Jaycees International. Ibid.

80. Ford oral history, May 9, 2000, 75.

81. Ibid., 75–76.

82. Ibid.

83. Ibid.

84. Adam Clymer, "Wendell Ford, 90, Dies; Kentucky Senator Pushed Voting Rights," *NYT,* January 22, 2015; oral history interview with Wendell H. Ford, July 11, 2000, LBNCOH, 11.

85. *The Public Papers of Governor Wendell H. Ford, 1971–1974,* ed. W. Landis Jones (Lexington: University Press of Kentucky, 1978), 4. At the time, Ford was also involved with a number of other civic groups, such as the American Legion, the Kentucky Council of Education, the Boy Scouts, and the Kentucky Chamber of Commerce. "Ford," Jaycees Foundation.

86. Ford oral history, June 6, 2000, 43–44; Jack Brammer, "Kentucky Democratic Icon Wendell Ford Dead at Age 90," *LHL,* January 22, 2015; Clymer, "Ford."

87. Brammer, "Kentucky Democratic Icon"; Clymer, "Ford."

88. Cross, "Legacy"; Ford oral history, June 6, 2000, 46–48.

89. Ford oral history, March 28, 1994, 17; Ford oral history, May 9, 2000, 72.

90. Oral history interview with Wendell H. Ford, November 16, 2001, LBNCOH, 13.

91. Landis Jones, "Wendell Hampton Ford," in *Kentucky Governors,* ed. Lowell H. Harrison (Lexington: University Press of Kentucky, 2004), 213; Stoddard, "Sen. Ford's Finger"; Gerth, "Ford."

92. Jones, "Ford," 213; Cross, "Legacy"; Gerth, "Ford."

93. Stoddard, "Sen. Ford's Finger."

94. *Politics in America: Members of Congress in Washington and at Home,* ed. Alan Ehrenhalt and Renee Amrine (Washington, DC: CQ Press, 1985), 581; see also Gerth, "Ford." Ford was known to say, "My daddy told me . . . never leave the table without winning at least something." Nathaniel C. Nash, "Man in the News: Wendell Hampton Ford; the No. 2 Man for the Democrats in the Senate," *NYT,* November 14, 1990.

95. Ford documentary.

96. Ibid.; King, "Ford." Ford and Ralph Nader clashed over tobacco so heatedly that their relationship ended altogether. King, "Ford."

97. Ford documentary.

98. Cross, "Legacy."

99. *Wendell H. Ford, United States Senator: Tributes Delivered in Congress* (Washington, DC: Government Printing Office, 1998), 16–17 (hereafter *Tributes*).

100. Emily Langer, "Wendell Ford, Democratic Governor and Senator from Kentucky, Dies at 90," *WP,* January 22, 2015.

101. King, "Ford."

102. Ibid.

103. Al Cross, "Democrats Pay Tribute to Senator Ford; Vice President Joins Thousands to Offer Praise," *LCJ,* July 19, 1998, in *Tributes,* 53.

104. *Tributes,* 31; see also James R. Carroll, "An Appreciation of Former Sen. Wendell Ford," *LCJ,* July 19, 2014.

105. *Tributes,* 25.

106. For more on this divide, see chapter 9.

107. Ford documentary; see also Lowell H. Harrison and James C. Klotter, *A New History of Kentucky* (Lexington: University Press of Kentucky, 1997), 415.

108. Ford documentary.

109. Al Cross, "What Ford's Life Meant," *LCJ,* January 5, 2015.

110. Cross, "Legacy."

111. Ibid.

112. Ford documentary.

113. Ibid.; Ford oral history, June 6, 2000, 35.

114. Ford documentary.

115. Ibid.; Cross, "Legacy"; Clymer, "Ford."

116. Oral history interview with Wendell H. Ford, August 24, 2000, LBNCOH, 9; Ford documentary.

117. Ford oral history, June 6, 2000, 61.

118. Ibid.

119. Cross, "Legacy."

120. Ibid.; Clymer, "Ford."

121. Kentucky's state constitution has since been amended to ensure that the governor and lieutenant governor are of the same party.

122. Ford oral history, June 6, 2000, 55–56.

123. Cross, "Legacy."

124. Harrison and Klotter, *New History,* 415.

125. Interview with Clyde Middleton, September 22, 1988, LBNCOH, accessed February 15, 2018, https://nyx.uky.edu/oh/render.php?cachefile=19880H233_LEG0008 _Middleton.xml.

126. Harrison and Klotter, *New History,* 415; Ford oral history, August 24, 2000, 18; Cross, "Legacy"; Michael Barone, Grant Ujifusa, and Douglas Matthews, *AAP 1976* (New York: E. P. Dutton, 1975), 311.

127. Ford oral history, June 6, 2000, 53; Ford documentary.

128. Jones, "Ford," 212; Ford documentary.

129. Clymer, "Ford."

130. Gerth, "Ford."

131. George Douth, *Leaders in Profile: The United States Senate; 1975 Edition* (New York: Sperr & Douth, 1975), 248.

132. Clymer, "Ford."

133. Ibid.

134. Ford oral history, March 7, 2013.

135. Gerth, "Ford"; Northern Kentucky University, Undergraduate Catalog, 2009–2010, 9, accessed February 15, 2018, http://docplayer.net/3722560-Northern-kentucky -university-undergraduate-catalog-2009-2010.html; Jones, "Ford," 212; oral history interview with Wendell H. Ford, October 23, 2001, LBNCOH, 27.

136. Ford oral history, July 11, 2000, 54–55; R. Quay Glass, "Plans to Celebrate Birthday of Martin Luther King Set," *LCJ,* January 3, 1975.

137. Cross, "Legacy"; Jones, "Ford," 213.

138. "Kentucky Derby Trivia," 365 Horses, accessed February 15, 2018, http:// www.365horses.com/kentucky_derby_trivia.html.

139. "Wendell Ford's Funny Kentucky Derby Story," *LCJ,* January 23, 2015.

140. Clymer, "Ford."

141. Ibid.

142. Ibid.

143. Ibid.

144. Ibid.

145. Ibid.

146. "Senate Race Announcement," in *Public Papers of Ford,* 597–99.

147. Jones, "Ford," 211.

148. Ford documentary.

149. Cross, "Legacy"; see also Ford documentary. ("Ford largely ignored the Senate's special role in foreign policy").

150. Ford oral history, March 7, 2013.

151. Michael Barone and Grant Ujifusa, *AAP 1998* (Washington, DC: Times Books, 1997), 596. For more on Ford's deft defense of the tobacco industry, see King, "Ford."

152. Barone and Ujifusa, *AAP 1998*, 596.

153. Michael Barone and Grant Ujifusa, *AAP 1992* (Washington, DC: Times Mirror, 1991), 479.

154. Gerth, "Ford."

155. Robin Kolodny, *Pursuing Majorities: Congressional Campaign Committees in American Politics* (Norman: University of Oklahoma Press, 1998), 224–25.

156. King, "Ford."

157. Ibid.; "Party Division," US Senate, accessed February 15, 2018, https://www.senate.gov/history/partydiv.htm.

158. "Party Division."

159. *Tributes,* 8 (Sen. Byrd).

160. Barone and Ujifusa, *AAP 1998,* 596.

161. Ibid.

162. Gerth, "Ford"; Ford documentary; Ronald D. Elving, "Democrats Fill Other Senate Posts: Cranston Beats Ford for Whip; Pryor Wins Secretary Position," *CQ Weekly,* December 3, 1988; Helen Dewar, "Sen. Ford to Seek Leadership Post," *WP,* September 28, 1988.

163. Nash, "Man in the News."

164. Ibid.; Timothy J. Burger, "Cranston Says He'll Be Back as Whip, but His Campaign Is on Hold for Now," *RC,* July 23, 1990; Timothy J. Burger, "Ford Outlines Plan to Use Rules Panel Chair to Boost His Agenda if He Is Elected Whip," *RC,* January 29, 1990.

165. Nash, "Man in the News."

166. Glenn R. Simpson, "Is Cranston Vulnerable to Whip Challenge?" *RC,* December 11, 1989; Burger, "Cranston"; Ford oral history, March 7, 2013, https://www.kentuckyoralhistory.org/catalog/xt79057cv82n.

167. Ford documentary; Ford oral history, March 7, 2013.

168. Ford oral history, March 7, 2013. Two noted authorities have written, "Byrd had refined the art 'of putting people under obligation' to him." Katherine Scott and James Wyatt, "Robert C. Byrd: Tactician and Technician," *in Leadership in the U.S. Senate,* ed. Colton C. Campbell (New York: Routledge, 2019), 82.

169. Ford oral history, March 7, 2013.

170. In 1969, Senator Edward Kennedy knocked off Russell Long (D-LA) as whip. Robert L. Peabody, *Leadership in Congress: Stability, Succession, and Change* (Boston: Little, Brown, 1976), 358–90. In 1971, Byrd defeated Kennedy and secured the position for himself. Ibid., 358, 391–421.

171. Ibid., 420 n. 35.

172. Ibid.

173. Oleszek, "Party Whips," 959–63.

174. Ibid., 960–61.

175. Walter Kravitz, "Party Organization," in "The United States Senate: A History" (unpublished manuscript on file with the authors), 122; Walter J. Oleszek, *Majority and Minority Whips of the Senate* (Washington, DC: Government Printing Office, 1985), 6 n. 26.

176. Kravitz, "Party Organization," 123; Oleszek, *Majority and Minority Whips*, 6 n. 26.

177. Oleszek, "Party Whips," 962–63; Kravitz, "Party Organization," 123.

178. The assistant floor leader and whip positions had been separate dating back to at least the 1920s, when Charles Curtis (R-KS) was assistant floor leader and Wesley Jones (R-WA) was majority whip. Garrison Nelson, "Leadership Selection in the U.S. Senate, 1899–1985: Changing Patterns of Recruitment and Institutional Interactions" (paper, 1985), 7; Oleszek, "Party Whips," 968. Over the years, the two titles were often, but not always, assigned to the same senator. Kravitz, "Party Organization," 123–24. In the 1930s, Alben Barkley served as assistant majority leader—but not whip—under majority leader Joe Robinson (D-AR). Yet in 1936, Democratic whip Lewis noted that the whip "is ex-officio assistant floor leader, and in the absence of the floor leader, and other assistants, may be called upon to represent the party." 80 *CR* 7046 (1936). From 1949 to 1951, Senator Francis Myers (D-PA) apparently held both the whip and the assistant leader titles. David B. Truman, *The Congressional Party: A Case Study* (New York: John Wiley & Sons, 1959), 101.

Even after the honorific "assistant leader" was formally attached to the whip position in the 1960s, some whips did not carry the title. Robert Byrd requested that he be called only whip, due to the title's historical pedigree. Byrd, *Senate*, 201. In the early years while Ford was whip, Wyche Fowler (D-GA) was deputized "assistant majority leader" by majority leader George Mitchell. Steven S. Smith, "Forces of Change in Senate Leadership and Organization," in *Congress Reconsidered*, 5th ed., ed. Lawrence C. Dodd and Bruce I. Oppenheimer (Washington, DC: CQ Press, 1993), 273. In 2016, Dick Durbin (D-IL) retained the position of Democratic whip but lost the title "assistant Democratic leader" to Patti Murray (D-WA). Burgess Everett, "Democrats Settle on Leadership Hierarchy, Murray Named Assistant Leader," *Politico*, November 16, 2016.

179. Oleszek, "Party Whips," 973–77.

180. Evans and Grandy, "Whip Systems," 207. The chairman of the relevant committee, James Eastland (D-MS), was a strong opponent of the civil rights legislation and was therefore not in a position to manage the bill on the floor.

181. "Nickles Calls for Vote on Lott," *UPI*, December 15, 2002, accessed February 15, 2018, https://www.upi.com/Top_News/2002/12/15/Nickles-calls-for-vote-on-Lott /37231039971714/.

182. For more on the episode, see McConnell, *Long Game*, 135–36.

183. Truman, *Congressional Party*, 117–21.

184. Oleszek, "Party Whips," 973–74; Byrd, *Senate*, 205.

185. Oleszek, "Party Whips," 970–77; Smith, "Forces of Change," 275–76; see also Scott and Wyatt, "Byrd," 86 (quoting Democratic cloakroom aide Martin Paone: the duties of the whip are "whatever the boss gives you").

186. Joel K. Goldstein, *The White House Vice Presidency: The Path to Significance; Mondale to Biden* (Lawrence: University Press of Kansas, 2016), 20–34, 66–91, 105–49; Michael Nelson, "Background Paper," in *A Heartbeat Away: Report of the Twentieth Century Fund Task Force on the Vice Presidency* (New York: Priority Press Publications, 1988), 67–69, 74–76; Paul C. Light, *Vice-Presidential Power: Advice and Influence in the White House* (Baltimore: Johns Hopkins University Press, 1984), 44–51; Oleszek, "Party Whips," 970–74.

187. Bowers, *Kern*, 351–52; Virginia F. Haughton, "John Worth Kern and Wilson's

New Freedom: A Study of a Senate Majority Leader" (PhD diss., University of Kentucky, 1973), 146–49.

188. Don Oberdorfer, *Senator Mansfield: The Extraordinary Life of a Great American Statesman and Diplomat* (Washington, DC: Smithsonian Books, 2003), 309; Randall Ripley, *Power in the Senate* (New York: St. Martin's, 1969), 93–94, 107 n. 12.

189. Oleszek, "Party Whips," 976; Ripley, *Power,* 94; see also Scott and Wyatt, "Byrd," 78–79.

190. Oleszek, "Party Whips," 976; Smith, "Forces of Change," 275–76.

191. Oleszek, "Party Whips," 964, 973; Byrd, *Senate,* 205.

192. Barone and Ujifusa, *AAP 1998,* 596; Cross, "Legacy." Of the two, Ford had a better relationship with Daschle. Cross, "Legacy."

193. Oleszek, "Party Whips," 965–69; Byrd, *Senate,* 198, 205. Much as the vice president temporarily fills in for the president, so too the whip fills in for the floor leader. Cf. Byrd, *Senate,* 198.

194. Oleszek, "Party Whips," 966–67, 973–74; Byrd, *Senate,* 198, 205.

195. Oleszek, "Party Whips," 968–69, 978; Byrd, *Senate,* 198.

196. Nelson, "Leadership Selection," 15.

197. Alexander Bolton, "Durbin and Schumer Prepare for Fight with Donations to Senate Colleagues," *TH,* February 2, 2010, accessed February 15, 2018, http://thehill.com/homenews/senate/79163-durbin-and-schumer-lay-ground-for-a-fight; Fawn Johnson and Sarah Mimms, "Chuck Schumer's Path to Democratic Leader Looks Clear," *TA,* March 27, 2015, accessed February 15, 2018, https://www.theatlantic.com/politics/archive/2015/03/chuck-schumers-path-to-democratic-leader-looks-clear/449454/.

198. Cross, "Legacy." For Ford's contemporary reflections about running for the Senate majority leader position, see Ford oral history, March 28, 1994, 1–2; see also Helen Dewar, "Ford Takes Self out of Race to Succeed Retiring Mitchell," *WP,* April 5, 1994.

199. Cross, "Legacy."

200. Ibid.

201. Oleszek, "Party Whips," 969.

202. Byrd, *Senate,* 204.

203. Ibid.

204. Lister Hill (D-AL) stepped down as whip in 1949 due to his disagreement with President Harry Truman over civil rights. Rowland Evans and Robert Novak, *Lyndon B. Johnson: The Exercise of Power* (New York: New American Library, 1966), 43 n*. Holding the Democratic whip position did not prevent Lyndon Johnson from repeatedly attacking the Truman administration for its conduct of the Korean War, however. Ibid., 47.

205. Ripley, *Power,* 94.

206. Oleszek, "Party Whips," 973.

207. 110 *CR* 6607–8, 6613 (1964); see also Floyd M. Riddick and Alan S. Frumin, *Riddick's Senate Procedure: Precedents and Practice* (Washington, DC: Government Printing Office, 1992), 1094. The authors would like to thank Elizabeth MacDonough for noting this point in a discussion about Senate procedure.

208. Later, Lewis was elected again to the Senate.

209. Byrd, *Senate,* 201.

210. Ibid.

211. Ibid.

212. Neil MacNeil and Richard A. Baker, *The American Senate: An Insider's History* (New York: Oxford University Press, 2013), 217.

213. McConnell, *Long Game,* 147–48.

214. Ibid.

215. Ibid.

216. Ibid.

217. Ibid.

218. Ibid.

219. Andrew J. Glass, "Mansfield Reforms Spark 'Quiet Revolution' in Senate," in *American Government and Public Policy,* ed. John F. Manley (New York: Collier-Macmillan, 1976), 277; Smith, "Forces of Change," 276; Ripley, *Power,* 93.

220. Glass, "Mansfield," 277.

221. Ibid.; Smith, "Forces of Change," 276.

222. Bradbury et al., "Senate Whip System," 6; Evans and Grandy, "Whip Systems," 207–8. During this time, Dole also relied on Republican White House legislative affairs offices for whip counts. Bradbury et al., "Senate Whip System," 6.

223. Bradbury et al., "Senate Whip System," 6; Evans and Grandy, "Whip Systems," 207–8.

224. Byrd, *Senate,* 202–3.

225. Ibid.

226. Ibid., 202; Steven S. Smith and Gerald Gamm, "Emergence of the Modern Senate: Party Organization, 1937–2002" (paper presented at the annual APSA meeting, August 29–September 1, 2002), 20.

227. "The Leader," *Time,* September 14, 1962.

228. Burger, "Cranston."

229. Winthrop Griffith, *Humphrey: A Candid Biography* (New York: William Morrow, 1965), 266.

230. 80 *CR* 7046 (1936).

231. *Tributes,* 3.

232. Ibid.

233. Michael Barone and Grant Ujifusa, *AAP 1982* (Washington, DC: Barone, 1981), 405; Ford documentary.

234. Barone and Ujifusa, *AAP 1998,* 597.

235. Michael Barone, Grant Ujifusa, and Douglas Matthews, *AAP 1980* (New York: E. P. Dutton, 1979), 330.

236. Ibid.; Barone and Ujifusa, *AAP 1982,* 405; Cross, "What Ford's Life Meant"; Gerth, "Ford."

237. *Tributes,* vii; Ford documentary.

238. *Tributes,* 40; oral history interview with Wendell H. Ford, December 4, 2012, accessed February 15, 2018, https://www.kentuckyoralhistory.org/catalog/xt7dnc5sb922.

239. *Tributes,* vii–viii; Ford documentary.

240. *Tributes,* 12 (Sen. McCain); ibid., 16 (Sen. Levin).

241. "Chairmen of Senate Standing Committees, 1789–Present," accessed February 15, 2018, https://www.senate.gov/artandhistory/history/resources/pdf/CommitteeChairs.pdf.

242. Joseph Gerth, "More than 400 Bid Farewell to Wendell Ford," *LCJ,* January 28, 2015; Ford oral history, February 17, 1994, 30.

243. Ford oral history, December 4, 2012.

244. *Tributes,* vii; ibid., 9 (Sen. Byrd).

245. Ibid., vii.

246. Charles R. Babcock, "Grand Jury Will Not Indict Senator," *WP,* December 22, 1981; Charles R. Babcock, "Sen. Ford's Name Surfaces in Ky. Probe," *WP,* February 5, 1981.

247. Cross, "Legacy"; Babcock, "Grand Jury."

248. Clymer, "Ford."

249. Cross, "Legacy"; Jones, "Ford," 215; Kim Mattingly, "Rules Chairman Eyes Ky. Governorship," *RC,* July 10–16, 1989.

250. Helen Dewar, "Sen. Ford Announces He Will Retire," *WP,* March 11, 1997. Ford later served as a part-time consultant at a Washington, DC, lobbying shop. Al Cross, "Ford Will Do Work for D.C. Legal Firm," *LCJ,* January 16, 1999; Gerth, "Ford."

251. Ford family interview; Ford documentary.

252. "Wendell H. Ford Government Education Center," accessed February 15, 2018, https://www.fordgovcenter.com/.

9. Senate Party Campaign Chairman

1. For the lead author's personal reminiscences of his own tenure as Senate party campaign chairman, see Mitch McConnell, *The Long Game: A Memoir* (New York: Sentinel, 2016), 107–10, 117–18.

2. Thomas Hamilton Syvertsen, "Earle Chester Clements and the Democratic Party, 1920–1950" (PhD diss., University of Kentucky, 1982), 2.

3. Ibid.; Thomas H. Syvertsen, "Earle Chester Clements," in *Kentucky's Governors,* ed. Lowell H. Harrison (Lexington: University Press of Kentucky, 2004), 185.

4. Syvertsen, "Clements" (2004), 185.

5. Syvertsen, "Clements" (1982), 3.

6. Ibid.

7. Willard Rouse Jillson, "Governor Earle C. Clements: A Biographical Sketch," *RKHS* 46 (1948): 375, 376–77.

8. John Ed Pearce, *Divide and Dissent: Kentucky Politics, 1930–1963,* 2d ed. (Lexington: University Press of Kentucky, 2006), 47; Syvertsen, "Clements" (1982), 5–6.

9. James C. Klotter, "Earle Chester Clements," in *The Scribner Encyclopedia of American Lives,* ed. Kenneth T. Jackson et al. (New York: Charles Scribner's Sons, 1998), 1:163.

10. Syvertsen, "Clements" (1982), 503.

11. Ibid., 21, 503; Pearce, *Divide and Dissent,* 59.

12. Syvertsen, "Clements" (1982), 125; Pearce, *Divide and Dissent,* 151–52, 227.

13. Pearce, *Divide and Dissent,* 48, 49, 59, 227. Former senator Wendell Ford said simply, "Earle was the best organizer in the political arena I've ever dealt with." Oral history interview with Wendell H. Ford, July 11, 2000, LBNCOH, 44.

14. Pearce, *Divide and Dissent,* 227; see also Lowell H. Harrison and James C. Klotter, *A New History of Kentucky* (Lexington: University Press of Kentucky, 1997), 400–401.

15. Syvertsen, "Clements" (1982), 19.

16. Ibid., 22.

17. Ibid., 24.

18. Ibid., 6–11.

19. Ibid., 11 (quoting Clements).

20. Ibid., 10.

21. Klotter, "Clements," 163.

22. Ibid.

23. Charles P. Roland, "Albert Benjamin Chandler," in Harrison, *Kentucky's Governors,* 168, 170.

24. Syvertsen, "Clements" (1982), 35–36; Pearce, *Divide and Dissent,* 36.

25. Syvertsen, "Clements" (1982), 35–36; Pearce, *Divide and Dissent,* 36.

26. Charles P. Roland, "Happy Chandler," *RKHS* 85 (1987): 138, 141, 143, 145; Syvertsen, "Clements" (1982), 3–6.

27. Syvertsen, "Clements" (1982), 23; Andy Mead and Jim Warren, "Kentucky's 'Happy' Chandler Dies," *LHL,* June 16, 1991.

28. Pearce, *Divide and Dissent,* 59–60.

29. Ibid.

30. Betty K. Koed, "Earle C. Clements: A Quiet Partisan Takes Control," *Unum* 19 (Winter 2015): 11.

31. Pearce, *Divide and Dissent,* 59–60.

32. Ibid., 48; see also Syvertsen, "Clements" (1982), 24.

33. Syvertsen, "Clements" (1982), 24; Stephen D. Boyd, "The Campaign Speaking of A. B. Chandler," *RKHS* 79 (1981): 227, 228–39.

34. Syvertsen, "Clements" (1982), 41–43; Pearce, *Divide and Dissent,* 90, 180, 189.

35. Pearce, *Divide and Dissent,* 4, 24, 28–29, 33, 38–39, 46, 59–62, 180, 183, 196–97, 227; Syvertsen, "Clements" (1982), 38; Harrison and Klotter, *New History,* 367–68, 400–401; Happy Chandler and Vance Trimble, *Heroes, Plain Folks, and Skunks: The Life and Times of Happy Chandler* (Chicago: Bonus Books, 1989), 247–48.

36. Mead and Warren, "Chandler Dies."

37. Syvertsen, "Clements" (1982), 197–98, 209 n. 55, 245–88. For more on Clements's House tenure, see ibid., 163–214.

38. Ibid., 305.

39. Ibid.

40. Jillson, "Clements," 378.

41. Pearce, *Divide and Dissent,* 2, 49–51; Harrison and Klotter, *New History,* 401.

42. Pearce, *Divide and Dissent,* 185–86; Harrison and Klotter, *New History,* 401.

43. "Earle Clements of Kentucky; Was Governor and a Senator," *NYT,* March 14, 1985.

44. Harrison and Klotter, *New History,* 401.

45. Syvertsen, "Clements" (2004), 187.

46. Ibid.; Syvertsen, "Clements" (1982), 384–93, 439–45.

47. Syvertsen, "Clements" (1982), 344–45, 350–53; see also Harrison and Klotter, *New History,* 385, 401.

48. Syvertsen, "Clements" (2004), 189.

49. Robin Kolodny, *Pursuing Majorities: Congressional Campaign Committees in American Politics* (Norman: University of Oklahoma Press, 1998), 224.

50. "Party Division," US Senate, accessed February 15, 2018, https://www.senate.gov/history/partydiv.htm.

51. Ibid.

52. For background on Clements's early appointment to the Senate Democratic Policy Committee, see Ernest W. McFarland, *Mac: The Autobiography of Ernest W. McFarland* (privately published, 1979), 127.

53. Rowland Evans and Robert Novak, *Lyndon B. Johnson: The Exercise of Power* (New York: New American Library, 1966), 53.

54. Ibid., 52–53.

55. Oral history interview with Lady Bird Johnson, October 19, 1976, Earle C. Clements Oral History Project, LBNCOH, accessed February 15, 2018, https://kentuckyoralhistory.org/catalog/xt7m3775vg0z; Evans and Novak, *Johnson,* 53, 97.

56. Evans and Novak, *Johnson,* 53.

57. Steven S. Smith and Gerald Gamm, "Emergence of the Modern Senate: Party Organization, 1937–2002" (paper presented at the annual APSA conference, August 29–September 1, 2002), 20; see also Evans and Novak, *Johnson,* 53.

58. Lady Bird Johnson oral history.

59. William S. White, "The Ten Who Run Congress," *NYT,* January 2, 1955.

60. Harry McPherson, *A Political Education: A Washington Memoir* (Boston: Houghton Mifflin, 1988), 30.

61. Evans and Novak, *Johnson,* 84.

62. Koed, "Clements," 11.

63. Ibid.

64. 101 *CR* 9834–37 (1955); see also Koed, "Clements," 11; Robert A. Caro, *Master of the Senate* (New York: Alfred A. Knopf, 2002), 628–29. Clements briefly filled in for Johnson a few months earlier when the latter had an operation to remove a kidney stone. Albon B. Hailey, "Johnson's Condition Reported More Stable," *WP,* July 4, 1955.

65. Caro, *Master,* 661.

66. Ibid.

67. John T. Shaw, *JFK in the Senate: Pathway to the Presidency* (New York: Palgrave Macmillan, 2013), 141.

68. Ibid. For more on the panel's work, see chapter 4.

69. Koed, "Clements," 11.

70. Ibid.

71. John N. Popham, "Clements Opens Attack on Rival," *NYT,* August 4, 1955.

72. Chandler and Trimble, *Heroes,* 248.

73. Ibid.; Pearce, *Divide and Dissent,* 62.

74. Mead and Warren, "Chandler Dies"; Harrison and Klotter, *New History,* 403.

75. "Chandler Claims Kentucky Control," *NYT,* July 1, 1956.

76. Sara Judith Smiley, "The Political Career of Thruston B. Morton: The Senate Years, 1956–1968" (PhD diss., University of Kentucky, 1975), 9, 20–21, 29–30; John N. Popham, "Old Feuds Warm Kentucky Issues," *NYT,* July 31, 1955; Harrison and Klotter, *New History,* 404; Pearce, *Divide and Dissent,* 73–74, 94.

77. Pearce, *Divide and Dissent,* 73–74, 94.

78. Ibid., 73, 200.

79. Ibid.

80. Transcript, Earle C. Clements oral history interview II, December 6, 1977, 1–2, Lyndon Baines Johnson Presidential Library.

81. Caro, *Master,* 678–81; Evans and Novak, *Johnson,* 156–59.

82. Caro, *Master,* 680–81; Evans and Novak, *Johnson,* 157.

83. Caro, *Master,* 680; Evans and Novak, *Johnson,* 157, 159.

84. Transcript, Clements interview II, 1–2; Caro, *Master,* 681; Evans and Novak, *Johnson,* 159.

85. Harrison and Klotter, *New History,* 405.

86. Ibid.

87. Ibid.

88. Democratic National Committee press release, February 6, 1957.

89. "Party Division." The largest net gain for a Senate party occurred in 1866, when Republicans gained eighteen seats. The largest net gain of Republican seats outside of the Reconstruction era occurred in 1946, when the Senate GOP picked up an even dozen. Ibid.

90. Evans and Novak, *Johnson,* 246, 259, 264.

91. "Kentuckian to Lead Drive for Johnson," *NYT,* December 6, 1959.

92. Pearce, *Divide and Dissent,* 135–39, 151, 152, 191–92, 214. Clements also faced tax difficulties after his Senate tenure. "Clements Faces $291,288 Tax Suit," *NYT,* September 23, 1960; "Clements Settled Tax Claims," *NYT,* February 12, 1963.

93. Syvertsen, "Clements" (2004), 190. In 1965, while in the employ of tobacco interests, Clements was criticized for using his privileges as a former member to lobby lawmakers on the Senate floor. Mark J. Green, James M. Fallows, and David R. Zwick, *Who Runs Congress?* (New York: Bantam Books, 1972), 44. Such activity is not permitted today under Senate Rule XXIII.

94. Pearce, *Divide and Dissent,* 228.

95. Ibid., 2–44, 59–62, 213–14.

96. Smiley, "Morton," 1, 8–9, 20–21, 29. For the Chandler-inspired divisions among Democrats, see ibid., 110, 114.

97. Kolodny, *Pursuing Majorities,* 22–23; Hugh A. Bone, "Some Notes on the Congressional Campaign Committees," *WPQ* 9 (1956): 116, 117.

98. Bone, "Notes," 117.

99. Kolodny, *Pursuing Majorities,* 3; Cornelius P. Cotter and Bernard C. Hennessy, *Politics without Power: The National Party Committees* (New Brunswick, NJ: Aldine Transaction, 2009), 13–14.

100. Kolodny, *Pursuing Majorities,* 3.

101. Ibid.

102. Ibid.

103. Ibid.

104. Richard H. Abbott, *The Republican Party and the South, 1855–1877* (Chapel Hill: University of North Carolina Press, 1986), 87; Detroit Post and Tribune, *Zachariah Chandler: An Outline Sketch of His Life and Public Service* (Detroit, MI: Post & Tribune, 1880), 312.

105. Gerald Gamm and Steven S. Smith, "The Senate without Leaders: Senate Parties in the Mid-19th Century" (paper delivered at the annual meeting of the APSA, August 30–September 2, 2001), 10–11; Abbott, *Republican Party,* 87; Jesse Macy, *Party Organization and Machinery* (New York: Century, 1904), 87–88; see also Ernest Paul Muller, "Preston King: A Political Biography" (PhD diss., Columbia University, 1957), 646–50.

106. Gamm and Smith, "Senate without Leaders," 10–11; Macy, *Party Organization,* 87–88.

107. Kolodny, *Pursuing Majorities,* 18–19.

108. Ibid., 4, 16–20; Macy, *Party Organization,* 87–88; *One Hundred Years: A History of the National Republican Congressional Committee* (Washington, DC: Republican Congressional Committee, 1966), 1, 8–17.

109. Kolodny, *Pursuing Majorities,* 4, 22–23; Abbott, *Republican Party,* 87; *One Hun-*

dred Years, 1, 8–17; Macy, *Party Organization,* 87–88. Robin Kolodny argues that 1866 is the best date of origin for the campaign committees. Kolodny, *Pursuing Majorities,* 22–23.

110. Kolodny, *Pursuing Majorities,* 33.

111. Ibid., 12, 15.

112. Ibid., 12–13.

113. See chapter 7, note 109; chapter 8, note 28.

114. Kolodny, *Pursuing Majorities,* 34; Macy, *Party Organization,* 88.

115. Gamm and Smith, "Senate without Leaders," 11.

116. Kolodny, *Pursuing Majorities,* 9.

117. Ibid.; Macy, *Party Organization,* 89.

118. Kolodny, *Pursuing Majorities,* 15.

119. Ibid., 68–72.

120. Ibid., 29, 33–35.

121. Ibid., 21–22; David J. Rothman, *Politics and Power: The United States Senate, 1869–1901* (Cambridge, MA: Harvard University Press, 1966), 3, 155, 159–90.

122. Kolodny, *Pursuing Majorities,* 33–34; Gerald Gamm and Steven S. Smith, "The Rise of Floor Leaders, 1890–1913" (draft book chapter), 20.

123. Kolodny, *Pursuing Majorities,* 35.

124. Ibid., 41.

125. Ibid., 68–69; Hugh A. Bone, *Party Committees and National Politics* (Seattle: University of Washington Press, 1968), 128.

126. Kolodny, *Pursuing Majorities,* 70.

127. Ibid., 72.

128. Ibid.

129. Ibid., 80.

130. Ibid., 78.

131. Ibid., 75, 79–80, 83.

132. Ibid., 80.

133. Ibid., 69.

134. Cf. ibid., 92.

135. Ibid.

136. Ibid., 265 n. 50.

137. Ibid.

138. Ibid., 11.

139. Ibid., 11–12.

140. Ibid., 93.

141. Ibid., 86, 93; Bone, "Notes," 125.

142. Bone, *Party Committees,* 145.

143. Neil MacNeil and Richard A. Baker, *The American Senate: An Insider's History* (New York: Oxford University Press, 2013), 34, 36–38, 44–46.

144. Ibid., 42–44; Kolodny, *Pursuing Majorities,* 125.

145. Kolodny, *Pursuing Majorities,* 126.

146. Ibid., 124–25.

147. Ibid., 126.

148. Ibid., 176–81, 195–96; Steven S. Smith, "Recent Senate Party Leaders in a Historical Perspective," in *Leadership in the U.S. Senate,* ed. Colton C. Campbell (New York: Routledge, 2019), 277.

149. Walter J. Oleszek, "Senate Leadership," in *The Encyclopedia of the United States Congress*, ed. Donald C. Bacon, Roger H. Davidson, and Morton Keller (New York: Simon & Schuster, 1995), 3:1268.

150. Kolodny, *Pursuing Majorities,* 152.

151. Ibid., 88, 89, 175–81, 224–25.

152. Ibid., 175–81, 195–96.

153. Ibid., 177, 193–95, 224–25.

154. Ibid.

155. Ibid., 191–92.

156. Ibid.

157. Ibid., 192.

158. Ibid.

159. Ibid.

160. Ibid.

161. Ibid.

162. Ibid., 185.

163. Ibid., 185–86.

164. Ibid., 186.

165. Smiley, "Morton," 1.

166. Ibid.

167. Ibid.

168. Ibid., 3.

169. Ibid., 1, 3.

170. Ibid., 3.

171. Roger Winship Stuart, *Meet the Senators* (New York: McFadden Books, 1963), 106.

172. Ibid.

173. Smiley, "Morton," 8, 60, 79; Harrison and Klotter, *New History,* 405; Pearce, *Divide and Dissent,* 200.

174. Stuart, *Meet the Senators,* 104; Smiley, "Morton," 1–2. Ballard & Ballard was acquired by Pillsbury in the early 1950s. Stuart, *Meet the Senators,* 106.

175. Stuart, *Meet the Senators,* 106; Byron Hulsey, "Thruston Ballard Morton," in *Scribner Encyclopedia of American Lives,* 1:580.

176. Smiley, "Morton," 1–2.

177. Hulsey, "Morton," 580.

178. Ibid.

179. Oral history interview with Thruston Morton, February 26, 1969, 1, Lyndon Baines Johnson Presidential Library, accessed February 15, 2018, https://www.discoverlbj .org/item/oh-mortont-19690226-1-74-224.

180. Smiley, "Morton," 14–15.

181. Ibid.

182. Ibid.

183. Evans and Novak, *Johnson,* 20–21.

184. Ibid.

185. Ibid.

186. Byron Hulsey, "Partisanship and the National Interest: Thruston Morton, Lyndon Johnson, and the Vietnam War," *WFMJ* 34 (1994): 28–30.

187. Hulsey, "Morton," 581.

188. Smiley, "Morton," 7.

189. Ibid., 3.

190. Ibid., 3–4, 7–8.

191. Assistant Secretaries of State for Legislative Affairs, US State Department, accessed February 15, 2018, https://history.state.gov/departmenthistory/people/principalofficers/assistant-secretary-legislative-affairs.

192. Smiley, "Morton," 4, 6.

193. Ibid., 13–14.

194. Ibid., 14.

195. Ibid., 12.

196. Robert L. Riggs, "Thruston Morton, the All-Purpose Republican," *TNR,* July 27, 1964; "Morton the Realist," *TN,* October 16, 1967.

197. Ford oral history, July 11, 2000, 36–37.

198. Former Democratic senator Wendell Ford had great respect for Morton, describing him as "a smart devil" and conceding that "he was likeable." Ibid.

199. Thruston B. Morton, "Senatorial Campaigning," in *The Senate Institution,* ed. Nathanial Stone Preston (New York: Van Nostrand Reinhold, 1969), 43–44.

200. Riggs, "Morton."

201. Smiley, "Morton," 27.

202. Ibid., 28.

203. Ibid.

204. Stuart, *Meet the Senators,* 106.

205. Smiley, "Morton," 31; Harrison and Klotter, *New History,* 405.

206. Smiley, "Morton," 32.

207. *History of the Committee on Finance* (Washington, DC: Government Printing Office, 1981), 155–57.

208. Smiley, "Morton," 78–79, 124, 140, 159–61; Neil MacNeil, *Dirksen: Portrait of a Public Man* (New York: World Publishing, 1970), 304; John H. Averill, "Weary Sen. Morton Calls It Quits," *BG,* February 24, 1968.

209. Smiley, "Morton," 35–37. Morton, at least publicly, disclaimed any interest in unseating Dirksen as Senate minority leader. "I don't want it. I'm too lazy to do the work he does. I've told him that if he has a contest for the leadership, I'll be his campaign manager." MacNeil, *Dirksen,* 304.

210. Smiley, "Morton," 35–39.

211. Ibid., 35–36.

212. Ibid., 48.

213. Ibid., 45–46, 116.

214. Ibid., 116.

215. Ibid., 171–72, 185.

216. Ibid., 44.

217. Robert Mann, *The Walls of Jericho: Lyndon Johnson, Hubert Humphrey, Richard Russell, and the Struggle for Civil Rights* (New York: Harcourt Brace, 1996), 257.

218. Ibid.

219. Ibid.; see also Russell Baker, "Johnson Expects 'Good' Nights Bill When Clash Ends," *NYT,* March 5, 1960.

220. Mann, *Walls,* 257; Baker, "Johnson."

221. Smiley, "Morton," 58.

222. Ibid.

223. Ibid.

224. *The Eisenhower Diaries,* ed. Robert H. Ferrell (New York: W. W. Norton, 1981), 377; see also Hulsey, "Morton," 581.

225. Daniel M. Berman, *In Congress Assembled: The Legislative Process in the National Government* (New York: Macmillan, 1964), 246.

226. Ibid.

227. Smiley, "Morton," 57.

228. Ibid., 64.

229. Averill, "Weary Sen. Morton."

230. Smiley, "Morton," 114.

231. Ibid., 78–83.

232. F. Clifton White with William J. Gill, *Suite 3505: The Story of the Draft Goldwater Movement* (New Rochelle, NY: Arlington House, 1967), 93, 305; Riggs, "Morton."

233. There had been some speculation that Clements might seek a rematch, but nothing came of it. Pearce, *Divide and Dissent,* 172.

234. Wilson W. Wyatt Sr., *Whistle Stops: Adventures in Public Life* (Lexington: University Press of Kentucky, 1985), 172–73.

235. Riggs, "Morton."

236. Ford oral history, July 11, 2000, 37.

237. Wyatt, *Whistle Stops,* 171.

238. Ibid.

239. Ibid.

240. "Goldwater Calls Regime Indecisive," *LCJ,* October 5, 1962.

241. Pearce, *Divide and Dissent,* 199–206.

242. Ibid., 183.

243. Ibid.; see also Wyatt, *Whistle Stops,* 169–71.

244. Smiley, "Morton," 113.

245. "Party Division."

246. Morton, "Senatorial Campaigning," 49.

247. Smiley, "Morton," 93.

248. Ibid., 95–96; "Thruston B. Morton," in *Political Profiles: The Kennedy Years,* ed. Nelson Lichtenstein and Eleanora W. Schoenebaum (New York: Facts on File, 1976), 372.

249. Smiley, "Morton," 97–100.

250. MacNeil, *Dirksen,* 293–95.

251. Ibid., 292.

252. Ibid.

253. Ibid.

254. Ibid.

255. Ibid., 292–93.

256. Ibid., 293.

257. Ibid., 293–95; Smiley, "Morton," 181–83.

258. Smiley, "Morton," 181; MacNeil, *Dirksen,* 293.

259. Smiley, "Morton," 182; Richard Pearson, "Thruston B. Morton Dies at 74," *WP,* August 15, 1982; MacNeil, *Dirksen,* 293.

260. Smiley, "Morton," 182–83; MacNeil, *Dirksen,* 294–95.

261. Smiley, "Morton," 182; MacNeil, *Dirksen,* 293–94.

262. Smiley, "Morton," 182–83; MacNeil, *Dirksen,* 294.

263. Smiley, "Morton," 183; MacNeil, *Dirksen,* 293.

264. Smiley, "Morton," 183; MacNeil, *Dirksen,* 293–95.

265. For more on informal Senate leadership, see chapter 10.

266. MacNeil, *Dirksen,* 317.

267. Ibid.

268. Ibid.

269. Ibid.

270. Gary Stone, *Elites for Peace: The Senate and the Vietnam War, 1964–1968* (Knoxville: University of Tennessee Press, 2007), 162.

271. MacNeil, *Dirksen,* 305; see also ibid., 294, 355.

272. "The Defection of Senator Morton," *NR,* October 17, 1967, 1105; "Morton the Realist"; see also Smiley, "Morton," 178–81.

273. Smiley, "Morton," 180–81. For Morton's cautious support of the Gulf of Tonkin Resolution, see Stone, *Elites,* 28.

274. "Morton the Realist"; "Defection of Senator Morton." Senator Eugene McCarthy (D-MN), when challenging Johnson for the Democratic presidential nomination in 1968, stated that he might nominate Morton for secretary of state if he won the White House. Dorothy J. Gaiter, "Thruston B. Morton Is Dead at 74, Served as Senator from Kentucky," *NYT,* August 15, 1982.

275. "Morton the Realist"; Joseph R. L. Sterne, "Sen. Morton Confirms He Will Retire," *BS,* February 24, 1968. The *Nation* applauded Morton's frankness: "This is the most effective way of avoiding fruitless discussion and the need for apologetics designed to prove that one can be right on both sides of a controversy." "Morton the Realist."

276. Gaiter, "Morton Is Dead."

277. Smiley, "Morton," 188.

278. Pearson, "Morton Dies."

279. Gaiter, "Morton Is Dead"; Hulsey, "Morton," 582.

280. Gaiter, "Morton Is Dead."

281. Ibid.

282. Ibid.; Smiley, "Morton," 4; Bob Johnson, "Former GOP Power Thruston Morton Dies: Tough Leader Pushed Party in Direction of Moderation," *LCJ,* August 15, 1982, in 128 *CR* 21209 (1982) (Sen. Huddleston).

283. Gaiter, "Morton Is Dead."

10. Senator as Informal Policy Leader

1. Steven S. Smith, "Informal Leadership in the Senate: Opportunities, Resources, and Motivations," in *Leading Congress: New Styles, New Strategies,* ed. John J. Kornacki (Washington, DC: CQ, 1990), 71–83; *Power in Congress: Who Has It, How They Got It, How They Use It* (Washington, DC: CQ, 1987), 43–56. Professor Steven Smith has rightly cautioned that "to speak of informal leaders as a special class in the U.S. Senate requires great care. After all, leadership in the Senate has traditionally come from informal sources." Smith, "Informal Leadership," 71. In Cooper's case, his informal leadership is fairly clear-cut, as it occurred in the modern era, when formal leadership organs were firmly in place, thus making his informal status evident.

2. In the Senate, the lion's share of lawmaking also takes place in committee, but panels by themselves lack the means of keeping floor amendments completely at bay. Lauros G. McConachie, *Congressional Committees: A Study of the Origins and Development of Our National and Local Legislative Methods* (New York: Thomas Y. Crowell, 1898), 118, 326.

3. Barbara Sinclair, "Congressional Leadership: A Review Essay and a Research Agenda," in Kornacki, *Leading Congress*, 98; John W. Kingdon, *Agendas, Alternatives, and Public Policies* (New York: Longman, 2011), 122–24.

4. Sinclair, "Congressional Leadership," 98.

5. Donald R. Matthews, *U.S. Senators and Their World* (Chapel Hill: University of North Carolina Press, 1960), 95–97.

6. Randall B. Ripley, *Power in the Senate* (New York: St. Martin's Press, 1969), 160–62, 170–72, 229; Matthews, *Senators and Their World*, 95–97, 249–50, 253.

7. C. Lawrence Evans, "Informal Leadership in the U.S. Senate" (paper presented at the Woodrow Wilson International Center for Scholars, May 2002), 1, 3. Malcolm Jewell noted: "the Senate respects the man whose interests, knowledge, and committee experience have equipped him to speak with some authority on a subject." Malcolm Jewell, *Senatorial Politics and Foreign Policy* (Lexington: University of Kentucky Press, 1962), 80; see also Robert L. Peabody, *Leadership in Congress: Stability, Succession, and Change* (Boston: Little, Brown, 1976), 5; *Power in Congress*, 43–56; George H. Haynes, *The Senate of the United States: Its History and Practice* (New York: Russell & Russell, 1960), 1:489–92. For more on issue leaders, see Ripley, *Power*, 84–89.

8. For other examples of informal Senate policy leaders in recent years, see Evans, "Informal Leadership," 18; *Power in Congress*, 43–53. For more on the lead author's personal reminiscences of Cooper, see Mitch McConnell, *The Long Game: A Memoir* (New York: Sentinel, 2016), 33–35, 72, 101–2, 138, 227.

9. Ray Hill, "The Independent from Kentucky," *KF,* March 2013; Paul F. Healy, "Battle of Giants in Kentucky," *SEP,* September 18, 1954, 32, 117; see also Clarice James Mitchiner, "Senator John Sherman Cooper: Consummate Statesman" (PhD diss., Indiana University, 1976), 6.

10. Richard Clayton Smoot, "John Sherman Cooper: The Paradox of a Liberal Republican in Kentucky Politics" (PhD diss., University of Kentucky, 1988), 3; Mitchiner, "Cooper," 6.

11. "Kentucky: Whittledycut," *Time,* June 5, 1954, 10, 11.

12. Ibid.

13. Robert Schulman, *John Sherman Cooper—The Global Kentuckian* (Lexington: University Press of Kentucky, 1976), 16.

14. Ibid., 98.

15. Richard C. Smoot, "John Sherman Cooper: The Early Years, 1901–1927," *RKHS* 93 (1995): 133, 138.

16. Ibid., 5–7; Mitchiner, "Cooper," 9–10, 14; Schulman, *Cooper,* 7.

17. Mitchiner, "Cooper," 15–16.

18. Ibid., 17.

19. Ibid.

20. Ibid., 17–18; Smoot, "Cooper: Paradox," 20.

21. Mitchiner, "Cooper," 17–18.

22. Ibid., 18.

23. Smoot, "Cooper: Early Years," 156.

24. Mitchiner, "Cooper," 18.

25. Smoot, "Cooper: Paradox," 30–31.

26. Schulman, *Cooper,* 20–21.

27. Smoot, "Cooper: Paradox," 41; "Kentucky: Whittledycut," 11.

28. Schulman, *Cooper,* 22, 24; Mitchiner, "Cooper," 22–23.

29. Schulman, *Cooper,* 23–25; Smoot, "Cooper: Paradox," 44–45.

30. Schulman, *Cooper,* 23–24.

31. Ibid.

32. "Kentucky: Whittledycut," 12.

33. Schulman, *Cooper,* 23.

34. Smoot, "Cooper: Paradox," 53–57; Lowell H. Harrison and James C. Klotter, *A New History of Kentucky* (Lexington: University Press of Kentucky, 1997), 404.

35. Smoot, "Cooper: Paradox," 54.

36. Schulman, *Cooper,* 25.

37. Ibid., 25–26.

38. Mitchiner, "Cooper," 24.

39. Schulman, *Cooper,* 28; Mitchiner, "Cooper," 24–26.

40. Smoot, "Cooper: Paradox," 83–84.

41. Ibid., 84–85.

42. Ibid., 84–85, 88.

43. Ibid., 84–85.

44. Ibid., 86.

45. Ibid., 85; Schulman, *Cooper,* 31–32.

46. Smoot, "Cooper: Paradox," 85.

47. Ibid., 85–86; cf. Schulman, *Cooper,* 31–32.

48. Smoot, "Cooper: Paradox," 85–86; Schulman, *Cooper,* 31–32.

49. Smoot, "Cooper: Paradox," 86; Schulman, *Cooper,* 31–32.

50. Mitchiner, "Cooper," 25–27.

51. Ibid.

52. Smoot, "Cooper: Paradox," 87–88.

53. Ibid., 94, 182, 211–13; see also C. David Heymann, *The Georgetown Ladies' Social Club* (New York: Atria Books, 2003), 119–20.

54. Smoot, "Cooper: Paradox," 94.

55. Ibid., 100–101.

56. Byron C. Hulsey, "Thruston Ballard Morton," in *The Scribner Encyclopedia of American Lives,* ed. Kenneth T. Jackson et al. (New York: Charles Scribner's Sons, 1998), 1:580, 581.

57. Healy, "Battle," 32; Schulman, *Cooper,* 65–66.

58. Smoot, "Cooper: Paradox," 169, 180. For Cooper and Chandler's friendship, see ibid., 245–47.

59. Neil MacNeil, *Dirksen: Portrait of a Public Man* (New York: World Publishing, 1970), 162–63.

60. Ibid.

61. Ibid.; Walter Kravitz, "Leadership, New Style: The Floor Leaders," in "The United States Senate: A History" (unpublished manuscript on file with the authors), 101.

62. Byron C. Hulsey, *Everett Dirksen and His Presidents* (Lawrence: University Press of Kansas, 2000), 113.

63. "John Sherman Cooper," in *Political Profiles: The Kennedy Years,* ed. Nelson Lichtenstein and Eleanora W. Schoenebaum (New York: Facts on File, 1976), 98.

64. Ibid.; see also Healy, "Battle," 33.

65. Schulman, *Cooper,* 56.

66. James C. Klotter, *Kentucky: Portrait in Paradox, 1900–1950* (Frankfort: Kentucky Historical Society, 1996), 327–28; Schulman, *Cooper,* 41.

67. Smoot, "Cooper: Paradox," 169, 180, 245–47.

68. Harrison and Klotter, *New History,* 374, 405.

69. *Tributes to the Honorable John Sherman Cooper of Kentucky in the United States Senate upon the Occasion of his Retirement from the Senate* (Washington, DC: Government Printing Office, 1972), 38.

70. H. Paul Jeffers, *How the U.S. Senate Works: The ABM Debate* (New York: McGraw-Hill, 1970), 55.

71. Mitchiner, "Cooper," 71–72 (quoting John Ed Pearce).

72. Schulman, *Cooper,* 51 (quoting J. Graham Brown).

73. Healy, "Battle," 119.

74. Bill Cooper, "John Sherman Cooper: A Senator and His Constituents," *RKHS* 84 (1986): 192, 207.

75. Ibid.

76. Ibid.

77. Matthews, *Senators and Their World,* 73–74; see also Mitchiner, "Cooper," 45–47.

78. Cf. Mitchiner, "Cooper," 45–47.

79. *Tributes,* 36.

80. Terry L. Birdwhistell, "An Interview with Jacqueline Kennedy Onassis on John Sherman Cooper," *KR* 10 (1990): 11, 12.

81. Interview with Senator Edward Kennedy, in *Gentleman from Kentucky: John Sherman Cooper* (documentary, Kentucky Educational Television, 1989), accessed February 15, 2018, https://www.ket.org/episode/KGENT%20000000/ (hereafter Cooper documentary). President Kennedy publicly lauded Cooper, terming him "an outstanding Republican." "John Sherman Cooper," in *Political Profiles: The Johnson Years,* ed. Nelson Lichtenstein et al. (New York: Facts on File, 1976), 133.

82. Birdwhistell, "Onassis Interview," 16.

83. Cooper documentary.

84. Ibid. (quoting Sen. Edward Kennedy).

85. Ibid.; Heymann, *Georgetown Ladies,* 94.

86. Heymann, *Georgetown Ladies,* 94.

87. Cooper documentary.

88. Birdwhistell, "Onassis Interview," 21.

89. JFK Assassination Records, title page and letter, National Archives, accessed February 15, 2018, https://www.archives.gov/research/jfk/warren-commission-report/letter.html.

90. "50 Top Washington Correspondents Rate Them: The Ablest Men in the Senate and House," *Newsweek,* June 20, 1960, 35.

91. Ibid.

92. Michael Barone, Grant Ujifusa, and Douglas Matthews, *AAP 1972* (Boston: Gambit, 1972), 283. Elsewhere, he has been described as one "of the unsung Senate giants." Ira Shapiro, *The Last Great Senate: Courage and Statesmanship in Times of Crisis* (New York: Public Affairs Press, 2012), 29. One professor ranked Cooper as one of the ten greatest sena-

tors of the twentieth century. Mark A. Lempke, "The Greatest Senators Post-1900," accessed February 15, 2018, https://www.ranker.com/list/greatest-senators-post-1900/marka-lempke.

93. John D. Feerick, *The Twenty-Fifth Amendment: Its Complete History and Applications,* 3d ed. (New York: Fordham University Press, 2014), 136; Smoot, "Cooper: Paradox," 243.

94. Smoot, "Cooper: Paradox," 242–43.

95. Eric Redman, *The Dance of Legislation* (Seattle: University of Washington Press, 2001), 157.

96. Ross K. Baker, *Friend and Foe in the U.S. Senate* (New York: Free Press, 1980), 196 (quoting a colleague).

97. *Tributes,* 7.

98. William S. White, "What Makes Johnny (Cooper) Walk?" *HM,* May 1962, 87, 91; Albin Krebs, "John Sherman Cooper Dies at 89; Longtime Senator from Kentucky," *NYT,* February 23, 1991, 13; Smoot, "Cooper: Paradox," 142–44.

99. McConnell, *Long Game,* 33–34.

100. Ibid., 34–35.

101. Ibid., 35; see also Timothy N. Thurber, "The Second Reconstruction," in *The American Congress: The Building of Democracy,* ed. Julian E. Zelizer (Boston: Houghton Mifflin, 2004), 539.

102. McConnell, *Long Game,* 35.

103. Ibid.

104. Ibid., 34; see also Cooper, "Cooper: Senator and His Constituents," 199–200.

105. Barone, Ujifusa, and Matthews, *AAP 1972,* 283.

106. Smoot, "Cooper: Paradox," 128–30.

107. Ibid., 163; see also Douglas A. Franklin, "The Politician as Diplomat: Kentucky's John Sherman Cooper in India, 1955–1956," *RKHS* 82 (1984): 28, 59; Schulman, *Cooper,* 72.

108. Smoot, "Cooper: Paradox," 163.

109. "A Guide to the United States' History of Recognition, Diplomatic, and Consular Relations, by Country, since 1776: East Germany (German Democratic Republic)," Office of the Historian, US Department of State, accessed February 15, 2018, https://history.state.gov/countries/german-democratic-republic.

110. Heymann, *Georgetown Ladies,* 323.

111. Ibid., 112–15. For more on Lorraine Cooper, see ibid., 93–117, 241–49, 263–68.

112. Ibid., 103–4.

113. Ibid., 106–8; Cooper documentary.

114. Schulman, *Cooper,* 68 (emphasis added).

115. Ibid., 72–74; Heymann, *Georgetown Ladies,* 100, 112–16.

116. Baker, *Friend and Foe,* 112, 115.

117. Ibid.

118. *Tributes,* 20 (Sen. Byrd).

119. Mitchiner, "Cooper," 21.

120. McConnell, *Long Game,* 37–38.

121. Ibid.

122. Ibid.

123. Cooper, "Cooper: Senator and His Constituents," 205–7.

124. "History," US Senate Select Committee on Ethics, accessed February 15, 2018,

http://www.ethics.senate.gov/public/index.cfm/history; *Tributes,* 17 (Sen. Javits); Smoot, "Cooper: Paradox," 210–11.

125. *Tributes,* 24 (Sen. Allott).

126. Cooper documentary.

127. Schulman, *Cooper,* 18; Klotter, *Kentucky,* 328; Heymann, *Georgetown Ladies,* 110.

128. Smoot, "Cooper: Paradox," 83; Healy, "Battle," 33.

129. Heymann, *Georgetown Ladies,* 110.

130. Schulman, *Cooper,* 18.

131. Ibid.; Healy, "Battle," 117.

132. Healy, "Battle," 33.

133. Schulman, *Cooper,* 18.

134. Bob Johnson, "Former GOP Power Thruston Morton Dies: Tough Leader Pushed Party in Direction of Moderation," *LCJ,* August 15, 1982, in 128 *CR* 21207, 21208 (1982) (Sen. Huddleston).

135. Ibid.

136. Ibid.

137. LeRoy Ashby and Rod Gramer, *Fighting the Odds: The Life of Senator Frank Church* (Pullman: Washington State University Press, 1994), 336–37, 381; McConnell, *Long Game,* 33; Healy, "Battle," 33.

138. Ashby and Gramer, *Fighting,* 336–37, 381.

139. Healy, "Battle," 33.

140. Ibid.

141. Schulman, *Cooper,* 7, 37; Heymann, *Georgetown Ladies,* 116; *Tributes,* 25 (Sen. Allott and Sen. Brooke), 26 (Sen. Boggs); Smoot, "Cooper: Paradox," 219–21.

142. Smoot, "Cooper: Paradox," 236–39. For a full-length treatment of these Cooper-led efforts, see Robert Kinder Lane, "The Cooper-Church Amendment: A Case Study of Senate Initiative and Influence in Foreign Policy" (MA thesis, Arizona State University, 1974).

143. For Cooper's hesitation about the Gulf of Tonkin Resolution, see Fredrik Logevall, "The Vietnam War," in Zelizer, *American Congress,* 589–90; Gary Stone, *Elites for Peace: The Senate and the Vietnam War, 1964–1968* (Knoxville: University of Tennessee Press, 2007), 29, 31.

144. Francis O. Wilcox, *Congress, the Executive, and Foreign Policy* (New York: Harper & Row, 1971), 30; Joseph A. Fry, *Debating Vietnam: Fulbright, Stennis, and Their Senate Hearings* (Lanham, MD: Rowman & Littlefield, 2006), 25; "Cooper," in *Political Profiles: Johnson Years,* 133–34.

145. Logevall, "Vietnam War," 596.

146. P.L. 91-121, §401(a). This was the first successful congressional effort to restrict the war. Earlier legislative attempts, such as a 1966 amendment to repeal the Gulf of Tonkin Resolution by Senator Wayne Morse (D-OR), had been easily defeated. Rowland Evans and Robert Novak, *Lyndon B. Johnson: The Exercise of Power* (New York: New American Library, 1966), 571.

147. Lane, "Cooper-Church," 70–80.

148. Ashby and Gramer, *Fighting,* 299; Gustaf J. Brock, "'Congress Must Draw the Line': Senator Frank Church and the Cooper-Church Amendment of 1970," *IY* 35 (1991): 27. The two senators had teamed up on issues related to the war in Indochina as early as 1967, when they lent their names to a public document alerting Hanoi that the United States would not pull out of the conflict unilaterally. Ashby and Gramer, *Fighting,* 300.

149. Jeffers, *How the Senate Works*, 55, 70–72, 78, 80, 86, 88; Smoot, "Cooper: Paradox," 233–34; Mitchiner, "Cooper," 212–17; Cooper documentary.

150. Lane, "Cooper-Church," 99, 107, 124, 177.

151. Mitchiner, "Cooper," 219–22; see also Amy Belasco et al., "Congressional Restrictions on U.S. Military Operations in Vietnam, Cambodia, Laos, Somalia, and Kosovo: Funding and Non-Funding Approaches," *CRS Report to Congress,* May 7, 2007, 5.

152. Ashby and Gramer, *Fighting,* 299–300 (citations omitted); see also Brock, "Congress Must Draw the Line," 30.

153. Ashby and Gramer, *Fighting,* 319.

154. Ibid.

155. Brock, "Congress Must Draw the Line," 30.

156. Lane, "Cooper-Church," 4; Ashby and Gramer, *Fighting,* 313.

157. Ashby and Gramer, *Fighting,* 304–5; Lane, "Cooper-Church," 39, 97, 100–101, 132.

158. Ashby and Gramer, *Fighting,* 308–10.

159. Ibid., 313.

160. Ibid.

161. Ibid.

162. Ibid., 313–14.

163. Ibid., 314.

164. Ibid., 324–26.

165. Don Oberdorfer, *Senator Mansfield: The Extraordinary Life of a Great American Statesman and Diplomat* (Washington, DC: Smithsonian Books, 2003), 383.

166. Ashby and Gramer, *Fighting,* 324.

167. Ibid.

168. Ibid., 326.

169. Ibid., 330.

170. Ibid., 319; see also ibid., 380–81.

171. Brock, "Congress Must Draw the Line," 35.

172. P.L. 91-652, §7. In 1971, the two senators rolled out an updated and enhanced Cooper-Church Amendment. This measure would have cut off funding for all US military activities in Southeast Asia, except to permit the armed forces to withdraw and protect themselves. Ashby and Gramer, *Fighting,* 336–40. Cooper, however, began to cool toward his own amendment, based partly on concerns about the return of prisoners of war. Ibid., 339–40. This amendment faced formidable obstacles and was never enacted. Ibid., 364; see also *Congress and the Nation, 1969–1972* (Washington, DC: CQ Service, 1973), 3:920–21.

173. Oberdorfer, *Mansfield,* 383; Julian E. Zelizer, "How Congress Got Us out of Vietnam," February 19, 2007, accessed February 15, 2018, http://prospect.org/article/how-congress-got-us-out-vietnam.

174. Ripley, *Power,* 168.

175. Barone, Ujifusa, and Matthews, *AAP 1972,* 283.

176. Peabody, *Leadership in Congress,* 5; see also notes 1 and 7.

177. Katherine Scott and James Wyatt, "Robert C. Byrd: Tactician and Technician," in *Leadership in the U.S. Senate,* ed. Colton C. Campbell (New York: Routledge, 2019), 88 (quoting Sen. Byrd: "A senator will be listened to if he is perceived by his colleagues to be the one who *knows* what the subject is about and who knows more about the subject than others").

178. Lane, "Cooper-Church," 99; see also ibid., 77.

179. Ibid., 99.

180. Ashby and Gramer, *Fighting*, 304.

181. Ibid., 322.

182. For Cooper's skepticism about more extreme antiwar measures, see ibid., 380–82.

183. Cf. C. Lawrence Evans, *Leadership in Committee: A Comparative Analysis of Leadership Behavior in the U.S. Senate* (Ann Arbor: University of Michigan Press, 1991), 42 n. 1.

184. Woodrow Wilson, *Congressional Government* (New York: Meridian Books, 1956), 141.

185. Ibid., 141–42.

186. Cf. Evans, *Leadership*, 70.

187. Ibid., 28–29, 87–88.

188. William C. Berman, *William Fulbright and the Vietnam War: The Dissent of a Political Realist* (Kent, OH: Kent State University Press, 1988), 128, 131, 199.

189. John Hart Ely, *War and Responsibility: Constitutional Lessons of Vietnam and Its Aftermath* (Princeton, NJ: Princeton University Press, 1993), 32–43; Wilcox, *Congress*, 35–36; Logevall, "Vietnam War," 596–98; *Congress and the Nation*, 900, 910–13. Characteristically, Cooper was not a knee-jerk supporter of all antiwar measures. "John Sherman Cooper," in *Political Profiles: The Nixon/Ford Years*, ed. Eleanora W. Schoenebaum (New York: Facts on File, 1979), 150; see also Ashby and Gramer, *Fighting*, 339–40.

190. *Tributes*, 9 (Sen. Allen), 16 (Sen. Symington), 17 (Sen. Javits), 42–43 (Sen. Church); Lane, "Cooper-Church," 37–39, 41–43.

191. Brock, "Congress Must Draw the Line," 36.

192. Belasco et al., "Congressional Restrictions," 5, 7.

193. Heymann, *Georgetown Ladies*, 325.

194. Ibid.

195. Ibid.

Conclusion

1. Woodrow Wilson, *Constitutional Government in the United States* (New York: Columbia University Press, 1961), 56.

2. Gerald Gamm and Steven S. Smith, "The Rise of Floor Leaders" (draft book chapter), 15–16, 84.

3. Ibid., 14–17.

4. Robert V. Remini, *Daniel Webster: The Man and His Time* (New York: W. W. Norton, 1997), 43 n. 1 (quoting Clay).

5. Lowell H. Harrison and James C. Klotter, *A New History of Kentucky* (Lexington: University Press of Kentucky, 1997), 49.

6. Ibid., 72–73; Merrill D. Peterson, *The Great Triumvirate: Webster, Clay, and Calhoun* (New York: Oxford University Press, 1987), 7.

7. Harrison and Klotter, *New History*, 72–73.

8. Ibid., 80–83.

9. For whatever reason, a number of senators profiled in this volume briefly tried their fortunes elsewhere before settling for good in Kentucky. John Crittenden went to Illinois, John C. Breckinridge to Iowa, James B. Beck to New York, Joseph C. S. Blackburn to Arkansas and Illinois, and John W. Stevenson to Mississippi.

10. More than a century ago, Kentucky was termed the "Mother of Senators," as well as the "Mother of Governors." Lauros G. McConachie, *Congressional Committees: A Study of the Origins and Development of Our National and Local Legislative Methods* (New York: Thomas Y. Crowell, 1898), 262; A. C. Quisenberry, "Kentucky—Mother of United States Senators and Representatives," *RKHS* 18 (1920): 77; John Wilson Townsend, "Kentucky, Mother of Governors," *RKHS* 8 (1910): 59.

11. William S. White, "Democrats' Board of Directors," *NYT,* July 10, 1955.

12. Christina Snyder, *Great Crossings: Indians, Settlers, and Slaves in the Age of Jackson* (New York: Oxford University Press, 2017), 14; Harrison and Klotter, *New History,* xv; James K. Libbey, *Alben Barkley: A Life in Politics* (Lexington: University Press of Kentucky, 2016), 132.

13. Harrison and Klotter, *New History,* xv.

14. Maryland and Missouri are occasionally considered southern states. Both senators from these states also voted for the act.

15. Thomas D. Clark, *Kentucky: Land of Contrast* (New York: Harper & Row, 1968).

16. McConachie, *Congressional Committees,* 90.

Afterword

1. Mitch McConnell, *The Long Game: A Memoir* (New York: Sentinel, 2016), 33–35, 72.

2. Jennifer Steinhauer, "Myanmar's Leader Has a Longtime Champion in Mitch McConnell," *NYT,* September 15, 2016.

3. Ibid.

4. Ibid.

5. Transcript of interview with Robert Novak, *Meet the Press,* NBC, August 23, 2009, accessed February 15, 2018, https://archive.org/details/MSNBC_20090823_180000_Meet_the_Press/start/3420/end/3480.

6. Joan Biskupic, "Amid Tension, Trump and McConnell Together on Judges," CNN, September 5, 2017 ("McConnell has continued to steer the stocking of the federal bench in a way that sets him apart from previous Senate majority leaders.").

7. Jordain Carney, "Senate GOP Breaks Record on Confirming Trump's Court Picks," *TH,* December 14, 2017, accessed February 15, 2018, http://thehill.com/homenews/senate/365011-senate-gop-breaks-record-for-confirming-trumps-court-picks.

8. Juliet Eilperin, "Trump Undertakes Most Ambitious Regulatory Rollback since Reagan," *WP,* February 12, 2017, accessed February 15, 2018, https://www.washingtonpost.com/politics/trump-undertakes-most-ambitious-regulatory-rollback-since-reagan/2017/02/12/0337b1f0-efb4-11e6-9662-6eedf1627882_story.html?utm_term=.dacd77fe3a7a.

9. Ibid.

10. "After Words with Senator Mitch McConnell," C-SPAN, May 23, 2016, accessed February 15, 2018, https://www.c-span.org/video/?408861-1/words-senator-mitch-mcconnell&start=3363.

11. Ibid.

12. Ibid.

13. Ibid.

Index